D1256769

WAYS AND MEANS

ALSO BY ROGER LOWENSTEIN

America's Bank:
The Epic Struggle to Create the Federal Reserve

The End of Wall Street

While America Aged: How Pension Debts Ruined General Motors,
Stopped the NYC Subways, Bankrupted San Diego,
and Loom as the Next Financial Crisis

Origins of the Crash:
The Great Bubble and Its Undoing

When Genius Failed: The Rise and Fall
of Long-Term Capital Management

Buffett:
The Making of an American Capitalist

WAYS

and

MEANS

Lincoln and His Cabinet and the

Financing of the Civil War

ROGER LOWENSTEIN

PENGUIN PRESS

NEW YORK

2022

PENGUIN PRESS
An imprint of Penguin Random House LLC
penguinrandomhouse.com

Illustration credits appear on pages 411 and 412.

LIBRARY OF CONGRESS CATALOGING-IN-PUBLICATION DATA
Names: Lowenstein, Roger, author.
Title: Ways and means : Lincoln and his cabinet and the financing of the
Civil War / Roger Lowenstein.
Description: First edition. New York : Penguin Press, 2022. |
Includes bibliographical references and index.
Identifiers: LCCN 2021029398 (print) | LCCN 2021029399 (ebook) |
ISBN 9780735223554 (hardcover) | ISBN 9780735223561 (ebook)
Subjects: LCSH: Lincoln, Abraham, 1809–1865. |
United States—History—Civil War, 1861–1865—Economic aspects. |
United States—History—Civil War, 1861–1865—Finance. |
United States—Politics and government—1861–1865. |
United States—Economic conditions—To 1865. |
United States—History—1849–1877.
Classification: LCC HC105.6 .L69 2022 (print) |
LCC HC105.6 (ebook) | DDC 973.7/1—dc23
LC record available at https://lccn.loc.gov/2021029398
LC ebook record available at https://lccn.loc.gov/2021029399

Printed in the United States of America
1   3   5   7   9   10   8   6   4   2

Designed by Amanda Dewey

To Judy

The Revolution did not create a nation.

— Robert Penn Warren

CONTENTS

WAYS AND MEANS

Greenback Plunges and Recovers
Value of $100 Greenback in Gold

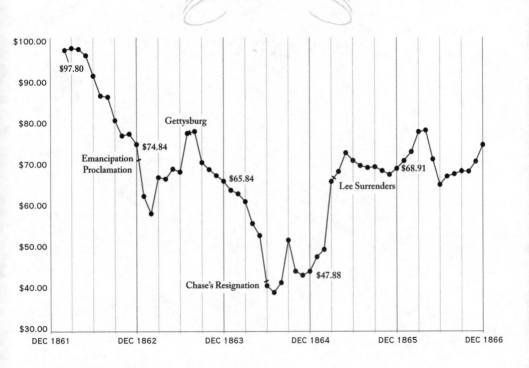

$100.00

$90.00

$97.80

$80.00

Gettysburg

$74.84

Emancipation
Proclamation

$70.00

$65.84

$68.91

Lee Surrenders

$60.00

$50.00

$47.88

Chase's Resignation

$40.00

$30.00

DEC 1861   DEC 1862   DEC 1863   DEC 1864   DEC 1865   DEC 1866

Source: Economic History Association

Hyperinflation in Dixie
Value of $1 of Gold in Confederate Notes

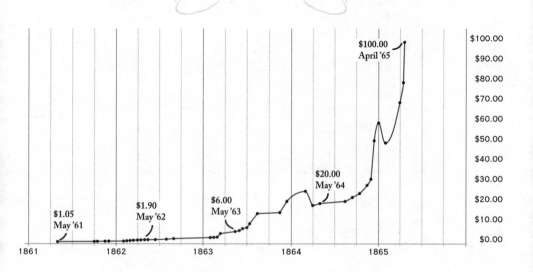

$100.00
April '65

$20.00
May '64

$6.00
May '63

$1.90
May '62

$1.05
May '61

1861   1862   1863   1864   1865

$100.00
$90.00
$80.00
$70.00
$60.00
$50.00
$40.00
$30.00
$20.00
$10.00
$0.00

Source: Richmond Civil War Centennial Committee via InflationData.com

Revolution Completed

O N CHRISTMAS EVE 1825, Thomas Jefferson let loose an anguished cry. The government of the country he had helped to found, half a century earlier, was causing him great distress. It was assuming vast powers, specifically the right to construct canals and roads, and to effect other improvements. Jefferson thought of the federal government in the most restrictive terms: as a "compact" or "a confederated fabric"—that is, a loose affiliation of practically sovereign states. He was roused at the age of eighty-two to issue a "Solemn Declaration and Protest" against what he termed the "usurpation" of power by the federal branch. Jefferson was so agitated that he declared that the "rupture" of the United States would be, although a calamity, not the greatest calamity. Even worse, reckoned the sage of Monticello, would be "submission to a government of unlimited powers."

This ideological debate had been raging since the Revolution itself. Federalists led by Alexander Hamilton had sought to establish a strong central government to marshal the country's finances and develop its infrastructure and commercial potential. Jeffersonians adamantly objected.

And by and large, Jefferson won. No fewer than six of his successors vetoed or thwarted federal legislation to build roads and canals, improve harbors and riverways, maintain a national bank, fund education, and even care for the indigent mentally ill. In 1860, just before the election of Abraham Lincoln, the latest of these, James Buchanan, struck down a project to deepen a water channel in Michigan and vetoed a bill for federal homesteads.*

Had Jefferson survived until 1860, the federal government of the day would not have displeased him. Its main vocation was operating the postal service and collecting customs duties at the ports. Its army consisted of a mere sixteen thousand troops scattered mostly among a series of isolated forts west of the Mississippi River. Those functions aside, the states were essentially on their own. The federal payroll was modest in the extreme. The civilian bureaucracy in Washington consisted of a mere two thousand employees. Its administrative scaffolding was threadbare, its financial capabilities primitive.

The modest federal purse was supported by tariff duties and a smattering of land sales. Federal taxes (an unpleasant reminder of the English Parliament) were reflexively scorned.

Then came the "rupture."

The Republicans—elected on the eve of the Civil War—vastly enlarged the government, not only to defeat the Confederacy but to carry out an agenda for industry and growth, and to foster opportunity, especially for those at the bottom. They accomplished a revolution that has been largely overlooked.

Though their purposes stretched well beyond those of the Founders, Lincoln and the Republicans did not think of themselves as countering the original American revolution. More nearly, they were completing it. These Republicans revered the Founders—Jefferson included—but they scarcely resembled them. They owned no plantations nor slaves, had not been born to wealth, generally had not traveled to England or France. For the most part, the Republican leaders were self-made men, many forged in a crucible of hard experience. John Sherman, a leading con-

---

* The others were James Madison, James Monroe, Andrew Jackson, James Polk, and Franklin Pierce.

gressman, was the son of a lawyer who had died when John was six, leaving his mother to raise eleven children in poverty. Salmon Chase, the Treasury secretary, on whom fell the Bunyonesque burden of raising more money than had been expended in total since the beginning of the Republic, had been plagued by hardship and personal losses. Horace Greeley was born to poor farmers in New Hampshire.

Prototypical was Thaddeus Stevens, born with a clubfoot in a remote hamlet in Vermont to a cobbler father who abandoned him. Confronted with prejudice as well as poverty, Thaddeus developed a protective shield of sarcasm, enrolled in Dartmouth, and established himself in Pennsylvania, where he practiced law and operated an iron foundry. Stevens typified both sides of the Republican rags-to-riches ethos—support for the common classes combined with mercantile ambition. Early in his career, he distinguished himself by fighting for free public schools, which Pennsylvania established before any other state. During the legislative fracas, Stevens mocked opponents of public education with the derisive barb that it was "easier to pass a bill to improve the breed of hogs than that of men." In Congress he became the scourge of the South, the bitter enemy of the slave masters.

Lincoln, Stevens, and most of the Republicans were former Whigs, disciples of Henry Clay (Lincoln's hero) and Daniel Webster. The basic thesis that a robust federal state could promote prosperity was a Whig idea. However, by tiptoeing around the slavery issue, the Whigs made themselves irrelevant. The Republicans were born, in 1854, out of the ashes of the Whigs.

The issue that brought the Republicans to power was slavery. Slavery—or the election of a party hostile to slavery—was the main reason the cotton states seceded. That is not quite to say that slavery caused the Civil War. Southern secessionists did not anticipate—certainly did not desire—a war. Quite the contrary, they believed their cotton was so essential to northern industry, and to its counterpart in Europe, that not a finger would be lifted against them. Southern plantations produced three-fourths of the world's cotton, and this cotton accounted for 60 percent of American exports. Confidence in its cartel led South Carolina's James Hammond to boast in the U.S. Senate, "No power on earth dares to make war upon it. Cotton is king." The comment came to stand for a kind of magical triumphalism, a belief that the South could afford to never compromise. And indeed, both before and after secession, northerners abjectly tried to placate the South, that is, to assure it that if only the Union were preserved, Washington would not, ever, interfere with slavery in the states where it existed. A frequently voiced corollary was that since Britain and France could not afford disruption to their textile industries, "the crowned heads" of Europe would not permit a war. Once it became clear that disunion could lead to bloodshed, southerners reacted with shock. Caroline Gilman, a writer living in Charleston, wrote after secession that the local women were "sad & frightened, some in tears," at the prospect of cannon fire from Fort Sumter. Gilman herself sounded stunned, for, as she put it, "civil war was foreign to the original plan."

Secession was a southern project; the war came mostly from the North. Even in the Union, the people, while appalled by secession, showed no interest in a war. Lincoln's cabinet, polled on whether to re-supply the federal garrison at Fort Sumter, voted five to two against. Yet just a month later, when Lincoln sent a fleet to reprovision the fort, prompting the South to fire the first shot, the northern public over-whelmingly supported war. The overnight change in northern sentiment dovetailed with the only justification that Lincoln gave for fighting: to preserve the Union.

To modern readers, that may seem a great hurrah at tragic cost. Of course, no one expected it to be such a long and costly war. But even had they glimpsed the torturous road to Appomattox, to Lincoln and his confreres, American democracy was a providential and worthy ex-periment. To them, democracy carried a unique promise to better the lives of its people. Disunion would shatter it.

Only later, after four years of brutal war, did Lincoln and the North embrace abolition. In 1861, although the Republicans were an antislav-ery party, antislavery did not imply all that it would today. The issue then was not abolition by the federal government, which not even Republicans believed was permitted under the Constitution, but whether to tolerate the extension of slavery beyond the fifteen states where it existed. Republicans opposed extension, and so, probably, did most northerners. However, few northerners evinced much feeling for the plight of the Black slave. It's important to remember that prior to the Civil War, Blacks accounted for scarcely more than 1 percent of the northern population. Few northern whites had much to do with Blacks, slave or free, and even fewer supported abolition. They were opposed to slavery's extension mainly because they preferred their own societies to the slave societies in the Deep South. Whigs, and later Republicans, advocated a system of "free labor," which connoted not just the absence of slavery, but a positive culture of small farms, cottage industries, and independent craftsmen. Free laborites contrasted the economic system in Massachusetts or Pennsylvania with that in Georgia or South Carolina, and judged the former vastly superior *from the vantage point of whites.* Education and transportation were more available, land more widely owned, the public square more vibrant, the society more fluid.

Yankee apostles advocated free labor not, principally, on behalf of the Negro, but out of concern for the welfare of future *white* settlers. They wanted to extend the culture of free labor that, as they saw it, had given rise to New England villages dotted with churches and schoolhouses because white pioneers would fare better in such places. They envisioned the territories as a safety valve for urban crowding—and few settlers would go west if it meant competing with slave labor.

The proof that the well-being of the Negro was not on the minds of most northerners is that the so-called free states went out of their way to proscribe Blacks from voting and other expressions of citizenship, such as jury privileges. The northwest states of Ohio, Indiana, and Illinois, as well as Oregon, passed laws or constitutional provisions to bar Black immigration. In Indiana, Black suffrage was put to a state convention and defeated 122 to 1. Only the New England states, where few Black people actually lived, permitted Blacks an unrestricted franchise.

David Wilmot, a congressman from Pennsylvania, unabashedly framed the antiextension movement in terms of white self-interest. "The negro race already occupy enough of this fair continent," he told a rally in 1848. "Let us keep what remains for ourselves, and our children—for the emigrant that seeks our shores." Lyman Trumbull, an Illinois Democrat and later Republican, endorsed this racially exclusive vision of "free" labor, saying, "I want to have nothing to do, either with the free negro or the slave negro. We wish to settle the Territories with free white men." Northern politicians abhorred slavery, but they expressed little sympathy for the slave.

What northerners truly abhorred was the South's economic and social backwardness. The South was less urban, less educated, woefully underindustrialized. Although the slave states accounted for just under 40 percent of the population, they accounted for less than 6 percent of the country's pig iron and leather—even of its cotton and woolen textiles. Total capital invested in manufacturing—per capita—was more than three times higher north of the Mason-Dixon Line. Transportation was far more extensive. Ohio, although a bit smaller than Alabama, had twelve times as many railroad miles. Free laborites also frowned on the great wealth disparities (among whites), the listless quality of southern farms, and the insularity of its villages steeped, as Representative Stevens put it, in "mournful decay."

Frederick Law Olmsted, a young, Yale-educated farmer from Staten Island (soon to tackle the design of New York's Central Park) made three trips across the South in the early 1850s, traveling by steamboat, train, stagecoach, and horse. Olmsted's letters on his travels began to appear in the recently founded *New York Times* in 1854, and in book form two years later, and his descriptions of southern society appalled his well-bred readers. Olmsted's central conclusion was that the cotton cartel had done the southern people more harm than good. The mass of its citizens were impoverished and "their destitution is not just material . . . it is intellectual and it is moral." Olmsted described the city of Norfolk as "a dirty, low, ill-arranged town. . . . It has a single creditable public building. . . . No lyceum or public libraries, no public gardens, no galleries of art."

Olmsted was dismayed to find acre after acre of uncultivated land, testifying to an attitude of wasteful "complacency." Inefficiency abounded. At one stop, he encountered six mules and five Blacks tugging a stuck wagon. He also meticulously described the condition of the slaves. Those in the steamy pine barrens worked in "coarse gray gowns" and heavy shoes while an overseer rode among them, "carrying in his hand a raw-hide whip, constantly directing and encouraging them." The slaves slept in windowless huts, unfit for animals. But—Olmsted's point—their condition was inferior only by degree to that of poor whites. Olmsted described some of the latter in North Carolina leaning vacantly against the sides of their hovels as he passed—saying nothing, only blinking, "as if unable to withdraw their hands from their pockets" and shade their eyes from the sun.

The South was bountiful but impervious to change. In the decade before the war, cotton production jumped from 2.8 million bales to more than 4 million, and the unit value of its four million slaves doubled. This industry was centered in four hundred mostly contiguous counties of loamy delta that was essentially a monoculture. In the North, farmers sought to improve varieties of wheat and corn. They invested in farm tools and machinery. Southern planters felt no need to innovate. There was scarcely any patent activity in cotton and little investment in machines. They scarcely invested in capital goods. It was cheaper to breed Negroes.

Southern writers warned that the South's dependence on northern manufacturing was a serious liability. At conventions across the South, speakers exhorted southerners to develop industry and scientific know-how. *De Bow's Review*, founded in New Orleans by James D. B. De Bow, beseeched the South to diversify. "The suicidal indifference on the part of the public should awaken the anxiety of reflecting citizens," *De Bow's* lamented in 1855, "for the whole south is now almost slavishly dependent on the north for the very necessaries of life." But zealous defenders of plantation culture rejected the call to industrialize. "We do not want it," said a customs collector in Charleston. "We are satisfied with our slave labor." John F. H. Claiborne, a Mississippi newspaper editor, declared that the South's place was to remain "sedentary and agricultural . . . among the reminiscences of the past."

The South was hostile to the Whig-Republican agenda for a stronger central government. Federal improvements threatened to impose an unwanted modernity, ultimately jeopardizing slavery itself. As early as the 1830s, Nathaniel Macon, an influential North Carolina politician, warned his fellow planters that "if Congress can make canals, they can with more propriety emancipate." The planters also feared the government's effect on the white, nonslaveholding majority. Raising the sights of the poor would disturb the social order. Lincoln had characterized his program as one "to allow the humblest man an equal chance to get rich with everybody else." Southern planters had no such social aspirations.

To southern statesmen, higher education existed to provide a sheen of refinement to young men of privilege, not to lift up those below. According to Jefferson Davis, who had learned planting from his father and been staked to a cotton plantation by his brother, "Agriculture needs no teaching by Congress." Such attitudes were deeply inbred in the planters' culture. As early as 1671, William Berkeley, governor of Virginia and a rice and tobacco farmer, denounced public schools as leading to disobedience and heresy, proclaiming publicly, "I thank God there are no free schools nor printing [in Virginia], and I hope we shall not have these for a hundred years."

The planters sought to persuade poor whites that slavery was also to their benefit—and generally, they succeeded. In 1857, Hinton Rowan Helper, the son of a small slaveholder in North Carolina, created a tempest with his book *The Impending Crisis of the South*. Helper argued that a cotton "oligarchy" had rigged the economy to benefit only itself and that, in fact, nonslaveholders were veritable serfs in a sham democracy run by planters. This idea was too dangerous to be discussed. The book was banned in several southern states. The planters disseminated an alternate economic thesis, that slavery, as John C. Calhoun had affirmatively put it, was "a positive good," by which he meant an enlightened system of labor. The plantation system was said to be superior to the crowded, potentially volatile factories up north, because it had abolished the potential for class conflict.

Once the war started, inequality in the South loomed as a potentially serious problem. Jefferson Davis needed more than passive acquiescence from white commoners. He needed them to fight. Since only a quarter of the white population owned slaves, and only a twentieth were large slaveholders, Davis's ability to wage a war depended on his ability to persuade poor southerners that slavery, and thus the Confederacy, benefited *all* whites.

Lincoln genuinely believed in popular government; he believed that ordinary laborers could rise above their births. Shortly after his nomination, he provided a sketch of himself to the journalist John L. Scripps, so that Scripps could write a campaign biography of the man known to the country as the "rail splitter" and Honest Abe. Lincoln made his account a tale of self-improvement. His father, he wrote, had been "a wandering laboring boy, and grew up literally without education." Lincoln himself had only attended "A.B.C. schools" and only for "short periods"; his formal education "did not amount to one year."

Many more hours, he recalled, he was made to devote to laboring. At a very young age, "an axe [was] put into his hands . . . and he was almost constantly handling that most useful instrument"—save when he was conscripted by his father to plow or harvest on the family farm, or was hired out by his father to work elsewhere. It was not only the taxing work that Lincoln remembered, but the challenging physical circumstances that encumbered the family's moves to a succession of plots in Kentucky, Indiana, and finally Illinois, and the rutted and barely navigable roads that hindered travel and trade.

Lincoln's early life was an object lesson in making the most of slim opportunities: Abe breaking free of his overbearing father; settling in the pioneer village of New Salem, Illinois; buying goods on credit for a store that "winked out"; serving in the Black Hawk War, during which he failed to encounter hostile Indians but—"to his own surprize"—was elected captain of his volunteer company. Encouraged by his "great popularity," this amiable striver was elected to the state legislature, studied lawbooks on the side, and before he turned thirty was familiar to the lawyers traveling the Eighth Judicial Circuit and had become the leader of the Whigs in the Illinois House.

Lincoln culled from his remarkable rise the liberal philosophy that government should make every effort to expand opportunities for others. As he declared in a campaign speech in New Haven, "I want every man to have the chance . . . in which he can better his condition." His decision to preserve the Union was informed by a sincere commitment to government as the engine of popular progress. Democracy, so he believed, was the world's best hope. Improved transportation, access to credit, and help for the pioneering farmer were issues he carried with him to the White House.

But the project of making a Hamiltonian government was a collective enterprise. In the nineteenth century, the executive was at most a co-equal branch. Republicans in Congress were as much, often more, responsible for the financial and legislative specifics and even some of the direction. These Republicans did not plan on a war in 1861, but their social vision prepared them for one. Their ideal of a stronger and larger central government not only enabled them to harness the necessary resources to win the war, it encouraged them to do so in a way that helped to bring about a modern and dynamic industrial society.

Under the emergency of war, Lincoln's party formulated a new notion of what the federal government could do. They raised and spent unprecedented sums. They launched the country's first truly national currency, pushing aside an inchoate system of thousands of disparate bills issued in the states. They created a national banking system and the first credible program for federal taxation. They inserted the government into railroads, education, agriculture, immigration, the sciences, financial regulation. The war government interposed a visible (and at times dubious) hand into industry by enacting a series of high protective tariffs. Most important, the Lincoln government ended slavery.

All this crystallized a feeling absent in 1776. It made the country more than just a union of the states, closer to what Lincoln called it at Gettysburg—a "nation."

The southern model was the exact antithesis—states' rights and social domination by a planter aristocracy. It would take four years to sort out ancillary elements, such as the two sides' relative military and strategic capabilities as well as the South's grim, cussed determination, and to put these competing visions to a true test. But while the North hardly found its way easily or without trial and error, the Union was innovating and, after a slow start, prospering, while the South was simply consuming its resources. The North finished the war stronger and richer in every respect; the South was completely depleted. Unlike economies had pitted two disparate civilizations against each other; they also determined the result and shaped the America that was to emerge.

One

Two Crises

The sinews of war are unlimited money.

— Cicero

EIGHT WEEKS AFTER HIS ELECTION AS PRESIDENT—New Year's Eve, 1860—Abraham Lincoln telegraphed an invitation to the Ohio Republican Salmon P. Chase to visit him in Illinois. Lincoln was home in Springfield, assembling his cabinet. He would not take office for another two months, but the postelection interregnum was already momentous. On December 20, a convention in South Carolina had voted 169–0 to break from the Union; the other cotton states seemed likely to follow. Parallel to the secession crisis, the United States was suffering a financial crisis.

It was the troubled state of the finances that Lincoln considered as he wrote to Chase. He had already picked William Seward, his closest rival for the Republican nomination, for the State Department. Lincoln had in mind Chase, a former Ohio governor and senator and also a defeated presidential rival, for secretary of the Treasury. Even before Lincoln took office, the United States was teetering on the edge of insolvency. With America on the verge of disintegrating, trade had slackened, plunging the country into a recession. This had serious fiscal repercussions. Duties on foreign trade were the primary source of government revenue. The prospect of secession cooled business confidence considerably—especially as President James Buchanan pronounced that he was powerless to stop southern states from bolting. His view was by no means unique. None less than Horace Greeley editorialized in the *New York Daily Tribune,* the most widely read paper in the country, that the cotton states had a right to secede, adding for effect, "we insist on letting them go in peace." With secession seemingly a fait accompli, duty receipts plunged by about 25 percent.

Making matters worse, Buchanan's government had lived well above its means, leading to a doubling of the federal debt. More worrisome than the absolute level of the debt—$65 million—was that Buchanan's secretary of the Treasury, Howell Cobb, had failed to place a sufficient volume of bonds when the opportunity availed. Instead, Cobb was meeting government expenses by selling short-term notes. This was government on a credit card.

Cobb's inadequacy was surpassed only by his disloyalty. Word had spread on Wall Street that Cobb, a Georgia planter and slave owner, was mocking investors who had subscribed to loans for underwriting a government likely to be dismembered. This did not exactly inspire confidence in the Treasury.

Cobb confided to a friend, "I regard submission to Lincoln as utter & irretrievable ruin and I trust with all my heart that a United South may be brought to regard it in the same way." In the month following the election, as Lincoln prepared to assume the reins, the finances of the country remained in the hands of a putative traitor, and faith in government securities evaporated.

George Templeton Strong, a New York lawyer who kept close tabs on the market and recorded his impressions in a diary, tracked the steady deterioration on Wall Street. "The financial crisis is already beginning in Charleston and Mobile. . . . Their terrorists [southerners] are confiscating Northern property and repudiating Northern debts. . . . Stocks have fallen heavily today. Southern securities are waste paper in Wall Street. . . . A most gloomy day."

Northerners were in disbelief that southerners would willingly jeopardize the country's material wealth. "The people are not yet all fools, even in South Carolina," *The New York Times* sighed with palpable frustration. Dividing the country ran counter to the bedrock American story of a new people forging a common prosperity. Ohio congressman John Sherman gave voice to the fear that disunion would interrupt America's forward saga, rhetorically pleading, "Who shall possess this magnificent capital, with all its evidences of progress and civilization?"

Throughout November and December, financial pressures spread like an advance signal corps of sectional conflict. Southern merchants refused to honor their debts to the North, and banks both north and south began to totter. The merchant Lord & Taylor returned goods from Dixie and peddled them at fire-sale prices. Georgia's governor advised that northern assets simply be confiscated. This was not a trivial threat. Planters and merchants in the South owed an estimated $200 million to the North. It was not clear if they would pay. It was not clear they *could* pay.

Panicked over the loss of the cotton trade, northern merchants demanded concessions to keep the South in the Union. In liberal Boston, a well-tailored mob—anxious to mollify southern slave owners—stormed a gathering of abolitionists at Tremont Temple. In New York City, business leaders appointed a committee to go south and give assurances of solidarity. The merchants insisted that the Union do the compromising. As August Belmont, a Democratic financier in New York, put it, "The first steps have to be taken by the north."

Ominously for the incoming Lincoln administration, lenders were backing away from government loans. Europeans were bailing out of American paper. This created a serious problem, for Cobb's notes were now coming due. The Treasury lacked the funds to meet either its notes or the government payroll. Since its credit was so damaged, Cobb recommended that it forgo even trying to sell bonds and seek authorization from Congress for yet more notes. Having thus consigned the Treasury to a treadmill of short-term paper, on December 8—citing his "sense of duty" to the State of Georgia—Cobb abruptly resigned.

Congress now authorized $10 million in notes, to be sold at auction; however, only $1.8 million worth of bids were deemed acceptable, and these at a punishing interest of 12 percent (6 percent had been typical). Other bidders demanded as much as 36 percent, signifying a complete lack of confidence in American credit.

With an interest payment due January 1, Cobb's successor frantically turned to John J. Cisco, the assistant secretary of the Treasury in New York, who was close to the city's bankers. Cisco persuaded John A. Stevens, president of the Bank of Commerce, the largest bank in New York, to seek a loan from the city's financial titans. On the evening of December 27, 1860, Stevens and a lieutenant, Henry Vail, drove in horse and carriage to the homes of leading financiers, begging them to stave off a government default. Appeals were made to duty and patriotism, but the syndicate pledged a mere $1.5 million, also at 12 percent. As if to emphasize the banks' utter lack of faith in the Treasury, Vail stipulated that the proffered funds were to be used "expressly to meet interest on Government debt due first January."

For Lincoln, naming a Treasury secretary was crucial. But having won the presidency with just under 40 percent of the popular vote, he was constrained by politics. He bore a large debt to Pennsylvania, a crucial battleground state that he had swept thanks to Republican support for the tariff, the decisive issue in the iron and coal districts in the western parts of the state. Lincoln was mindful (at times overly) of the demands of patronage, and his convention managers had promised Treasury to Simon Cameron, a political hack who was one of the state's senators. When Lincoln telegraphed Chase, he did not quite have a job to offer.

Chase arrived in Springfield a few days later. Weary from riding four different railroads over two days, he booked a room and sent his card to Lincoln's home with the message that he would call at a convenient time. The President-elect, dispensing with formalities, immediately called on his guest, a friendly gesture that struck Chase as slightly undignified. Oddly, given their prominence in Republican circles, the two had never met. Lincoln seemed every bit the prairie lawyer, his clothes disheveled, his manner lighthearted. Chase was tall, striking, aloof. At the outset, Lincoln sheepishly confessed, "I have sent for you to ask whether you will accept the appointment of Secretary for the Treasury, without, however, being exactly prepared to offer it to you." For the second time, Chase's tender sensibilities were pricked.

The visit did not go poorly even if it did not go well. Chase and Lincoln got acquainted and did much talking. Chase stayed through Sunday and accompanied the Lincolns to church. He did not exactly loosen up, though his host prodded him with self-effacing humor. The two might have struck a rapport had they realized all they had in common: both reared on the frontier (although Chase had been born in New Hampshire) and both lawyers who had overcome difficult beginnings. Chase's lineage, unlike Lincoln's, was distinguished: an uncle was a senator and his father was a successful farmer and legislator and a friend of Daniel Webster. However, his father had died when Salmon was nine. His mother had sent him to live with another uncle, an episcopal bishop in Ohio—who by all accounts was a stern and cold guardian. Perhaps resentment over his fall from privilege had nurtured in Chase such an acute sensitivity to affronts.

Even for that era, the fifty-two-year-old Chase had suffered uncommonly bad luck. He had buried three wives as well as three children, and seemed to harbor a survivor's anguish. As if to protest an unjust fate, he lamented to a friend, "The lord hath dealt very bitterly with me." Lincoln, of course, knew sorrow as well. Before courting Mary Todd, he had been deeply smitten with Anne Rutledge, who died suddenly of typhoid. He had lost his mother when young, and later one of his sons. But in Lincoln, personal losses nurtured a stoic acceptance.

There were other differences. The pious Chase tended to see right and wrong in absolutes. Lincoln appreciated that political issues were often matters of degree. Once, during his single term in Congress, defending an internal improvement bill against a withering attack, Lincoln observed, "There are few things *wholly* evil, or *wholly* good. Almost everything, especially of government policy, is an inseparable compound of the two." Gradualism was in his nature.

Improbably, given the job he was preparing to offer, it was Lincoln—not Chase—who had spent his political life immersed in economic issues. As a westerner, his formative experiences were of growing up in country deprived of good roads and bereft of banks. He had never forgotten his family's painstaking journey to Illinois, when he had driven an oxen team across the muddy flats. The store where he had clerked, which subsequently failed, had schooled him to the social necessity for banks. "Money," Lincoln recognized, "is only valuable while in circulation"—a significant insight. Ever since his first campaign, for the Illinois legislature, at age twenty-three, he had advocated a federal bank to modernize the financial system and furnish the people with a workable currency.

During his four terms in the legislature, Lincoln had tirelessly supported the Whig program of government improvements. He had proclaimed that his "highest ambition" was to be the DeWitt Clinton (builder of the Erie Canal) of Illinois. His waterway and rail projects had resulted in overbuilding, and the state bank failed but—important for a future wartime president—his expansionist fiscal tendencies survived. Lincoln's goal for what the federal government could accomplish was essentially a national version of the activist program he had pushed in Illinois.

Above all, Lincoln was fixated on promoting prosperity. As an attorney earning $3000 a year when he ran for president ($98,000 in today's money), he rejected efforts to demonize the rich and foreswore "any war upon capital." His railroad clients, a big part of his law practice, steeled him against the common prejudice against the corporation. Lincoln was hardly an apologist for business—he also took cases against the rails, and he always identified with working people. The point is that his work sensitized him to the Whiggish idea that business was a constructive force, conducive to material progress. Once, when defending the Rock Island Bridge Company (the owner of the first bridge to span the Mississippi River) against a steamship owner who had collided with the bridge and wanted it taken down, Lincoln nearly cried, "Must the products of the boundless fertile country lying west of the river for all time be compelled to stop on the western bank?!" This was a plea not only for his client but for American prosperity.

Chase's economic knowledge was limited, and what views he held were, from the Republican point of view, suspect. Like most of the Republican leaders, Chase had started out as a Whig. But early in his career, he flipped, joined the Democrats, and adopted Jacksonian economics, essentially a set of prejudices against high finance and paper money, and against federal interventions. Chase's innate suspiciousness darkened his view of bankers, a crucial constituency for the Treasury. He also disdained the tariff—the standard position of Democrats, who were hostile to federal interference and protective of farming interests. It would be a simplification to call Chase's philosophy the opposite of Lincoln's, but not entirely wrong.

Despite their differences, each man saw much to admire. Chase scribbled in his diary after the visit, "He is a man to be depended upon." Expanding on this favorable impression, he confided to a colleague, "Our conversations were free & unreserved. All I saw & heard impressed me with a high idea of his ability, sincerity, fidelity to political principle & absolute integrity of character."

Lincoln had expected to be impressed. He was grateful that Chase, almost alone among Republican leaders, had come to Illinois in 1858 to support his bid for the Senate. And he was familiar with Chase's trailblazing work in antislavery. In the 1840s, Chase had written platforms for a pair of third parties, Liberty and Free Soil, whose doctrines were ultimately absorbed by the Republicans.

Lincoln's and Chase's experiences in antislavery were a mirror image of those in economics: Chase had been more engaged. Chase had attended Dartmouth and, thanks to his guardian uncle, studied the law under a U.S. attorney general. He had set up practice in Ohio, where he distinguished himself by compiling the three-volume *Ohio Statutes*.

Deeply religious, Chase was ripe for a crusade, and Ohio turned out to be a "volcanic fault line," as the modern-day writer and political operative Sidney Blumenthal aptly put it, in the slavery crisis. Northern Ohio, settled by New Englanders, was heavily antislavery, a reliable depot on the Underground Railroad. Cincinnati, in southern Ohio, where Chase established himself, had inherited the prejudices of nearby Kentucky. In 1836, a mob destroyed the printing press of an abolitionist publisher in Cincinnati named James Birney, tossing it into the river. When the mob went looking for Birney at a local hotel, Chase hurried to the entrance and blocked their path. Told he would pay for his actions, Chase coolly replied, "I can be found at any time."

Now engaged in antislavery, he took the case of an Ohio farmer accused of sheltering runaways from Kentucky. He argued incisively that the defendant was innocent because once a slave crossed into a free state he ceased to *be* a slave, not because the law of Ohio freed him, "*but because he continues to be a man*, and leaves behind him the law of force which made him a slave." His penetrating briefs, even if of limited success in antebellum courts, quickly became part of the canon of antislavery lawyers. Moreover, Chase buttressed his legal arguments with persuasive scholarship. Researching Jefferson's contribution to the 1787 Northwest Ordinance, which forbid slavery in the future Great Lakes states, he spread the gospel that the Founding Fathers had all along been opposed to slavery, and hoped for its extinction.

Lincoln, the son of pioneers born in western Virginia, and reared for his first seven years in Kentucky, a slave state, had a more intimate knowledge of southerners—which is to say, he recognized that abolitionism would tear the country apart. There is no doubt that slavery morally offended him. As a young legislator, he had made infrequent but courageous stands against slavery. In 1841, after a steamboat voyage to St. Louis, he was tormented by the sight of bound captives "strung together precisely like so many fish upon a trot-line . . . being separated forever from the scenes of their childhood, their friends, their fathers and mothers, and brothers and sisters." Lincoln could not, if he wished to have a political future in Illinois, advocate equal rights for Blacks, or even the right to vote. He refused to make a claim for social equality among the races. But Lincoln's commitment to opportunity led him to a politically salable antislavery that focused on the Black man as an economic actor. In the first of the seven Douglas debates, in Ottawa, Illinois, in 1858, Lincoln asserted of African Americans, "In the right to eat the bread, without leave of anybody else, which his own hand earns, *he is my equal and the equal of Judge Douglas, and the equal of every living man.*" Lincoln's brief for Black opportunity sprang from his general credo that the government's job was to help people get a foothold on the economic ladder. He returned to this theme in Hartford, in 1860, when he was preparing to run for president. "We think slavery is morally wrong," he asserted. "We *all* think it wrong." The next day, he pinpointed the immorality as economic. After asserting that everyone deserved the chance to rise, he pointedly added, *"And I believe a black man is entitled to it."*

Lincoln had been nominated largely because he was deemed to be safer than his rivals on the slavery issue (although his antislavery views were clear). Horace Greeley had spoken for many in Chicago, site of the Republican convention, when he had warned that voters would "only swallow a little Anti-slavery." The editor urged the party to sweeten its appeal by adopting economic planks—a tariff, river improvements, a Pacific railroad, homesteads—which it promptly did. For similar reasons, the Republican platform defended the right to slavery in the states, while firmly opposing its spread into the territories.

Although Chase would not have been nominated in any case, he viewed these efforts at conciliation with bitterness. Even in offering congratulations to Lincoln, Chase volunteered that he regretted not carrying the Ohio delegation, signaling he had not forgiven the convention for choosing Lincoln rather than himself. Chase's serious flaw lay not in his political economy but in his emotionally fragile character. If Lincoln saw this, he thought it offset by Chase's intelligence and diligence. Besides, Lincoln wanted balance in his cabinet: not North and South, which was beyond his reach, but Democrat and Whig. When Chase departed Springfield, the President-elect wrote Senator Trumbull that it was *necessary* for Chase to get Treasury due to his "ability, firmness and purity of character." But as no job was yet on offer, Chase loftily declined to confirm his interest.

As Lincoln pondered his choices for Treasury, Buchanan named John A. Dix, a pro-Union Democrat and retired army officer, to be his third Treasury secretary in a month (Cobb's replacement had also resigned). Dix found the Treasury in a state of chaos. "Public business had been neglected," his son, the later editor of his papers, recounted. "Letters from merchants and capitalists remained unanswered, and complaints from all parts of the country had been unheeded." The department's disarray was manifest in the unfinished condition of its building, the western expansion of which had been abruptly abandoned. Seen from Pennsylvania Avenue, where unused slabs and columns of stone lined the perimeter, the Treasury bore a faint resemblance to a Roman ruin.

Worse, the cash register was empty. The Treasury had a nominal balance of barely $2 million, and unpaid bills were mounting. Dix sold the notes authorized in December, and at a slightly lower interest rate of 10⅚ percent. But that hardly dispelled the crisis. The budget was awash in red ink and government employees were going without pay. Lincoln was said to have joked that Stephen A. Douglas, the Illinois Democrat he'd defeated for the presidency, had gotten the best of him by losing the election, for he, Lincoln, had been left to face "an empty Treasury and a great rebellion."

Dix was the first official to recognize the grave threat to the finances posed by secession. Of the 152 ports collecting duties, fully a third were located in the future Confederacy. Charleston's custom house was already in Rebel hands. And customs receipts were crucial. The United States had no authorization to tax its citizens, no government bank, no currency. The private banking system was atomized and weak, comprised of sixteen hundred banks, each answering to disparate state regulations. In a financial sense, there was no Union.

Dix immediately took preemptive steps to delay a collapse. He was residing in this interim at the White House as Buchanan's guest, but he seems to have acted on his own initiative. First, he advised Representative Sherman, the chair of the Ways and Means Committee, that he would need authorization for an additional $25 million in bonds. The War and Navy Departments were already delaying requisitions for lack of funds. Dix warned Sherman, "Time is very short."

When Dix got his bond approval, he made an unusual request—that the individual states use their funds to bolster the Treasury's credit. This was an extraordinary sign of the federal government's weakness. Nothing came of it.

Meanwhile, secession was spreading. Mississippi seceded on January 9, 1861. Over the next three weeks, it was followed by Florida, Alabama, Georgia, Louisiana, and Texas. Following South Carolina's lead, they seized federal forts, navy yards, arsenals, custom houses, and post offices. Federal collectors willingly surrendered receipts to state officials. Georgia raided the custom house and seized three ships in Savannah. Louisiana took possession of the mint and custom house, laying claim to $599,303 in gold and silver.

Dix was incensed that, as he put it, "no effort had been made by the government to secure its property." A particular concern for Dix were the revenue cutters, the fleet of small, armed Treasury craft that enforced customs and other maritime laws. During previous wars, these swift-moving vessels had been recommissioned by the navy into a nimble auxiliary fleet. Barely had he taken the job than Dix realized that revenue cutters in New Orleans, Mobile, and Galveston were vulnerable to seizure. On January 18, his fourth day at work, Dix sent a special agent south with orders to reprovision the three cutters and speed them to New York.

Eleven days later he received, from New Orleans, an alarming dispatch: Captain John Brushwood, the Virginian in command of the five-gun *Robert McClelland,* had refused his order. Dix immediately penned a second order, demanding Brushwood's arrest. Dix closed with a flourish: "If any one attempts to haul down the American flag, shoot him on the spot." Then, he handed the incendiary note to the telegraph clerk.

Dix's war telegram jolted the sleepwalking northern people. They suddenly awakened to the reality of conflict. Belmont, the Democratic Party financier, and previously an appeaser, wrote spirited letters to the southern governors, pleading restraint. "Secession," he warned, "means civil war." Southerners had confidently, if recklessly, interpreted north-ern efforts to conciliate to mean that business interests would prevent the North from ever employing force. Their miscalculation was simple: the South's leverage lay in the *threat* of secession. Once the South se-ceded, northerners would have no reason to placate.

In February, Rebel delegates gathered in Montgomery, Alabama, to set up a provisional government. Given that the Republicans did not advocate abolition, the southerners' logic was puzzling to many con-temporaries. Frederick Douglass said the South was overreacting. John Sherman's brother William, hastily departing the Louisiana military academy where he was superintendent, brusquely concluded, "Men here have ceased to reason." But an explicit reason was in fact tendered. The Republican strategy of squeezing slavery by preventing its expansion, forbidding it in federal territory and, potentially, banning the interstate slave trade would pop the bubble in the slave market. Southern slaves had a market value of $2.7 billion ($675 per man, woman, and captive child)—more than the combined capital invested in the country's rail-roads and manufacturing. This value would plummet if slavery were to be hemmed in, even if, for a while, the institution staggered on. As a Mississippian had written to Representative Justin Morrill of Vermont, "a panic of fear seized upon [the people]. It was an honest fear that their slave property, which is dearer to them than all other property, was endangered."

The South itself was divided. Outside of the cotton delta, no economic interest favored secession. In the western highlands and the commercial hubs of the Upper South, secessionists were a decided minority. In the northern slave states, soil depletion had narrowed the appeal of slaving and commerce was intertwined with the North.* Virginia, North Carolina, and Tennessee—three of the four most populous southern states—sent no delegates to Montgomery.

Even within the cotton belt, many people opposed, or perceived no self-interest in, secession. Georgia's governor, Joseph E. Brown, tried to rally small farmers under the banner of white solidarity. Slavery, he asserted, was "the poor man's best Government." But the planters did not consult the poor man. Alfred Aldrich, a South Carolina legislator, warned that "if the question must be referred back to the people . . . it will be an utter failure." Of the seven Rebel states, only Texas submitted secession to a popular vote. Otherwise, secession was decided by convention, and the conventions were stacked with planters. In Mississippi, half of the delegates to the state convention owned at least fifteen slaves. Montgomery was giving birth to revolution from above.

Former Treasury secretary Cobb, who had his hopes on the Confederate presidency, had to settle for the temporary post of president of the Provisional Congress. Jefferson Davis got the prize. He was inaugurated February 18, 1861, two weeks before Lincoln was scheduled to take the oath in Washington. In an unlikely coincidence, Davis had been born in 1808 in Kentucky, 125 miles west of where Lincoln would be born eight months later, in a log cabin, albeit more comfortable than the Lincolns'. The future presidents had little else in common. Davis's father, a Revolutionary War veteran, owned six slaves. The family moved when Jefferson was an infant to Louisiana, then to Mississippi, just as leadership in the South was shifting from tobacco to cotton. Given a boost by his successful attorney brother, Davis enrolled at West

---

* From 1840 to 1860, the slave population in the cotton belt nearly doubled; it barely budged in Virginia, Maryland, and Kentucky.

Point and became one of the wealthiest planters in Mississippi. He served with distinction in the Mexican War, a turning point in his career. Entering Congress, he became a messianic proponent of slavery, an institution he adjudged in the interest of the slaves—for its Christianizing influence. As early as 1848 he was predicting civil war. As a young man, Davis lost a wife and spent a biblical seven years in isolation. He also suffered from a painful neuralgia. He battled such travails with courage but was possessed of neither humor nor self-knowledge. He was hypersensitive to affronts. He had read deeply in American history and "revered" the U.S. Constitution, which, to his reading, assigned no powers to the federal government except for those that the states delegated to it.

The constitution framed in Montgomery made Davis's preferences explicit. It was not democracy to which the Confederates objected, but the Hamiltonian ideal of centralism. Federal involvement in the economy was off limits. Protective tariffs were barred, ditto outlays for internal improvements. The memorable goal in the preamble of the original Constitution—"to form a more perfect union"—was scotched, for union was not the goal. It was to be, literally, a confederation—"each state acting in its sovereign and independent character." If the object of Philadelphia had been government of the people via the limited instrumentality of federalism, in Montgomery the people spoke through the states. And this time, there was no euphemistic reference to "persons held to service." The framers retained the Bill of Rights but explicitly protected "the right of property in negro slaves."

According to Davis, not only was the Confederacy beyond revocation, it was "permanent." Yet Davis recognized that as an agricultural region, the South would be dependent on trade, thus on maintaining open ports. This would require a vigorous military. Foreseeing trouble, he confided to Varina, his wife, "We are without machinery, without means, and threatened by a powerful opposition." Davis saw the likelihood of war, but missed the irony that it would require a degree of centralism inconsistent with the Confederate ethos.

Even as the secessionists convened, another set of representatives, at a so-called peace convention in Washington, were drafting pro-slavery "compromises" to preserve the already shattered Union. Separately, Congress sent to the states an amendment to the U.S. Constitution barring Congress from *ever* interfering with a "domestic institution" within a state. Although largely symbolic, given that virtually no one claimed that the government had the power to abolish slavery, Representative Morrill anguished, "No vote I ever gave has caused me so much serious thought."*

Lincoln paid heed to the discussions to the limited, but important, extent of warning Republicans not to bend on the pivotal issue of extending slavery into the territories. On February 11, the day before his fifty-second birthday, he made a short, emotional address to a crowd of familiar faces at the Great Western Depot in Springfield and boarded an eastbound train.

En route to the nation's capital, Lincoln rode on twenty different railroads through the panoramic country he wouldn't see again. The trip gave him time to think. The Union as a coherent place—its texture and its physicality—was much in his mind. In Indiana, where Lincoln had grown to young manhood, nostalgia gave way to profound awe at the scope of development since he had left. "When I first came to the west, some 44 or 45 years ago," he told the gathered crowd, "at sundown you had completed a journey of some 30 miles which you had commenced at sunrise and thought you had done well. Now, only six hours have elapsed since I left my home in Illinois . . . and I find myself far from home surrounded by strangers." Still, he added meaningfully, "We are bound together."

In Cincinnati, the rail-splitter spoke in favor of homesteads. "The wild lands of the country should be distributed," he said, "so that every man should have the means." Hearing foreign accents in the crowd, he added that immigrants, too, should qualify. In Pittsburgh, he spoke to

---

* Once the Civil War began, this proposed amendment died.

the issue that had first claimed his attention in politics, and which Congress was now reconsidering—the tariff. Without belaboring the economic merits, Lincoln noted that a higher tariff was needed to meet the budget crisis, for "the treasury of the nation is in such a low condition."

During his journey, the tariff bill, sponsored by Morrill, sprang to life, given new possibility by the desertion of southern senators. The New York Chamber of Commerce protested that higher tariffs would make secession irrevocable. That ship had sailed, and as Greeley pointed out, the Republicans had been elected "with direct reference to giving us a tariff." Henry Carey, a quackish and ardently pro-tariff economist who had been read by Lincoln, even claimed that "protection [had] made Lincoln President."*

Morrill proposed a revenue tariff (a modestly higher duty on imports), not a sharply higher "protective" tariff to wall out foreign goods. But his bill was a gift to home industry. Among the items subject to an increased duty was wool. Not coincidentally, Vermont's 315,000 inhabitants tended a million sheep, whose spun fleece Morrill would now protect. The new tariff also rewarded Pennsylvania by raising duties on iron, with an eye toward prohibiting British imports. (The state's powerful congressman, Thaddeus Stevens, owned an iron forge). It is estimated that the average rate on dutiable imports jumped from 19 percent to 27 percent. Buchanan signed the Morrill tariff two days before leaving office.

When Lincoln arrived in New York, ships at the piers were decked in red, white, and blue, a patriotic homage that scarcely disguised the city's sullen mood. Wall Street had suffered a renewed market panic and a plunge in luxury imports such as silk. Capitalists wanted a reassuring word. For all his belief in enterprise, Lincoln was not about to let Wall Street hijack his agenda. After the panic in November, he had written

---

* Carey's claim is defensible. While Lincoln received 32 percent more votes than the Republican ticket had in 1856, in tariff-happy Pennsylvania the party's total rose 82 percent and in neighboring New Jersey it doubled. Without the thirty-one electoral votes he garnered from those two states, Lincoln would have fallen just short of a majority.

privately, "Nothing is to be gained by fawning around the '*respectable scoundrels*' who got it up." Now, on Lincoln's visit to lower Manhattan, William E. Dodge, a prominent merchant and metals dealer, implored the President-elect to save the country from a collision that would lead to bankruptcy and to grass growing in the monied streets. Lincoln said he would defend the Constitution; then, he impatiently added, "Let the grass grow where it may." At City Hall, when the southern-friendly Mayor Fernando Wood pleaded that commercial interests were endangered, Lincoln pledged to defend the Union—"not only the commercial interests of New York but the whole country."

On the anniversary of Washington's birth, Lincoln was in Philadelphia; he was wildly cheered at Independence Hall. The presidential party, now swelled to include Mary Todd Lincoln and staff, traveled on in two well-appointed cars, a reporter noting that Lincoln slept while his "peripatetic" wife was restlessly awake. In Harrisburg, Lincoln got word of potential assassins awaiting him in Baltimore. The President-elect and an armed companion rushed ahead that night. They entered an unguarded Washington at six a.m. He had been traveling for twelve days.

Lincoln planted himself at the Willard Hotel, a sprawling fixture of antebellum Washington, where he was deluged by job seekers. When Chase called, Lincoln was still undecided on whom to appoint to the bleeding Treasury. This added to the awkwardness between them. Two influential Pennsylvanians, Stevens and Carey, urged Lincoln to appoint Chase rather than their fellow Pennsylvanian, Cameron, who was known to be corrupt. But Lincoln was getting serious pushback from Seward, who threatened not to accept a position if Chase were included. Remarkably, Lincoln's cabinet was divided even before he took the oath.

"Everybody longing for the Inaugural," wrote Strong, and thirty thousand came to hear it. The address was lengthy and lawyerly and almost torturously fair-minded. Lincoln dismissed secession as "legally void" on the grounds that "perpetuity is implied, if not expressed, in the fundamental law of all nations." Yet he sought to reassure the South of his respect for the legal framework of slavery where it existed, awk-wardly pledging to "confirm to and abide by all those acts which stand unrepealed."

He blended two seemingly contradictory points: conciliation toward southerners and inflexibility where he was determined to draw the line. There would be no "invasion," no attempt to force "obnoxious strangers among the people." On the other hand, customs would be collected, federal property defended. For all its labored balance, the address was studded with happy phrases—the "mystic chords of memory," the "better angels of our nature." Lincoln's theme was that the angels favored union, a word he employed no fewer than twenty-one times. He regretted the destruction of the "national fabric," doubted there were a better or equal hope to American democracy. Drawing on his recent journey, he distilled the impracticality of division, the topographic wholeness of the country, its natural and economic linkages. "Physically speaking," he noted, "we cannot separate."

Two

Exigencies of War

In a war, money loses its value and human
beings themselves become the currency.

— ALAN MOOREHEAD

OTH THE NORTH AND SOUTH reckoned that if a war came,
money would be decisive. And each side had an economic strategy for winning. The South hoped to leverage its control over
the world's cotton supply to force an early peace. The North, more simply, hoped to convert its superior wealth into an overwhelming fighting
force. The idea was to starve the South into submission. Abraham Lincoln told a White House visitor that "resources" would decide the war;
the side where the money held out longest would win. Yet at the outset,
neither government had a financial system even marginally adequate to
support a major conflict.

On March 6, 1861, Lincoln's second day in the White House, he
resolved a critical uncertainty in his cabinet, nominating Salmon Chase
for the Treasury. Chase protested—nothing between the two came
easily—but he was promptly confirmed. Lincoln then asked for a report
on the state of the finances.

Chase had inauspicious news. The United States was advancing toward a major war with no currency and no ability, under the law, to
borrow in the currency that did exist (the notes of private banks). Chase

had no funds to tap, and since Congress did not meet until December, no way of obtaining funds. The United States had no taxing mechanism except for the tariff, and an armed conflict would surely have a depressing effect on trade. The government's financial system, in other words, resembled that of a primitive state. Chase's only scant resources were the unused portions of loans authorized under President Buchanan.

The immediate issue was Fort Sumter, the federal installation in Charleston harbor and the last significant Union property in the cotton states. Major Robert Anderson, its Kentuckian commanding officer, reported to Lincoln that Sumter could not be defended without at least twenty thousand troops. The entire U.S. army had approximately sixteen thousand men, scattered over scores of outposts. Without fresh supplies, Sumter's food would be gone in a matter of weeks. But the public (similar, as we have seen, to Lincoln's cabinet) did not consider secession a reason to go to war. Chase favored resupplying only after torturously reckoning that it would not lead to war anyway.

While Sumter hung in the balance, Lincoln was careful not to provoke the South. If war came, he wished not to be seen as having caused it. He let southern judgeships lie vacant; he did not attempt to retake forts and custom houses in Rebel hands. But the notion of ceding part of the government he had inherited sat poorly with the President. As he would say to Congress (histrionically referring to himself in the third person), "He felt that he had no moral right to shrink; nor even to count the chances of his own life, in what might follow."

Toward the end of March, the seventy-four-year-old Lieutenant General Winfield Scott, who had served under every president since Thomas Jefferson, recommended evacuating Sumter, and also Fort Pickens in Florida. But Lincoln had resolved not to give in. He reacted in the spirit of what he had written to Lyman Trumbull, after his election: "The tug has to come, & better now, than any time hereafter." The cabinet fell in line and (with the exception of Secretary of State William Seward) now supported reprovisioning. Lincoln gave the

South to know that the Union would supply food, not arms, as long as its ships weren't fired on.

But Jefferson Davis wanted the border states, most especially Virginia. He calculated that only bloodshed would rally them to the Confederacy. Sumter was the obvious target. Charleston was swarming with excited Rebels, including Edmund Ruffin, a seventh-generation Virginia planter, heir to his grandfather's slave plantation, who after the election had hastened to South Carolina. It is evidence of the South's boiling temper that Ruffin, an erudite farm journal editor credited with improving crop yields, had abandoned his earlier moderation and was seen about town in flowing white locks and blue cockade, beating the drum for secession. The sixty-six-year-old widower was accorded the honor of firing the first shot. "The shell struck the fort, at the northeast angle of the parapet," Ruffin mechanically recorded in his diary on April 12, 1861—hardly moved at having begun the Civil War.

The attack hit the North like a shock wave. Patriotic spirit was suddenly awakened. "The northern backbone is much stiffened already," George Templeton Strong wrote the day after Ruffin's parapet shot. Days later, the New Yorker spoke of the heightened awareness that accompanies moments of great purpose. "We are living," he said, "a month of common life every day. The national flag is flying everywhere!"

The North's purposes would evolve over the course of the war, but when Strong wrote those words, his compatriots were fighting to defend the "Union." Americans felt their sense of identity threatened. If the South went, there were fears of California going too, perhaps New York and a general dismemberment. Nationhood was not universal (neither the Italian nor the German peoples had unified). Strong felt "ashamed" to hail from a country that was "decomposing."

In truth, the United States had scarcely any national government to disintegrate. Outside of its small standing army, its military was decentralized. So-called volunteer (but in fact, paid) regiments would be organized under the control of individual states, led by often inexperienced politicians or other local dignitaries. Militia were funded by private

citizens, cities, and states on the uncertain expectation of federal reim-
bursement. The troops took an oath of allegiance to the United States,
but the line between federal and state responsibilities was blurred. Units
retained close affiliations with their hometowns. State governors had
the power to appoint generals and states competed with Washington to
sell bonds. William Dennison Jr., the governor of Ohio, virtually conducted his own foreign policy. Dennison cut off supplies to Kentucky
and imposed an information blackout by seizing telegraph lines—
actions at odds with Lincoln's desperate efforts to conciliate Kentucky,
lest it defect to the Confederacy. Then, like a feudal baron menacing a
neighboring duchy, the governor massed troops on the Ohio River facing Wheeling, Virginia, in an effort to spark a Unionist uprising in the
western part of that state. He did all this without federal direction.
Union tactics at this early stage of the war were highly improvised.

The supply chain was chaotic and impractically—almost absurdly—
decentralized. Each state furnished its own uniforms and equipment, of
varying quality and color. Governors turned to business cronies to supply their needs. New York State awarded a contract for twelve thousand
uniforms to a single manufacturer—Brooks Brothers—which misled
officials over the weight of its broadcloth. A New York City merchant,
months away from being elected mayor, won a lucrative contract for
himself to supply nearly five thousand blankets. The governor of Massachusetts was forced to send an agent to England to procure nineteen
thousand Enfield rifles. In the first few months of the war, individual
states and localities, often with legislative approval, raised $31 million
(nearly as much as the United States government had ever spent on the
military in a full year).

Yet from the first hour of fighting, the national government—
Lincoln especially—assumed a larger role. Two weeks after Sumter, in
response to sniper attacks on Union troops in Baltimore, the President
suspended the power of the courts to review arrests of civilians along
the vital rail corridor south of Philadelphia. In view of the constitutional provision for suspending habeas corpus "in Cases of Rebellion,"

Lincoln's actions were probably legal. But they represented a significant accretion of executive power. Over time, they would lead to sweeping arrests of, in the words of one scholar, both "real and imagined" threats, including a third of the Maryland General Assembly. The emergency of war was supplanting deep-seated traditions of limited government. Seward was to say, "I can touch a bell on my right hand and order the imprisonment of a citizen of New York; and no power on earth except the President can release them."

Without waiting for congressional approval, Lincoln called for seventy-five thousand volunteers to serve ninety days, a tenure that was to prove abjectly inadequate. In May, exercising his power as commander in chief, he asked for sixty thousand three-year enlistments. He also ordered Congress into emergency session to convene July 4, for the urgent task of raising funds.

In response to Lincoln's call, northern states rushed to fill troop quotas. Now that war could not be prevented, business leaders swiftly closed ranks and contributed funds. August Belmont, once the leader of the anti-Lincoln forces in New York, organized a regiment. A soldier in New York's Seventh, parading down Broadway before his transfer to the country's undefended capital, soon recalled, "It was worth a life, that march. Only one who passed, as we did, through that tempest of cheers, two miles long, can know the terrible enthusiasm of the occasion."

Antislavery, it was asserted, was not the North's reason for fighting. Edmund Clarence Stedman, a journalist and poet living in New York, insisted in a letter to his mother in Italy that the war "is not waged by abolitionists, is not the result of abolitionism." Yet some on either side sensed that slavery was unlikely to be unaffected. The *Atlantic Monthly* queried, rhetorically, "Are we indeed only fighting . . . for the control, by the interest of free labor or of slave-labor, of certain remaining national territories?" The implication was that the war was too great for a purpose so small.

Slavery, as Lincoln would say, was "somehow" at the heart of it, even if emancipation was not the overt goal. In late May, General Benjamin

Butler, the commander of the Union-held Fort Monroe, which guarded Chesapeake Bay, gave refuge to three Black runaways. When a Rebel colonel, approaching under a flag of truce, sought to reclaim his human property, Butler replied that the men were "contraband of war" and would not be returned to their master. Although Butler acted on his own, without authorization from Lincoln, his action signaled that the South's economic system would be at risk in the war, for other Blacks were sure to seek their freedom as well. Thaddeus Stevens, the brilliantly caustic progressive congressman, grasped that the North's full purposes could not yet be spoken or perhaps even imagined. "Our object," he said tartly, "is to subdue the rebels." Beyond that, he thundered, "Ask those who made the war what its object is. Do not ask us!"

The South had two purposes—to win its independence and to perpetuate slavery. Although it was generally assumed that these aims were mutually reinforcing, the war had put slavery in jeopardy. And a minority of southerners sensed that the peculiar institution would not survive a long war. "Slavery has to go, of course, and joy go with it," Mary Chesnut, a Charleston society hostess whose husband was an aide to Jefferson Davis, scribbled in her diary. Chesnut was just enough of an outsider to bear witness to the slow fraying of the genteel southern society that depended on slave labor. Unable to bear children (she was thirty-eight when the war began), her childless status rendered her something of a misfit in proper Charleston, with its rigorous social expectations. The war and her diary gave her a sense of purpose. She wrote of her fellow southerners, their rituals of courtship, and men in general with a jaundiced eye. In July, still early in the war, she recorded having attended a sumptuous dinner watered with white port wine at Jefferson Davis's table, while the President, the commander Robert E. Lee, and her husband were closeted in fervent discussion. Did Mary wonder about the gist of the conversation—and whether the distant war drums might come to envelop her and her well-heeled friends? All we know is that three weeks after the occasion at the Davises, she decided to wrap her gold and diamonds for a speedy escape—just in case one were needed. "I thought it injudicious to leave it lying loose," she explained. "So I have sewed it up in a belt, which I can wear upon an emergency." In contrast to Chesnut's careful taking of precautions, many of her compatriots seemed willfully—even exuberantly—deluded. LeRoy Pope Walker, the Confederate secretary of war, swaggeringly boasted that separation would be effected with so little violence that he would be able to wipe away any blood with his handkerchief.

The shelling of Fort Sumter put paid to the hope of avoiding war, but it enlarged the Confederacy to a plausibly viable scale. Once Lincoln called for troops, Virginia's delegates flipped and ratified an ordinance of secession. Arkansas, North Carolina, and Tennessee followed. The addition of these four states doubled the nonslave population of the Confederacy, which could not have lasted long without them. Virginia brought with it a navy yard, rifle works, and an industrial base that dwarfed those of the other southern states. Among Richmond's gifts was the Tredegar Iron Works, sitting astride the James River and linked to the interior by five railroads, the only facility in the South capable of producing heavy arms. Even with the added states, the South faced an enemy more than two times as great (twenty-two million people against nine million, Black and white), and an industrial base perhaps five times larger.

In Richmond, where the Confederacy established a "permanent" capital, and in Nashville and Raleigh, joyous crowds swarmed through the streets. A traveler in the South noted well-equipped troops "everywhere accompanied with cheers, smiles and bouquets." The general feeling was, they were "forever rid of the Union." As materials and supplies were diverted to the troops, a few shops in Charleston closed; a pair of spinster sisters in Virginia found they were "in want of many things," including flour. Such early tidings of economic strain were generally ignored. Their significance was not considered.

Davis's closest adviser, Judah Benjamin, injected a singular voice of realism into the southern cabinet. A short, heavyset shopkeeper's son, Benjamin was born in St. Croix in 1811 and raised in Charleston, a city reputed for religious tolerance. After attending Yale, he sought his fortune in the multicultural entrepôt of New Orleans. He married into a Creole family, trained in the law, and was highly successful at the bar. Yet Benjamin was convinced the future lay in sugar and purchased a three-hundred-acre plantation on the Mississippi River. The Jewish slaveholder was wittily derided by an Ohio politician as "an Israelite with Egyptian principles." President Millard Fillmore offered to appoint him to the Supreme Court, where he would have been the first Jewish associate justice, but Benjamin, who had just been elected to the U.S. Senate, declined the honor.

Benjamin was only lukewarm on secession, probably recognizing the risk, including to his thriving plantation. Davis recognized his brilliance and appointed him attorney general. Benjamin's shining black eyes and black beard were compelling to women, including to Varina Howell Davis, who wrote that her husband's consigliere had the peculiar quality of never being depressed. In fact, he was merely taciturn. Benjamin's wife, a local beauty, treated him with "callous indifference," eventually abandoning him to live in France. Benjamin's ability to bury disappointment suited the role of adviser. According to the diarist Mary Chesnut, who penetrated the highest circles of the Confederacy, "Everything Mr. Benjamin said, we listened to. . . . He is a Delphic oracle."

The oracle did not subscribe to the exuberance prevailing in Richmond. As a lawyer, even when handling a difficult case, Benjamin had habitually addressed the court as if it were impossible for him to lose. He knew the penalty for bluffing and the South, he felt, was bluffing with too much at stake. Early in 1861, Benjamin proposed that the South hedge its risk by purchasing 100,000 bales, or even more, of cotton and ship it to England, where it could be stockpiled and gradually sold to finance the war. This eminently sensible plan would have bankrolled the government for a long while. But the suggestion that the Confederacy faced a protracted struggle, much less a financial deficit, was laughed off by others in Davis's inner circle. With the region basking in prosperity, economic want was hard to imagine. Statesmen in Richmond indulged in fantastical debates, such as whether the Confederacy should admit *northerly* states, such as Pennsylvania, when (as they expected) such became disenchanted with the Union. In any case, with regard to cotton, a counterplan emerged: the South should withhold its cotton and force England and France to their collective knees. The origin of the strategy is unknown, but Davis embraced it. Robert Toombs, plucked from Georgia to be Confederate secretary of state, insisted to a dissatisfied southerner that England and France depended *absolutely* on the cotton trade. In England, the textile industry provided employment for close to a half million workers, with more than three-quarters of the cotton derived from the American South. Thus, the theory took wing that when the great mill cities of England and France ran out of fiber, their industries would buckle, and the war would be made untenable.

Exactly how a depression in Lancashire or Lyon would force a ceasefire in America was never spelled out, a stunning oversight given the reliance the South put on it. But the strategy was clear. Halting cotton exports would foster intolerable economic pressure in Europe, even a "revolution." According to Alexander Stephens, the new government's vice president, cotton was to be "the tremendous lever by which we can work our destiny."

Psychologically, the strategy smacked of a delusion that could only have sprung from a cloistered cocoon such as Dixie. In economic terms, the plan was naïve. The South was the world's low-cost cotton producer, but not its only one. "Monopolists are always blind," the *Atlantic Monthly* surmised that spring. The Confederacy heard, through an envoy in Thebes, confirmation of that truism from Mohamed Sa'id Pasha, de facto ruler of Egypt, who patiently explained, "If your people stop the cotton supply for Europe, my people will have to grow more and furnish them."

Unfortunately for Richmond, the harvest of 1860 had produced a record crop, satisfying England's needs for the moment. The South's embargo, which took practical effect against the crop of 1861, was not legislated, but it was informally adhered to, and some southern governors issued proclamations forbidding shipments. Exports plunged to a tiny fraction of the prior year's. By one tally, shipments from New Orleans plummeted 99 percent, from 1.5 million bales in the 1860 crop to a mere 11,000 in the next.

The surest sign that suspending the cotton trade was contrary to the South's economic interests was that the North was pursuing the same goal. Days into the war, Edward Bates, Lincoln's attorney general, proposed an economic blockade, arguing that strangulating the South could win the war without the shedding of blood. As he outlined in a memorandum to the cabinet, cotton and sugar were the South's only staples: "They *must sell* or sink into poverty and ruin." On April 19, 1861, Lincoln answered with a blockade of southern ports.

Lincoln's policy was not immediately enforceable. The small Union navy could scarcely patrol thirty-five hundred miles of southern coastline. It was flawed in another respect, as Thaddeus Stevens hastened to explain to the President. "Nations do not blockade their *own* ports," Stevens noted. A blockade, in short, was a tacit recognition of southern independence. The problem was more than merely semantic. According to international law, it was legal for third-party nations to circumvent a blockade as long as it wasn't tightly maintained. By contrast, had Lincoln proclaimed that southern ports were *closed*, potential trading partners would have been greatly discouraged, because trading with a closed port constituted smuggling—a just cause for war. Lincoln had acted precipitously, without understanding the issues. But this did not detract from the irony that while the North sought to deprive the world of southern cotton, the job was actually being accomplished by the South itself. Catastrophically for the Confederacy, the forgone revenue amounted to well over one hundred million dollars.

D avis sent three representatives to London and Paris to enlist the
Europeans' help in ending the war. But with surplus cotton piled
in warehouses on the continent, their bargaining power was limited.
And Davis's commissioners were ill chosen. The leader was an Alabama planter and ardent secessionist named William Lowndes Yancey,
who seemed to think the Confederacy's mere request for recognition
would be sufficient. He and the other commissioners obtained an audience with the British foreign secretary, Lord Russell, who, however,
was careful to receive them as private citizens, not official envoys. Yancey's attempt to persuade the British of the beneficence of slavery was
particularly unwise. Parliament had abolished slavery within the British
Empire a generation earlier, and the British public, when it thought
about slavery, generally opposed it. Nor did it help that Stephens, the
Confederate vice president, publicly renounced Thomas Jefferson's assertion that all men were created equal. As Stephens put it in a speech
in Savannah, "Our new Government is founded on exactly the opposite
ideas." Such cavalier remarks, when published in England, could only
inflame Victorian sensibilities. Charles Darwin observed in private correspondence, "I have not seen or heard of a soul who is not with the
North."

Yet British opinion soon turned. The prime culprit was the Morrill
tariff. Having adopted free trade for itself in the 1840s, Britain viewed
the tariffs of other nations as both unenlightened and offensive. That its
former colonies would restrict British exports was simply unpardonable.
Even though seven states had seceded by the time the bill was enacted,
many Britons assumed that the Morrill tariff had caused the Civil War,
which inclined them to side with the South.* Among the free-trade

---

* "Morrill caused the War" must be regarded as somewhere between a gross overstatement and conspiracy theory. Southerners certainly objected to the tariff, but they objected to many other Union
policies as well.

Britishers was Charles Dickens, who published savagely antitariff articles in his literary magazine, *All the Year Round*. The prime minister, Lord Palmerston, neatly summarized England's conflicted sentiments, telling Charles Francis Adams Sr., the U.S. envoy to London, "We do not like slavery but we want cotton and we dislike very much your Morrill tariff."

Both North and South needed Europe because it had the hard currency that each side hoped to borrow. Foreign loans would pay a political dividend as well. Secretary of the Treasury Chase knew that floating bonds in England would help to align its political sympathies with the Union. The South hoped to elicit recognition, after which it counted on Europe to act as a peacemaker. Edmund Ruffin's diary was peppered with forecasts that England, perhaps in concert with France, "will not long delay" formal recognition of the Confederacy. Conversely, Strong worried in mid-May, "We are a little uneasy today about the position England may take."

Strong could not know that at that moment, on the advice of her ministers, Queen Victoria was issuing a proclamation declaring British neutrality. By recognizing North and South as belligerents, it entitled the Confederacy (as well as the United States) to purchase arms and contract for loans in neutral states—even to purchase ships that were not plainly equipped for war. The royal edict tended, in other words, to level the field—greatly offending the North. When the news reached America, Strong reacted with dismay, writing, "Disappointment and exasperation are universal and deep." In London, Adams delivered to Lord Russell an ominous-sounding message from Seward that recognition of the Confederacy would mean an end to friendly relations with the United States. By presenting the message verbally, Adams conveyed the appropriate sternness without confronting Russell with Seward's written words, which would have required an equally stern reply. Lincoln was fortunate to have Adams representing him. The son and grandson of previous American envoys (each also a U.S. president), he understood Britain as well as any living American. Gently warned by

Adams, Lord Russell did not close off his options, but he did nothing to further antagonize the North.

France was more eager to get involved. The court of Emperor Napoleon III felt an aristocratic kinship with Richmond and greatly objected to the Union blockade. The French hoped to mediate a cease-fire—which would fix the respective armies in place and probably ensure the South's independence. But Paris was leery of acting alone. For the moment, it mimicked London by declaring itself neutral. Meanwhile, rival diplomats conducted a shadow war on the continent. Confederate agents pressed their case in foreign salons and churned out pro-southern publicity. Meanwhile, Belmont, the American agent of the Rothschilds, the European banking family, wrote to well-placed contacts in Britain, emphasizing that the entire North—Democrats included—supported the war effort. Belmont's Union fervor carried weight since, prewar, he had been a leading Douglas supporter. Employing a stinging analogy, Belmont inquired of Lionel Nathan de Rothschild, a member of Parliament, how England would feel if America were to show support for a rebellion in Ireland. In June 1861, Belmont sailed for Europe, tasked by Chase to scope out interest in Union loans. This was more tactful than dispatching a Treasury official, which would risk a formal rejection. Belmont pleaded with the London Rothschilds, who had bankrolled the British during the Napoleonic Wars, not to subscribe to Confederate loans, assuring them they were a foolish investment.

While the two sides parried each other in Europe, each faced a dire need for revenue. Richmond's raids on federal custom houses had furnished it with a onetime bounty of $6 million. It also sold $15 million in bonds, capitalizing on the spirit of its people, who parted with the gold they had laid away in banks and lockboxes. However, the South needed much more to pay for arms overseas. Its momentary prosperity fell far short of resolving its need for recurring income. And its biggest revenue source, slave-grown cotton, was not getting to market.

Davis's secretary of the Treasury was Christopher Gustavus Memminger, who had been brought to America as an infant from Württemberg and raised, after his mother's early death, in an orphanage in Charleston. Memminger was a lawyer with a useful expertise in banking. After the bond issue, he requested a modest tariff, which the Confederate Congress promptly enacted. Even in the South, laissez-faire took a backseat to the exigencies of war. But the tariff was pitiably small and never produced much income.

Having tried both taxes and bonds, Memminger now turned to a third option: issuing short-term notes. These were readily accepted and circulated in the South like money. Memminger was well aware of the potential for such issues to become habit-forming and inflationary. Indeed, before secession, he had earned a reputation as a fierce advocate of sound money. Memminger could not have imagined how little of that reputation would survive the war. As of June 1861, the disciplined, German-born secretary reassuringly reported that he had limited note issuance to just $1.1 million.

Chase faced the same options as Memminger—indeed, as any sovereign. He could tax, he could borrow, or he could print money. The financial narrative of the war was essentially the story of how the opposing camps chose from among these alternatives. Each of the three financing options affected the potency of the other two. A government that taxed, and thus collected income, saw its credit enhanced and was more able to borrow. A government that overran the printing press would ruin its credit.

Chase had less experience in finance than Memminger, and the Treasury he inherited was essentially bankrupt. The government did not have sufficient funds even to pay for stationery. Even Chase's physical circumstances were challenged, with the Fifth Massachusetts Regiment drilling on the Treasury grounds and a parade of office seekers besieging him inside the building, which remained unfinished. Chase, however, was a dogged and disciplined worker, often staying at the Treasury late into the night. "Certainly," he confided, "I never worked nearly so hard." Late in March 1861, he sold some of the bonds that had been authorized under Buchanan. Bankers offered a good rate. Wall Street was buoyant and enveloped in its own patriotic mist.

Once the shooting started, bond prices plunged (meaning that lenders demanded a higher interest rate to compensate for the heightened risk). As the Union commenced to spend on a never imagined scale, it became clear that the fiscal demands of the war would gallop ahead of the government's revenues. Troops had to be fed, clothed, and equipped. During Chase's first three months, the Treasury collected just shy of $6 million, while spending four times as much.

Chase could close the gap only by borrowing, but borrowing how? Antebellum law* put him at a disadvantage—that is, it forbid him from borrowing anything but gold, silver, or Treasury notes, a Jacksonian restriction intended to insulate the Treasury from speculative bank notes. The Treasury was insulated, all right—and unable to deal in the country's principal currency. Sensibly, Chase turned to John Cisco, the veteran assistant Treasury secretary in New York, who had cobbled together the emergency loan the previous winter. Cisco, a Democrat, had offered his resignation, but Chase invited him to Washington, putting him up at his home, at Sixth and E Streets. They talked into the night, Cisco agreeing to stay on the job and advising Chase to salt away a war chest by selling long-term bonds. This was sound advice, for long-term financing would relieve the Treasury of the insistent pressure for cash.

But Chase was reluctant to borrow long term. He had the classic debtor's disease of thinking he could get through a present emergency by borrowing short, counting on long-term rates to fall to more attractive levels later. Also, he imagined that the war would be short. In April, he placed $3 million in bonds and rather more—about $5 million—in short-term notes. (The latter sum was worth about $154 million in 2021 dollars.) In May, he had to borrow again. Contrary to his expectations, markets were not more friendly; in fact, the loan

---

* The Independent Treasury Act of 1846.

wouldn't sell. Chase pleaded with a group of Wall Street financiers, including Belmont, Moses Taylor, who controlled City Bank of New York (later Citibank) and John Jacob Astor, to round up buyers. This followed the pattern of earlier American wars, in which the government had relied on a small circle of elite bankers. With the bankers' help, Chase managed to sell $7.3 million in bonds, although the bidders insisted on hefty discounts. Chase could have sold more but he rejected bids that he thought too cheap. His motivation was admirable—not wanting the public to be overcharged—but his rigidity did not sit well with bankers. Chase presumed that *he* should be able to dictate the terms and that the bankers, out of patriotism, would meekly submit. In fact, governments were considered poor credit risks. The bankers expected to be compensated. By June, the Treasury's credit had deteriorated so much that even its short-term paper was being discounted. As he fell behind on paying bills, Chase had to lean on government suppliers to accept short-term notes, which at least paid 6 percent interest and, in any case, were all he had to give.

This was finance on a shoestring—or rather, a tightrope, strung over a monetary abyss. Chase reassured himself that since the war would end soon, the harm could not be great. On the other hand, his fellow Ohioan, the budding politician James Garfield, foresaw "a long and sanguinary war." The point is not that Chase guessed incorrectly—many others did as well—but that finance is always the art of planning for the worst.

Lincoln provided none of the counsel Chase would have welcomed. The President was busy organizing the army and its generals (a task that was to burden him nearly the entire war). He was greatly concerned with the government's fiscal position, as evidenced, early, when he implored Chase to crack down on any tariff evaders. But he trusted his Treasury secretary to manage the details. The ultrasensitive Chase misinterpreted Lincoln's confidence in him as signaling a lack of interest. Craving Lincoln's approval, he boasted that he had obtained a lower interest rate than his predecessor, transparently adding: the "decided improvement in finances will gratify you." When no word of presidential gratification arrived, Chase, in late April, frantically urged Lincoln to protect the custom house in Baltimore from the city's active Rebels. Chase could not resist offering the unsolicited and disparaging judgment that "as yet we have accomplished nothing but the destruction of our own property." He made matters worse by enclosing an editorial by Henry Raymond of *The New York Times,* an erstwhile Lincoln supporter, accusing the government of having fallen well short of the South's "ardor and action" by prosecuting the war with "incompetence and indifference." Chase could not help adding, "It has too much truth in it." Lincoln was a master at disregarding such little pinpricks, but the Treasury secretary was already formulating the corrosive idea that his partnership with the President would function better were their roles reversed.

Left to his own, Chase grew resentful of the bankers. When they declined to lend at advantageous rates, he was quick to suspect a "concerted effort" against him. This was his old Jacksonian suspicion of financiers. His instincts steered him toward a more democratic ideal— bypassing Wall Street and selling loans directly to "the people." He nursed a romantic vision of placing bonds with, as it were, "a farmer at the country crossroads." He tried to sell bonds to the public, but the Treasury had no organization for administering a popular loan—much less for finding farmers willing to lend. Perhaps for this reason, Chase came to closely consult with a like-minded banker, the Philadelphian Jay Cooke.

Cooke was an American archetype—a born promoter and proselytizer. He was exceptionally cunning in pursuit of his self-interest, and brash in the way that has led many financiers to grief. But he glimpsed earlier than his peers that American investors, if led by the right shepherd, could become a decisive factor in the war. Reared in Ohio by a lawyer father involved in canal building, Cooke came naturally to the Whig belief in progress. He was born in 1821, just as the Erie Canal went into service and the steamboat graced Lake Erie. The optimism of that time never left him. Episcopalian duty was important to Cooke, but the church did not lead him to contemplation. He was not a critical thinker, according to an early biographer, but possessed a retentive mind that soaked up practical details like a sponge.

In antebellum days, the leading financiers tended to be merchants. Cooke began his career in a transitional moment, when merchants were facing challenges from purely financial players—that is, banks. He was hired at age eighteen by Clark, Dodge & Company, a Philadelphia concern that traded in financial assets such as gold and bank notes. Eventually, the firm broadened into investment banking. Critically, Cooke cut his teeth distributing a Mexican war loan as well as a bond for the Republic of Texas, demonstrating the latent potential in banking to the government. "I have got on the right side of fortune in Philadelphia," wrote the optimistic junior partner. Alas, the firm overextended; during the Panic of 1857, it collapsed.

Cooke, who still possessed a "fair fortune," landed on his feet. In January 1861, as war drums threatened, he set up Jay Cooke & Co. in a brownstone on South Third Street in Philadelphia. Thirty-nine and ambitious, Cooke viewed the incoming Lincoln administration with beady eyes. His brother, Henry, was a publisher in Ohio who had earlier promoted the careers of both John Sherman and Salmon Chase. When Chase landed such an influential job, it seemed the answer to Jay Cooke's dreams. "I see Chase is in the Treasury and now what is to be done?" he wrote to Henry. Not waiting for an answer, he directed Henry to cultivate his powerful contact—and to think about selling his newspapers and launching a banking operation in Washington, "whereby we can all safely make some Cash."

Meanwhile, Cooke participated in the government loans of both April and May and began to offer counsel to Chase—gratefully received perhaps because Cooke, too, was an outsider to the New York financial world. Chase offered Cooke a Treasury job, but Cooke had a more enterprising role in mind. He hopefully suggested that Chase might recruit him as a "secret agent." Nothing came of the hint, but Cooke was cultivating a friendship with the secretary, opening his home to Chase and to his two daughters—a great comfort to a solitary widower who was often traveling. In June 1861, Cooke marketed $3 million in war bonds for Pennsylvania, using newspapers to advertise the loan throughout the state. Despite predictions that Pennsylvania would have to settle for a discount, Cooke sold the bonds at par. Although he ludicrously overbilled his feat as "an achievement as great or greater as Napoleon's crossing the Alps," it was notable that he had circumvented bankers and sold the bonds via agents, to a wider public. This was an early attempt at investment banking. He was careful to let Chase know.

Chase was impressed, particularly as his own efforts to raise capital were failing. At the end of June, he confessed to John Stevens, head of the Bank of Commerce, "The Treasury is now rather hard run." This was a blunt request for charity. "It would be a great comfort," Chase went on, "if you New York gentlemen could be patriotic enough to take some Five Millions of the Treasury Notes." The bankers agreed to lend—but this time only for sixty days. Six months earlier, the treasonous Howell Cobb had quit after failing to get the Treasury off of the opium of short-term credit. The loyal Chase was in the same position.

Three

Ways and Means

All taxes are odious.

—THADDEUS STEVENS

L INCOLN HAD SUMMONED CONGRESS into emergency session in
July to raise both men and money. Of these, the financial burden
was seen to be tougher. The United States had fought in other
wars, and in this one, the North had a great edge in manpower. But even
if the war lasted only a short while, as most people (including the President) thought it would, the Union's financial needs dwarfed any prior
expense or governmental undertaking. Its demands for the first year
were six times as much as its previous annual budget. As John Sherman
was to recall, "We were physically strong but financially weak."

While Lincoln faced these challenges, he also had in mind a broader
purpose—to cohere the Union into a stronger whole. He needed to
strengthen the Union to fight the war, but also to serve the ends for
which, as a young man, he had entered politics. To Lincoln, the Union
had been conceived to assure the people with "liberties" more fully than
could the individual States, and ever since his apprenticeship as a Whig,
he had defined those liberties in economic terms. The test of a democracy was that it provide the people a better shot at advancing on the

economic ladder. He told Congress, on July 4, 1861, that the *chief purpose* of the Union, and thus of the war, was to promote opportunity and a fair chance to all.

> This is essentially a People's contest. On the side of the Union, it is a struggle for maintaining in the world, that form, and substance of government, whose leading object is, to elevate the condition of men—to lift artificial weights from all shoulders—to clear the paths of laudable pursuit for all—to afford all, an unfettered start, and a fair chance, in the race of life.

Lincoln referred to the Union forty times, but three times in his address he referred to the United States as something new: a "nation." A union was composed of many parts; a nation was integral. It was one country.

The President's address was delivered in written form—a tradition established by Thomas Jefferson, who thought appearing before Congress in person was too monarchial, redolent of the British king. For Lincoln, respect for Congress was more than merely symbolic. The Whigs had always had a parliamentary tilt. Their great leaders— Lincoln's heroes, Webster and Clay—had been senators. The chief executives of Lincoln's time had been weak. Not one of the eight presidents preceding Lincoln had been reelected. On his journey to Washington before his inauguration, Lincoln had emphasized his Whig lineage, telling a crowd in Pittsburgh, "My political education strongly inclines me against a very free use . . . by the Executive, to control the legislation of the country." Although Lincoln noted that the Constitution permitted the president to "recommend measures which he may think proper," and also to veto improper ones, he referred to presidential influence over legislation in a highly pejorative manner, as "external bias."

This did not mean Lincoln was timid. In his first four months, he stretched the limits of presidential authority, suspending habeas corpus and expanding the regular army and navy without the approval of Congress.* The thought that he might have overreached troubled him, though he believed that the urgency of the war required it. In a private talk with his friend Senator Trumbull of Illinois, Lincoln volunteered that he did not know of any law to authorize some things he had done, but he thought that to save the Constitution and the laws generally, "it might be better to do some illegal acts, rather than suffer all to be overthrown."

The President aired his dilemma in his message to Congress, wondering, philosophically, whether republics were doomed by the need to permit so much liberty as to make them vulnerable to rebellion. As he put it: "Is there, in all republics, this inherent, and fatal weakness?" While allowing that some of his own actions may have lacked a legal basis, he had acted, he said, "under what appeared to be a popular demand, and a public necessity; trusting, then as now, that Congress would readily ratify them." He added that Congress had the "competency" to ratify his measures; in other words, he had acted, he hoped, as Congress's agent.

This legislative bias set the tone for Lincoln's administration. With the significant exception of his constitutional role as commander in chief of the armed forces, and the partial exception of slavery policy, where he and Congress alternated in playing leading roles, Lincoln allowed Congress to set the blueprint. It was in Congress—comfortably Republican and ideologically Whiggish—where major legislation was crafted and often conceived. Lincoln guided the broad policy.

This was especially true in the crucial area of government finance. The President's message to Congress did not mention taxes, tariffs, or loans; it merely requested that Congress appropriate the vast sum of $400 million. Knowing that this was many times any previous budget, Lincoln tried to soften the blow with a historical grace note. The requested sum, he noted, was less per person than the total debt accumu-

---

* Under Article I, Section 8, of the Constitution, only Congress had the power "to raise and support Armies" and to "provide and maintain a Navy"—and even Congress could not do so for longer than two years.

lated during the Revolutionary War. "Surely," he added, "each man has as strong a motive *now*, to *preserve* our liberties, as each had *then*, to *establish* them."

Nonetheless, $400 million was a frightful sum—far more than the United States had spent on any previous war—indeed, adjusting for inflation, the first-year budget was more than the country had spent on three previous wars combined. America had no obvious way of raising such a sum. To put it mildly, Salmon Chase faced an overwhelming task. The Treasury secretary was so daunted, he trimmed Lincoln's request by a fifth, asking Congress, over the coming year, for only $320 million—still more than Buchanan had spent over his entire term.

Aware that Americans loathed taxation, Chase asked that Congress raise only a quarter of his requested budget, or $80 million, through taxes—still, this was double the previous year's revenues. He put the rest on borrowing. This formula was not unreasonable. No government could defray such extraordinary expenses from current income. They would have to be paid off over time, like a family's mortgage.

Nonetheless, Chase might have been bolder. His forecast of the government's needs would turn out to be well short of the mark. As with a man wary of delivering bad news, overoptimism would be a chronic problem. There was, in addition, a touch of arrogance in the precision of Chase's spending forecast—$318.5 million. It was false precision, or rather, foolish precision.

Thaddeus Stevens, chairman of the Ways and Means Committee in the House (John Sherman, the previous chair, had moved to the Senate), spearheaded legislation to give Chase the necessary borrowing authority. By virtue of the committee's control over revenue, Stevens was a powerful figure. He moved fast, and he was not above using his tongue to intimidate members who stood in his way. Once, when a representative was pacing the floor while presenting an argument, the dyspeptic Stevens called out: "Do you expect to collect *mileage* for that speech?" His sarcasm aside, the Pennsylvania congressman was the rare loyalist who did not underestimate the South or the difficulty of the contest. He predicted "a protracted and bloody war," and he was willing to say that "many thousand valuable lives will be lost, and that millions of money will be expended." Within three days of being appointed chair, Stevens reported a bill authorizing $250 million in loans. The next day, when the bill went to the House, Stevens suspended the floor rules and limited debate to one hour. That was July 10. One week later, the bill was signed. The legislation gave Chase authority to sell twenty-year bonds as well as three-year notes. These, of course, would have to be marketed to investors. In addition, Chase was authorized to sell $50 million of Treasury notes in small denominations. These last were a very different sort of security. They did not pay interest, but were re-deemable for coin by the assistant treasurers in New York, Philadelphia, and Boston. Since the notes were redeemable on demand, they were called "demand notes." In practical terms, Chase did not expect ordi-nary citizens to travel to a government bureau; his idea was that people would accept the notes with the expectation of circulating them, like money. Without fully realizing it, Congress had authorized Chase to experiment with a new currency. In finance, necessity is the mother of improvisation.

Chase immediately used some of the demand notes to pay wages to the army and navy, to government clerks and—to demonstrate their reliability—to himself. The secretary promised to exercise the "greatest care," lest overissuance of this monetary candy lead to "degradation" (i.e., inflation). But the demand notes made bankers nervous. They were well aware that Britain's resort to paper money during the Napo-leonic Wars had resulted in rampant inflation, and that American "Continentals" issued in the Revolutionary War had become practically worthless. The bankers feared that Chase's notes would dilute the value of the various bank notes (the country's primary currency)—which, of course, were issued by the banks themselves.

Chase hoped to dampen inflationary pressure by placing loans over-seas for hard currency (the British pound sterling was considered as good as gold). But the reception in London was chilly. When Belmont, the American banker, called on Lord Palmerston, the prime minister skeptically inquired: Where did Chase expect to raise such enormous sums? The English press betrayed a rather too obvious pleasure in the strains suffered by their American cousins. The *Economist* said smugly, "It is utterly out of the question, in our judgment, that the Americans can obtain, either at home or in Europe, any thing like the extravagant sums they are asking, for Europe *won't* lend them; America *cannot.*" Belmont then traveled to France and the German-speaking states but heard the same discouraging response.

Belmont's reports took time to reach America (on both sides of the Atlantic, ships were awaited at dockside for late editions of the press).* But worse news struck a mere twenty-five miles from the capital. Lincoln had been under tremendous pressure to mount an offensive before the expiration of ninety-day troops. One of the most relentless critics was Horace Greeley. The mercurial publisher, having abandoned his previous pacific tendencies, tried to goad the President into launching an attack. Heedless of the unready state of the North's volunteers, Greeley's *New York Daily Tribune* published the incendiary headline FORWARD TO RICHMOND. More such stories followed, some of them aimed directly at Lincoln.

On July 21, with the President's reluctant authorization, raw recruits under the command of Brigadier General Irvin McDowell struck the Confederate army at a stream in northern Virginia known as Bull Run. So confident were the brass of victory that Lieutenant General Winfield Scott sent passes to congressmen, forty dollars for a carriage ride to observe the battle. Senator Sherman, who recently had shepherded the loan bill through the Senate, rode horseback over a pontoon bridge at Georgetown, continuing past Arlington until he heard distant cannon fire. He asked a sentinel if the sound had been present all day. Came the reply: "Yes, but not so loud as now."

---

* Cyrus W. Field, a paper baron, had laid a transatlantic telegraph cable in 1858, but weeks after communications began the cable failed. During the war, Field was at work on a new cable.

The battle became a rout. The sorriest part was that Union discipline collapsed. As if to dramatize the disorganized state of the government, enlisted men and officers broke ranks in a panicked retreat. Benjamin Brown French, Lincoln's commissioner of public buildings, described the scene the next morning: soldiers "straggling into the city . . . some without guns—some with two. Some barefooted, some bareheaded, & all with a doleful story of defeat."

The debacle exposed the Union army as laden with patronage and way too decentralized. Unfamiliar uniforms led (on both sides) to tragic instances of friendly fire. The battle also exposed the sorrowful state of wartime medical facilities. George Templeton Strong had helped to found the United States Sanitary Commission, a private relief agency to help sick and wounded soldiers. Hastening to Washington after Bull Run, the refined Strong was shocked by the unsanitary medical conditions. He found the Potomac "hotter and more detestable than ever," aggravated by a "plague of flies and mosquitoes." The underlying ill, thought Strong, lay in "our volunteer system with its elected colonels and its political major-generals." His condemnation of the military's medical department—"Its superannuated officials are paralyzed by the routine habits" of dealing with a threadbare organization—summarized the underdeveloped state of the federal government itself.

Bull Run spurred immediate changes in the army. George B. McClellan, a dashing, thirty-four-year-old soldier acclaimed for his gallantry in the Mexican War, was summoned by Lincoln to replace McDowell as head of the renamed Army of the Potomac. Lincoln signed a pair of bills that, in total, called for a million three-year volunteers. These actions were mirrored by similar measures in the Confederacy.

Financial reinforcements were equally urgent. With expenses on the Union side surpassing $1 million a day, Chase's budget was effectively busted two weeks after it had been proposed. Jacob W. Schuckers, Chase's personal secretary and his eventual biographer, said later that Bull Run shattered the hope of a quick or inexpensive war. But if this was so, Chase did not think to revise his request. The Treasury secretary put the burden of revenue collection where it had always been—on the tariff. Congress had raised duties in the Morrill tariff, but with trade depressed due to the war, duty receipts had plunged. The only option was to raise them again. Chase's purpose was to furnish revenue, as distinct from protecting domestic goods (thus, he sought duties on coffee and tea, which were not grown domestically, as well as sharply higher duties on sugar, liquor, and luxuries). Nonetheless, Henry Carey, the tariff evangelist who had assisted Morrill, carefully sought to loosen Chase from his free-trade moorings. Carey's vehicle was one of his disciples, William Elder, who, he suggested to Chase, would make a splendid hire at Treasury. At first, the appointment was to have been temporary, but Elder made himself useful. Soon, he was ensconced in the Treasury's "Tariff region" as a key assistant. The nimble aide drafted legislation while secretly reporting on his progress to Carey. The hardpressed Chase, grateful for the help of Carey's protégé, began to turn to Carey for advice, which the economist happily provided. Covering all bases, Carey also lobbied Lincoln. By July, Morrill reported to Carey that Chase had been won over.

Stevens had no trouble getting a tariff bill through the Ways and Means Committee, whose members included a banker, an ironmaster, a coal transporter, and only two free traders—both from farm states. Opposition on the floor was considerable. Congressmen who had breezily voted to let the government borrow were not so quick to let it tax. Stevens had to force the measure through, by a vote of 82–48. There was also opposition in the Senate, including from Charles Sumner, the worldly (and ardently antislavery) Bostonian, who worried about the effect of the tariff on relations with Britain. William Pitt Fessenden, the irascible chair of the Senate Finance Committee, only just cajoled a majority, 22–18. Together with the Morrill tariff, the war tariff of August 1861 nearly doubled previous duties. In five months of secession and war, Republicans had accomplished more for protection than Whig politicking had over decades.

But tariffs were only part of the story. To reach the $80 million projected for federal revenue, "internal" taxes (levied on homegrown goods and services) were needed as well. America's antipathy to internal taxes cannot be overstated—indeed, antitax agitation had been the original spark that lit the American Revolution, and it had remained a flash point ever since.

Chase was only too familiar with this history. He asked Congress for only $20 million of internal taxes—really a fraction of what he needed. He didn't even specify what sort of internal taxes he had in mind, preferring to leave such unpleasant details to Congress. Stevens, fearless as usual, was willing to go beyond Chase's request, arguing that revenue was necessary for its own sake and—a subtler point—to bolster faith in the government's credit. When his colleagues objected, Stevens mockingly observed that if taxes were disagreeable, the Rebels had forced on the Union "many disagreeable things. It is unpleasant to send your sons and your brethren to be slaughtered in this unholy war." He also made a more trenchant point. After the Revolutionary War, the failure to create a federal taxing authority had undone the original American framework, the Articles of Confederation, by leaving the government, financially, at the mercy of the states. "It was mainly on account of this great defect that a convention was called, and the present Constitution framed," Stevens said. Thus he identified the need for a vigorous taxing power as central to the origins of the government that the North, now, was fighting to defend. His colleagues were unmoved.

The most obvious source of internal revenue was a so-called direct tax (levied on states in direct proportion to their populations). Stevens's committee drafted a direct tax modeled on that of Albert Gallatin, who had been secretary of the Treasury under Jefferson and James Madison. Western legislators opposed it, for the simple reason that the west was closer to the east in *population* than it was in wealth. Direct taxes were typically assessed on land. The west had plenty of land. What the west had less of, and what it wanted taxed, were liquid assets: stocks, bonds, and mortgages. Representative Schuyler Colfax of Indiana led the charge. Anticipating future progressives, Colfax said, "I cannot go home and tell my constituents that I voted for a bill that would allow a man, a millionaire, who has put his entire property into stock, to be exempt, while a farmer who lives by his side must pay a tax."

Once again, Stevens worked fast. The direct tax was reduced (though not eliminated). Since something had to be conjured in its stead, Congress designed what was, for America, a new sort of tax: on income. Britain had experimented with an income tax, but few other nations had. Congress set the U.S. rate at a modest 3 percent of incomes above eight hundred dollars. Few households reached that threshold, but a "millionaire" stock trader would, which was the point. Stevens conceded he had "no way of ascertaining" how much revenue the novel tax would raise. Certainly, Congress had no income data to go on. Yet, with typical insouciance, Stevens declared that he would vote for it regardless of what his constituents thought. His goal was to win the war.

The income tax in America thus was born as the lesser of evils. Signed into law, along with the tariff, on August 5, it was regarded as provisional. Congress was scheduled to reconvene in December, before the tax was due, when it was expected that Congress would craft a more permanent tax (and establish a means for collecting it). Nonetheless, it was the country's first income tax, an extension of federal authority that eventually would redefine the average citizen's interactions with government.* Congress adjourned the next day.

Chase now had the difficult task of marketing the loans that Congress had authorized. Needing advice, he turned to Jay Cooke. The Philadelphia financier had prepared the ground in July with a letter, at turns both brazen and obsequious, offering to start a Washington banking house, in partnership with a more experienced firm, Drexel & Co., to handle the Treasury's bond sales. "We propose to give personal attention to the business at Washn. with a view of making our services

---

* August 5, 1861, is still considered a red-letter date in the history of American taxation. Modern Tea Partiers have savaged the legislation online (e.g., "Blame Abraham Lincoln for the nation's first national income tax").

valuable to yourself during the coming 3 or 4 years," Cooke began. That Cooke had in mind profiting from his and his brother Henry's increasingly cozy relationship with the Treasury secretary cannot be doubted, for he wrote that the operation would trust in "those natural advantages that would legitimately and honestly flow towards us from your personal friendship." He added unctuously, as if his willingness to do business with the government were itself a great favor, "we could not be expected to leave our comfortable homes and positions here without some great inducement & we state frankly that . . . we would . . . if we succeeded expect a fair commission from the Treasury." One may wonder that Cooke's oily self-promotion did not put Chase off. But the Philadelphian appealed to the secretary's vanity by cloaking his appeal in patriotism. And Chase must have sensed that Cooke possessed a battlefield vigor that other bankers lacked.

The plan that Chase worked out, in consultation with Cooke, was to enlist the banks to lend $150 million, in gold, in three installments of $50 million each. In theory, the loans would be financed by selling three-year notes to the public (if such sales did not occur, the banks would be stuck with the notes). Brightening the prospects for bank participation was the fact that banks in the east were flush with cash, buoyed by a familiar cycle of crop failures in Europe and bountiful grain exports.

Negotiations with the bankers were held in New York, but Chase had to go a roundabout route, via Annapolis on the Eastern Shore, to avoid capture by the Rebel general P. G. T. Beauregard. In Philadelphia, Chase was joined by Cooke and the two traveled on together, arriving in New York August 9.

The leader of the "Associated Banks," as the group was styled, was City Bank's Moses Taylor. Modern readers may think of banks as huge bureaucracies whose shareholders are diffuse and anonymous. In 1861, banks were small and entrepreneurial. Taylor had started out as a merchant, importing Cuban sugar, and branched into banking. Typically for bankers of his time, he was City's largest shareholder. When Chase sought bank loans, he was asking the bankers to lend their personal assets, and those of a close circle of investors.

The bankers were daunted by the scale of Chase's requests and uneasy about the Treasury's skimpy tax base. Chase responded to their concerns with his customary brittleness. He tended to view negotiations less as a business discussion than as a test of principle. He insisted that the Treasury's notes be valued at full price (par), as if any lower price would be disrespectful.

The most contentious issue concerned the form of the bridge loan. Chase wanted to be paid in gold, delivered to the sub-Treasury, as the department's branches in New York and elsewhere were known. Until recently, this archaic and cumbersome form of exchange was the only one permitted. But Congress, in its brief session, had amended the law precisely to give the Treasury flexibility. The bankers now preferred to lend in the form of bank checks. This more nimble method would let the Treasury draw on accounts at the banks, while the actual gold remained in their vaults. The banks in New York, Boston, and Philadelphia had gold reserves of just over $60 million. To commit to loan the Treasury $50 million would severely constrict their liquidity. The banks would need to hope that each gold coin they loaned was spent and then quickly redeposited, in time for the next loan—a precarious arrangement. In finance as in engineering, the most stable structures are those with a margin for error.

Chase would have none of it. Paper money had a history of depreciation, and in Chase, true to his Jacksonian roots, suspicion of paper was second nature. Not only did he deny that Congress had amended the law as others interpreted it had, he threatened the banks that if they didn't lend, he would issue his own paper—the Treasury demand notes—in such quantities, if necessary, to drive the price of breakfast, he said, to $1000. This aroused the bankers' gravest fear: inflation. Beneath all the jousting, the bankers and Chase were fighting over the definition of money. There was not enough specie (gold or silver coin) to satisfy a modern war economy. Clearly, paper would be needed. The banks preferred that it consist of bank notes—their own IOUs. Chase was emotionally attached to gold, but if paper were needed, he preferred that it be a government issue, that is, Treasury notes.

For all his woodenness, there was something persuasive about Chase. Some of the bankers resisted, but City's Taylor felt the group could not refuse the government in such an emergency. In mid-August, the bankers agreed to guarantee the first $50 million—in gold, at the sub-Treasury door. Five million would be delivered immediately, the rest as needed, in return for the three-year Treasury notes. New York bankers pledged $35 million, Boston's and Philadelphia's the remainder. (Western bankers had also been invited, but could not safely travel east.) Thus, the loans followed the pattern of earlier wars, in which the government relied on a small coterie of eastern financiers. This cozy arrangement was likely to be strained if the war persisted.

Chase did not get all he wanted. The notes carried a hefty interest rate, 7.3 percent. Thus, they were dubbed seven-thirties. And the banks refused to commit to the second and third $50 million installments, stipulating that the additional tranches would be lent, at their option, later. They were overwhelmed as it was by the first loan. At a celebratory dinner at the Willard Hotel in Washington, John Stevens, the Bank of Commerce president, warned the Treasury secretary not to count on the banks for more. "Mr. Chase," he said, "you have received from the Associated Banks the vast sum of $50 million. We earnestly hope that will be sufficient to end the war." Ultimately, it was to be spent sixty times over.

Lincoln had to be pleased with Chase's resourcefulness. At the same time, the Treasury secretary could not resist sowing small seeds of dissatisfaction with the chief. Writing to Belmont in Europe, he characterized the Bull Run defeat as "more an Administration than a military disaster," a none too subtle dig at Lincoln. Chase then excused his only partial success on the financial front on the grounds that he did not have "an Emperor Napoleon to sustain me."

As if he harbored Napoleonic fantasies himself, Chase was also carrying on a private correspondence with several Union generals, including William Tecumseh Sherman, George McClellan, and John C. Frémont, freely dispensing military advice irrespective of whether it concurred with policy. Lincoln courted Chase's opinions on military matters because his war secretary, Simon Cameron, was weak, and because he respected the Ohioan's expertise on neighboring Kentucky, a constant worry for the President. Still, in Chase's frequent and often pandering letters to the generals there was an odor of private alliance, of mildly conspiratorial engagement.

Chase diverged from Lincoln most consequentially over the latter's measured approach on slavery. The backdrop for Chase's frustration, and that of the so-called Radical Republicans, was the failure of either the administration or Congress to make abolition a formal goal of the war. Four days after Bull Run, Congress took a decided step backward, approving (over Thaddeus Stevens's withering objection) the Crittenden Resolution, named for a Kentucky congressman and slave owner. Its Senate sponsor was also a border-state slave owner, Andrew Johnson. The Crittenden Resolution explicitly affirmed that the war "is not waged . . . for any purpose of . . . interfering with the rights or established institutions of those [Confederate] States." Thus, Congress—by an overwhelming majority—went out of its way to reassure wavering border states as well as war mothers that their sons' lives were not being risked for the freedom of the Negro. This surely comported with the wishes of most white northerners.

Chase was extremely unhappy with Congress's reactionary declaration. He was hardly mollified when, in August, Congress passed the Confiscation Act, legalizing the seizure of southern property (including slaves) employed in the rebellion. What he and Thaddeus Stevens regretted was that the Confiscation Act was toothless. In contrast, Lincoln took note that even this weak antislavery measure received virtually no support from Democrats or border-state representatives. What the President distilled, in other words, was that an explicit antislavery policy would further divide the Union, which he sought to avoid at all costs.

Slaves had begun to self-emancipate, fleeing singly and in small groups to Union lines. The ad hoc nature of these escapes did not involve a question of policy and, therefore, did not require a response from Lincoln. What General Frémont did on August 30, 1861, was different. With the State of Missouri wracked by guerrilla fighting, Frémont declared martial law and authorized the confiscation of Rebel property and emancipation of Rebel slaves. Various westerners, including Lincoln's oldest friend, Joshua Speed, warned the President that Frémont's order would weaken Kentucky's hard-won loyalty to the Union. Lincoln did not want that, and he did not want to yield control of slavery policy to a general. After asking Frémont to modify the order, on September 11 Lincoln revoked it. This was the beginning of a split between Republican moderates and Radicals—with the latter rebuking Lincoln for his gradualist approach. "How many times," lamented James Russell Lowell, the Cambridge poet and scion of a textile fortune, "are we to save Kentucky and lose our self-respect?"

Chase was greatly disturbed by Lincoln's reversal of Frémont's order. He understood slavery as a profound moral wrong, and he had less patience for the pragmatic aspects of policy making. Chase corresponded with a coterie of antislavery crusaders, including Joseph Medill, the editor of the *Chicago Daily Tribune*, who (unfairly) likened Lincoln's order to the worst deeds of his White House predecessor, James Buchanan. Chase tried to keep a foot in both camps. He avoided any direct contravention of the President, but his feelings were with the Radicals.

Nearly as vexing as slavery, and more in Chase's turf, was the problem of regulating trade with Union-occupied areas of the South. In a normal war, commerce with the enemy would be strictly prohibited. It was not so simple in the Civil War. As military lines shifted, southern communities came under Union control. Neither Chase nor Lincoln had any wish to punish the people in those areas. As Chase noted, "The exchange of provisions and supplies [arms excepted] would be more useful than injurious." The problem was, trading in occupied areas would inevitably risk supplying cash or goods to the Rebels. The issue was controversial within the cabinet, but Lincoln, typically, was concerned with the broader effects on morale.

At the President's direction, the Treasury secretary wrote a bill, enacted in July, authorizing the government to issue "such trading licenses as the public good might require." Lincoln had several motivations for this surprising policy. Bringing cotton out of the South would allow the Union to ease the shortage on the continent—and therefore, relax the pressure on England and France to get involved in the war. It would relieve mill owners in New England, who were equally desperate for raw material. Finally, it would garner gold for the Treasury. And Lincoln seems to have rationalized that the northern blockade was not effective, anyway. Two weeks after the legislation, when his longtime friend Orville Browning dined at the White House, Lincoln said, as the Illinois senator recorded in his diary, that the foreign powers were "determined to have the cotton crop as soon as it matured—that our coast was so extensive that we could not make the blockade of all the Ports effectual."

Nonetheless, the President's policy offered an economic lifeline to the enemy. For a region desperately in need of supplies and cash, this was no small matter. Cotton remained the South's biggest crop,* but little of it was getting to market (thanks to the South's self-imposed embargo). Scarcity had elevated the price of cotton on the New York wharf to 15⅝ cents a pound, up from a prewar level of only 10 ¼ cents. This furnished a powerful incentive for traders on either side to ship cotton north. Chase's mandate was to write the rules governing the issuing of licenses, and then award them to traders who were not involved

---

* According to the nineteenth-century authority B. F. Nourse of Boston, the 1861 cotton harvest, though down from the prewar level of 4.9 million bales, was still a robust 3.8 million.

with the enemy. This required threading a needle of improbably small eye. The Treasury secretary, perhaps underestimating the challenge, adopted a spirited maxim, "Let commerce follow the flag." As the flag moved to and fro on the battlefields, northern traders became increasingly entangled with the Confederacy.

Early in August, Chase worked out a plan to borrow the northern banks' gold. The key was to sell the seven-thirties notes, and thus replenish the banks' stockpile, so they could commit to the second gold loan and then the third. No banking syndicate existed, but with Cooke's encouragement, Chase recruited marketing agents across the country. For a while, the chain-letter scheme worked. Chase hired nearly 150 agents, typically local bank presidents, working on commission.

Cooke was the most resourceful agent. He advertised in a score of newspapers and arranged for "editorial" copy every bit as favorable as paid publicity. One of his selling points was that at the 7.3 percent rate of interest, a buyer of a hundred-dollar note would collect two cents in interest every day. To a public new to investing, this was an exciting prospect. Cooke's description of investors lining up at his office on South Third Street was catnip for Chase, who had been so eager to market to "the people." Cooke reported that investors of all stripes— "clergy, draymen, merchants, girls, boys"—clamored for Chase's notes "almost with tears in their eyes." Even when crafting this treacly report, Cooke could not help smacking his lips. "We bagged over $70,000 as the day's work," he gloated. In a September 13 article penned for the *Philadelphia Inquirer*, Cooke planted the singular idea that investors in Treasury securities were as vital to the Union as infantry. "In the last six days about 800 persons have subscribed"—nearly as many, he noted, as in a regiment. "Their charge of money bags is quite as efficient as a charge of bayonets." Cooke also conceived of a fund-raising technique later beloved by the organizers of charity drives—publishing the names of willing subscribers.

When Cooke blew through his advertising budget, Chase refused to up his allowance, but the banker kept spending, cutting into his profits but burnishing their relationship. Cooke sold $4.2 million of the first tranche of notes—that is, a quarter of the total sold by the other 147 agents combined. His commission was a paltry $6680, a trifling fee for raising such a sum.

The problem was that the Treasury spent the money as fast as Chase could borrow it. As expenses outpaced Chase's forecasts, he had to resort to issuing demand notes to government suppliers. But not everybody wanted these notes. Some railroads, and some hotels, refused them. James Gallatin, a banker in New York and the son of Jefferson's Treasury secretary, ordered his tellers to turn them away. Chase and the banks were engaged in a sub-rosa war over which paper should properly circulate—over the character of money.

In late September 1861, Chase journeyed to New York to ask the banks for the second $50 million. By now, relations between him and the bankers were fraying. The first note issue had not been a complete success; the banks had been stuck with $5 million of the seven-thirties that the public didn't want. Gallatin demanded that for the second loan, the Treasury accept the banks' paper rather than their coin. Chase, who felt the bankers were being selfish, again refused. But the bankers' ability to sustain the government in gold was increasingly in doubt. From August 17 to September 21, the New York banks saw their specie balance plummet by $13 million. And after the debacle at Bull Run, the Union army's expenses had mushroomed. An Ohio colleague of Chase begged him to accept the banks' paper. It would draw more lenders into the market, and there was simply not enough gold to finance what was rapidly becoming a wider war.

However, Chase was the beneficiary of a small miracle. As the Treasury accelerated its spending, the government's gold was delivered to suppliers, who redeposited in banks. So quickly did the Treasury spend that the banks' balances began to recover. As long as the gold moved through each stage in near perfect synchrony, a precarious balance obtained. On October 1, the bankers wearily agreed to Chase's demands and guaranteed the second $50 million, once again in gold. However, the public had little interest in more seven-thirties, nor did it have the gold to buy them, and the public sale was abandoned. This meant the entire second tranche fell on the banks. By late October, Chase's chain-letter operation was seriously strained.

In the South, Bull Run had produced an opposite and uplifting effect. Victory was followed by confident assurances that recognition from Britain was at hand. *The Times* of London fanned the enthusiasm, opining that southern independence was inevitable. British leaders were, in truth, worried about a cotton shortage, but they also remained determined to avoid a conflict with the United States.

While the South waited for Lord Palmerston and his cabinet to act, the Confederacy faced considerable difficulties raising funds. Unlike the Union, Richmond did not have the option of bank financing. Southern banks had nothing to offer but paper, having suspended gold redemptions months earlier. Treasury Secretary Memminger begged the Confederate Congress for a tax. Despite its laissez-faire bent, Congress agreed. But the tax, enacted in August 1861, was minuscule, only 0.5 percent on real estate and other property. And there was serious doubt whether even this paltry tax would be collected. Enforcement was left to the states (as was typical in America before the war), but only South Carolina made a serious effort to collect it. Some states paid the tax by printing notes, a game of paper for paper. Others did not even bother to assess the property rolls, on which collection was to have been based. The southern people were willing to part with blood; with treasure, not so much.

Memminger then sought a long-term loan, pledging war bonds for twenty years at 8 percent. Knowing that the people's appetite for a loan was flagging, he conceived a clever scheme, allowing farmers to subscribe to the bonds by pledging crops. He dubbed this the "produce

loan." At first, produce bonds sold briskly, but after a while, sales petered out. Cotton planters preferred to hold their cotton for cash. The
produce loan was effectively a form of barter. What Memminger needed
was a currency. Congress obliged, authorizing $100 million in short-
term notes. Issuing notes violated the secretary's conservative instincts,
but he had no alternative. The Confederacy had no hard cash, no real
taxing system, and its only marketable assets (cotton and other crops)
were marooned in the South. The new notes were optimistically designed to mature six months after the adoption of a peace treaty between Richmond and the United States. Until then, they circulated like
money.

Sensing that finance would be a vital front in the war, northerners
followed the South's distress with consummate interest. Information
about money and prices in both North and South circulated freely on
either side. Newspaper subscribers in Richmond were well versed with
Salmon Chase's strategies, and the northern press scoured the southern
papers for signs of Richmond's financial woes. *The New York Times*
judged, perhaps not unfairly, that "the Confederates feel the need of a
Salmon P. Chase" even more than they did additional troops.

An ominous sign emerged shortly after the Rebel Congress authorized the additional notes: inflation. Mary Chesnut observed that
"Lawrence," a Negro man she and her husband held as a slave, "asks for
twice as much money now when he goes to buy things." This was an
exaggeration (expressing exasperation with slaves was a staple of southern parlors). However, the inflation was real. By September, prices had
risen an estimated 25 percent since the start of the war. This had a
gradual, but discomfiting effect on the psychology of the people.

As prices rose, the government needed more money to pay for the
war, and so Richmond authorized, and Memminger issued, another
$50 million in notes. Richmond even issued postage stamps to supple-
ment the circulation of small bills. Yet more bills only pushed prices
higher. The *Nashville-Louisville Courier* noted, "The currency question
perplexes us exceedingly."

By the fall of 1861, newspapers were reporting not only rising prices but periodic shortages. Commodities such as leather were in urgent demand; butter, reported the *Richmond Examiner*, was "very scarce"; of coffee, there was "none in market." Edmund Ruffin, the Virginia diarist, grumbled at having to pay "enormous prices for all the ordinary necessaries & comforts of life." Of course, Ruffin was lucky that he could afford the "comforts"; he even exchanged five hundred dollars of his depreciated Rebel currency for a Confederate bond, a patriotic inflation-hedge. Higher prices were especially hard on working families whose usual breadwinners were away at war. A soldier from Mississippi who overstayed his furlough wrote to the governor, "We are poor men and are willing to defend our country but our families [come] first."

The planters at the top of the economic pyramid still indulged in material comforts. But the shortages, and the inflation, spawned a sense of foreboding. Even among the rich, growing scarcity presaged a frightening economic instability, a threat to the cherished social order.

Four

The Window Shuts

The lowest abyss is not the absence of love,
but the absence of coin.

– E. M. FORSTER, *Howards End*

J UDGED FROM THE BATTLEFIELD, the Confederacy was holding
its own or better. It was winning its share of the battles and in the
crucial eastern theater, the North had made no progress against
General Joe Johnston's Army of Northern Virginia.* In the parallel war,
the economic contest, the South was losing.

The inescapable fact was that the South's slave-based economy had
been designed for agriculture. It could not quickly adapt or switch to
industry. For manufactures it was dependent on imports. In wartime,
this became a crushing weakness.

For ammunition and other supplies, as well as vital information cou-
riers, the South was dependent on safe passage from Europe. The South's
utter reliance on imports vaulted the naval war to a theater of crucial
importance.

The Union navy was weak, but northern shipyards were working
overtime to build ships and tighten the blockade. As early as the fifth

---

* It was not called the Army of Northern Virginia until 1862.

month of the war, LeRoy Walker, the Confederate war secretary, complained to the governor of South Carolina that the blockade was interfering with his efforts to import uniforms. The danger of capture forced a roundabout voyage, in two steps, that limited cargo sizes and also the hours when passage was safe.

Sleek, fast-moving "runners" made quick trips from Charleston, Mobile, and other southern ports to nearby Bermuda and Nassau; from there, larger merchant ships sailing under the British flag crossed the Atlantic. By one estimate, during the first year of the war, some six hundred runners successfully evaded the blockade. Northern captures were relatively rare.

Scarcity and high prices created enormous incentives for blockade runners. On a successful journey, shippers could rake in profits of 500 percent. Inevitably, shippers began to trade in the most valued commodity—cotton—violating the southern embargo, though necessarily in far smaller quantities than the tonnage before the war. Running was a private enterprise, often financed with British capital, and ship captains were free to transport whatever paid. However, on return trips, Richmond directed its agents in London to concentrate on military needs. Small arms, powder, and saltpeter were given top priority. For example, the *Fingal*, chartered strictly on the Confederate government's account, left England in October 1861 with 7520 Enfield rifles and 17,000 pounds of cannon powder.

Since the South had little gold and its currency was worthless overseas, Richmond made remittances in cotton, often via Fraser, Trenholm, & Co., a Charleston firm with a branch in Liverpool. George Trenholm, a native Charlestonian, had been a leading cotton broker, based in New York. When the war broke out, he relocated to the Bahamas and Bermuda. Trenholm became a principal financier of the Confederacy and adviser to Memminger.

Shippers procured swift, shallow-draft vessels to run the blockade. These operated at night on the short haul between the mainland and island ports. The South was helped by Britain's liberal interpretation of the rules regarding the provision by neutral states of ships intended for use in warfare. And it was greatly helped by Britain's willingness to tolerate colonial ports that were little more than Confederate depots.

Among the South's most vital cargo in 1861 were a pair of Rebel diplomats. President Jefferson Davis, who was desperate to win recognition in European capitals, appointed two new envoys, James Mason and John Slidell, respectively to England and France, to replace the previous commissioners. Mason and Slidell were widely respected in the South, had some experience in foreign affairs, and were considered an important diplomatic upgrade. By October 1, 1861, the pair were in Charleston, awaiting passage on a blockade runner. The Mason-Slidell mission was something of an open secret, and in the South greatly anticipated. Edmund Ruffin was encouraged when he learned from James De Bow, the publisher, that the pair had successfully departed Charleston. He was further cheered by the news that another ship, the *Bermuda*, had sailed from Savannah with 1500 bales of cotton, on which Trenholm, the chief owner, could expect a profit of $100,000—in precious hard currency. Ruffin noted with satisfaction, "These enormous profits, *with the easy evasion of the blockade*, will doubtless induce many other adventurers to pursue the same course."

Ruffin's diary entries had become so defiant one almost feels the clenching of his teeth in the act of writing. The old planter, who had lost his wife before the war, was increasingly lonely. The South's isolation—and his own—may have contributed to an emotional strain. His scribblings oozed with contempt for the world outside the South. Even *Julius Caesar*, a favorite from his childhood, evoked his sour disapproval.

While southerners like Ruffin anxiously awaited news of Mason and Slidell's safe passage, Lincoln's cabinet was also tracking the envoys. Secretary of the Navy Gideon Welles ordered the Union fleet to intercept them as they departed Charleston, but their vessel eluded capture and safely reached Havana. Three weeks later, when the British mail ship RMS *Trent* steamed out of the Cuban port, a veteran U.S. captain, Charles Wilkes, surmised that the diplomats would be on board. Wilkes was incautious despite his forty-three years of service, and he was hoping to atone for the navy's previous failure and doubtless to win laurels for himself. On November 8, 1861, Wilkes intercepted the *Trent* on the high seas and, after a summary search, put Mason and Slidell under arrest.

In the North, Wilkes became an instant hero. Americans had been seething over what they regarded as Britain's insults to the Union, and the war had widened the chasm between northerners and the mother country. In September (two months before the *Trent*'s interdiction), the high-toned *Atlantic Monthly* had bristled at the assertion of *The Times* of London that southern states had a "right" to secede. The *Atlantic* was especially piqued by the repeated British assertion that the Confederate goal of independence was similar to that of the original thirteen colonies, as if Jefferson Davis were a latter-day George Washington. "Why has the North felt aggrieved with England" the *Atlantic* rhetorically wondered. Surveying the newspaper accounts filled with vituperations, misrepresentations, and prophecies of doom, which arrived with "every steamer," the magazine concluded: "This Nation . . . has just cause of complaint."

Yet Secretary of State William Seward and other American officials recognized that Captain Wilkes had grievously overstepped. He had offended British honor and probably violated international law. Potentially, he had given the Confederacy its greatest gift—a reason for Britain to intervene. "Not a dozen battles lost," Belmont worriedly wrote to Chase, "could have damaged our good cause as much as the *ill-judged & over-zealous* Capt. Wilkes." It took time for London to learn of the offense and formulate a response. Meanwhile, Ruffin spoke for all Dixie when he prayed that "the insult" would spur the British lion into the war.

The Union navy made a more judicious attack the day before detaining the *Trent*. After bombarding Confederate defenses, it seized Port Royal, Hilton Head, and other outcroppings in the Sea Island chain extending south from Charleston. This capture was commercially significant, because the salty air and Sea Island soil produced a fine, long-fibered cotton among the most valuable in the world. Shortly after the attack, *The New York Times* reported "interesting intelligence from Port Royal." The slave population, approximately ten thousand, "seem to have remained behind when their masters fled, and welcomed our men with rejoicing."

The Blacks on Port Royal had been cruelly mistreated. Many spoke of abuses at the "whipping tree," a place of notorious punishments. One woman recounted how, while pregnant, she had been tied with a rope and beaten so brutally she lost her child. As the Union forces approached, the planters had attempted to frighten the slaves into fleeing with them, warning that the Yankees intended to sell them to Cuba. But the young daughter of an abusive planter rebelled against the savagery of her society and assured the slaves the story was false. As the whites bundled their belongings and fled, the Negroes stayed and welcomed their presumptive liberators. The story of the defiant Port Royal Blacks spread, evoking in white planters a latent fear of slave revolt. Ruffin was shocked. Having personally overseen scores of slaves, he had deluded himself into believing that they were content. (He had once written that American slaves were "the most comfortable, happy and cheerful of all laboring and poorer classes.") He now admitted, "This seems to me to indicate a mutinous disposition which was not suspected."

Salmon Chase took over administration of the Sea Islands (abandoned property fell under the domain of the Treasury). This put him in charge not only of a valuable swath of the Carolina economy but of the largest community of Blacks to have, practically speaking, freed themselves during the war. Chase had been yearning for a way to further the cause of antislavery; suddenly, he had one.

On the recommendation of a family friend, Chase deputized Lieutenant Colonel William H. Reynolds, an officer in the First Rhode Island Artillery and a successful cotton trader before the war, to go to

Port Royal and harvest the cotton. Reynolds proposed that the plantations be leased to private operators who would employ the freedmen at a modest wage and provide some rudimentary schooling for the children. As Reynolds hastened to South Carolina, another Chase friend, Edward L. Pierce, vehemently protested. Pierce, a Boston lawyer and ardent foe of slavery, feared that private growers would manage the cotton fields purely for profit. He argued that, if given the chance—and proper education—the Blacks would prove "no less industrious" than the whites and set an antislavery example for the country. These views were strongly aligned with Chase's. Pierce's concerns for the freedmen's well-being were amplified during the first weeks of occupation, when the army consumed most of the food on the islands, leaving little for the freedmen, who wanted for doctors, teachers, and ordained ministers. Meanwhile, the Yankee conquerors faced few restraints. One Union adventurer gleefully reported, "I found 41 bales of the best Sea Island cotton . . . and made four negroes put it on two wheels" to transport it to the harbor. Such reports confirmed that Union soldiers were not much focused on the welfare of the Blacks. To his credit, Chase recognized that the freedmen would require a period of adjustment, including training and support. He directed Pierce to go to Port Royal to prepare the freedmen "for self-support by their own industry." Chase now had two emissaries, Reynolds and Pierce, pursuing the not necessarily consistent goals of cotton collection and Negro edification.

As Chase struggled to provide for the freedmen, he continued to wrestle with the banks. When he traveled to New York in mid-November 1861, he found the bankers more reluctant to lend than ever. James Gallatin warned that to insist on further gold loans would completely deplete their gold reserves, wreck the dollar exchange rate in Europe, and "inaugurate a depreciated paper currency." A paper currency couldn't work, he admonished, citing evidence of "disastrous failures in other countries."

But Chase needed loans. Expenses were now running at more than $1.5 million a day (up from $1 million at the time of Bull Run). The Treasury was late in paying bills. Government contractors were peddling receivables at a discount. Chase had hoped to keep the delicate pinwheel of gold loans, government purchases, and deposits in balance but the country's gold reserves did not stretch far enough. Given the delay in collecting, shipping, and disbursing hard coin, only a fraction of the existing metal was actually in use at any time. The country needed a more pliant currency.

To the bankers, the solution was simple. Let the gold in their vaults be the basis for an expanded issue of bank notes. To Chase, this would be "undemocratic," a term equivalent to "elitist" today. He regarded bank notes as an interest-free loan that benefited the issuing banks. Chase's suspicion of bankers was essentially Jeffersonian. In the agrarian society of the early 1800s, it was possible to argue that banks and bank notes were hardly needed. That no longer held. Even Chase was coming to recognize the need for paper. But if the government was to rely on a bank currency, the Treasury secretary wanted a different sort of bank—responsible, as he saw it, not to wealthy private investors, but to the people.

While Chase was pondering how to reinvent the banking system, in mid-November he bludgeoned the banks into committing to a third loan of $50 million. Once again, they agreed to part with gold, but this time, they forced Chase to value the government's paper at a discount and refused to take seven-thirties (which they knew were unsalable). Instead, they took bonds, which they hoped to resell to investors in Europe.

However, confidence in the government's credit was plummeting. Government contractors were demanding a surcharge, so Horace Greeley's *Tribune* reported, merely "to cover the expense and delay of getting paid." Part of the problem was rampant corruption. Contracts were dished out to politically connected suppliers, resulting in supply bottlenecks and higher prices.

And the Union was plagued by continuing competition between state and federal quartermasters. Since the war was mainly fought in the South, the North had longer supply lines and therefore more complex logistics. The demands of the Union army were immense. According to the historian James M. McPherson, each 100,000 men required 35,000 animals and 2500 supply wagons. Only a centralized bureau could marshal and organize such convoys. Anxious to assert control, the War Department ordered the states to stop making individual procurements. Montgomery C. Meigs, a Georgian West Point graduate who had remained loyal, had been appointed the army's quartermaster general. Meigs performed herculean labors, but he grew frustrated as the states refused to give way. He claimed that procurement officers in the states were driving up prices. The persistence of local supply lines testified to the powerful hold of the states' rights doctrine even in the North. As Meigs protested in a telegraph to Seward, "The public service has suffered . . . from the conflict between the State and Federal authorities here. . . . As the matter stands now there is no unity of action."

Military troubles ate into Chase's ability to fund the war. Chase could not sell bonds if the army didn't move on Richmond, but General George McClellan, while highly capable at drilling and organizing, and popular with his troops, essentially refused to do the job he was appointed for: attack the enemy in Virginia. Even when commanding superior forces, he vastly overestimated enemy strength, even falling for the old ruse of "Quaker guns" (logs painted to look like weaponry). Such lapses only seemed to heighten his Napoleonic self-regard. The general privately flaunted disrespect for Lincoln, referring in correspondence to the "imbecile administration." One night, the President and Secretary of State Seward called on McClellan in hopes of persuading him to get his army moving. The general was out; when he arrived home and was told of his important guests, he ignored them and went upstairs. Eventually, Lincoln's party was informed that the general had retired. The President good-naturedly sloughed off this disrespectful treatment. But he could not ignore that in the latter part of 1861, the

Union lost most of the important battles, with consequent harm to the purse.

When Lincoln delivered his Annual Message to Congress (forerunner of today's State of the Union) on December 3, Union morale was low. The President was still on probation with the northern people, underappreciated by easterners in particular. George Templeton Strong, the Wall Street diarist, had met Lincoln in October and was unimpressed. Unable to look past Lincoln's unrefined manners, and not bothering to conceal his racist sensibility, Strong described the President as "lank and hard-featured, among the ugliest white men I have seen." Although Lincoln did impress him as perceptive and good-hearted, he did not earn his affection, for Strong had crudely added, "his laugh is the laugh of a yahoo, and a wrinkling of nose that suggests affinity with the tapir and other pachyderms; and his grammar is weak."

Lincoln's Annual Message fairly recounted the most cataclysmic year in American history. "A disloyal portion of the American people," he began as if in wonder, "have during the whole year been engaged in an attempt to divide and destroy the Union." The rambling speech was not among his best—one historian called it "tedious." But it was remarkable, nonetheless. Lincoln noted that the South's attempt to force the hand of foreign nations by "the embarrassment of commerce" (the cotton embargo) had failed to have effect, and that the disputed states of Kentucky, Missouri, and Maryland now fielded forty thousand active Union troops. Lincoln commended Chase for managing the Treasury "with signal success." He was especially gladdened that "citizens of the industrial classes" had invested in the seven-thirties, testifying to the people's faith in the democracy.

As if to validate the people's faith, Lincoln asked for a pair of economic measures—a new department of agriculture, to compile statistics on the nation's farm economy and to distribute seeds to farmers, and a railroad to link Kentucky to other loyal regions. Promoting agriculture would be an unprecedented step toward activist government—a visible hand to support what Lincoln termed "the largest interest of the nation." Forty percent of the northern population was involved in farming, and they had always been on their own. But even in the private sector, Lincoln maintained, government could work to the "general advantage." Congress interpreted his request as a signal to restart the dormant Whig agenda. The following day, the House reported a homestead bill; several days later, Justin Morrill, the congressman from Vermont, reintroduced a bill for land-grant colleges. Both bills aimed to create opportunities for people on the rise. They affirmed Lincoln's belief that, even during the war, economic progress couldn't wait. The present struggle, he said, was not only for today, "it is for a vast future also." The President forecast that—*if* the Union were preserved—some of those alive would see it grow to 250 million people, a figure that must have dazzled his contemporaries.*

Lincoln also delivered a more personal economic message, launching into a discourse on one of his favorite topics, the relationship between capital and labor. This philosophical detour, ventured during the chaos of the still early stages of the war, struck some of his audience as strange. (Thaddeus Stevens, declining to take up this portion of the President's remarks in Congress, sarcastically observed, "There is no appropriate committee on metaphysics.") But to Lincoln, political economy was close to the purpose of the war. He regarded the Confederacy as a rejection of "the rights of the people." Workers in the South were in chains, and not only its slaves. Richmond's was not a popular government; it was a planters' aristocracy. In contrast, the North, as he idealized it, exhibited "the just, and generous, and prosperous system, which opens the way to all." Reprising his 1860 New Haven speech, Lincoln maintained that even a "penniless" northern worker would labor for "awhile," and save a surplus "with which to buy tools or land for himself" and progress to a condition of self-employment, then earning the capital to hire others.

---

* Lincoln was right on the substance, but wrong on the timing. The U.S. population did not reach 250 million for another two life spans, or until 1990.

Lincoln saw labor less as a competitor to capital than as its partner. This vision, rooted in the preindustrial society of his youth, was somewhat out-of-date. By 1861, a worker on the Pennsylvania Railroad was unlikely to rise to manager. Perhaps for this reason, while continuing to assert that capital had rights, and that those rights "were as worthy of protection as any other rights," Lincoln affirmed the priority of labor. Labor existed first; capital was but the fruit of labor. Therefore, "labor is the superior of capital, and deserves much the higher consideration." Lincoln was asserting a political economy of freedom and distinguishing northern society from its rival. The North, and only the North, offered upward mobility for those at the bottom.

Lincoln's pronouncements on the future of enslaved people dovetailed with prevailing white prejudices. He emphasized his intent to keep the war from becoming a "revolutionary struggle," meaning, presumably, one whose purpose was a general emancipation. Recognizing that the Confiscation Act, and the war itself, would lead to instances of emancipation, he recommended that Congress provide for "such persons," but also that it adopt a "plan of colonization" including, he specified in painful detail, "the acquiring of territory, and also the appropriation of money beyond that to be expended in the territorial acquisition." Recent commentators have seen these remarks as classically Lincoln, a gradual step toward the Emancipation Proclamation. But that is hindsight. At the time, Lincoln was intent on keeping the loyalty of the border states and advocated a (voluntary, to be sure) exodus of Black Americans, with the added selling point that "the emigration of colored men leaves additional room for white men remaining or coming here." Eight months into the war, Lincoln resolutely condemned slavery, but his America, as yet, had scarcely any room in it for the people who were enslaved.

One week after Lincoln's message, Chase submitted his annual report to Congress. This document was eagerly awaited, for it provided the public with its first glimpse of the country's finances during the war. Fearing that the public was losing patience with the war's mounting expense, Chase made a rather transparent attempt to sugarcoat the numbers. His tone was reassuring, but his figures were alarming. In the apt description of the financial historian Bray Hammond, he cloaked gloomy facts in "a fog of calm and confidence." Due to the rising number of troops, as well as increased soldier pay, Chase had raised his spending forecast a whopping 70 percent from his meticulous forecast the previous July. He now forecast an annual budget of $540 million, approximately ten times the government's annual revenues. Such a gap was not, or seemed to be not, sustainable. But he had equally bad news on the revenue side. Rather than the $57 million he had hoped to raise from the tariff, the Treasury secretary forecast only $32 million.

By now, Chase might have realized that his forecasts were little more than guesses, and that he should seek all the revenue he could. Yet the cautious Chase still feared to increase taxes, except very modestly.* He was constrained by the knowledge that Americans, as citizens in a democracy, were uniquely able to reject taxes at the ballot box. (McPherson observes that Americans were among the most lightly taxed peoples on Earth.) Chase, more drily, said, "It will be seen at a glance that the amount to be derived from taxation forms but a small portion of the sums required for the expenses of the war." In a report that soldiered on for a ponderous twenty-nine pages, this single sentence horrified Wall Street. Bankers realized that what Chase proposed in lieu of taxes was to close the gap by borrowing. The amounts were stupendous. By June 30, 1863, assuming the war was then still on, Chase would need to borrow an additional $650 million. As recently as June 1861, the total government debt had been $90 million. Although Chase did not say so explicitly, he was planning to rely on taxes for not quite a sixth of the budget, with loans to cover everything else. That was considerably

---

* Chase did seek an increase in duties on sugars and coffee, which Congress approved. He did nothing to implement the income tax and even expressed doubt "whether the probable revenue affords a sufficient reason for putting [it] in operation."

more than in the Confederacy, which had relied on taxes for less than 2 percent of its first-year expenses (and on the printing press for 75 percent!), but it was not sufficient for Wall Street. As with an overmortgaged family, the government was at serious risk of seeing the credit window shut.

The Treasury secretary had been stewing over this, and his report divulged a plan. It was nothing if not complex, for that was how his mind operated, with a lawyer's love of detail. He would not finance the war through Treasury notes, the path to dreaded inflation. Nor did he want to rely on the banks, and see the gains go to private financiers. Rather, Chase proposed to organize a new system of banks, privately owned but chartered by the federal government. These banks would be required to invest in government bonds—bolstering the government's credit. The notes of these new banks would become the country's money—uniform, stable, secure.

Chase had a larger purpose in mind. Issuing currency, he insisted, was the job of the *federal* government. He questioned whether bank notes were not illegal. Actually, the Constitution forbade the *states* from coining money or issuing paper bills. It said nothing about whether banks could do so. But the Constitution had been written in a simpler time, when only a handful of banks existed. Chase was trying to adapt it to the industrial age. In a stroke worthy of Hamilton, he was trying to reclaim exclusive monetary authority for the national government.

Chase's solution was elegant, and as an abstract blueprint it was masterly. But his plan entirely ignored the present emergency. The government needed loans immediately. It could not wait to restructure the banking system, much less engage in constitutional disquisitions. Bankers completely shunned his plan—hardly a surprise, since the Treasury secretary made clear that his intent was to drive existing bank notes out of circulation. Congress also was hostile. It had not occurred to Chase to cultivate legislative allies, and with the exception of John Sherman, he had none.

Chase had prepared his plan under mounting personal stress. He was overworked and complained that he was underappreciated. The Treasury secretary was a strange mix, at once imperious and emotionally needy. He griped to his elder daughter, Katherine (always "Kate"), a beguiling woman serving as mistress of his household, that due to his miserly salary and mounting personal expenses, he might be forced to resign. His duties as a father, including supporting Kate's taste for luxuries, merely added to his stress.

The banks had been hoping to refinance their loans with bond sales in England. After receiving news of the seizure of the *Trent*, Britain reacted with outrage at this American violation of British sovereignty. Suddenly, the question became not whether Britain would buy American bonds but whether it would go to war. The British government demanded the release of Mason and Slidell, now imprisoned in Fort Warren in Boston harbor. America and Britain had been through this before, in 1812, when James Madison had protested British interference with American ships. This time, it was Britain that felt its honor at stake, egged on by a bellicose British press. Lord Palmerston dispatched troops to Canada and warships steamed into the Atlantic. "We know that a message is on its way from England to America," the *Richmond Daily Dispatch* wrote hopefully, "which may change the civil war into a great and world-wide struggle." European intervention was a serious threat, especially as France (with British and Spanish support) had invaded Veracruz to force repayment of Mexican debts. It was easy to imagine that a European force south of the Rio Grande might seek common cause with the Confederacy.

The loss of potential British financing exposed the banks as vulnerable. Investors knew that during previous wars, governments had gone off gold and the paper currency had wildly depreciated. People who feared suspension now sought to redeem their notes before others did so—the classic recipe for a bank run. Chase's strategy actually aggravated the risk. By demanding the banks' gold, he had whittled away their reserves, leaving every other customer at greater peril.

On December 16, the news that Britain was threatening war sparked a panic in the stock market. Cisco, the stalwart assistant secretary, wired Chase, "Stocks have experienced a heavy decline." Rumors of suspension were rife. The *New York Herald* concluded, "The only question . . . is when our banks should take the step of suspending specie payments." The following day, representatives from the banks met at the American Exchange Bank in New York. City Bank's Moses Taylor, once again coming to Chase's rescue, persuaded the group they had nothing to fear. The group reckoned that the banks were safe, because England needed American grain, which would, perforce, be paid for with British coin.

Nonetheless, bank balances continued to erode. The New York sub-Treasury's gold stock was shrinking as well. Incredibly, in the midst of the crisis, Chase demanded the next installment on his loan. Some of the banks refused. Cisco sent his boss an alarmed note: "Our total payments today over receipts have been about Two Million Dollars . . . it will be necessary to replenish it immediately." In truth, the currency crisis had little to do with any possible war with Britain. No sane person will deposit gold if they fear that the bank is imperiled. Rather than deposit gold and silver coins, people were hoarding them—a pattern reputedly observed by the sixteenth-century merchant Sir Thomas Gresham.* Coins disappeared from circulation at lightning speed. According to Lucius Chittenden, a Treasury official, "They seemed to vanish in a day."

Chase was actually pressing the banks to commit to a *fourth* loan. The bankers rejected this brazen and wholly impractical request, recognizing it as suicidal. They invited the Treasury secretary to New York, hoping he would offer an alternative. But Chase was out of ideas. On December 23, the banks reported sharp declines in deposits and in gold. The New York banks were hardest hit. What ailed the New York

---

* "Bad money drives out good" was an oft observed principle; it was dubbed Gresham's law by the nineteenth-century Scottish political economist Henry Dunning Macleod.

institutions was less a lack of assets than a lack of liquidity. Gotham banks had sunk $54 million of their capital into normally safe government bonds. These they could not sell without incurring steep losses—practically, they could not sell at all.

On Christmas Day 1861, Lincoln and the cabinet resolved to return the Rebel prisoners from the *Trent*. They did not want a second war, and Britain's ambassador, Lord Lyons, who was staunchly pro-Union, had softened the tone of the British ultimatum, allowing America to back down without losing face. The two Confederates were transferred to Provincetown, on the far shore of Cape Cod, and quietly released to British custody and to freedom—in which condition they would be hard-pressed to do as much for their cause as they had as hostages.

But the currency crisis now had a momentum of its own. The *Trent* no longer mattered. Chase believed that the loyal states held $250 million in specie (the total was probably closer to $200 million). The problem was getting people to lend it. And Chase was powerless. The Treasury was a modest operation, lacking the facilities to galvanize an industrial war economy. A delegation of New York financiers traveled to Washington, to warn Lincoln that suspension was inevitable. The President had seven hundred thousand men in uniform but he had few financial weapons. America had not had a government bank since the 1830s (when Andrew Jackson had abolished the Second Bank of the United States). Since then, private banks had been forced to suspend three times.[*] Throughout those years, Lincoln had advocated reestablishing a national bank, without success. His government had nothing to lend, and no influence over the private banks that did. Suspension, the bankers were drily informed, "was not a question for the Government to decide."

On the final weekend of 1861, the Associated Banks reported another drop in gold. The forty institutions in New York had lost nearly 30 percent of their specie in less than a month. They still had gold re-

---

[*] The banks suspended in 1837, when the Second Bank lost its charter, in 1841, and in the depression year 1857.

serves of $29 million, but it was plain that if the spigot remained open, their vaults would empty. On Saturday, December 28, they voted to suspend—to cease redeeming notes for gold. Depositors who wanted coin would have to go outside the metropolitan area—a logic that forced suspension to spread to every other city.

Not only the gold standard fell, but also the illusion that the banks could finance a major war. In truth, the banking system was outmoded. The banks were entrepreneurial private lenders. The America of iron and railroads had outgrown them. The government as well as industrial corporations needed bigger institutions that could sell vast sums of securities and pool larger reserves of capital.

Lincoln's Treasury secretary immediately recognized that the government, too, would be forced to go off gold. A despondent Chase alerted Cisco, "I deplore exceedingly the suspension . . . it is certain that the Govt cannot pay coin unless the Banks do." Chase had fought harder than anyone to stay on specie. Now, he would have to fight the war with paper.

Five

Legal Tender

The absence of the precious metals will,
it is believed, be a temporary evil, but until
they can again be rendered the general
medium of exchange, it devolves on the
wisdom of Congress to provide a substitute.

—JAMES MADISON

I N THE DESPERATE WINTER OF 1861–1862, the financial crisis threatened to halt the Union armies. The Treasury was empty; the banks had suspended; the government had no currency. Chase had few ideas, other than a labored program for bank reform. Almost by default, the Republican Congress seized the initiative. The most likely vehicle for financial resuscitation was the House Ways and Means Committee. Ways and Means had two subcommittees. One dealt with revenue, but revenue legislation was unlikely to provide help in the near term. The other subcommittee, on currency, was chaired by Elbridge Spaulding of New York State. Spaulding had been working on Chase's proposal to reform the banks, but when the banks went off gold, Spaulding realized there would not be time. He himself was an investor and director in Bank of Attica and the Farmers and Mechanics' Bank, both in Buffalo. In the 1860s, it was not uncommon for representatives to tailor legislation affecting personal investments. Spaulding, who had been a popular Whig mayor before running for Congress, was untroubled by any idea of conflict of interest. He simply reckoned that the banking channel was stuck and it was in the public interest—also in his private interest—to unstick it. On December 30, 1861, with the Union nearly overwhelmed by fiscal problems, Spaulding reported another bill—for a government currency.

In theory, Spaulding could have proposed more of the Treasury demand notes, but as we have seen, the demand notes were refused in some quarters. Spaulding wanted a universally acceptable currency that the Treasury could use to pay for the war. His bill was revolutionary. As if by a conjurer's trick, it authorized the Treasury to print United States Notes to distribute to soldiers, suppliers, and others. The catch was that, unlike virtually every other bill in circulation, Spaulding's notes would not be redeemable for silver or gold. This meant the government would not be constrained by the supply of metal; it could print as much as it liked, or at any rate as much as Congress authorized.

And Spaulding's notes would not pay interest. Today, we scarcely pause to consider that the money in our wallets does not yield a return. After all, it is "money." In 1861, virtually all government paper did pay interest. That was the inducement for holding it. Finally, Spaulding's paper would not have a maturity date. This, too, was unusual. A maturity date was a pledge that the paper could be exchanged for something of value at a specified time. But these notes would not be redeemable. They were issued for perpetuity.

To the Civil War mind, these features were both shocking and blasphemous. Several years before the war, a Boston merchant named Samuel Hooper had published *Currency or Money*, a tract that had considered—and denounced—such a currency. Hooper did not mince words. "They [paper bills] are not money," he wrote disdainfully. "They are, in fact, only *promises* to pay money." The son of a shipper in Marblehead, Massachusetts, Hooper had learned finance at a countinghouse on State Street in Boston, and then become a prosperous businessman, trading in the Pacific Northwest and China. A savvy appraiser of financial risk, he had written that paper money was no more like the real thing than a contract to deliver flour was flour itself. "Paper money possesses no intrinsic value," Hooper had patiently explained. "It has only a derivative or secondary value, founded upon the good credit of those who issue it."

What, then, was Spaulding proposing to offer—if not an interest payment and not redemption at a maturity date—to induce people to take his currency? Spaulding's U.S. Notes would be "legal tender"— they would be money by proclamation, that is, by government fiat. They would suffice for all debts and commercial exchanges; acceptance would be compulsory and universal.

Secretary of the Treasury Chase had also considered legal tender but had rejected it as subversive as well as inflationary. This had also been Hooper's view. When bills cannot be converted to coin, he had written, "depreciation [inflation] is one of the consequences." Yet on January 15, 1862, as Chase noted in his diary, he was visited by Hooper, who was now a member of Congress—and also by Spaulding. Hooper, despite his adamant earlier warning that paper was no more money than it could be flour or bread, "expressed his decided opinion that the U.S. notes must necessarily be made legal tender." Evidently, the emergency had changed his mind. Chase promised to consult with Thaddeus Stevens, the Ways and Means Committee chair, but did not commit himself.

Chase was also conferring with a cabal of big-city bankers, some of whom were as horrified as he was. The bankers feared that the new U.S. Notes would replace the multitudinous private bank notes that were the country's primary currency. They were shocked at the notion of a paper money unhinged from gold. Gold and silver had a market price around the world. As long as the dollar was tied to gold, Americans could seamlessly trade with other nations. Spaulding's bill would sever the link—not only to gold but to foreign currencies.*

---

* Typical of the era's reverence for gold, Hugh McCulloch, a banker who would become Lincoln's third Treasury secretary, was to write that precious metals had been devised by the Almighty to give civilizations a standard of value.

Over the first few weeks of 1862, the bankers attempted to cobble together a substitute bill—revolving around their own notes. But the banks' position was weak. Their notes were trading at a discount (inevitably, since they were no longer backed by coin). On January 20, a Boston banker telegraphed Chase that the effort to confect an alternate solution had collapsed.

The government had now superseded the banks as the responsible party for issuing currency. Within the government, initiative had shifted from Treasury to the House committee. Spaulding, however, needed Chase's support. When Chase returned the bill to Spaulding, he noted he was "regretting exceedingly" the legal tender aspect. That fell short of the endorsement Spaulding wanted, nonetheless he reported the revised bill to the House.

Even Spaulding, whose paternal grandfather had served as a captain at Bunker Hill, seemed wary of his bill. He defended it as an accommodation to war—"a measure of necessity, and not of choice." Yet he challenged his colleagues to act on the emergency: "Will Congress have the firmness and the courage?" The call to courage also referred to his demand that Congress support the new currency with higher taxes.

The legal tender debate was among the most profound of the war. Opponents maintained, and firmly believed, that issuing paper would cause a ruinous inflation. Thus far, inflation in the North had been relatively modest. But legislators were well aware that war currencies had come a cropper in the past, including in America during the Revolutionary War and in Britain and France during the Napoleonic era. Congressmen frequently quoted the Founding Fathers; all had been skeptical—if not dead set against—paper money. None other than Alexander Hamilton himself had warned:

> The emitting of paper money by the authority of Government is wisely prohibited to the individual States, by the national Constitution. And the spirit of that prohibition ought not to be disregarded, by the Government of the United States.

But paper was unavoidable. The only practical issue was whether to make the Union's paper legal tender, and thus compel its acceptance. Democrats, the party of Andrew Jackson, with their long suspicion of paper currency, were naturally opposed, but not a few Republicans were troubled as well. Stevens was the most forceful advocate. When a member objected that if the notes were legal tender they would depreciate, Stevens responded savagely: "How do gentlemen expect that using the same amount of notes without the legal tender will inflate it less?"

There was extensive debate over the law's constitutionality. (The Constitution did not explicitly permit, nor did it prohibit, such a currency.) The most heartfelt objections were moral. Legal tender struck many as a fraud—an attempt to pass off as "money" what was merely paper. George Pendleton, a Democrat from Ohio, called it a "shock" to the mind. Most upsetting, people who had contracted a debt under the gold standard would now be able to repay it with paper. Roscoe Conkling, an upstate New York Republican, warned that legal tender would proclaim "a saturnalia of fraud; a carnival of rogues. Every agent, attorney, treasurer, trustee, every debtor of a fiduciary character, who has received for others money—*hard* money . . . will forever release himself from liability by buying up, for that knavish purpose, at its depreciated value, the spurious currency we will put afloat." Supporters promised that this one authorization would be the last, but they were disbelieved. Conkling invoked the French maxim on virtue: it was the first wayward step that assured the rest. This was not all theatrics. Legislators genuinely feared that legal tender would be a stain on the nation's honor. They feared that if such ignoble paper circulated, gold, as per the famous law of Gresham, would be forever hidden away. Morrill, one of the most powerful Republicans in the House, denounced his party's bill: "It is of doubtful constitutionality; it is immoral; a breach of the public faith; it will banish all specie from circulation; it will degrade us in the estimation of other nations. . . . *I protest against making anything a legal tender but gold and silver.*" The Vermonter, who incidentally was a shareholder in a state bank, dolefully predicted that within sixty days, the government would seek to authorize more.

Morrill's fear was not unreasonable. The bill authorized only $150 million of notes.* At the present rate of federal spending, nearly $2 million a day, such a sum would be exhausted by spring. But the bill also authorized $500 million of twenty-year bonds. The Republican sponsors maintained that people would use the legal tender notes to purchase the bonds. In such a way, the notes would be returned to the Treasury, which could then reissue them. In effect, the legal tender notes would serve as a conduit to funnel public capital into long-term bonds, which would finance the war.

There was something defensive about this theory—as if even the sponsors doubted that people would carry notes yielding 0 percent rather than bonds yielding 6 percent. Even Stevens allowed that, but for the war emergency, he would never willingly abandon "that circulating medium which, by the common consent of civilized nations, forms the standard of value."

Grievously for the bill, Chase had deep reservations regarding the probity of legal tender. He also had constitutional worries, although Lincoln may have mollified those. According to one visitor, the President said, "Go back to Chase and tell him not to bother himself about the Constitution. Say that I have that sacred instrument here at the White House, and I am guarding it with great care." The comment was probably apocryphal. Although Lincoln was willing to adapt the Constitution to his purposes, he was not cavalier about it. What we know is that since his apprenticeship as a legislator, the President had supported liberal banking and currency arrangements. And earlier that month, he had visited Montgomery Meigs, the quartermaster general, in his office, settled himself in a chair by the open fire and, according to Meigs's later recollection, pleaded woefully, "General, what shall I do? The

---

* Fifty million of the new legal tender notes simply replaced the old demand notes.

people are impatient; Chase has no money and he tells me he can raise no more. . . . The bottom is out of the tub."

Lincoln surely favored the Legal Tender Act, but he left it to Chase to formulate the administration position. Chase sought counsel from John Cisco, his deputy, and John Stevens, president of the Bank of Commerce; each was strongly in favor. George Harrington, Chase's assistant secretary, advised him, "It is impossible to get along without it [legal tender]."

By the end of January, Chase had come around to the idea, but he hesitated to say so. Spaulding complained that the Treasury secretary's silence was undermining the bill. On January 29, Chase sent a dense letter to the Ways and Means Committee, admitting his "great aversion" to declaring anything but coin as legal tender, but conceding that the bill would, at least, put all citizens "on the same level." This was too tortured a formulation to turn any votes. On February 3, Chase finally wrestled his demons to the floor and assured Spaulding of his unconditional support. "It is true that I came with reluctance to . . . the legal tender clause," the Treasury secretary acknowledged, "but I came to it decidedly. Immediate action is of great importance. The Treasury is nearly empty." Spaulding read this letter aloud on the House floor. Two days later, Chase wrote Spaulding with the urgency of a convert: "The public exigencies do not admit of delay."

Chase was not exaggerating. Federal quartermasters had been paying for goods with vouchers, creating serious cash flow problems. As detailed by the historian Mark Wilson, the vouchers passed hand to hand like money, illustrating people's need to devise a currency when none exists. Edwin Stanton, newly installed as secretary of war (replacing the inept Simon Cameron) was besieged with demands for payment. Without a standard currency, neither government contractors nor their workers could be paid. A textile maker in New London, Connecticut, who had delivered $18,000 worth of woolens to the army poignantly pleaded with Stanton: "My help, who are poor, want their pay."

Even with Chase's lobbying, the vote was expected to be close. Bankers were divided, but they had nothing else to offer. The press was mostly favorable. Proponents argued that more currency would boost wages and be good for workers, similar to liberal arguments for lower interest rates a century later. The publisher of *The New York Times*, Henry Raymond, who was a leading figure in the Republican Party, was adamantly in favor. The notes had to have the legal tender sanction, according to the *Times*, otherwise "selfishly inclined" bankers could refuse them. Most persuasive was the simple point that tender would be good for the troops. Soldiers in that era were often dependent for supplies on so-called sutlers—self-styled merchants who peddled provisions to troops in the field, often from the back of a wagon or a makeshift tent. "It would be absurd," observed the *Times*, "to compel the soldiers to take their pay in money that Sutlers" could refuse. On February 6, 1862, the House passed the bill by a party-line vote of 93–59; immediately, it went to the Senate.

The chair of the Senate Finance Committee, William Pitt Fessenden, was a former colleague of Chase. In the 1850s, the two were fellow crusaders in the Senate against the "slave power." Pitt's father, Samuel Fessenden, had been a state legislator and celebrated abolitionist lawyer. Pitt showed traces of his father's passion when he ascended to the Senate, in 1854. In his first appearance, Senator Andrew Butler of South Carolina had threatened secession if the North persisted with its antislavery agenda; Fessenden's sarcastic response—"Do not delay it on my account!"—thrilled northerners who had been longing for a spirited leader. Like other antislavery Whigs, Fessenden was not an abolitionist but a commerce-minded politician. Born in 1806, three years before Lincoln, and educated at Bowdoin, he had married Ellen Deering, daughter of a wealthy shipowner, who provided the couple with a federal-style home on Portland's fashionable State Street. Married into the commercial elite, young Pitt "lavished praise," so his biographer said, on the city's merchants. At twenty-five, he was elected to the legislature, with support of Maine businessmen who were lobbying for a charter to build a railroad to Montreal. Fessenden's mentor was Daniel Webster, with whom, in 1837, he memorably journeyed to the west, a three-month expedition via stage, steamboat, and muddy canals, the sorry state of which threw him into "a perfect rage" over President Jackson's opposition to internal improvements. Like Lincoln, Fessenden focused on the Whig economic issues—transportation, banking, and tariffs. He grew apart from Webster over the slavery issue, and denounced the Compromise of 1850, which Webster strongly supported. Nonetheless, Fessenden's opposition to slavery was rooted in a pragmatic belief that it stained the nation and its politics by empowering southern slave owners, as distinct from personal empathy for the enslaved. He opposed the expansion of slavery, he said publicly, "not on the ground of humanity, not on the question, whether slavery is right or wrong itself . . . but on the question of political power."

Fessenden's wife, Ellen, long in poor health, died in 1857, after which he fulfilled his Senate duties with joyless resolve. Rooming at a boardinghouse on Seventh Street, he took solace in card games and pursued an intimate correspondence with a younger female cousin. But he missed Portland and his home on State Street, with its overstocked library, its garden, and his circle of friends. With three of his four sons off to war, Fessenden was a lonely legislator. In July 1861, he was named chair of the Finance Committee, responsible for appropriations as well as revenue.

No sooner did the Legal Tender Act land in Fessenden's committee than Chase scribbled a personal letter, stressing the Treasury's need for more notes—*with* the legal tender proviso. Among those with whom Fessenden conferred, such as the Boston businessman John Murray Forbes, Representative Hooper, and Senator Sherman, all were strongly in favor. So, by now, was Chase, who emphasized that with the Treasury's debts mounting and its bonds trading well below par, borrowing was not a practical option. Yet Fessenden had doubts—in fact, he was plagued with doubt. The fact that he was the swing vote on the committee might have roused him to a decision, but in Fessenden's case, it merely heightened his agony. "I have been engaged all day in consulting with the Secretary and others, and no two men can be found to agree," he said in frustration. "This legal tender clause is opposed to all my views of right and expediency. It shocks all my notions of political, moral, and national honor." Fessenden was beset with constituent letters, but their conflicting counsels only deepened his crisis. He fitfully protested, "This thing has tormented me day and night for weeks."

It is important to recognize that to Fessenden and his colleagues, the legal tender notes would constitute a "debt." True, they bore no interest, and carried no maturity; nonetheless, it was widely assumed that, after the war, they would be redeemed for gold. Today, people think of "money" as having inherent value. In 1862, even proponents of legal tender thought of the paper as provisional, casting a debt upon the future.

Worse than a loan, the notes would be a *forced* loan (none could refuse them). This offended Fessenden's sense of commercial propriety. He questioned whether the emergency required such a drastic step. The government, after all, could pay its soldiers in any notes it chose. "If the soldier sends the notes to his wife to be passed at a country store," the senator reckoned, would not they be accepted? His greatest fear was mercantile and Whiggish—that legal tender would dishonor America among foreign creditors. This fear was not ungrounded—from London, the *Economist* quickly pronounced that the federal finances were heading toward "ruin."

Such were the divisions within the Senate Finance Committee—perhaps within the person of its chair—that it sent the bill to the floor without a recommendation. However, Fessenden orchestrated a critical change. In the original bill, the legal tender notes were to be lawful money "in payment of all debts, public and private." *As amended*, holders of government securities, and they alone, would be paid in coin, rather than in notes. Fessenden made this change to reassure investors, both domestic and overseas. The *London Morning Post*, the mouthpiece of Lord Palmerston, had already warned its readers that with legal tender the Union was "effecting its own ruin." Fessenden, whose Portland community was steeped in the transatlantic trade, was sensitive to British opinion. The amendment protected investors against a likely depreciation, but it blemished the bill with an unegalitarian bias. Soldiers in the field, and others, were to get paper; bondholders were to be paid in coin. The Whig commercial lawyer had declared his allegiance.

In the full Senate, business support was pivotal. Henry Wilson of Massachusetts, a shoemaker turned newspaper publisher, rebutted a proposal to strip the legal tender provision by pointing out that Boston merchants wholeheartedly favored the bill as a stimulant to business. Chambers of commerce in New York and other cities also supported it.

Sherman, who was being forcefully prodded by the financier Jay Cooke, sponsored the bill in the Senate. The Ohioan pointed out the United States would face obligations totaling more than $300 million by July 1—of which $100 million were due immediately. "How are we going to get this amount?" Sherman rhetorically quizzed the floor. It could not be from borrowing; the interest rate would be exorbitant. It was dubious, in any case, that people had the money to lend. Sherman also defanged the argument that government notes amounted to a forced loan. Perhaps in a technical sense, a soldier who was paid with a ten-dollar note was "lending the Government money," Sherman observed, but that was not the view that people took of it. For the soldier, even for the senator, "We receive notes as money." Legal tender would endow common practice with the force of law.

Fessenden wouldn't budge. The chairman voted *for* an amendment to kill the legal tender designation—which narrowly lost, 22–17. On the bill itself, he voted in favor, reckoning that the provision for interest payments in coin (which still needed House ratification) would reassure creditors. The Senate passed it overwhelmingly, 30–7. All but one of those opposed hailed from the east; all but one of the western senators voted in favor, hinting at an emerging regional split on monetary policy. After the Civil War, eastern legislators would favor tight money, while western states, and farm states in general, would tilt toward expansive currency.

Three days after the vote, Brigadier General Ulysses S. Grant captured Fort Donelson, on the Cumberland River in Tennessee—the biggest prize in the western strategy of choking the South by seizing major waterways. Coming on the heels of the capture of Roanoke Island, off North Carolina, the victory permitted opponents of legal tender to mount a last-ditch argument that the bill was no longer needed, since the war would be over soon.

During the debate, Washingtonians were subject to a spate of terrifying fevers, including smallpox. Chase's daughter Nettie contracted scarlet fever, and Kate, her older sister, took a severe cold. Thankfully, the girls had been staying with Jay Cooke in Philadelphia. Chase would have sent for them, he explained to Kate, "if I did not fear that Wash. just now must be considered an unhealthy place." Cooke's hospitality presumably tightened his bond with Chase. But it was truly an act of mercy. At a time when the capital was overrun with thousands of ragged soldiers, and conditions in the Potomac resembled those of a cesspool, Chase's girls were protected from further exposure. Lincoln was not so fortunate. Early in 1862, Willie and Tad, the President's eleven- and eight-year-old sons, suddenly became ill. The brothers were known for their mischievous play (they had delighted in pulling their father's lawbooks off the shelves) and their sudden quietude threw a pall over the President and First Lady, who years earlier had suffered the loss of their second son, Edward. Tad was only mildly afflicted, but Willie, whose deliberate way of puzzling through a problem Lincoln had likened to his own, and whom one writer was to call "a miniature Abe Lincoln," became seriously ill with typhoid. He died on February 20. The President sobbed as he related the news to John Nicolay, his private secretary. He was calm when Willie was laid to rest. Mary Todd Lincoln was plunged into an absorbing grief, from which she did not truly recover.

Lincoln was unavailable as the tender legislation reached a climax. The House ringleaders—Spaulding, Hooper, and Stevens—were apoplectic over the Senate's deference to bondholders. Their idea had been to contrive an equality, so that $100 of U.S. Notes were valued the same as $100 of specie. It was "simple in its machinery, and easily understood"—so claimed Stevens. The Senate provision for interest payments in coin upset the balance, because it created a greater demand for gold than for notes. What infuriated Stevens about the Senate's "cunning scheme" was the disequilibria it introduced between the financial class and everyone else. The closest among the Republican leaders to a genuine revolutionary, Stevens thundered, "It creates two classes of currency, one for bankers and brokers, and another for the people."

Hooper was so upset he tried to kill the entire bill. Preferring to compromise, Stevens fashioned an amendment requiring that tariff duties, as well as federal land sales, also be paid in gold. The idea was to restore some balance by furnishing the government with the coin it would need to make interest payments. Lincoln signed the Legal Tender Act on February 25. It introduced the country to fiat money and launched the first truly national currency since the 1830s.*

The bill seemed to have an immediate and invigorating effect. Business conditions in the North were noticeably perkier even during the legislative debate. An English correspondent in New York reported "little of any popular distress, or of hard times." The port and wharves were crowded with ships; Broadway was "impassable" due to the fleets of carts and carriages. The Britisher's only rebuke concerned the repression of Blacks, whom he dubbed "a class apart," unwelcome on many streetcars. In a damning reproof of northern racism, he added sadly, "I have never yet seen a Negro walking with a white man."

To fund operations while the tender notes were being engraved, Chase resorted to a variety of expedients. One of these bears special mention. On March 1, Congress gave Chase authority to issue certificates to approved creditors (that is, to contractors with audited claims) who preferred not to wait for cash. The certificates would run for a year and pay 6 percent interest. While clearly different from legal tender—they were not "lawful" money—contractors gobbled them up, either circulating them, using them as collateral for loans, or selling them to

---

* Notes of the Second Bank of the United States had circulated widely until the Bank was destroyed by Jackson.

investors, usually at a small discount from face value. Congress set no
limit on Chase's ability to issue the certificates, which were ready for
distribution almost immediately. As the *New York Daily Tribune* recognized, Chase had managed to turn claims against the Treasury into a
"first-class" financial instrument.

Within weeks, Chase was issuing nearly $2 million worth of cer-
tificates a day. Spaulding noted that the power given Chase was "broad
and unlimited." Effectively, it was the power to print money. Over the
course of the war, the Treasury issued just over $500 million of these
certificates—an enormous sum. As Chase was discovering, the demar-
cation between money and credit was vanishingly thin. Any debt or
IOU that was viewed as creditworthy could, in theory, circulate. It was
latent money.

The Confederate Congress was also debating legal tender. Numerous critics had pointed out that its failure to establish a trusted
currency was undermining its positive results on the battlefield. According to the *Nashville Union*, the sinking currency "threatens greater
dangers" than the federal armies. The *Richmond Enquirer* asserted similarly that currency depreciation "was more to be dreaded than all of
Lincoln's legions." The problem went deeper than inflation. Advanced
societies need a currency. Where a good one does not exist, people resort to a bad one. Since Confederate currency did not suffice, individual
states began to issue notes. Early in 1861, even before the shooting
began, Alabama authorized $1 million in state notes (a sum quickly
deemed to be insufficient); Virginia, Florida, and Georgia followed,
then Mississippi and North Carolina. When the war started, the city of
Richmond issued $300,000 in small bills; Charleston did so as well.
Not only states and cities but southern railroads and corporations issued
IOUs—essentially, private money. Small businesses and some individuals did the same. Innkeepers, grocers, milk dealers, and barbers hoarded
their silver and issued notes redeemable in goods and services. The

South experienced an explosion of monetary instruments, a spontaneous eruption of bills of every description. Bills of smaller and more familiar issuers proliferated because they were considered more trustworthy (the baker could always redeem his IOUs for bread, whereas the solvency of the Confederate government was rather in question). But the overall effect was chaos. A babel of currencies could not finance a national project such as a great war.

The rapid deterioration in the currency took a serious toll on Jefferson Davis's attempts at nation-building. Merchants in the South treated the supposed national money with disdain. They much preferred the notes of local banks (those that remained tolerably solvent), on the theory that the banks had customers, who might one day repay them with coin. One of the most popular southern bills was the red-tinted Citizens Bank of Louisiana ten-dollar note, known by its French appellation, *Dix*—or "Dixie." It spread so swiftly that the term became synonymous with the entire South. Bank notes such as the Dixie threatened to upstage Confederate money—and so did United States money. To Davis's ire, merchants in disputed terrain showed a clear preference for Union paper over Confederate notes. The latter were discounted as much as 75 percent. Southern loyalists excoriated those who dealt in Yankee money as traitors. A Memphis newspaper lambasted "persons in this city—traitors at heart, base and cowardly—[who] refused Confederate Treasury Notes in payment of debts due them." But calls to patriotism will rarely persuade a merchant to decline a good note in favor of a bad one.

A bill for Confederate legal tender was formally introduced weeks after Lincoln signed the U.S. Legal Tender Act. But the instinct of the Rebel Congress was originalist: to forbid anything the Rebel constitution didn't explicitly permit. And Treasury Secretary Memminger feared that a law making Rebel notes compulsory would backfire by inviting further suspicion of them. In March 1862, in a memo to the Confederate House Judiciary Committee, he explicitly forswore legal tender. He warned that printing notes was "the most dangerous of all methods of raising money."

But that did not still his hand. With military expenses escalating sharply, Memminger had no choice. Although historians have difficulty keeping track of the precise total, by March the note issue in the South may have been as high as $200 million (at the end of 1861 it had been only $100 million). At that rate of increase, it did not matter what the notes were called, or what their legal designation was: inflation was a dead certainty. Edmund Ruffin grumbled about percolating coffee prices and fumed that his son Julian had exchanged $100 in Confederate notes for only $30 in gold. Memminger requested a tax hike, hoping that it would stem the money printing. But even the modest existing tax was unpopular. The Treasury secretary's plea went unheeded.

Exercising central authority was a delicate matter for the Confederacy. States' rights was its founding credo, yet the war fostered a need for unitary control. Davis increasingly stretched the bounds of the Jeffersonian model. In the first winter of the war (1862), the President won authorization from Congress to suspend the writ of habeas corpus and to declare martial law in areas endangered by the enemy. Davis quickly used this authority in Richmond and in other Virginia cities. This was a bold step toward centralism. Infringements on civil liberties in the South were generally milder than in the North; nonetheless, they were bitterly opposed. Resentment was keenest in the poorest areas, such as the North Carolina hill country, whose farmers, eking out a meager living on rocky soil, had showed scant enthusiasm for joining a rebellion of wealthy cotton planters. Richmond's authoritarian edicts threatened to inflame the latent tension between planters and ordinary foot soldiers. Even Charleston, the cradle of the Confederacy, was sensitive to the terrifying possibility of a class schism. Mary Chesnut reported that "ladies in their landaus [enclosed carriages] were bitterly attacked by the morning paper for lolling back in their silks and satins, with tall footmen in livery, driving up and down the streets while the poor soldiers' wives were on the sidewalks."

Davis sought help on economic problems from his trusted lieutenant, Judah Benjamin. Benjamin, unpopular with the planters, had been forced out as war secretary after the loss of Roanoke Island—but Davis immediately made him secretary of state, in which role the two worked even more closely. As Richmond's top diplomat, Benjamin's focus was obtaining British and French support. Benjamin urged James Mason, one of the envoys seized on the *Trent* and now representing the Confederacy in London, to spread the word that peace would bring a bonanza in cotton and other southern trade. And Benjamin quietly contacted foreign agents in New Orleans to feel out the possibility of a European loan. He floated a more audacious proposal to Napoleon III, offering one hundred thousand bales of cotton plus access to southern markets *if* France recognized the Confederate States of America—or even better, broke the blockade. The emperor, whose uncle Bonaparte had sold Louisiana to the United States, was surely tempted. But France remained reluctant to act without Britain.

When the U.S. legal tender notes were issued, the inferior status of Rebel notes became clear. As John Christopher Schwab, a scholar born the week the Civil War ended, was to observe, "Wherever the Northern troops advanced, the Federal 'greenback' followed, and found its way into general circulation." Yankee bills crossed into disputed border regions and penetrated deep into Dixie, an early warning sign that the Confederacy was in trouble. Southern merchants needed no knowledge of the fine points of the legislation to discern that greenbacks were meeting with popular favor.

The term "greenback" emerged spontaneously. The bills were indeed green on the reverse side, and featured a portrait on the front (the one-dollar bill bore the likeness of Chase). Word of the efficacy of the new currency traveled quickly. In the first week of April 1862, *The Alleghanian* reported from Pennsylvania iron country that "Greenbacks are in demand—$1 of 'Lincoln currency' being equivalent to $1.25 in Tennessee bills." The *Holmes County* (Ohio) *Farmer* observed that when the federal paymaster made an overdue visit to the troops, he "set some of his Greenbacks afloat, which has gladdened many a heart. Some of them have not had any pay for the last six months." Even in Union-occupied Memphis, according to the *Chicago Daily Tribune*, stores were hawking clothing, groceries, and other "necessaries and luxuries" at greatly reduced prices—but only in exchange for gold, silver, or "the Lincoln greenbacks."

From the outset, greenbacks were exchanged at a 2 percent discount to gold. This was hardly runaway inflation, but it was a sign that the critics had not been all wrong. The depreciation was progressive; before year end, the greenback value in gold fell to only seventy-five cents. Its purchasing power also suffered. During 1862, prices in the North rose 12 percent, something of a shock to a generation that had not seen even modest inflation (prices in the three decades prior had been flat). The greenback contributed to the inflation, but so did the huge demand for military goods. When demand rises, higher prices are an appropriate response.*

Moreover, any reckoning of the inflationary harm must be balanced by the considerable benefits. The Treasury could pay soldiers' wages and purchase supplies. The government's credit, rather than suffering further injury, as many had predicted, immediately improved. Washington was now able to borrow vastly greater sums at slightly lower interest rates than at the time of Lincoln's inauguration. The lubricant of ready money revived the banks and elevated morale. Legal tender performed all of the expected functions of a currency, and it was accepted by the entire loyal population (and by much of the disloyal population). It also stretched the federal mandate, asserting public sovereignty over the money supply, previously the domain of private banks. It pushed the United States appreciably further in the direction of a centralized state. The Union's southern adversary, steeped in the ideology of states' rights,

---

* Since consumer prices were flat in the first year of the war (before the Legal Tender Act), the temptation is to blame the greenback for the entire inflation in 1862. However, wholesale prices rose at a steadier rate, even before the greenback. That suggests that war demand contributed to the inflation.

could not have been more different. From 1862 on, there were "Lincoln dollars," but never "Davis dollars."

Enactment of legal tender did not still the debate. Massachusetts senator Charles Sumner, a reluctant supporter, worried that Congress would fall into the dangerous habit of printing paper whenever it ran short of funds. "The medicine of the Constitution," he warned, "must not become its daily bread." Even John Sherman, who avidly favored the bill, pledged not to repeat the experiment, as if legal tender were a dangerous virus capable of infecting the entire nation. Retrospectively, he was more favorable. When Sherman wrote his memoirs decades later, he concluded that "the legal tender act was the turning point in our physical and financial history."

╭─────────╮
│   *Six*   │
╰─────────╯

Forgotten Congress

For me there is no greater name in
American education than that of
Senator Justin Smith Morrill.

— ROBERT FROST

I N THE DECADE BEFORE THE WAR, the U.S. Capitol underwent a
great expansion. The enlarged building required a higher dome
(the original, wood sheathed in copper, was also a fire hazard).
Work was suspended when the war broke out, but in 1862, building
resumed, and a new, cast-iron dome, modeled on St. Peter's Basilica in
Rome, rose over the Washington skyline.

The old dome had admitted a meager shaft of light through a single
oculus. The new one was ribboned with windows and capped by a
nineteen-foot-six-inch statue of a sword-bearing female defending freedom. It was a brilliant sight—to Lincoln a symbol of national unity that
seemed to affirm, as well, the Madisonian concept of legislative preemi-
nence.* It was during this time that the Thirty-Seventh Congress—the
most consequential yet—enacted a blizzard of legislation that made the
federal government, for the first time, a visible presence in the lives of
ordinary Americans. It inserted the government into economic develop-

---

* Federalist No. 51.

ment; it greatly expanded the federal bureaucracy; it reshaped the government's relationship to the American people, and it shifted the nexus of political power to Washington. All this occurred during its second session—a mere eight months, from December 1861 through July 1862, as the Union and Rebel armies waged a series of increasingly savage battles over Virginia in the east and Mississippi River towns and valleys in the west.

The Thirty-Seventh Congress, today scarcely remembered, was when American politics finally caught up to the legacy of the Whigs. It broke from the "governing least" philosophy of Jefferson and legislated in the spirit of the "more perfect union" advanced by Lincoln. It abandoned laissez-faire and interposed a visible hand in the hope that, also in Lincoln's words, "every man [might] have the chance." Congress enacted a protective tariff worthy of Henry Clay and enabling legislation for a transcontinental railroad. It involved the federal government in agriculture, education, and land policy. It legislated an income tax and refocused the war's purposes to include a frontal attack on slavery. It could almost be said that it created the government itself.

Walter A. McDougall, an American historian, called the Thirty-Seventh Congress the most prolific in history. Others said its actions amounted to a "second American revolution." "Counterrevolution" might be more apt. The Founding Fathers' animating idea was to impose checks on the government by dividing its power among the various branches and limiting its authority relative to that of the states. In the years since, their small-government bias had scarcely been challenged. The former Whigs in the Thirty-Seventh set the pendulum swinging in the other direction. They legislated boldly, and to the perceived edge of constitutional license. A San Francisco newspaper approvingly declared, "Constitutions are made for peace. We are at war." In fact, the Republicans in Congress remained firmly committed to the Constitution. But their interpretation of it was substantially liberalized. In the spring of 1862, their consistent impulse was to centralize.

Few of the members thought of themselves as revolutionaries. Many were motivated by the emergency of the moment rather than ideology. But it should not be forgotten that the Thirty-Seventh, unlike the Founding Fathers, was led, for the most part, by self-made men. On the whole, they were less intent on preserving, more on building and improving. They espoused a more national concept of patriotism—fidelity to the country rather than to their states.

With southerners absent, the Republicans comfortably controlled both chambers. Galusha Grow was Speaker of the House (he had been nominated by Stevens and was, like him, a New Englander resettled in Pennsylvania). Grow moved fast on a pair of bills that typified the Republican credo of furthering prosperity while thwarting the spread of slavery. The first of these, the Homestead Act, was a cornerstone of the Republican platform. A version of the idea had been around since 1775, when Jefferson had proposed that the Virginia constitution furnish 50 acres to each white male owning less than that amount. Congress passed a federal homestead law in 1860, but President Buchanan vetoed it. The 1862 version would provide settlers with 160 acres and give title to those who worked the land for five years. It perfectly blended Lincoln's two contrasting impulses regarding labor: his belief in self-reliance and his leavening conviction that the government should help to foster opportunity, even a dose of redistribution. It also heralded a change in land policy—land being what America held in abundance. Since the beginning of the Republic, land sales had been a prop to the federal budget. Remarkably, in the midst of a protracted budget crisis, the Republicans were willing to forgo the revenue and use the land to promote development as well as immigration. Even for the government to *think* of broader economic goals was new. As Lincoln eloquently put it:

> It has long been a cherished opinion of some of our wisest statesmen that the people of the United States had a higher and more enduring interest in the early settlement and substantial cultivation of the public lands than in the amount of direct revenue to be

derived from the sale of them. This opinion has had a controlling influence in shaping legislation upon the subject of our national domain.

The second bill would create an Agriculture Department. Although
the department's agenda would be modest, distributing seeds and statistical information and promoting improved cultivation, the idea was
truly revolutionary. For the first time, the government was to assist a
specific sector of private enterprise. Skeptical observers fretted over the
latent potential for bureaucratic expansion. If the government could distribute seeds, or underwrite one industry as opposed to others, what could
it not do? *The New York Times* churlishly groused, "Why not a Department of Manufactures?"

The answer, for the moment, was the need to mollify the farm states.
The new bill would establish an independent farm lobby with, for start-
ers, a commissioner at a $3000 annual salary and a chief clerk. The bill
was introduced by an Illinois congressman-farmer and friend of Lincoln, Owen Lovejoy. Lovejoy's brother Elijah had been a well-known
abolitionist printer—until, one night in 1837, he had been murdered by
a pro-slavery mob, as his horrified brother looked on. Owen adopted
abolitionism, energetically assisted runaway slaves, and championed
government support for agriculture. In the antebellum era, these causes
went hand in hand. Independent small farmers were considered the best
prophylactic against the spread of slavery.

By 1860, agricultural improvement was a big issue in the west—
where Lovejoy's bill found favor. Easterners were wary of the expense
and skeptical of the purpose. Farmers in the east were situated closer to
towns and had more farming know-how and more capital. Fessenden,
whose knowledge of farming was limited to New England (he had not
traveled west since the 1830s) said he doubted that one in a hundred
farmers had expressed any desire for government support. Westerners
were not so smug. Fessenden succeeded in paring the proposed department's budget; even then he voted against it. Lincoln, who knew the
west firsthand, envisioned that the Agriculture Department would be-

come a valuable prop for farmers. He signed the measure on May 15, 1862, and the Homestead Act five days later. The *Cleveland Morning Leader,* brimming with Republican faith in the new art of policy making, predicted that western lands would be improved and, what's more, "great encouragement and assistance will be given to the industrious poorer classes."

Another bill, proposed by Representative Morrill, expanded notions of the government's purposes. Morrill, the son of a blacksmith, had deeply regretted his inability to afford higher education. He had run a store, prospered (through lucrative investments in bank and railroad stocks), and become an inveterate reader. Eventually, he built his own library, but the missed education gnawed at him. Morrill thought tuition should be free and college democratized—an extraordinary notion at a time when less than a quarter of 1 percent of the population was enrolled in college. Indeed, few Americans had finished high school. Even among intellectuals, college was relatively rare. Walt Whitman hadn't attended college, nor had Mark Twain. Higher education was mainly for doctors, lawyers, and ministers. Morrill wanted colleges to teach more practical courses, befitting a man whose library was stocked with not only the classics but gardening and architecture books, which he had used to design his home and garden (the latter was a local showpiece, blooming with one hundred varieties of trees, shrubs, fruits, and nuts). He proposed a bill in 1857 to endow state public colleges that would specialize in "agricultural and mechanic arts." A highly practical man, Morrill was worried about soil depletion and declining productivity in Vermont's rocky terrain. His bill passed in 1859 but—like the Homestead Act—Buchanan vetoed it.

Morrill reintroduced the college bill in December 1861. Since he intended to fund the new colleges with grants of federal land, his bill was another example of using America's vast natural resources toward a public good. States would have five years to sell the land and use the proceeds to endow a college. The size of land grants was proportional to population (thirty thousand acres for each member of a state's congressional delegation); thus, the largest grants would go to New York and Pennsylvania. This biased westerners against the bill, especially since the largest tracts of federal land were located west of the Alleghenies. Westerners were hardly excited about seeing "their" land used to fund education in richer states back east. A Wisconsin Republican, John F. Potter, chair of the House Committee on Public Lands, determinedly shelved the bill. In May, however, Morrill pulled an end run, persuading Benjamin Wade of Ohio to introduce the bill in the Senate. Opponents insisted the land was needed for other uses, such as homesteads. In truth, the government had hundreds of millions of untapped acres; scarcity was not the issue. What slowed the bill was sectional rivalry and Congress's preference for giving land to railroads, where the potential for payoffs was considerably greater. Morrill made a plea on patriotic grounds: colleges, he said, would strengthen the Republic and prove a blessing for the ages, "wronging nobody." After an amendment limiting the acreage to be taken from any one state, even western Republicans were induced to go along. The Vermonter would prove prescient. Over time, the Morrill Act (formally, the Land-Grant College Act of 1862) would spawn approximately seventy institutions of higher learning. They ranged from Cornell University, founded in 1865, in the east (Morrill Hall still anchors the Cornell Arts Quad) to Oregon State University in the west. From the outset, admission was coeducational and, outside the South, racially integrated. For the first time, large numbers of nonaffluent students attended college. Practical curricula were emphasized, but not to the exclusion of liberal arts. The Morrill Act did indeed bring blessings through the ages.

Lincoln's contribution to the legislation was modest, although he heartily supported it. Few purposes were closer to Lincoln's heart than broadening opportunity for commoners, which had been his focus in his years in the political wilderness.

Lincoln was somewhat more involved in the Pacific Railway Act. Both his early struggles on the frontier and his later years as a railroad attorney conditioned him to think of railroads as a force for the national good. In particular, the legislation met Lincoln's test that government should do what private citizens couldn't. The expense and risk of building across the Rocky Mountains and the vast expanse of the Great Plains, where virtually no white settlers lived, was simply too great for private capital. The rail had been extensively debated during the 1850s, but legislation had foundered due to disputes over the route (north or south). When Lincoln, shortly before running for president, said, "The iron horse is panting, and impatient," he betrayed his own eagerness.

Business as well as ordinary travelers wanted a speedier and safer route through Indian territory and over the Rockies than the perilous trip by stage or the months-long voyage by sea. The territory had been surveyed; the rebellion added a fresh rationale for connecting California to the east. During the war, railroads had come to symbolize the national purpose. The Union's superior rail network gave its armies a tactical edge. One of its unsung heroes was General Herman Haupt, who had been drafted by Stanton to supervise the military's use of railroads. Haupt was an organizational genius. He knitted myriad railways into what was, in effect, the country's first mass transportation system. In May 1862, using untrained recruits, Haupt astounded generals by erecting a four-hundred-foot bridge over Potomac Creek, clearing a route to Fredericksburg. When Lincoln saw it, he called it "the most remarkable structure human eyes ever rested upon." Perhaps no less surprised were the raw troops, many of whom, prior to enlistment, had never traveled with the aid of machines. None of this figured in the details of the legislation, but it burnished the public impression of the railroad as a patriotic enterprise, one that would further the "march of civilization." As Thaddeus Stevens said of the railroad bill, "Few will doubt its utility as a great national work." What could be more straightforward?

As it turned out, practically anything. In the first place, the "transcontinental railroad" wasn't one railroad but several. The federal government had no authority, or so it was asserted, to charter a railroad *within the states*. It could only do so within the territories. (Once again,

Congress was restrained by the very doctrine of states' rights in whose name the rebellion was being waged.) Thus, Congress proposed to charter a new enterprise, patriotically dubbed the Union Pacific Railroad Company. The Union Pacific was to run from the eastern edge of Nebraska Territory to the western boundary of Nevada Territory. From its eastern terminus, the Union Pacific would link up with various feeder railways running along the Missouri River and points east. In the west, the Central Pacific, chartered by California, would lay track from the Golden State until it bumped into the Union Pacific in Nevada or Utah.

The first question was whether ownership should be public or private. Fearing that a government monopoly would wield too much power, Congress opted for private ownership under federal supervision. The difficulty was that private capital would not build without assistance; the terrain was simply too difficult and too remote. Congress had to provide an incentive, and once again, it offered land grants, with the added rationale that a railroad would raise the value of surrounding terrain. But land grants were not enough. To induce investment, legislators offered developers a special plum—U.S. bonds, delivered on the completion of each forty-mile section of track, with the number of bonds to be trebled for the most challenging terrain. This formula was essentially guesswork. Congress had no experience in chartering railroads; it had not, actually, chartered a corporation of any sort since the Second Bank of the United States, in 1816.

As Congress was wrestling with this complicated issue, lobbyists descended. The most artful of these was Thomas Ewing Jr., a Kansas Republican, a real estate speculator, and a director of the Leavenworth, Pawnee and Western Railroad Company (LP&W). The LP&W had been chartered by the Kansas territorial legislature in 1855, but remained a "paper railroad," without track and practically speaking without assets. Moreover, its potential path was blocked by a Delaware Indian reservation. Ewing advanced the nearly bankrupt line's prospects by securing a treaty with the Delaware (ostensibly an agreement between the tribe and the United States) ceding rights-of-way and more than one hundred thousand acres of mortgageable territory, on exceptionally favorable terms. When a group of Delawares, backed by a government Indian agent, protested that the negotiating chiefs were unschooled in the ways of contracts and were likely drunk when the deal was cut, Ewing hurried to Washington, toting affidavits testifying to the chiefs' sobriety. Ewing met with Lincoln several times. The President came to doubt the treaty's fairness and insisted on provisions that he hoped would protect the tribe. Nonetheless, the treaty that Lincoln sent to the Senate for ratification remained a railman's dream.

When the Pacific Railway Act was introduced, Ewing turned his energy to securing a main branch line for the LP&W. Shares were promptly distributed to relatives or cronies of the two Kansas senators, Samuel C. Pomeroy and James Lane. Ewing reported gleefully, "We have friends in all the delegations."

His friends treated Ewing kindly. Ignoring objections from Iowa, which had the stronger geographic claim, the House bill positioned the main spur in Kansas. Ewing chortled that if the bill were enacted, "my interest will be worth a half million dollars" (more than $13 million today). The Senate was not so pliable. Senator Daniel Clark of New Hampshire called the bill "a great scheme to get the Government's money." His blood rising at the brazen corruption of party principles, the senator thundered:

> I am willing to build a Pacific railroad; I am willing to start near Fort Kearney [Nebraska] or at some proper point, and build it through the deserts and over the mountains, so as to give a national road; but I am not willing to give the Government's money to aid the people in particular states to build branches to it.

Ultimately, the Senate version authorized the Union Pacific to build the main spur from the boundary of Iowa, with the precise terminus to be chosen by the President of the United States. The LP&W was downgraded to feeder branches from Kansas City and Leavenworth.

The final bill included significant safeguards. Congress narrowed the financial incentive by deferring a portion of the bonds. It tasked the President with picking two nonshareholders to serve on the Union Pacific board, as public watchdogs. And it retained the right to reduce fares along the Union Pacific if profits exceeded 10 percent of costs. Perhaps most crucially, to prevent the companies from shilly-shallying at public expense, if the line wasn't completed by 1876, all the pieces of the transcontinental road would revert to federal ownership.

Fessenden so objected to the bill's corporate tilt he declined to cast a vote. It was also arguable that the Senate erred in the other direction—by being too parsimonious. The law authorized the Union Pacific to organize a board and commence operations only after it had sold $2 million of stock (out of a total authorized capitalization of $100 million). Whether the act offered a sufficient carrot to entice private capital would not be clear for some time. While the next move was up to investors, the quartet of land bills marked a highpoint of Whiggish legislation. For the first time, the government assumed responsibility for transportation, farming, development, and education.

The legislative burst was accompanied by generally encouraging war news. General Grant had taken not only Fort Donelson but also Fort Henry in Tennessee, and the Union had secured its hold in Missouri. By late winter 1862, the Union seemed to have entered a more conventional phase of "organized war" in which one campaign predictably followed another. That April, Grant turned back a fierce attack at Shiloh. More consequential in economic terms were the successes of the Union navy. The sea was the South's economic lifeline, and naval battles, though they received less fanfare than the bloody encounters on land, assumed paramount importance. In a harbinger of the Union's growing strength at sea, it intercepted the side-wheel steamer *Magnolia*, which was transporting four hundred bales of cotton, off Mobile. (The engineer tried to destroy the ship but succeeded only in killing himself.) Ruffin, the Virginia diarist, glumly reflected, "The continuation of the Yankee blockade threatens more danger to our cause, by the consequent scarcity & high prices of necessaries of life, than do the Yankee arms & armies & fleets."

Weeks after Shiloh, Union Commander David C. Farragut invaded the lower Mississippi and captured New Orleans. This seriously constrained the Confederacy's inland river network. Cotton producers in the lower watershed were cut off from the market. Mary Chesnut was dejected, lamenting, "New Orleans gone and with it the Confederacy."

The Confederacy's survival was further imperiled by falling enlistments. Fearing a crisis, its Congress took up a controversial proposal from a career soldier with the ignominious distinction of having previously been offered the command of the army he had chosen to fight against—Robert E. Lee. Now serving as adviser to President Davis, Lee, one of America's most esteemed career soldiers, blue or gray, proposed a compulsory draft. Conscription faced strident opposition from states' rights adherents, who disliked rule from Richmond nearly as much as from Washington. But with Davis's strong support, Congress enacted a draft on white males ages eighteen to thirty-five, with exceptions for government officials and people in vital trades. A more controversial exemption was granted to one male in each household owning more than twenty slaves. Due both to its intrusive nature and its rank inequity, the draft was immediately unpopular.

The Confederacy lacked for supplies even more than men. It lacked machinery, spare parts, clothing—and food. Plantations switched from cotton to corn and grain, but not enough to alleviate shortages. Richmond, formerly a stately city, now looked harried and threadbare. A visitor described the capital as "tired and tawdry." Whiskey was in short supply. Gambling houses closed—"excepting the select few which were frequented by the higher officers of the Government."

No one kept closer tabs on daily life in the capital than John Beauchamp Jones, a Maryland journalist and southern sympathizer who went south at the start of the war, having written Jefferson Davis and obtained a job as a senior clerk in the War Department. Jones made daily entries in his diary on economic indicators such as food supplies and prices. At the beginning of 1862, he recorded that beef was selling at 30 cents a pound, up from 12 cents at the start of the war. By May, beef as well as bacon had jumped to 50 cents. Coffee had surged to $1.50 a pound, ladies' shoes to an exorbitant $15, and boots to a stratospheric $30 a pair.

General John Winder, who was governing Richmond under martial law, tried to maintain a semblance of a normal economy by imposing price ceilings on foodstuffs. However, farmers refused to sell at the controlled prices. Winder quickly acknowledged the failure and lifted controls.

With the Confederacy reeling financially, the Union had a seeming chance to deliver a knockout blow. New Yorkers took bets on when General McClellan would be dining in Richmond. But rather than make a direct advance, the general insisted on a drawn-out maneuver, transporting his troops by water down the Chesapeake Bay to Fort Monroe, then embarking on an arduous march up the Virginia Peninsula. While moving at a glacial pace, the would-be Napoleon ceaselessly complained that his army (which greatly outnumbered the one it faced) lacked for supplies and men. Lincoln's message of April 9 showed his mounting irritation:

> I think it is the precise time for you to strike a blow. By delay the enemy will relatively gain upon you—that is, he will gain faster, by *fortifications* and *re-inforcements*, than you can by re-inforcements alone. . . . I always insisted, that going down the Bay in search of a field, instead of fighting at or near Manassas, was only shifting, and not surmounting, a difficulty—that we would find the same enemy, and the same, or equal, intrenchments, at either place.

Republicans in Congress were equally impatient. Frustration with the stalled campaign in Virginia spurred them to move against slavery.

In the minds of the antislavery Radical wing,* the war and emancipation were joined at the hip. Thaddeus Stevens noted that freed slaves could become a potent force in the Union army. At very least, he recognized that the Union had an economic imperative, and therefore a military imperative, to eliminate the South's supply of unpaid labor. "If the slaves no longer raised cotton and rice, tobacco and grain for the rebels," Stevens declared, "this war would cease in six months." On a moral plane, he said it was time to "carry out to final perfection" the principle of all men created equal. The Pennsylvanian had the soul of an abolitionist. Not every Republican did, but as the war dragged on, they naturally felt the stakes were rising. The mounting cost in treasure and blood seemed to demand a larger purpose. As early as the start of the Thirty-Seventh Congress, in December 1861, William Holman, an Indiana Democrat, proposed that the House reaffirm the resolution of the previous summer that abolishing slavery was *not* a war aim. This time, the House refused to go along.

Congress followed with a flurry of antislavery measures. In March, it acted on Lincoln's request for a resolution granting aid to any state that adopted a program of gradual emancipation. The same month, it forbade army officers from returning fugitive slaves, a pressing issue as thousands of Blacks in the South were fleeing to the shelter of Union camps. In April, Congress abolished slavery in the District of Columbia. Although the United States compensated slaveholders ($300 per slave), abolition in the capital was freighted with symbolic power. George Templeton Strong, the diarist, marveled, "The federal government is now clear of all connection with slaveholding." In June, the Thirty-Seventh banned slavery in every U.S. territory, resolving the issue that, above all others, had led to the war.

Radicals such as Charles Sumner and Thaddeus Stevens prodded and provoked Lincoln to declare a general emancipation. Exuding the

---

* To modern readers, it may seem odd to call antislavery hard-liners "Radical," but that was the contemporary term, reflecting the verité that the northern public was not generally abolitionist.

Whiggish credo for legislative direction, Sumner said of the President, "He is only the *instrument* of Congress." Lincoln, however, regarded slavery policy as well within his domain. His views regarding emancipation were inching toward those of the Radicals, but he insisted that he would control both the policy and its timing.

With all the talk of emancipation, few had thought about how freed Blacks would manage or what assistance they would need in transition. In the blinkered view of white Americans, it was an open question whether emancipated slaves would be willing to work. The liberal *Atlantic Monthly* deemed this "the social problem of our time." The progressive Mary Peabody Mann, a teacher and the widow of the education reformer Horace Mann, ridiculed the latent racism embedded in such a formulation. In a letter to Chase, she urged both him and Lincoln to move ahead of public opinion and take "definite action." Specifically, she asked the Treasury secretary to reject "the chronic but absurd prejudice that the freed slaves will never be able to take care of themselves." Chase received such counsel warmly. He was supervising a test case, the South Carolina Sea Islands, where former slaves resided on two hundred abandoned plantations. Potentially, the islands could showcase economic opportunity for the freedmen.

However, Chase's agent on the islands, the former cotton trader William Reynolds, was mostly interested in the islands' profit potential. On January 1, 1862, Reynolds assured Chase that all was well with his new charges. "The Negroes seem very well disposed," he reported, "& quite well pleased with the new order of things here, most of them preferring to remain on the Plantation where they were raised, if they can receive something for their Labor." Chase got a more thorough report from Edward Pierce, the headstrong Boston lawyer he had dispatched to look after the Negroes' welfare. Soon after disembarking in Port Royal, Pierce dispatched a remarkable thirty-six-page letter—the first detailed report on the condition of freed African Americans. Pierce was perceptive, compassionate, only rarely patronizing, and decidedly optimistic regarding the fate of the former bondsmen. He had no doubt that, "when properly organized . . . they will, as freemen, be as industrious as any race of men are likely to be in this climate."

Pierce gave an unvarnished account of the freedmen's lifestyle, emphasizing that slavery had distorted their social relations. Visiting the sixteen-by-twelve-foot shacks, one to a family, where the Blacks resided, he reported:

> Except on Sundays, these people do not take their meals at a family table, but each one takes his hominy, bread, or potatoes, sitting on the floor or a bench, and at his own time. They say their masters never allowed them any regular time for meals.

Pierce emphasized to Chase, a most prudish man, that the freedmen's loose pattern of sexual congress was similarly the result of years of bondage:

> Notwithstanding their religious professions, in some cases more emotional than practical, the marriage relation, or what answers for it, is not, in many instances, held very sacred by them. The men, it is said, sometimes leave one wife and take another—something likely to happen in any society where it is permitted or not forbidden by a stern public opinion, and far more likely to happen under laws which do not recognize marriage, and dissolve what answers for it by forced separations, dictated by the mere pecuniary interest of others.

Pierce stressed that the freedmen wanted to earn their keep, but he warned that the Treasury was behind in their wages. "This delay of payment . . . has made the laborers uneasy, and affected the disposition to work." The former slaves were also impatient for their children to get schooling. Yet despite ample basis for complaint, the freedmen demonstrated a surprising lack of rancor. Pierce noted, "They make no universal charges of cruelty against their [former] masters."

Thanks to runaways, who were fleeing the mainland in small craft, mostly at night, the Black population on the islands was steadily climbing. Pierce urged that Chase make haste in providing an administrative structure for this swelling community, as well as schools, ministers, and doctors. Pierce also warned that Colonel Reynolds's plan to lease the plantations would encourage "the worst vices of the slave system" and, as in British East India, attract men whose paramount interest would be "self-interest." If, on the other hand, the Treasury could adopt a "beneficent system" staffed by progressive administrators, Chase could settle "a great social question."

This plea resonated with Chase, who hoped to fuse the social mission with economic goals. After getting authorization from Lincoln, he organized the plantations under a network of superintendents. No federal money was available to help the freedmen, but Pierce was given carte blanche to raise funds from sympathetic charities. Benevolent societies in Boston and New York sent teachers and other recruits. The first delegation of pilgrims, a zealous group of forty-one men and twelve women, many from Harvard, Yale, and divinity schools, departed New York on the steamship *Atlantic* March 3. They likened their voyage to that of the *Mayflower*, journeying to a strange new world. One said fatalistically of the mission, on which three teachers would perish, "Success or defeat might be in store for us." They found the Blacks already planting corn in private patches, but disinclined to grow cotton, a hated "badge of servitude." Nonetheless, forty-five hundred acres of cotton were brought into cultivation, and workers were given side plots to grow food. Chase's experiment seemed to be off to a good start. Thirty schools were organized; two thousand children attended, most of whom, previously, had not been able to identify a single letter.

Yet, the Blacks were effectively tenants on the land and highly vulnerable. Northern textile brahmins exhorted Chase to ramp up cotton production, while cloaking their message in high-minded talk of racial betterment. Some of the businessmen were genuinely interested in demonstrating that paid labor performed better, but the "free" Blacks had no say over wages or other living conditions.

Inevitably, Chase's two emissaries on the islands clashed. Pierce was outraged over the Blacks' mistreatment. Their pay was inadequate, and Colonel Reynolds was overcharging them for coffee and sugar. Soldiers cavalierly stole the freedmen's livestock and farm animals. Pierce's concerns were echoed by Mansfield French, a Methodist minister and racial egalitarian. French warned Chase, "I have not found under Colonel Reynolds one man whose heart, I think, is right towards the colored man's moral intent." After barely a month of trying to coexist with Reynolds, Pierce added troubling details. The cotton agent appointed by Reynolds was "a most unsuitable man . . . so far as the welfare of the negroes is concerned." This agent, Colonel William H. Nobles, was scheming to make $40,000—a fantastic sum, equivalent to $1 million in today's money—from cotton harvested by hired Black labor. Colonel Reynolds, for his part, bridled at the outspoken do-gooder's efforts to meddle in his plantations. He assured Chase he had done all he could do facilitate Pierce's efforts, but tellingly added, "I must say frankly, he has made himself *personally* obnoxious to me, by assuming authority over those employed by me." Reynolds denied he had come to Port Royal for "pecuniary considerations," but crudely added of his Black charges that seven-eighths were "totally unfit for the positions which they attempt to occupy."

In a final salvo, Pierce responded that "the Government has not treated the laborers as a good master or as a good employer." Some were going "ragged, and even naked." Colonel Nobles, aggrieved by Pierce's nonstop complaining, accosted Pierce and struck him a violent blow to the head, knocking him to the ground. By then, the War Department had had enough. It took over the islands' administration, under the command of General Rufus Saxton, a Massachusetts progressive to Chase's liking. Chase encouraged Pierce to stay on, but the lawyer left in June. Chase continued to take a proprietary interest in the Sea Islands, but for the moment, his involvement in the experiment had ended.

Just as Chase's role in South Carolina was ebbing, Lincoln invited Chase and Secretary of War Stanton to accompany him on a revenue cutter to Fort Monroe, at the southeast tip of Virginia, to investigate the military situation and hopefully spur General McClellan to more decisive action. Chiefs of state in that era could still see a war firsthand, and the distinguished entourage witnessed stirring battle scenes. At one point, Lincoln feared for their safety. The brush with danger quickened Chase's pulse and livened his prose. He recounted to his daughter having seen the ironclad USS *Monitor*, which had battled a Rebel ironclad to a ferocious draw. Suddenly, he reported, they saw a belch of smoke curling over Sewell's Point, "and each man, almost, said to the other, 'There comes the Merrimac.'"* Somewhat anticlimactically, "the great rebel terror" avoided a repeat engagement and steamed back to berth. After witnessing the capture of Norfolk, Chase fretted aloud that he had forgotten to write an important letter before leaving the capital. Lincoln soothed his feelings with a philosophical aside. Having in the past suffered when his words were later used against him, the President mused. "A man was sometime lucky in forgetting to write a letter," lest it appear in the future "and confront him with an indiscreet word or expression."

While they were on shipboard, the simmering dispute over who controlled slavery policy burst into the open. Union General David Hunter, an ally of the Radical wing in Congress, abruptly decreed that, as "a military necessity," all the slaves in his department (encompassing South Carolina, Georgia, and Florida) were "forever free." Hunter's decree was partly a response to the increasing numbers

---

* The USS *Merrimack* (misspelled by Chase) had been rechristened, by Richmond, the CSS *Virginia*.

of Blacks who were escaping into Union lines. But it preempted Lincoln. Back in Washington, Chase advised Lincoln, "It seems to me of the highest importance . . . that this order be not revoked." Lincoln tersely rebuked his Treasury secretary: "No commanding general shall do such a thing, upon *my* responsibility, without consulting me." Two days later, Lincoln annulled Hunter's order. Lincoln, typically, was concerned about the effect of such a decree on the border states, and adamant that generals not be permitted to hijack a major policy decision. Chase could not suppress his frustration. Corresponding with Hunter and with Horace Greeley, Chase indulged his habit of surreptitiously criticizing Lincoln.

However, Lincoln's annulment did not take issue with the substance of Hunter's decree; the President merely stated that he reserved such questions to himself. He further softened the effect of the annulment by issuing an "earnest appeal" to the border states to accept the federal government's previous offer of compensation in return for gradual emancipation. Even Chase, in a letter to Jay Cooke, seemed ready to accept the ultimate wisdom of Lincoln's course. "We are certainly too lenient [to slave owners]; but the President hates to be harsh, even when harshness is deserved," the Treasury secretary noted. "I must say, I have always found his judgment wonderfully good." Those were the most generous words about Lincoln Chase ever wrote. Frederick Douglass said much the same, remarking in an address in Rochester, New York, that a "blind man can see where the President's heart is." Senator Sumner echoed Douglass, replying to a friend who criticized the President's gradualism that if he knew Lincoln as Sumner did, even with all his caution, "you would be grateful that he is so true to all that you have at heart."

On the financial front, the Union's condition had been improved by the new greenbacks. Duty receipts were also higher. At least temporarily, the government had money to spend. Newspapers celebrated a bull market in Union bonds and the seeming success of Chase's financial regime. Particularly gratifying were reports that American bonds were in brisk demand in London.

Yet the Union's credit still depended on the premise that Congress would shore up the Treasury with revenue. All through the feverish legislative spring, the House subcommittee on revenue, chaired by Justin Morrill, burrowed away on a tax bill. The Vermonter painstakingly laid out 119 sections whose object was to extract an unprecedented slice of the national income for the government.

The revenue bill superseded the never implemented tax of 1861 and was far more extensive. Maunsell Field, a Treasury official, said the intent was to tax "every thing under the sun." A constituent of John Sherman in Dayton, Ohio, went one further: "Every thing on the earth and *under* the earth is to be taxed." For a people who had thrown off the yoke of England on account of relatively minor levies, the breadth of the legislation was eye-popping. Morrill's bill imposed excise taxes on scores of professions and commercial activities. It taxed interest, dividends, and inheritances.* It superimposed a personal income tax, which resulted in double taxation. Radically for its time, the income tax was progressive—the rate was greater for higher earners. In another modern touch, it mandated withholding from government employees. To ensure collection from everyone else, it created a Bureau of Internal Revenue within the Treasury Department, which was to divide the nation into 185 revenue districts and dispatch assessors and collectors into every commercial nook of the country. The commissioner of the new bureau started with three clerks; within a year, he would preside over a staff of four thousand.

Congressmen vociferously protested that tax collection would be intrusive. Even Morrill, in bringing the bill to the floor, apologized for its

---

* A legislative draft gives a vivid sense of the nineteenth-century business landscape. It included taxes on spiritous liquors, ale and beer, stem or leaf tobacco, cigars, lard, linseed oil, coal oil, gas, banknote paper and printing paper, soap, salt, sole leather and upper leather, flour, railroad passengers per mile, steamboat passengers, omnibuses, ferryboats and horse railroads, advertisements, carriages, gold and silver watches (later deleted), gold plate, billiard tables, slaughtered cattle, hogs, and sheep. The bill imposed license fees on bankers, auctioneers, wholesale and retail liquor dealers, retail dealers in goods, pawnbrokers, "rectifiers" (distillers), brewers, hotels, inns and taverns, eating houses, commercial brokers, other brokers, theaters, circuses, bowling alleys, wholesale and other peddlers, and coal oil distilleries.

"inquisitorial" character. Ohio representative George Pendleton warned, "When this vast system goes up into operation, and these tax gatherers are abroad in the land, there will go up a voice in the country that will make this legislature tremble."

Pendleton was to prove prescient. Although assessors relied primarily on "personal declarations" by taxpayers, the new bureau had the power to issue summonses and search homes. It also relied on informers to rat out their neighbors, a practice Americans found odious. In an attempt to compel compliance, the bureau disclosed lists of taxpayers and their incomes, which were published in local newspapers, in the hope that it would discourage cheating. Far more than a tax on tea, this was an unprecedented intrusion in Americans' lives.

But there was no doubt the revenue was needed. Under existing law, taxes for fiscal 1862 (ending in June of that year) would amount to only $52 million, far less than the $80 million Chase had forecast. Opposition was less to taxation per se; rather, opponents urged that collection be left to the states, which they imagined people would find less objectionable. The attachment to federalism ran deep, even in the North. Predictably, Thaddeus Stevens pushed back. "Why, sir," old Thad said mockingly, "will there be any more officeholders if they are appointed by the United States than if they are appointed by the States? Would they go to any more houses? Would they frighten any more people?" Far from apologizing for creating a federal machinery, Stevens, the quintessential Republican, was proud of it.

Business energetically lobbied to weaken the bill.* Some sixty lobbyists swarmed in and about the Capitol. "Everybody wants to see his neighbor taxed," the *Chicago Daily Tribune* noted, "but is anxious that his own burden shall be light." Congress secured the tax by protecting

---

* Sherman's files for the spring of 1862 are stuffed with pleas from lobbyists representing—among others—the iron, railroad, publishing, whiskey, milling, tobacco, banking, gas light and coke, insurance, wine, leather, and mitten and gloves industries. Let one letter speak for their general character: "The undersigned, manufacturers are wholesale dealers in perfumery, cosmetics and fancy soaps in the City of Philadelphia respectfully represent that . . . the proposed tax bill is in regard to our peculiar industry so onerous and cumulative in its provisions as to cause the ruin of our business."

key constituencies. The income tax was imposed only above $600 of earnings per year (about $16,100 in today's money)—too high to affect the vast majority of wage earners. The bill also treated farmers more kindly than manufacturers. Finally, the debates persuaded investors that, without a tax, inflation would result and bond values would suffer. Thus, the poor and many farmers had little to lose from the tax, and the rich were persuaded to embrace it.

The members conducted an interesting debate on whether to tax property in slaves. They decided not to, for fear of legitimatizing slavery. Progressivity was also an issue. The House set the income tax at a flat 3 percent. In the Senate, where farm states had greater proportional strength, there was more resentment of eastern wealth. Not coincidentally, it was the upper chamber that raised the tax to 5 percent for income above $10,000.

The Revenue Act, all twenty thousand words, was the longest and most detailed statute the country had ever seen. It was widely reported on (even in Richmond), and it had some obvious flaws. It failed to tackle the thorny question of whether "income" would mean "net income"—but at the same time, it was needlessly complex. The Senate tacked on no fewer than 315 amendments. Yet it was still a watershed. It enlarged the scope of the national government; it bolstered the government's credit, and it contributed to a dawning sense of nationhood. Its underlying rationale was also important: as the people's government, the United States had a call on the public income. Lincoln signed the bill on July 1, 1862.

To level the field for domestic firms targeted by new taxes, Morrill sought—once again—higher tariffs. He spun the increase as a necessary shield; otherwise, "we shall have destroyed the goose that lays the golden eggs." In truth, American industry was thriving. But northern manufacturers sensed that the war was providing political cover for higher tariffs. A coal operator unabashedly informed Morrill that if he raised the tariff, "it will influence thousands of votes." War fervor had also whipped up nationalistic feeling. The public resented Britain for its blockade running and was willing to countenance greater barriers to British goods.

Henry Carey, the proselytizer for higher tariffs, again helped Morrill write the bill. By the time it reached the floor, members were wilting in the steamy Washington summer and anxious to finish. The "second Morrill tariff" was enacted on July 14. It raised duties to record levels—on average, 37 percent. The bill also sliced the "free list" by nearly half. Even farm products were slapped with higher duties, though few nations could hope to compete with American agriculture.

Perhaps out of embarrassment that trade policy had morphed from its previous purpose of furnishing revenue to, in addition, sheltering industry from competition, the official language of the 1862 tariff described it as "an Act increasing, temporarily, the duties on imports"—as though the higher levies were merely a wartime adjustment. But the act did not contain a sunset provision, and its tariffs would prove remarkably durable. Under the pretext of war, a curtain of protection had been draped over the country, a more rigid version of the "American system" pursued by the Whigs and Henry Clay.

Paradoxically, while Congress was legislating new taxes, the Treasury was running out of money again. The drawn-out fighting in Virginia was dreadfully expensive, and it would be some while before the new taxes furnished revenue. The Union's debt had ballooned to $514 million (eight times its prewar level): borrowing would be difficult. The easiest solution was to print more greenbacks. Chase, fearing inflation, was reluctant. Lincoln lightheartedly urged him to "give your paper mill another turn." With Lincoln's support, Chase went to Congress. Although congressional leaders had promised that they would stop with a single issue, greenbacks were popular and they seemed to be working. On July 11, Congress authorized an additional $150 million.

Even as the new tenders were being considered, the market value of the greenback tumbled. When the bills first appeared, in April 1862, they traded at a discount to gold of 2.5 percent (one greenback dollar fetching 97.5 cents in gold). The discount steadily widened, to 4.5 percent in May and 9.5 percent in June. The currency fell further in July.

It is tempting to think that the excess supply prompted traders to mark down the price. This was almost certainly not the case. In the long run, the greenback fluctuated according to its purchasing power, but in the short run it was as much a military indicator as a financial one. In the late spring of 1862, the Confederacy had been on the ropes. McClellan had pursued the Rebels to within six miles of Richmond. Mary Chesnut despaired that they were to be "starved out." In June, Davis's government made plans to evacuate the capital. Then, the wheel turned. Rebel General Stonewall Jackson engineered a brilliant diversion, invading the Shenandoah Valley and paralyzing the Union command. The Rebels gained precious time to concentrate their forces. Significantly, Lee was installed as head of the Army of Northern Virginia. Late in June, Lee counterattacked. Both sides suffered horrendous casualties, but the result was a disaster for the Union. Lee flung the Yankees back toward Washington, and the Union's ill-fated Peninsula campaign was abandoned.[*]

The likely explanation for the sell-off on Wall Street is that financial markets were dismayed by the Union retreat and the prospect of a longer war (delaying any eventual redemption of greenbacks). Strong, who was close to the pulse of markets, wrote on June 30, "The darkest day we have seen since Bull Run."

Wall Street's verdict was ominous for Chase. It signaled that investors would support the Union only so long as it was winning. The Treasury secretary contemplated resigning. He was distraught over the renewed financial troubles and frustrated by Lincoln's continued sufferance of McClellan, whom he had demoted but kept in command. Chase vented

---

[*] Had the South surrendered at this point—before Lincoln committed to emancipation—the war might have ended without a clear mandate to abolish slavery.

his despair to Cooke on July 4. Lamenting the "sad state" of the nation on Independence Day, he could only wonder: "Is it the darkest hour before the dawn? God grant it."

Congress was furious over the military fiasco and seized the initiative again. All spring it had been pressing Lincoln to tighten the knot on slavery. As frustration with McClellan reached the breaking point, the Radicals demanded a second Confiscation Act—stronger than the similarly named bill of a year earlier. The aim was to take the economic war to the plantation, by authorizing, on military grounds, the seizure of property (including slaves) of Rebel officials. While some property had already been seized, the bill sought to institutionalize this practice, by making it a duty of the President to initiate confiscations, subject to legal proceedings in U.S. courts. Slaves escaping into Union lines were also to be freed.

Lincoln had serious qualms about the bill, legally and as a matter of policy. The President and the Radicals divided over a defining issue: Was the South to be simply defeated, or was its society and economic structure to be remade? Stevens was warming to the idea of an economic upheaval, uprooting the oligarchy and confiscating plantations. The fiery congressman had said earlier, "I would seize every foot of land, and every dollar of their property as our armies go along, and put it to the uses of the war and to the pay of our debts." Lincoln also was thinking about emancipation. But he habitually subjected proposed legislation to a lawyerly screen. The broad license in this bill to seize property seemed of dubious legality. To the fury of the Radicals, Lincoln prepared a veto message. Congress was forced to placate the President by adding a moderating "explanatory resolution" that shielded heirs of treasonous offenders from forfeiture of real estate. On July 17, 1862, Lincoln, still with some misgivings, signed the Confiscation Act. In practice, neither Confiscation Act freed many slaves. Its exhaustive work now done, Congress adjourned.

Congress's attack on slavery resembled its economic program in that each sprang from the Republican vision of an expanded national government. The partisan *New York Times* applauded the growing federal sector for its apparent connection to the North's more advanced civilization. "The people of the North," the *Times* exulted, "seek a consolidated Government because this is the only Government which can give a field for industry and enterprise." Contrariwise, in the South, the central state had few responsibilities other than the military and defending slavery. Unlike economies had yielded contrary philosophies of government:

> The two sections have therefore always been at issue upon questions of tariff and internal improvements. The construction of a railroad to the Pacific would, necessarily, inure more to the benefit of the North than the South; to intelligence than ignorance; consequently it is strenuously opposed by the latter. In almost every question that could arise, the two sections were diametrically opposed—the North seeking to secure the aid of the Government in promotion of its objects, by what may be termed a liberal construction of the Constitution—the South to hold its rival in check by restricting the functions of Government to as few subjects, and within as limited a range as possible.

At a distance of a century and a half, the Thirty-Seventh Congress remains a landmark. The government founded in 1789 had been little more than a centralized coordinating body; in 1862, it began to exercise real power.

Seven

Proclamation

Chase is a good man, but his theology is
unsound. He thinks there is a fourth
Person in the Trinity.

— SENATOR BENJAMIN WADE

D URING THE SUMMER OF 1862, the Union army fell into a
slump. The army's reverses moved Britain closer than ever to
recognizing the Confederacy and pushing for a peace settlement. These two factors—disappointments in battle and the growling
British lion—weighed like a millstone on the Union's credit. Military
and financial stagnation served as a backdrop for two major Union ini-
tiatives. One was Lincoln's decision to finally tackle the question of
emancipation. The other, more purely financial, involved a major effort
by the President and his Treasury secretary to get cotton out of the
South. Lincoln thought more about the purse than is credited; he considered a robust Treasury vital to winning the war. And until the war,
cotton had been America's biggest export, playing much the role of oil
in a modern petrostate. Congress had authorized trading in occupied
southern territory, under Treasury regulations, in 1861. By 1862, Lincoln had come to believe that exporting cotton could significantly relieve the strain on the Union finances. He and Salmon Chase were each

extremely anxious to procure cotton because its sale for gold or other hard currency would shore up the greenback and the Union's credit.

The President was also eager to revive business in the Union-occupied South. The potential for trade with southern communities spoke to the vision he had articulated at his inaugural—that America was one country, with no natural boundaries or divisions. However, this lofty vision ran smack into the fractious reality of civil war. Trade within the South would inevitably deliver funds into enemy hands. It would prop up the Confederacy at its weakest link—its hollowed-out economy.

At a cabinet meeting in February 1862, Chase presented a plan for issuing licenses to traders to purchase cotton and other goods. The same day, Lincoln issued an order permitting "a partial restoration of Commercial intercourse" *within* the rules to be prescribed by the Treasury secretary. Thus, significant responsibility lay with Chase. The regulations obtained practical significance after the Union's victories in the spring, when Yankee troops came in close contact with southern populations. Chase issued permits to carefully selected buyers, who were supposed to trade only with Southerners who pledged an oath of loyalty to the United States. However, Lincoln and Chase overestimated the degree of loyalty in the occupied South. A mere oath was hardly to be relied upon. Even assuming the best of intentions, once a payment passed into the South, there was no way to prevent it from flowing into the war effort.

The Confederacy had its own problems with enemy trade. Officially, Richmond proscribed "all trade with the enemy." Newspapers defended the policy and heaped scorn on those who dared to conspire with Yankee profiteers. However, the South was too dependent on obtaining vital supplies to completely banish commercial relations. Despite the official policy, the Confederate War Department allowed that "some barter or trading for the supply of [people's] necessities is almost inevitable." President Jefferson Davis himself, while personally incorruptible, conceded that "as a last resort" trading with the Yankees might be justified.

On either side, supply and demand pressures often trumped policy. Interruption of normal trade had left the South with a huge surplus of cotton and forced four out of five northern textile mills to close. Anyone who could get cotton out of the South stood to reap a fortune. The Union had a further and important rationale: relieving the depression in English and French manufacturing districts. Both countries were seeking to develop other sources of supply; meanwhile, laid-off mill workers were begging for bread. *The New York Times* reported a quarter of a million unemployed in Lancashire and "physical symptoms of starvation." Secretary of State Seward keenly wanted to get cotton to Britain to temper the pressure on Britain to intervene in the war. As Edward Bates, Lincoln's attorney general, neatly summarized, "We want Cotton badly, for both home use and European supply." Lincoln realized that the policy was problematic, but judged that on balance it helped the Union cause.

General William Tecumseh Sherman, who in late July arrived in Memphis as military governor, vehemently disagreed. Sherman discovered a commercial entrepôt linked northward to Mississippi River towns thirsting for a revival of trade, and southward to the cotton deltas of Arkansas and Mississippi. On the Confederate side, cotton could be procured for as little as ten cents a pound, but any cotton that traversed into Union territory was worth upward of sixty cents. Given the potential for profit, financial inducements outweighed patriotism.

Barely a week after his arrival, Sherman grasped the essential truth: "We cannot carry on war & trade with a people at the same time." Chase should have reckoned with this insight. Sherman protested that the flourishing trade in enemy territory was founded on a bald misconception. The war, he heatedly advised the Treasury secretary, "has been complicated with the belief . . . that all on the other [side] are *not* enemies."

In fact, it was safer to assume that local populations were hostile. Sherman discerned that Memphis and outlying districts were honeycombed with Confederate sympathizers. Many were illicitly supplying vital goods to the Confederacy, smuggling salt, bacon, powder, and arms into the South. There were cases of contraband smuggled in a hearse during a funeral procession, and of women sashaying past respectful Union guards with forbidden goods hidden in the folds of their crinoline skirts. Smugglers also supplied the dangerous guerrilla forces that menaced Union troops. According to Sherman, none could venture "beyond the sight of the flag-staff without being shot or captured."

Sherman viewed the merchants trading across lines as a fifth column propping up the enemy. He thought the cotton order was "worse to us than a defeat." General Grant, who had briefly passed through Memphis, was similarly seething with frustration over the "great disloyalty manifested by the citizens of this place."

Both Union generals were horrified that profiteers were putting their troops at greater risk, and used their authority to block them. Sherman directed that all travel into and out of Memphis be conducted during daylight, and on specified roads, where sentries were authorized to search at will. Grant directed traders to stay in the rear as his army moved south. Perhaps because they realized that physical barriers were ineffectual, they tried to prevent northerners from spending hard currency. As Sherman pithily noted to Grant, "Money is as much contraband of war as powder." Effective August 1, Grant ordered that no gold or silver be used in exchanges; those who did would suffer arrest. Sherman went further, banning the use of gold, silver, or Treasury notes; speculators, he decreed, could procure cotton with "obligations" to be settled after the war. This would have halted the cotton trade outright, which is what Sherman wanted. However, the monetary restrictions violated the Treasury's policy, as well as that of the War Department, and were quickly rescinded.

Sherman blamed the black- and gray-market trading on a familiar scapegoat: Jews. He fumed that "the country will swarm with dishonest

Jews who will smuggle powder, pistols, percussion-caps, &c., in spite of all the guards and precautions we can give." Sherman similarly protested to Chase that "the commercial enterprise of the Jews" was undermining military objectives. And he advised Grant, "I found so many Jews & Speculators here trading in cotton . . . that I have felt myself bound to stop it." In all likelihood, Sherman had no idea which traders might have been Jewish. His phraseology suggests that he axiomatically associated the two.

Antisemitic stereotypes were as commonplace in the military as they were in civilian life. At least four other Union generals explicitly blamed Jews for the cotton trade, and a distinguished Illinois colonel reportedly expelled "a dozen Jewish cotton buyers" for dealing in southern money. Who knows how many of them actually were gentiles?

Jews had been a microscopic portion of the U.S. population until the 1850s, a period when European immigration (gentile as well as Jewish) increased sharply. By 1860, America had approximately 150,000 Jews (roughly half of 1 percent of the population). They were concentrated in cities, and many were engaged in commerce. Although 10,000 Jews fought in the Civil War, seven of ten for the Union, prejudice was widespread, and resentment of speculators fused into antisemitism on both sides of the Mason-Dixon Line. Many Jewish émigrés who had settled in the antebellum South claimed, previously, that they had been received more hospitably than their northern cousins. At very least, their whiteness placed them on the favored side of the race line. Moreover, merchants were in scarcer supply and therefore welcomed. However, as the war went on, shortages and higher prices awakened the same antisemitic tropes as in the North. The *Richmond Examiner* evidenced an offhand antisemitism in its casual observation that "native Southern merchants have outdone Yankees and Jews" with "the lust of extortion." John Beauchamp Jones, the Confederate War Department clerk, frequently blamed unnamed Jews for supposedly rapacious commercial practices. The most troubling expression of antisemitism occurred in December, when General Grant, who was wintering in Holly Springs,

Mississippi, in preparation for an assault on Vicksburg, and had become incensed at the persistence of black-market trading, issued General Orders No. 11, banishing Jews from his military department, a vast area consisting of parts of Tennessee, Kentucky, and Mississippi. Lincoln revoked this prejudicial order two weeks later. Afterward, Grant seemed to regret having issued it; as president he went to great lengths to appoint Jews to his administration.

The trade across lines was most flagrant in New Orleans. Beginning in May 1862, the city was placed under the command of a military governor, General Benjamin Butler. A Massachusetts politician with significant textile investments, Butler reaped large profits through the sale of heavy cloth to the army. Chase, who was hoping that Louisiana could be reintegrated into the Union in time to support a presidential bid in 1864, cultivated Butler as a politically useful ally.

Soon after Butler arrived in New Orleans, Chase revealed his desire for "Louisianans to make haste back into the Union." The Treasury secretary was also receiving private reports on the outlook for building a Republican Party in Louisiana loyal to him. In July, he sent Butler his most indiscreet note, in which he urged the general to go beyond Lincoln's policy on slavery. "If some prudential considerations did not forbid I should at once, if I were in your place, respectfully notify the slaveholders of Louisiana that henceforth they must be content to pay their laborers wages," Chase advised. But of course, a "prudential consideration" did exist. Chase was advising Butler to interfere with slavery—the very step taken by General Hunter and countermanded by Lincoln. In other words, the Treasury secretary was urging a general to defy his commander in chief. Lest there be any doubt, Chase added, "It is plain enough now that the annulling of Hunter's order was a mistake."

Butler improved the civil administration in New Orleans and cleaned the streets. But he failed to grasp that profiteering was undermining his administration. Under his watch, trading with the enemy reached epidemic proportions, as Treasury agents and others fanned out along Mississippi River tributaries in search of cotton. In many cases, cotton was purchased with salt—a forbidden currency for which the South was desperate. A Treasury agent and distant Chase relative, George S. Denison, who effectively served as Chase's spy, sent a stream of letters warning that trade in New Orleans, fully sanctioned by Butler, was aiding the rebels.

By the fall, Denison was reporting that the Union had sent at least five thousand sacks of salt to the Rebel army and that the trade was demoralizing honest soldiers. "Many officers and soldiers," he reported, "want to go home, not wishing to risk their lives to make fortunes for others."

Butler tried to shift the blame to the usual suspects. When traders were apprehended for smuggling, he commented contemptuously, "They are Jews who betrayed their Savior, & also have betrayed us." In fact, the worst offender was a gentile—one Colonel Andrew Jackson Butler. As Denison informed Chase with alarm, "Col. Butler is a brother of Gen'l. Butler and came out with the army, and immediately commenced doing business. He is not in government employ. He is here for the sole purpose of making money, and it is stated by secessionists— and by some Union men—that he has made half a million dollars."

Although Chase had heard disquieting reports about Butler since June, he seemed willfully oblivious to their implications. Denison, though, kept hammering away. In October 1862, he warned Chase of Butler's extreme tolerance in granting permits and endorsing military passes. Denison noted that eight or nine riverboats under military authority had been carrying on a "constant" trade and that "large quantities of salt crossed Lake Pontchartrain to rebels." In the blunt words of a Rebel officer, the Yankees "will do anything for money."

Reports eventually reached Chase imputing not only Butler's brother but Butler himself. In late October, Chase was forced to admonish General Butler: "So many and seemingly such well-founded charges against your brother, Col. Butler, have reached me and other members of the admin, as well as the president, that I feel bound to say to you that . . . you owe it to yourself not to be responsible, even by toleration, for what he does." The Treasury secretary reminded his ally that trade with the enemy was "expressly forbidden." While General Butler's personal involvement was unproven, Chase warned his friend that "many" expressed the conviction that Butler and his officers were involved.

Butler finally realized that his situation was precarious. He admitted to Chase, "My brother has been indeed engaged in commercial adventure in New Orleans, and has been successful." He contended, however, that his profits had been overstated and that he had not aided him "officially"—although, he admitted, he had given him "the use of my name at the North, and drawing on my bankers where I had some means before the war." Perhaps recognizing that this amounted to a confession, Butler asked his brother to leave New Orleans. Nevertheless, Butler's efforts to clean house were unsuccessful. In late November, Denison again complained to Chase of flagrant profiteering. With the trade so lucrative, it was impossible to suppress. Denison also disclosed that he had been offered a $50,000 bribe (equivalent to $1.35 million today) to look the other way. "People here think if a man has a chance to make money, however dishonorably—that he will avail himself of it. I again express the hope that no trade of any kind, with the enemy, will be authorized from Washington."* The President recalled Butler at the end of the year.

Throughout the summer, Chase and the Radicals in Congress prodded Lincoln to take action on slavery. In the Treasury secretary's mind, emancipation could be a spur to the sputtering Union army. And lack of progress in the war was hurting the North's finances. These issues are usually thought of separately, but to contemporaries, the fate of the slaves, the Union's credit, and the war itself were ingredients in the

---

* Denison was later accused of taking a bribe, but a scholar who looked at his case concluded that if Denison was corrupt, "it was apparently on a very minor scale." Nothing came of the charges.

same simmering stew. Despite the recent financial legislation, the government remained strapped. Chase's clerks, ensconced in the basement of the Treasury, were busily printing the second run of greenbacks. But the issue was limited and being expended fast. One floor up, the head of the new Bureau of Internal Revenue was reading the tax law to formulate an impression of how to carry it out. Revenue was clearly a ways off. Meanwhile, the Treasury was again falling behind on payments and Chase was having no luck marketing the bonds authorized by Congress as part of the Legal Tender Act. Since these bonds were redeemable after five years, and matured in twenty, they were known as five-twenty bonds, or, colloquially, five-twenties.

Chase's efforts to sell the five-twenties were essentially hostage to General McClellan. After the disastrous Virginia campaign, the cautious general had withdrawn his forces and settled into a waiting game on the banks of the James River.* In early July, when Lincoln went to inspect McClellan's army, the general handed the President a memorandum on the war's aims and conduct, explicitly ruling out any "forcible abolition of slavery." This was, of course, well beyond his charter, and in keeping with his often disrespectful treatment of Lincoln. Two weeks later, Chase visited the White House and implored Lincoln to remove the imperious general. As he recorded in his diary, "I also urged General McClellan's removal upon financial grounds." The Treasury secretary asserted that if the President were to dismiss McClellan, and to take decisive action on slavery, he, Chase, could "insure" that the price of United States bonds would soar within ten days, enabling the government to borrow. This forecast was exceedingly brash. But Chase was deeply worried about the government's lagging bond sales. And with the people's faith in the Union's paper greatly diminished, many were hoarding gold and silver coins, heightening the pressure on the greenback. The Treasury secretary argued that sacking McClellan would renew public confidence and therefore the public credit. Lincoln was

---

* Earlier in 1862, Lincoln had quipped that if General McClellan did not want to use the army, he, Lincoln, would like to *borrow* it.

noncommittal, but the appeal to the finances surely made an impression on him.

At the same time, the President was edging toward a watershed decision on slavery. Early in July, Senator Pitt Fessenden made a strong plea not only for freeing the slaves, but also for arming them. So did Thaddeus Stevens, who stated unambiguously, "Slavery was the cause of this war." Such comments helped to recast popular notions not only of the war's causes but of its aims. Lincoln, who had one eye on the fall elections, did not support enlisting freedmen, but he was beginning to reckon with the war's broader purposes. It has been argued that he felt compelled to act against slavery to preempt more radical action by Congress. But there is ample evidence that Lincoln, of himself, was becoming impatient with the continued persistence of slavery in the face of such a brutal war. The greater the toll in blood, the greater must be its compensation. In July, the President was forwarded a letter from a correspondent in New Orleans suggesting that the war would end if the North agreed to restore the country "as it was"—meaning with slavery intact. "Broken eggs cannot be mended," Lincoln replied with uncharacteristic irritation. "This government cannot much longer play a game in which it stakes all, and its enemies stake nothing."

During the summer, he told a group of visitors he was considering emancipation "as a practical war measure." So it was on July 13, 1862, riding in a carriage to a funeral with two members of his cabinet, William Seward and Gideon Welles, that Lincoln (as Welles recorded in his diary) said he was thinking of emancipating the slaves "by proclamation." The President spoke of it as "a military necessity absolutely essential for the salvation of the Union."

Nine days later, on July 22, Lincoln divulged his plan for a proclamation to the full cabinet. In a sign of deference to Congress, he said he would base it on the recent Confiscation Act. Like the act, his proclamation would apply only to slaves in states (or parts thereof) engaged in rebellion. Somewhat lost to history, Lincoln intended the proclamation to be proffered as an inducement, however unlikely, for southern surrender. In any states that laid down arms before it took effect, emancipation would not occur.

In the context of the congressional agitation, Lincoln's news struck Chase as more evolutionary than we think of it today. The Treasury secretary recorded drily that the President was unwilling to countenance arming the slaves, "but proposed to issue a Proclamation, on the basis of the Confiscation Bill, calling upon the states to return to their allegiance," followed by emancipation. Chase offered his "cordial support," though he regretted, he said in cabinet, that Lincoln planned to renew his offer to compensate loyalists who freed their slaves voluntarily. And Chase said he thought emancipation could be better accomplished by generals in the field. The soldiers had arms; Lincoln's proclamation would be mere parchment. What Chase and others missed was the rhetorical power of a presidential decree. Two and a half centuries after the first settlement at Jamestown, a president of the United States was proposing to free the slaves.

Montgomery Blair, the postmaster general, was the only cabinet member who objected. Blair, the son of a Kentucky slave owner who had turned against slavery before the war, feared that the proclamation would hurt the Republicans in the fall elections.* Secretary of State Seward objected only to Lincoln's timing. Seward had the British reaction in mind, and urged the President to wait until the Union army notched a significant victory, so that the proclamation would not seem an act of desperation. Lincoln agreed. These deliberations were kept confidential, but the President's drift was clear. Mary Chesnut acidly observed, "The Yankees, since the war has begun, have discovered it is to free the slaves that they are fighting. So their cause is noble."

In mid-August, his proclamation still under wraps, Lincoln hosted a delegation of Black leaders—the first Black guests ever invited to the White House. The President's personal interactions with African Americans were cordial and respectful. Sojourner Truth, the abolition-

---

* Blair had represented Dred Scott, and argued for his freedom, before the U.S. Supreme Court.

ist, who was to meet him later, remarked that Lincoln showed "as much respect and kindness to the coloured persons present as to the white." Frederick Douglass expressed a similar sentiment, noting that the President addressed him as "Mr. Douglass." But however respectful, his purpose in the August 1862 meeting was dismaying: to ask the delegation for help in recruiting African Americans to immigrate to a prospective Black colony in Central America, which he intended to be Chiriqui, in western Panama. Lincoln told them that slavery was "the greatest wrong inflicted on any people," yet he added that Blacks had little chance to achieve equality in the United States, due to the unwillingness of "our" people to accept them.

Colonization was a tired prescription (it had long been proposed by white moderates, including Lincoln's hero, Henry Clay) and was deeply offensive to free Black Americans. James McPherson has argued that Lincoln fixated on colonization in order to defuse the backlash he expected to his proclamation. And the President was hardly wrong about the level of racism in the North. As recently as June, while Lincoln was beginning to consider a proclamation, voters in Illinois, his home state, overwhelmingly passed referenda to bar Blacks from settling in Illinois or (for those already there) voting.* Still, few American Blacks gave serious thought to emigration, and Negro spokesmen dismissed Lincoln's colonization scheme, which was widely reported, as a fantasy.† Chase spiritedly rebuked the President, writing in his diary, "How much bet-

---

* Illinoisans voted to bar Negro settlement by more than two to one; the measure to prohibit Blacks from voting passed by an even more lopsided 219,920 votes to 35,139—that is, by more than six to one. The *New York Times* correspondent, unable to contain his outrage, said, "We doubt whether any corner of Jeff. Davis' dominions would much exceed this decided expression."

† Thaddeus Stevens, who opposed colonization on principle and argued that Blacks be recruited to fight the "oppressors of their race," reported to Chase that Lincoln had been gulled by land speculators who owned property in Panama—which Stevens described as so unhealthy as to be "wholly uninhabitable" and "not worth a dollar." Chase read Stevens's letter to Lincoln, who promised to probe further before going ahead. But the President's interest in colonization proved stubbornly resilient. He floated it publicly as part of his preliminary proclamation in September 1862, and again in his Annual Message in December. By then, several Central American countries had made clear that American colonies would not be welcome. In 1863, the U.S. government sponsored the resettlement of 450 Blacks on an island near Haiti, but the experiment was short-lived. Enthusiastic Black enlistment in the Union army reaffirmed that, to Black Americans, America was home. By 1864, Lincoln had dropped the idea.

ter would be a manly protest against prejudice against color!—and a wise effort to give freemen homes in America!" This was high-minded if a trifle naïve. Lincoln understood, as his Treasury secretary did not, that "manly protests" rarely succeed in curing people of their prejudice. But in this case, Lincoln's support of colonization was wrong and persisted far too long.

On August 20, less than a week after the group's visit, Horace Greeley accused the President of bending to the will of border-state politicians in failing to use the new law to emancipate. "We think you are strangely and disastrously remiss . . . with regard to the emancipating provisions of the new Confiscation Act," Greeley wrote. "We complain that the Union cause has suffered . . . from mistaken deference to Rebel Slavery." Greeley headlined his piece THE PRAYER OF TWENTY MILLIONS. Lincoln, skirting the main issue, replied that his purpose remained to save the Union. "If I could save the Union without freeing *any* slave I would do it, and if I could save it by freeing *all* the slaves I would do it; and if I could save it by freeing some and leaving others alone I would also do that." Although Greeley exaggerated in claiming that twenty million whites favored emancipation, public opinion did seem to be shifting. Four days after the editorial, Senator John Sherman wrote his brother William, the general, "You can form no conception at the change of opinion here as to the Negro Question. Men of all parties who now appreciate the magnitude of the contest . . . agree that we must seek the aid and make it the interests of the negroes to help us."

As the "Negro Question" percolated and the war raged, Chase was doggedly trying to raise money. His efforts at selling the five-twenty bonds continued to flounder. The banks were the only natural customers, and they would purchase only at a discount. In desperation, Chase sold a small volume of bonds at a markdown—a bitter pill. Such sales were merely a stopgap. He needed a comprehensive and more enduring solution. He therefore revived his proposal from the previous year (which he had been chafing to resubmit) to create a new system of national banks designed, by charter, to lend to the government. However, Congress was not due back until December, so banking reform was on a slow fuse. It had been Chase's hope that, meanwhile, people would convert their greenbacks into bonds, but people preferred to hang on to the popular new notes as walking-around money. So the bonds languished. These financing difficulties led the Treasury secretary to return to his earlier idea of circumventing the banks and selling bonds directly to the people. But how could he sell the public on U.S. bonds when its armies were flailing? Chase despaired to his friend Sherman, "The future does not look promising to me."

Frustrated on the finances, Chase tried to force his way in the military command. He wrote to an ally at the New York port that he was going to see Major General Joseph Hooker, "hoping to find him well enough to take a command forthwith"—notwithstanding that Chase did not have a command to offer. He tirelessly cultivated military sources and tried to insert himself in high-level strategy discussions. For Friday, August 1, he noted in his diary, "Wrote to Genl. [John] Pope and Genl. Butler, touching, in both letters, the Slavery question. Called on Genl. [Henry] Halleck in the evening, and talked a good while with him." That was three generals in a day.

The hard truth was that Chase was shut out of the decision tree. Within Lincoln's counsels, Chase was a rival, and decidedly second, to Seward. The Treasury secretary tried to win points by flaunting his intelligence, a tactic unlikely to win the President's favor. Seward was also ambitious, but his relaxed manner put Lincoln at ease. That Lincoln relied on Seward for a host of matters outside his formal responsibilities only stoked Chase's jealousy. The Treasury secretary bitterly complained that his advice on military matters was ignored, and repeatedly intrigued against the President and his leadership style. Chase fumed to John Sherman, "We have as little to do with it . . . as if we were the heads of factories supplying shoes or clothing." As Lincoln declined to act on his repeated advice to sack McClellan, Chase seemed to nurse an interior grudge against the President. In private conversations he portrayed the administration as weak and bungling. He criticized its "half measures" militarily and against slavery. To his daughter Kate, he groused, "We have trifled with our opportunities . . . and kidgloved [the] rebellion."

The Union doldrums seemed to proffer a tantalizing opportunity to the Confederacy—a chance to contrive a quick peace. In a long letter to Jefferson Davis, Gazaway Lamar, a Georgia banker, argued that the time was ripe for negotiations. Underlying Lamar's suggestion was a keen sense that the opportunity, while real, might be fleeting. Richmond's financial capability was less sustainable than Washington's. Its ability to export cotton was increasingly constrained—as Lamar, who owned an interest in three blockade runners, well knew. Lamar's idea was that by negotiating now, Richmond might influence the elections up north and create a groundswell for peace. Absent that, he warned, "our resources are being exhausted."

Dixie's economic muscle was already breaking down. With the war mostly fought on southern soil, Yankee troops engaged in economic warfare, wrecking factories and bridges in their path. Hints of the disintegration were recorded by the Virginia planter Edmund Ruffin. His two plantations, Beechwood, which lay to the south of the James River, where his family raised wheat, corn, and tobacco, and Marlbourne, north of Richmond, which served as a laboratory for Ruffin's soil experiments, had supported his numerous descendants and afforded him the comfort for writing and reflection. But his carefully arranged domestic organization was fraying. He wrote in June of "a fruitless attempt made to fix the reaping machine. . . . The new parts will not fit to the old." Proper replacements were either unavailable or horrendously expensive. It was only a reaper, but Ruffin understood its significance. "With such high prices & increasing scarcity of the necessaries of life," he wrote with an edge of panic, "I begin to lose hope of our Confederacy being able to carry on the war much longer." Marauding Yankee troops commented admiringly on his well-stocked library (at Beechwood) but nonetheless trashed the home, smashing furniture, tearing mattresses, defacing walls. The most stinging setback arrived from his overseer, who "came across the river to report the additional loss of 21 negroes [making 89 in total], who went off last night, in boats." When the slaves fled, the fields could not be plowed.

Economic scarcity, previously an inconvenience, now began to pose a threat to survival. Prices of wood and coal were soaring, beckoning a shortage of heating fuels and, potentially, a winter of suffering. Coffee shortages were, at very least, a great hardship. When last we checked, in May 1862, John Beauchamp Jones had recorded a coffee price of $1.50 per pound. By October it fetched $2.50 (a leap of 67 percent in five months). Such a destabilizing inflation undid any cheer that southerners might have derived from their successes in battle. Inflation punished saving—that is, it discounted the future. Only for one "commodity" was the price declining: Negro slaves. It's a measure of the South's continuing delusion that people were buying slaves at any price, but the pronounced drop was a signal that the planter economy was in trouble.

The New York Times cited the bankrupt condition of the Confederate treasury as "the chief cause" of what it asserted was Dixies's "approaching collapse." Closer to home, the *Richmond Examiner*, which under the editorship of John M. Daniel was the leading dissenting voice in the Confederate capital, scored the Davis administration's relentless note printing, the total of notes now having topped $210 million. However, it cast the chief blame not on the government but on "an evident indisposition on the part of our people to make [longer-term] investments," in bonds. The actual problem was more fundamental, and it challenged the Confederacy's founding premise that it could thrive (or even survive) on its own: the South had no liquid capital. In the years before the war, the planters had built a system of seigneurial wealth. They had *fixed* capital: slaves, land, houses. Some modern critics have argued that modern American capitalism is an evolved form of slaveholding.[*] Actu-

---

[*] "The 1619 Project," *New York Times*, August 14, 2019.

ally, for all its faults, present-day capitalism is the antithetical inverse of the southern system. Modern financial capitalism is dynamic and transactional: everything is mutable, no business (or employee) is worth retaining a minute more than the market imperative. Because each firm is engaged in a mortal struggle in which losing spells liquidation, *nothing is fixed*. Adaptive change is a constant. The slaveholders had built their fortresses for an improbable perpetuity. Labor was locked in place, as surely as with medieval serfs, and given the difficulty of converting property to cash on any scale or with any dispatch, assets were practically immobile.

The South's inability to adapt, to shift capital to more vital industries, or those that might substitute for scarce supplies, severely hurt its prospects. During the second year of the war, the *Atlantic Monthly* recalled that the Dixie of 1860 was "literally overrun with goods," thanks to the sixteen steamers running between Savannah and New York and an equal number to Charleston, not to mention the countless boats bearing "their tribute of flour, lard, and corn" down the Mississippi. This trade masked the South's utter dependence on the outside world. Now, the South had to feed itself, not least by replanting millions of acres of export crops with grain and corn. But the southern soil wasn't as well suited; its farmers weren't experienced or skilled in their production, they had less investment in machinery, and their yields were consequently meager.

The industrial deficit was even more glaring. The stores in Charleston, formerly "overflowing with merchandize," the *Atlantic* recalled, now were "utterly empty. In Mobile we hear . . . not a carpet can be found on the floor of any resident; they have all been cut into blanket for the army." Curtains and drapes were repurposed into shirts. The magazine conceded that the South boasted one great advantage—its stock of fighting men. The planter's son, it noted in condescending tribute, had been "accustomed from childhood to the use of the horse and rifle." While southerners were well suited for fighting, in the estimation of the elite Boston periodical, their armies still needed an economy to support them. For that, Dixie needed, at very least, a degree of centralization. It needed taxing power, it needed liquid financial assets, and it needed a modern infrastructure. Much of Virginia was dependent on a single railroad, the East Tennessee and Virginia, for both hay and salt, which were absolutely essential to the war effort. Transport was similarly vital to distribute lead, copper, and salt from western Virginia. The *Richmond Examiner* judged that the Confederacy's struggle to protect the railway, which Union troops were constantly attacking, was a question of "vast and pressing importance." On the preservation of such scarce and diminishing commercial routes depended the South's chances of survival.

Despite such significant handicaps, in August 1862 the Confederacy notched another triumph. McClellan had been ordered to reinforce General John Pope's Army of Virginia, which was operating to the north, near Washington. McClellan was unduly casual in getting there, and Pope suffered a terrible defeat on the previously disputed battlefield at Bull Run, at the hands of Stonewall Jackson. Not only did Pope's army sustain heavy casualties, it withdrew toward the capital in confusion. Chase ordered Treasury clerks into the field to nurse the wounded. Northern morale swooned again, further dispiriting the market for the five-twenty bonds.

Chase blamed McClellan—indeed, he thought McClellan's tardiness was deliberate. Modern historians have concluded that Henry Halleck, the supervising commander, was more at fault. What matters for our purposes is that Lincoln's patience with McClellan finally cost him. There was a strong tide of northern opinion that faulted the President himself. George Templeton Strong wrote despairingly, "Abe Lincoln is not the style of goods we want just now. . . . He is unequal to his place." Senator Fessenden called the President "the slave of McClellan." This was unfair, but Fessenden had just lost his youngest son, twenty-one-year-old Lieutenant Samuel Fessenden, at Bull Run. In any case, the dissatisfaction was widespread.

On September 1, Chase and Stanton sought to force the issue. They drafted a communiqué to Lincoln demanding McClellan's resignation, and procured signatures from four of the seven cabinet members. Navy Secretary Welles was in rough accord but unwilling to sign a paper he thought disrespectful to the President. Chase insisted both to Welles and to posterity (in his diary) that he "disclaimed any movement against the President"—though that was precisely what he had instigated. Perhaps he could not abide McClellan because he, Chase, had been one of his early supporters.

The following day, the cabinet was stunned to learn that Lincoln had repositioned McClellan, giving him command of Pope's vanquished army to defend the capital. The President was supremely distressed to find the majority of the cabinet aligned against him. He was not naïve about McClellan, but he knew that "Little Mac" was popular with the rank and file and his reinstatement boosted morale. "He is a good engineer, all admit; there is no better organizer," Lincoln told the cabinet, "but he is troubled with the 'slows' and good for nothing for an onward movement." With that balanced appraisal, the President went ahead.

The Confederate success in moving the front from the outskirts of Richmond to the doorstep of Washington was big news in Britain. "The Federals got a very complete smashing," Lord Palmerston wrote to Lord Russell, the foreign secretary. If General Lee were to extend his winning streak, the British prime minister suggested, it might be time for "an arrangement upon the basis of separation." Barely a week later, on September 24, Palmerston revealed a plan under which, in October, the cabinet would draft a joint proposal with France to the *two* American governments for "an Armistice" with the aim of negotiation "on the basis of Separation."

Throughout September, as Europe looked on, the Rebels extended their gains. Lee daringly invaded Maryland and took the fight to the North. The Rebels occupied Frederick, Maryland; their brothers-in-arms notched victories in the west. The graycoats recaptured territory in Tennessee and threatened Chase's hometown, Cincinnati, as well as Louisville, unleashing terror among civilians.

On form, this was the moment for Britain to seek an end to the slaughter. Its stockpiles of cotton were exhausted. Its largest industry, textiles, was in a shambles, and tens of thousands of its people were unemployed. William Gladstone, the most pro-southern member of the cabinet, told a gathering in Newcastle, "There is no doubt that Jefferson Davis and other leaders of the South have made an army"; what's more, he said, it appears "they have made a nation."

Southerners were thrilled by such talk, yet they were mistaken to think they had Britain's sympathies. It is true, among the British gentry, there was an antidemocratic strain that wished for a comeuppance for the United States and for its coarse experiment in democracy. But this was offset by a general distaste for slavery. Despite the terrible hardships endured by textile workers, British labor sided with the Union. Labor activists saw the war as an American version of the class struggle, with the plantation owners playing the part of the exploitative capitalist class and the Union forces, as one put it, the "down-trodden people of Europe."

What Lord Palmerston weighed, ultimately, was not Britain's sympathies but its interests. He was reluctant to provoke the United States without a clear sign that Richmond was prevailing. According to Edwin De Leon, a freelance adventurer-diplomat who managed to get an audience in England with the prime minister, and reported back to Jefferson Davis, "England will insist on a masterly inactivity as she regards it." France, where a discouraged De Leon headed next, was little different—it certainly was unwilling to provoke Washington on its own.

By mid-September, Lee was camped in northern Maryland, menacing Pennsylvania. On September 17, McClellan engaged him at Antietam Creek—stunning the nation with its bloodiest ever day of fighting (3650 dead), D-day included. Lee was forced to retreat to safety across the Potomac. Though not decisive, the battle was consequential across the Atlantic. News of Antietam cooled Palmerston's interest in mediating the war.

At home, Lincoln chose to interpret the qualified victory as the good omen he had been waiting for. The following Sunday he declined to see visitors, leaving word he was busy writing. Chase recorded, "Thought to myself, 'Possibly engaged on Proclamation.'" On Monday, September 22, Lincoln summoned the cabinet at noon. According to Chase, the President read aloud from a book he considered highly amusing, guffawing heartily as he read. Then, he adopted a graver tone. "Gentlemen," he began, "I have, as you are aware, thought a great deal about the relation of this war to Slavery." That was the crux of it. The "relation" to slavery would now be central—the Union's purposes, as they had evolved, now would include emancipation. "I think the time has come now," he said.

Lincoln's proclamation, published the next day, declared that, in states still under rebellion on January 1, slaves would be "forever free." Lincoln pledged in the second paragraph that the effort to colonize "persons of African descent" would continue—that discordant note aside, there was no mistaking its revolutionary character. Joyous citizens serenaded Lincoln at the White House and then moved on to Chase's residence, where the Treasury secretary marveled at the insanity of the slaveholder class for starting the revolt—absent which, "they might have kept the life in their institution many years." Frederick Douglass, writing in his antislavery journal, said, "We shout for joy that we live to record this righteous decree."

Northern newspapers were mostly positive. Even the *Atlantic*, founded by the literary lions of New England three years before Lincoln's election, and the voice of liberals who were well tired of the administration's gradualism, saw a decisive step forward. True, the magazine cautioned, the proclamation was not "self-enforcing"; without victory, it would be a scrap of paper. And the editors remained anxious about the lives that awaited the freedmen, particularly their ability to acquire property. Yet the *Atlantic* took the full measure of what Lincoln had achieved. Pausing to mark the moment for its thirty-thousand-plus subscribers, it commented, "The Twenty-second of September, 1862, bids fair to become as remarkable a date in American history as the Fourth of July, 1776."

Southerners furiously denounced Lincoln for (as they saw it) economic plunder. The Confederate Congress called it a "gross violation of the usages of civilized warfare, an outrage on the rights of private property [that] should be held up to the execration of mankind." The *Richmond Enquirer* excoriated Lincoln for seeking "to destroy four thousand millions of our property at a dash of the pen."

Emancipation did not make Chase's life any easier. Northern investors reacted with dismay—perhaps because they sensed that with the stakes raised, the chance for an early peace had vanished. "Stocks have declined," Lincoln noted dejectedly, stung by the market's verdict. Gold rose to a 20 percent premium to the greenback, that is, 120 greenbacks for $100 in gold. In October, the premium widened further, to 30 percent. With the government's appetite for men and arms now seemingly insatiable, the Treasury fell four weeks behind in payments. Chase was burning through $37 million a month—for that era, a frightful sum—compared with revenue of barely $12 million a month.

Chase again inquired about the prospects of placing bonds with bankers but received the same response: to buy in any volume, the banks demanded a hefty discount. Then, late in September, the Treasury secretary was visited by Jay Cooke. Nothing was accomplished, but the meeting seems to have crystallized Chase's growing faith in the Philadelphia banker. Cooke had been nurturing their relationship from the moment of Chase's appointment. Not only had he opened his home to Chase and his daughters, he had been investing the Treasury secretary's personal funds, regularly sending him checks from railroad speculations selected by Cooke. When Cooke launched a streetcar company in Washington, Chase became a stockholder. When Chase's daughter needed an enclosed carriage, Cooke offered to buy one (Chase wisely declined the offer). With rare exception, such as when Cooke furnished the Chase home with bookshelves, or when Chase asked the banker for a $2000 loan, in each individual encounter the Treasury secretary behaved properly. Yet the web of intimacies was in their sum disturbing. Chase had come to regard Cooke as an invaluable backstop—for himself personally and for the public credit. Cooke routinely purchased scraps of public financings that the Treasury secretary was anxious to unload, and he comforted Chase with the pleasing daydream that Jay Cooke & Co. could be a safe haven if he chose to leave the government.

Cooke had opened a Washington branch, conveniently situated on Fifteenth Street, opposite the Treasury, with the explicit aim of exploiting this relationship. Subsequently, according to Cooke's first biographer, Ellis Paxson Oberholtzer, Jay's brother Henry came and went at Chase's home almost with the license of a private secretary, "and in this way learned much that was of the greatest value to a banking house." Chase recognized that the public would not look kindly on such coziness. In the wrong hands, the details of his relationship with Cooke could be political dynamite. Therefore, the Treasury secretary repeatedly asked the banker to restrict their personal business to private correspondence. On August 8, he curtly implored the financier, "Please keep out of private letters to me all references to public matters."

Today, we would deem such a relationship highly improper, no matter Chase's attempts to compartmentalize its private and public aspects. There is no evidence that Chase crossed an ethical line, only that he allowed himself, the nation's chief financial officer, to become a supplicant to an increasingly important private banker. Chase was a self-righteous man, too self-absorbed to realize when he had incurred a debt. He reassured himself that his and Cooke's values were similar but lost sight of the difference in their roles. Both men thought of themselves as tribunes of the people, the vessels of a patriotic virtue absent on Wall Street. But Cooke was a tribune for himself—a highly ambitious financier. Chase could have worked with Cooke while keeping a distance. But he saw that Cooke was effective. The Philadelphian had quietly been placing a small amount of bonds with good results. Chase believed Cooke's assurances that he could sell the five-twenties "among the people" at par, while the other bankers were requiring a discount. And no one matched Cooke's energy and resourcefulness.

Chase had survived his first crisis, in 1861, with private bank loans, but the bankers were balking at more. He had weathered a second storm, reluctantly, with legal tender. What options remained? The political balance was far too delicate for the Treasury secretary to seek more taxes. This wisdom was confirmed on October 14, when the Republicans were hit with devastating news from early-voting states. They were trounced in Ohio, Chase's home state, which sent fourteen Democrats to the House, out of a delegation of nineteen, and they lost their advantage in Pennsylvania. Democrats had seized on the proclamation, arousing white voters' fears of being overrun by Negro freedmen. The lack of military progress hurt Lincoln's party as well. To James Blaine, a Republican from Maine, the early results were "utterly discouraging."

The day after the October election, gold hit a high (that is, the greenback hit a low) of 132.5, or a premium of 32.5 percent. Chase told Union General John Cochrane he was out of financial tricks. "By miracles," the Treasury secretary wrote with characteristic immodesty, "I have been able to get this far, notwithstanding our [military] disasters. But the miracles cannot be repeated; and I see financial disaster imminent." Chase was not being wholly candid. He had one trick left.

Five days later, on October 23, Chase penned the letter Cooke had been waiting for—offering the Philadelphian the exclusive agency for marketing the government's five-twenty bonds. Recalling Cooke's success in helping to place the smaller "National Loan" of the previous year, Chase ventured boldly, "It has seemed to me possible that by enlarging your sphere and increasing your compensation," the government, with Cooke's assistance, could finally market the much larger sums that it needed to finance the war now. Some $500 million of the five-twenty bonds were authorized; almost none had been sold. The United States had never embarked on a campaign of such scale before. "Can this be done?" Chase urgently asked his friend. "Are you willing to undertake it?"

Eight

Chase's Plan

The people demand uniformity in currency.

– SALMON P. CHASE

B Y THE END OF OCTOBER, Chase had authorized Jay Cooke to be the exclusive agent for the five-twenty bond. The Treasury would also sell the bonds directly, but among private dealers Cooke had an exclusive franchise. Chase agreed to pay a commission of 0.375 percent, of which it was expected that Cooke would spend a third on subagents and a third on publicity, keeping the remainder as his profit.* In addition, Cooke had to post security and was responsible for the funds until the government received them. These terms were reasonable but, fearing that the arrangement could become a political liability, Chase did not put it in writing, a casual approach that would lead to quarreling later.

Cooke immediately converted Jay Cooke & Co. at South Third Street, Philadelphia, into the nerve center of a national brokerage. The firm relied on the telegraph to execute orders—the first "wire house," a species of brokerage that was to proliferate on Wall Street. Cooke recruited agents (often local bankers) to canvass Pennsylvania, New

---

* This rate applied on sales after the first $10 million in bonds. Up to that threshold, Cooke's gross commission was 0.5 percent.

England, and the upper Midwest. As early as the second week of November, advertisements aimed at "Farmers, Merchants, Mechanics, Capitalists" started appearing in northern newspapers.

Although investors had been discouraged by the Union's dismal showing on the battlefield, the five-twenty was an attractive product. People could acquire bonds by converting U.S. Notes (greenbacks) on a one-for-one basis. Yet the interest on the bonds would be paid in gold. It was also expected that, at maturity, the principal would be paid in gold. This amounted to an alchemy machine, a device for turning paper into specie. The interest rate, 6 percent, was also attractive. For anyone who expected the United States government to remain in business, the five-twenty was a good investment.

The challenge was that few Americans thought in such terms, for few had experience investing. Cooke's marking amounted to a primer for people for whom building a nest egg was a novel concept. While gilding his pitch with appeals to patriotism, Cooke emphasized the bonds' security. He blithely declared that the five-twenty was "payable in gold" (which was expected but not guaranteed). He framed the bond as a call on the entire productive power of the loyal states or, as Cooke gaudily advertised, "a FIRST MORTGAGE upon all Railroads, Canals, Bank Stocks and Securities and the immense products of all the Manufacturers, &c., in the country." This was a subtle but important point. Since the federal government had taxing power, its bonds were backed by the wealth of the people. This was not nearly so true for Richmond.

Cooke goaded publishers to run favorable editorials (many of which he wrote) on what he deemed the wisdom of investing. He essentially extorted them by threatening to withhold advertising. A master salesman, Cooke challenged towns not to be surpassed in subscriptions by their neighbors. The lift to the Treasury was immediate. As of June 1862, only $14 million of the bonds had been sold. With Cooke on board, Chase unloaded another $10 million by the end of November. Unable to contain his enthusiasm, the Treasury secretary exclaimed, "I am gratified by the success which has attended your efforts thus far."

He was especially pleased that Cooke was spending more on advertising and local agents than Chase had "suggested."

Chase's wording reflected the troubling informality in their arrangement. Later, when their relationship came under public scrutiny, the Treasury secretary asserted that the banker was "bound" to spend the stipulated sums on publicity and agents, but at the time Chase has it merely as a "suggestion." In the same letter, he virtually apologizes to Cooke for keeping records of his payments. "You must not think me parsimonious because I keep an eye on outgoes," he writes. "The People trust me . . . and I want to preserve a full record of [the loan's] progress and results."

Jay Cooke was barely forty-one when he became the government's banker. Now that his business depended on the Union's military progress, Cooke developed a personal interest in seeing General McClellan put to pasture. Late in October, Cooke visited Lincoln at the Soldiers' Home, a former banker's cottage perched on a high elevation in Washington, where Lincoln went to escape the heat. Cooke and Lincoln talked until late into the night, and the financier stressed that the Union's credit could conceivably collapse—"unless McClellan was sent away very soon." Much later, in a memoir composed in the 1890s, Cooke said he always felt that his appeal was "the immediate cause of Mr. Lincoln's prompt action."

The President had his own reasons for wanting to be rid of the indecisive general who, for all his popularity with the troops, had turned out not to be a Napoleon after all. When McClellan complained that his horses were weary, Lincoln spat back, "Will you pardon me for asking what the horses of your army have done since the battle of Antietam that fatigue anything?" After further fruitless efforts to goad him into action, the President had come to fear, as he told his private secretary, that the general was "playing false." On November 5, Lincoln finally dismissed McClellan, replacing him with yet another major general, Ambrose Burnside. Clearly, the dismissal had been long in coming. But the timing suggests that Cooke's plea may have been the final straw.

The President often acted with deliberation. The prospect of a break-down in the Union's fragile credit may have tipped his hand.

Contrary to Chase's prediction, McClellan's firing failed to steady the markets. Speculators bid up the price of gold, depressing the green-back and greatly perturbing Wall Street. Cooke's more nervous brother said, "The infection of despair is becoming general." Chase, as well as Lincoln, viewed the gold speculators as unpatriotic, a fifth column poi-soning the Union's credit. But mostly the speculators' motivation was profit, not politics. The Treasury was behind on soldiers' pay and other bills. And prices of consumer goods were rising at an unprecedented clip, leading to serious inflation worries. Such problems drove the gold premium to 38 percent, its highest yet.

The financial industry responded in the worst way. In late October, the Board of Brokers in New York prohibited gold trading at the stock exchange. Gold continued to trade informally but now, as the *New York Herald* explained, "its fluctuations will not be placed twice a day before the eyes of outside speculators to tempt them." Soon after, the *Herald* reported that the "experiment" in censoring markets was going well, speculation having abated. Then, the evil genie returned. "Large quantities of gold are held here on speculation," the *Herald* ruefully said. "Public confidence is very sensitive indeed." A few days later, on November 16, the Board of Brokers admitted that "the exclusion of gold from the Board had not diminished speculation in it." Throw-ing in the towel, it restored gold to the official list. Predictably, the at-tempt to suppress trading had backfired, heightening fears of financial instability.

Economic insecurity hurt the governing party in the off-year elec-tions. Democrats sought to arouse fears that—post-proclamation—freed Blacks would threaten northern whites. A campaign notice in New York ungraciously avowed, "We are unwilling to lose our free-dom at the North for the purpose of bestowing it upon the negro slaves of the South." The appeals to racism worked. Republicans lost their majority in the House, although they retained a plurality. Mortifyingly to Lincoln, the party was thrashed in Illinois, and lost the important post of governor of New York, to Horatio Seymour, a relentless Lincoln critic.

To Lincoln, the remedy for ethnic rivalry could only be a resurgent commerce. Even amid the war, he put stock in a business revival as a salve for the nation's wounds. He wistfully envisioned the Union Pacific Railroad and federally sponsored canal improvements. He was excited by the potential of the new Agriculture Department, and by the mineral wealth being unearthed in the territories. These projects would need the approval or further encouragement of Congress, and in his annual address, the President formally sought legislative action.

His December 1 message to Congress was his most focused yet on economics. In the opening sentence, he offered thanks for the "bountiful harvests" of the past year, dismissing the lack of peace almost as a detail to be remedied later. Throughout the war, Lincoln's vision of America as a great, interwoven enterprise bolstered his belief in the Union. Only as a single nation, he essayed, were America's cornfields and cotton deltas and the whole of its commercial output truly viable. As part of one nation, each and every merchant was connected to Europe, South America, Asia, and Africa. Yet, he went on, "Separate our common country into two nations, as designed by the present rebellion, and every man of this great interior region is thereby cut off from some one or more of these outlets." New borders would bring new restrictions and "embarrassing and onerous trade regulations." No, there could be no severing of the national homestead. For how would the separation be drawn? "There is no line, straight or crooked, suitable for a national boundary, upon which to divide," opined the former Sangamon County surveyor. "Trace through, from east to west, upon the line between the free and slave country, and we shall find a little more than one-third of its length are rivers, easy to be crossed, and populated, or soon to be populated, thickly upon both sides. . . . No part of this line can be made any more difficult to pass, by writing it down on paper, or parchment, as a national boundary."

Lincoln waffled on slavery, suggesting that slave states loyal to the Union be given until the remote year 1900 to adopt compulsory emancipation. But as often, when he considered slavery in economic terms, he radiated with understanding. The great fear in the North had nothing to do with whether Blacks remaining in the South were enslaved or free. The people who voted for Seymour in New York, and others like him, worried that, once free, those Blacks would head north, inhabit their cities, and compete with whites for jobs. While few Blacks lived in the North (just over 1 percent of the population), racial animosity dovetailed with economic anxiety. Lincoln sought to allay it with his trademark logic. "It is insisted that their presence would injure, and displace white labor and white laborers," the President noted. "It is dreaded that the freed people will swarm forth and cover the whole land. Are they not already in the land? Will liberation make them any more numerous?" Even if equally distributed throughout the country (which Lincoln considered unlikely), there would be but one freedman to seven whites, hardly a daunting proportion. The heart of his argument was that Blacks were already working, and after emancipation their labor would still be needed as it was needed now. It was a powerful point, apprising white America as if for the first time that Blacks were, indeed, "already in the land."

In his first address to Congress, Lincoln had referred to "these United States"—as a plural or collective project. Now, he referred to *the* United States; it had become one thing—a unitary nation. Yet its preservation was hardly assured. Since the Union would require massive financial support, the President urged Congress to give "diligent consideration" to the finances. He praised Chase's administration and stewardship of the public credit. Yet the scale of Chase's needs demanded the legislators' "best reflections" on how to provide the necessary revenue without, as Lincoln cautioned, harming either business or labor. Between the lines, he wanted the revenue but not its inflationary side effects.

While Lincoln praised legal tender (his first public comment on the greenback), he nonetheless looked to a return to a gold basis at the earliest possible moment, presumably after the war. Paper money had proved a brilliant expedient, but it was still an expedient. Some more permanent currency was needed. Yet Lincoln, like Chase, knew there was no going back to the old mix of gold and silver coins plus Treasury and assorted state bank notes. With the postwar world coming into view, the President recommended Chase's long delayed banking reform. Indeed, Lincoln said, "I know of none which promises so certain results [of] a safe and uniform currency."

The *Annual Report of the Secretary of the Treasury on the State of the Finances*, typically released after the President's Annual Message, was usually a dry document, a run of figures and projections. Chase had those, as well as a request that Congress authorize the breathtaking sum of $900 million in borrowings over the next eighteen months. But the heart of his thirty-page report was a treatise reimagining the American system of currency. Chase's scheme was revolutionary, yet it reflected his innate conservatism. It was clear to him that the country needed more currency, to buy his bonds and to conduct its business. Yet his instincts remained Jacksonian, colored by an undying affection for gold. Congress could not simply undam the river of greenbacks—"as injurious as it would be easy." Nor could the source of the new money be the 1600 state-chartered banks (1400 in the loyal states), each of which issued at least six bills, making eight *thousand* bills in circulation. They were too numerous and cacophonous, too dissimilar in value and in the differing state regulations to which they were subject. Their disparate physical appearance even gave rise to widespread counterfeiting. And Chase unfairly blamed these bank notes for inflation.

The Treasury secretary was just modern enough to adopt the heresy that government, as distinct from private banks, should control the circulation. Yet he was too much a Jacksonian to countenance a central bank. That left the possibility of a hybrid, a new note regulated by the federal government yet issued by a private source, a collection of newly organized national banks. These banks would be "national" in the sense that Washington would grant their charters, but they would operate as independent, for-profit associations. Their notes would be backed by their private assets, commercial loans as well as gold. Thus the new currency, Chase hastened to add, would be "no mere paper money scheme."

Finally, the national banks would be required to invest a portion of their capital in U.S. bonds, furnishing Chase with a market for the government's credit. The private banks would thus forge a vital connection to the federal purse. Every national bank, and every individual who held a dollar of the new circulation, would feel a shared interest with the government. This was a very Republican and un-Jacksonian idea—promoting the authority of the central state. War begat an itch to centralize and Chase was not immune. In time, he envisioned that the national notes would displace those of the state banks, giving rise to a single currency under federal control.

Chase insisted that this was the "central idea"—to establish "one sound, uniform circulation, of equal value throughout the country." Yet it was a complicated scheme, with overlapping objectives. Moreover, as Chase acknowledged, his banking reform was unlikely to bear fruit right away—perhaps not even during the remainder of the war. For these and other reasons, enacting it would not be easy. The nation's bankers, who ran the state banks that Chase was hoping to displace, were naturally opposed. And bankers were well represented in the House of Representatives.

Chase did have the support of Lincoln. However, even as the President lobbied for Chase's plan, the Treasury secretary continued to nurture an undercurrent of opposition to Lincoln's leadership. Chase had been covertly expressing his unhappiness with Seward, whom he held responsible for the administration's failed military strategies and for insufficient enthusiasm for the Union's purposes, including antislavery. Seward and Chase had entered the cabinet as rivals, and their relations since, according to Welles, had been governed by "cold courtesy." The President valued both, but had warmth only for Seward, whose nature was as convivial as Chase's was rigid, and whose company he genuinely enjoyed. As Welles devastatingly put it, Lincoln was "fond of" Seward; he respected Chase.

While Lincoln made only selective use of the cabinet as an advisory group, he freely confided in Seward. The others were plainly irked that the wily secretary of state held such sway, though probably not to the degree that Chase was. And the Radicals in Congress held an exaggerated view of Seward (who previous to the war had been a leader in the Senate) as a Machiavellian conniver leading the king astray. Thaddeus Stevens confided to a friend in mid-November, "It were a great blessing if Seward could be removed." The bill of charges was always vague, but Seward was said to be the muse for all of the President's failings and especially for his excesses of moderation. Was Lincoln too patient with McClellan? Too slow to move on slavery? It was all on account of Seward. "All the wires at the command of Mr. Seward, he is actively pulling," sniped the radical-leaning *Chicago Daily Tribune*, as if the secretary were a malevolent Oz. "His influence over the President, as well as his associates, he is silently but skillfully exerting."

Chase stoked these fears, deliberately feeding gossip on the cabinet to the Radicals and winning their tacit endorsement for his possible candidacy in 1864. Senator Sherman, in a letter to his general brother, declared that if the Union required it, he would prefer "an abolitionist like Chase . . . to guide our counsel." The problem for Chase was that, unlike Lincoln's congressional detractors, he owed his loyalty to the President. Meanwhile, in numerous whispered sidebars, he encouraged the view that Lincoln's cabinet was controlled, as Chase put it to Pitt Fessenden, by a "back-stairs influence." This greatly misread the President; indeed, it amounted to a charge that he was Seward's helpless pawn.

These simmering rivalries might have continued to fester under the surface, more or less benignly. But in mid-December (a week after Chase proposed his banking program) the Union was routed at Fredericksburg, despite holding a big edge in numbers. Casualties were horrific and hugely disproportionate on the Union side. That the fault for its bungled attack lay with General Burnside—the most recent of Lincoln's promotions—highlighted the President's mismanagement of the war.

Egged on by Chase, Republican senators caucused after the defeat and voiced great displeasure with the administration. After further deliberations, on the evening of Thursday, December 18, a delegation of nine mostly Radical senators paid a call on Lincoln. Vermont senator Jacob Collamer, who acted as chair, read a prepared text demanding changes in the cabinet, owing to its alleged lack of cohesion and commitment. Others made clear they considered Seward to be the culprit, for wrecking the cabinet's putative harmony, for indifference in pursuit of the war and other goals, and for influencing Lincoln in such directions. This was a blunt attack on the executive branch.

Lincoln was shocked and deeply grieved. He told his private secretary that the senators "appeared to think that when I had . . . any good purpose or intention Seward contrived to suck it out of me unperceived." His whimsical humor notwithstanding, the President was greatly upset at the mutiny within his party. He handled it with supreme skill. While gently deflecting the charges, he asked the senators to return to his office Friday evening. On Friday morning, he summoned the cabinet. Lincoln directed his ministers (save Seward, who had responded to the protests by submitting his resignation) to return that evening for a joint parlay with the dissatisfied senators.

That evening, eight senators (one had bowed out) trooped back to the White House. They were greatly surprised to see the cabinet waiting in Lincoln's anteroom. The President ushered them in and spoke in defense of the cabinet, not as a perfectly harmonious group but as a functioning council that collectively supported policy once a decision had been made. He also defended Seward. Lincoln spoke for a while and then asked Chase whether he agreed. Chase's position was beyond awkward; he either had to betray his fellow cabinet members, in their presence, or disappoint his putative coconspirators in the Senate. He weakly stammered that the cabinet had "not suffered for a want of unity." The senators saw that he was unmanned. After this humiliation, Lincoln polled the senators on whether they wished Seward to be dismissed. Now, half responded in the negative or refused to say. Still, the President retired in a despondent mood.

The next morning, Lincoln summoned Chase, candidly telling him, "This matter is giving me great trouble." Stanton and Welles were present, so once again, the Treasury secretary felt the awkwardness of facing the President in front of witnesses. Chase stiffly replied that he had brought an offer of resignation. On hearing this, Lincoln brightened. "Let me have it!" he said. He snatched the paper, which Chase seemed reluctant to hand over. Turning to Welles, Lincoln said gleefully, "This cuts the Gordian knot!" They sat by the fire a little, Lincoln's mood suddenly improved. The second resignation had furnished him with a plan. "Now I can ride," he supposedly said, in his homely style. "I have got a pumpkin in each end of my bag." The President was definitely back in the saddle, for now he could retain both Seward and Chase (neither of whom he wanted to lose) without seeming to favor either. He promptly wrote identical letters requesting that each of the rivals rescind their resignations. Seward immediately returned to work. Chase responded with a tortured disquisition, as if his proffered resignation was too grave a matter to be so easily set aside. But within a day he, too, was back on the job.

Henry Cooke, who had written Jay of "a terrible row in the cabinet," and was worried for Chase's job security (and its effect on bond sales), was greatly relieved. Of course, there were aftereffects. Lincoln emerged in greater command of his government while Chase had been exposed as a bluffer. The Treasury secretary was fortunate that his boss was not a man to swell in triumph. Just over a week later, the President accepted Chase's lawyerly revision of the Emancipation Proclamation, adding the key phrase that it was "sincerely believed to be an act of justice, warranted by the Constitution, upon military necessity." Invoking the Constitution (unmentioned in Lincoln's draft) was a deft attempt to head off potential legal challenges. Just as important, in the final version, issued January 1, 1863, the President dropped all reference to col-onization and declared that freed slaves would be welcomed into the armed services. Before the war was over, 179,000 Black Americans would serve in the U.S. army, and another 19,000 in the navy.

In the months between the preliminary proclamation and the final draft, Lincoln had more fully embraced its magnitude, its effect on the evolving purposes of the war. According to the Lincoln scholar Harold Holzer, as he prepared to sign the document, he steeled himself, rub-bing his hands together to calm his nervous tremors, and remarked, "If my name ever goes into history it will be for this act." A bit later, when congratulated by the lawyer Simon Wolf, Lincoln is said to have re-plied, "It was not only the Negro that I freed, but the white man no less." Americans continued to debate the proclamation's practical util-ity, but overseas, its effect was immediate. Public assemblies were held across Britain lauding the President. Support was strongest among the hard-hit British working class. In Manchester, where so many textile workers had lost their jobs, a large meeting was held at the Free Trade Hall, where numerous speakers, many of them mill workers, congratu-lated Lincoln on his "humane and righteous policy." Lincoln, who knew that the American war had cost Britons dearly, was deeply touched. Responding to "the workingmen of Manchester," the President praised their support "as an instance of sublime Christian heroism which has not been surpassed in any age or in any country." More than good feel-ing was at stake. Popular support for emancipation ended any realistic hope that Britain would intervene for the Confederacy. Henry Adams, a young Harvard graduate who was serving as secretary to his ambas-sador father in London, said, "The Emancipation Proclamation has done more for us here than all our former victories."

However, the proclamation did nothing to calm Wall Street. Con-fidence in the government's paper was damaged by more dispiriting news from the front. General Grant, the Union army's most accom-plished soldier, had stalled in front of Vicksburg. Markets were also worried by the gaping federal deficit. Most critically, soldiers' pay on extended arrears was reaching alarming proportions. Congress was forced to consider the forbidden topic of a third series of greenbacks. According to Senator John Sherman, talk of more greenbacks "operated like magic" (black magic). Expanding the money supply inevitably juices speculation, be it the Federal Reserve lowering interest rates today or dumping legal tender on markets then. Fearing depreciation, investors rushed to exchange notes for real estate or stocks. The opening of stock subscriptions for a gold-mining company triggered a veritable mania. According to the *Philadelphia Inquirer*, "The people did not care apparently whether they [the company's mines] were located in Colorado or in the clouds. What they wanted was shares, shares, shares."

As faith in the greenback ebbed, people hoarded gold, and as gold became scarce, the greenback slid further. By mid-January 1863, a gold dollar fetched nearly a dollar and a half in greenbacks. The depreciation exacerbated wartime inequality; workers on fixed salaries especially suffered. "Gold has risen fifteen percent in a fortnight," the *New York Herald* reported grimly. "Where is the depreciation to end?" For Chase, the speculation had a lethal effect: investment in government bonds came to a crashing halt.

Hoping to enlist the help of bankers, the Treasury secretary made a hurried visit to New York. According to the *Herald*, Chase learned that no loan could be obtained "on any terms." Having forecast that he expected the Union's debt to reach twenty-seven times its prewar level, Chase should have not been surprised that creditors were wary. Prior to the war, the federal debt had scarcely risen at all (the debt in 1860 had been less than under General Washington after the Revolutionary War). The Civil War debt explosion was altogether new. Predictably, Chase interpreted the dismal response as proof that the country needed his new banking currency. He wrote to Joseph Medill, the Chicago editor: "Give us the plan and I can borrow."

Congress could not fathom why the secretary of the Treasury was pushing a long-range reform that did not, in any immediate sense, address the revenue crisis. On a motion by Thaddeus Stevens, both chambers approved a resolution for an immediate printing of $100 million in legal tender. Representative Morrill, who had opposed greenbacks a year earlier, rationalized that the patient had gotten used to "opiates" and now could not be denied. But the added dose of greenbacks was only a stopgap. According to Chase, arrears to the army and navy were approaching $60 million. At an army wage of thirteen dollars per month, the new greenbacks would be exhausted by springtime.

Lincoln signed the legal tender resolution on January 17, 1863—specifying that he did so "for the prompt discharge of all arrears of pay due to our soldiers and our sailors." However, he expressed "sincere regret" that the measure had been needed. Greenbacks had to be kept "within due limits," the President warned, or they would produce "disastrous consequences," particularly for working families. Lincoln reprised his endorsement of Chase's banking reform and asked Congress to promptly approve the bill. For a president, especially a Whiggish one, to intervene in the legislative process was considered practically a violation of Church and State. *The New York Times* labeled it "extraordinary" and "injudicious." Lincoln, though, felt "bound" to intervene because the topic of the currency was "so important." Banking had been his maiden subject. As a Whig, he had struggled, unsuccessfully, to reestablish a central bank. He felt it was the government's job to provide a worthy currency. And he was anxious to give "every possible support" to the public credit. Chase's plan would require the national banks to invest in U.S. bonds, as security for their notes. Thus, once the system was up and running, the new banks would become the Treasury's customers. Chase seems by now to have persuaded himself, as well as the President, that these benefits would come quickly.

Yet even with Lincoln's endorsement, Chase's plan was given little chance. Opposition in the House was fierce. Representative Spaulding (highly respected for his role in passing the Legal Tender Act) was against it. The Buffalo banker defended the state system of which his two banks were members. Seemingly without irony, Spaulding told the chamber, "Immense interests are involved in the banks."

The entire concept of the bill was to squeeze the notes of state banks out of existence. It pushed this process along by taxing these notes. Ultimately, the aim was to encourage state banks to convert to national charters, unifying the system. However, the so-called circulation privilege was highly prized. The license to issue notes was (literally) a license to print money. Bankers such as Spaulding naturally sought to retain the privilege.

Spaulding noted that in New York, the banks functioned well. This was true; in fact, Chase had used the Empire State as a blueprint for his national system. In other states, regulations were looser, the banks less worthy. This furnished the Treasury secretary with a persuasive argument. The persistence of splintered currencies, a relic from colonial times, struck many Republicans as antithetical to the purposes of the Civil War. Gradually, the fight over banking morphed into a battle over state versus federal authority. Chase's opponents condemned what they termed an unprecedented grab of federal power. Collamer, the Vermont senator, quoted Montesquieu on the abuse of power and fretted that the bill would furnish the Treasury secretary with enough authority to "make himself President any day" (a thought that did not displease Chase). Spaulding protested, in language that any Confederate would have applauded, that Chase's banking bill would "contravene the State sovereignty."

While Chase lobbied for banking reform, the House proceeded on a parallel track, legislating to give the Treasury greater flexibility in borrowing. Both Chase and Congress recognized the need for modifications in loan terms to make the government's paper more marketable. But even there, the two camps were at odds. Chase wanted authority to issue *interest-bearing* notes, which he thought people would hold, rather than spend—thus restraining the inflationary effect. Legislators, on the other hand, favored more greenbacks. As the *Times* observed, "The choice is really between the issue of legal tender notes and the national banking scheme of Secretary Chase."

Through January and much of February, Chase continued to spar with Congress. Meanwhile, the greenback hit new lows. The gold premium soared to 54 percent on January 20 and 60 percent at the end of the month. Chase took his campaign to the press, exhorting Horace Greeley, "Why don't you—who can so well point out the path which others ought to walk—do your part?" He warned Pitt Fessenden that the only remedy for gold fever was the banking bill.

Chase had not been able to enlist the support of Cooke. But the latest financial crisis had decimated bond sales. Cooke came to think that the Chase plan, by contriving a market for bonds, might be a tonic. In January, he flipped, and once he supported the bill he did so with his usual pluck. Cooke had purchased ads for the five-twenties in so many newspapers that he felt they could hardly refuse him a few columns to promote the banking bill. Presently, pro-reform articles flooded the press. "The dollar of America should be as valuable in New York as in Wisconsin," the Philadelphia *Press* (possibly ghostwritten by Cooke) persuasively argued. The paper attacked the existing system for its "sectional character," which made it sound like an offshoot of secession. Since most newspaper readers did not have well-formed opinions on banking, such publicity was invaluable. Of equal importance, the Cookes lobbied Congress. The bill was still moribund in the House, and in the Senate, a majority of the Finance Committee, including Fessenden, was opposed. However, on January 22, at Chase's request, Henry Cooke, who had managed one of John Sherman's political campaigns, visited his old friend in the Senate. Sherman had been cool to the banking plan, but Henry patiently pressed his case. As Sherman explained to his wife, "Chase appealed to me through Cooke to remodel the bill to satisfy my views and take charge of it in the Senate." Four days later, Sherman introduced the banking bill.

The plan had little support in the east, where the banks were generally strong and their notes circulated at close to face value. West of the Alleghenies it was a different story. Of the 2200 state banks established by 1863, more than a quarter had defaulted on notes. Moreover, banking strength was exceptionally lopsided, with currency and credit concentrated in the east. At the outbreak of the war, Chicago had precisely 1 bank compared with 55 in New York City, which boasted no less than 32 percent of the nation's deposits. Even in Ohio, an industrial state, bank circulation amounted to only $9 million, compared with $50 million in New England, whose population was not much greater. Zachariah Chandler, a senator and merchant from Michigan, upbraided eastern colleagues who professed to see little attraction in Chase's new currency. "Very little demand will arise in the eastern States for this circulating medium," Chandler prophesied. "It will be different in the West."

On February 10, Sherman gave a lengthy peroration, stressing the proposed system's national character. As opposed to the thousands of bills presently in circulation:

> This currency . . . will be printed by the United States. It will be of uniform size, shape, and form; so that a bank bill issued in the State of Maine will be current in California; a bank bill issued in Ohio will be current wherever our Government currency goes at all.

Sherman cleverly linked his argument to patriotic feeling. The "higher motive" of the banking act was that it would promote "a sentiment of nationality," he said. "The policy of this country ought to be to make everything national as far as possible, to nationalize our country, so that we shall love our country."

Sherman did not mean "nationalize" in the modern sense of acquiring a state-owned enterprise. He meant, rather, to prioritize the federal government over the states. No public statesman since Hamilton had made such a strident case for federal power. If the war was being waged to deny the right of states to secede, then the federal government should also reign supreme in banking and, indeed, in "everything." Sherman turned the banking act into a war bill.

The Ohio senator was an adroit salesman. While promoting the Hamiltonian concept of national banking, Sherman deftly attacked the state banks for their alleged corruption and for undersupplying currency to ordinary people, a populist theme that resonated with Jacksonians and western Democrats. Suspicion of banks was an American birthright, as old as Jefferson (it survives today). Yet, while nodding to the problem of currency scarcity, Sherman, like Chase, regarded the potential for *excessive* note printing as far more worrisome. In many states, the regulations governing note circulation were quite lax and, in Sherman's phrase, promoted a "facility for excessive expansion."

The new system was designed to restrict excesses. Banking exists on a spectrum, risk at one end versus safety at the other. Chase's plan did not fail to choose sides. The plan was remarkable for its safeguards—requirements on capital (a daunting $100,000 to start a bank, except in very small towns, where the minimum was $50,000), onerous reserve requirements, a prohibition on real estate loans. Banks had to submit to rigorous federal examinations, plus there was the requirement that they secure their notes with the safest of assets—Treasury bonds. *In addition*, shareholders in failing banks faced double liability. Sherman insisted on the most restrictive clause, a cap on the total of National Bank Notes of $300 million. Rarely has a revolution been so prudent.

The reform would reinsert the federal government into banking, where it had been absent for a generation. Under the old system, the government could not so much as handle bank notes—the country's currency. Now, the banks and the government would be permitted to seamlessly traffic in each other's paper. Effectively, they would be partners. The role of banks would be elevated, for now they would serve as depositories for federal funds. Few Americans understood this. Sherman preferred to stress the benefits of a uniform currency. Appealing to Americans' pride, he emphasized that each bill would be identically engraved, and the country's money would be internationally convertible, like notes of the Bank of England.

Sherman made major compromises to win support from eastern colleagues. He agreed to let the national banks in New York, Philadelphia, and Boston be assured of a privileged role in redeeming notes (one modern writer has called this a "bribe"). The tax on state bank notes was held to only 2 percent, arguably trivial and certainly a level at which state banks could continue to operate. Despite such concessions, Sherman remained several votes short. He and Chase had to arm-wrestle Republican holdouts. Lincoln also lobbied for the bill—a rare departure from custom. An assistant secretary to the President, William O. Stoddard, told Wisconsin senator Timothy Howe that Lincoln felt very deeply about the bill. Howe instantly agreed to vote in favor. Chase and Lincoln also put pressure on Fessenden, who reluctantly agreed as well. Banking reform came to a vote on Lincoln's birthday, February 12. Chase nervously attended the roll call. In the first poll, the bill went down, but two more senators flipped and it won by the narrowest of margins, 23–21. In the House, Chase and Lincoln again helped, and so did nationalistic feeling. Spaulding switched from opposing the bill on state-sovereignty grounds to declaring that Hamilton's strong central government was, in fact, "the true policy." This was the emerging Republican credo of centralism. On February 25, 1863, Lincoln signed the National Banking Act,* the most far-reaching financial reform in the country's history.

National Banking got off to a slow start. Establishing such an intricate and tightly regulated system would take time. Chase unnecessarily slowed its growth by insisting that national banks be denoted numerically; thus, the first institution to organize in a city would be dubbed the "First National Bank of ——," followed by the Second National, the Third National, etc. Presidents of state banks were reluctant to give up their names, which discouraged them from converting. Chase nominated Hugh McCulloch, an Indiana banker, to be the system's first regulator. McCulloch personified the financial conservatism that Chase sought to institutionalize. His title, comptroller of the cur-

---

* The legislation was officially known as "An Act to Provide a National Currency." Most newspapers in 1863 referred to it as the "currency bill." In time, the legislation and an add-on bill in 1864 became known as the National Banking Acts.

rency, reflected the framers' primary concern—to control the money supply.

By the time National Banking passed, Congress was debating a bill to authorize additional loans—contentious due to Stevens's insistence on a further injection of legal tender. With Wall Street speculators predicting a panic if Stevens got his way, the gold premium surged to 72.5 percent (put differently, the greenback, which had been intended to trade at parity, plunged to only 58 cents). The final bill, enacted March 3, was notable in two respects. The sums approved were gargantuan. Congress—as requested by Chase—authorized $900 million in loans, just to finance the Treasury through June 1864. And Chase was given wide latitude in tailoring the securities, a mark of the respect he had earned on Capitol Hill. This included authority to issue long-term bonds for up to forty years, unthinkable to a less stable credit (such as Richmond).

Throughout the war, both North and South struggled to issue paper that would fund their operations without spurring inflation. The trick for Chase, as well as for his opposite number Memminger, was to persuade people to take longer-dated paper and squirrel it away. But their respective citizens preferred to use government bills as money—i.e., to spend them—either for convenience or out of a self-protective desire to not get stuck with depreciating paper. In the March 1863 act, Congress also authorized short-term notes, but at Chase's urging, most of the new notes would pay interest, which Chase hoped would make them attractive to investors. Nonetheless, Congress provided an escape hatch, giving Chase the authority to issue $150 million in greenbacks.*

The loan bill was a second triumph for Chase. Among its many features, at Chase's request, Congress put a deadline of July 1 on the

---

* The "Nine Hundred Million Loan Act" authorized the Treasury to borrow $300 million in fiscal 1863 (through June) and another $600 million in fiscal 1864. Chase, as noted, was given great discretion to tailor these loans. Rather than require that bonds be sold at par, as was common, Congress gave the Treasury secretary latitude to sell at market prices. It also left to Chase to determine whether the Treasury notes would be legal tender. Of the $900 million authorized, up to $400 million could be Treasury notes and $150 million U.S. Notes (greenbacks). The latter sum included the $100 million already approved in January.

right to convert greenbacks into the five-twenty bonds. This gratified Chase, who hoped that investors might now rush to convert *before* the deadline. Jay Cooke immediately pounced, trying to spur investors with the warning "Those who neglect these Six per cent. Bonds . . . may have occasion to regret it."

Both the loan bill and the banking bill expanded the horizons of the federal government and the Treasury secretary in particular. Ideologically, they conformed to a pair of non-economic bills enacted in a similar federalizing spirit. Congress (also on March 3) approved a military draft, subjecting every male citizen aged twenty to forty-five to conscription, for the first time.* Congress also gave the President authority to suspend the writ of habeas corpus—as Lincoln, of course, had already done. Under this policy, hundreds of suspected Rebel sympathizers were summarily arrested. The collective effect of such measures was to augment federal power. Centralism had begun as a necessity of war, but it was now Republican doctrine. Even John Sherman sounded awed, and a tad circumspect. With Congress recessed, he wrote his brother William, "The laws passed at the last session will be a monument of evil or of good. They cover such vast sums, delegate and regulate such vast powers, and are so far-reaching in their effects, that generations will be affected well or ill by them."

---

* During the Revolutionary War, states were urged to draft militiamen into the Colonial army; this first effort at conscription was irregular and unsuccessful.

Nine

Cotton for Cash

Money is the great power in war and will
conquer at last.

— *St. Louis Daily Evening News*

Shall we starve?

— JOHN BEAUCHAMP JONES

B Y EARLY 1863, Salmon Chase's financial architecture was essentially complete. His biggest obstacle, he complained to President Lincoln, wasn't financial—it was military. In the western
theater, Ulysses S. Grant's attack on Vicksburg was literally stuck in
mud. In the east, at a desolate Virginia crossroads known as Chancellorsville, Robert E. Lee dealt the Union army a disastrous loss despite
being outmanned more than two to one. Lincoln turned a ghostly gray
when he heard the news. Noah Brooks, a newspaperman close to Lincoln, was to say, "Never, as long as I knew him, did he seem to be so
broken." The President worried how long the country would support
such a war. He worried about the potential for civilian discontent or
even disloyalty—a "fire in the rear." Early that year, Lincoln's worst
suspicions were confirmed when prominent northern Democrats began
to call on the British to intervene and mediate a peace. In May, as the
fighting raged in Virginia, a company of Union soldiers arrested Clem-

ent Vallandigham, a leader of the Copperheads (antiwar Democrats) at his home in Dayton, Ohio—setting off a rampage of rioting by his supporters. Even among loyalists, pessimism over the war was widespread. Joseph Medill, one of the most doggedly pro-Union newspaper editors, predicted an armistice before the year was out. After the rout at Chancellorsville, Senator Charles Sumner barged into the office of Navy Secretary Gideon Welles, raised his hands, and bewailed, "Lost, lost, all is lost."

Only from one perspective did the war seem not only not lost but, in fact, already won. The Union was increasingly productive and prosperous, while the southern economy was slowly imploding. The Union had taxing power, a new banking system, a vibrant commercial life. "But for the daily news from the war in the papers & the crowds of soldiers you see about the streets *you would have no idea of any war,*" the businessman William Dodge wrote from New York. "Our streets are crowded. Hotels full . . . the Road ways & manufacturers of all kinds except cotton are doing so well." As if to emphasize the normalcy in his life, the diarist George Templeton Strong noted that he passed an agreeable afternoon listening to the New York Philharmonic rehearse Beethoven's Fourth, "a very noble symphony."

In the South, such cultural amenities were fast disappearing. Every resource was devoted to guns, scarcely any to butter. Shortages were becoming pervasive, and prices were climbing on the order of 10 to 15 percent *per month.* "All the necessaries of life in the city are still going up higher in price," noted the peevish John Beauchamp Jones, the Confederate War Department clerk. "By degrees, quite perceptible, we are approaching the condition of famine."

In a moonshot effort to rescue their finances, southern agents in Europe had been searching for a banker to float a loan denominated in cotton. In the fall of 1862, they came to rough agreement with a young financier who understood its potential even better than they. That banker was Frédéric Emile d'Erlanger, a precocious and worldly thirty-year-old who ran the French arm of a German banking house, Erlanger et Compagnie. The basic idea was simple: Richmond would sell bonds, backed by the value of a store of cotton, for hard currency (pounds sterling or francs) that the Confederates could use to purchase weapons and other supplies on the continent.

The main difficulty was that cotton in the South was essentially inaccessible. Erlanger believed that European investors—if offered sufficiently attractive terms—might be willing to lend now and wait to claim the cotton until after the war. Erlanger's connections made him a natural go-between. He was close to the French court, and also to John Slidell, the Confederate minister to Napoleon III. (He was also rather fond of Slidell's stunning daughter Mathilde, whom he would marry before the war was out.)

Richmond urgently needed such a deal. Three-quarters of its arms were supplied in Europe, and the Confederacy suffered acutely from the lack of foreign exchange. Investors had purchased bonds in the first year of the war—but after that, they had lost interest. Richmond's only alternative source of hard currency was running the blockade, which provided only a trickle. Cotton shipments to Great Britain had plunged to 4 percent of their prewar level. (The South by now had given up all thought of embargoing cotton, but with Union frigates patrolling the waters, shipping had become perilous.)

Erlanger demanded an exorbitant fee for underwriting the loan. The Confederates didn't balk; where else were they to turn? But, oddly, while Erlanger offered to lend £5 million (or its equivalent in francs), Richmond authorized only £3 million, the prewar equivalent to $15 million U.S.

Intent on persuading the Confederate leadership to borrow more, Erlanger took the somewhat reckless step of running the blockade from the Bahamas, daring the Union cruisers that lay in wait off Nassau. The banker arrived in Richmond late in 1862. One peek at the shops, where goods were few and prices high, and at the haggard look of the citizens, must have reaffirmed his conviction that the Confederacy was in no position to resist his offer. Treasury Secretary Christopher Memminger was desperate to slow the inflation. The total of Confederate notes had swelled to more than $400 million. Including bank notes and other forms of currency, there was plausibly $600 million of paper in circulation. This explosion of bills had lifted inflation far above what was customary even for a nation at war. The South had reached the funhouse-mirror stage, in which prices cease to bear much relation to the thing itself—only to the ever increasing supply of paper. As reported in the *Richmond Daily Dispatch*, the increases were truly astronomical.

COMMODITY	JANUARY 1863 MULTIPLE OF PREWAR PRICE
Flour	Two and a half X
Meal	Four X
Butter	Seven X
Bacon	Eight X
Candles	Eight X
Lard	Eight X
Soap	Eleven X
Sugar	Fourteen X
Tea	Sixteen X
Pepper and salt	Twenty-five X
Coffee	Forty X

Memminger knew he was presiding over one of history's great inflations, but he was helpless to stop it. The Confederate bonds sold at the start of the war had plunged to 33 cents in gold, that is, a two-thirds devaluation. No further loans were forthcoming. All that remained was the printing press. At the rate Richmond was spending, Memminger calculated, he would need to issue $200 million more in notes just during the next six months—which would drive prices higher still. Robert M. T. Hunter, the Virginian chairman of the Confederate Senate Finance Committee, realistically surmised, "Bankruptcy stares us in the face."

Richmond's purchasing agents overseas were desperately short of cash. James Bulloch, a former U.S. naval officer who became the Confederacy's chief purchasing agent in Liverpool, notified his masters at home that to execute pending arms contracts he had no alternative but to try to borrow cash from expat southerners. That was a strategy born of desperation. The opportunity presented by Erlanger, to mortgage cotton stockpiled throughout the South, was a gift. As word of the prospective Erlanger bonds began to circulate, Bulloch and other agents pressed Richmond to borrow all it could. Lieutenant James H. North, Bulloch's colleague in Paris, alerted Secretary of the Navy Stephen Mallory that he was "very, very anxious" for the bonds to be issued "knowing that in a short time I would have a large payment to make."

Even the cautious Memminger acknowledged that, given the war's longevity, "it would be well for us to increase the credit of our government in Europe to the largest possible sum." Inexplicably, when actual negotiations commenced, Memminger insisted that $15 million was the maximum he would borrow. This figure must be compared with the annual value of cotton exports before the war—$190 million. In correspondence, the Treasury secretary attributed his caution to Congress's reluctance to authorize more. This is hardly credible, since the Rebel Congress was essentially President Davis's tool. Erlanger appealed to Davis, who surely discussed the matter with his adviser Judah Benjamin. The latter did succeed in modestly reducing the interest rate. But Benjamin, unusually for him, failed to appreciate the loan's potential. He viewed the loan mostly as a lever to pull the French into the war—a possibility he should have recognized was now remote.* Neither he nor Davis was willing to override Memminger on the $15 million ceiling. This was a monumental blunder.

Congress debated the bond deal in secret and ratified it January 29. Word soon leaked to the European press. The terms immediately aroused the appetites of speculators, for Erlanger, who returned to Paris in February 1863, had devised a clever carrot. The bonds were twenty-year instruments, with 7 percent interest payable in sterling. However,

---

* Many southerners clung to this unlikely hope. John Beauchamp Jones wrote excitedly on January 20, 1863, of a rumor of French recognition, adding, "We all pray for the Emperor's intervention."

investors could at any time claim an equal value in "New Orleans middling cotton," valued at the *prewar* price of six English pence per pound. On a £100 bond, that amounted to 4000 pounds of cotton.* But the price of cotton had soared. In Liverpool, middling cotton now fetched approximately *twenty-two* pence.

This meant that the Erlanger bonds obligated Richmond to deliver a quantity of cotton valued at nearly four times the loan value. This was not a concern to the government, which had more than enough surplus cotton, having purchased large stockpiles on credit from planters. To investors, the premium price represented a huge windfall. In theory, they stood to quadruple their investment.

The catch, of course, was that they had to collect their prize within the Confederacy. For the duration of the war, Richmond was obligated only to deliver the cotton to a point within ten miles of a navigable river or railway depot. It was up to the investor to run the blockade. For investors willing to wait until peace was restored, Richmond would deliver to port.

The offering was wildly popular—indeed, it was oversubscribed. Erlanger's firm purchased the bonds at 77 (23 percent less than face value) and sold them at 90, pocketing the difference. It also claimed a commission. Subscriptions were offered on March 18 in Paris, Frankfurt, London, and Amsterdam. They sold out immediately, the great majority in London. Both *The Times* of London and the *Economist* rated the bonds more highly than securities of the United States, remarkable testimony to the mania that greeted the issue. Wealthy merchants, gentlemen of property, and military men were among the investors—as were the future prime minister William Gladstone and, reportedly, Napoleon III's private secretary. The total pledged by investors was $13.5 million, leaving, after Erlanger's hefty fee, $11 million for Richmond. But the demand would have absorbed five times that amount—a vast potential treasure lost to the Confederacy. In the aftermath, Rebel officials, perhaps too quickly, permitted themselves to exult in triumph.

---

* The old English pound was equal to 240 pence, so £100 equaled 24,000 pence.

James Mason, the envoy in London, jubilantly exclaimed to Benjamin, "I think I may congratulate you. . . . Cotton is King, at last!"

The South's purchasing agents eagerly prepared to receive the funds, which were to be paid in Paris and transmitted to Fraser, Trenholm & Co., the depository for the Confederate Treasury in Liverpool. Erlanger, which was not remiss in seeking opportunities for profit, established a shipping line to run the blockade to cater to investors who wanted the cotton right away. How many investors succeeded in getting their cotton isn't known, but it could not have been many. The rest were willing to wait, buoyed by rumors (spread by Richmond) that Grant's forces were being set back at Vicksburg. The investors do not seem to have considered that the Rebels might lose the war and that, if they did, their bonds would be worthless.

It is staggering to recall that the same British investment community had been selling American (that is, Union) securities. Now, they were lending hard cash to Richmond. Investors are cautious when modest sums are at stake, but presented with the potential for vast profit, they lose their heads. Even the potential profit was an illusion, for it was based on the wartime cotton price. Any cotton shipped when the war ended would be worth a great deal less.

The bonds surged in the aftermarket from the offering price of 90 up to 95½. They traded like a gambling stock, rising or falling on the war news. The Union hit on a clever counterstrategy. During the 1840s, various American states had defaulted on bonds held by European investors. Mississippi had been one of them, and Jefferson Davis had defended Mississippi's right to default. Now, egged on by Union agents, newspapers in England spread the story that the Confederate president was a "repudiator." This gave investors a fright, and the Erlanger bonds began to slide.

The banker now had a problem, for only a deposit, representing 15 percent of the total price, had been required of investors in March. The rest was due in stages over the ensuing months. As the price slid, investors began to consider forgoing their deposits—leaving Erlanger, potentially, on the hook for the balance. This was not what he had envisioned.

Richmond, however, could not afford to lose the offering. By now, its financial unraveling was producing a serious political and social crisis, greatly worsening public morale. The government was forced to take draconian measures to ensure that food and supplies were diverted to the army. People began to go hungry; not surprisingly, they were increasingly resentful of the authorities.

Although Richmond was loath to admit it, the government was commandeering food from civilian stores to feed the troops. As early as 1862, the army's meat ration was cut from twelve to eight ounces. Lee's soldiers were scavenging for wild onions. Military authorities stepped up the practice of "impressment" (requisitioning crops and other supplies at artificially low prices). The *Richmond Whig*, the most critical of Davis of the newspapers in the capital, excoriated the administration for "set[ting] aside all law and justice" with its exercise of "tyrannical power." The government established commissions to oversee prices, for the supposed purpose of making them fair, but in practice, farmers regarded impressment as little better than theft.

During the early months of 1863, Jones's family suffered as prices of staples such as butter, bacon, and sweet potatoes outstripped his income. Jones grimly described the meager contents of a dinner for seven, which included their "servant" (presumably a slave): twelve eggs, a little corn bread, some rice and potatoes. He sadly recorded, "My youngest daughter put her earrings on sale to-day—price $5." His tone was increasingly accusatory. He bitterly charged, "None but the opulent, often those who had defrauded the government, can obtain a sufficiency of food and raiment."

Early in March, the food crisis boiled over. Authorities in Richmond seized flour from warehouses and mills. Quickly, shops ran out of bread. Women began to beg in the streets. On March 30, Jones summarized the state of affairs, operatically but not inaccurately: "The

gaunt form of wretched famine still approaches with rapid strides."
Then, on April 2, several hundred women gathered in the "African"
church to present demands to Governor John Letcher. When the governor failed to respond, hundreds of women, many wielding axes, went
on a rampage, breaking into stores and seizing provisions. Letcher now
troubled himself to talk to the rioters, but in a scolding manner. Eventually, President Davis hurried to the scene, jumped on a cart, and
urged the crowd to focus on their common enemy. Someone shouted,
"We are starving." Troops arrested forty demonstrators—wives and
mothers of Confederate soldiers. A similar women's food riot erupted in
Salisbury, North Carolina. Some states passed laws to limit the production of nonfood crops, but they were generally ignored.

The "Richmond Bread Riot" was a serious affair. The sons of Virginia would not long fight for a government holding its women in a
stockade. Butter was deciding the war as much as bullets. The need for
relief was so acute that Edwin De Leon, the Confederate diplomat,
who had come to recognize that neither Britain nor France would ever
join forces with a slave state, lobbied Davis to consider a truly radical
reform—emancipation. Davis knew the planters would reject it out of
hand; he never mentioned it in public.

The financial collapse exposed the inadequacy of states' rights as a
guiding principle of government. The central state was simply too
threadbare. In the spring, the Confederate Congress adopted a rash of
measures purportedly to strengthen the finances. To shrink the volume
of notes, Congress enacted a bill to induce southerners to (voluntarily)
surrender notes for long-term bonds.* The idea was to replace currency
with permanent funding. Less than 15 percent—a "lamentably small
portion," in the words of the *Richmond Examiner*—of the Confederacy's
debt was long-term, for the simple reason that investors did not know
how long the Confederacy would endure. That is why Memminger
kept issuing notes. Trying to inculcate faith by suasion, Memminger

---

* The government offered a high exchange rate on notes surrendered immediately and a progressively
lower rate thereafter.

lobbied governors to pledge their states to meet investment quotas. Another bill barred southerners from accepting greenbacks. This was based on the delusion that a law could regulate the people's preference.

In normal times, prices translate the essentials of supply and demand into a practicable number for commerce. Richmond's monetary chaos distorted the idiom, turning ordinary transactions into risky speculations. The *Richmond Examiner* observed with dismay, "Every man in the community is swindling everybody else." Congressmen engaged in food speculations, some of them proscribed by the very laws they had enacted. State governments speculated in cotton. "Cotton banks" lent to planters who pledged their crops as security. Dixie reverted, at least in part, to a prefinancial age in which cotton was the most effective currency. Some businesses began to refuse Confederate bills, demanding payment in goods. A manufacturer said, "Money will buy little or nothing here and unless I can find some means of getting food for my workers, I fear I shall lose them."

Congress's other remedy, enacted at Memminger's pleading, was a variety of taxes—on income, agriculture, and business. Its intent was to shore up the government and restrain inflation, and the press generally supported it. Edmund Ruffin, writing on a gloomy winter's day, predicted that the people would bear the "proper remedy—heavy taxation." However, enforcement was inconsistent and many of the taxes were far from "heavy."* Moreover, taxpayers had considerable ability to delay collection—which given the inflation rate was a form of avoidance. Partly to surmount this problem, Richmond levied a tax of one-tenth of all agricultural products payable *in kind*. To enforce the in-kind tax, it dispatched three thousand agents to canvass the countryside, seizing crops. This allowed the government to sidestep the crumbling financial system. The in-kind tax was far more intrusive than anything southerners had endured from the government of the United States. Farmers bore most of the burden—and of these, poor farmers were hit the

---

* The income tax began at 1 percent, compared with 3 percent for a similar tax in the Union.

hardest, because slaves and land, which were exempt, were owned in greater proportion by the rich. Davis would observe, with the jarring frankness that characterized the slave-owning class, that Congress "sought to reach, so far as was practicable, every resource of the country except the capital invested in real estate and slaves."

Officials in Richmond defended their increasingly heavy hand as an exigency of war. The *Richmond Enquirer*, the mouthpiece of Jefferson Davis, went so far as to say that if the war persisted for several years, it might "compel the country to invest its Executive, as commander-in-chief, with dictatorial power." Richmond's growing power was resented, in particular, because its application was so unequal. Davis spoke of a common cause, but the tax regime exposed the Confederacy as an oligarchy of planters. Not surprisingly, opposition to the taxes was keenest outside the cotton belt. Richmond's "tyranny," not infrequently, was likened to Lincoln's or to that of the British king. At a public meeting in North Carolina, a resolution was adopted "to resist, to the bitter end, any such monarchial tax." Resentment among poor soldiers led to increasingly high rates of desertion. One woman in North Carolina wrote to the governor, requesting a discharge for her husband. She said, "I would like to know what he is fighting for. I don't think that he is fighting for anything, only for his family to starve." Small farmers decried the "rich man's war," a sentiment inflamed by the provision in the draft exempting large slave owners. In fact, slave owners were more likely to fight than others, not surprising since they had a greater interest in the perpetuation of slavery. Nonetheless, the preponderance of foot soldiers were drawn from the poor.

Impressment, taxes, and the draft wakened the Upper South to the insights of Hinton Rowan Helper, who had warned before the war that under southern slavery, poor whites were the unseen victims. Nowhere was this feeling more acute than in the Tar Heel country of Helper's youth. Infuriated by the law that permitted President Davis to suspend the writ of habeas corpus, *The North Carolina Standard* of Raleigh bridled with a sense of aggrievement, as if finally reckoning that North

Carolina (the last state to secede) had been foolish to ever have joined the rebellion. The *Standard* fumed like a man betrayed: "We were told, when the old government was broken up by the States south of us, that the contest was to be for liberty."

It was just as the economic vise was tightening that Erlanger went to Mason, the Confederate envoy in London, in a bit of a panic. The cotton bonds, he said, were in jeopardy; barring some action to prop up the bonds' prices, he feared that subscribers would cancel their orders. Erlanger's solution, rather convenient for his firm, was that the Confederate government use some of the proceeds from the bond sale to go into the market and repurchase bonds. Since this would have to be done incognito, Erlanger further proposed that Richmond authorize his firm to (covertly) buy bonds on its behalf. Most likely, Erlanger et Compagnie was among the sellers. After some resistance, Mason agreed. The operation did stabilize the bonds, roughly at the offering price—but only after the Confederacy had expended far more coin than it could afford. In mid-May, Mason confided to Slidell that the purchase of cotton bonds on government account, "as reported by Mr. Erlanger this morning, somewhat exceeds one and a half million pounds." In other words, Rebel officials had blithely agreed to a financial manipulation that ended up squandering approximately half of the receipts of the bond sale. It was an unforced and catastrophic error.

Seemingly blind to the consequences of the repurchases, Mallory, the head of the Rebel navy, excitedly directed Bulloch, "We want ironclads, ironclads, ironclads." The government's grand design was to build an invincible armada to safeguard its supply chain. Bulloch, who was more realistic than the cloistered grandees in Richmond, tersely replied, "I fear the Treasury Department is overstating the amount to be realized from the Erlanger loan." Treasury subsequently admitted that the Confederacy netted only about 40 percent of the face value, or about $6 million (its ultimate take may have been even less). Richmond's agents on the continent were left still desperate for funds. By mid-summer,

Mallory had confessed to "a grievous disappointment." The only party who came out ahead was Erlanger.

As Richmond was struggling to save the cotton bond, Chase was reviving his efforts to sell the five-twenties. Sales had sagged during the winter financial scare, but in the spring they revived. Jay Cooke redoubled his marketing and ramped up his use of the press. His agents tirelessly lobbied newspaper editors and warned them against printing Copperhead or other dissenting views. Cooke's efforts produced a deluge of articles as well as ads promoting the bonds. To make the bonds seem less forbidding, he took pains to describe the people lining up at his office for subscriptions—a studied collection of humble citizens and moneymen, thus a "nursery maid," a "hale old farmer," a wounded Union officer, an "old lady" with her money stashed in a handkerchief, and a "portly gentleman" who was one of the "solid men" of Philadelphia. Cooke's treacly, sentimentalized description of "A Day at the Agency for the 'Five-Twenty' Loan," was printed without attribution in his hometown *Philadelphia Inquirer*, and widely reproduced.

Like the World War I–era marketers of Liberty Bonds, Cooke emphasized that investing was a small way for people on the home front to emulate the sacrifice of soldiers. He marketed to the troops, too, dispatching agents to solicit them on paydays. One soldier in the Army of the Potomac enclosed his surplus earnings to the subscription agent with the words "If I fight hard enough, my bonds will be good."

Cooke's campaign spurred sharply higher sales. In late March 1863–when a Confederate envoy was bragging that cotton was king—*The New York Times* reported that due to "extraordinary demand" the Treasury was employing a large force of clerks to speed bonds to the engraver. Meanwhile, Cooke's agents were canvassing the country, buttonholing subagents and editors and posting flyers in hotels, courthouses, railroad stations, and post offices. Thanks to this network, Cooke could boast of customers in "almost every town and village throughout the country." An agent in Illinois, J. E. Zug, confirmed that in many cases, "farmers who live in a little cabin, wear their home-spun clothes and ride to church and town in their two-horse wagons" had purchased bonds to the tune of several thousand dollars. Bonds sold briskly even in border areas of Maryland, West Virginia, and Kentucky. Business was hot in Baltimore, once rabidly secessionist.

President Lincoln purchased the five-twenty bond; so did Treasury Secretary Chase, Navy Secretary Welles, James Garfield (the future president), Admiral David Farragut, and a score of congressmen. Other investors included Nathaniel Hawthorne, P. T. Barnum, and the diarist Strong.

Lincoln sorely wanted the bonds to be popularly subscribed. Wide ownership would translate to support for the war. The bonds, which were available from fifty dollars up to ten thousand, were available in two forms. The simplest were "coupon" bonds, which came attached to perforated coupons that could be turned in to the Treasury in Washington, and at other offices, for the semiannual interest. These bonds were easy to trade; whoever had the coupon could collect the interest. The other variety, more secure but more difficult to transfer, were "registered" bonds, for which only a registered buyer was entitled to payment. The government kept records on registered bonds, and these show large numbers of relatively modest purchases, consistent with Lincoln's aim. Perhaps surprisingly, a quarter of registered bonds were purchased by women (some, presumably, whose husbands were at war). The average investment by women was $2400; the average by men was $5500. Those were considerable sums in an era when lieutenants earned $105.50 per month, and testifies to the growing confidence in the Union.

Cooke's publicity featured investment "questions" to which his writers supplied staged and reassuring replies. Knowing that people thought of gold as safer, he sought to rupture the metal's mystique, emphasizing the "utter folly" of hoarding gold, which was static and inert, whereas his bonds would provide a positive return. Cooke despised gold because it acted as a check on paper finance. "There are those who would make gold the barometer," he wrote disdainfully after a defeat on the battlefield failed to stem his sales, "but it seems that after all it indicates nothing."

Newspapers regularly published sales totals, nationally and by city, which had a powerfully suggestive effect. Beginning in April 1863, the Treasury sold more than $1 million per day; during May, sales often topped $2 million. Combined with the government's new taxes, five-twenty sales were paying for the war. To the *Chicago Daily Tribune*, the bond drive presaged eventual victory. Noting in its left lead column that five thousand people had subscribed over the previous twenty-four hours, the *Tribune* enthused, "The people do not believe the Government is going to fall." A more stirring testimony was offered by Spencer Kellogg Brown, a twenty-one-year-old Union sailor awaiting execution as a spy in a Richmond prison. In his final hours, the condemned sailor asked both his father and his sister, in letters home, to invest his pay, for the benefit of his soon-to-be-widow, in "United States six per cent bonds." Soon after his death by hanging, Brown's letters were publicized and he was glorified as a martyr.

Cooke worked closely with Chase and burnished their relationship by stroking the needy Treasury secretary with praise. He emphasized that Chase's policies were boosting confidence in the government. This was good for sales, because people believed that Chase's personal virtue would secure their investment. The Philadelphian also worried about protecting the bonds in the aftermarket. In a parallel to Erlanger, he persuaded Chase to let him use a government fund to support the price. But the similarity ended there. By the end of June, five-twenty sales over the past year had swelled to $175 million, a fabulous boon to the Union. Of the total, three-quarters were sold by Cooke and the rest directly by the Treasury.

Despite the heady figures, members of Congress (as well as envious bankers) criticized Chase for having granted Cooke a lucrative monopoly. The Treasury secretary came under political fire and repeatedly prodded Cooke to reduce his fee. Cooke responded in the worst way—by coming dangerously close to offering his patron a bribe. In May, he sent a check for $4200 (more than the annual income of a United States senator), representing the profit on three hundred shares in the Philadelphia and Erie Railroad. Chase had hoped to pay for the stock through the sale of a farm in Ohio, but had not gotten around to it. "As I had not paid for the stock," Chase noted, "I cannot regard the profit as mine." Adding that he was "determined to avoid every act which could give occasion to suspicion," he returned the check by the same post. Cooke replied that he was "quite astounded" by the Treasury secretary's show of scruples. He added that he didn't regard the money as his and would "lay it aside for future consideration"—putting Chase on notice that the plum would remain on offer. Barely a week after his show of conscience, Chase unwisely asked Cooke to advance $1000 to the widow of an abolitionist supporter of his previous campaign. Most likely, he was already thinking about lining up support for the next campaign, and it clouded his judgment. Political ambition was Chase's Achilles' heel.

The spring of 1863 should have been a glorious moment for Chase. The financial picture was rosier than ever. The Union's debt had soared to $1.1 billion (up from $65 million before the war), but the Treasury was more than able to service it. Revenue from customs and the still fledgling tax system totaled $107 million, double that in the preceding year. This was enough to meet the civilian budget and to pay the interest on the war debt. Chase's government was now self-sustaining, giving the Union a decisive financial advantage. Moreover, the Union's funding was increasingly long-term, relieving Chase from having to constantly beg for funds. In the middle of May, he was able to brush off reports from Europe that continental financiers were unwilling to lend. "There is not at this date in the Treasury Department a single unsatisfied requisition," he boasted, adding with characteristic immodesty, "My financial measures have thus been crowned with more than expected success."

Improbably and, with his knack for poor timing, coincident with the recovery in the Treasury, Chase submitted his resignation. Lincoln and

Chase had been receiving complaints regarding the behavior of Victor Smith, a Chase ally whom Chase had appointed collector of customs in Puget Sound in Washington Territory. A grand jury had charged Smith with corruption, and while the charges were dropped (under pressure from Chase), Lincoln had concluded that "the degree of dissatisfaction . . . is too great for him to be retained." Explaining his decision, the President wrote Chase a kindly note intended to soothe any bruised feelings. "I believe he is your personal acquaintance and friend," Lincoln noted, "and if you desire it, I will try to find some other place for him." Chase's response was to resign. Patronage jobs were the currency of politics, and he was peeved at losing a supporter. Moreover, he was hurt that Lincoln had questioned his judgment—which indeed had been faulty. Smith was a crony of Chase from Cincinnati, and his removal, he wrote Lincoln, "greatly pained me."

Though troubled by this latest outburst, the President viewed Chase's prickly pride as an acceptable price for his Treasury secretary's considerable skills. Knowing that he would need Chase to sell plenty more bonds, and to establish the new banking system, Lincoln was not about to let him go. The President also recognized, as he sensitively confided to a Springfield chum, that he had hurt Chase's feelings, and he was anxious to set them right. Although he would not reinstate the offending Smith, he trooped over to Chase's house in a conciliatory mood and promised to let Chase name a successor to Smith. Draping one lanky arm on his shoulder, Lincoln with the other handed Chase his resignation letter, and pleaded with his sulky minister, "Chase, here is a paper I want nothing to do with; take it back, and be reasonable."

Ten

Gettysburg Summer

We are the poor rabble, and the rich rabble
is our enemy.

— RIOTER IN NEW YORK CITY, July 1863

I N THE THIRD YEAR OF THE WAR, the North fully recovered from the depression caused by the loss of southern markets and experienced a genuine boom. The ground had been laid during the antebellum years, when a mania for railroads and river improvements had fostered a burst of transportation spending. As the war economy picked up steam, the Union's infrastructure and industrial might gave it an overwhelming edge.

Factories in emerging lakefront cities such as Milwaukee, Toledo, and Detroit churned out machine tools, leather goods, and processed foods. Iron boomed in Pennsylvania. Of more than incidental interest, the North produced twelve times as many firearms per capita as the South.

The great engine of this industrial colossus was transportation. Tonnage over the Great Lakes (beneficiaries of painstaking harbor improvements) nearly doubled over the course of the war. The North's lead in railroad track gave it a decisive edge. While railroads in the Confederacy were increasingly hampered by equipment shortages, tonnage between New York City and the Midwest grew 75 percent. Railroad dividends and stock prices rose in step. By the latter part of the war, ninety trains entered Chicago every day, where none had gone as recently as 1850.

Most surprising, as the historian Bruce Catton has stressed, even with a million men in uniform, northern farms effortlessly met the increased demand. Wheat and corn production set records, thanks to bumper crops in the breadbasket states. From 1860 to 1863, U.S. grain exports more than trebled, bailing out Europe, which had suffered repeated crop failures, and cementing Britain's attachment to the Union.

In North and South alike, soldiers were replaced in the fields by women. But northern farms also turned to mechanization. Mowers, reapers, an improved plow, and a steam-powered thresher led to leaps in productivity. In contrast, on southern farms, people worked longer hours and conscripted children into the fields.

And the North—and only it—was bolstered by immigration. In 1863, 176,000 newcomers immigrated to the United States, in large part single young men. The pace quickened as the war went on. Many of these newcomers pushed westward—indeed, westward expansion continued almost as if the war were occurring in another country. Thousands of new acres were put under cultivation, and populations in the western states registered heady increases. Illinois added 430,000 inhabitants during the war, a gain of 25 percent. Minnesota, a new state, added 78,000 people—a gain of nearly half. Sparked by gold and silver discoveries, pioneers trekked across the Great Plains to Colorado, Nevada, and Idaho. Hundreds of prairie schooners (caravans of covered wagons) ferried would-be prospectors and families into the territories.

The North's prosperity came with a sizable caveat: many workers didn't share in it. With women and migrants swelling the labor pool, wage increases were muted. By 1863, prices were rising at an annual clip of 23 percent. Adjusted for inflation, wages had fallen 15 percent. Laborers in cities, working at large factories and crammed into foul tenements, had scant opportunity to better their conditions. Workers began to organize, and strikes were increasingly common. Inequality in northern cities amounted to a serious social problem, undermining support for the war. For many poor whites, economic anxiety was inflamed by the Emancipation Proclamation, which aroused fears that freedmen would compete for their jobs.

Confederate leaders, Robert E. Lee in particular, sought to kindle the discontent of northern workers and chisel away at the public's willingness to fight. The general's strategy was aimed at forcing the North to the negotiating table. Richmond did not need to win, merely to outlast the North's appetite for war.

Given its economic and demographic disadvantages, the South's stick-to-itiveness, militarily, was nothing short of remarkable. "The Yankees did not whip us in the field," one Confederate leader said. "We were whipped in the Treasury Department." In fact, the ragged and outnumbered Confederate troops were more than holding their own. In the west, the Rebels were stoutly defending against Ulysses S. Grant's attackers. On the eastern front, Lee's victory at Chancellorsville had demoralized the North and cleared the path for his army to cross the Potomac. Washington, Baltimore, and even Harrisburg, Pennsylvania, lay within striking distance—sowing confusion about Lee's intentions and alarm among civilians.

By June, Lee was on the march. Salmon Chase wrote to James Garfield, by then a brigadier general, "Rumors are rife of a movement in Lee's army." The New York diarist George Templeton Strong fretted on June 17, "Nothing definite yet as to Lee's programme. Hooker seems to be after him, and troops . . . are pouring into Pennsylvania." As Lee had hoped, northerners were not so relaxed when a battle beckoned on their own turf. Among the first to reckon with the significance of Lee's advancing columns were the gold speculators. Some, like the poet Edmund Clarence Stedman, put their chips on "Fighting Joe" Hooker, commander of the Union Army of the Potomac, to thwart the invaders. "Stocks must *rise* and gold *fall*," Stedman confidently predicted. But

Hooker was slow to move. Stedman's partner, a railroad investor named Samuel Hallett, grew increasingly anxious. "Great interest, as you seem to understand, attends the movements of Hooker," Hallett wrote with more restraint than he surely felt, "and if you can give us early intelligence of the results, we should so use it [to benefit] ourselves and you." When Lee's army was reinforced, gold surged and Hallett telegrammed in a state of panic: "Extra *Herald* with statement that Lee has been reinforced. Please instruct me in regard to your shorts." By now, most northerners (not just speculators) were tracking the rival armies with intense interest and mounting concern. By June 25, Lee's entire force had crossed the Potomac. "Matters are becoming more serious," Chase alerted his daughter, adding that Washingtonians were alarmed by the nearness of the Rebel cavalry. Chase did not know Lee's objective, though he guessed it was Maryland.

Lee's goal—outlined at a war council in Richmond—was to invade virgin Pennsylvania, stun the North, and spread panic among civilians. This would rouse the Peace Democrats (those who opposed the war either from horror at its costs or sympathy with the Confederacy), catch the attention of the European powers, and upset the northern consensus for war. Fighting and winning on Yankee soil, in Jefferson Davis's phrase, would make the locals feel "the evils of war."

Among the first to feel the evils was Thaddeus Stevens, who (when Congress was out of session) had been in Washington, pressing the cause of colored troops. Returning home to Lancaster, the Pennsylvania congressman paid a visit to the Caledonia Iron Works, and was pleased to find that his business was turning a profit. On June 16, he was conferring with John Sweeney, his business manager, when breathless scouts reported that Rebel cavalry were approaching. The firebrand Stevens was advised to leave and hurriedly boarded a northbound coach. Hours later, a "marauding party" commandeered the factory's horses. Soon after, the factory was seized by Jubal A. Early, one of Lee's commanders. When Sweeney pleaded with the Rebel general to spare the plant for the sake of the employees, Early snapped, "That is not the way

Yankees do business." The general looted the premises, then set it afire. The destruction was an act of vengeance: Early viewed Stevens as an enemy of the South, bent on seizing its property and slaves.*

While Lee's forces were plundering south central Pennsylvania, Hooker telegrammed that he could exploit the vacuum in Virginia by marching on Richmond. Lincoln checked him: "I think *Lee's* Army, and not *Richmond*, is your true objective point. . . . Fight him when opportunity offers." But Hooker worried (unnecessarily) that he was outnumbered. Lincoln despaired that yet another of his generals had fallen under Lee's intimidating spell. On June 27, Lincoln relieved Hooker, replacing him with General George G. Meade. The change of command seemed to spark the Union forces. Four days later, a Rebel detachment in search of shoes clashed with Union cavalry at a bustling crossroads town named Gettysburg. From July 1 through July 3, over eighteen square miles of mostly open plain, two giant armies fought with astonishing bravery. At first, the Rebels appeared to be winning. Then, Colonel Joshua Chamberlain led the Maine Twentieth in a counterattack at Little Round Top. With the tide turning, Lee ordered a reckless charge on the Union center that resulted in an appalling sacrifice of his own men. Total Rebel casualties were a horrific 28,000—more than a third of Lee's army. Union casualties were also frightful—23,000. Meanwhile, on July 4, as Gettysburg fell silent, Grant captured Vicksburg, and with it control of the Mississippi River. This split the Confederacy in two.

Strong judged Gettysburg "one of the great decisive battles of history" (easterners underplayed the significance of Vicksburg). Wall Street was also impressed. The gold premium narrowed and Union securities rose.† "People downtown very jolly today," Strong observed,

---

* Stevens's furnace, two forges, and a rolling mill were burned; he also lost considerable supplies—horses, mules, 4000 pounds of bacon, $4000 worth of bar iron and other stocks. He estimated his losses at a minimum of $75,000 ($1.6 million in today's money). A public subscription in Lancaster raised funds to reimburse him, but Stevens declined it (the money was eventually donated to the poor). Unbowed, Stevens said if the war were won and slavery eliminated, "I shall deem it a cheap purchase."

† During June 1863, gold's premium to the greenback ranged from 40 to 48 percent. By July 28, the premium had collapsed to 23 percent.

rather callously. When word of the battle reached Europe, the Erlanger cotton bonds plunged sharply, falling from 90 to the low 60s.

Yet the war was far from won. While New Yorkers toasted the presumptive end of hostilities, Strong advised his "deluded friends" that there remained, as yet, "battles by the score." Strong was chagrined—and Lincoln extremely upset—that General Meade had rested his exhausted troops (as probably was necessary) rather than pursue Lee's retreating army. With the end not nearly in sight, Chase would need to raise more funds. The Union army would, similarly, need an injection of fresh troops—a matter of urgency, because many enlisted soldiers' terms were expiring, and new enlistment was flagging. This is why, despite serious civilian opposition, Lincoln implemented a federal draft.

Lincoln asked for three hundred thousand call-ups. But the conscription law, enacted in March, was notably unegalitarian. By long tradition, draftees could "hire" a substitute to serve in their place. One who did so was Theodore Roosevelt Sr., a wealthy glass importer and father of the future president. In addition, the Civil War law permitted draftees to buy their way out for a three-hundred-dollar fee to the government. These loopholes did not strike Lincoln or other Republicans as unfair. The government had paid bounties to encourage voluntary enlistment; payment in lieu of service was a converse application of the same principle. Various communities raised funds to underwrite exemptions for the poor and did not encounter serious opposition.

Nonetheless, Lincoln should have heeded the French traveler Alexis de Tocqueville, who had predicted in 1835 that, in a democracy, voluntary recruitment would not suffice. The key to making conscription work, the Frenchman argued, was fairness: "The government may do almost whatever it pleases, *provided* it appeals to the whole community at once: it is the unequal distribution of the weight, not the weight itself, which commonly occasions resistance."

These words were remarkably prophetic. The actual "weight" of the Union draft was modest. Although three quarters of a million men were drafted, excluding those who hired a substitute, paid the fee, were deemed unfit or exempted on other grounds, such as being the sole support for an indigent parent, as well as those who failed to report, only about 50,000 draftees actually served. (A somewhat greater 120,000 conscripts served in the South.) Nonetheless, the draft was highly controversial. Recruitment had always been a *state* responsibility. Democrats opposed the federal draft as another Lincolnian abuse of power. Through the spring of 1863, as the government was preparing to implement conscription, the draft became a touchstone for Copperheads, who attacked it as unfair to the poor. "In a Republic neither riches, nor office, nor social position, should furnish any ground for exemption from military service," an army officer proclaimed in a leading New York daily. This sentiment was warmly received in the city's poor Irish Democratic districts, where many families lived in squalid conditions and teemed with resentment over lagging wages.

Feelings of class antagonism were greatly inflamed by appeals to racism. The Copperhead press accused Lincoln of fighting for "abolition," a term used as a slur even after the proclamation. It was often paired with the baseless charge that poor whites were fighting and dying so that Black freedmen could come north and take their jobs. The *New York Herald,* a leading Democratic organ, inveighed in April, "All this folly [help for freedmen] is consummated at the expense of Uncle Sam, and Sambo begins to think he is not only as good as a white man, but a great deal better." The next month, the *Herald* exhorted, "The blood of white men has been shed very copiously in the cause of the negroes. Let the negroes themselves now bleed a little, if only for sake of variety." It urged that Blacks be conscripted and sent South, for then, "their places will be well supplied by the sturdy and more intelligent labor of healthy Irish and German emigrants." Such racist screeds nourished a poisonous belief among poor whites that the blame for their hardships lay with the Black man. Horace Greeley, editor of the liberal *New York Daily Tribune*, frequently pointed out the inconsistency of arguing both that Blacks were indolent and shiftless Sambos and that they were eager to take white people's jobs.

In fact, there did exist a rivalry between African American and Irish workers in New York, although Blacks had mostly been on the losing end of it. Before the waves of immigration in the 1840s and '50s, many of the brickmakers, whitewashers, dockworkers, coachmen, stablemen, porters, bootblacks, waiters, domestic servants, laundresses, and seamstresses were drawn from the city's twelve thousand Blacks, who represented about 1.5 percent of Manhattan's population. As immigration accelerated, many of their jobs were taken by Europeans, in particular poor Irish. Frederick Douglass, advising his comrades they had better learn a skill, dolefully observed, "Every hour sees the black man elbowed out of employment by some newly arrived emigrant."

Working-class anxiety, along with race prejudice, was intentionally whipped up by Democratic politicians. The Irish American leader Richard O'Gorman organized a mass meeting against "abolitionism." After the preliminary proclamation in September 1862, O'Gorman had provocatively asked, "May not these poor people, enjoying their newly acquired freedom here, swarm on us here in the North?"

But there was no swarm. A trickle of freedmen ventured north, but the number who settled in the northeast during the war appears to have been negligible. What made the draft a looming tinderbox was not, as was alleged, any horde of Negroes from the South. It was the tense labor conditions on the wharves and elsewhere in lower New York.

The longshoremen's trade in New York was mostly Irish. Wages were low, and from the 1850s through the early years of the war, workers repeatedly struck against the going rate of $1.50 a day, and against the irregular hours. Many workers congregated in the bars near the docks, veritable cauldrons of working class antagonisms. Tensions escalated in 1861, when the Republicans awarded federal patronage jobs in the custom house to Blacks—replacing "good Irish Democrats," so said partisan newspapers. Then, in August 1862 (as Lincoln was preparing to announce the proclamation), Irish workers in a tobacco factory in the neighboring city of Brooklyn raided an adjacent and smaller tobacco plant, which employed Black women and children. Later that day, a large mob of whites stormed the plant and prepared to set it afire, as terrified Blacks cowered on the second floor. A voice cried out, "Burn the damn niggers," and they would have, had not police intervened. In the weeks after the attempted lynching, several solitary Blacks in other parts of Brooklyn and across the East River in New York were attacked by Irish mobs.

The longshoremen struck in October and again in January 1863. Some had suffered pay cuts and bitterly complained about inflation. In supporting the strike, the *Herald* editorialized against the supposed threat of an invasion of Black labor. In March, dockworkers at the Erie Railway struck, and Black replacements were hired to move bales of cotton. They were attacked by a mob of Irish, and the regular workers were rehired with their previous $1.50 wage restored. The next month, the Black stevedores, who were paid the same wages as whites, were driven from the waterfront by a mob chanting "Kill the niggers!" Greeley remonstrated that the latest outrage was "the natural climax of the persistent effort of the Pro-Slavery press of this city to strengthen the prejudices, and embitter the hate of its readers." Railing, further, against the mob's "insane and inhuman bigotry," Greeley admonished, "Dislike the negro if you must, but he and you equally are *under* the law."

No sooner had the embers cooled than, in June 1863, labor leaders called a massive work stoppage. Five hundred dockworkers marched from pier to pier, attacking any workers still on the job until police were summoned. The federal government, alarmed because the strike was interrupting military shipments, brought in a detachment to load the ships—while troops stood guard with fixed bayonets. On June 18, various firms settled for a $2 wage and a nine-hour day. By July, although the longshoremen had achieved significant gains on their bread-and-butter economic issue, emotions were running high and white labor on the waterfront, as a later scholar summarized, was "obsessed with a fear of competition from Negroes."

There had long been murmurings that Democrats might try to block the draft. On July 4, Horatio Seymour, New York State's Democratic governor, publicly denounced Lincoln for trampling on the people's rights—a clear reference to the draft. Copperhead politicians added an inflammatory charge—that "niggerheads" (Black sympathizers) wouldn't carry their share of the load: "They will lie and steal and tyrannize over the people, but never fight," so one agitator said.

With the army running short of fresh recruits, the draft went ahead. On Saturday, July 11, draft officers in New York started drawing names while protesters menacingly toted NO DRAFT placards. Hundreds of workers gathered at the waterfront and at nearby saloons to plot resistance. Longshoremen canvassed the piers to recruit would-be rioters. On Monday, a mob from the waterfront, joined by factory and railroad workers, attacked the draft office on Third Avenue and Forty-Sixth Street, pelting it with "clubs, stones, brickbats and other missiles." Police appeared but were overwhelmed by the mob. Blacks were randomly attacked on the street; some were pulled off streetcars and beaten. "The mob was in no hurry; they had no need to be; there was no one to molest them or make them afraid," recorded Strong. "The beastly ruffians were masters of the situation and of the city." Tracks were destroyed, telegraph wires cut. The mob proceeded to the armory, burst it open with sledges and seized a cache of weapons.

Mayor George Opdyke, a wealthy importer, pleaded with loyal citizens to report to police headquarters. His home was attacked. Late in what the *Times* called the "day of infamy and disgrace," the mob set fire to the Colored Orphan Asylum on Fifth Avenue. Then, it went after Greeley and the *Tribune*. Rioters threw rocks and attempted to storm the premises. Greeley was warned to leave for his own safety. He calmly worked to get out the next day's edition.

By the second day of rioting—Tuesday, July 14—the work of loading and unloading ships had ceased and Blacks had disappeared from the docks. Those who ventured too close were beaten or murdered. Black waiters at hotels and downtown restaurants were attacked and forced to flee. One establishment attempted to protect itself by posting a sign with the blunt message NO NIGGERS IN THE REAR.

Rioters seized control of downtown neighborhoods; some erected barricades, imitating the Parisian rabble of Victor Hugo. Many were mere boys, giving the riots the aspect of spontaneity. But in fact, the attacks were orchestrated by dockworkers, with assistance from other trades and southern sympathizers. One ringleader was John Urkhardt Andrews, who, according to the *Times,* was a man "of fine personal appearance," a Virginian who had been residing in New York since before the war. He was a gifted orator who specialized in inciting crowds.

As the rioting raged into a third day, railroads and carriages were made to halt and shops in lower Manhattan and along its perimeter were shuttered. The owner of a printing shop demanded by what authority he was being ordered to close; came the reply: "By the authority of the mob." Officials now realized they were dealing with an organized resistance for which the draft was little more than a pretext. The discerning Hamilton Fish, who had served as governor in the late 1840s, grasped that the rioters' underlying motivation was economic. "The idea has been industriously impressed upon them," he wrote to Treasury Secretary Chase, "that it is a part of the Emancipation policy of the Administration to bring the emancipated negroes from the south into the Northern States. . . . 'Employment & profits of labor,' say they, will thus be interfered with & the dignity of labor be degraded."

Resentment against wealthy Republicans—today, they would be called elites—was manifest in incidents of plunder and in deliberate attacks on finer retail establishments, such as Brooks Brothers. The best evidence for the mob's state of mind comes from a rioter, who exclaimed in a mood of aggrieved self-righteousness:

> We are the poor rabble and the rich rabble is our enemy by this law [conscription]. Although we got hard fists, and are dirty without, we have soft hearts, and have clean consciences within, and that's the reason we love our wives and children more than the rich, because we got not much besides them; and we will not go and leave them, at home for to starve.

Never before had America seen such an extreme of civil unrest. And never, in the North, had the Black man received such violent and prolonged notice of his unwelcomeness. On Wednesday night—the third evening of rioting—an African American laborer dressed in a tarpaulin work suit made the mistake of walking past a "groggery" and was pursued by a group of longshoremen. They caught him, beat him, pulled him down, and slit his throat. Miraculously, he survived. The same day, a waiter at a downtown restaurant was beaten and killed. Also that day, a mob of drunken men attacked a Black man and threw him into the river, where he drowned. The same day, a Black man named Peter Hubsted, sixty-three, suffered a beating that left his head and face "horribly mangled"; he was transported to Bellevue Hospital, and was reported to be dying. Thomas Lewis, thirty-three, was treated at the same hospital after his skull had been fatally fractured. The mob not only beat, it beat with savagery. A reporter noted: "One could not help wondering at the unparalleled depravity and barbarity" of the mob. Blacks were lynched and hung from lampposts. Rioters attacked the tenements and rooming houses where African Americans lived. The mob swelled into the hundreds and at times to several thousand. William Henry Yates, a forty-one-year-old Black man, frantically tried to defend his wife and children from this terrifying spectacle and offered such stout resistance, according to the *Times*, that the mob vowed to burn him alive. In desperation, Yates hanged himself.

An elderly African American whitewasher, a native New Yorker who was accosted by a crowd and beaten, voiced the harrowing question that hung over the city: "I entertain no malice and have no desire for revenge against these people," the man said. "Why should they hurt me or my colored brethren? We are poor men like them; we work hard and get but little for it."

Democratic politicians in New York did little to discourage the rioters. Governor Seymour denounced the violence but also told a crowd (while the rioting raged) that he had sent his adjutant general to Washington to ask for a suspension of the draft, thus offering the rioters a carrot. Terence Farley, a city alderman, blamed the ongoing disturbance on supposed invaders from New Jersey. His own constituents, he averred, "are as orderly and law abiding as any community in the whole country."

Local police and citizen militia were unable to quell the mob. They were supplemented by thousands of troops, some fresh from Gettysburg. Authorities fired small howitzers and field pieces on the crowd. Despite heavy casualties, the mob repeatedly regrouped. The disturbances lasted four days and left more than a hundred rioters dead. Approximately a dozen Blacks were murdered, and many more injured. "The Left Wing of Lee's Army," as the rioters were called, inspired copycat disturbances in other cities but failed to slow the Union military effort. And Lincoln refused to suspend the draft. In September, partly to thwart Democratic judges who were dismissing draftees from service, the President suspended the writ of habeas corpus.

For Lincoln, the riots brought back the memory of lynchings and vigilante justice common to the frontier. He had always reviled the "mobocratic spirit," which he had renounced in an address at the Springfield Lyceum at the tender age of twenty-eight, after a horrific burning of a Negro man in St. Louis. The mob was a threat to democracy itself, for "whenever the vicious portion of population shall be allowed to gather in hundreds and thousands" and wreak mayhem and murder, "at pleasure, and with impunity; depend on it, this Government cannot last . . . the feelings of the best citizens will become more or less alienated from it." Ultimately, Lincoln's aversion to mob rule was the reason for his attachment to the law. The President did not, then, comment on the New York riots, but Frederick Douglass visited the White House soon after. He and Lincoln spoke, it seems, mostly about another urgent concern of northern Blacks—the treatment of Negro troops. Douglass, who was critical of many of the President's policies, later remarked that Lincoln was the first "great man" in the United States "who in no single instance reminded me . . . of the difference of color." Douglass chalked it up to the fact that he and Lincoln were both self-made men. The riots were painful to the President because they upended his Whiggish notion of a harmoniously rising lower class. They implied that one group's progress might stand in the way of another's. The following year, Lincoln broke his silence, addressing a delegation of workers from New York City. Echoing the elderly whitewasher, Lincoln said, "The most notable feature of the disturbance in your City last Summer was the hanging of some working people by other working people. It should never be so."

When labor actions occurred, Lincoln generally sided with the workers—even though strikes disrupted the war effort. He told one group of strikers, "I know that in almost every case of strikes, the men have just cause for complaint." Nonetheless, as a social prescription, he rejected attacks on property and class conflict. "That some should be rich shows that others may become rich," the President somewhat patronizingly advised the workers' delegation. Lincoln was reared in a less contentious era, in which laborers in small shops worked alongside their bosses and might one day hope to replace them. That era was already fading, but the giant factories in which thousands of workers toiled anonymously were a page from a future he never saw. The riots themselves seem like a harbinger of a later time, when Blacks were excluded from labor unions and rival ethnic gangs jousted for control in urban slums.

The President did jot down thoughts on the draft, shortly after the riots, in a memorandum he never published. He was pained by the charge of unfairness, and his lawyerly disquisition set out to establish that the draft law, like much legislation, was good even if imperfect. "Much complaint is made of that provision of the conscription law which allows a drafted man to substitute three hundred dollars for himself," he noted, "while, as I believe, none is made of that provision which allows him to substitute another man for himself." Yet given that substitution was permitted, Lincoln argued correctly if somewhat tendentiously that permitting men to opt out for a fee "modifies the inequality which the other introduces." It put a ceiling on the price of substitutes. Therefore, Lincoln argued, "It allows men to escape the service, who are too poor to escape but for it."

New York City promptly defused the issue by appropriating funds to exempt draftees. A year later, when the outcry still had not quieted, Congress revoked the three-hundred-dollar escape hatch. In any event, workers suffered far more egregious examples of inequity—lagging wages, for instance—than conscription. It is hard to escape the conclusion that the so-called draft riots resulted from economic hardship stoked by racial prejudice. After the riots, many Blacks who had lost their jobs were not rehired. A committee of merchants, recognizing the unfairness, pledged to use its influence to protect the rights of Blacks "to pursue unmolested their lawful occupations." But job discrimination persisted.

The riots highlighted the smoldering issue of how to integrate unprecedented numbers of freedmen after the war. When Lincoln proclaimed that slaves were free, there was no federal bureau to oversee the transition, no government social services of any kind—and no funding to provide them. Salmon Chase did what he could in a small way. He fired a clerk who, in refusing to subscribe to a fund to help raise a Black regiment, had defended his refusal with crude, racist remarks. The Treasury secretary also agitated for equal treatment—and equal pay—for Black servicemen.[*] In September, shortly after the riots, Chase unleashed his righteous anger on his friends the Cookes. Chase and the Cookes were investors in the capital's new street railroad, which used horses to pull carriages along a side-rail. When Chase learned that Blacks were barred, he fumed at Jay Cooke, "Why cannot colored people

---

[*] Early in 1863, Chase vented to George Opdyke, "American blacks must be called into this conflict, not as cattle, not even as contrabands, but as men." Not until June 15, 1864—nearly eighteen months after the Emancipation Proclamation—did federal law equalize pay for Black and white soldiers.

ride in the Washington & Georgetown Street Railroad Cars? . . . Their exclusion is a shame & disgrace." The railroad had announced that it was procuring cars for Blacks, but Chase, suspecting that Black-only carriages would be inferior, was not mollified. "What kind of cars?" he persisted. Noting that Generals Ulysses S. Grant and Nathaniel P. Banks had each declared their "colored regiments" to be indispensable— this despite their lower wage—Chase added bitterly, "If the colored people are to be confined to special cars, let them be *better* than the others." Rethinking this, he concluded equitably, "But have no such cars. Let all cars be free to all."* Race prejudice always brought out the best in Chase. As noble as his protest was, the Treasury secretary was seeking a more systematic remedy to ease the transition of freedmen into the market economy. Independently, the idea gained traction among Boston radicals, including John Andrew, governor of Massachusetts, who urged Senator Sumner to establish a commission to study "the main question"— how to establish "just and normal relations between the labor of so many poor men without capital." Sumner conferred with Chase and Edwin Stanton, and in March 1863 the war secretary established the American Freedmen's Inquiry Commission. Though purely investigative, the Inquiry Commission was a significant step toward widening the scope of the federal government. It was the first federal body tasked with promoting economic opportunity, the distant progenitor of so many antipoverty programs in the future.

One purpose of the commission was to help freedmen prosper on the ground and deter migration north. Self-help was to be the goal, not charity. One of its backers, reflecting the era's social Darwinism, boasted that he would "treat poor blacks as we would poor whites"— that is, let them starve if they were not self-sufficient. Stanton's commission was not quite so harsh. Its preliminary report emphasized land policy and encouraged the idea that freedmen be assisted, with funds

---

* Thanks largely to Senator Sumner, Washington streetcars—unlike those in Virginia and throughout the South—were fully desegregated in 1865. Unlike those throughout the South, they remained integrated all through the Jim Crow era.

derived from the sale of confiscated cotton, to acquire pieces of former plantations. Practically, it advocated creation of a federal bureau. For the moment, this was too radical a step for Congress. However, Chase had persuaded Lincoln to restore control to the Treasury of a wide swath of abandoned property, including in South Carolina. This returned Chase to a supervisory role at Port Royal, where freedmen, supported by northern friends, had come to the same conclusion: to succeed as free citizens, they needed to acquire land. Chase sent his friend Edward Pierce, the crusading Boston lawyer, back to Port Royal with a special charge to supervise the freedmen's economic progress.

The idea of providing cheap land to freedmen faced a serious challenge. Congress had authorized federal commissioners to sell confiscated land at auction for back taxes, and investors, including some of the same liberal Bostonians, were converging on Port Royal to buy plantations. This greatly worried the teachers, clerics, and nurses, commonly referred to by the biblical appellation Gideonites, who were working with the freed people. The minister Mansfield French protested that "sharp sighted speculators are on hand & with larger purses than those of the friends of humanity. If the plantations fall into their hands—most of the colored people will suffer greatly." No doubt, he was thinking of Edward Philbrick, a savvy businessman who had organized an investment syndicate. Philbrick was a fervent abolitionist who, all the same, believed that newly freed slaves had to prove their worth in the market, as distinct from being favored with government assistance. He took a dim view of Black people's ability to stand on their own. Soon after arriving on the island, he reported to Pierce, "We find the blacks as dependent as children." Fearing that the freedmen would be shut out, Governor Andrew urged Chase to delay the auction. But in March 1863, the government went ahead and sold the first sixteen thousand acres of its vast holdings—half of it to Philbrick, who scooped up eleven plantations for $7000, a ludicrously cheap price of less than one dollar per acre. As Andrew feared, only two thousand acres went to freedmen. Philbrick maintained that his venture was committed to hu-

manitarian goals—indeed, he insisted that his purchase had been necessary to keep the land from "speculators." In practice, it was hard to tell
the difference.

The social mandate wasn't entirely forgotten. Amos Lawrence, another abolitionist textile magnate, donated much of his early profits to
freedmen's education. Philbrick opened stores for the freedmen, who
demonstrated the capitalist spirit by purchasing trunks and padlocks to
protect their new possessions. Pierce, who daily observed Blacks on
his rides through the fields, reported to Chase that he was "entirely
satisfied" with the freedmen's progress. "The negroes will work for a
living . . . with no one to force them," he said, as if resolving a great
anthropological mystery. Pierce was understandably pleased that Black
children were enrolled in schools. But his optimism was premature.
The investors were concerned with profit, and the workers he espied
were employed as subsistence labor. Chase was reminded by William
Curtis Noyes, a New York trial lawyer, "The way to secure the colored
people & give them a real interest in our institutions is to confer upon
them titles to small parcels of land." French, the minister, went further,
warning the Treasury secretary that the freedmen were counting on
acquiring titles. "Many have laid up, little sums, from their hard & scanty
earnings. . . . They have been told that the lands would be in market,
and on such conditions that they could purchase homes." Appealing to
Chase's sense of history, French argued that by helping the freedmen he
could salvage the lives not only of today's newly freed Blacks but of "the
millions yet to be borne."

Securing titles for the freedmen should have been a priority for both
Lincoln and Chase. For the Treasury secretary, it was a simple matter
of racial equity. For the President, land distribution was the surest way
to realize the Whig dream of opportunity for all working people, regardless of race. Taking a small step in the direction of Black home
equity, in September 1863, Lincoln, on advice from Chase, instructed
the tax commissioners on the Sea Islands to sell another batch of sixteen thousand acres, in twenty-acre plots, to the freedmen at the going

rate of $1.25 per acre. He also ordered the commissioners to set aside land for schools and, prior to the auction, to conduct necessary surveying. However, the President (again on Chase's advice) approved one and a half times as much land for sale to investors. The set-aside for freedmen wasn't nearly enough to accommodate the Black population, which had swelled to fifteen thousand.

Lincoln and Chase didn't properly focus on the crucial question of freedmen's land, perhaps because they were subject to a vortex of conflicting demands. They were obliged to treat federal lands as a revenue source, and Port Royal was only one aspect of the vexing puzzle of what to do about the considerable part of the cotton industry now within reach of Union troops. Merchants along the Mississippi were clamoring for a revival of trade, and the British were putting strong pressure on the State Department to let the cotton out.

The President, with his Whiggish faith in commerce as a healing solvent, was perhaps too eager to normalize trade relations. Chase similarly felt that restrictions should be "as moderate as possible." After Vicksburg fell, he telegraphed customs officials at Ohio River cities and at St. Louis: "Clear boats and cargoes except of prohibited articles to New Orleans if desired." But it was not so simple. Grant sent a scorching letter, strenuously protesting. "No matter what the restrictions thrown around trade," the general sniped, "if any whatever is allowed it will be made the means of supplying . . . the enemy." He cynically added that no law-abiding merchant would realize a profit, "hence none but dishonest men go into it." However, pressure from business interests was too strong for even Grant to overcome. Attorney General Edward Bates protested in cabinet that the restrictions were far too onerous. (Not coincidentally, Bates hailed from St. Louis, where the merchant lobby was most insistent.) Over the summer, Chase worked at the thankless task of revising the regulations. His new scheme would divide occupied territory among five districts, known as Agencies, each supervised by a special agent of the Treasury. His aim was to widen the funnel for trade while still preventing supplies from reaching the Rebels, a hopeless assignment. No wonder that when Lincoln signed the new rules, he self-protectively added, "You understand these things; I do not."

The President was well tiring of the cotton question, but he was scarcely done with it. He was besieged by requests from merchants and others seeking special trading permits, including from his friends and his (or Mary's) family. In August, he had to review the record of twenty-seven officers charged with improper cotton dealing, a painful affair. Earlier in the summer, he had been pestered by William Kellogg, a former Illinois congressman, who wrote to Lincoln after Chase had turned down his request for a permit to trade cotton out of Helena, Arkansas. The President's irritation leapt off the page:

> I have received, and read, your pencil note. I think you do not know how embarrassing your request is. Few things are so troublesome to the government as the fierceness with which the profits of trading in cotton are sought. . . . The matter deeply affects the Treasury and War Departments, and has been discussed again and again in the cabinet. . . . I know it is thought that one case is not much, but how can I favor one and deny another.

In fact, Lincoln did grant exceptions. On this matter, Grant had the surer grasp of priorities. Trade with the South (regulated or not) extended Dixie a vital lifeline, especially because fewer supplies were arriving by sea. According to Confederate naval records, from the start of the war through October 1863, only 200,000 bales of cotton had successfully run the blockade. That was roughly the amount shipped during *one month* before the war. And the Union's grip was tightening. While only one vessel in ten was caught in the early months of the fighting, by 1863 the capture rate had climbed to an estimated one in four. Rebel purchasing agents were growing desperate. In one missive, John Tory Bourne, the agent in the Bermudan port of St. George's, darkly warned his English counterparts, "I do not think it prudent to hire ships to bring cargoes . . . and let them lie in the harbor." In the fall his warning was vindicated: "I regret to state that the Yankees have made wholesale captures—5 out of 7 of our blockade runners have fallen into their hands." By December, the Union navy had notched more than a thousand captures.

Union seizures aggravated the Rebels' shortage of machinery and spare parts. This led to serious roadblocks in factories, machine shops, and rail traffic. Union captures also led to highly embarrassing press. Northern newspapers delighted in printing sensitive correspondence seized on shipboard. De Leon, the Confederate diplomat, indiscreetly wrote Davis from his comfortable lodgings in Paris, "It is useless to disguise the fact that the men around you do not inspire confidence." The world soon read of his criticism of the Davis cabinet in *The New York Times*. The unwanted publicity cost De Leon his job.

Successful runners still reaped fabulous profits, however, the heightened risk led them to alter the composition of their cargoes. Captains favored lighter goods that might fetch a windfall but did not take much room. Counterintuitively, as the Confederacy grew poorer, runners stuffed their holds with pricey luxuries such as silk but frowned on bulkier goods such as machinery. (Later scholars termed this the Rhett Butler effect.) Quinine, morphine, expensive fabrics, ribbons, laces, brandy, and playing cards got through, according to Thomas E. Taylor, who threaded the blockade twenty-eight times, the most of any sea captain. But, Taylor said flatly, "it did not pay merchants to ship heavy goods."

Jefferson Davis was furious that scarce cash was being squandered on luxuries and frills. The government engaged a British partner to start its own blockade-running venture, though it envisioned only five ships, not enough to make a difference. But neither private nor government agents prioritized ordinary consumer goods. Shortages for the common man grew steadily more acute. By the fall of 1863, a pair of boots in Richmond fetched $100—a 300 percent increase in only a year. Jones, who had complained of famine the previous spring, now reported that his rations had been reduced. He recorded with his usual meticulous precision, "I have lost 20 pounds, and my wife and children are emaciated to some extent." He added woefully, "We are a shabby-looking people now."

Eleven

Chase for President

Under the sharp discipline of civil war the
nation is beginning a new life.

— ABRAHAM LINCOLN

B Y THE FALL OF 1863, two-term presidencies seemed a relic of
the past. No president had won reelection in over thirty years;
remarkably, none of the previous seven had even been *renominated*.* Many thought Lincoln would follow in this pattern. The war's
unexpected duration had led to a great despondency among the people.
The President's trademark patience, given the terrible hardships of the
war, had also led to criticism in Congress and to a common misunderstanding of his character. People thought him waffling or weak. Despite the Union's many advantages, he did not seem able to finish the
job. None of his commanders had been able to corral Lee, whose army
remained formidable. The frustration extended to the western theater,
where William Rosecrans—one of a string of generals Lincoln had
anointed—lost a major battle at Chickamauga, Tennessee. Such defeats
inspired criticism of the President as inept and slow-footed, an opinion

---

* The seven were William Henry Harrison, who was elected in 1840 and died in office, John Tyler,
James Polk, Zachary Taylor (also died in office), Millard Fillmore, Franklin Pierce, and James Buchanan.

pervasive among the party Radicals. And the sole terrain where the Union was proving its advantage, the public finances, was precisely the domain of Salmon Chase, Lincoln's putative rival.

Chase had been dropping hints of his availability in 1864 almost since losing to Lincoln in 1860. Outwardly, he deflected any admission of interest, sometimes with a pious assertion that the choice would be up to the people. But Chase was too vain to conceal his ambition. In October 1863, he traveled home to Ohio, and to Indiana, where he delivered a series of speeches—widely seen as campaign stops. In Columbus, he arrived at the rail depot at two a.m. and was greeted by hundreds of supporters and a brass band. Some in the crowd affectionately shouted hurrahs to "old Greenbacks!" In Cincinnati, Chase applauded the Emancipation Proclamation as "the right thing at the right time," but could not resist swiping at Lincoln—"It would have been even more right, had it been earlier." In Indianapolis, Chase narcissistically recounted that he had put his own portrait on the one-dollar greenback because "the engravers thought me rather good looking." He returned to Washington in a fog of self-delusion, convinced that the masses would swarm to his campaign.

Radicals such as Horace Greeley, Thaddeus Stevens, Henry Ward Beecher (brother of Harriet Beecher Stowe, author of *Uncle Tom's Cabin*), and the Boston abolitionist Wendell Phillips encouraged Chase to run. They approvingly cited his outspokenness on slavery and the effectiveness of his policies, in seeming contrast to Lincoln's halting progress in the war. With such sentiments in mind, a Pennsylvania politico dropped by the Treasury secretary's and all but promised Chase the state's delegation. Jay Cooke & Co. contributed money—hardly a disinterested favor, since Cooke knew that when the five-twenties sold out, Chase would need to peddle a new loan, for which Cooke was eager to be the agent. (This blatant conflict of interest was further aggravated by the fact that Chase and Cooke were still squabbling over Cooke's fee on the five-twenty.) For now, the bonds continued to sell briskly—on average, nearly $2 million a day. Chase's reputation had never been higher. Cooke added gloss to the Treasury secretary's image by planting newspaper stories that depicted Chase as a financial wizard who had mastered the complexities of a billion-dollar budget. Even the Democratic *New York Herald* overpraised Chase as "a sort of genius." Moreover, the new national banking system was getting going, albeit slowly. Chase could be fairly depicted as the architect of revolutionary change. None less than the *Richmond Examiner* favorably contrasted Chase with the stewards of the Rebel fisc, acknowledging that he "has conducted the finances of his Government with consummate ability."

Publicly, Chase said nothing afoul of the administration, but his correspondence was lined with veiled criticisms. On September 21, he wrote to Murat Halstead, an Ohio editor and war reporter, that the administration suffered from great differences as to the temperament, goals, and intellectual traits of its members—a "condition" that could "only be remedied by the President &c, as yet, he fears the remedy most." Feigning disinterest in being Lincoln's usurper, he often protested that the only job he coveted was chief justice of the Supreme Court but, as he confided that October, "I really feel as if, with God's blessing, I *could* administer the Government of this country."

Yet Chase was also generous to Lincoln. He reminded Greeley that no matter how impatient progressives were to move forward on Black rights, the President "advances slowly but yet advances." Chase added, in a truly magnanimous statement, "On the whole, when we think of the short time, and immense distance in the matter of Personal Freedom . . . the progressives cannot be dissatisfied with results." Lincoln presumably had not been thinking of his cabinet when he coined the phrase "better angels of our nature," but his Treasury secretary was clearly wrestling with his. To William Sprague, a powerful Rhode Island politician and textile manufacturer who was to marry Kate, Chase's elder daughter, in November, Chase frankly acknowledged the President's kindness. "I can never permit myself to be driven into any hostile or unfriendly position as to Mr. Lincoln," Chase wrote. "His course toward me has always been so fair & kind." Yet in the same letter, Chase vented, in the passive voice he typically employed to disguise the provenance of uncharitable views, the wishful opinion that Lincoln's reelection was neither feasible nor desirable. Thus, "I doubt the expediency of reelecting anybody, and I think that a man of different qualities from those the President has will be needed for the next four years." It was almost laughable that Chase added, "I am not anxious to be regarded as that man."

Perhaps had he been more willing to acknowledge his ambition, Chase might have realized that his bid faced difficult challenges. He counted on the Radicals, his natural base, but some of them, including Ohio's Benjamin Wade, personally detested him. Other seeming supporters, including Greeley, had been careful not to commit. In Union-occupied Louisiana, where Lincoln and Chase partisans were waging a proxy war to control the prospective new state government, the president's forces were gaining the upper hand. Chase gave his detractors fresh ammunition by indulging in a needless political struggle at the Custom House in New York. Moderate Republicans were eager for the Treasury secretary to dispose of the Collector of the Port, Hiram Barney, who was entrenched with the Radicals and, what was worse, tarnished by reports of corruption. Chase, who could never recognize malfeasance on the part of political allies (he was similarly overlooking reports that the internal revenue collector in Columbus was involved in a cotton ring), dug in his heels, at the risk of alienating influential New York Republicans, including Greeley and Secretary of State William Seward.

Lincoln let Chase keep his man, but the President's inner circle was becoming alarmed. Chase plainly intended to use his army of Treasury clerks as foot soldiers in the campaign. Mary Todd Lincoln warned her husband to be wary, but Lincoln is said to have laughingly replied, "Mother, you are too suspicious!" He was also warned by John Hay, his secretary, that Chase would try to make political capital out of "this Rosecrans business."* The President grinned and said, "I suppose he will, like the bluebottle fly, lay his eggs in every rotten spot he can find." Another time, so the story goes, Lincoln likened Chase's presidential bug to a "chin-fly" that irritated a horse but also stirred it to plow harder. Beneath his humor, the President was truly annoyed. Rumors were swirling that General Grant, the shining star in the Union constellation, would also challenge Lincoln and run for the White House. When Grant disdained any interest, via letter, Lincoln was greatly relieved and, choosing yet another insect metaphor, heartily exclaimed, "You don't know how deep the Presidential *maggot* can gnaw into a man's brain." He was surely thinking of Chase. Lincoln was secure enough not to let his irritation lead him to question Chase's fitness for the Treasury, but the relationship between the two was becoming strained.

Chase gave away the beautiful Kate on the second Thursday in November. He had raised her single-handedly and lately been blessed by a reversal of roles, as Kate adroitly assumed the management of the household, a great comfort during his crowded years at Treasury. Their affections ran deep, and as Chase confessed to his future son-in-law, a fortnight before the betrothal, his pleasure "mingled not a little sadness." His daughters—Kate and the younger Nettie—provided him the uncomplicated joy that was absent in his other relations. Perhaps overcome with emotion, he lost sight of the fact that extravagance was unseemly during wartime. Kate was married in a white velvet dress and a tiara of matched pearls and diamonds that William Sprague, the groom, was said to have purchased for the fabulous sum of $50,000. Jay Cooke sent ten boxes of Lake Erie grapes. The wedding, at the Chase residence on Sixth Street, was the social event of the season, attended by a flood of dignitaries.

---

* Rosecrans was relieved of his command in October, a month after his defeat at Chickamauga.

Sprague's rise in politics had been swift—governor of Rhode Island at age twenty-nine and now, at thirty-three, a senator. He was a useful ally for Chase. Sprague was a large campaign donor and politically connected. But he was trailed by whispers that illicit payments had greased his rise. More grievously, he may have been involved with a former Texan, Harris Hoyt, in a blockade-running scheme to trade guns for cotton, which Sprague needed for the family textile business.* There is no reason to think that Chase had any knowledge of this treasonous business, but his naïveté underscored that Chase was unprepared for the seedy underside of a campaign.

Mary urged Lincoln not to attend the wedding, probably because she resented the idea of Washington's leading men fawning over Kate. The President knew he could not afford to offend his sensitive cabinet member and put in a brief appearance. Several days later, he thoughtfully dispatched a personal note inviting Chase to join the presidential railcar to Gettysburg, where, on November 19, he was to give a commemorative address. Chase inopportunely declined. "I should like to go," he explained to Kate, "but cannot leave my work."

At least thirty thousand people—spectators, government notables, and a military procession—assembled at the battle site, according to the *Chicago Daily Tribune*, "and the spot on which they stood is one of the most beautiful on earth." The day being clear, South Mountain was visible at a distance and so, closer in, was Little Round Top, scene of the Union infantry's gallantry. Lincoln spoke briefly, reading from a sheet he held in his hand, deliberately, and with emphasis. Newspaper coverage focused on the solemnity of the occasion rather than the President's brief remarks. Lincoln reverently remembered the dead but addressed himself to the living. He spoke patriotically about the country

---

* In 1864, cotton seized by the navy was traced to Hoyt, who fingered Sprague as a partner. The charge against Sprague, a political hot potato, was referred to Secretary of War Edwin Stanton but dropped after Lincoln's assassination. The Senate later investigated, and William Belknap, secretary of war under Grant, reported "additional information in relation to the traffic with rebels" by Sprague, Hoyt, and others. However, Belknap himself was forced to resign over corruption charges. The charge against Sprague was never proved.

that was to emerge when the fighting ceased—"*a new birth of freedom.*" He harked back to his Whiggish conception of the United States as a singular thing, a "nation"—a word that among his two hundred and seventy-two he uttered five times, while mentioning "union" not at all. It is interesting to note that Jefferson Davis, who had been laboring to foster greater unity among the Confederacy, nonetheless observed, in his annual message, that its constitution required him "to protect each *State* from invasion." Davis's government was a compact of states; Lincoln's one of individuals—"government of the people, by the people, for the people." His audience applauded heartily at these words. There was nothing remarkable about the first part—"of the people, by the people." It was the bit that followed, the "*for* the people," concisely adapted from Daniel Webster, that distinguished his conception of the American experiment.* The United States would govern "for" its people; it would enact laws, create departments, make available homesteads, build roads, establish a currency, endow universities, raise armies, and impose taxes, *for* them.

The day before traveling to Gettysburg, Lincoln had attended to one of his fondest projects, the transcontinental railroad, issuing an order fixing the western boundary of Iowa as the eastern terminus of the Union Pacific. Ground was broken (amid an orgy of land speculation) two weeks later.† The President gave two other addresses, one before and the other just after Gettysburg, reaffirming that he had begun to think about the shape of the country after the war, and the potential for economic growth to speed the recovery. In October, responding to a plea from the author Sarah Josepha Hale, Lincoln proclaimed a day of Thanksgiving on the last Thursday of November (the

---

* In his famous Second Reply to Hayne, in 1830, Webster rejected the claim of South Carolina that the Constitution permitted it to nullify a federal law with the ringing words: "It is, Sir, the people's Constitution, the people's government, made for the people, made by the people, and answerable to the people."

† Lincoln was apparently distracted when he fixed the terminus; his order also alluded to Omaha, just across the state line in Nebraska. The following March he more clearly situated the terminus on the Iowa boundary.

holiday was already observed; Lincoln made it official). He acknowledged the horrendous civil war in progress—an odd time, one might
think, for expressing thanks. But he found cause in the remarkable
bounty of American workers, their progress seemingly unchecked by
the war or, as Lincoln put it:

> Needful diversions of wealth and of strength from the fields
> of peaceful industry to the national defence, have not arrested
> the plough, the shuttle or the ship; the axe has enlarged the
> borders of our settlements, and the mines, as well of iron and
> coal as of the precious metals, have yielded even more abun-
> dantly than heretofore. Population has steadily increased, not-
> withstanding the waste that has been made in the camp, the
> siege and the battle-field; and the country, rejoicing in the con-
> sciousness of augmented strength and vigor, is permitted to ex-
> pect continuance of years with large increase of freedom.

Thanksgiving as Lincoln perceived it (and as we perceive it today)
had a material aspect. The fruits of "the plough" and "the axe" were
"great things"—material things. Lincoln thought it "fit and proper that
they should be solemnly, reverently and gratefully acknowledged." He
returned to this theme on December 8, 1863, in his Annual Message to
Congress. The Republicans had registered victories in the fall elections,
and Lincoln could now anticipate a second term. He envisioned the nation "beginning a new life," girded by its farms and factories. The President expounded on his belief that government should help to foster
opportunity. He trumpeted the new federal banking system, the homestead law, the projected Pacific railroad, and the telegraph. He asked
Congress to approve a new project to enlarge the waterways from the
Mississippi to the Eastern Seaboard, which, he noted, it had considered
and failed to do in the previous session. Lincoln had added to the spectrum of government functions, recently, by signing a bill to create the
National Academy of Sciences, establishing a federal role in research.

Weeks after his election, the newly bearded Lincoln posed for the Bavarian-born photographer Samuel G. Alschuler, who operated a studio in Urbana, Illinois. Lincoln soon fretted that he faced "an empty Treasury and a great rebellion."

Salmon P. Chase worked tirelessly to fund the Civil War—a challenge in a country that loathed taxation. As Secretary of the Treasury under Lincoln and a would-be president himself, he schemed against his chief.

Justin Smith Morrill had been pained by his inability to pay for college; during the war, he spearheaded legislation to endow universities for the middle class.

The financier Jay Cooke had the unblushing temerity to compare himself to Moses. He realized sooner than anyone else the latent power of selling bonds to the public.

Thaddeus Stevens crusaded for economic, as well as political, justice for the slaves. He warned his fellow legislators that if they failed to provide the freedmen with plots of land, they would meet "the execration of history."

In 1860, Horace Greeley warned his fellow Republicans that voters would "only swallow a little Anti-slavery." He urged them to focus on economic development.

The greenback was a new kind of money—"legal tender" created by government fiat. Chase had philosophical reservations but nonetheless put his picture on the one-dollar note.

William Pitt Fessenden was tapped to run the Treasury as the greenback plummeted to its low. Fessenden refused. Lincoln insisted.

The Capitol's graceful new dome, depicted in a drawing by its architect, Thomas U. Walter, symbolized the revolutionary agenda of the 37th Congress.

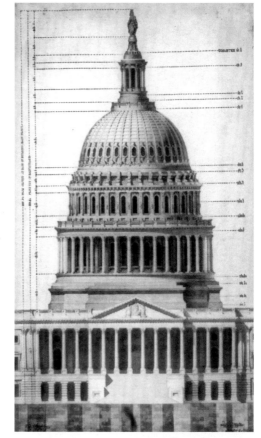

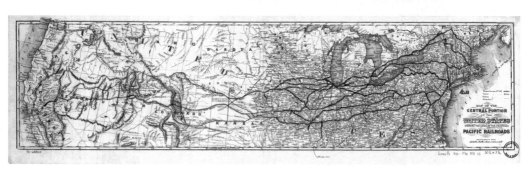

The public wanted the transcontinental railroad, but Congress could not agree on a route. This map, drawn in 1857, located the start at Council Bluffs, Iowa—where the railroad lawyer Lincoln was to visit two years later.

George Templeton Strong's copious diary testified to the New Yorker's seesawing faith in the Union's prospects and to his growing reverence for Lincoln. He is shown early in the war at Fortress Monroe, seated second from left.

Contrasting economies North and South: A New York shipyard (below) evokes the vitality of Northern industry; a slave market (left) on a desolate street in Atlanta is guarded by a lone man with a rifle. Note the lettering on the facade: "Auction & Negro Sales."

Jefferson Davis, President of the Confederacy, improbably struggled to create a robust central government in a nation pledged to slavery and states' rights.

Within the Confederate cabinet, Judah Benjamin was a lone voice urging Richmond to export cotton early in the war.

When cotton revenue flagged, the Confederate treasury had no choice but to issue paper, like the two-dollar note shown. Note the explicit promise of redemption "six months after the ratification of a treaty of peace" with the United States.

Mary Boykin Chesnut, who chronicled the disintegration of southern planter society, dolefully predicted that slavery would become a casualty of the war.

Edmund Ruffin, a Virginia agronomist, combined modern farming techniques with bitter hatred of the Yankees. When war beckoned, he hastened to Charleston.

The slaves at Port Royal, South Carolina, chose to live under Union troops rather than flee with their former masters. Ruffin was astonished by their "mutinous disposition." Shown are the slave quarters.

African American workers at a cotton warehouse in Charleston. This 1879 photograph suggests that for the freed people, improvements in living conditions were slow in coming.

The President also called for immigration legislation, asking Congress to help the "destitute" who, by the tens of thousands, were "thronging our foreign consulates, and offering to emigrate to the United States if essential, but very cheap, assistance can be afforded them." This idea seems to have been Lincoln's own. The Grand Old Party's not-distant roots had been watered in the Know-Nothing Party (a nativist movement in the mid-1850s), snobbishly Protestant and pro-temperance. Lincoln, unlike many of his Whig and later Republican partisans, felt no disdain for the waves of poor Irish coming to America. Part of his greatness was to see the humanity in people, and he recognized that in a vast continent whose interior was not, remotely, settled, the scarce and therefore essential economic ingredient was *people.** He rebranded immigration as an asset, rather than a threat: a "source of national wealth and strength." At Lincoln's urging, Congress promptly drafted a bill, the first of its kind, to encourage alien settlement.

More controversial was Lincoln's Proclamation of Amnesty and Reconstruction. Trying to seize the initiative before Congress did, the President offered a full pardon to any participant in the rebellion (Confederate officers excluded) who pledged allegiance to the United States and to its laws, including to the Emancipation Proclamation. Once a tenth of the voters in a state took the oath, they could reestablish a state government and reenter the Union. As the historian Marc Egnal points out, the proclamation said nothing about the right of Blacks to vote or even their equality under the law. The abolitionist Wendell Phillips groused of Lincoln's decree, "It frees the slaves and ignores the negro." The President also promised, in most cases, "restoration of all rights of property, except as to slaves." The prospect of permitting southern gentry to keep or reclaim their plantations was deeply troubling to the

---

* When a delegation of anti-immigrant Know-Nothings visited Lincoln, during the party's heyday in the mid-1850s, he bluntly told them, "Your party is wrong in principle." He emphasized his objection with a rhetorical barb: Did not the true native Americans "wear the breech-cloth and carry the tomahawk"?

Radicals, including Thaddeus Stevens, who favored an overhaul of southern society. It failed to address the bedrock economic demand that land be made available to the freedmen. For this to occur, in Stevens's view, "the foundation of their institutions, both political, municipal, social, must be broken up and relaid. . . . This can only be done by holding them as a conquered people."

Chase and Lincoln contested these competing visions in Louisiana, where Reconstruction was already in process. The Radical wing, with the Treasury secretary's quiet encouragement, was pushing to guarantee the franchise for freed slaves. This was indeed regarded as radical (Blacks could not vote in most northern states) and the President did not endorse it. Chase's more progressive view of race relations constituted the essence of his appeal—his reason for running. However, the gap between the two was less than was often supposed. Lincoln moved cautiously but (as Chase had acknowledged) always in the direction of greater liberality. And his sympathies were clear. As early as October 1863, the President confidentially told Hay that despite the trouble they caused him, the Radicals were closer to his heart. When Louisianans elected a new governor, Lincoln offered a private and, for the time, progressive suggestion: since the state was about to draft a constitution that would determine voting eligibility, the governor ought to consider "whether some of the colored people may not be let in—as, for instance, the very intelligent, and especially those who have fought gallantly in our ranks."

Both Lincoln and Chase were avatars of Republican progress. Chase expressed a more modern notion of equal rights, but their significant difference lay less with policy than with temperament. The President was a pragmatist, with a deep appreciation for the limits to which other people might be pushed. He achieved his ends by working within, and slowly advancing, the guide rails of political potential. His Treasury secretary was far more the ideologue, possessed with genuine passion for antislavery yet freighted by his not always considered prejudices (for instance, his antique reverence for gold). Neither his ambition nor his political opinions were bounded by any humility.

By the fall of 1863, Chase had his eye firmly on Baltimore, site of the next year's Republican Party convention. Hay was warned that Chase was busily "at work night and day, laying pipe." That was true almost in a literal sense. The ringleaders of Chase's campaign were intimately involved in the railroads spawned by the Pacific Railway Act. No matter how visionary was the act's purpose, the prospect of government grants was a tempting vehicle for corruption. Since the act's passage, there had been much jockeying by promoters but little actual development. The law required that two thousand shares be subscribed for the Union Pacific to elect a board and begin operations, a high hurdle. For fourteen months, nothing happened. Finally, in September 1863, Thomas C. Durant, a professor of surgery who had abandoned medicine to become a railroad promoter, offered illicit cash and guarantees (under the table) to stock subscribers. The Union Pacific was promptly organized, with Durant as its vice president and controlling party. Durant telegraphed Lincoln, seeking a military escort for his engineers over the Rocky Mountains. Lincoln, impatient for the work to start, agreed to see Durant when he came to town.

Interest now perked up in the Kansas spur of the system, the Leavenworth, Pawnee and Western Railroad (LP&W). Senator Samuel Pomeroy of Kansas had taken, as we have seen, a powerful interest in the road, coincident to which shares were liberally distributed to a friend and also a relative of Pomeroy. The controlling investor was the Wall Street speculator Samuel Hallett. Hallett had a shady past; previously, he had been charged in a bond forgery. Once he gained control of the LP&W, he renamed it Union Pacific, Eastern Division—a ploy to make it appear that it was the principal route—and reneged on the company's obligations to its principal contractor. Construction continued—now supervised in-house and without the services of a competent engineer. Not surprisingly, the work was shoddily done.

Hallett's only concern was grading forty miles of track (in whatever condition), this being the legal requirement for receiving federal bonds.

It was up to the Treasury secretary to authorize the bonds, and luckily for Hallett, his investing partner, the poet Clarence Stedman, was a friend of Chase's personal secretary. In November 1863, Hallett tasked Stedman to "proceed immediately to Washington" and persuade Chase to release the bonds. As the Pacific Railway Act provided for $16,000 for each of the forty miles of track, Stedman recorded in his diary, with arithmetic precision: "Received my commission from Hallett to go to Washington and procure $640,000." Chase was surely impressed by the dashing Stedman, a thirty-year-old, Yale-educated poet who had written dispatches from Bull Run and was already highly regarded in literary circles. (William Dean Howells, a dean of American letters, was to say, "I stood very much in awe of him, as I should of Lowell or of Longfellow.")

What thickened this stew considerably was that Senator Pomeroy, even as he plugged ahead with the railroad, was chairing a committee to raise funds for Chase's campaign. Included on the committee were Chase cronies Senator John Sherman and James Garfield, as well as various politicos with grievances against Lincoln. Pomeroy seems to have been motivated by his desire for more patronage than he could wrest from the President, including favored treatment of the railroad. His war chest was stacked with railroad money. There is no evidence (and no reason to suppose) that Chase thought of the committee as trading campaign support for railway loans. The Treasury secretary had a rigorous sense of personal honor that paralleled his astonishing blindness to conflict of interest. He certainly became aware (exactly when is uncertain) of Pomeroy's support of his campaign. And he surely knew that the cheerful, side-whiskered senator, who combined abolitionist politics with unfettered pursuit of self-interest, was the political patron behind the Union Pacific, Eastern Division. Pomeroy had a history of unseemly coziness with Kansas railroad men, who had greased, if not substantially accomplished, his ascension to the Senate. Chase had made a poor choice of a political benefactor.*

In December, Chase released the bonds—worth $13.8 million in today's money—to Hallett's railroad. Stedman was reassigned to New York, where the railroad men instructed him to establish a "Bureau of Action" for the Chase campaign. Now on salary, the poet devoted himself full-time to the campaign; he also sent word of his activities to Jacob Schuckers, Chase's secretary, who surely relayed such information to Chase. The Treasury secretary had not declared his candidacy in public, which would have been awkward, but his annual report to Congress was patently promotional. Boasting of his success in distributing the five-twenty loan, Chase reported, "The history of the world may be searched in vain for a parallel case of popular financial support to a national government."

In truth, the five-twenty loan did catch the public's imagination. Patriotism was a factor, but so was Chase's leadership. Chase had an idea of extending the five-twenty beyond its original $500 million authorization; however, Jay Cooke, in his marketing, had assured investors that no more bonds would be forthcoming. "Our reputation is therefore at stake," Cooke informed the Treasury secretary, by which he meant *his* reputation. Chase relented. The loan closed in January 1864. By the time Cooke's army of approximately twenty-five hundred subagents suspended operations, sales totaled just shy of $515 million. Cooke placed 70 percent of that total, and pocketed a general agent's fee of $435,000, just over a tenth of 1 percent of his sales. To Chase's delight, once bond production ceased, the formidable five-twenty rose to a premium, casting an aura of success over the entire offering.

In a sour aftermath, Congress grew suspicious of Chase's comfy relationship with the Cookes, and their arrangement came under heavy fire. Greeley's *New York Daily Tribune* tartly observed, "The entire ne-

* Pomeroy would be the model for Senator Abner Dilworthy, a comically corrupt politician in Mark Twain's *The Gilded Age*. According to Justin Kaplan, a Twain biographer, the fictional Dilworthy was "Pomeroy undisguised."

gotiation has not been creditable to the Treasury Department." Henry
Cooke had traded on inside information, gleaned from Chase (without
his knowledge). Although this was hushed up, in January, the House
voted to seek a full accounting from Chase of his dealings with Jay
Cooke & Co. Chase was on solid ground in responding that the fee was
reasonable, indeed, the bond sale "could not have been as successfully
performed, nor, indeed, performed at all, by the Treasury Department
[alone]." But the inquiry was troublesome for the Treasury secretary.
Potentially, it precluded his future use of his best salesman. And Chase
was hardly done borrowing. He forecasted that the United States
would run a deficit of close to half a billion dollars, so he would need to
float the equivalent of a new five-twenty loan for every year the war
continued.

These vast financial needs kept the gold market worrisomely frothy
(at year end, the premium to the greenback hovered around 50 percent).
To keep gold at bay, Chase—who had already issued approximately $1.5
billion in Union notes, bonds, and other instruments—was anxious to
keep future borrowings to a minimum. Thus, he asked Congress for a
large tax hike. In unusually direct prose, Chase warned Pitt Fessenden
that the Senate Finance Committee had to move fast.

Chase tried to keep his Treasury work untainted by politics, but his
campaign was beginning to stir up dust, if not exactly dirt. The Cookes
had paid a large advance to a Philadelphia magazine to publish a profile
of the Treasury secretary, accompanied by a handsome portrait. In other
words, having paid a fee to Cooke & Co. of $435,000 to distribute the
government's bonds, Chase then accepted a large campaign contribution from the same family. No doubt, he expected to keep his funding
private, but the magazine, *American Exchange and Review*, used the
Cookes' subscription to solicit others. Inevitably, Lincoln got wind of it,
and let Chase know that he knew. This was highly embarrassing for
Chase. Trying to talk his way out of it, he explained to Lincoln that he
had no involvement in the profile, which had been published by a "respectable periodical." In fact, *American Exchange and Review* was any-

thing but reputable; it was "yellow-covered-literature" whose stock in trade was hawking tawdry patent medicines. Chase should have ended his letter there but, perhaps from some nagging sense of guilt, added that had he been consulted he *would* have stopped the Cookes from subscribing—"Not that any wrong was intended or done; but because the act was subject to misconstruction. . . . Mr. Jay Cooke is a friend, & though he did not subscribe to the sketch, doubtless sanctioned the subscription, of his brother Henry who is also a friend." Chase did not realize how inculpatory this explanation was, or at least he buried whatever were his fleeting doubts. Within a couple of weeks of this exchange, he got himself involved with another hack writer, John T. Trowbridge, a Bostonian who penned inspirational boys' fiction. Once again with backing from the Cookes, Chase began writing laborious letters to Trowbridge, supplying grist for a laudatory campaign biography to be excerpted in *Atlantic Monthly*.

Chase's publicity forays were remarkably amateurish, and it is doubtful that Lincoln was too troubled by them. The President was, however, more than irritated by his Treasury secretary's unwillingness to clean up the port of New York. Early in January, detectives arrested Albert M. Palmer, the personal secretary to Collector of the Port Barney, for helping to smuggle contraband via Nassau to the South. His patience exhausted, Lincoln asked Chase whether he now was ready to fire Barney—who had been, at best, ignorant of shenanigans in his own port. The Treasury secretary refused, replying that his confidence in Barney was "undiminished." This was ill considered of Chase. His stubbornness weakened him within the city's Republican organization, and at a crucial moment. Stedman disgustedly confided in his diary: "Find that Mr. Chase has shockingly mismanaged all his patronage. The Custom House, etc., is in the hands of his enemies, and of many disloyalists."

The President now began to show unsuspected strength in the state legislatures, which controlled the selection of party delegates. Chase admitted to a confidant that reports "*seem* to indicate the re-nomination of

Mr. Lincoln." Chase tried to blunt this opinion with an awkwardly phrased but uncharitable kicker: if the President were reelected, "he will be likely to close his first term with more honor than he will the second." Chase also expressed gratitude that a group of elected officials and others had "organized a Committee here with the purpose of bringing forward my name," demonstrating that he was fully aware of the Pomeroy group.

The trouble was, Lincoln had more support. He had used his patronage adroitly, and he was increasingly popular with the people. Alfred Stone, a Chase protégé in Ohio, dispiritingly reported that a majority of the legislature considered Lincoln's renomination to be inevitable and were inclined "to go with the current." It hardly helped that Stone added, "They nearly all say, 'if we could only elect Chase, he would make the best President . . . but Old Abe is popular with the Masses.'"

The Treasury secretary continued to be vexed by the gold premium, which in mid-February climbed above 60 percent—not a ringing endorsement of his fiscal policies. And he still had to confront the unresolved question of the economic status of the freedmen in Port Royal. As one of the first freed communities, the Sea Islands became a laboratory for testing Chase's, as well as Lincoln's, commitment to providing former slaves with economic opportunity.

Among the whites on the islands, two schools of thought predominated. Adherents of laissez-faire held that the Blacks should be left to compete in the marketplace, while progressives argued that small plots should be set aside, at reasonable prices, to facilitate what was, after all, an unprecedented social transition. General Rufus Saxton, the military governor on the Sea Islands, led the charge for land distribution. Saxton had been raised in a Unitarian and strongly abolitionist family in Greenfield, Massachusetts. While not, like some radicals, demanding free land for the Negro, Saxton argued that decades (and centuries) of hard labor entitled them to a generous settlement. "As a mere question of wages withheld and accumulated for generations," Saxton pointed out to Secretary of War Stanton, "they would seem to have paid for it many times over."

General Saxton had an ally in Mansfield French, the Methodist minister working with the former slaves. Toward the end of 1863, the two had agreed that the government should divide the land seized for nonpayment of taxes and distribute small parcels to freedmen. Saxton lobbied for an official policy of "preemption"—i.e., squatter's rights. Not waiting for an official response, Saxton and French encouraged freedmen to stake claims and build cabins, apparently in the hope that freedmen-farmers holding presumptive claims would deter northern investors. According to a witness who heard Saxton lay out his plan to a gathering of freed people, the latter reacted with eager enthusiasm. Within days, 160 freed people turned up at Saxton's headquarters to register preemptive claims.

At Saxton's request, French, who had known Chase in Ohio before the war, went to Washington and serenaded him on the virtues of preemption. Chase agreed, annulling the previous plan for an auction. On December 31, Lincoln gave official sanction to Chase's volte-face, in a modestly titled memorandum, "Additional Instructions to Direct Tax Commissioners." Lincoln's edict instructed the trio of tax commissioners in Port Royal to "allow any loyal person of twenty one years of age, or upwards, who . . . now resides upon, or is engaged in cultivating any lands in your district owned by the United States to enter the same for preemption." Specifically, up to forty acres previously held for auction would be offered to freedmen at the affordable price of $1.25 per acre. This heralded a small revolution. Prevailing doctrine worshipped the marketplace as the only route to progress. But freed slaves, lacking both capital and experience, were effectively shut out of the market. Lincoln's instructions utilized government to fill in the gap. It was girded in an older, Jeffersonian faith in a small, independent yeomanry as the bedrock of democracy. Willie Lee Rose, a historian of Reconstruction, has suggested that Chase did not fully understand the monumental implications of the order, and it is possible that this was also true of Lincoln. His directive went far beyond the vague assertion of goodwill in his recent amnesty decree. At least on the Sea Islands, it effectively extended the Homestead Act and the Republican promise of opportunity to African Americans. It was the boldest stroke, then or during the subsequent period of Reconstruction, for land reform for freed slaves.

On New Year's Day, 1864, Saxton dared to speak to the freedmen of a not-distant future when "we may see these islands covered with neat cottages, each the centre of a happy home, little farms well tilled." Recognizing that the battle was far from won, he urged the freedmen "to lose no time" in filing claims. Former slaves now believed that the long promised humble plots were finally to be theirs.

The backlash came swiftly. Two of the three tax commissioners delayed and in some cases refused to accept preemption claims. They disputed the legality of preemption and urged investors to bid for the land anyway. Seeking a high road, the antipreemptionists claimed that Lincoln's order would shelter African Americans from the test of the marketplace and impede their social development. Of course, it was ludicrous to contend that, after centuries of slavery, Blacks could compete on a level field. Edward Philbrick, the Boston businessman and abolitionist who had purchased plantations on the islands, argued that, rather than preempt, it was more realistic for freedmen to work for hire while slowly attaining capital and skills (obviously a self-serving view). He pointed to the superior productivity of his employees, compared with their former output as slaves. In a public letter, Philbrick boasted that his four hundred freedmen employees were earning, on average, fifty-five cents per day, and also received free housing and personal plots for growing their food. He bragged about the schools attended by three hundred of their children. In reality, Philbrick was championing not a market economy but a benevolent plantation, a company town that paid its best wages to capital. Even under wartime conditions, he was cultivating choice Sea Islands cotton at a cost of only 37½ cents a pound, compared with a market price of $1.50, yielding a lucrative gross profit margin of 75 percent. Somewhat preposterously, Philbrick objected that preemption would grant "special privileges to negroes, to the exclusion of whites."

Sensing that preemption was still in doubt, French desperately appealed to Chase. "Never have I seen such joy" he wrote to the Treasury secretary, "as when your instructions were declared to the people." But preemption turned out to be difficult to put in practice. The business of staking and filing claims was haphazardly done. Surveying was incomplete. By the end of January, African Americans had managed to claim only six thousand acres, a small portion of the available land, and opposition to preemption was mounting. The *Cleveland Morning Leader* judged that Philbrick took "a correct view of the future civilization of the freedmen. If they are to become industrious, self-reliant and civilized, it must be done under the guidance of the white man." At very least, the proposal to establish a Freedmen's Bureau to assist in the transition from slavery recognized a duty to offer such guidance. But the Freedmen's Bureau was facing stiff opposition in the U.S. Senate. And although Congress had begun to consider a Thirteenth Amendment to abolish the peculiar institution, the fate of slavery after the war remained uncertain.

Port Royal offered a preview of this debate, and its resolution fell squarely on Chase. General Quincy Adams Gillmore, who commanded the Department of the South from nearby Hilton Head, urged the Treasury secretary to flat out rescind preemption. Gilmore warned that if preemption stood and Blacks were thrust into competition with white speculators, "the colored man will be the sufferer." Contrarywise, General Saxton protested to Chase, in anguished tones, that two of the commissioners were refusing to implement his instructions. One of the two, William Henry Brisbane, a former planter, dismissed preemption as a "wild scheme, that out radicals all the radicalism I ever heard of." Brisbane was an abolitionist who, prior to the war, had moved north and freed his inherited slaves. He objected to preemption because he disputed its legal validity and due to paternalistic sentiments similar to Philbrick's. And possibly, because the notion of distributing land to Black men simply "out-radicaled" him.

Described as "beside himself with anger," Brisbane wrote a scorching critique of preemption to his superior, the commissioner of internal revenue, who reported to Chase. Brisbane's missive clouded the Treasury secretary's already overburdened mind with largely trivial objections—for instance, that Lincoln's loosely written order would permit all sorts of undeserving folks, such as white missionaries and teachers, to take title and speculate. He also pointed out that by selling land cheaply to Blacks, the government would forgo revenue (this was also true of the Homestead Act, which had been intended principally for white settlers, and no one had seemed to mind). Brisbane's weightiest assertion was that preemption would not be legal without an act of Congress. This was debatable, but assuming it were true, it would not have been the first time that Lincoln, during the emergency of war, had expanded executive powers. Unfortunately for the freedmen, the one commissioner who supported preemption, Abram D. Smith, a former judge, was a notorious drinker, and his bouts of drunkenness undercut his effectiveness with Chase. The Treasury secretary was caught between his genuine desire to help the former slaves and his uncertainty regarding the law, and perhaps distracted by his campaign. Buckling under the pressure, on February 11, 1864, Chase suspended Lincoln's instructions—that is, he canceled preemption, retaining only a small set-aside for freedmen. French tried to shame the Treasury secretary with a plaintive verse from Psalm 137, "The willows bend again under the weight of broken harps." He urged the freedmen to stay on the land. One week later, before a mixed crowd of investors, freedmen, and missionaries, the auction went ahead. Whites purchased most of the land, at an average price of $11 an acre. Philbrick's assistant concluded, with unflinching candor, "Did you know we had long ceased to be philanthropists or even Gideonites? We are nothing now but speculators." One hundred and ten Black families managed to acquire, in total, a tiny fraction of the land, at the $1.25 price. Some of the others refused to leave and (over Saxton's protests) were bodily evicted by the army. The revolution was over.

The Pomeroy committee for Chase, meanwhile, shifted into full throttle. Just as Chase backtracked at Port Royal, the committee released a slashing document, "The Next Presidential Election," denigrating Lincoln as vacillating and inept. This nasty screed was most likely written either by James Winchell, a Republican politico and war correspondent who had been active in the Kansas branch of the Union Pacific, or by Stedman. Chase's friends, including Sherman, mailed it under official postage—thus linking the Treasury secretary, at least by association, to the attack on the President. Now ready to promote its man, the committee distributed a second document, laying out its brief for Chase for president. This second epistle, signed by Pomeroy, became known as the Pomeroy Circular. It was supposedly confidential, but as it was distributed to more than one hundred political operatives it quickly became public—indeed, it was published on February 23 in *The New York Times*. The Pomeroy Circular baldly stated that Lincoln's reelection was neither possible nor desirable, due to the President's "manifest tendency toward compromises and temporary expedients of policy." It argued that these presumptive character flaws would become more egregious during a second term, to the detriment of "the cause of human liberty" and to "the dignity and honor of the nation." Presenting what it hoped was a clear contrast, the circular feted Chase as a statesman "of rare ability," who was in possession of "more of the qualities needed in a President during the next four years, than are combined in any other available candidate."

If Chase had hoped this would ignite his campaign, he was profoundly disappointed. The Pomeroy committee was out of sync with Republicans on the ground. It had moved too far, too fast, and thus things became much worse for Chase than had it not moved at all. Several legislatures promptly adopted resolutions endorsing Lincoln. Devastatingly for Chase, Ohio's was among them. The popular reaction seemed to be one of umbrage that a member of Lincoln's cabinet would target the executive in such a conniving fashion. George Templeton Strong, a reliable bellwether, scribbled in his diary, "I should bet on Uncle Abe." Many newspapers rushed to Lincoln's defense. The *Chicago Daily Tribune* mocked the circular as "A Game That Won't Work," as if it were a ploy by a mischievous child. The *Pittsburgh Gazette* was incensed:

We do not hesitate to say that we do not like its *tone*. More than this, we do not like its *assertions*. It is not *manly*. It is not *truthful*. . . . This base attack upon Mr. Lincoln and his administration will not make any friends for Mr. Chase among honorable men.

Chase tried to distance himself from the embarrassing circular, but he could scarcely disavow what his friends had done in his interest. He wrote Lincoln that he had no knowledge of the circular—but felt compelled to add, truthfully, that he had given his permission to the Pomeroy gang to put his name forward. Once again, he offered to resign. The President, who had been tipped to the committee in advance, responded with a brief note, promising a fuller response later. After letting his Treasury secretary stew for a week, Lincoln coolly replied, "Now, on consideration, I find there is really very little to say." In a deft, and what for Chase must have been a humiliating, coda, Lincoln added, "I have not yet read it, and I think I shall not"—as though Chase's entire bungled campaign was not even worth the bother. Having demonstrated his utter political mastery of his cabinet member, the President then offered him a lesson in statesmanship, deflecting Chase's offer to resign with the apt observation that it depended on "my judgment of the public service; and, in that view, I do not perceive occasion for a change."

Lincoln, with sublime self-assurance, had not even conditioned Chase's continuance in his administration on a cessation of his campaign. But how much campaign did Chase have left? One of his patronage recipients in Cleveland warned the Treasury secretary, "You can have no idea of the [ill] effects produced by that 'Circular.'" Representative Francis P. Blair Jr., a Missouri moderate, attacked Chase on the House floor as contemptuous to "every honorable man"—a serious charge because of its source. Blair's brother Montgomery was postmaster general and Chase's rival in the cabinet. A friendly journalist, Henry Villard, warned Chase that his "enemies" were intent on forcing him not just out of the race but also out of the cabinet, implying that his

Treasury position was not worth sacrificing for a quixotic run at the White House.

Early in March, Chase withdrew. There is no sign that he accepted any blame for his horribly inept campaign. Probably, he convinced himself of the white lie that he had foisted on Nettie, that he had withdrawn so as not to impair his "usefulness as Secretary." In fact, he still hoped to return to the race. But now was not the time. The Treasury still faced a growing cash and credibility crisis. He could scarcely revive his candidacy when the greenback was in free fall.

Twelve

Roast Mutton
and Partridge

To trade with the enemy either directly or
indirectly is an admitted evil: But a
seeming attempt to starve a people is a
greater and a more disastrous evil—

— JACOB THOMPSON TO JEFFERSON DAVIS

As CHASE SOUGHT TO RESCUE the greenback, and perhaps his
political fortunes, the economic collapse in the Confederacy
was accelerating. By late 1863 and into early 1864, the plight of
ordinary southerners was turning desperate. This was so even while the
Rebel armies were holding their own; indeed, Richmond was doing better by its soldiers than by ordinary civilians. Rationing and currency
problems are common to wartime, but they were aggravated in the Confederacy by egregious errors: the failure to export cotton early, when it
could have bankrolled the war economy for years; overreliance on money
printing, rather than taxation; a lopsided allocation of men and matériel
to the military, which drained the civilian sector; resistance to centralized direction. And finally: resistance to recruiting African American
troops, a step that would have forced the aristocracy to choose whether
they were fighting for independence or to keep their slaves.

These miscues were evidence that the economic model of the Confederacy had been wrong all along. The insistence on preserving the South as an agricultural society, the "King Cotton" model, had doomed the South to a dependent status. It was now too late to develop railways and infrastructure, too late to build factories or establish homesteads. President Davis, therefore, tried to command the southern economy to go where he wanted it. He became a convert to centralized rule, including economic controls. It is not a stretch to say that Davis adopted many of the tactics of the hated Republican philosophy of Hamiltonian central government he was fighting against.

Davis knew these measures would be received poorly, but he felt he had little choice. He had been a popular leader at the outset of the war, but after nearly three years of fighting and widespread hardship, his popularity had worn thin. He was criticized by southern intellectuals, such as Edward Alfred Pollard, an influential editor of the *Richmond Examiner*, for despotic tendencies. States' rights advocates said his policies were unconstitutional. He was rebuked by the Rebel Congress for his tendency to declaim, rather than engage. He meddled with his generals and, while that could also be said of Lincoln, he was, unlike his northern counterpart, disinclined to delegate or even to consider dissenting views. His mien was aristocratic and chilly. A historian born during Davis's lifetime said he was a leader of a cause, not of men. Davis himself recognized, belatedly, that the Confederacy could not succeed unless its people were united. In an echo of Lincoln, he warned the governor of Arkansas that it was a fatal error to suppose "that this great war can be waged by Confederate States *severally* and not *unitedly.*" Weeks after Lincoln's Gettysburg Address, in December 1863, Davis proclaimed that sacrifice had joined his people into a single bloody fabric. "We have been united as a people never [as] before," he said. This was wishful thinking. In staggered elections for the Confederate Congress, in 1863, the opposition gained significant strength, leaving Davis with only a slim majority. John Beauchamp Jones even expressed concern for Davis's personal safety, voicing alarm that he had some "few deadly enemies in the city" and ought not to go on rides unaccompanied.

Davis's most urgent problem was relieving people's hunger. Generally, food scarcity was more acute in cities. In normal times, market economies solve for such disparities. But markets depend on prices, and prices require a currency. Farmers in Dixie didn't trust the currency. As the well-informed George Templeton Strong observed, "The famine [in Richmond] is caused not so much by actual deficiency of hog and hominy as by the unwillingness of Virginia farmers to sell anything for which they must be paid in rebel paper."

During 1863, the Rebel Treasury Secretary, Christopher Memminger, printed notes at the fastest rate of the war and probably in American history. Over the first nine months of the year, government revenues amounted to $601 million, of which only a pitiable $5 million were raised from taxes. Bonds accounted for just a quarter of the total, while a horrendous $442 million were issued in short-term notes. Runaway inflation was the inevitable result. From October 1861 to March 1864 retail prices rose by a staggering 10 percent per month. Flour, which had fetched $5.50 per barrel before the war and $38 before the Richmond food riot, in April 1863, soared to $220 the succeeding winter. This inflation was disastrous and far faster than the rise in wages. Nothing conveyed the desperate currency straits so vividly as a financial snippet in the *Richmond Whig*: "It is nothing unusual to see a stout negro going through the streets of this city with a load of Confederate treasury notes fresh from the stamping press." It would be hard to imagine a greater contrast: in northern cities, currency was now supplemented with modern bank checks; in the South, enslaved captives were dragging sacks of notes through the streets. Memminger even saw fit to transport a printing press to the far side of the Mississippi, so that the western arm of the Confederacy, whatever else it lacked, would be well supplied in notes.

The best estimate for the growth in the money supply is that during the Confederacy's first three years, the money in circulation multiplied eleven times. The deluge of notes was actually worse than the figure suggests, because Union armies were continually reducing the area where the notes were accepted—and as they did, *residents shipped notes back into areas where they still circulated*—thus, more notes piled up over a smaller and smaller terrain.

With the currency so out of control, normal business became impossible. Merchants felt compelled, under the influence of inflationary expectations, to raise prices even faster than the underlying accelerant (the money stock). Thus, the eleven-fold increase in actual bills produced, by late 1863, wholesale prices that were *eighteen* times higher. The best indicator of monetary instability is found in the exchange rate in gold for Confederate notes, which before Gettysburg stood at seven to one. Within a couple of months, the notes plummeted to twelve to one, and by the end of 1863 crashed to eighteen to one. This was a collapse of epic proportions.

To alleviate the hardship for civilians, the government posted price controls for essential goods. (Many states also imposed controls.) But it was hard to find supplies at the official prices. Richmond's efforts to control distribution didn't help and probably hurt. Since the army was mostly interested in impressing edible crops, farmers switched to cotton and tobacco; thus, the policy exacerbated the food shortage. Controls were also accompanied by bureaucratic bungling and waste. Jones noted despairingly, "We have accounts of corn, and hay, and potatoes rotting at various depots!"

Inevitably, controls fostered efforts to evade the regulations. Right under the President's nose in Richmond, butchers were obtaining beef from commissary agents at 45 cents a pound, yielding a gaping illicit profit, since the government permitted a retail price of up to $1.25 a pound. Sugar was commandeered at 50 cents, with commissaries pocketing the difference, up to $2.50. People complained about middlemen although—or perhaps because—many depended on middlemen for food. As one observer noted, anyone with a product to sell was accused of being a "speculator." Under such conditions, speculation was inevitable and probably salubrious. With food rotting at rail depots, speculators helped to allocate commodities where they were needed. Even Jones did it. While blaming high prices on Jewish traders, he confessed to his diary that he had obtained twenty-four pounds of bacon from a commissary that he promptly resold at a "saving" (i.e., a markup) of 150 percent. "Without such 'short cuts,'" he rationalized, "it would be impossible to maintain my family."

A related problem was that the crashing currency incentivized people to behave in nonsensical and nonproductive ways. People paid extravagant prices for secondhand junk just to be rid of bills. The wealthy purchased property they had no use for. Farmers refused to accept money. They stopped selling meat and refused to market grain. The distortions multiplied.

Private informers warned Davis that the southern economy was becoming enthralled with gambling. He heard from a surgeon in the First Arkansas Cavalry, "The cotton trade is carried on to such an alarming extent that I feel it to be my duty to inform your excellency of its magnitude." Davis was warned of the futility of trying to suppress illicit trade— even with the enemy. In a climate of "destitution," when a pound of cotton could purchase three pounds of bacon, a Mississippi politician counseled, "You cannot consider it [trading] strange or peculiar or disloyal." Davis was hardly mollified. "The passion for speculation," he thundered, "has become a giant evil. It has seemed to take possession of the whole country, and has seduced citizens of all classes from a determined prosecution of the war to a sordid effort to amass money."

Civilian conditions were considerably worsened by the government's persistent favoring of the military. With the army reduced to half rations, forced requisitions (impressment) broadened to include horses, cows, wagons, railroad cars, and enslaved workers—whatever the army needed. Jones noted, "Everywhere the people are clamorous against the sweeping impressments of crops, horses, etc." To keep the army's horses from starving, Davis decreed that forage be diverted to the military "in preference to anything else."

A similar military bias sapped the strength of industry, as men and

matériel were rerouted to the army. Lack of tradesmen such as metal-
workers and machinists led to serious bottlenecks. A mill in Selma,
Alabama, reported "a number of our most important tools are idle . . .
for want of mechanics." In Manchester, Virginia, production at a cotton
mill ceased when a few skilled hands were called into the militia—
putting two hundred women and children out of work.

The government similarly exerted practical control over the rails. As
rolling stock was destroyed by Union armies, southern generals demanded priority use of trains and equipment. Civilian transport became a logistical nightmare, spawning lopsided food distributions. In
an extreme case, corn fetched $40 a bushel in Richmond when, in Ala-
bama and western Georgia, the same commodity was going for only
$1.25.

This economy was hardly sustainable. It was threatened not only by
bankruptcy but by popular revolt. Refugees were streaming north to
Cairo, southern gateway to Illinois, where they recounted tales of famine. In North Carolina, the *Raleigh Daily Progress* rang in the year declaring that the people faced a choice: peace or starvation. Cities were
suddenly insecure and crime ridden, as if shorn of the patina of civilization. Richmond was plagued by robberies. Thanks to human scavengers, the streets were bare of garbage. A sea captain who had run the
blockade and was in Charleston over the sorry Christmas of 1863 was
appalled. The city's lone hotel served the most meager and unappetiz-
ing fare. According to this traveler, tobacco was "the only solace." Fort
Sumter was in ruins. "Some of their leaders," the captain mused, "should
have foreseen that the catastrophe was coming." Perhaps, had the aristocracy shared more of the pain, the Rebel Congress would have been
quicker to repair the finances. It is incredible, even at a distance of a
century and a half, to read that Mary Chesnut, the society hostess and
intimate in Davis's circle, laid a Christmas dinner of oyster soup, roast
mutton, ham, turkey, wild duck, and partridge, then a plum pudding,
watered by Burgundy, sherry, and Madeira, as if the destitution all
around her were happening someplace else. There were no hearty

repasts, and in many cases no meat at all, for common folk in the capital. "It is a sad Christmas," Jones lamented, "cold, and threatening snow."

Ordinary southerners deeply resented the ability of planters' sons to escape the draft. That many did try to opt out is clear from the steady inflation in the price of substitutes—which rose from $100 early in the war to $6000 by late 1863. One gentleman was so desperate that he offered a 230-acre farm, in Hanover County, outside Richmond, to avoid serving. But most of the wealthy did fight—and as in the Union army, Confederate officers died in slightly higher proportion than enlisted men.[*]

Just as worrisome to the southern elite, there were stirrings of resistance among the poor whites on whom they depended. The ravages of the war economy exposed the uncomfortable truth that slavery, and the Confederacy itself, had never been much use to whites outside the slaveholding class. Poor men were irate that planters continued to grow cotton rather than foodstuffs. There was more than a hint of class warfare in the correspondent who cried to the Savannah *Morning News*, "The crime is with the planters." Desertions became endemic. In backcountry Florida, Georgia, North Carolina, Alabama, Arkansas, and Texas, bands of deserters congealed and became a law unto themselves, in many cases barring passage to Confederate soldiers. In North Carolina, resisters formed defensive militias and even set up networks to warn of encroaching graycoats. Such resistance was scattered but considerable. An editor who toured southwest Georgia during 1863 and early 1864 claimed, "We are fighting each other harder than we ever fought the enemy," surely an overstatement but just as surely a reflection of the tattered state of the southern union.

Discontent was most pervasive in the Tar Heel State, where support for secession had been tepid at best. *The North Carolina Standard* prodded the governor to protect the people against incursions from Richmond, pointedly reminding him that he presided over "a sovereign

---

[*] A guest at an upper-crust tea party hosted by Mrs. Davis noted, "The ladies were all dressed in deep mourning; some (the greater part) for the sad reason that they had lost near and dear relatives in the wretched war."

State." The *Standard* demanded that the governor thwart Confederate officers from distilling the state's "precious grain," refuting the presumption of military priority. It struck a note of defiance, proclaiming, "the army can do without whiskey better than our women and children can do without bread." In eastern Carolina, the *Wilmington Journal* reported that the talk of the troops was of their wives and children suffering at home, their smokehouses locked, their bellies empty. One battle-scarred Tar Heel veteran claimed that rather than slowly starve, "We might as well be under Lincoln's despotism."

North Carolina's governor, Zebulon B. Vance, a fervent states' rights advocate, found himself mediating between the increasingly authoritarian central government and resisters at home—the latter including the editor and proprietor of the *Standard*, William W. Holden, who called for a state convention to demand peace talks. "I fear we are on the eve of another revolution & civil war in the State," Vance fretted in December 1863. The governor pleaded with Davis to alleviate the causes of popular discontent, among which he cited "the evils and abuses of the impressment system" and "ruthless" conscription. He also urged the Confederate president to try harder for a negotiated peace. Davis, knowing full well that Lincoln's terms included reunification as well as emancipation, refused. Seeking to quash the rebellion before it started, Davis warned Vance not to hesitate in suppressing antisecessionists out of "an over-earnest desire to reclaim [them] by conciliation." In January, Davis received a delegation from the state, whose members threatened that if Congress proceeded with authoritarian legislation (including suspension of the writ of habeas corpus), North Carolina would become "the bloodiest field of the South." Davis must have winced at the irony when his visitors pleaded, "Mr. President, trust North Carolina *& let her alone.*" These were the precise sentiments Davis had expressed toward Lincoln. When Vance seemed to express support for the rights of anti-secessionists, Davis signaled he would not tolerate more. "I warned you," he replied sternly, "of the error to warming *traitors* . . . by ill-timed deference or timid concession."

The common thread among southern deserters and resisters was poverty. As with the draft rioters up north, war aggravated class inequities. On both sides of the Mason-Dixon, deprivation begat resentment and resentment curdled into prejudice. Somewhat surprisingly, Davis also lost support among the Confederate leadership. General Robert Toombs, Davis's first secretary of state, and a founder of the Confederacy, delivered a scorching rebuke, charging in the Augusta (Georgia) *Constitutionalist* that the Confederacy's woes were due to financial mismanagement: "In all else we have had the advantage." Specifically, Toombs upbraided the Davis-Memminger regime for the "folly" of attempting to finance an expensive war "solely on credit, without taxation." Early in 1864, Toombs declared in utter frustration that he had "seceded" from the Confederacy and now maintained allegiance only to the State of Georgia. Although Toombs was an extreme case, the anti-Davis wing included Alexander Stephens, the Confederate vice president.

With the Confederacy nearly at war with itself, some of its officers quietly suggested an unthinkable reform: expanding the pool of soldiers by recruiting slaves, who would ultimately be offered freedom. An Arkansas general named Patrick Cleburne advocated a more sweeping idea: universal emancipation. Cleburne reasoned that freeing the slaves would furnish Dixie with legions of fresh troops and more zealous workers, and perhaps renew the rebellion's purpose. Breaking with the South's most inviolate taboo, he read a paper to his fellow officers arguing that emancipation would raise its Black population from "a dreaded weakness to a [source] of strength." Indeed, Dixie could emancipate more effectually than the North, "for we can give the Negro not only his own freedom, but that of his wife and child, and can secure it to him in his old home."

Cleburne's paper was read in Richmond, and Davis was not insensitive to its merits. While slavery had been a prime reason for secession, Davis and the other Confederate leaders had invested hard years in building what they construed to be an independent republic. Their priority now was to keep it. Privately, Davis told his wife he did not think slavery could survive the war. This opinion was validated early in 1864, when his servant Cornelius managed to escape, boldly running off with a sack containing cold chicken, ham, preserves, and bread, as well as cash.* Over the course of the war, hundreds of thousands of slaves bolted for Union territory, sapping the home front of vital workers. Emancipation would stem the exodus.

Nonetheless, the fixity of southern racial attitudes was such that Davis feared to do what Lincoln had done. Emancipation would have shocked the white population. Mere discussion of it would have torn his government apart. Cleburne's proposal elicited outrage from his fellow officers. One of them labeled it a "monstrous proposition . . . revolting to Southern sentiment, Southern pride, and Southern honor." We also have the testimony of Edmund Ruffin, who had just reached the disconcerting milestone of his seventieth birthday. His customary sourness now aggravated by a catalog of physical infirmities—rotting teeth, tremulous hands, failing hearing—he laid into Thomas Jefferson for "his most dangerous & abominable principles of govt, . . . the dogma of the equal rights of all men to govern, & its corollary, universal suffrage." To Ruffin, and to the preponderance of planters, the Confederacy was indivisible from white supremacy, and therefore slavery. Davis could not afford to lose the planters. On Davis's order, the war secretary commanded Cleburne to quash his incendiary brief and suppress all mention of it. Davis would not touch slavery.

Davis concentrated on financial reforms, which the planters might abide. He and his overmatched Treasury secretary imagined that they might imitate Chase and sell a popular loan. Hoping to whip up interest, Memminger urged that at town meetings across the breadth of Dixie, committees be formed to solicit subscriptions. "There is no reason for distrust as to our currency," Memminger insisted.

---

* Cornelius was captured and jailed. However, his zeal was undiminished. He asked for water, and when the lone jailer opened the door, Cornelius knocked him down and fled, this time, evidently, with success.

Addressing the Confederate Congress when it convened in December 1863, Davis pleaded that the finances required immediate attention. He had been bombarded by demands for currency reform, notably from Moses Mordecai, a prominent steamship owner in Charleston, who averred that "severe diseases require severe remedies." In the spirit of Mordecai, Davis and Memminger proposed an extreme fix—note "repudiation" (i.e., cancelation). The government would replace the canceled notes with bonds, that is, forcibly convert the people's money into loans. This was a new strategy only in its particulars. The Davis government had been forcing the farmers to part with crops and forcing communities to offer conscripts. Now, it would force the people to lend.

But what would persuade the people to invest in long-term government paper, for which they had shown scant interest since early in the war? Chase had a tax base; Memminger didn't. Isidor Straus, a savvy young southerner who had slipped the blockade to New York City that year with gold sewn by his mother into his underclothes, saw enough of the Union's muscle to advise the family in Georgia to put its assets into anything *but* Rebel paper. "Buy real estate, land, houses and lots," counseled the future owner of Macy's department store. He specifically warned against buying slaves.

Perhaps the clearest measure of Richmond's deficiency was that while Salmon Chase was wrapping up a gargantuan bond campaign, the original Rebel bonds, marketed in 1861, had plunged to nine cents to the dollar. Even the Erlanger cotton bonds, floated in April at close to par, plummeted to less than forty cents. Neither the southern people nor investors in London (where the bonds traded) had faith in Richmond's credit. As they were well aware, the Confederacy's debt amounted to $1.2 billion, equivalent to 80 percent of the Union's debt, although the United States controlled vastly greater resources. Therefore, Davis settled on "compulsory funding"—a forced loan.

Since even a forced loan must be supported by revenue, Davis advocated a seminal change—taxing slaveholders. Opposition was vehement, often couched (as in the northern tax debates) on constitutional grounds. Critics accused Davis of being a "dictator." His response was that if he waited, the Confederacy would expire. The Rebel Congress met in a surly mood and debated Davis's agenda in secret. However, they had no alternative.

On February 17, 1864, Richmond enacted a currency bill bearing the wishful title An Act to Fund, Tax and Limit the Currency. The bill aimed to compel holders to give up notes in return either for twenty-year bonds or for a new series of notes that would not be redeemed until after the war. Holders could swap their notes for bonds until April 1; any notes not exchanged would be subject to a 33 percent tax or (the equivalent) replaced by "new" notes at the rate of three old dollars for two new ones. In theory, the legislation would reduce the total of Confederate notes, of which more than $700 million were in circulation, by at least one-third.

Simultaneously, Congress legislated a tax of 5 percent on property, including, as quaintly described by the *Richmond Enquirer*, "land, ne-groes, horses, mules, cattle and all live stock on plantations," as well as farm tools, furniture, houses, kitchen utensils, cotton and tobacco, gold and silver, jewelry, and financial assets such as bank shares. This was bolder than anything Richmond had attempted before. It permitted the tax collector to assess (although at a low rate) land and slaves—which amounted to two-thirds of the Confederacy's taxable property, so Jeff Davis calculated. Congress also imposed a steep tax on profits.

The new laws amounted to a serious effort to repair the government's financial condition. The immediate reaction to the currency law was bewilderment. Prices of food and merchandise jumped, this being the reflexive response in the South to any pending disruption. After a few days' reflection, prices of sugar, corn and cornmeal, even beef and pork began to decline. The *Augusta Chronicle & Sentinel* gratefully noted "a sensible decline in the price of the necessaries of life in this market." Before long, people were swapping their notes for the new bonds. By

March 21, the government office in Petersburg, Virginia, had processed $2.2 million worth of note cancelations; in Columbus, Georgia, $1.35 million. The *Lynchburg* (Virginia) *Republican* complained that money in the city was "tight" (scarce). Even *The New York Times* conceded, "prices are tumbling all over the Confederacy." A later reconstruction reckoned that the annual rate of inflation fell from 700 percent to less than 200 percent. The *Richmond Whig*, as if to settle the matter, declared "our currency, under the salutary provisions of the last Congress, must grow better and better daily."

It was not so simple. The reform did accomplish a general deflation, beginning some time in spring. But prices remained substantially higher than in prewar days. And the contraction in the money supply—a one-time event—did not resolve the Confederacy's ongoing fiscal imbalance. Until, and unless, taxes were actually collected, the government had no way to fund the war except by issuing new paper notes. The February law authorized Memminger to issue these notes without limitation. Thus, the currency reform's fleeting success could be made to last only if, and as long as, taxes were collected or expenses pared.

The tax law boosted government receipts (although, adjusted for inflation, the money was worth less). The share of revenue raised from taxes also rose. One scholar termed it "a remarkable achievement," and under the circumstances, perhaps it was. The war severely hampered collections. Richmond could not spare thousands of bodies to serve as assessors and collectors; moreover, as the Union seized territory, the tax base progressively shrank. The people, who were anyway hostile to taxation, were disinclined to support a losing effort. Evasion was rampant, and taxes never came close to defraying more than a small fraction of the budget.

Military expenses could not be economized, especially when Grant's spring campaign against Lee went into high gear. Troops had to be paid, arms and supplies requisitioned, and these required fresh emissions of the dreaded notes. Distribution of the new notes started in earnest as early as April (two months after the act). The underlying problem with the reforms was foundational. No program of paper swaps can substitute for economic productivity, nor can a "tax" deliver beyond the means of the people subject to it.

The greatest effect of the financial package may have been to heighten popular resentment. It and other legislation made the central government an invasive presence without delivering palpable relief. Richmond suspended the writ of habeas corpus—to southerners, an odious infringement—and widened draft eligibility up to age fifty. It also eliminated exemptions. It banned the use of greenbacks and other U.S. bills save for the risible exception of permitting their use by Confederate officials—and only them! For official purposes, Memminger could not afford to be stuck with his own currency.

The most extreme proposal, suggested to Davis by Alexander Clayton, a Mississippi district judge, was that the government seize all the cotton in the South in exchange for bonds. Clayton's logic was that cotton had become the South's real currency, and Richmond ought to control it. Davis would not antagonize the planters, and the proposal died. But Congress did give him authority, which he was to use with alacrity, over cotton shipments and blockade running in general. Congress was prompted by dispiriting news from Europe. Britain and France had definitively shut the door on further deliveries of ironclad ships, giving the North a free hand to tighten the blockade. Moreover, Richmond's agents in Europe reported there was no appetite for more cotton bonds. Davis felt he had no choice but to control the diminishing freight still able to slip past Union ships, and Congress acquiesced. The new law compelled blockade runners to reserve half of their space, outgoing as well as incoming, for government account. Luxury and other high-priced imports were prohibited, and the government gained a virtual monopoly over exports of cotton, tobacco, sugar, molasses, and rice, subjecting private shipments to strict regulations devised by the President. Cotton in Liverpool fetched ten times the price within the Confederacy. Seizing this low-hanging profit seemed Davis's only hope.

Opposition was fierce. The new shipping regulations federalized what had been a state responsibility. Several states were already in the shipping business, in partnership with private capital. North Carolina's blockade runners were so successful that its units enjoyed a surplus of shoes, blankets, and uniforms. Recognizing that Richmond was intent on cutting him out, Governor Vance vehemently protested that in light of the emergency, states should be *increasing* imports. President Davis refused to budge. If exceptions were made for state ventures, he noted, "then all the ships engaged in running the blockade would ere long be owned in part by States; and there would be nothing left for the Confederate Government to regulate."

The new law was probably self-defeating. War profiteers had been Richmond's lifeline, and they were loath to risk their capital merely to work on government account. The experience of Augustus Charles Hobart-Hampden, a retired Royal Navy captain, may have been illustrative. Hobart-Hampden, the son of the Earl of Buckinghamshire, was a seafaring Victorian with a romantic's flair for adventure and a businessman's thirst for profit. He showed no interest in the moral issues of the war (indeed, he wrote up his exploits with a Kipling-like contempt for nonwhites). In 1863 and 1864, piloting a 180-foot steamer with an English crew of thirty-four, he threaded the blockade a dozen times, escaping capture by the narrowest of margins. Once, he slipped by an unseeing Union cruiser outside the harbor in the dark, passing so close, he claimed, "I could have dropped a biscuit into the boat with ease." When the new law required that he work on government account, the captain saw his prospects considerably diminished. "The profit to their owners, who had been put to an enormous expense and risk in sending vessels in," he would write, "was so much reduced that the ventures hardly paid." Soon after the law went into effect, Hobart-Hampden called it quits.

Jeff Davis was not a quitter. He determinedly pursued the war unfazed by the gradually eroding military outlook, nor by the rather faster erosion of the currency, nor by the severely painful neuralgia that afflicted him throughout. He was a tireless servant, who despite his image as an aloof loner was occupied, much as Abraham Lincoln was, by streams of supplicants in addition to his duties administering the war and economic policy and maintaining his voluminous correspondence. He sought to instill among white southerners a loyalty that superseded that to the individual states—what the Civil War historian Frank Vandiver called "a sense of Confederateness." But his conception of the state and its powers remained tentative and blinkered. He never challenged the planters, or not enough and not soon enough. He lacked the leadership to make the Confederacy a "nation" for all its people, rich and poor, much less Black and white. He was too timid to loosen the doctrine of white supremacy, even when the survival of the Rebel army depended on it. The same fidelity to planters prevented him from seeking, with all his regulations, one that would have required farmers to devote sufficient acreage to foodstuffs. Davis was much criticized for mismanaging the Confederate armies, but his economic errors hurt his cause more. He "overmobilized" by hoarding the South's resources in the military. He failed to feed its people. The historian David Williams points out that the Rebel army did not, ever, lose a major battle due to lack of arms. But the erosion of the civilian economy cost it plenty, both in the fields and in the straining of its threadbare industry. This eroded popular support and accelerated the government's financial collapse.

Thirteen

Exit Secretary

The greatest financial Secretary . . . since Hamilton.

—Lincoln's private secretaries, John
George Nicolay and John Hay,
on Salmon Chase

THE SPRING OF 1864 BROUGHT fervent hopes that, as the snows melted, the Union army would finish Lee and end the war. In March, Lincoln promoted Grant to the rank held previously only by George Washington, lieutenant general, in charge of all Union troops.* With U. S. (aka "Unconditional Surrender") Grant at the helm, many thought victory was in reach. Traders did not agree. The gold price, an inverse barometer of Union fortunes, ticked steadily higher.

Once again, Salmon Chase had to demonstrate that the United States had sufficient revenue to fight the war. This time, he did not have his full arsenal. Since his abortive campaign for the White House, his relationship with Lincoln had frayed to the breaking point. He could not risk tapping his master bond salesman, Jay Cooke, who had become a political liability. And in the late spring, as Grant's offensive slowed and then stalled, the Union's credit seriously weakened.

---

* Winfield Scott had won a brevet promotion to lieutenant general in 1855; however, a "brevet" promotion typically did not confer the authority of the rank.

Chase faced these pressures with his customary verve, attacking on multiple fronts as if conducting his own civilian war. He pressed to increase taxes, sell more bonds, and complete his bank reform. But his credibility and thus his entire program depended on fighting inflation and—what was nearly the same—suppressing gold. By April, the price of gold had climbed to 169½ (a premium to the greenback of 69.5 percent). The Treasury secretary was extremely concerned—desperate is not too strong a word. Demanding that Congress act, he pleaded with Thaddeus Stevens: "To arrest this depreciation is an absolute necessity."

In northern cities and towns, the gold price did not affect most ordinary business. Within the Union's borders, greenbacks were a perfectly acceptable currency. One may ask, then, why did Chase care about gold? The Treasury secretary was a bullionist, committed to restoring the gold standard (the condition under which the Treasury could redeem every paper bill for coin). Every spike in the metal reflected waning public confidence in Chase's ability to bring the greenback and gold into parity. Even his ally Senator John Sherman considered it a stain. "Chase is a man of ability," he confided, "but in recent measures he has failed." More practically, the gold price determined the dollar exchange rate overseas, while at home, turbulence in gold fostered a climate of inflationary expectations.

The New York Times reported in April that the appreciation in breadstuffs, provisions, and other goods was *"influenced by the rapid rise in Gold."* Coffee was quoted at 40 percent higher than a year earlier; sugar, 50 percent; and pork, 70 percent. Representative James Brooks toted up prices of thirteen "articles of necessity," such as iron, salt, and gunpowder, and computed an average rise of 63.5 percent over the preceding three years. Brooks was a Democratic critic of Chase and was thought to have exaggerated, but modern research shows he was not far off.* There is no doubt that the inflation in consumer goods was signifi-

---

* Ethel D. Hoover, a mid-twentieth-century Department of Labor economist, calculated 39 percent inflation from December 1860 to December 1863, the period for which Brooks computed his homemade index. While Brooks was certainly on the high side, the tools available to him were far cruder.

cantly higher than in wages. Over the entirety of 1864, prices rose by 20 to 25 percent, faster even than the torrid pace of 1863. This became a crisis for workers, soldiers, and their families.

Chase might have alleviated some of the pressure by demonstrating a little flexibility. The best way to soak up surplus currency would be to borrow it in exchange for bonds—as he had, so successfully, in the five-twenty drive. He tried to market a new bond—this time, a *forty-year* bond, which required considerably more confidence from investors than the twenty-year variety. (This new bond was known as the ten-forty.*) The new campaign met with little success. The absence of Cooke was one factor, but Chase was also to blame, having cut the interest rate from 6 percent to 5, a rate that did not excite investors. The Treasury secretary was too stubborn to accept that investors demanded more, and sales languished. The excess currency had to go somewhere and—not going into bonds—it went into gold. Wall Street was badly unnerved. George Templeton Strong drew a clear connection. "The war languishes, and makes no progress," the diarist groused. "*People naturally turn their thoughts, therefore, to questions of finance, taxation and prices.*"

Chase did not want to be a northern Memminger. To rein in gold and inflation, he made three demands of Congress. His first object was raising revenue. In March 1864, Congress had tripled the tax on spirits.† Chase wanted a more sweeping increase and boldly proposed that the total contribution of tax revenues should *double*. No government had ever asked the American people for so much.

Chase also asked Congress to amend the National Banking Act. His dream of creating a single currency was being stymied by the continued circulation of state bank notes. Technically, the Treasury secretary sought only a tax on these notes, but his intent was to tax them out

---

* Ten-forties were payable at the government's option in ten years and redeemable in forty.

† Whiskey was an easy target. Thaddeus Stevens quipped that in their fervor to tax spirits, "men on the temperance side of this question became as intoxicated as if they had been drinking liquor for a month."

of existence. He wrote to Joseph Medill that he sought to "criminalize" these notes. Chase's justification was that only "an exclusive National Currency" could save the finances. "What can I do?" he asked Horace Greeley in a philosophical vein. "The Army must be paid—the Navy must be paid—the public creditors must be paid. We *cannot* pay unless we can keep gold down." Since the volume of government issues had soared and that of banks was little changed, Chase's contention that banks had created the inflationary bubble had little basis. But he had staked his reputation on creating a new banking system and stubbornly stuck with it.

Telegrams poured into the Treasury demanding that Chase suppress the gold price, not through some slow-moving banking reform but right now. Speculation was spreading like a fever. Not only traders, but ordinary citizens were hoarding coins. The mania extended to the White House, where William Stoddard, a secretary who handled the First Lady's mail and other clerical tasks, was embarrassed by the revelation that he was playing the stock and gold markets. As Stoddard admitted later: "Stock and gold gambling was the mania of the day, and for a time I had it very badly." President Lincoln exclaimed, casually, that he would like to see the gold speculators' heads shot off, but when the opportunity presented itself, he treated Stoddard with compassion. Chase was less forgiving. He misread speculators as the cause of inflation, rather than the messenger.

Chase's eagerness to suppress speculation spurred his third ask from Congress—legislation permitting the Treasury to intervene in the gold market. Thanks to robust duty receipts, the Treasury was accumulating gold coin. Chase proposed to sell the surplus—to flood the market with metal and, as he hoped, drive down its price. As the Treasury secretary's bill worked its way through Congress, he was said to be exceedingly anxious that it passed.

The primary supporter was Thaddeus Stevens. In contrast to the bullionist Chase, Stevens detested the common veneration for gold as an anachronism of bankers. His aim was not so much to achieve paper parity with gold as to drive the metal from official embrace, almost as the

First Amendment precluded an official religion. "When a man asks five dollars for a hat," Stevens lectured his colleagues in the House, he did not mean five dollars in bullion but in "the actual [paper] currency, the lawful money, of the United States." Stevens took great offense to the premium that gold commanded in the market, which he ascribed to the antique belief that paper currency was merely promissory—a form of credit. Noting that greenbacks, his pet creation, paid no interest, he insisted, "They are not debts. They are the *money* of the country." This was a very Republican argument—that federal paper was as good as gold. Of course, Stevens's rhetoric did not make it so.

With Stevens leading the charge, Congress gave Chase authority to sell the Treasury's gold. John Cisco, his trusty assistant treasurer, advised that, out of prudence, the Treasury continue to hold a large reserve. Cisco argued that the threat of intervention would carry more weight than its execution. Jay Cooke advised the opposite course (Cooke viewed the yellow metal as a detestable rival to his bonds). Aiming at Chase's vulnerable spot, Cooke insisted that if Chase deployed him to use his new powers, he could, as he put it, "hold the whip over these speculators" and break the price. The Treasury secretary could not resist. On April 10, 1864, Chase asked Cooke to confer with Cisco in New York, and that the two devise a plan. He stressed, "It is of immense importance to bring down the price of gold."

Chase was stepping into a minefield. Markets had been unusually volatile—just how volatile emerges from the papers of Stedman, the poet-gambler. After starting the month with blazing profits, Stedman reported despairingly on Tuesday, April 5, "Panic in stocks this morning. Took all my courage . . . in holding on to stock." On Wednesday, his fortunes revived with that of the surging Reading Railroad, but on Thursday it was more gloom: "Terrible fall in Ft. Wayne [Railroad] and panic in the market." Stedman ended the week with a trader's faith: "Market all better. The sheep again crazy to buy." One almost hesitates to deliver Stedman's report a week following: "Terrible panic in stocks."

It was at this point that Chase gave Cisco the order to sell. Chase had already made a desperate pronouncement in cabinet—that because the national debt had risen to more than $1.6 billion, neither the Navy nor Interior Departments should make further calls on the Treasury for coin. (Bills, of course, Chase could happily furnish.) He begged Lincoln for help on two measures of "great importance"—elimination of state bank notes and the tax hike.

On April 14, Chase joined Cooke and Cisco in New York. By then, the gold premium had soared to 90 percent. Cisco, acting in consultation with Cooke, furiously unloaded the Treasury's bullion. Under the pressure of government selling, the premium fell sharply. Not all investors were pleased. "Gold has been oscillating madly today," Strong reported. "Things look very bad." Strong's desperation may sound strange, since prices of breadstuffs and other foods were falling, just what consumers wanted. But neither inflation nor its cure affects all parties equally. By paying out gold and draining the market of cash, Chase was rewarding people on fixed incomes to the detriment of the stock market. By April 18, the New York banks were desperately short of greenbacks, producing panicky selling in railroad shares and a sharp break in commodities. A well-known speculator, overloaded on railroad shares, went belly up. Chase had expended $11 million of the Treasury's gold, simulating the larger interventions of modern central banks. He would discover, as did they, that controlling a price is not so easy. The monetary tightening beckoned a slowdown. "There is panic and smash in the stock market," Strong wrote drily, after five days of selling. "Large fortunes gained by gambling . . . evaporated suddenly and quietly." Chase did not want a recession. With the gold premium having retreated to 67 percent, the Treasury secretary called a halt. Cooke protested that with only a little more selling he could break the gold bulls for good. (He unctuously boasted, "It seems to me that I am the only one unselfish enough to desire the government to get the entire upper hand.") This judgment was shortsighted. The only sure result of the operation was a reduction in the Treasury's gold reserve; continued selling would empty its vault. This would damage—not strengthen—the Treasury's credit. Cisco had been right: the threat would have been better.

Chase could have benefited from this lesson, but he had yet to learn it was fruitless to wrestle with markets, as if they were a dragon to be slayed with only a bit more pluck. He now sent a truly draconian bill to Congress—to ban gold trading and authorize jail terms for speculators. Chase naïvely lobbied Lincoln that if only the requested medicine were prescribed, "there will be no need to fear financial disasters."

It is ironic that the crisis was unfolding while the Treasury was collecting record tax receipts. The Bureau of Internal Revenue, now in its second year, was raking in three times the taxes collected in 1863. Tariff collections had surged to their highest level of the war. Yet it was not enough. The Treasury's expenses, inexorably rising as the fighting entered a particularly savage phase, climbed to $2.5 million a day. With bond sales having plunged, Chase again fell behind on requisitions. He pleaded that Congress act on his tax request, and the Republican press supported him.

For most of the nation's history, duties on foreign trade had been the government's primary source of revenue. In 1864, for the first time, internal revenue eclipsed the tariff. Emboldened by this experience, Congress sought to squeeze more from manufacturing, the professions, securities, and numerous other industries. Effectively, it tried to adapt tax policy to the more modern industrial economy north of the Mason-Dixon.

Concerns with inequality loomed large in the debate. There were cries for the rich to pay a greater share. Luxury items such as silks and fine brandy were a natural target. Chase's commissioner of internal revenue urged that the income tax be made more progressive. The House Ways and Means Committee, dominated by Thaddeus Stevens, refused. It endorsed a flat tax, 5 percent for all. This sparked a heated debate in the House that presaged modern critiques of inequality. Representative Augustus Frank, a banker from upstate New York, proposed sharply higher taxes on the rich. Frank's amendment, offered in April, would raise the tax to 7.5 percent on income above $10,000 and 10 percent above $25,000. These, however, were very high incomes. Nationwide, between 10 and 15 percent of Union households paid some tax by the war's end.* Very few people were in the highest bracket. Even a successful corporate attorney, such as Lincoln previous to his election, had earned only about $3000. In short, Frank's tax above $25,000 was a tax that hardly anyone would pay.

Nonetheless, leading Republicans didn't like it. Pitt Fessenden, whose roots were in mercantile Portland, protested that higher taxes would discourage the wealthy from working, foreshadowing conservative arguments of more than a century later. Stevens, a firebrand on racial issues, argued that progressive taxes were unjustly discriminatory. Even Justin Morrill, father of the egalitarian Land-Grant College Act, objected to the supposed "inequality" of higher brackets. The self-made congressman denounced the whiff of farmland populism, what Morrill called the "spirit of agrarianism." He bitterly added, "It is seizing property of men for the crime of having too much."

Arguments over the income tax demonstrated the limits of the Republican revolution. To be "liberal" in the mid-nineteenth century meant, among other things, to favor freedom of trade. It meant to encourage enterprise as distinct from restricting trade by guilds, cartels, monopolies, or, for that matter, slavery. Liberals were committed to laissez-faire, not to greater government controls. Lincoln's economic crusade was about extending opportunity—not cashiering it for a homegrown Jacobinism. Pointedly, he had remarked to a workers delegation, "Let not him who is houseless pull down the house of another, but let him labor diligently, and build one for himself." Likewise, his fellow Republicans had no interest in a war on wealth. But westerners were clearly more populist than the old money back east. Thus, in the

---

* During the war, Internal Revenue reported the total tax *collected*, but not the number of filers. Estimates on the percentage of people who filed range widely—from 1 percent to (an unlikely) 20 percent.

House, dominated by big population centers, Republican legislators were more concerned with revenue than redistribution. In the Senate, farm states had greater sway and sentiment was more progressive. These differences were not easily reconciled.

Congress simultaneously took up the tariff. As before, Morrill argued that steeper duties were necessary to balance the expected tax increase on domestic firms. The protectionist camp benefited from wartime nationalism and resentment of Britain. But the tariff remained highly sectional, eagerly sought by manufacturing states and equally detested in farming regions.

As Congress wrangled over these issues, Chase grew increasingly impatient. Seemingly forgetting his recent, and disparaging, campaign against Lincoln, he again became the loyal servant and sought the President's help. "If you concur with me in these judgments," he wrote in April, "may I not hope that you will and for such members [of Congress] as are disposed . . . to be lukewarm or opposed . . . *urge them to give their needful support* to the bills." There is no record that Lincoln did so. In May, Lincoln volunteered a suggestion: that Chase close the revenue gap by sweetening the terms of his bonds: "Suppose you change your five per cent loan to six," Lincoln advised. It was one of the only times the President offered specific advice. But Chase found it difficult to reverse a decision, and he bridled at the implied criticism from his boss. The Treasury secretary did not realize how badly he needed Lincoln's support. His political enemies, some of them close to the President, were eager to destroy Chase's political base and remove him from power. As usual, Chase himself provided an opening.

Late in April, Lincoln rewarded Representative Blair (the brother of Chase's cabinet rival) with a coveted commission as major general. It happened that, as Lincoln was granting the commission, Blair was delivering another scorching attack on Chase, accusing him of lax supervision of the Treasury, which he asserted was riddled with corruption. Blair timed his attack at a sensitive moment, when Chase was trying to fend off rumors of malfeasance within the department and, mortifyingly for Chase, of a sex and champagne bacchanalia among a handful of Treasury employees. (Subsequently, two Treasury officials were accused of accepting bribes and, in the argot of the day, "corrupting" young females.) None of this reached the level of Chase, but Blair's clear aim was to destroy Chase's reputation, and his assault prompted a House investigation of the Treasury. Lincoln's award of a commission could be interpreted by a suspicious mind as evidence that the President was conspiring with the Blairs against his own Treasury secretary. This was not the case, but Lincoln, employing another cracker barrel metaphor, said that when he read of Blair's speech, he "knew that another beehive was knocked over." He considered withdrawing Blair's commission to spare Chase's feelings—but decided not to. Perhaps he was tired of always being the one to give in.

Chase erupted when he learned of the appointment—beehive indeed. According to Albert Gallatin Riddle, an Ohio lawyer who shared a private railcar with Chase, the latter flew into "a frightful rage. . . . The spacious car fairly trembled under his feet." Weeks later, Chase was still sore over the imagined alliance of Lincoln and the Blairs. Denigrating Lincoln's intention of running for reelection on a "National Union" ticket (a more inclusive label than "Republican"), Chase said bitterly, "the Convention will not be regarded as an Union Convention; but simply as a Blair-Lincoln Convention." This unpleasant episode further eroded their mutual trust.

Senator John Sherman said the Congress of 1863–1864 was "perhaps the busiest and most important one in the history of our government"—probably an overstatement. This Congress was mostly tasked with strengthening and preserving what the Thirty-Seventh Congress had achieved in 1862. One exception was the immigration bill requested by Lincoln—the first official act to encourage what would become a tidal wave of foreign settlers. As modest as were its provisions,* the bill was laudable for countering the xenophobia that was already a feature of American society. Waspish prejudice was so ingrained that *The New York Times* felt compelled to reassure readers that immigration had not diluted the dominant Anglo-Saxon blood stock. The new law implicitly countered prevailing prejudices. Its most controversial aspect, suggestive of the Republican Party's drift toward business, was that it sanctioned the practice of employers paying an immigrant's passage in return for up to a year's wages, similar to indentured servitude. Labor unions protested that the reform would lead to a deluge of cheap labor. Lincoln did not see it that way. He expected that, over time, immigrants would spur the country's growth, and in this he was surely right. In another bill that expanded the federal agenda, Congress granted Yosemite Valley (already a tourist site) to California, under the condition that it be protected as a public park. This was a precursor to the national park system.

Congress's most revolutionary step was initiated in the Senate, which in April debated the Thirteenth Amendment, abolishing slavery. Some Senators objected that codifying emancipation would backfire against Republicans in the fall elections. But three years of war had hardened the majority against compromise. Charles Sumner, passionately antislavery, observed that if a stranger from "another place" were to visit Earth, his first surprise would be that in a land of such plenty "four millions of human beings [were] held in the most abject bondage, driven by the lash like beasts," and his second would be that this wickedness was uninhibited by the Constitution of the United States. Senator John Hale of New Hampshire said it was a day he had longed for—"the day in which the nation was commencing its real life" and awakening to the sublime truths of its founders. The Senate approved

---

* The Act to Encourage Immigration established a commissioner of immigration in the State Department, who was to circulate information in European consuls and annually report to Congress. It also set up an office in New York to protect immigrants against frauds and facilitated the purchase of railroad tickets (paid for by the newcomers) to regions needing labor.

the amendment overwhelmingly. It faced a stiffer challenge in the House due to opposition from Democrats, one of whom, from New York, declared that slavery was the optimal condition of the Negro.

Lincoln wasn't involved in the debate, but ten days later, when he spoke in Baltimore, emancipation was on his mind. The occasion was the launching of a "sanitary fair" to raise money for sick and wounded soldiers.* Glancing at the detachment of troops present, the President observed that, when the war commenced, Baltimore was so ardently secessionist that Union soldiers could not safely enter it. Noting that the city was part of "a far wider change," he switched his focus to the gradual dislodgment of slavery, not only prospectively by the amendment or by his proclamation, neither of which he mentioned, but by the thousands of Blacks who were fleeing their overseers. "When the war began, three years ago, neither party, nor any man, expected it would last til now," he said. "Neither did any anticipate that domestic slavery would be much affected by the war." These remarks confirm the only plausible interpretation of the war's beginnings: when Lincoln had given the order to resupply Fort Sumter, he did not have a notion of uprooting southern slavery. But the war's horrors had surpassed all bets, and his purposes had evolved.

Lincoln spoke of slavery, as he often did, as an *economic* system that cheated men of the fruits of their labor and divided the American people.

> We all declare for liberty; but in using the same word we do not all mean the same thing. With some the word liberty may mean for each man to do as he pleases with himself, and the product of his labor; while with others the same word may mean for some men to do as they please with other men, and the product of other men's labor. Here are two, not only different, but incompatible things, called by the same name—liberty.

---

* Sanitary fairs were held across the North to support the U.S. Sanitary Commission (for which Strong served as treasurer) and other relief organizations. The abolitionist author Louisa May Alcott served as a Sanitary Commission nurse. Her poem "The Sanitary Fair" paid homage to nurses who cared for soldiers "even while they mourn."

Lincoln referred to God as the ultimate arbiter of these disputes. One more thing that had evolved was Lincoln's sense of humility as a mortal man. More and more, as the casualties mounted, he ascribed the war's terrible toll to the unseen purposes of the Almighty.

Congress was not in so humble a mood. The war had sanctified the federal purpose, and to Republican eyes, virtually any federal action served the military objective. National and martial aims had merged— abolition, war finance, immigration. In promoting a larger state, Congress was also more willing to advance the interests of capital—to partner with business, as long as business advanced the national agenda. These Republicans seemed less the prairie rebels of their origins and more the party of the eastern business establishment.

A prime example was Chase's bid to amend the National Banking Act. Chase framed his crusade in Republican terms, arguing that the country's money ought to be a national concern. However, the politically powerful state banks still outnumbered national banks by a wide margin. Those in the east were prospering and had no incentive to convert. In fact, the higher interest rates permitted by some states provided an incentive *not* to convert.

The job of recruiting state banks fell to Hugh McCulloch, the Indiana-bred comptroller of the federal system. McCulloch was an exceptionally prudent banker, intent on keeping National Banking free of what he called "adventurous speculators." Under McCulloch's cautious stewardship, the system made slow progress. By the end of 1863, only a hundred or so national banks had formed, mostly small ones. These hardy pioneers had issued only $4 million worth of bank notes—a laughable sum for a supposedly national currency.

New York banks posed the biggest obstacle to reform. Business was good and the city's financial titans were disinclined to change.* In the west, banks were tempted to convert so they could issue the new currency—a means of borrowing—whereas, in New York, with its

---

* In the decade prior to the war, the New York banks processed an average of $22 million of clearings daily; by 1864, volume had soared to $115 million.

monied population, banks were able to borrow by taking deposits (as they do today).

Most important, the New Yorkers saw National Banking as a threat. Institutions in the city acted as banker to the nation by taking deposits from larger banks outside New York and lending these funds to the stock market. Under National Banking, banks in large cities were required to keep, as a reserve, a quarter of their assets *in their vaults*. A similar, if less onerous, restriction applied to rural banks, known as "country banks." Funds that were frozen in local vaults would not be available for deposit in New York. Thus, the new system could upset Gotham's role as the primary funnel for the country's capital.

Duly alarmed, the New Yorkers actively conspired to stop National Banking. In September 1863, Augustus Ely Silliman, president of Merchants' Bank, one of the largest in the city, circulated an incendiary manifesto to his peers, imploring them to reject National Bank Notes. Silliman thundered, "Let the Associated Banks in the three great cities of New York, Philadelphia, and Boston decline all recognition of these [national] institutions." Refusing to deal in the new notes was patently subversive. As the New Yorkers understood, without the participation of the country's financial center, National Banking was dead in its tracks.

Chase promptly counterattacked. The Treasury secretary inquired whether the Cookes, who had organized a pair of national banks, one in Philadelphia and one in Washington, might start one in New York City. Jay Cooke, always happy to do a favor for Chase, quickly raised $5 million, a formidable sum, largely from outside the city, in start-up capital. "New York opposes the scheme," Jay breezily informed his brother, "but we will triumph over them."

Their position strengthened by Cooke's new bank, Chase and McCulloch issued a threat: the Treasury would deposit federal funds only in *national* banks. This put a scare into the Gothamites, who sensed that the momentum was shifting. As one of them warned, "They think they can now get along without us." New York bankers now switched tactics. With legislation to amend the system moving through the

House Ways and Means Committee, the New Yorkers offered their cooperation as the price for influence. McCulloch and Representative Samuel Hooper, who was drafting the bill, found themselves in delicate negotiations in which the aim was to offer just enough, and no more, to entice New York into the system. Significantly, Chase's draconian plan—to eliminate the state notes—was shelved. As one historian noted, these negotiations were no longer mainly about war finance; they would have consequences "far beyond the end of the Civil War."

What Wall Street wanted for the future was to be the nation's depository. Warning of the dangers of "a vast moneyed power," Representative John Steele, a Democrat, sounded like a reincarnation of Andrew Jackson. Hooper, a Boston Republican, was similarly wary of "an immense accumulation of . . . funds" in New York. The Hooper bill was far too restrictive for Wall Street, and the Senate followed Hooper's lead. However, over the first weekend in May, Chase and McCulloch buttonholed Sherman, the pivotal senator on the Finance Committee. They surely argued that without more give, the system would lose New York and probably fail. Sherman promptly flipped and submitted a new bill. This one strengthened Gotham's edge by preserving its access to the country's capital. Writ large, Sherman's flip was a recognition that for any national system to operate efficiently, funds had to flow—and the natural destination could only be Wall Street. Reserve requirements were reduced, meaning that more of the balances of banks in the interior could be siphoned to New York. The Bank of Commerce won a special plum—a clause onto itself—excusing its shareholders from a noxious provision subjecting them to double liability.* McCulloch wrung from Chase a trivial-seeming but actually important concession: the Treasury would allow banks that converted to keep their names. A rose was not always a rose.

---

* Under double liability, when a bank fails, shareholders are required to put up additional capital.

The framework for National Banking was now in place. If the old system suffered from chaotic dispersion, the new one would be anchored firmly on Wall Street. As the historian David Gische put it, the National Banking Act of 1864—enacted in a party-line Republican vote—"gave legal status to the pyramiding of reserves." New York banks would finish the war in a far stronger position than before, poised to dominate finance during the Gilded Age.

The Pacific railroad posed many of the same questions as banking: How involved should the federal government be, and with what support to business? But the rail was far more a bedrock Republican issue, in particular for Lincoln. As a young attorney, he had ridden the Eighth Judicial Circuit on horseback and horse and buggy, an endurance test stretching hundreds of miles across rutted roads and rushing streams through the small towns of central Illinois. But he had practiced long enough to see great changes. By the late 1850s, Lincoln could reach every county seat by rail, a technological improvement that he sought to extend over the whole of the United States.

By the time of his presidential run, the transcontinental rail was central to Lincoln's vision of what government could accomplish. Like the vast majority of Americans, he had never been to California nor even to the Rocky Mountains. Visiting Council Bluffs, Iowa, the prospective eastern terminus, in 1859, Lincoln had remarked, "There is nothing more important before the nation than the building of the railroad to the Pacific Coast." Since the 1862 legislation, he had fixed the site of the terminus and given the project hearty encouragement. He told one of the promoters that if they could hurry the road to completion he, Lincoln, would ride it after he retired from the White House, adding that this journey would make his signing of the bill the proudest achievement of his life.

But two years later, the transcontinental rail existed almost exclusively on paper. By the spring of 1864, thirty-one miles had been completed in California, but over more than seventeen hundred miles of desolate prairie and soaring Rockies, nothing. The project spooked investors. Costs remained prohibitive; inflation had raised the price of supplies, and the war had raised the price of labor.

The Union Pacific Railroad Company had obtained the required number of investors thanks only to under-the-table payments from Thomas Durant, the stock promoter who controlled the management. And although the Union Pacific had some illustrious directors, none of the major industrialists of the era had been willing to invest.* This is not so surprising—established capital rarely bets on the new thing. Its would-be rival, the Union Pacific, Eastern Division, which was to build through Kansas, was in even worse shape. This feeder line still entertained hopes of supplanting the main branch, but it was controlled by the roguish Samuel Hallett (who had been mixed up in the Chase campaign). Hallett and his partner, General John Frémont (now inactive in the army), had been squabbling over control, leaving the corporation mired in lawsuits. "I hardly know what to do with the Union Pacific R.R. Especially the Kansas branch, as we have no authentic suggestions from the Genl [Frémont]," noted Thaddeus Stevens, who was chair of the House Committee on the Railroad and, as it happened, an investor in the Kansas line. "Indeed, we yet do not know which is the true company."†

Perhaps the best thing going for the upstart branch was that Durant was also an investor in it. The wily doctor was able to argue that both lines—the entire transcontinental project—needed congressional help. Cornelius Bushnell, a Union Pacific director, met with Lincoln, and according to Bushnell's testimony nearly a decade later, the President said his experience was that every railroad attempted in the west had failed before it was completed. He urged the company to seek ample

---

* The directors included John Dix, the former Treasury secretary, and J. Edgar Thomson, president of the Pennsylvania Railroad. Another was the Mormon crusader Brigham Young.

† In a brutal coda, a former railroad engineer wrote to Lincoln that the Kansas line was being shoddily constructed. Hallett got wind of it and had the man whipped, severely. On July 27, 1864, the man caught up with Hallett in Wyandotte County, Kansas, aimed a Spencer rifle at Hallett's back, and shot him dead.

federal assistance. Bushnell's account cannot be verified, but it jibes with Lincoln's lifelong support of internal improvements. Sherman captured the spirit of the Republican commitment when he said, "I am willing to appropriate *any* amount necessary to aid in building a Pacific railroad."

But Durant, who operated out of a suite at the Willard Hotel in Washington, was taking no chances. The promoter hired a well-connected lobbyist, Joseph Stewart, who was entrusted with $250,000 (equivalent to more than $4 million today) to get the law amended. Stewart never accounted for how he spent this fantastic sum, but much of it was devoted to placating the querulous investors in the Kansas line.

The earlier law had granted developers 6400 acres of public land for each mile of track. Given the risks, investors wanted more. Aside from increasing the acreage, Durant had two main objectives: sweetening the terms of the federal bonds and loosening various restrictions. Due to the fear (well-grounded) that Congress would cave to the companies, the legislation was extremely controversial. For instance, there was strong sentiment in the Senate that the government should guarantee the bonds. Elihu Washburne, a Republican congressman from Illinois, countered that the Union Pacific operators were "bad . . . unprincipled men" and, therefore, the public should have nothing to do with them. Washburne noted that the reputable directors were removed from the operations "while the real management is in the hands of a set of Wall Street stock-jobbers who are using this great engine for their own private ends." Washburne was hardly wrong. He urged that Congress save its resources for winning the war.

Stevens defended the probity of the Union Pacific, a bit too emphatically. He said, almost wittily, "I believe the company is composed of pure men." Early in his career, Stevens had not been above directing legislative support for a railroad near his iron forge, and in Congress he had consistently pushed for higher iron tariffs. One understands why a 1942 biography of this champion of antislavery, in many ways a heroic figure, bore the suggestive subtitle *A Story of Ambition*. In the spring of 1864, as Congress was amending the railroad act, he unabashedly worked to quash a provision to allow the rail to use cheaper imported iron.

Legislating in one's self-interest was not unusual; the test was whether one pursued the public good. By Stevens's lights, the chief public interest was building the road. As with Lincoln, he thought the railroad "one of the greatest enterprises of the age." Stevens rejected the Senate formulation of a federal guarantee, which would expose the government to potential losses. Stevens preferred a more modern approach— sweetening the pot for private capital *if* the rail succeeded. He was willing to double the land grant because, as he pointed out, without a railroad most of the land was worthless.

In a sarcastic rebuke to Washburne, Old Thad pointed out, "If the bill passes . . . the Government is not one dollar poorer, at any rate until after the war is ended." The bill gave the companies nothing "except some little land, and as to that land, I ask the gentleman [Washburne] what he is going to do with it, how he is going to feed soldiers on it?"

> The gentleman lives in the West, and knows all about this matter. He knows that after we get beyond the one hundredth degree of longitude the land is hardly worth holding. . . . When you get to the other side of the Rocky Mountains, to what is called the plains, you find a barren valley that bears nothing but sage of the bitterest kind, and that never can be made fertile. Then you come upon the Sierra Nevada, and when you pass over that range of mountains you find no land worthy of anything until you get into California.

Stevens's priorities mirrored those of most Americans, who had heard the tales of glittering gold and wanted the railroad built. But the plums for developers were richer than Stevens let on. They consisted not only in doubling the land to 12,800 acres per mile and, now, granting title to any coal and iron on the land, but also in permitting the

Union Pacific to issue first-mortgage bonds (thus relegating the government bonds to a second lien). This enhanced the Union Pacific's credit. Furthermore, bonds were to be delivered on a faster basis. Stevens aimed to protect the public by increasing the number of directors appointed by the President. Perhaps he suspected that such safeguards were insufficient. The congressman refused to print the final conference report, preferring to deliver an oral version of the changes, which he summarized, with masterly laconicism, as "all in favor of the United States."

Congress preserved the Union Pacific's position as the favored line. However, it opened a door to serious corruption within the Union Pacific. The key to the line's vulnerability, and to much future misery, was that Durant, who was not persuaded that the railroad would ever be profitable, was hatching a scheme to make a killing from its construction. Durant and a promoter named George Francis Train, who had his fingers in the drafting of the bill, were establishing a parallel company to build the road, owned by many of the same investors and run by the same Durant. The theory was that this shadow company could reap a quick return by billing for construction costs, and billing at inflated levels. This company was called the Crédit Mobilier.* Congress, in its haste to amend the act without either reading or hearing the terms of the amendment, did not impose requirements for open bidding (nor even that the railroad accept the lowest bids). Stevens also rammed through legislation to charter the Northern Pacific Railway, a speculative route through the thinly populated northwest, also with federal land grants. As the historian Heather Cox Richardson has pointed out, by chartering a road within state lines, Congress significantly expanded the federal

---

* Crédit Mobilier was one of the worst scandals in U.S. history. In 1872, during President Grant's first term, it was revealed that the railroad had been crippled by vastly inflated billings, accompanied by payoffs to more than a dozen congressmen. Schuyler Colfax, Speaker of the House in 1864 and vice president when the scandal came to light, and Henry Wilson, elected that year to succeed Colfax, were among those accused of receiving bribes; so was the current Speaker of the House, James Blaine. Thaddeus Stevens, by then deceased, was not implicated.

government's mandate. The two railroad acts put the government firmly into partnership with business.

As the Republicans approached their party convention, they had legislative accomplishments aplenty but neither financial stability nor momentum in the field. Belying their National Union brand, the Republicans were far from united. Greeley's *Tribune* had continued to mutter that the Republicans would be better served by nominating Chase or a Radical general. The party was badly split over the shape and speed of the looming Reconstruction of the South. The Radicals insisted that Congress control the process, and they wanted to subject disloyal states to a tougher, and lengthier, test for readmission. Lincoln favored a quicker, less onerous process. Particularly offensive to the Radicals, the new constitution in Louisiana extended suffrage only to whites. Although slavery was abolished, at the behest of Lincoln's commander, Nathaniel Banks, Blacks in Louisiana were being forced to work at wages set by the government—not exactly "freedom."

The party chasm flared into the open when a handful of Radicals gathered in Cleveland and nominated Frémont (who was also busy with his railroad) on a third-party ticket. The tension resurfaced at the convention, held in Baltimore in June. Thaddeus Stevens strove for a plank affirming that the southern states were legally out of the Union and would be treated as conquered fiefs. But Stevens failed. The platform was penned by Henry Raymond, publisher of *The New York Times* and Lincoln's campaign biographer. It avoided the forbidden topic of land reform and focused on the (safer) Whiggish economic planks—the Pacific rail, immigration, a "national currency."

Raymond's text unambiguously declared that slavery had caused the rebellion. However—an important distinction—it did not say slavery caused "the war."

To the generation of 1860, the North had waged war to keep the Union intact. Slavery led to secession, disunion led to war. But now, as Robert J. Breckinridge, honorary president of the convention, observed, they were "prepared to go further." The war had acquired a larger purpose. When a plank endorsing the Thirteenth Amendment (still pending in the House) was introduced, the convention broke into thunderous cheers and the waving of hats, a moment joyfully recorded by the abolitionist William Lloyd Garrison, who covered the convention for *The Liberator*, the newspaper he had founded thirty years earlier. The nearly six hundred delegates ratified Lincoln's policy of pursuing the war to an unconditional surrender and renominated Lincoln by acclamation.

The party nominated Andrew Johnson as Lincoln's running mate. No evidence survives that he was Lincoln's preference—but it seems likely. Johnson was the only senator from a seceding state who had remained loyal, and it was like Lincoln to favor a Tennessee Democrat to broaden the ticket's appeal. Stevens warned the President that Johnson was a "rank demagogue" and a "scoundrel." Lincoln stuck with him; it would prove to be a mistake.

In a portent of the power of electronic communications, the American Telegraph Company transmitted news bulletins directly from the convention. Still, the party adhered to custom and sent a delegation to Washington to personally notify Lincoln of his selection. He humbly expressed gratitude and went on record, for the first time, in support of the amendment abolishing slavery. He understatedly told his visitors, "I now perceive its importance and embrace it."

The convention was held under the shadow of some of the grimmest fighting of the war. The Army of the Potomac, commanded by General George Meade and supervised by Grant, was "grinding away" in Virginia—not isolated engagements but relentless carnage. Captain Oliver Wendell Holmes Jr., reflecting on the ceaseless brutality, said, "Many a man has gone crazy since this campaign began." Northern newspapers, eager to sell extra editions, professed to see the end in sight. The *New York Herald* published the boldface headline GRANT!—beneath which it exulted, "Things are approaching . . . a glorious victory." Lincoln fretted that such bulletins were fostering unrealistic expectations. And, indeed, heavy rains slowed Grant's advance, giving the Rebels time to gather a formidable opposing army. As the Union momentum stalled, the public

tasted the bitterest fruit: disappointment. The battle of attrition produced appalling casualties. Inevitably, morale sagged. The strain on the
President was very great. George Templeton Strong traveled on Sanitary
Commission business to the War Department in May 1864, and while
waiting to see Stanton, he caught a telling glimpse of the chief. In
Strong's words, "the long, lean, lank figure of Uncle Abraham suddenly
appeared at the door. [He] uttered no word, but beckoned to Stanton in
a ghostly manner with one sepulchral forefinger, and they disappeared."
When their conference ended, Strong saw Lincoln in the telegraph room,
grimly waiting for dispatches—which would report a violent counterattack by Lee. By the time Strong returned to New York, a gloom had
settled on Wall Street. Strong reported, "the feeling downtown today is
despondent and bad." Contrary to recent suppositions, "the 'backbone' of
the 'Rebellion' is not 'broke at last.' . . . Lee still shews [sic] fight."

With financial markets hostage to the war, Salmon Chase entered
an especially difficult time. John Cisco had predicted that nothing but
a sustained advance by Grant would check the gold price; he was proving correct. As Grant's progress slowed, gold speculation reignited.
Chase confided to the governor of Ohio, "My anxiety is very great." By
the end of May, gold had rebounded to 180, recouping much of the
ground lost during the Treasury's selling spree. Chase responded predictably, ordering Cooke and Cisco to resume the gold selling. The
Treasury secretary was also harried by Gideon Welles, the dissatisfied
navy secretary, who complained that his department was "seriously embarrassed" by the want of coin to meet requisitions. Still worse news for
Chase—Cisco announced that, owing to poor health, he would retire at
the end of June. Chase replied with genuine, if awkwardly expressed,
affection for his lieutenant: "Your letter of yesterday," he wrote on May
24, "gave me the first real pain I have experienced from any act of yours
since we have been connected by official relations."

By June, Grant had doggedly advanced to Cold Harbor, within ten
miles of Richmond. On June 3, seeking to establish a base on the James

River, he ordered a direct assault on fortified Rebel earthworks. It resulted in a lopsided slaughter. Over a twelve-day siege, the Union suffered a horrific thirteen thousand casualties. In his memoirs, Grant would regret the attack, of which he admitted, "no advantage whatever was gained to compensate for the heavy loss we sustained." Lincoln stuck by his determined general, but after Cold Harbor, financial markets turned completely despairing. By June 9, gold had risen to 197. "People are blue," said Strong, adding drily, "They have found somehow that Grant will never get into Richmond after all."

In desperation, Chase began to ponder a foreign loan, which due to his pride was difficult for him. He admitted, "It galls me." The truth was that London was no more eager to lend than was New York. The Treasury secretary had been struggling to sell barely $10 million of the ten-forty bonds per *month*. His expenses were running at more than $70 million a month. He was even considering heeding Lincoln's advice and raising the interest rate on U.S. bonds. Meanwhile, finding a replacement for Cisco was presenting a serious problem. The job of assistant treasurer in New York was a significant patronage plum, and Chase's earlier battle over the New York port had hardened party bosses against accepting another Chase loyalist. Under a mounting strain from the combined pressure of the gold price, fiscal pressures, and Cisco's impending departure, Chase cried out, "The price of gold must & shall come down or I'll quit and let somebody else try."

In June, Lincoln visited a sanitary fair in Philadelphia. Fifteen thousand locals thronged to the festivities; the President spent two hours shaking hands amid a swarming crowd. At an evening banquet, he praised Grant, who, he noted approvingly, had reached a position "from whence he will never be dislodged until Richmond is taken." The guests cheered. Lincoln also acknowledged the war's toll on the nation's purse—it had "deranged business . . . destroyed property . . . produced a national debt and taxation unprecedented, at least in this country." When he alluded to the war's cost in human lives, the President found his deepest muse, somberly observing, "It has carried mourning to almost every home, until it can almost be said that 'the heavens are hung in black.'"

Grant crossed the James River on June 15; two days later, Strong joyfully reported the taking of Petersburg. The report turned out to be premature. After a series of failed assaults, Grant's troops were forced to dig trenches, the beginning of a lengthy siege. With the Union's progress halted, and gold rising, Chase became frantic. In a psychological sense, he was also a prisoner. He railed against the speculators; he berated Congress for failing to approve his tax with an air of one whose patience has been unmercifully tried by having to depend on men less clear-sighted than he. "Why won't Congress see it?" he wailed to a businessman in Boston. He urged Senator Fessenden to consider a tax of 10 or even 20 percent on incomes. Publicly, and for dramatic effect, Chase said he would submit to a tax of 50 percent! He insisted to friends in New York, "There is not the slightest reason for any rise in the price of gold," as if the market required Chase's validation.

With Congress bickering over the tax, the Treasury secretary's bill to ban gold futures was brought to the floor. Sherman, doing Chase's bidding, said the aim was to prevent "gambling." Even members who voted aye realized it was a desperate attempt to interfere with supply and demand. Thomas Treadwell Davis, a New York congressman, sardonically proposed an amendment to suspend not only the laws of trade but also the law of gravity. The *New York Evening Post* called the bill the work of "ignoramuses." Still, it passed, and on June 17, Lincoln signed it. The gold room in New York was shuttered; similar restrictions were placed on foreign currency. But trading off-exchange continued. By June 21, gold had risen to 200, meaning the greenback had fallen to fifty cents. The deeply discounted greenback represented an enormous opportunity for anyone who believed that the U.S. Treasury would, eventually, redeem its paper at full value. At the moment, though, it seemed a repudiation of Chase's years of labor. The trading ban wasn't helping; it was hurting. Bankers begged the government to let the market function. Chase could not see it. An unhappy Strong despaired, "Pauperism probably awaits me."

Chase suffered a further embarrassment in international markets. As cotton climbed to $1.20 per pound, twelve times its prewar price, the price of the Confederate cotton bonds (the Erlanger bonds) rose in step. London investors mentally converted the bonds into their value in cotton, even though the cotton itself remained stockpiled in warehouses about the South. Over the first half of 1864, as European interest in the bonds revived, they rallied from 37 percent of par to, in June, more than 60, then to more than 70. As if in a topsy-turvy universe, Richmond's bonds traded higher than Chase's greenback. Investors were, remarkably, untroubled by any thought that after the war ended, when they planned to take possession of the cotton, there might be no Confederate government to deliver it.*

It is true that the Erlanger issue was small. Still, it tarnished Chase's image to see his paper trade at a discount to Richmond's. "I am daily more dissatisfied with the Treasury management," Welles wrote acidly. "Chase has not the sagacity, knowledge and ability of a financier. He is a man of expedients." Agonizingly, the greenback kept falling. Gold surged to 230, a greenback equivalent of only forty-three cents. A delegation of New York financiers called on Chase and begged him to rescind the ineffectual gold-trading ban. Quite quickly—June 22, or five days after passage of the shortsighted ban—a bill was introduced for repeal. The gold price slightly receded. But repeal was far from a certain tonic, and Congress was mired in weightier discussions over the tax, tariff, and railroad bills. And Chase had other problems.

Cisco, who had served every president since Franklin Pierce, was a remarkably able functionary. Chase had presumed, given how closely they worked together, that he would have free rein in choosing a successor. Lincoln had other ideas. The moderate wing of the party was smart-

---

* One credulous English investor in the cotton bonds explained that "an able international lawyer" had assured him that "whenever peace came the debts of both belligerents must be recognized."

ing over the Treasury secretary's habit of hiring Radicals loyal to him. The President could not afford to split the party; moreover, he was tired of Chase's stubbornness on patronage questions. Just weeks earlier, Chase had again resisted removing Hiram Barney, the New York port collector (to whom Seward had offered an ambassadorship), prompting Lincoln to sigh, "Well, I backed down again." The President had similarly relented during a squabble over the San Francisco port the previous year.

This time, Lincoln told his Treasury secretary to submit any name that was acceptable to Edwin D. Morgan, senator from the Empire State and chair of the Republican National Committee. A onetime small grocer, Morgan had made a fortune as a merchant and investor. In politics, Morgan was the face of the party's moderate faction. He was no great intellect, but he was a capable organizer and loyal to Lincoln.

On June 27, Chase called on Morgan. The senator offered several names, but they were not to Chase's liking. No doubt, Chase was more than a little distraught over the prospect of losing Cisco. He said he wanted to appoint Maunsell Field, his assistant Treasury secretary in Washington. Morgan understood that Field's chief qualification would be personal loyalty to Chase; he begged the Treasury secretary not to submit Field's name. That evening, Chase did so anyway. He did not realize how stubbornly he was behaving. Lincoln, the most compromising of men, was at wit's end. He had spoken with Morgan, and when he saw Chase's recommendation, he knew it would topple another "beehive."

The President wrote Chase, "I can not, without much embarrassment, make this appointment." His patience obviously tried, Lincoln said—again—"it will really oblige me" if Chase were to pick a name acceptable to Morgan. Chase, however, had fallen into the trap of confusing a personal crusade with a matter of principle. In his diary, he scribbled, "Oh, for more faith & clearer sight!" Chase now asked the President for a personal interview. Lincoln masterfully declined— because, as he put it, "the difficulty does not, in the main part, lie within the range of a conversation between you and me." The President added that it had been "a great burden" to retain Barney at the port. Selecting Field would prompt "an open revolt" within the party.

It was now late afternoon on June 28—two days before Cisco's scheduled retirement. Refusing to back down, Chase telegraphed Cisco, "begging" him to consider temporarily staying on. Advising Lincoln of his latest gambit, he added that, if Cisco declined, Field would remain the "best qualified" and "I trust you will act without delay." This was extremely insolent of Chase.

Cisco promptly telegraphed his reply: he could not resist Chase's "appeal," and would temporarily defer retirement. With a sigh of relief, Chase relayed the welcome news to Lincoln. This was June 29. But he belatedly sensed—perhaps from the President's refusal to see him—that a coolness had entered their relations. In his message to Lincoln he also enclosed a letter of resignation—his fourth such offer—which he presumed would be rejected with earnest avowals of Lincoln's renewed affections.

Even amid this melodrama, Chase was waging his great battle to defray the ever rising costs of the war. It filled him with angst. The public debt had swelled—it would be $1.74 billion when the books closed in twenty-four hours, up from $1.1 billion only a year earlier. "The day has been one of great anxiety and distress," he lamented miserably. He dusted off some of the old five-twenty bonds, but the market was unmoved. He played for time by paying contractors with temporary certificates. Purchases of artillery horses had been delayed—vendors would not accept the government's paper—and pay to the army was in arrears. Although Congress was closing in on the tax and tariff bills, Chase was writing the committee chairs, Stevens and Fessenden, and consulting with Representative Morrill, on the need for an *additional* revenue measure, which the Treasury secretary had in fact prepared. He huddled with the Senate Finance Committee. But the military stall was wrecking his plans. It sent the gold price soaring to 238—a record. Traders were dazzled by the stubbornness of Lee's forces. *The Times* of London exclaimed, "The Confederates give no sign of yielding." The speculators were correct inasmuch as the Rebels were firmly entrenched, but they failed to appreciate that the Rebs were immobilized, hemmed in by the James River and the capital. Grant's army had freedom to maneuver.

Lincoln spent Thursday, June 30, receiving visitors and signing a rush of bills habitually churned out at the end of session. He was not called to lunch until three p.m., which he later ascribed to the fact that "my wife happened to be in the way." As he was waiting, his stomach growling, he determined to answer Chase's letter, with its positive news on Cisco, but which Lincoln had yet to finish. He picked up the enclosure—but as he did, another leaf wafted out of the envelope. The President turned and saw, to his surprise, that Chase had submitted his resignation. Without reflection, but with considerable relief, Lincoln accepted.

> Your resignation of the office of Secretary of the Treasury, sent me yesterday, is accepted. Of all I have said in commendation of your ability and fidelity, I have nothing to unsay; and yet you and I have reached a point of mutual embarrassment in our official relation which it seems can not be overcome, or longer sustained, consistently with the public service.

When Lincoln's thunderbolt reached the Treasury, Schuckers, Chase's assistant, burst out of the inner office exclaiming, "We no longer have a Secretary!" Chase's first reaction was shock; his second was self-pity. Reading Lincoln's gracious words, he fumed, "I had found a good deal of embarrassment from him but what he had found from me I could not imagine, unless it had been created by my unwillingness to have offices distributed as spoils or benefits with more regard to the claims of divisions, factions, cliques and individuals, than to fitness of selection." He added bitterly, "He had never given me the active and earnest support I was entitled to." Chase's frustration then turned to fantasy—had the President only asked, he would have "cheerfully withdrawn" his resignation. He could see only "one reason" for Lincoln's eagerness to dismiss him—"that I am too earnest, too antislavery, and, say, too radical."

As he cleaned out his papers, the fifty-six-year-old lawyer observed that his "official life" was closing, but Chase didn't truly believe that. He was already thinking that Lincoln might tap him for the chief justiceship, if the position, occupied by the octogenarian Roger Taney, finally became vacant—or even that an opening might yet emerge in the presidential race. He continued to fret—up to his last moments at the Treasury—that Congress had yet to raise taxes. Only to a friend, the Radical publisher William Cullen Bryant, did Chase relax and permit himself a fitting valedictory. "My grand objects," he reflected, "have been, first, to provide for the vast demands of the war, and second, the substitution of a national bank-note currency for State bank-note currency, and through the last resumption of specie payments, and so permanence and strength in our financial order."

The capital was unnerved by the sudden news of Chase's exit. Hooper was so depressed he did not see how the financings could be done. Gold soared to 245. Lincoln, as if eager to be rid of any and all Treasury business, hurriedly picked a successor. His choice, David Tod, a former governor of Ohio, was supremely unqualified. Fortunately, Tod refused. Lincoln next sent Pitt Fessenden's name to the Senate. The crotchety Maine senator also refused, but the President told him, "If you decline you must do it in the open, for I shall not recall the nomination." Fessenden, "utterly exhausted" by his labors, accepted with reluctance. He hardly had Chase's energy, but in financial circles he was a known quantity. Official Washington—also the gold market—greeted his confirmation with relief.

Fourteen

Staggering Transformation

A centralization of power, such as
HAMILTON might have eulogised as
magnificent.

— *The New York Times*

SALMON CHASE DEPARTED just too soon to see his labors bear fruit. On the Treasury secretary's final day, Lincoln signed a monumental tax hike. Finally persuaded by Chase's unrelenting pleas, Congress adopted a graduated income tax—with earnings above $10,000 subject to a stiff 10 percent levy. This was the tonic Chase had been seeking.* The bill gave a tremendous boost to the Union's finances. During Chase's last year, internal taxes—not even a line item before the war—had furnished $110 million. Under the new law, the take would double. As a companion bill, Congress enacted a steep increase in the tariff, raising the average duty to 47 percent. This tariff was a Republi-

---

* The bill created a three-tier structure, beginning with a 5 percent tax for incomes above $600. Many other taxes were raised or imposed: on "manufactures and productions," on ships, barges and stages, on theaters, operas, and circuses, on auctions and brokers, licenses and breweries, spirits, and more. Sherman said, "It provided for an increase of all internal taxes contained in previous laws, and added many new objects of taxation, so as to embrace nearly every source of revenue provided for by American or English laws."

can gift to business and a veritable assault on free trade. However, the combined revenue produced by the tax and the tariff (the latter paid in coin) brought the North a degree of self-reliance the South could only dream of. Over the entire war, the Union supplied fully 21 percent of the federal budget from taxes, decisively above the 5 to 6 percent mustered by the Confederacy and virtually identical to the 22 percent share achieved later, during World War I.

A t the end of its session, Congress sought to build on the Union's strength by authorizing $400 million in additional debt. According to Senator Sherman, the United States could now tap "almost unlimited sources of revenue." Fessenden's challenge was to persuade investors to buy his notes and bonds.

Economic signs were auspicious—indeed, industry in the North was thriving. Iron and coal production were blazing to new heights, and there was a spike in the rate of business incorporation. New mines opened in the west and prospectors jockeyed for oil leases in Pennsylvania. Remarkably, despite the severe decline in cotton textiles, total manufacturing was greater in 1864 than at the start of the war. Exports were vibrant, demonstrating that American industry was capable of competing in a global market. Economic growth suggested new possibility for finance in pooling the country's capital. Twenty-seven-year-old J. P. Morgan tested this premise by launching a new banking firm on Wall Street. Farther uptown, New York opened the lower section of Central Park, a vast, sculpted meadow that rivaled the civic purposes of Paris. Commercial technology also advanced. Grover & Baker Company boasted two "distinct" sewing machines for fine and coarse fabrics—available, thanks to the company's liberal credit arrangements, to "the poorest sewing girl."

The North's economic vitality gave it an unimpeachable edge. The mystery is that Fessenden could not seem to exploit it. The Union's advantages were many—financial, economic, technological. Yet markets were not quite attuned to the Union's strength. Prices of government securities skidded lower, while investors were unwilling to lend, or nearly so. Their reluctance is better understood when one considers the truly vast scale of the Treasury's needs. Thus far, the United States had expended more money during the war than in all of the years prior since George Washington's first inauguration. Its interest expense alone was more than the entire prewar budget. Since the government had to borrow to survive, financing the Treasury remained something of a confidence game. The very profusion of Union paper, some thirty-two varieties of notes, bonds, and other instruments, gave it the casual appearance of a bankrupt. In the long view, this appearance was misleading. A country's economic strength hinges not on its paper but on its productivity.

But northern investors had trouble looking past the war, and the battle news was not auspicious. A week into Fessenden's tenure, the Rebel General Jubal Early, having stormed the Shenandoah, stunned the Union by charging across the Potomac. Just when northerners were praying for decisive news from Richmond, Rebel troops advanced to within five miles of the White House. A pitched battle was fought within District of Columbia lines; Lincoln witnessed the fighting from Fort Stevens, carelessly exposing himself—in a stovepipe hat—to live fire. The threat to Washington shook morale and caused a panic in the capital and, naturally, in the gold market. (Congress had repealed the gold trading ban after only two weeks.) On July 11, gold spiked to a record 285 ($2.85 in greenbacks for only $1 in gold).

Fessenden by then was in New York, pleading for bank loans. Tapping the banks had been Chase's initial tactic. But the banks had lent their cash to the harvest; Fessenden returned to Washington empty-handed. His next idea was to float a popular loan. Chase had tried that, too. In what could hardly have been a welcome comment, a correspondent upbraided Fessenden, "I am pained to see that you are treading already in the steps of the former Secretary." The truth was that Fessenden had the same tools to work with. Congress had authorized the Treasury to issue notes but the new secretary, fearing inflation, declined to do so. He could have issued more of the popular five-twenty bond, but these paid interest in gold coin, and he was wary of pledging too much gold.

Fessenden, therefore, attempted to market a medium-term note—the three-year seven-thirty instrument that Chase had pushed early in the war. The seven-thirty carried an attractive interest rate (7.3 percent), and though payment was in currency, the notes were ultimately convertible into the gold bonds. Fessenden's thought was that the seven-thirty could sustain the government until, as he hoped, the war ended and investors might convert into longer-term securities. His problem was, he had to sell a lot of them. Not only did he have to finance current needs, he had to refinance old notes that were expiring. He might have done more to tout the investment merits of the seven-thirty, but he chose, rather, to appeal to investors' patriotism. "It is *your war*," he publicly proclaimed, as if scolding the people to do their duty.

Fessenden also consulted with Jay Cooke, who was eager to be reappointed general agent. But Fessenden was aware of the criticism suffered by Chase for having handed Cooke a monopoly. He listened politely and demurred.

Fessenden had been a fiery antislavery orator in the Senate and its leading financial expert. But the war years had wearied him, and he had not developed a close relationship with Lincoln. He had been considering retiring before his appointment, and his chief ambition now was to return to Maine. All July was heavy for him. His bone-dry marriage had ended, before the war, with his wife's death, and he had not recovered from the loss of his son Sam at Bull Run. In the sweltering Washington heat, the new Treasury secretary felt physically incapacitated—overwhelmed by the demands for funds. A correspondent told him gravely, "More depends on you than on either General Grant or Sherman." Such a summons would have thrilled Chase; it caused Fessenden to cringe. The Treasury's debts mounted by the week. The gold price, though receded from its high, hovered in the still dizzying range of 250, a greenback value of only forty cents. Pitt was as powerless against speculation as his predecessor. As a partner of Jay Cooke succinctly put it, Fessenden could not break gold: "Grant must do that." Nearly crippled by fatigue, the unhappy cabinet official wrote to an intimate in Portland, "I sigh for State Street, a sniff of salt air, and a good long talk."

Barely a month into the job and dogged by rumors he was quitting, Fessenden absconded to Maine. He was overjoyed to return to his garden, and he was comforted by his widowed cousin Elizabeth "Lizzy" Warriner, with whom he was increasingly intimate. The sea breezes were a tonic. But he could not shake the feeling of an ever present burden. After a fortnight, he sulkily caught a return train for Washington. It was already clear that sales of the seven-thirty were falling well short of what he needed. As Fessenden alerted Assistant Treasury Secretary George Harrington, "The people are not awake to the urgency of the case."

Investors did not trust the seven-thirties; what they wanted were the gold bonds. Fessenden reckoned that he needed to raise on the order of $3 million per day. He was forced to resort to stopgaps, a series of short-term artifices. He kept his promise not to issue currency—in a technical sense. However, he papered the country with securities that were currency in all but name, including that Chase favorite, the "certificates of indebtedness"—pieces of paper attesting that the holder was owed money by the United States. Meanwhile, he permitted unpaid bills to accumulate and soldiers to go unpaid. According to Harrington, "The pressure for money was unceasing."

Lincoln tried to resuscitate the Union's finances by ramping up efforts to bring cotton out of the South. This long contentious issue heated up in July, when Congress authorized the Treasury secretary to regulate trade in occupied territory, and to purchase products on government account. It was up to Fessenden to rewrite the rules governing this thorny trade, subject to Lincoln's approval.

The President hoped that cotton sales would ease the Union's financial problems. His secretary, John Hay, recorded in his diary, "The President told me yesterday he had a plan for relieving us to a certain extent financially: for the government to take into its own hands the whole cotton trade and . . . sell for Gold." The plan was also intended to restore the country's international balances. Thanks to the absence of cotton exports, the Union's trade balance had steadily declined. The bullion held in New York banks and in the sub-Treasury in New York had also declined, despite the steady production of ore in California. No doubt, Lincoln blamed diminishing gold reserves for the plummeting price of the greenback.* His solution was to reclaim a portion of cotton exports for the Union. He seems to have been overly impressed with the self-serving arguments of the Boston cotton merchant Edward Atkinson, who wrote Lincoln over the summer. Atkinson argued that were the Union to market Dixie's cotton, it would so depress the price that the Rebels would be none the richer.

Union commanders emphatically objected—General William Tecumseh Sherman was to write War Secretary Edwin Stanton that all cotton was "tainted with treason." While northern politicians focused on the financial trouble at home, generals in the field recognized that the South was on the verge of economic collapse. Hoping to hasten the war to a finish, they increasingly resorted to economic warfare—targeting factories and bridges, burning crops, stealing horses and cotton, destroying canal locks. Grant was trying to starve Lee into

---

* Gold movements during the Civil War were a complicated business—more than Lincoln acknowledged and more than may interest the lay reader. From the time the shooting started, large volumes of metal left San Francisco for foreign ports, much of it ultimately reaching China and other countries that were filling the void of southern cotton. Since the United States maintained a positive (though declining) trade balance, one would have expected the gold to return—but through the war, the Union exported significantly more bullion and coin than it imported. Fessenden admitted to being puzzled. "What direction the gold product takes to avoid assay and coinage it is not easy to state," he wrote in 1864. "This diversion of treasure from its usual course [New York] is large. . . . Much of it may be, and probably is, held as undrawn deposits abroad, or used when the market favors." This suggests that, amid the great financial uncertainty of the war, speculators preferred to hold assets overseas rather than in the United States.

submission. In August, the Union general cut the railroad linking Petersburg, Virginia, to Wilmington, North Carolina—a vital blockade-running port. He ordered Major General Philip Sheridan to turn the Shenandoah into "a barren waste," helpfully elaborating that the valley should not be left with sustenance even for crows. (Sheridan complied with brio, destroying crops, tools, barns, and dozens of flour mills.)

While northerners were frustrated with the standoff in Virginia, southerners were stricken by the impoverishment on the home front. "One can almost hear the death-rattle!" exclaimed Mary Chesnut. The rattle was audible in the shops and homes of civilians, who were strained to the point of collapse by the failure of the Confederacy's financial reforms. The new taxes, enacted in February, were already falling short due to popular resistance (aided by some state governors), and by advancing Union armies. Treasury Secretary Memminger was forced to concede that "no material aid will be derived" from taxes that year other than those in kind. Taxes in kind (food seizures) were deeply resented. They highlighted Richmond's priority for provisioning the military. An unidentified Confederate correspondent brutally confirmed this. "The army," he noted, "is abundantly furnished with food. . . . But there is real suffering among the people, and there will be more." This inequity was not sustainable. Memminger resigned—coincidentally, within a fortnight of Chase. Memminger was succeeded by George Trenholm, a sensible choice, since his firm specialized in what was now the South's leading industry—blockade running. He had barely settled into office when Union Admiral David Farragut captured Mobile Bay, one of the South's few significant remaining ports.

With the South so desperate, Union generals were incensed that northern traders were supporting the enemy. The cabinet approved Fessenden's cotton-trading policy, but with serious reservations. Attorney General Edward Bates dolefully surmised that the Union was furnishing the enemy with "the sinews of war." In truth, the cotton trade did help the South. During a two-month stretch in 1864, imports into Wilmington and Charleston supplied nearly nine million pounds of meat, two million pounds of lead, half a million pair of shoes, a like number of pounds of coffee, and twenty-six hundred packages of medicine. They were paid for with cotton profits.

Fessenden was the crucial link, implementing directives that permitted southerners to bring cotton to designated Treasury agents for sale to the United States at a discount to the New York price. There were several problems with this policy. The Treasury had little ability to trace the cotton, whose provenance was usually a Rebel planter. Virtually every sale aided the Confederate government, which now owned much of the cotton directly. On the northern end, cronyism often determined access. Many of the Treasury agents running the trade were corrupt. Confronted with evidence of malfeasance, Fessenden naïvely expressed his shock. Navy Secretary Welles sighed, "Fessenden certainly knows as little of men as Chase."

However, responsibility for the policy wasn't Fessenden's; it was Lincoln's. Some credit is due the President for recognizing that, in economic terms, organized trade would supply the North more efficiently than the black market. And Lincoln was aware that profiteers would capture much of the spoils. But he dismissed such concerns as secondary, breezily concluding, "Let us be thankful that so much good can be got out of pecuniary greed."

The President went out of his way to personally endorse requests for cotton permits, whether as favors to friends or politicos or simply to send supplicants with sob stories on their way. Lincoln's endorsement helped his Illinois confidant, the former senator Orville Browning, as well as Lincoln's longtime friend Leonard Swett. Similarly, Lincoln urged military protection, within the regulations, for James Hughes of Indiana—"a worthy gentleman and a friend, whom I wish to oblige." The President had to deal with supplicants even within his own family. He endorsed a permit in the west to trade "all kinds of Merchandize" for a poor relative by marriage of Nancy Hanks, his late mother.

More surprisingly, and more questionably, Lincoln requested safe transport for James Harrison, a Missourian also endorsed by Attorney

General Bates, "to pass our military lines, once and return, at his plea-sure" even though Harrison's application divulged that he was making "arrangements with the Confederate authorities to bring out cotton." In other words, Lincoln and Bates were assisting a cotton trader who was openly dealing with Rebel officials.

Lincoln also made life difficult for generals trying to tighten en-forcement. He complained to General Edward Canby that he was get-ting "frequent complaints" that people trying to trade in accordance with Treasury regulations were being "frustrated" by civil or military authorities. Lincoln asked Canby to stop the "abuses"—meaning, to let the cotton through. Another Union general, Napoleon J. T. Dana, or-dered a colonel in Memphis to investigate whether applicants were "bona fide" or "mere speculators and adventurers." Dana's order prompted a quick rebuke from the chief.

Lincoln had no wish to prolong the war. He hoped to normalize a system that was veering on lawlessness. He was correct that haphazard enforcement by military authorities often enlarged the opportunities for corruption. As he explained to Fessenden in September, "extensive re-gions lay open where neither party was in possession . . . but the mo-ment the cotton appeared . . . it was . . . seized and appropriated by our own soldiers and others. It was plunder." Lincoln also recognized the military imperative, assuring Canby, "I do not wish [cotton] to take precedence of the military." But practically, the President and Fessen-den enforced the rules in a way that kept the cotton moving.

Only with Grant, his favorite general, was Lincoln willing to defer. Having approved a large shipment of southern produce to pass Grant's lines, the President left the ultimate decision to Grant. Lincoln stressed, "You [Grant] must be allowed to do as you please in such matters." Grant took him at his word. He notified Stanton of a steamer "loaded with sugar and coffee," approved by Treasury to go south. Grant sarcas-tically informed the secretary of war, "I have positively refused to adopt this mode of feeding the Southern army unless it is the direct order of the President."

Lincoln could not resolve the tension in the cotton trade, which counterposed two heartfelt goals—victory and economic renewal. He was under severe pressure to make progress on both fronts. By the summer of 1864, the Union's military and financial problems had led to a serious problem with civilian morale. The Confederacy was losing hope of winning on the battlefield; its plan was to survive through the November election when, potentially, a peace party might throw Lincoln out of office. This scenario terrified Lincoln, who feared that defeat at the polls would be followed by a negotiated settlement. Grant's army was stopped before Richmond; Sherman was mired in the hill country of northwest Georgia. With the military picture cloudy and the Treasury overwhelmed, Lincoln's political prospects were not auspicious. At the end of July, the Rebels stormed Chambersburg, Pennsylvania, and burned the town. The public mood sank on the news of yet another incursion onto Yankee soil. Even the Pollyannaish Jay Cooke wrote his brother, who was in Europe, "Grant has lost prestige and people begin to doubt even his success."

Copperheads tried to tar Lincoln with financial dirt, alleging that he took his salary, which was $25,000 per year, in gold while ordinary citizens were stuck with inflated paper. Harrington, who administered the President's salary, emphatically refuted the charge. Lincoln was paid in greenbacks (like the troops), and his surplus funds were invested in government securities. Indeed, Honest Abe was paying income taxes, even though the law was unclear whether, in the President's case, they were required. After his death, his estate received a refund.

Peace Democrats got more traction by charging that Lincoln's obsession with freeing the slaves was blinding him to the possibility of ending the war. His opponents trafficked in overtly racist claims—for instance, that Lincoln's priorities were distorted by his "negro mania." Alarmingly for the President, not only Democrats but also stalwart Republicans demanded that he sound out Jefferson Davis on peace terms. Davis, in fact, had reiterated his terms to a northern journalist who had traveled to Richmond on a military pass that summer. "We are not fighting for slavery," Davis told him. "We are fighting for independence, and that, or extermination, we *will* have." Since the Republican platform demanded unconditional surrender and allegiance to all United States laws, including the Emancipation Proclamation, no meeting of minds was possible. Yet the fantasy persisted that peace was attainable if only the subject of emancipation were deferred. Horace Greeley, who in 1862 had rebuked Lincoln for not moving quickly enough on emancipation, now insisted that Lincoln engage in peace talks without preconditions.

Greeley was the most credulous of a group of Republican appeasers who mistook vague rumors emanating from the South as representing a willingness on the part of Davis to pursue reunification. On July 7, Greeley privately wrote Lincoln that "our bleeding, bankrupt, almost dying country also longs for peace—shudders at the prospect of fresh conscriptions, of further wholesale devastations, and of new rivers of human blood." In mid-July, Greeley involved himself (with Lincoln's grudging permission) in a dubious diplomatic errand to the Canadian side of Niagara Falls to meet with supposed Rebel envoys—who, as it turned out, were not authorized to negotiate for Davis's government, or to do anything else. The only result of this ill-advised mission was damaging publicity, permitting Copperheads to charge that Lincoln was unwilling to negotiate.

Dissatisfaction with the war, coupled with the Union's "wretched finances" (Strong's phrase), gave rise to a serious anti-Lincoln movement. Republicans openly called for another candidate, many mentioning Chase. Thurlow Weed, a power broker in New York, proclaimed in early August that Lincoln's reelection was "an impossibility," because the people were "wild for peace." Even Thaddeus Stevens declined to support Lincoln.* With gold remaining above 250, bond sales at barely

---

* Senator Sherman, another leading Republican, confided to his brother William in late July, "The conviction is general that Lincoln has not the energy, dignity, or character to either conduct the war or to make peace."

$1 million per day—less than half what Fessenden needed—and Grant's army hemorrhaging blood, it did seem as if Lincoln were in trouble. A despondent Strong wrote on August 8, "One of the bluest of any blue days." Twenty-four hours later, Greeley, the Union's most celebrated journalist, penned a frantic-seeming letter in which he "begged" the President to end the war. On August 19, the mercurial editor stated, as if it were fact, Lincoln "is already beaten; he cannot be elected."

Democrats hoped to force the President to choose between peace and emancipation. Seeking to avoid this trap, on August 17, Lincoln tried to rebut the charge of a Wisconsin editor and War Democrat* that emancipation represented a broadening of his original war aims. This required delicate footwork, because Lincoln's purposes *had* evolved. Lincoln portrayed his emancipation policy as merely a military expedient. In pursuing victory, he explained, he had used the lure of freedom to tempt Negroes to flee their masters and join the Union cause. And flee they had—at least 130,000 were serving as soldiers, seamen, and laborers. To renounce emancipation now would "ruin" the Union cause—for "negroes, like other people, act upon motives." Why would they risk their lives with "full notice of our purpose to betray them"? Lincoln's assertion that African Americans were driven by the same human motives as whites was, for its time, enlightened. But Lincoln went further. Blacks, he said, had enlisted on the "promise of freedom. And the promise being made, must be kept." This was not a pragmatic argument, but a moral one.

Lincoln didn't send this letter; perhaps he recognized that to do so would furnish his opponents with fresh ammunition. In any case, the President received devastating news from Henry Raymond, chairman of the Republican National Committee. Raymond had polled party members around the country, based on which he reported, "The tide is setting strongly against us." Under the weight of so much pessimism, Raymond suggested dispatching a commissioner to Richmond "*on the*

---

* War Democrats were members of the opposition party who supported the Union.

sole condition of acknowledging the supremacy of the constitution." Raymond did not expect Davis to accept; he saw his gambit as a political ploy. But even offering it, absent any condition on slavery, would be a concession. And Lincoln, undoubtedly worn down as well, accepted. On August 24, he directed Raymond himself to travel to Richmond to offer peace "upon the restoration of the Union and the national authority . . . all remaining questions to be left for adjustment by peaceful modes." It was a momentary lapse. The next day, a refreshed Lincoln met with Raymond and, in the words of the President's private secretary, persuaded his visitor that sending a delegation to Richmond "would be worse than losing the Presidential contest—it would be ignominiously surrendering it in advance." Lincoln expected to pay a heavy price for his refusal to waver on emancipation. He penned the thought that he expected to lose in November, preserving the moment for history by sealing his memorandum and asking his cabinet to sign it unseen.

Treasury Secretary Fessenden's efforts to market notes to the public continued to sputter. On rare days, sales of the seven-thirty broke the $1 million mark; more commonly, they languished in the high six figures. "Money comes in very slowly," Pitt despaired to Lizzy, "and not half so much as I need." One day toward the end of August, sales plunged to $565,000—the next, to $312,000, a pitiable sum.

Salmon Chase could not refrain from whispering to Jay Cooke, "I do not think, perhaps I may be overvain, that Mr. Fessenden quite draws my bow." Chase was overvain, but he offered his care-worn successor sound advice—that Fessenden abandon his qualms and reenlist Cooke. While Fessenden ruminated over this suggestion, he let bills pile up and issued certificates to suppliers. Like his predecessor, Fessenden was drowning the market in short-term paper.

Perhaps no cabinet secretary was ever so miserable. He was forced to let the total of outstanding certificates swell to $247 million, a staggering sum, and as he did, the certificates were peddled in the aftermarket at an embarrassing discount. Canny investors now scooped them up in preference to the government's investment securities. Thus, the deluge of Treasury certificates depressed bond sales, threatening the entire scaffolding of government finance. *The Times* of London judged that U.S. bonds were inferior to the Erlanger cotton bonds—which were trading above 80 percent of par. It is hard to know which to make more of—England's utter credulity vis-à-vis Richmond, or its complete loss of confidence in the United States.

On the final day of August, the Democrats nominated General George McClellan to run against Lincoln. The threat to the Union, and to its securities, leapt off the page of the Democratic platform. The party of Jackson adopted the resolution of Clement Vallandigham (the patently disloyal Copperhead) advocating, without *any* preconditions, "immediate efforts . . . for a cessation of hostilities." Fessenden now understood that only the Union army could salvage his bonds, for only it could keep Lincoln in office. He wrote home in a plaintive mood, "Oh, for a great victory."

And then, there was one.

Sherman captured Atlanta on September 2. Atlanta was a vital manufacturing center and railroad hub, the nerve center of the southern economy. Its loss was devastating. Transporting supplies became next to impossible. Factories could not source materials. The Confederacy tried to mitigate the loss of economic output the only way it could—by printing notes. The volume of Rebel notes had shrunk after the February monetary reform, but as the physical economy imploded, Richmond had no choice but to issue the "new" notes. Seventy million were printed by the end of August, nearly $300 million by October. Needless to say, the new notes produced exactly the same effect as the old. Their value collapsed to thirty to one to gold (i.e., three cents on the dollar). By winter, they traded at sixty to one. The government manufactured so many bills that it resorted to printing notes on wallpaper. With Grant closing in on Richmond, the Note Bureau was forced to halt operations, but still the money printing continued. A hundred or so of the bureau's clerks, mostly women, boarded a train south and set up makeshift printing in Columbia, South Carolina. Since its inception through October 1864, the would-be nation had raised nearly 60 percent of its "revenue" by printing it (compared with only one-sixth in the Union). This was a formula for monetary collapse.

Trenholm, the new Treasury secretary, tried to abandon notes where possible, preferring to deal in bills drawn on cotton. Notes were not a real currency anymore. Farmers and tradespeople refused them; the rich hurried to convert bills into property at stratospheric prices. Even schoolteachers demanded wages in edible provisions. The lack of a trusted currency eviscerated trade, which further depleted food supplies in the cities. The southern press had for months denied the evidence, but after Atlanta, even the *Richmond Enquirer*, the government's trusty defender, glumly reported that "the wealthy consume their capital, the middle classes retrench and hunger in silence, the poor rely on charity and public means of support."

Up north, Atlanta revived Lincoln's political fortunes. The Republican mutiny ended. Greeley did a volte-face and editorialized for the President. Chase campaigned for his former boss. Stevens, recognizing that emancipation rode on the election's outcome, ardently canvassed for Lincoln. Old Thad urged his disciples to forget that the President had "ever erred." He publicly thanked God for Lincoln.

The greenback rallied as if a fog had lifted; it soon surpassed fifty cents. Fessenden had reluctantly decided to market gold bonds—the five-twenties—an acknowledgment that simply more paper wouldn't do. In mid-September, in the flush of the enthusiasm over Atlanta and over Sheridan's triumphant march through Shenandoah, the Treasury secretary offered $32 million worth. Investors snapped them up. A larger offering followed. Fessenden wrote home, "It is a great success"—as joyous a remark as one finds from him in cabinet. The biggest purchaser was Jay Cooke, but demand was also strong in Europe. Fessenden still had to plug a gaping deficit. And he faced the essential quandary that American investors were wary of bonds that did not pay interest in coin. Fessenden's thoughts turned to Europe, where demand for American bonds had gradually accelerated. In October, he had an intriguing idea: why not send Chase overseas as his agent? The two had fashioned a working relationship, and in European capitals Chase commanded enormous respect. He was certainly eager to be in the thick of things. But the partnership was not to be.

The idea collapsed when Roger Taney, who had reigned over the Supreme Court for twenty-eight years and in 1857 delivered the notorious *Dred Scott* decision, denying that Blacks could be United States citizens, died at the age of eighty-seven. Chase waited a week, then wrote Sumner lobbying for the chief justice job. Lincoln deftly deferred any decision until the election.

Lincoln won in a landslide. He captured 55 percent of the popular vote, winning every nonslave state except New Jersey, McClellan's home. Remarkably, given the soldiers' affection for Little Mac, three-quarters of active soldiers cast their ballots for Lincoln. The Republicans gained fifty seats in the House, giving them commanding majorities in both chambers and a clear shot at passing the Thirteenth Amendment.

The results seemed to vindicate the view of James Russell Lowell, the resident poet and professor of languages at Harvard, that Lincoln's stature had grown in office. In 1860, the former rail-splitter had been nominated on the basis of his "availability" and carnival appeal on the stump. Sophisticated easterners had found his lack of refinement almost repellent. "Mr. Lincoln has steadily drawn the nation over to him," Lowell reflected in a lengthy essay in the *North American Review* early in 1864. While he was "not handsome nor elegant . . . we cannot say that we like him any the worse for it." As president, Lincoln had demonstrated a firmness and wisdom absent which the nation would have tumbled into chaos; he had compromised without conceding; he had proved his mettle at statecraft "by so gently guiding public sentiment that he seems to follow it." Lowell predicted, "History will rank Mr. Lincoln among the most prudent of statesmen and the most successful of rulers."

Yet the President's support was confined to the same political base as in 1860. He carried old-line Whigs, prosperous and Protestant farmers, merchants, and professionals. His larger vote share was almost entirely due to the absence of the South. The regional vote tallies were similar to those of four years earlier. In his first campaign, Lincoln won 62 percent of the vote in New England; now 63 percent. In the industrial heartland (Ohio, Indiana, Illinois) he improved from 51 to 55 percent; in the Mid-Atlantic region, he captured a fraction over half both times. American political geographies are hard to budge. Lincoln's appeal continued to be weakest among poorer farmers, unskilled laborers, and Catholic immigrants—many of whom viewed freedmen as threats. These racial and economic fissures suggested looming trouble as the country headed toward Reconstruction.

After his victory, Lincoln turned to the vacant chief justiceship. With General Sherman commencing his march to the sea, and General Grant having pinned Lee at Petersburg, Lincoln could focus on the Supreme Court's potential impact after the war. He was concerned that the court validate two of his most cherished achievements: the Emancipation Proclamation and the Legal Tender Act. Chase would presumably support him on each. And tapping Chase would mollify the party's Radical wing, whose support Lincoln would need to effect his views on reconstruction. Various naysayers warned that the Ohioan's still simmering presidential ambitions could impair his ability to lead the court. But Lincoln hardly needed counsel. He was more aware of Chase's presidential fever than anyone. And he sensed that financial markets would welcome Chase's selection as a sign of continuity. On December 6, he nominated Chase to become only the third Chief Justice in sixty-four years. John Nicolay, one of Lincoln's secretaries, wrote his fiancée, "Probably no other man than Lincoln would have had . . .

the degree of magnanimity to thus forgive and exalt a rival who had so deeply and so unjustifiably intrigued against him."

Lincoln's Annual Message to Congress also looked to the postwar future. Echoing his theme of economic renewal, he evinced a hope that the country would resume its "high career of commerce and civilization." He enthused over the general "condition of prosperity" in the territories. He devoted but two paragraphs to the progress of the war—and even there, he took an economic view, basking in the Union's "material resources," which furnished it, he believed, with an unimpeachable, and theoretically unending, advantage.

The President "venture[d] to recommend" that the House approve the Thirteenth Amendment banning slavery, the sooner the better. In an era in which Congress did not lightly take direction from the executive, Lincoln's politely worded suggestion demonstrated a resolve to rid the country of slavery forever. It was a very Republican amendment, in style as well as substance. All twelve of the previous amendments had *limited* federal powers. The Thirteenth would expand them.

Lincoln's most extended discussion concerned the public debt, now more than $2 billion—thirty times larger than under his predecessor. Lincoln exalted the debt as "a substantial branch of national, though private, property"—a phrase evocative of Alexander Hamilton's dictum that the debt could be a "national blessing." But Lincoln's meaning was slightly different. Hamilton had prized government bonds as a stimulant to business and markets. Lincoln praised the debt because, to the extent that it was owned by individuals, it would bind them to the government and to its purposes. As he put it, "Men readily perceive that they cannot be much oppressed by a debt which they owe to themselves."

To the Log Cabin President, popular investment in government securities was a complement to democracy. "The more nearly this property can be distributed among all the people," he said, "the better." This led him to a radical suggestion: that, within limits, Congress make government bonds held by individuals tax-free. In the folds of Lincoln's proposal was a hint of the modern notion of social security. The President's suggestion was too vague to interest Congress during wartime, but his purpose was clear: to "enable every prudent person to set aside a small annuity against a possible day of want."*

Lincoln also ventured a more timely proposal: that the country move beyond its mélange of currencies and make national banks the exclusive issuer. National Banking had been sold as a war measure; Lincoln dropped the pretense. In contending that the Treasury could not satisfactorily conduct its operations while in competition with the states, the President was asserting a more expansive notion of what the Treasury's proper function was. Only the federal government could, or should, control the money supply. State banks being beyond the reach of Washington, their notes warranted extinction.

Lincoln did not explicitly suggest legislation (though the inference was clear). But Treasury Secretary Fessenden asked Congress to impose a punitive tax on state currency. Senator Sherman spearheaded this legislation, which imposed a 10 percent tax on state notes—enough, in time, to achieve their elimination. It was enacted on March 3, 1865. By then, momentum had shifted toward National Banking. Five hundred and eighty-four banks had joined the new system by the end of 1864—including one hundred in New York State, previously the heart of the resistance. National Banking even had footholds in the former Rebel strongholds of Norfolk and Memphis. While National Bank Notes remained a minority, the legislation sealed the fate of the old state monies. The new law epitomized Republican ideology, establishing federal primacy over banking.

However, the banking law did not address the government's urgent need for cash. After the election, Fessenden reversed himself and invited Jay Cooke to return to the fold as the Treasury's agent. Cooke visited Washington on November 24, after which Fessenden continued

---

* In 1913, Congress exempted interest on state and local securities from federal taxation.

the discussions with Jay's brother Henry. The negotiations were difficult. Cooke, miffed at being kept at bay, demanded a more lucrative commission than he had received before. The Treasury secretary was wary of being exploited by the canny banker and proposed, as a precaution, that Cooke share the assignment with a rival financier. This condition was supremely distasteful to Cooke. The banker recruited Sherman to lobby Fessenden for an exclusive agency—the very monopoly that critics had objected to.

The Treasury secretary agreed—but then, as if suspecting a rat, changed his mind and decided to see if he could enlist the new national banks to sell bonds, both the seven-thirties and the ten-forties. Their sales amounted to a trickle. An informer in the Treasury reassured Cooke he had no cause for worry. "I have very little doubt that the Secretary [will] find it desirable to avail of your services as agent," he remarked—patronizingly with respect to his boss. The gold market underlined his point. Gold closed the year at 226, a greenback value of only forty-four cents. Not even a second coup by General Sherman—the capture of Savannah—could buoy the Union currency. Either there was too much paper or the northern people did not trust it. During the first week of 1865, Congress authorized more seven-thirties, but Fessenden did not have an agent to market them. Sales by national banks were "disappointingly small." By then, the Treasury secretary was a spent force. Looking for a face-saving escape, Fessenden quietly arranged for his allies in the Maine legislature to vote him back to the Senate for the term commencing in March.

Richmond by now was in extremis. There is ample evidence, at this late stage, of a classic hyperinflation. The price of wheat had risen 1700 percent just since 1863; bacon, 2500 percent. A barrel of flour had cost 220 Rebel notes early in 1864; by the second week of 1865, it cost 1000 notes. Such astronomical rates of increase reflected not just a worthless currency (which it was) but an extreme scarcity of supplies.

One scholar calculates that prices reached ninety-two times their pre-war base. The South was suffering both a monetary and an economic catastrophe.

As supply lines frayed, hunger became a commonplace. In Georgia, a northern writer sadly recounted the withered look of the people, "the thin and haggard cheek, the sunken eye." We have a picture of despair from Edmund Ruffin, whose diary reveals a gnawing psychological depression. In the spring of 1864, the Yankees (having already trashed Beechwood, his primary source of income) set up headquarters at his other plantation, Marlbourne. His anguish deepened with the losses in battle of a grandson and his son Julian. Ruffin now fled to the estate of Edmund Jr., southwest of Richmond. All around he confronted a vanishing world. Sensing the downfall of his cherished planter aristocracy, he stoked his bitterness reading Victor Hugo's recently published novel of the popular uprising in France, *Les Misérables*. He suffered recurring doubts about the worth of going on. The more resilient Mary Chesnut hid her silver. She left posterity a pithy and prophetic appraisal: "The deep waters are closing over us."

President Davis had shielded the army from the worst effects of the economic collapse, but this was no longer possible. It is never a case of guns or butter, for the one is needed to support the other. Trenholm, the Confederate Treasury Secretary, had to stop paying the troops; General Lee's army, already on tight rations, now wanted even for soap, a serious deprivation for soldiers who spent their days caked in mud. The army responded to shortages by ramping up impressment, generally paying one-seventh of the market price and sometimes a good deal less. Farmers, when they could, refused to sell. The price in notes became almost meaningless. As the South devolved toward a state of barter, *things* were a better barometer. People resorted to monetary substitutes—the classic response to a worthless currency. Newspaper classifieds were choking with offers of secondhand jewelry and watches. Goods were solicited in exchange for "Cotton, Bacon or Salted Pork." St. Mary's School in Raleigh advertised board for the term with a salary of fifty dollars "payable in provisions, or in cotton cloth, or cotton yarns."

With impressment agents scavenging the countryside, antigovernment feeling reached a boil. "Our whole male population was freely tendered," the *Charlottesville* (Virginia) *Chronicle* protested, as if enumerating the causes of its grievance. "We have allowed [the government] to impress horses, wagons, cattle, grain, at nominal prices, until it has left the country almost bare." James Seddon, the secretary of war, warned Trenholm that his policy of deferring pay and other obligations was "prolific of mischiefs" including poor soldier morale, internal theft, and desertion. Trenholm had no alternative, but he was more frank than his predecessor. He acknowledged that the recent reforms had been a failure. He pleaded with the Rebel Congress for a more effective tax and, importantly, one that would be perceived as equitable. He also sought to restore the currency. Memminger had also tried that, but Trenholm was more inspired. He aimed to confect a new currency out of agricultural credits. Rather than pay farmers with worthless notes, he sketched a plan to pay in corn certificates, or those backed by other commodities, to be redeemed after the war. "We want a measure of value"—normally the function of money—he noted in a public letter. Trenholm's underlying premise was correct: southern agriculture, what remained of it, was a better basis of commercial exchange than Confederate credit. Corn was more valuable than paper. But he needed the Congress to act now. As he warned the House Ways and Means Committee late in the year, come January 1, "the Treasury will be completely empty."

Amid the runaway inflation, only one "commodity" was falling: the price of human chattel. Classified columns were rife with notices of auctions of a dozen or more enslaved Negroes, sometimes offered alongside pianos, billiard tables, or other merchandise, or with securities, gold, and silver. The only buyers in bulk were railroads, who were desperate to replace white employees conscripted into the army. The ads bore headlines such as NEGROES FOR HIRE AND SALE. Some "owners" offered rewards for runaways—typically three to five hundred dollars. Similar rewards were quoted for horses. In February 1865, John Beauchamp Jones confirmed that the price for an able-bodied male had crashed to the equivalent of four barrels of flour. In gold, the price was one hundred dollars, a 90 percent drop from peacetime.

The plunging slave market shows that southerners were increasingly fearful of losing the war. The outlook was so dire that the topic of Black recruitment could no longer be avoided. President Davis had squelched such talk in the past, but as Sherman's army knifed through Georgia, General Lee advised that Blacks be recruited into noncombat roles, tartly adding that Blacks who did not fight for the Confederacy would end by fighting against it. The planters remained firmly opposed, as if a world without slaves was too terrible to contemplate. The *Richmond Enquirer* said flatly that slaves were unfit for soldiering. Union regiments had disproved that, but even in the South, it was thought unfeasible to re-enslave a man who had carried a gun in the service of his masters. Thus, enlistment was equated with emancipation. *The North Carolina Standard* denounced Black recruitment as "abolition doctrine." Howell Cobb, the Georgian planter who had abandoned the U.S. Treasury in 1860 to join the rebellion, was among the staunchest foes. Cobb advised the war secretary, with unconscious irony, "If slaves will make good soldiers our whole theory of slavery is wrong." Perhaps it was not surprising that the impetus came from army officers, who saw the need for recruits firsthand. By the fall of 1864, southern newspapers were openly debating the question. "One thing is evident," opined the liberal Wilmington *Carolinian:* "more men must be had."

Davis's priority now was preserving independence. Without it, slavery was doomed in any case. He therefore began to consider emancipation "as a reward for faithful service." Early in 1865, Lee publicly endorsed Negro soldiery *with* a general emancipation. The issue still proved exceptionally controversial. With Davis's support, the Confederate Congress approved Black enlistment—but without a promise of freedom, and too late to make a difference in the fighting. The State of

Virginia organized two companies of Blacks, who drilled in gray but remained unfree.*

Thousands of slaves were taking matters into their own hands by fleeing north, many taking refuge in the skirts of Sherman's army. However, troubling reports of mistreatment percolated up to Washington. Stanton traveled to Savannah to investigate, and irritated the general by insisting on questioning Blacks without Sherman present. The freedmen gave the general high marks. They expressed a strong desire to live among themselves—not with whites—and to have their own land. Stanton raised the issue with Sherman, who had a history of crude and prejudicial remarks. But on January 16, Sherman issued Special Field Orders No. 15, providing for forty acres to freedmen heads of households from land confiscated along the coast of Carolina, Georgia, and Florida. Sherman wrote the order at Stanton's prodding, but there is little doubt that Sherman grasped its sweeping purpose. As he succinctly summarized, "The negro is free, and must be dealt with as such." The military edict by this seemingly bigoted soldier provided the freedmen with an economic foothold. Thousands of Blacks on the Sea Islands were settled on individual plots. However, pending federal legislation, Sherman's order provided only for possession, not for permanent legal title. It was a foothold and no more.

If slavery was one trembling pillar of the Rebel economy, trade with Britain and Europe was the other. On January 15, Union forces, including thousands of Negro troops, stormed the Rebel stronghold on Cape Fear, on the Carolina coast. At daybreak the next day, observers awoke to the novel sight of "Federal troops, white and colored, strolling on the ramparts of Fort Fisher." The fort guarded Wilmington, the last seagoing port in the South's hands. Difficult to blockade, Wilmington had been the terminus for a near constant parade of fast steamers to the West Indies and England. Now, with its capture, the *Richmond Enquirer* observed as if stunned, "No more cotton goes out of the confed-

---

* Lincoln was unimpressed. Speaking to troops from Indiana, he said Black enlistment in Dixie was unlikely to matter for they "cannot fight and stay at home and make bread too."

eracy." Nor would supplies enter into it. Isolation beckoned, and the economic system of the Rebel nation was finished. The *Enquirer* ventured the preposterous hope that the South (though depleted of capital, tools, and machinery) could develop manufacturing. The truth was that the South was completely cut off. By March, Richmond was suffering widespread hunger. The society doyenne Mary Chesnut was reduced to accepting charity—rice, potatoes, and a sack of flour—from a kindly colonel, while adopting an itinerant life, moving ahead of Yankee troops. The Rebel currency was quoted at one seventy-sixth of nominal value, evaporating the savings of millions of southerners. General Lee himself was ruined. Even the cotton bonds, which had long denied reality, fell into the midthirties.

Lincoln knew he could end the war by destroying what remained of the South's economy. As he put it, "We have to reach the bottom of the insurgent resources." But his own Treasury was under terrific pressure. With the need for funds to pay the troops uppermost in mind, Lincoln urged his Treasury secretary to reengage Jay Cooke, with whom negotiations had lagged. On January 28, Fessenden signed Cooke as general agent. Days later, Fessenden submitted his resignation, effective March 3, which gave him precisely a month to right the finances. Perhaps embarrassed at having awarded Cooke a generous commission, he reserved the right to cancel Cooke's agency at any time—which the sensitive Cooke found highly offensive but accepted, in view of his certain large profits.*

The mere news of Cooke's recruitment excited sales of the seventhirty, as if buyers wanted in on a rising tide. Three days later, the House of Representatives, after vigorous arm-twisting by Lincoln, approved the Thirteenth Amendment, abolishing slavery. The evening after the vote, joyous celebrants serenaded the President at the White House. Lincoln appeared at the upper window, under a portico, and

---

* Fessenden agreed to three-quarters of 1 percent on the first $50 million and five-eighths of 1 percent on the next $50 million, from which Cooke would pay marketing and other expenses, with the commission on additional sales to be negotiated later.

declared that ratification was necessary lest the Emancipation Proclamation face a legal challenge and to root out "the original disturbing
cause" of the "great difficulty." The President was in a jovial mood, noting proudly that Illinois had already ratified the amendment. Chief Justice Chase took the sympathetic step of swearing in John Rock, a Boston
lawyer, and the first Black accredited to practice at the Supreme Court.

The clarification of Union purpose gave a jolt to bond sales, and the
reemergence of Cooke unlocked a reservoir of private capital. Demand
for Union paper soared in Europe, especially in the German states, spurred
by enthusiasm for emancipation. At home, Cooke contacted former agents
and rebooted his publicity machine. He had the help of the national
banks, which acted as subagents. Within a week, Cooke was besting
Fessenden's target. Cooke literally bought favorable newspaper coverage
by dangling options to select editors (a corrupting offer). As with the
five-twenty loan, he emphasized the campaign's democratic color. His
writers mythologized investors as simple folk—"needlewomen" and
"mechanics." His publicity notwithstanding, Cooke elicited large sums
from the wealthy. Congressmen were avid buyers; Chase purchased
$20,000 worth. Big investors may have helped to broaden the market.
On February 15, sales reached the extraordinary sum of $8.7 million,
including single subscriptions of $1 million from New York and
$300,000 from Cleveland. The following day, more than three thou-
sand small investors subscribed for $50 or $100 each. One hundred and
fifty Black recruits in Pennsylvania purchased the seven-thirties, as did
Spanish settlers in Santa Fe and southerners in occupied Arkansas and
Louisiana. "Night agencies" in New York peddled bonds to workers
while plying them with coffee and doughnuts. The seven-thirty reached
many more small investors than the five-twenty. When Cooke's wife
and children traveled by steamer to Fort Monroe, where they met General Grant, the Union commander supposedly remarked that Cooke
was doing "more than all the generals in the army." Although the source
for this compliment was obviously biased, the *Richmond Examiner* was
hardly less flattering:

The efforts of the Yankees to sustain this explosive and inflated paper system has, so far, been marked by great ingenuity,
resolution and success. Whether they will succeed in conquer-
ing the South, depends, in a great degree, upon their continued
success in upholding this paper system.

The "paper system" was the beginning of an organized capital market. Cooke had demonstrated that, without significant participation
overseas, the American market could support a broad underwriting.
The future Wall Street with sales offices in every city, eventually
every town, was initiated in those hard-bitten final months of Lincoln's
first term. Sales of the seven-thirty skyrocketed from $771,000 per day
prior to Cooke's appointment to just over $3 million during February
and March. This was sufficient to pay the troops and other government
creditors. On March 3, Congress authorized a further $600 million in
loans. As Grant's army waited for the rains to cease, the Union Treasury
was flooded with cash.

Lincoln was inaugurated March 4. Fittingly, it was Chase, the architect of the financial reforms and Lincoln's most passionate antislavery minister, who swore him in for his second term. An estimated thirty
thousand people stood to hear him, many wading in mud after a brief
but angry storm. In the words of Walt Whitman, who covered the inauguration for *The New York Times*—"Mud, (and such mud!)" In contrast to four years earlier, when cavalrymen with drawn sabers stood
eight deep to protect him, an unguarded Lincoln rode to the Capitol "in
his own carriage, by himself, on a sharp trot." The poet observed that
he looked very much worn and tired, showing lines of "vast responsibilities." Lincoln spoke briefly and beautifully, seven hundred words in
which he asked for God's deliverance from the war, evidencing to the
historian Walter McDougall a spiritual journey driven by his burdens
over the last four years.* It was a speech of reconciliation, offering charity to the vanquished, but it completed that other journey, Lincoln's

---

* Lincoln predicted that the address would "wear as well as—perhaps better than—any thing I have
produced."

evolving reckoning of the war's purposes. "All knew," he observed, that slavery was "somehow" the cause of it. In 1861, the Union had merely sought to limit its "territorial enlargement." Even that overstated slavery's role in the North's calculations, which had been concerned only with preserving the Union. Now, before a racially mixed gathering, which included Frederick Douglass, Lincoln reframed the war as divine retribution for the economic crime of slavery. Lincoln described the peculiar institution distinctly in the terms of a laboring man—as the South "wringing their bread from the sweat of other men's faces." Yet divine retribution also extended to the North, perhaps an unspoken acknowledgment of the North's long trade in cotton. Both sides, north and south, had bled for the ill-gained loot of slavery, and if God willed it so they would continue to bleed until the theft was expiated—"until all the wealth piled by the bond-man's two hundred and fifty years of unrequited toil shall be sunk."

After the inauguration, Lincoln appointed Hugh McCulloch, the comptroller, to replace Fessenden. Anxious to ensure that the spigot of bond sales remained wide open, the new Treasury secretary raised Cooke's fee to three-quarters of 1 percent on every bond as an incentive for speedy performance. "Hurry up the sales," McCulloch pleaded. Part of his anxiety stemmed from the fact that, while the Treasury was reaping a bonanza in seven-thirty sales, the gold price had barely budged. Before Cooke's appointment as sales agent, the metal had stood at 212. Four weeks later, it had eased only to 199, or a greenback value of fifty cents. Wall Street mavens hypothesized that the Union simply had too much paper. "We must accept the fact," one explained soberly, that "no great fall must be immediately expected." In the way that Wall Street is wont to confer on recent experience predictive power, the 200 level was held to be a natural, or an economic, barrier, nearly impervious. Yet if the Union was winning, and philosophically committed to redeeming greenbacks at parity, why were they trading at 50 percent off?

Through the first week of March, as Grant made ready to renew the assault, gold held firm. As late as March 8, the metal traded at 196.

Then, it sank like a stone. Wall Street cried "panic," for everything went down—gold, bacon, cotton, flour, wheat. In a mirror image of the Confederacy, only the currency went up. Seven-thirties—calls on future dollars—sold like hotcakes, $4 or $5 million worth a day. By late March, with the weather clearing and the roads at Petersburg improving, gold traded below 150. This was painful for the gold bulls, but not to anyone else. It was a sign that the Union had the taxing power to support its paper—as the *New York Post* observed, that "the nation is able to bear its own burdens." This was a staggering transformation.

The federal government had not only acquired a taxing power to pay for the war, but a banking system and a viable currency. Before the war began, every state had had its own money; presently, the United States would have only two: greenbacks and National Bank Notes. Its debt, a measure of the public investment, had reached the towering sum of $2.68 billion—forty-one times as much as at the onset of secession. Yet with all its borrowing, America's credit was strengthened. It now borrowed much bigger sums than under Buchanan at much lower interest rates. The federal government had not only paid for the war, it had emerged from it financially stronger.

The government was also enlarged, shed of its Jeffersonian confines. It was subsidizing a railroad to the Pacific, processing thousands of claims for homesteads, deeding the acreage for public colleges. The changes were sufficiently profound for an editor in North Carolina to dub the Lincoln government a "New Deal," a lexical coincidence that accurately foreshadowed the welfare state of the twentieth century. In general, the changes both responded to the emergency and expanded the mission of government that, previously, had been distinguished by its limitations. From Jefferson to Buchanan, the government had been bound to the principle of limited federal power. The Republicans reversed this bedrock dogma.

It was now, as it had not been before, the federal government's business to help educate farmers, to preserve natural lands, to fix the standard railway gauge, to nurture the sciences, to operate an expanded postal service, to regulate banks, to encourage immigration. Even abolition, on the surface a stand-alone event, was enabled by the new ideology of centralism.

It is impossible not to notice that the losing side in the war was committed to the contrary ideology—to states' rights. If Salmon Chase had helped the North to win, the lack of central coordination, in particular in finance, and the absence of a culture fostering economic mobility surely contributed to the South's defeat—it may even have caused them to lose.

Lee surrendered at Appomattox April 9, the effective end of the war. Reconstruction ranked high on the agenda for the second term. The Radicals wanted a complete overhaul of the conquered South; Lincoln, typically, counseled patience. He had accomplished profound changes by moving gradually on slavery, and this was the approach he intended in Reconstruction. Two days after the surrender, he spoke to a large crowd from his upper window. Jubilant citizens had lit the city with bonfires, but the country, though newly at peace, was seething with hatred. Recognizing these deep fissures in American society, Lincoln said, "We simply must begin with, and mold from, disorganized and discordant elements."

Temperamentally, he put stock in a business renewal as an indirect curative for the country's wounds. His roots as a Whig crusader for banking and canals would signal the path toward resurrection. He had no interest in retribution; he intended (perhaps naïvely) to treat conquered southerners with forbearance. He had no wish, he told an Alabaman, to harm a hair on any head; he wanted southerners back at work, at their farms and in their shops. He was thrilled by the "great enterprise" of connecting the Atlantic and Pacific by railroad, and by the project to span the ocean via telegraph; he took special pride in the Department of Agriculture, which he imagined would foster a direct connection to farmers. He was eager to implement the immigration law and envisioned that migrants would settle not in crowded eastern cities but farther west. The west excited him as nothing else. The fateful morning of April 14, on which evening Lincoln and Mary had plans to attend the theater, the President entertained Schuyler Colfax, the Speaker of the House, who was set to journey westward. Lincoln implored him to carry a presidential message to miners. Transfixed by visions of vast natural resources, Lincoln said he intended to steer the immigrants who arrived from "overcrowded Europe" to the wealth in America's mountains. "Tell the miners for me," he said, "that I shall promote their interests to the utmost of my ability; because their prosperity is the prosperity of the nation." The President himself, who had never been west of Iowa, was thinking of relocating to California after his presidency. He often spoke of it. It would be a healthier place for his two surviving sons, a place for them to mature and prosper, a place to participate in the country's growth, which was now overseen by the strengthened and reunited government that had been his life's work.

Fifteen

Epilogue

AMERICANS WERE STILL TAKING Lincoln's measure when the war ended. This was especially true of educated easterners. George Templeton Strong, an admirer, sheepishly remarked on April 11, 1865, "It must be admitted that he sometimes tells stories of the class that is 'not convenient' and does not become a gentleman." The debt to his class now having been paid, Strong offered a fitting tribute. "But his weaknesses are on the surface," he conceded, "and his name will be of high account fifty years hence, and for many generations thereafter." Three days later, on April 14, John Wilkes Booth froze Lincoln's legacy with a .44 caliber pistol. Strong was overcome with grief: "I am stunned, as by a fearful personal calamity."

Lincoln's generation mourned him as a self-made leader who believed in democratic government as the tribune of the people. Ralph Waldo Emerson, who noted Lincoln's common manners while praising the "weight and penetration" in his letters, messages, and speeches, thoughtfully eulogized the slain president as a self-achiever in a country of self-improvers. According to the sage of Concord, "The middle-class country had got a middle-class President."

Later generations revered Lincoln for emancipation but forgot his connection to the middle class. They recalled Lincoln's commitment to the Union, but not the purposes for which he insisted on its preservation. To the son of the unlettered farmer, national progress was mostly a material quest. Government's job was to foster opportunity for the less fortunate; as the historian Richard Hofstadter put it, "for Lincoln the vital test of a democracy was economic."

The assassination interrupted the work of securing four great legacies: a larger and more essential federal government, emancipation and Black rights, federal currency and banking, and the establishment of the Republicans as a party of opportunity. These goals had been pursued jointly during the war, but in peacetime old coalitions frayed.

The battle over the greenback dominated postwar politics. Cheap money, necessary in wartime, became the scourge of Republican elites, even as it was desperately sought by farmers and laboring people as a prop to prices, wages, and credit. The struggle between these camps was exceptionally bitter.

Over the course of the war, the greenback had suffered 80 percent inflation. Bankers could not conceive of operating in a world in which the dollar depreciated at such a rate. They demanded a return to gold.

However, the ledger on the greenback was hardly all bad. It had not led to the apocalypse opponents had predicted. Its issue had been relatively restricted (greenbacks amounted to only a sixth of the federal debt). Thanks to such prudence, northern inflation was no worse than America's later experience during the two world wars. By contrast, inflation in the South was 9000 percent.

Soon after Appomattox, Treasury Secretary McCulloch, a fiscal conservative, moved to retire greenbacks, some $431 million of which were outstanding at the war's end. McCulloch quickly reduced the float by one-sixth. But deflation was highly unpopular. The Radical Republicans, reneging on their wartime pledge to return to gold, enacted a law to stop McCulloch. As grain and other commodity prices tumbled, populists demanded the issuance of more greenbacks. Eventually, farmers and some socialists founded the Greenback Party to advocate for cheap money.

Americans' feelings about the greenback split along class and geographic lines. To bankers and eastern businesspeople, gold was the path not merely to prosperity, but to morality and salvation. When Wall Street demanded a sound currency, it meant a scarce currency. Farmers preferred that money be abundant. They were more interested in high wheat prices than high bond values. The debate over the greenback became something larger, a debate over which interests would be served and what kind of country America would become. Republican consensus gave way to rancorous divisions that would cleave the party into progressive and pro-business factions, and whose outlines, in broad form, are still recognizable today.

Salmon Chase had never been more than a reluctant sponsor of legal tender, a point Lincoln overlooked when he appointed him chief justice. Fourteen months into the peace, Chase began to fulminate against the notes that, formerly, he had used to pay the Treasury's bills. "A fearless and sagacious secretary," he confided to Horace Greeley, "would have resumed [the gold standard] a year ago, and let contraction take care of itself." As Treasury secretary, Chase had stated firmly that the tender act was lawful. After leaving the Treasury, he began to migrate toward the more blinkered view of government he had held before, as a Democrat, and to his Jacksonist attachment to hard money. By 1868, Chase had persuaded himself that, ideologically, he had never (except on slavery) left the Democratic fold at all. He asserted to August Belmont, the Democratic politico, "For more than a quarter of a century, I have been in my political views and sentiments, a Democrat; and I still think that, upon questions of finance, commerce, and administration generally, the old democratic principles afford the best guidance."

Chase was soon in the thick of the controversy. Before the war, a wealthy Kentuckian named Henry Griswold had extended a loan to one Susan Hepburn. Griswold had expected to be repaid in gold or silver—the only lawful money in the United States. After passage of the

Legal Tender Act, Hepburn repaid the loan in the new paper money. Griswold refused to accept, and the high court in Kentucky upheld him, ruling that Hepburn had to pay in coin. Hepburn appealed, pointing out that Congress had made the greenback acceptable for "all debts." In November 1869, the U.S. Supreme Court heard *Hepburn v. Griswold*, challenging the legality of the tender act.

Chase, leading a four-to-three majority (two seats were vacant), issued a surprising and disruptive ruling that legal tender was an unconstitutional "taking" of value. This contradicted the Republicans' broad reading of Congress's powers. It also invalidated a currency that bore his own image! President Grant, dismayed by the outcome, quickly filled the vacant court seats. Presented with two more greenback cases, the reconstituted court reversed *Hepburn*. It now found, with Chase in the minority, that legal tender had been constitutional after all. This court said that requiring a creditor to accept legal tender was not an illegal "taking," but merely a substitution of valued coin for a different kind of value—the pledge of the nation's credit.

The court cases buried for good the Jacksonian relic of a decentralized financial system. Congress's authority not just to coin, but also to create, money, a landmark of the Civil War Congress, was judicially confirmed. Contemporary money in the United States is very much a descendant of the original greenbacks—paper bills with no intrinsic value other than the full faith and credit of the U.S. government. The "greenback era" lasted until 1879, when Congress made the notes redeemable in gold.

Chase never shook the curse of presidential ambition, what Lincoln had humorously likened to a "chin-fly" that kept a horse agitated and pulling a plow. In 1868, after presiding over the impeachment trial of Andrew Johnson, Chase unsuccessfully sought the Democratic nomination for the White House. Four years later, though in failing health, the chief justice made a bid to head the ticket of the breakaway Liberal Republican Party, losing again. He died in 1873.

Chase lived to see his other creation, National Banking, firmly established (Chase National Bank, a forerunner of JPMorgan Chase, was named in his memory). The notes of the national banks proved to be the uniform and universally accepted currency Chase had promised. Defaults were rare, and when they occurred, note holders were protected. The system put American banking on solider ground, and the system endured for fifty years—remarkable given that it was conceived as an emergency war measure. Even today, the faded inscription, "National Bank of ——" can be read in many cities on the façades of venerable bank buildings.*

As with other capitalist transformations, the fruits of National Banking were distributed unevenly. Wall Street was favored with low interest rates while the interior suffered money shortages. Growth was rapid but marred by painful depressions. Banks became the veritable engine of an increasingly industrialized America, but banking capital gravitated to cities in the east and the manufacturing belt rimming the Great Lakes. Rural communities suffered from a lack of credit and perpetually depressed grain prices.

The system's flaw was its rigidity. Chase had designed National Banking to cure the unpredictable gyrations of the old state notes. Under the new system, note issuance was tightly controlled, and the inflation that had loomed so large in the mind of its creator was not a problem. Instead, the postwar era was marked by thirty years of *deflation*.

By 1870, financial assets were more concentrated in New York than they had been before the war. The system was literally rigged to pull deposits from rural areas into the larger cities, and thence to New York, where banks earned high rates of return by lending to the stock market.

---

* Chase's brainchild failed to eliminate state-chartered banks, which soldiered on even though they no longer issued notes. This perpetuated the country's odd patchwork of federal banks and state banks answering to distinctive regulators.

It did not take long for the Republicans, the upstart reformers of the 1850s, to mature into defenders of the financial elite. The party made preservation of the tariff its singular objective. Even more than with banking, the protective tariff was good for manufacturers and harmful to farmers and other consumers. Big Business contributed lavishly to the dominant party; heeding its patron, the Republicans solidly aligned against free trade.

After the war, the government reaped large surpluses, which threatened the tariff by eroding its supposed rationale. Business lobbied, instead, to discontinue the income tax. In 1872, the Republican Congress let the income tax expire, a choice that epitomized the party's retreat from middle-class ideals.* Repeal of the tax and maintenance of the tariff padded the fortunes of Gilded Age barons. As the scale of business grew, the party's priorities were increasingly corporatized. Lincoln's colleagues had been store clerks and single proprietors. Their world appreciably vanished. In 1877, a Republican president used federal troops to crush the Great Railroad Strike (supported by 100,000 workers), aligning the party of Lincoln with capital. Republicans increasingly championed laissez-faire. The party emphasized less the nationalism of Sherman than social Darwinism, which asserted that business tycoons represented the economically fittest, against whom any intervention would interfere with the natural order.

For all that, there was no turning back on Lincoln's larger state. The federal government, previously a collection of custom houses and postal carriers, was entrusted with vast new responsibilities. The Lincoln administration bequeathed to the country a permanent bureau (which morphed into the Internal Revenue Service) for tax collection and a cadre of banking and currency supervisors. Its growth continued after the war. By the early 1870s, the government was allocating $30 million annually to public works, and a swiftly escalating sum to war pension-

---

* Members of Congress introduced dozens of bills to reinstate the income tax. It was reenacted in 1894 but struck down as unconstitutional. In 1913, the Sixteenth Amendment established its constitutionality.

ers. Federal budgets in the 1870s hovered around $250 million, four times as large as those in the 1850s. By 1890, with the United States at peace and the frontier officially closed, the federal budget topped $350 million. To pay for this expanded state, internal and external taxes remained multiples higher than before the Civil War.

The purposes of the government were also elevated in the minds of Americans. They looked to it, as they hadn't before, to solve national problems. Since the government had freed the slaves, people expected it to address other pressing issues, such as low farm prices, labor disputes, the power of the railroads, and monopolies. Lincoln and the Republicans had advanced a mostly new idea—nationhood and national sovereignty—and this idea stuck. Winning, and financing, the war had demonstrated the federal government's potential. The seven-thirty Treasury drive raised $830 million, the largest financing in the country's history. Postwar, the seven-thirties were refinanced into bonds, and much of the debt was repaid early.* As Jay Cooke had predicted, Union paper was redeemed in gold. Washington's ability to service its war debt offered further proof of federal strength. Fiscal soundness was a mark of political maturity. In contrast, the Erlanger cotton bonds collapsed. (Improbably, they continued to trade, at pennies on the dollar, for years after the Confederacy ceased to exist.)

The Thirty-Seventh Congress had enduring effects on American life. The transcontinental railroad, a striking success, transformed freight, passenger, and mail service and brought the western states fully into the nation. No more was the far west accessible only by means of a perilous, several weeks' journey by stagecoach. Beginning in 1869, regular service from Omaha to Sacramento was completed in four days. The rails made possible the emergence of a national market in business. Politically as well as economically, they validated America as a territorial whole.

---

* The U.S. debt peaked in 1866, a year after the war, at $2.77 billion. By 1880 it had fallen to $1.9 billion.

The Homestead Act did not provide the urban "safety value" that proponents had advertised. Few impoverished city dwellers took up the government's offer. Many homesteaders were, in fact, established farmers relocating farther west. Nearly half of those who began the process were unable to fulfill the two main requirements for taking title, improving the land and living on it five years. Nonetheless, the program had a profound influence. It accelerated the country's westward expansion and nurtured the self-reliant spirit that is often presumed to be an American birthright. It lasted more than a century and by the time it ended, in 1976 (later in Alaska), the government had deeded 270 million acres to 1.6 million homesteaders—equivalent to a tenth of all the land in the United States. Homesteading helped to establish a national ethos of home ownership, still visible in the federal tax code and in the federal mortgage agencies. Indeed, it was a forerunner of the modern policy of subsidizing home ownership—with considerably less risk. Title was conveyed free of debt, and it never caused a bank run.

The legacy of the Morrill Act was greater still. The original act spawned 68 colleges and universities, including flagship institutions such as Pennsylvania State University and Ohio State. The so-called second Morrill Act (1890) added federal funding and prohibited racial discrimination. The latter clause was honored in the South only by the establishment of a network of Black colleges, such as Tuskegee University and Florida A&M. Although the insistence on segregation was deplorable to say the least, Morrill's dream of a college education for Americans of modest means was realized for substantial numbers of whites and a not insignificant number of Blacks. Tribal colleges were added in 1994—a sadly overdue recompense for the fact that much of the original land was seized from Native tribes. Today, 1.7 million students are enrolled in 109 land-grant colleges, still an affordable path to higher education.

After the Civil War, the government became a more conspicuous—some would say meddling—presence. The Department of Agriculture, founded in 1862 with a single desk in Washington, set up extension offices in every state. Railroads, following the model established in banking, were placed under the scrutiny of a federal regulator. In 1890, Congress assigned to the government the task of policing monopolization. One is struck, a generation after the war, by the number and diversity of line items in the federal budget: the Treasury, mints and assay office, territorial governments, immigration, revenue cutters, a marine hospital, lighthouses, engraving and printing, public buildings, fish hatcheries, steamboat inspections, a national museum, the Smithsonian Institution, salaries for justices and marshals, colleges for agriculture, the Interstate Commerce Commission, a tiny Department of Labor.

The greatest purpose undertaken by the federal government was the guarantee of legal protections for African Americans. The Thirteenth Amendment, ratified eight months after Lincoln's death, truly ended slavery. Two other amendments purportedly granted equal protection and due process under the law, and male suffrage—but these were rendered ineffectual by white resistance, much of it violent. An ethos of white supremacy persisted, in the Deep South especially.

The Civil War did not resolve the urgent business of land for the freedmen. Various acts of Congress, beginning with the Confiscation Act of 1862, failed to provide clear title to confiscated lands. In 1864, Illinois senator Lyman Trumbull, who coauthored the Thirteenth Amendment, proposed a constitutional reform to permit confiscation of plantations; it went nowhere. Then, a month before Lee's surrender, Congress established the Freedmen's Bureau as a sort of social welfare agency to help emancipated Blacks get on their feet. The legislation came close to codifying General Sherman's edict for forty acres, but its language was vague, asserting the right of any male citizen to occupy confiscated land for three years, after which he could purchase "such title as the United States can convey."

Thaddeus Stevens, who championed land for the freedmen, battled mightily to extend and expand the Freedmen's Bureau's powers. On

December 18, 1865, he thundered in the House, "If we do not furnish them with homesteads from forfeited rebel property, and hedge them around with protective laws . . . we had better left them in bondage." Stevens concluded presciently that were Congress to fail in this "great duty . . . we shall deserve and receive the execration of history of all future ages."

The legislation faced two difficulties. First, the Republicans were divided. They believed in nurturing opportunity, much less in confiscation. In the words of a later chronicler of Stevens, they believed that "government existed to protect property, not redistribute it." Self-reliance was as much a part of Whig doctrine as expansive government. Even the Radical Republicans were divided over whether suffrage or land ought to take precedence. Charles Sumner, as stalwart an enemy of slavery as ever sat in the U.S. Senate, preferred to focus on political freedom. Economic development would be a longer haul. Even Republicans who recognized the moral argument for suffrage often failed to see that "freedom and famine," in Frederick Douglass's phrase, would not suffice. Freed slaves would require more than ballot access, namely, a material stake. Land reform forced the Republicans to choose between competing ideals: opportunity and property.

The second stumbling block was President Johnson, the Tennessee Democrat who did not, ever, evince sympathy for the freedmen. Whatever its own qualms, Congress moved cautiously on land reform due to its desire to avoid a presidential veto. The Republicans enacted a moderate bill, in 1866, which Johnson vetoed all the same. Stevens did not let up, warning, "We shall not approach the measure of justice until we have given every adult freedman a homestead on the land where he was born and toiled and suffered." That summer, Congress enacted a bill over Johnson's veto, extending the Freedmen's Bureau until 1868 and assigning it more powers, including that of selling certain forfeited lands to freedmen. However, few plantations were seized, and the administration restored lands to previous owners. "With help and striving, the Negro gained some land," observed a sympathetic *Atlantic Monthly*, but not much. In the decade after Appomattox, Blacks in Georgia acquired 350,000 acres, less than 2 percent of the state's farmland.

In the 1870s, support for Reconstruction faded, even among Republicans. White Americans were largely indifferent to the plight of the freedmen, and even many who were sympathetic did not support maintaining a permanent military presence in the South. In 1872, some of the staunchest Radicals—including Sumner, Chase, Trumbull, and Horace Greeley—defected to the Liberal Republican Party. Although still supportive of Black rights, the Liberals had tired of sectional struggle, and called for an end to Reconstruction.

Stevens had died in 1868, leaving land reform without its most energetic advocate. As the Freedmen's Bureau expired, millions of Blacks remained on farms, mostly as tenants or sharecroppers. Sharecroppers were free citizens de jure, but, owing to the lack of credit facilities coupled with harsh terms at rural stores, practically they became locked into cycles of debt peonage and poverty. With the establishment of Jim Crow, sharecroppers were effectively stripped of legal protections. Only about 10 percent of southern Blacks became landowners, which they achieved without federal assistance and often in the face of white hostility.

The Blacks at Port Royal and elsewhere on the Sea Islands constituted a special case, thanks to their isolation from the departed whites. By the war's end, most of the land had been seized for back taxes and was in a state of legal adjudication. Some plots had been sold to Negroes; some was held by the tax commissioners. However, on May 29, 1865, President Johnson granted a blanket amnesty to all persons "directly or indirectly" involved in the rebellion, "with restoration of all rights of property, except as to slaves." Technically, restitution did not apply to land already subject to confiscation proceedings. However, Johnson's order made clear that the administration would give a sympathetic hearing to the old slave masters. The planters began returning to the islands, confidently asserting ownership rights. Laura Towne, a Pennsylvania abolitionist who had come to the islands to found a school, noted with dismay, "Secesh are coming back thick."

General Rufus Saxton tried to convey land titles to freedmen in a hurry, to make "forty acres" an accomplished fact. For a while, he had the support of the head of the Freedmen's Bureau, the evangelical Union general Oliver Howard. But the planters complained to Washington. Johnson ordered Howard to go to the islands and work out a "mutually satisfactory" solution. As Willie Lee Rose notes in her history of Port Royal, the President's meaning was clear. At a large church meeting, a freedman cried out, "Why, General Howard, why do you take away our lands? This is not right." Unsold land was slated for return to white owners, who were required merely to settle their tax bills and swear a loyalty oath. In 1866, U.S. military forces—the same army that had liberated the South the previous year—supervised the restoration of land to the old plantation owners.

Freedmen in the islands closest to Port Royal retained more land than elsewhere. Schools were established and the Blacks became self-supporting, if far from wealthy. They lived, as they preferred, apart from whites, and were a force in local politics until late in the nineteenth century. In 1895, a new constitution in South Carolina paved the way for Jim Crow and voter suppression. Salmon Chase's hope that Port Royal could serve as a model for freed people across the South ended in failure. It did not even succeed in Port Royal.

Given the passionate resentment of white southerners, it is possible that land confiscation would have made Reconstruction even bloodier and uglier than it was. But the federals never tested the South's potential for reform by offering generous economic support. Quite the opposite: northerners, with reason, thought former Confederates were lucky to avoid treason charges after what they had done. Thus, federal policies toward the defeated South were neglectful at best. After the income tax expired, the government relied mostly on tariffs and excise taxes on whiskey and tobacco, a regressive formula that disproportionately burdened the South. Federal spending was no less lopsided. During the first eight years after the war, the South received less than 10 percent of public works—less in fact than New York State alone. The United States established a generous military pension that extended to soldiers' wives and dependents but excluded Confederate soldiers—that is, it excluded the region destroyed by the war. This was a Marshall Plan for the winners.

The missed opportunity was the failure to see that the entirety of southern society needed reform. It needed Whig modernizations and economic bootstrapping, without which the gap between North and South—the essential precondition for the war—persisted. The scale of the South's needs may well have been too vast for any nineteenth-century government, but the United States never even tried.

In the absence of federal relief, the economic chasm between North and South grew wider. Billions of the South's wealth had been vaporized by the destruction of railroads and other property and the looting and burning of cotton. This loss was not recouped anytime soon. By 1870, the region's total agricultural and manufacturing capital had fallen to half that of 1860—without counting the loss of its slaves. The effect on wealth distribution was severe. Over the same decade, the southern share of the national wealth plunged from 30 percent to merely 12 percent. The plantation system was destroyed, replaced by an inefficient system of smaller farms and sharecroppers. Commodity production, which rose in the North, plunged in the South by 40 percent. Many nations defeated in war have bounced back quickly, but no phoenix arose from the ashes of the Confederacy. Before the war, personal income per capita in Dixie equaled 70 percent of the national average; in 1880, it was only half. It remained at that level through 1900. This represented an enormous drop in relative living standards. The collapse was, by far, greatest in the Deep South cotton states, the heart of the former rebellion. Growth in per capita income in North Carolina and Virginia held its own with the North; however, in Alabama, Mississippi, Georgia, Louisiana, and South Carolina, incomes grew at only half the rate in the United States as a whole. The regions didn't converge—they grew further apart.

Through the end of the nineteenth century, most southerners worked on farms. Output inevitably shrank as women and children (former slaves) withdrew from the fields. By 1870, agricultural output in the Deep South was 30 percent less than in 1860. Southern farmers worked with inferior tools and little or no machinery—just as they had before the war. Lacking substantial investment and in the absence of slave labor, cotton production did not return to its previous high for nearly twenty years, or until 1879. American farms in general remained surprisingly primitive. Many farmers continued to plow on foot and milk by hand, mostly cut off from industrialization. This underdevelopment was most extreme in Dixie. As late as 1920, fewer than 10 percent of American farms had electricity; in the South, fewer than 5 percent did. It was almost as if the war had never been fought.

Southern industry made up lost ground, but not nearly enough to close the gap. Three decades after the war, Ohio boasted 21 miles of railroad track per each 100 square miles; Alabama had 7 and Mississippi under 6. Even rural Vermont boasted more track per square mile than Virginia. Despite the introduction of National Banking, southern business was handicapped by a paucity of credit. At the turn of the century, national banks in the eleven former Confederate states had fewer loans outstanding than the single city of Boston. In social measures, the region treaded water at best. Three-quarters of northern children ages five to eighteen were enrolled in school, compared with only 60 percent in the South. Most southern schools were open fewer than 100 days a year (in Arkansas only 70 days), while northern schools, even in farm states, were in session 130 to 190 days. And the North provided better materials and paid their teachers higher wages. Even decades after the war, the Whig revolution had yet to arrive.

The South also lost (in relative terms) population. The great immigrant waves settled mostly in the North. There was relatively little in-migration from other parts of the United States. In other words, the South was deprived of the ferment, industry, and creative energy of newcomers. The formula for renewal offered by the invisible hand—

that people and capital attracted by low prices will spark a recovery— works only to the degree that a region is not isolated and shut off. But the postwar South was characterized by a lack of social mobility, not dissimilar from southern society antebellum. Historians have treated the South's continuing poverty as a mystery, and a proper analysis is beyond the scope of this book. But we will observe that, for many decades, the South ignored the economic verdict of the war era, first set forth by one of its own. It was the North Carolinian Hinton Rowan Helper, author of the 1857 blockbuster *The Impending Crisis of the South*, who laid out the thesis that slavery, aside from oppressing Blacks, was retarding the majority of poor whites. They each existed in a condition of backwardness, and if poor whites were not as downtrodden as the enslaved, they enjoyed few of the possibilities open to northern strivers and settlers and pioneers. And for as long as the South perpetuated Jim Crow, as a quasilegal refinement of slavery, it remained an economic backwater. Some diversification occurred in the twentieth century, due to improved roads, urbanization, the appeal of nonunionized industry— and the boll weevil, which destroyed cotton plants and pushed farmers to experiment with peanuts and other crops. But the low wages, under-development, rural torpor, and lack of mobility that characterized the South before the war persisted, particularly in the Deep South. In 1940, per capita income in the South was less than two-thirds of the national average, about the same as in 1860. Only after the sweeping changes wrought by the civil rights movement in the 1960s did a more fluid, modern, and prosperous southern economy emerge. Only then was the South restyled as the Sun Belt, a fast-growing region with sleek airports, vibrant cities, top-ranked universities, and leading corporations. Only a century after the war, that is, when the South was forced to abandon the pervasive racial injustices of Jim Crow, and when it outgrew the corrosive social strategy of placating poor whites by keeping Blacks in an even more inferior position, did the South become a place where Americans moved *to* rather than fled from, and begin to catch up with the history it had missed.

Jefferson Davis publicly admitted after the war that he had erred in not heeding his closest adviser, Judah Benjamin, by stockpiling cotton in England while he could. He claimed it would have "more than sufficed all the needs of the Confederacy during the war." Davis was indicted for treason, along with other former Rebel officials. President Johnson issued a blanket pardon, absolving them. Neither Davis nor any Confederate official stood trial. Benjamin fled to England, where he pursued a second law career. According to Ruth Bader Ginsburg, who developed a curiosity about Benjamin (who before the war had turned down the chance to become the first Jewish Supreme Court justice), Benjamin "cheerfully start[ed] all over" in England and reinvented himself as a distinguished and high-earning barrister. Christopher Memminger, the hapless German who ran the Rebel Treasury but never figured out how to sustain the fisc, in retirement helped to develop the segregated school system in Charleston. Memminger's dashing successor, George Trenholm, returned to his cotton firm, but his luck had run out. The firm dissolved in bankruptcy.

William Pitt Fessenden remained in the Senate until his death, in 1869. Fessenden is remembered for his fiery antislavery oratory before the war. In the cabinet, he was a capable if unimaginative secretary, managing the finances during a difficult hour. Jay Cooke, who came to Fessenden's (and also Chase's) rescue, glimpsed the potential of American investors, preparing the ground for the vibrant capital markets of the postwar period. He attributed his success to divine intention. "Like Moses and Washington and Lincoln and Grant I have been—I firmly believe—God's chosen instrument." His inflated self-estimation soon caught up with him. After the war, Jay Cooke & Co. was named the exclusive agent for the Northern Pacific Railway, which had been chartered by Congress to link the Great Lakes to the Pacific northwest. The route was sparsely populated, and Cooke had trouble attracting investors. Cooke & Co. tried to backstop the road, stockpiling bonds the public didn't want. In 1873, the firm failed, triggering a panic and a long-lasting national depression.

John Sherman eclipsed his wartime companions, at least in longevity, persevering on the national stage until the start of the Spanish-American War. He was a major figure in public finance, serving as Treasury secretary and also secretary of state. In the Senate, he was largely responsible for passing the Sherman Antitrust Act, a groundbreaking law. He was a diligent public servant, not a shining star. History better remembers his charismatic brother.

George Templeton Strong had begun keeping a diary at age fifteen, in 1835. He religiously wrote in it nearly every day for forty years. Its 2250 raw pages, now housed in the New-York Historical Society (and excerpted in four published volumes), provide an unvarnished, if patrician view of the Civil War era and beyond.

John Beauchamp Jones, the Maryland journalist who became a Rebel war clerk, stayed in Richmond to the bitter end. He survived the assault on the city, copiously recording official gossip and the price of flour, but was weakened from illness and slow starvation. He died less than a year after Appomattox. Mary Chesnut lost her capital, which she and her husband had invested in Rebel bonds. Although they kept the family plantation in South Carolina, now bereft of slaves, they could not escape from financial pressures. Mary was as unprepared for ordinary work as was Margaret Mitchell's fictional heroine Scarlett O'Hara, to whom, later, she was often compared. She continued to speak of Blacks in a superior tone, but her own station was much reduced. She eked out a living selling butter and eggs; she tried sewing, she wrote novels that she didn't finish. In the late 1870s and early 1880s, she worked exhaustively on her diary, recasting and embellishing but preserving a tone of womanly defiance. As the work dragged on, she willed her papers to a friend. *A Diary from Dixie* was published, posthumously, in 1905; it was later reissued as *Mary Chesnut's Diary*. The memoir has been criticized as reworked and novelized but also acclaimed, deservedly, for its literary record of a tart Southern woman in the upper echelons of the Confederacy.

Edmund Ruffin, the seventy-one-year-old agronomist and radical secessionist who fired the first shot at Sumter, was present for the war's final act. Yankee troops had forced him to abandon his plantations, and the old widower was residing at Redmoor, the tobacco plantation of his eldest son. As Rebel troops retreated toward the Appomattox Court House, Redmoor lay in their path. Just before Lee's surrender, Ruffin fled from Sheridan's onrushing cavalry into the woods. Days later, the fighting was over, but Ruffin was scarcely at peace. He had lost eight of his eleven children, a favorite daughter-in-law, and, before the war, his wife. His "whole remaining capital," loyally invested in Rebel securities, was gone, and so was his dream of an independent South. Facing the prospect of living under the despot Lincoln, he contemplated whether death would not be merciful. His diary musings turned dark and bilious. He saw little future for himself, no means of support, no place of refuge. He reflected that his Rebel notes would not pay even for breakfast, yet he would not "consent to live a pauper on the charity of strangers abroad." Worse than material deprivation was the specter of living with the "evils of emancipation . . . the general intrusion & mastership of swarms of Yankee immigrants . . . the negroizing of the people." He could not admit that slavery had been the evil, nor even that the southern system had been its own undoing, especially in Virginia, where the acidic Tidewater soils had increasingly forced the planters to sell their chattel to the cotton and sugar barons in the Deep South, and therefore, that Lincoln's unwelcome invaders were destroying a system that was impeding the South's own progress. The final entry in his twenty-five volumes of manuscript, dated June 16, 1865, meditated upon the biblical prohibition "Thou shalt not kill," which, at some length, he endeavored to show proscribed only the killing of others. He had prepared the "mechanical means" and made the necessary arrangements, a musket and ball and forked trigger. In his room upstairs, where ordinarily he did his writing, he draped a Confederate flag about his shoulders and then, as he recorded, he felt his doubts and his fears melt. Grasping the pen that he had wielded as a secessionist sword, he affirmed, once more, "I here repeat, and would willingly proclaim, my unmitigated hatred to Yankee rule." Then he placed the muzzle in his mouth and departed a changed world he wanted no part of.

Acknowledgments

Many people helped me with this book (words that I have written before, and no less true for the repetition). First of all, my wife, Judy, tended to the manuscript, and to its author, with editorial skill and sustaining care. I think of this project as one we shared. My editor, Ann Godoff, again demonstrated unmatched skills. As with a great coach, she simply refused to settle for less than her grudging pupil's best. Melanie Jackson was so much more than a literary agent. She was a reader and a supportive counselor and, during the long months of COVID lockdowns, a welcome voice on the telephone.

The Civil War was new terrain for me, and two extraordinary scholars did their best to guide me through it. Frank J. Williams, the retired chief justice of Rhode Island and one of the country's foremost Lincoln scholars, was endlessly encouraging and consummately helpful. He generally responded to queries in minutes, often from memory, and always with grace. (For such traits, in Providence, Frank is known simply as "The Chief.") Adam Rowe, a newly minted Civil War historian (and law school student, too), similarly read—and reread—my every word and responded with comments and suggestions that reflected his profound understanding of nineteenth-century America. I'm also grateful to my friend Ron Chernow, who introduced me to Frank and was as supportive (and knowledgeable) as a friend could be.

Several accomplished scholars provided suggestions and help when I was starting out or along the way; I'm grateful to Marc Egnal, Jane Flaherty, Douglas Irwin, and Marc D. Weidenmier. And I'm profoundly grateful to numerous librarians who shepherded me through the vast archives, as well as the truly immense published collections, on the Civil War. Michelle A. Krowl, PhD, the Civil War and Reconstruction specialist in the Manuscript Division at the Library of Congress, seems to be on an intimate basis with every significant and lesser work and archive on the Civil War. She was generous with suggestions and with her time. I am grateful, as well, to the LOC's Juretta Jordan Heckscher, a reference specialist for early American history. Various librarians selflessly pitched in with on-site help when the pandemic or a deadline precluded travel. I'm grateful to Anita Clary, special collections librarian, and to Kara L. Robinson, associate dean, at Kent State University Libraries—and to Carol Heller at KSU Press. I'm grateful as well to Traci Patterson, an archivist and special collections librarian at Rice University; to Aron Bowers, a senior library associate at Mississippi State University; to Amie Freeman, scholarly communication librarian at the University of South Carolina, and to her colleague Edward Blessing; and to Christine L. Hernandez, curator of special collections at the Latin American Library at Tulane University. And I owe a debt to the staff at Widener Library and other branches in the Harvard system. These book-loving professionals work for the rest of us, readers and writers.

I also benefited from a terrific supporting cast at Penguin Press, notably associate editor Casey Denis, copy editor Trent Duffy, and my longtime publicist, Sarah Hutson. All three are as talented as they are careful and patient. Within the House of Lowenstein, Scott Steinhardt (my cousin) proved a whiz at gathering historical photographs online. Jacob Paul uncomplainingly morphed from answering a question or two about my outdated laptop into my on-call IT rescue service. Without Jacob, it was back to pencil and foolscap. I also want to thank Michelle L. Eureka at the Weatherhead Center at Harvard, and I want to thank my cousins David and Anna Fierst for their warm hospitality during research stays in Washington. Back home, Philip Sadler pitched in as only a good neighbor can, during crises editorial and other.

I'm especially grateful to the team of readers who interrupted their own work to read mine. Neil Barsky, with me from book one, Jeffry Frieden, Geoffrey Lewis, Mitch Rubin, Jeffrey Tannenbaum (another lifer), and Mark Williams read every word. All are close friends (I choose my critics with care). Some offered trenchant suggestions that enriched, focused, or—mercifully—trimmed the prose; some offered encouragement and support. I am grateful to all. Almost snarky Alex Beam, Hal Belodoff, my cousin Fred Fierst, my editor-sister Jane Ruth Mairs, David Moss, and Sam Waldron, who first critiqued my work a world ago in Caracas, read parts of the manuscript, some in its roughest early stages. Some offered sharp suggestions; some just said keep going. Thank you to all. Zachary, Matthew, and Allison Lowenstein (reversing the alphabetization seems fair) each read major portions and/or were unfailingly supportive. My mom, Helen Lowenstein, going strong after seven books, and my in-laws, Janet and Gil Slovin (now up to five), were unapologetically biased—that is, in my corner. My family, including my sister Barbara Pearl and others already mentioned and unmentioned, showed up at a difficult moment. Not least, on an otherwise quiet summer evening when I needed some help, Jonny Levenfeld and, as always, Judy, showed their mettle.

Roger Lowenstein
Tenants Harbor, Maine, August 2021

Notes

Unpublished Papers

The principal archives consulted for this book can be found in these locations:

Belmont Family Papers: Rare Book and Manuscript Library, Butler Library, Columbia University, New York, N.Y.

Salmon P. Chase Papers: Manuscript Division, Library of Congress, Washington, D.C. To avoid confusion with the five-volume *Salmon P. Chase Papers*, containing key documents (see *SPCP*, p. 342), these are referred to in the notes as "Chase Papers (LOC)."

Howell Cobb Collection: New-York Historical Society, New York, N.Y.

William Pitt Fessenden Papers: Manuscript Division, Library of Congress, Washington, D.C.

James A. Garfield Papers: Manuscript Division, Library of Congress, Washington, D.C.

Justin S. Morrill Papers: Manuscript Division, Library of Congress, Washington, D.C.

John Sherman Papers: Manuscript Division, Library of Congress, Washington, D.C.

Edmund Clarence Stedman Papers: Rare Book and Manuscript Library, Butler Library, Columbia University, New York, N.Y.

Published Primary Sources

The following abbreviations are used for some of the more frequently cited primary sources.

Chesnut   Mary Boykin Chesnut. *Mary Chesnut's Diary*, New York: Penguin Classics, 2011. (Originally published as *A Diary from Dixie*: New York: D. Appleton, 1905.)

CWL   Abraham Lincoln. *The Collected Works of Abraham Lincoln*. Edited by Roy P. Basler. 8 vols. New Brunswick, N.J.: Rutgers University Press, 1953.

Davis Papers   *The Papers of Jefferson Davis*. Edited by Haskell M. Monroe Jr. and James T. McIntosh. 14 vols. Baton Rouge: Louisiana State University Press, 1991–2015. Cited herein are vol. 10, *October 1863–August 1864*, edited by Lynda Lasswell Crist, Kenneth H. Williams and Peggy L. Dillard (1999), and vol. 11, *September 1864–May 1865*, edited by Lynda Lasswell Crist (2003).

RWCD   J. B. Jones. *A Rebel War Clerk's Diary*. Edited by James L. Robertson Jr. 2 vols. Lawrence: University Press of Kansas, 2015. I used this edition until the pandemic struck, after which I had to consult the original edition, a two-volume set published as *A Rebel War Clerk's Diary at the Confederate States Capital* (Philadelphia: J.B. Lippincott, 1866), online. These two editions have differing paginations, so all citations of Jones's *Diary* give the year as well as the abbreviation *RWCD*.

Ruffin   Edmund Ruffin. *The Diary of Edmund Ruffin*. Edited by William Kaufman Scarborough. 3 vols. Baton Rouge: Louisiana State University Press, 1972–1989.

SPCP   Salmon Chase. *The Salmon P. Chase Papers*. Edited by John Niven et al. 5 vols. Kent, Ohio: Kent State University Press, 1994–1998.

Stevens Papers   *The Selected Papers of Thaddeus Stevens*. Edited by Beverly Wilson Palmer and Holly Byers Ochoa. Pittsburgh: University of Pittsburgh Press, 1997.

Strong   George Templeton Strong. *The Diary of George Templeton Strong*. Edited by Allan Nevins and Milton Halsey Thomas. 4 vols. New York: Macmillan, 1952.

In addition to the above, I greatly benefited from published collections of letters, including those of Edward Bates, August Belmont, Benjamin Butler, Jefferson Davis, Ulysses S. Grant, John Hay, John Sherman, William Tecumseh Sherman, and Edmund Clarence Stedman. It was not uncommon in the nineteenth century for offspring of notables to publish accounts of their father's careers, including their correspondence. Two shining examples were compiled by heirs of Johns Adams Dix and William Pitt Fessenden, the secretaries of the Treasury, respectively, just before and during the final year of the Civil War.

The diary of Salmon P. Chase, Treasury secretary for most of the war, edited by David Herbert Donald, was invaluable. So were the published memoirs or diaries of George S. Boutwell, L. E. Chittenden, each of the two Shermans, William O. Stoddard, and Navy Secretary Gideon Welles. The diaries of people who held *no* official rank were enormously helpful in shedding light on the effects of the war on the economies and living standards north and south. Later published diaries of Mary Chesnut, John Beauchamp Jones (a minor Confederate clerk), Edmund Ruffin, and George Templeton Strong, told the story of the war, often vividly, from the home fronts.

Historians have written so many stellar books on the Civil War that it seems hopeless to attempt a list, but a handful were exceptionally useful to me, either because they offered such a trove of information, or because they helped to shape my thoughts during the research. I happily acknowledge a debt to Sidney Blumenthal for his multivolume biography, *The Political Life of Abraham Lincoln*, to Marc Egnal for *Clash of Extremes*, to James McPherson, for his comprehensive and masterly *Battle Cry of Freedom*, to Gabor S. Boritt, for the groundbreaking *Lincoln and the Economics of the American Dream*, and similarly to Eric Foner for *Free Soil, Free Labor, Free Men*, and to Heather Cox Richardson, for *The Greatest Nation of the Earth*. The endnotes that follow are studded with others too numerous to name. On Civil War finance, I greatly benefited from the work of David M. Gische, Bray Hammond, Matthew S. Jaremski, Christopher Schwab, David K. Thomson, and Marc Weidenmier, among others. Among the biographies of lesser-known but significant figures, Robert J. Cook's profile of Fessenden, *Civil War Senator*, is first-rate. There are many more.

Introduction: Revolution Completed

1   **Jefferson thought of the federal government:** Gordon S. Wood, *Friends Divided: John Adams and Thomas Jefferson* (New York: Penguin Press, 2017), 415.

2   **In 1860, just before the election:** Among the presidential vetoes, Madison in 1817 nixed legislation to build roads and canals throughout the United States; Jackson in 1830 vetoed a bill for a federal turnpike in Kentucky, and Pierce in 1854 vetoed a bill to set aside federal land for the benefit of "indigent insane persons." See Marc Egnal, *Clash of Extremes: The Economic Origins of the Civil War* (New York: Farrar, Straus and Giroux, 2009), 40. Buchanan's veto of the Michigan water channel improvements cited Madison's veto of 1817; for the former, see http://www.presidency.ucsb.edu/ws/index.php?pid=68392.

2   **Its army consisted:** Richard Franklin Bensel, *Yankee Leviathan: The Origins of Central State Authority in America, 1859–1877* (New York: Cambridge University Press, 1990), 118.

2   **had not traveled to England or France:** John Sherman, a rare exception, had vacationed with his wife in Europe in 1859.

3   **Early in his career:** "A Look at Public Education in Pennsylvania: Thaddeus Stevens; An Early Advocate for Pennsylvania's Public Schools," https://hourglasslancaster.org/wp-content/uploads/2020/06/March-2002-Forum-A-Look-at-Public-Education-in-Pennsylvania.pdf, 1.

3   **"easier to pass a bill":** Fawn M. Brodie, *Thaddeus Stevens: Scourge of the South* (New York: W. W. Norton, 1959), 59.

3   **three-fourths of the world's cotton:** James M. McPherson, *Battle Cry of Freedom: The Civil War Era* (New York: Oxford University Press, 1988), 39.

4   **"No power on earth":** Sven Beckert, *Empire of Cotton: A Global History* (New York: Alfred A. Knopf, 2015), 244.

4   **"the crowned heads"**: See, e.g., *New York Herald*, Dec. 13, 1860.

4   **"sad & frightened, some in tears"**: Kristin Claire Carlson, "Christian Duty in the Crisis of Seces-sion" (master's thesis, Virginia Polytechnic Institute and State University, 2015), 63.

4   **"civil war was foreign"**: Gavin Wright, *The Political Economy of the Cotton South* (New York: W. W. Norton, 1978), 147.

5   **abolition by the federal government**: See art. IV, sect. 2, clause 3, known as the "fugitive slave clause." It begins, "No Person held to Service or Labour in one State, under the Laws thereof . . ."

5   **scarcely more than 1 percent**: According to the Bowdoin College "Data Analysis: African Ameri-cans on the Eve of the Civil War" (https://www.bowdoin.edu/~prael/lesson/tables.htm), approxi-mately 225,000 Blacks lived in the New England, Mid-Atlantic, Midwest and far west states out of a total population of just under 19 million. The percentage of Blacks was higher in the so-called Upper South states (what became, during the Civil War, the loyal slave states).

5   **a system of "free labor"**: This is the "free labor" thesis of Eric Foner, beautifully rendered in *Free Soil, Free Labor, Free Men: The Ideology of the Republican Party Before the Civil War* (New York: Ox-ford University Press, 1970).

5   **In Indiana, Black suffrage**: Egnal, *Clash of Extremes*, 143.

5   **Only the New England states**: Richard C. Rohrs, "Exercising Their Right: African American Voter Turnout in Antebellum Newport, Rhode Island," *The New England Quarterly* 84, no. 3 (2011): 402. Connecticut, an exception, withdrew the franchise from African Americans in 1818. Blacks in New York could vote only if they met special property requirements.

6   **"The negro race already occupy"**: Egnal, *Clash of Extremes*, 148.

6   **"I want to have nothing to do"**: Egnal, *Clash of Extremes*, 148.

6   **The South was less urban**: Wright, *The Political Economy of the Cotton South*, 110; McPherson, *Battle Cry of Freedom*, 40.

6   **6 percent of the country's pig iron**: Benjamin T. Arrington, "Industry and Economy During the Civil War," National Park Service, https://www.nps.gov/articles/industry-and-economy-during -the-civil-war.htm.

6   **Total capital invested in manufacturing**: Wright, *The Political Economy of the Cotton South*, 110; Arrington, "Industry and Economy During the Civil War," says the North produced 90 percent of the manufacturing output in 1860; McPherson, *Battle Cry of Freedom* (p. 91), looking at 1850, says the North had 82 percent of manufacturing capacity.

6   **Ohio, although a bit smaller**: G. Lloyd Wilson and Ellwood H. Spencer, "Growth of the Rail Network in the United States," *Land Econom*ics 26, no. 4 (1950): 337–45; "Our American States: Alabama; Part I," *De Bow's Review* 18, no. 1 (1855): 21–28.

6   **"mournful decay"**: Samuel W. McCall, *Thaddeus Stevens* (Boston: Houghton Mifflin, 1899), 77–78.

6   **Frederick Law Olmsted**: Biographical details in Arthur M. Schlesinger, introduction to Frederick Law Olmsted, *The Cotton Kingdom: A Traveler's Observations on Cotton and Slavery in the American Slave States* (New York: Da Capo, 1996).

6   **done the southern people more harm**: Olmsted, *Cotton Kingdom*, 8.

6   **"their destitution is not just material"**: Olmsted, *Cotton Kingdom*, 12.

7   **wasteful "complacency"**: Olmsted, *Cotton Kingdom*, 11.

7   **six mules and five Blacks**: Olmsted, *Cotton Kingdom*, 141.

7   **"coarse gray gowns"**: Olmsted, *Cotton Kingdom*, 161.

7   **"carrying in his hand"**: Olmsted, *Cotton Kingdom*, 162.

7   **windowless huts, unfit for animals**: Olmsted, *Cotton Kingdom*, 161.

7   **"as if unable to withdraw"**: Olmsted, *Cotton Kingdom*, 135–36.

7   **cotton production jumped**: "Southern Wealth and Northern Profits," *De Bow's Review*, Aug. 1860, 197.

7   **unit value of its four million slaves**: Edward Baptist, *The Half Has Never Been Told: Slavery and the Making of American Capitalism* (New York: Basic Books, 2014), 271, 352, 359.

7   **invested in farm tools and machinery**: Wright, *The Political Economy of the Cotton South*, 54–55, 109.

7   **scarcely any patent activity**: Wright, *Political Economy of the Cotton South*, 54–55.

7   **"The suicidal indifference"**: "Our American States: Alabama; Part I."

8   **"We are satisfied"**: McPherson, *Battle Cry of Freedom*, 99.

8   **"sedentary and agricultural"**: Egnal, *Clash of Extremes*, 159.

8   **"if Congress can make canals"**: Egnal, *Clash of Extremes*, 198.

8   **"to allow the humblest man"**: *CWL*, 4:24.

8   **"Agriculture needs no teaching"**: Williamjames Hoffer, *To Enlarge the Machinery of Government: Congressional Debates and the Growth of the American State, 1858–1891* (Baltimore: Johns Hopkins University Press, 2007), 28.

8   **"I thank God"**: David Hackett Fischer, *Albion's Seed: Four British Folkways in America* (New York: Oxford University Press, 1989), 347; see also "Virtual Jamestown," http://www.virtualjamestown .org/exist/cocoon/jamestown/fha/J1062.

8   **Helper argued**: Hinton Rowan Helper, *The Impending Crisis of the South* (New York: A.B. Burdick, 1857), 23, 25.

9   **banned in several southern states**: Ralph Korngold, *Thaddeus Stevens: A Being Darkly Wise and Rudely Great* (New York: Harcourt, Brace, 1955), 100–101; McPherson, *Battle Cry of Freedom*, 200.

9   **"a positive good"**: Richard Nelson Current, *Old Thad Stevens: A Story of Ambition* (Madison: University of Wisconsin Press, 1942), 53.

9   **The plantation system**: See, e.g., James Ford Rhodes, *Lectures on the American Civil War* (New York: Macmillan, 1913), 12.

9   **Since only a quarter**: Olmsted, *Cotton Kingdom*, li.

9   **"a wandering laboring boy"**: *CWL*, 4:61–62.

10   **"winked out"**: *CWL*, 4:64–65.

10   **"I want every man"**: Lincoln speech in New Haven, Mar. 6, 1860, *CWL*, 4:24.

Chapter One: Two Crises

13   **"The sinews of war are unlimited money"**: Oxford Essential Quotations, https://www.oxfordrefer ence.com/view/10.1093/acref/9780191826719.001.0001/q-oro-ed4-00003011. The quote is sometimes given in English as "The sinews of war, unlimited money" (as it is in this source).

14   **the most widely read paper**: Mark R. Wilson, *The Business of Civil War: Military Mobilization and the State, 1861–1865* (Baltimore: Johns Hopkins University Press, 2006).

14   **"we insist on letting them go"**: "Going to Go," *New York Daily Tribune*, Nov. 9, 1860.

14   **duty receipts plunged**: *Annual Report of the Secretary of the Treasury on the State of the Finances* [hereinafter, Treasury Secretary, *Annual Report*], 1860, pp. 3–4, and 1861, p. 30; the drop refers to receipts in the December 1860 (fiscal 1861) quarter compared with the corresponding period a year earlier.

14   **doubling of the federal debt**: Treasury Secretary, *Annual Report*, 1860, p. 22; Treasury Secretary, *Annual Report*, 1857, p. 11.

14   **Word had spread**: *Strong*, 3:55. For background on Cobb, see John Eddins Simpson, *Howell Cobb: The Politics of Ambition* (Chicago: Adams Press, 1973), esp. 26–27, 113, and Richard H. Timberlake Jr., "The Independent Treasury and Monetary Policy Before the Civil War," *Southern Economic Journal* 27, no. 2 (1960): 101.

14   **"I regard submission to Lincoln"**: Howell Cobb to unknown recipient, Nov. 11, 1860, Howell Cobb Collection.

14   **faith in government securities evaporated**: Treasury Secretary, *Annual Report*, 1860, p. 9.

14   **"The financial crisis is already beginning"**: *Strong*, 3:62, 63, 64.

15   **"The people are not yet"**: "Commercial Relations Between the North and South," *New York Times*, Dec. 10, 1860.

15   **"Who shall possess"**: Rachel Sherman Thorndike, ed., *The Sherman Letters: Correspondence Between General and Senator Sherman from 1837 to 1891* (New York: Charles Scribner's Sons, 1894), 92–104.

15   **honor their debts**: *Strong*, 3:62; Philip Foner, *Business and Slavery: The New York Merchants and the Irrepressible Conflict* (Chapel Hill: University of North Carolina Press, 1941), 195, 212, 220–23; Edward K. Spann, *Gotham at War: New York City, 1860–1865* (Wilmington, Del.: Scholarly Resources, 2002), 7, 11; *Western Democrat* [Charlotte, N.C.], Nov. 20, 1860.

15   **banks both north and south**: See, e.g., Allan Nevins, *The War for the Union*, vol. 2, *War Becomes Revolution, 1862–1863* (Old Saybrook, Conn.: Konecky & Konecky, 1960), 485; James Ford Rhodes, *Lectures on the American Civil War* (New York: Macmillan, 1913), 71; "The Stock-Market," *New York Times*, Nov. 16, 1860.

15   **Lord & Taylor**: Foner, *Business and Slavery*, 208.

15   **Georgia's governor advised**: Foner, *Business and Slavery*, 218.

15   **an estimated $200 million**: Jane Flaherty, "The Exhausted Condition of the Treasury on the Eve of the Civil War," *Civil War History* 55, no. 2 (2009): 258.

15   **northern merchants demanded concessions**: Aside from banking and textiles, the railroad industry also demanded southern-friendly concessions; see Peter Maynard, *Baltimore's Great Railroad King: John Garrett of the B&O* (Brunswick, Md.: Brunswick Historical Press, 2012), 57–58.

15 **In liberal Boston:** Richard H. Abbott, *Cotton and Capital: Boston Businessmen and Antislavery Reform, 1854–1868* (Amherst: University of Massachusetts Press, 1991), 67.
15 **appointed a committee:** Spann, *Gotham at War*, 5.
15 **"The first steps":** Foner, *Business and Slavery*, 238.
15 **Europeans were bailing:** Flaherty, "The Exhausted Condition of the Treasury," 271.
15 **The Treasury lacked:** See Robert T. Patterson, "Government Finance on the Eve of the Civil War," *The Journal of Economic History* 12, no. 1 (1952); Wesley C. Mitchell, "The Suspension of Specie Payments, December 1861," *Journal of Political Economy* 7, no. 3 (1899): 292; Flaherty, "The Exhausted Condition of the Treasury."
15 **"sense of duty":** "The Resignation of Secretary Cobb: The Correspondence," *New York Times*, Dec. 14, 1860.
16 **Congress now authorized:** Patterson, "Government Finance on the Eve of the Civil War," 40; Mitchell, "The Suspension of Specie Payments," 292.
16 **Cisco persuaded:** Edith Vail Taylor, "Saving America from Bankruptcy: An Intimate Story of the First Civil War Loan," *New York Sun*, Mar. 31, 1917 (reprinted as a pamphlet that year by National Bank of Commerce, New York); Patterson, "Government Finance on the Eve of the Civil War," 40; Mitchell, "The Suspension of Specie Payments"; Maunsell B. Field, *Memories of Many Men and of Some Women* (New York: Harper and Brothers, 1874), 251–52.
16 **"expressly to meet interest":** Taylor, "Saving America from Bankruptcy."
16 **Republican support for the tariff:** There is a rich literature on the role of the tariff in the 1860 election. See, for instance, Coy F. Cross II, *Justin Smith Morrill: Father of the Land-Grant Colleges* (East Lansing: Michigan State University Press, 1999), 49; Reinhard H. Luthin, "Abraham Lincoln and the Tariff," *The American Historical Review* 49, no. 4 (1994): 612, 614–15, 617, 621; "Western Pennsylvania and the Election of 1860" (paper, Historical Society of Western Pennsylvania, May 31, 1922), file:///C:/Users/ElRog/Downloads/1311-Article%20Text-1159-1-10-20120925.pdf; Richard Hofstadter, "The Tariff Issue on the Eve of the Civil War," *The American Historical Review* 44, no. 1 (1938): 50–55. See also Republican National Committee to Justin S. Morrill, Sept. 25, 1860, Justin S. Morrill Papers, reel 5; Arthur M. Lee, "Henry C. Carey and the Republican Tariff," *The Pennsylvania Magazine of History and Biography* 81, no. 3 (1957): 300; Marc Egnal, *Clash of Extremes: The Economic Origins of the Civil War* (New York: Farrar, Straus, and Giroux, 2009), 240–44, 249; Charles H. Levermore, "Henry C. Carey and His Social System," *Political Science Quarterly* 5, no. 4 (1890): 553–82. Thaddeus Stevens said the tariff issue was more important in the election in his state than slavery—see Richard Nelson Current, *Old Thad Stevens: A Story of Ambition* (Madison: University of Wisconsin Press, 1942), 135.
16 **convention managers had promised:** John Niven, *Salmon P. Chase: A Biography* (New York: Oxford University Press, 1995), 222.
17 **The visit did not go poorly:** *SPCP*, 3:44–46; Niven, *Chase: A Biography*, 222–24; Albert Bushnell Hart, *Salmon Portland Chase* (Boston: Houghton Mifflin, 1899), 202; J. W. Schuckers, *The Life and Public Services of Salmon Portland Chase* (New York: D. Appleton, 1874), 201.
17 **"The lord hath dealt":** Chase to Charles D. Cleveland, Oct. 1, 1845, in *SPCP*, 2:121.
17 **"There are few things *wholly* evil":** *CWL*, 1:484.
18 **"only valuable while in circulation":** Gabor S. Boritt, *Lincoln and the Economics of the American Dream* (Memphis: Memphis State University Press, 1978), 64.
18 **"highest ambition":** Sidney Blumenthal, *The Political Life of Abraham Lincoln*, vol. 1, *A Self-Made Man, 1809–1849* (New York: Simon & Schuster, 2016), 92.
18 **$3000 a year:** Albert A. Woldman, *Lawyer Lincoln* (New York: Carroll & Graf, 2001), 236.
18 **"any war upon capital":** *CWL*, 4:25. In the same 1860 address in New Haven, Lincoln also said, "I don't believe in a law to prevent a man from getting rich; it would do more harm than good."
19 **"Must the products":** Woldman, *Lawyer Lincoln*, 183–84.
19 **"He is a man":** Salmon P. Chase, *Inside Lincoln's Cabinet: The Civil War Diaries of Salmon P. Chase*, ed. David Herbert Donald (New York: Longman's Green, 1954), 8.
19 **"Our conversations were free":** *SPCP*, 3:44–46.
19 **He was grateful:** See, e.g., Lincoln's comment, "As to Governor Chase, *I have a kind side for him*," in *CWL*, 3:395. See also Frederick J. Blue, *Salmon P. Chase: A Life in Politics* (Kent, Ohio: Kent State University Press, 1987), 119.
19 **Chase had written platforms:** Eric Foner, *Free Soil, Free Labor, Free Men: The Ideology of the Republican Party Before the Civil War* (New York: Oxford University Press, 1970), 78, 79, 83.
20 **"volcanic fault line":** Blumenthal, *A Self-Made Man*, 306.
20 **a mob destroyed:** Niven, *Chase: A Biography*, 48–49.

20   **"law of force which made him a slave":** John Niven, "Lincoln and Chase: A Reappraisal," *Journal of the Abraham Lincoln Association* 12, no. 1 (1991): 1–15 (emphasis added). The farmer was John Van Zandt, later a model for the fictional John Van Trompe in *Uncle Tom's Cabin.* Zandt's case went to the Supreme Court, where he lost.

20   **infrequent but courageous stands:** In 1837, Lincoln and another legislator had voted in the minority against a resolution denouncing abolitionists (not that Lincoln was one). Soon after, the pair introduced their own resolution defending the right of Congress to abolish slavery in the District of Columbia and declaring that slavery was founded on "injustice."

20   **"strung together precisely":** *CWL,* 1:260; Blumenthal, *A Self-Made Man,* 228.

21   **He refused to make a claim:** In Peoria in 1854, Lincoln said he was not "contending for the establishment of political and social equality" of the races. He said of the territories, "We want them for the homes of free white people" (*CWL,* 2:266, 268). Four years later, during his Senate campaign, Lincoln, in the fourth debate with Douglas, repeated, "I am not, nor ever have been in favor of bringing about in any way the social and political equality of the white and black races"—a comment met by prompt applause. (*CWL,* 3:145).

21   **"In the right to eat":** *CWL,* 3:16.

21   **"We think slavery is morally wrong":** *CWL,* 4:9.

21   *"And I believe a black man":* **CWL,** 4:24 (emphasis added).

21   **"only swallow a little":** Luthin, "Abraham Lincoln and the Tariff," 615. John Sherman similarly tried to downplay the slavery issue, asserting a month ahead of the convention that the Republicans had "other purposes in view": "Republican Meeting: Large Gathering at the Copper [*sic*] Institute; Addresses by Hon. John Sherman and Ex-Gov. Ford, of Ohio," *New York Times,* Apr. 14, 1860.

21   **Republican platform defended the right:** For the 1856 party platform, see http://www.presidency.ucsb.edu/ws/index.php?pid=2961.

21   **Even in offering congratulations:** *SPCP,* 3:28.

22   **"ability, firmness and purity of character":** *CWL,* 4:171.

22   **"Public business had been neglected":** Morgan Dix, *Memoirs of John Adams Dix* (New York: Harper & Brothers, 1883), 1:364.

22   **The department's disarray:** For U.S. Treasury history, see https://www.treasury.gov/about/history/collections/Pages/West_Wing.aspx.

22   **cash register was empty:** Mitchell, "The Suspension of Specie Payments," 293; James G. Blaine, *Twenty Years of Congress, from Lincoln to Garfield* (Boston: Avery, 1884), 1:397.

22   **Dix sold the notes:** Mitchell, "The Suspension of Specie Payments," 294.

22   **awash in red ink:** Treasury Secretary, *Annual Report,* 1861, pp. 37, 42.

22   **going without pay:** Flaherty, "The Exhausted Condition of the Treasury," 244–45.

22   **"an empty Treasury":** Don E. Fehrenbacher and Virginia Fehrenbacher, eds., *Recollected Words of Abraham Lincoln* (Stanford, Calif.: Stanford University Press, 1996), 170–71.

22   **fully a third:** Flaherty, "The Exhausted Condition of the Treasury," 257.

22   **already in Rebel hands:** *New York Herald,* Dec. 29, 1860.

22   **sixteen hundred banks:** Hart, *Salmon P. Chase,* 274; Ellis Paxson Oberholtzer, *Jay Cooke: Financier of the Civil War* (Philadelphia: G.W. Jacobs, 1907), 1:326; David M. Gische, "The New York City Banks and the Development of the National Banking System 1860–1870," *The American Journal of Legal History* 23. no 1 (1979): 24.

23   **already delaying requisitions:** Flaherty, "The Exhausted Condition of the Treasury," 245.

23   **"Time is very short":** John Sherman, *Recollections of Forty Years in the House, Senate and Cabinet* (Chicago: Werner, 1895), 1:252–53; see also Flaherty, "The Exhausted Condition of the Treasury," 244.

23   **an unusual request:** Dix's plea came in two forms. The first was that states pledge their surplus deposits as security for federal borrowing. The second was that the larger industrial states (of the North) co-endorse federal obligations. See Patterson, "Government Finance on the Eve of the Civil War," 41. Ultimately, Dix would place only $8 million, or about a third, of the bonds Congress authorized. See also Mitchell, "The Suspension of Specie Payments," 294, 297.

23   **Federal collectors willingly surrendered:** Flaherty, "The Exhausted Condition of the Treasury," 257.

23   **Georgia raided the custom house:** Sherman, *Recollections,* 1:210.

23   **"no effort had been made":** Dix, *Memoirs of John Adams Dix,* 1:371.

23   **Dix sent a special agent:** Dix, *Memoirs of John Adams Dix,* 1:371.

24   **"If any one attempts":** Dix, *Memoirs of John Adams Dix,* 370–71. Some sources (including Secretary Dix) use an alternate spelling for the revenue cutter captain, "Breshwood." Newspapers of the era did

not agree, and he signed his name "Brushwood." See John G. Brushwood to Captain Brown, Oct. 6, 1859, Series 2, box 1, folder 12, Callender I. Fayssoux of William Walker Papers, 1856–1860, Latin America Library, Tulane University, New Orleans, La.

24 **Dix's war telegram:** See, e.g., "The National Troubles," *New York Times*, Feb. 8, 1861; Dix, *Memoirs of John Adams Dix*, 1:370.

24 **"Secession . . . means civil war":** Irving Katz, *August Belmont: A Political Biography* (New York: Columbia University Press, 1968), 86–87.

24 **confidently, if recklessly, interpreted:** See, e.g., Robert Neil Mathis, "Gazaway Bugg Lamar: A Southern Businessman and Confidant in New York City," *New York History* 56, no. 3 (1975): 309.

24 **Frederick Douglass said the South:** David W. Blight, *Frederick Douglass: Prophet of Freedom* (New York: Simon & Schuster, 2018), 327.

24 **"Men here have ceased":** Sherman, *Recollections*, 1:238.

24 **bubble in the slave market:** Gavin Wright, *The Political Economy of the Cotton South* (New York: W. W. Norton, 1978), 129–30, 144.

24 **Southern slaves had a market value:** Douglas A. Irwin, *Clashing over Commerce: A History of U.S. Trade Policy* (Chicago: University of Chicago Press, 2017), 211.

24 **"a panic of fear":** C. C. Campbell to Justin S. Morrill, Jan. 15, 1861, Morrill Papers, reel 5.

25 **"the poor man's best Government":** James M. McPherson, *Battle Cry of Freedom: The Civil War Era* (New York: Oxford University Press, 1988), 243.

25 **"if the question must be referred":** Mario Chacon and Jeffrey Jensen, "The Institutional Determinants of Southern Secession," Working Paper #0001, March 2017, https://papers.ssrn.com/sol3/papers.cfm?abstract_id=3091512, 7.

25 **Of the seven Rebel states:** Egnal, *Clash of Extremes*, 274, 279, 281.

25 **at least fifteen slaves:** Edward Baptist, *The Half Has Never Been Told: Slavery and the Making of American Capitalism* (New York: Basic Books, 2014), 390.

25 **hopes on the Confederate presidency:** Cobb insisted to his wife he had no interest in the job—probably when he realized it would go to Davis. See Ruby Sellers Davis, "Howell Cobb, President of the Provisional Congress of the Confederacy," *The Georgia Historical Quarterly* 46, no. 1 (1962): 27.

25 **Davis had been born:** The biographical sketch of Davis has been drawn from Burton J. Hendrick, *Statesmen of the Lost Cause: Jefferson Davis and His Cabinet* (Boston: Little, Brown, 1939), 12–20, 24–30, 32, 41–43, 48; Walter A. McDougall, *Throes of Democracy: The American Civil War Era, 1829–1877* (New York: HarperCollins, 2008), 448; McPherson, *Battle Cry of Freedom*, 366, 429; Fawn M. Brodie, *Thaddeus Stevens: Scourge of the South* (New York: W. W. Norton, 1959), 108; Blumenthal, *A Self-Made Man*, 379–80.

25 **slave population in the cotton belt:** Adapted by United States Citizens Recovery Initiative Alliance from *Historical Statistics of the United States*, https://uscria.com/slave_pop_by_state.pdf.

26 **The constitution framed in Montgomery:** For the Confederate constitution, see https://en.wikisource.org/wiki/Constitution_of_the_Confederate_States_of_America.

26 **it was "permanent":** Davis's inaugural address is available at https://jeffersondavis.rice.edu/archives/documents/jefferson-davis-first-inaugural-address.

26 **"We are without machinery":** Jefferson Davis to Varina Davis, Feb. 20, 1861, in Frank E. Vandiver, "Jefferson Davis—Leader Without Legend," *The Journal of Southern History* 43, no. 1 (1977): 14.

27 **so-called peace convention:** "Monthly Record of Current Events," *Harper's*, April 1861. The convention was attended by delegates from twenty states.

27 **Congress sent to the states:** "Affairs of the Nation," *New York Times*, Feb. 28, 1861; "The Peace Movement," *New York Times*, Mar. 1, 1861; Ralph Korngold, *Thaddeus Stevens: A Being Darkly Wise and Rudely Great* (New York: Harcourt, Brace, 1955), 114.

27 **no one claimed:** Adam Rowe, conversation with author.

27 **"No vote I ever gave":** Justin S. Morrill to Ruth Morrill, Mar. 1, 1861, Morrill Papers, reel 5.

27 **Lincoln paid heed:** Baptist, *The Half Has Never Been Told*, 392.

27 **En route to the nation's capital:** McDougall, *Throes of Democracy*, 404.

27 **"When I first came":** *CWL*, 4:192.

27 **"The wild lands of the country":** *CWL*, 4:202–3.

28 **"the treasury of the nation":** *CWL*, 4:211–12.

28 **New York Chamber of Commerce:** Arthur M. Lee, "Henry C. Carey and the Republican Tariff," *The Pennsylvania Magazine of History and Biography* 81, no. 3 (1957): 299.

28 **"with direct reference to giving us a tariff":** *New York Daily Tribune*, Feb. 16, 1861.

28 **Henry Carey:** Egnal, *Clash of Extremes*, 257; see also Lee, "Henry C. Carey and the Republican Tariff," 297–98.
28 **a million sheep:** Cross, *Justin Smith Morrill*, 43. The Morrill tariff passed the House (already under Republican control) in 1860; the Senate passed it in 1861. See also Theodore E. Burton, *John Sherman* (Boston: Houghton Mifflin, 1908), 68–69.
28 **the average rate on dutiable:** Irwin, *Clashing over Commerce*, 210.
28 **When Lincoln arrived:** Spann, *Gotham at War*, 7.
28 **plunge in luxury imports:** "Commerce of the United States," *New York Times*, Mar. 15, 1862, reporting of a year earlier, "People felt uneasy . . . they did not buy so many luxuries."
29 **"Nothing is to be gained":** Adam Rowe, "The Paradox of Union: The Civil War and the Transformation of American Democracy" (PhD diss., University of Chicago, 2018), 75.
29 **"Let the grass grow":** Rowe, "The Paradox of Union."
29 **"not only the commercial interests":** Spann, *Gotham at War*, 7.
29 **his "peripatetic" wife:** "The Presidential Progress," *New York Times*, Feb. 25, 1861.
29 **rushed ahead that night:** "The Incoming Administration: All About the Change of Programme; The Secret History of the Great Conspiracy; Scenes After the Discovery; Moral Reflections," *New York Times*, Feb. 26, 1861; Benjamin Brown French, *Witness to the Young Republic: A Yankee's Journal, 1828–1870*, ed. Donald B. Cole and John J. McDonough (Hanover, N.H.: University Press of New England), 342.
29 **known to be corrupt:** Lee, "Henry C. Carey and the Republican Tariff," 294. Carey said of Cameron, "In both private & public life he has been a politician, intent upon the accumulation of fortune."
29 **serious pushback from Seward:** Niven, *Chase: A Biography*, 237.
29 **"Everybody longing for the Inaugural":** *Strong*, 3:105.
29 **The address was lengthy:** Lincoln's inaugural address is available at http://avalon.law.yale.edu/19th_century/lincoln1.asp.

Chapter Two: Exigencies of War

31 **"In a war":** Alan Moorehead, *A Late Education* (London: Hamish Hamilton, 1970), 113.
31 **Lincoln told a White House visitor:** Don E. Fehrenbacher and Virginia Fehrenbacher, eds., *Recollected Words of Abraham Lincoln* (Stanford, Calif.: Stanford University Press, 1996), 106.
31 **Lincoln then asked:** Heather Cox Richardson, *The Greatest Nation of the Earth: Republican Economic Policies During the Civil War* (Cambridge: Harvard University Press, 1997), 32.
32 **twenty thousand troops:** Message to Congress, July 4, 1861, in *CWL*, 4:423.
32 **The entire U.S. army:** Richard Franklin Bensel, *Yankee Leviathan: The Origins of Central State Authority in America, 1859–1877* (New York: Cambridge University Press, 1990), 118.
32 **a reason to go to war:** James M. McPherson, *Battle Cry of Freedom: The Civil War Era* (New York: Oxford University Press, 1988), 268.
32 **Chase favored resupplying:** *SPCP*, 3:53–54.
32 **"no moral right":** Message to Congress, July 4, 1861, 4:440.
32 **recommended evacuating Sumter:** John Niven, *Salmon P. Chase: A Biography* (New York: Oxford University Press, 1995), 243.
32 **"The tug has to come":** *CWL*, 4:150.
32 **The cabinet fell in line:** Niven, *Chase, A Biography:* 243–47; *SPCP*, 3:55; Fawn M. Brodie, *Thaddeus Stevens: Scourge of the South* (New York: W. W. Norton, 1959), 148; William E. Gienapp and Erica L. Gienapp, eds., *The Civil War Diary of Gideon Welles* (Urbana: University of Illinois Press, 2014), 1:691.
33 **Edmund Ruffin:** For biographical details, see *Ruffin*, 1:xvii, 496.
33 **flowing white locks:** "South Carolina," *New York Times*, Nov. 16, 1860.
33 **accorded the honor:** *Ruffin*, 1:xvi.
33 **"The shell struck the fort":** *Ruffin*, 1:586.
33 **"The northern backbone":** *Strong*, 3:119.
33 **"We are living":** *Strong*, 3:123.
33 **If the South went:** Bensel, *Yankee Leviathan*, 60–62.
33 **Strong felt "ashamed":** *Strong*, 3:109.
33 **So-called volunteer:** Mark R. Wilson, *The Business of Civil War: Military Mobilization and the State* (Baltimore: Johns Hopkins University Press, 2006), 9.
33 **control of individual states:** Bensel, *Yankee Leviathan*, 118.

33 **Militia were funded:** Wilson, *The Business of Civil War*, 9.

34 **Units retained close affiliations:** McPherson, *Battle Cry of Freedom*, 326.

34 **State governors had the power:** Wilson, *The Business of Civil War*, 8.

34 **states competed with Washington:** Niven, *Chase: A Biography*, 251.

34 **William Dennison Jr.:** Richard H. Abbott, "Ohio's Civil War Governors," Ohio State University Press for the Ohio Historical Society, https://kb.osu.edu/bitstream/handle/1811/6332/OHIOS _CIVIL_WAR_GOVERNERS_txt.pdf?sequence=1&isAllowed=y.

34 **furnished its own uniforms:** Wilson, *The Business of Civil War*, 5–24.

34 **Brooks Brothers:** *The Business of Civil War*, 19.

34 **A New York City merchant:** Edward K. Spann, *Gotham at War: New York City, 1860–1965* (Wilmington, Del.: Scholarly Resources, 2002), 49. The merchant and soon-to-be mayor was George Opdyke.

34 **nineteen thousand Enfield rifles:** Wilson, *The Business of Civil War*, 16.

34 **In the first few months:** "Monthly Record of Current Events," *Harper's*, June 1861. The previous peak annual spending on the army was $36 million in 1847: see Theodore E. Burton, *John Sherman* (Boston: Houghton Mifflin, 1908), 89.

34 **"in Cases of Rebellion":** U.S. Const., art. I, sect, 9.

35 **"real and imagined" threats:** Bensel, *Yankee Leviathan*, 141.

35 **"I can touch a bell":** Bensel, *Yankee Leviathan*, 141.

35 **In May, exercising his power:** McPherson, *Battle Cry of Freedom*, 322.

35 **organized a regiment:** Irving Katz, *August Belmont: A Political Biography* (New York: Columbia University Press, 1968), 90.

35 **"It was worth a life":** "New York Seventh Regiment: Our March to Washington," *Atlantic Monthly*, June 1861, 744.

35 **"is not waged by abolitionists":** Laura Stedman and George M. Gould, *Life and Letters of Edmund Clarence Stedman* (New York: Moffat, Yard, 1910), 1:242.

35 **"Are we indeed":** "The Reign of King Cotton," *Atlantic Monthly*, Apr. 1861, 451.

36 **"Ask those who made the war":** J. A. Woodburn, "The Attitude of Thaddeus Stevens Toward the Conduct of the Civil War," *The American Historical Review* 12, no. 3 (1907): 570.

36 **"Slavery has to go":** Chesnut, 66; the entry was penned on June 29, 1861, soon after the start of the war.

36 **diary gave her a sense of purpose:** Anna Braunscheidel, "Will the Real Miss Scarlett Please Stand Up: How the Life of Mary Boykin Chesnut Can Be Considered a Model for Margaret Mitchell's Scarlett O'Hara" (master's thesis, Clemson University, 2012), 18.

36 **attended a sumptuous dinner:** Chesnut, 73.

37 **"So I have sewed it":** Chesnut, 88.

37 **swaggeringly boasted:** Rollin Osterweis, *Judah P. Benjamin: Statesman of the Lost Cause* (New York: G.P. Putnam's Sons, 1933), 119; Walker made this claim before the shelling of Fort Sumter.

37 **doubled the nonslave population:** 1860 U.S. Census. The white population of the original seven Rebel states was a surprisingly small 2.7 million. The quartet of late-joining states added nearly 3 million more.

37 **twenty-two million people:** 1860 U.S. Census. Including Kentucky, Maryland, Missouri, and Delaware, the total population of the slave states was considerably larger—12.2 million—but those four states, of course, stayed loyal to the Union.

37 **an industrial base perhaps five times larger:** Estimates vary. McPherson, *Battle Cry of Freedom*, 322, estimated eight times as large.

37 **joyous crowds:** McPherson, *Battle Cry of Freedom*, 278.

37 **"everywhere accompanied with cheers":** William Henry Hurlbert, "Fifteen Months at the South," *New York Times*, Sept. 11, 1862.

37 **"in want of many things":** Anne S. Frobel, *The Civil War Diary of Anne S. Frobel* (1986; repr., McLean, Va.: EPM Publications, 1992), 39.

38 **Judah Benjamin:** For biographical details on Benjamin, see Osterweis, *Judah P. Benjamin*, esp. 25, 36, 38, 42–74; Burton J. Hendrick, *Statesmen of the Lost Cause: Jefferson Davis and His Cabinet* (Boston: Little, Brown, 1939), 154–78; Robert Douthat Meade, "The Relations Between Judah P. Benjamin and Jefferson Davis: Some New Light on the Working of the Confederate Machine," *The Journal of Southern History* 5, no. 4 (1939): 468–78; Robert N. Rosen, *The Jewish Confederates* (Columbia: University of South Carolina Press, 2000), 57–58, 63, 80.

38 **"an Israelite with Egyptian principles":** Hendrick, *Statesmen of the Lost Cause*, 172.

38   **Millard Fillmore offered:** Ruth Bader Ginsburg, "Four Louisiana Giants in the Law," Memorial Lecture Series, Loyola University New Orleans, Feb. 4, 2002, http://www.laed.uscourts.gov/court -history/law-giants.
38   **the peculiar quality:** Meade, "The Relations Between Benjamin and Davis," 474.
38   **"callous indifference":** Hendrick, *Statesmen of the Lost Cause,* 168.
38   **eventually abandoning him:** Rosen, *Jewish Confederates,* 58.
38   **"Everything Mr. Benjamin said":** *Chesnut,* 243.
38   **Benjamin had habitually addressed:** Ginsburg, "Four Louisiana Giants in the Law."
38   **Benjamin proposed that the South:** Osterweis, *Judah P. Benjamin,* 120.
39   **a counterplan emerged:** Mark Thornton and Robert B. Ekelund Jr., *Tariffs, Blockades, and Inflation: The Economics of the Civil War* (Wilmington, Del.: Scholarly Resources, 2004), 31; Hendrick, *Statesmen of the Lost Cause,* 205–7.
39   **Davis embraced it:** Thornton and Ekelund, *Tariffs, Blockades, and Inflation,* 31.
39   **insisted to a dissatisfied southerner:** Hurlbert, "Fifteen Months at the South."
39   **textile industry provided employment:** Stanley Lebergott, "Labor Force and Employment, 1800–1960," in *Output, Employment, and Productivity in the United States After 1800,* ed. Dorothy S. Brady (Cambridge: NBER, 1966), 5.
39   **three-quarters of the cotton:** Gene Dattel, "The South's Mighty Gamble on King Cotton," *American Heritage* 60, no. 2 (2010).
39   **"revolution" . . . "the tremendous lever":** McPherson, *Battle Cry of Freedom,* 383.
39   **"Monopolists are always blind":** "The Reign of King Cotton," *Atlantic Monthly,* Apr. 1861, 451.
39   **"If your people stop":** Edwin De Leon, *Secret History of Confederate Diplomacy Abroad,* ed. William C. Davis (Lawrence: University Press of Kansas, 2005), 1–2.
40   **some southern governors issued:** Hendrick, *Statemen of the Lost Cause,* 210.
40   **shipments from New Orleans:** Thornton and Ekelund, *Tariffs, Blockades, and Inflation,* 32. The "1860" crop refers to the crop harvested in 1860 and 1861.
40   **"They *must sell*":** Edward Bates, *The Diary of Edward Bates, 1859–1866,* ed. Howard K. Beale (Washington, D.C.: GPO, 1933), 183–84.
40   **"Nations do not blockade":** Congressional Globe, 37th Cong., 2nd Sess., 180–81. See also *Stevens Papers,* 236–37; Richard Nelson Current, *Old Thad Stevens: A Story of Ambition* (Madison: University of Wisconsin Press, 1942), 146.
41   **cotton piled in warehouses:** Niven, *Chase: A Biography,* 263.
41   **Yancey, who seemed to think:** Hendrick, *Statesmen of the Lost Cause,* 140.
41   **receive them as private citizens:** De Leon, *Secret History of Confederate Diplomacy Abroad,* 53.
41   **"Our new Government is founded":** De Leon, *Secret History of Confederate Diplomacy Abroad,* 42.
41   **"I have not seen or heard":** James Ford Rhodes, *Lectures on the American Civil War* (New York: Macmillan, 1913), 154.
41   **The prime culprit:** Coy F. Cross II, *Justin Smith Morrill: Father of the Land-Grant Colleges* (East Lansing: Michigan State University Press, 1999), 50–51, quotes John L Motley, an American historian in London, who wrote, "That measure [the tariff] has done more than any commissioner from the Southern republic . . . to alienate the feelings of the English public toward the United States." For Britain's—and Dickens's—feelings on the Morrill tariff, see Marc-William Palen, "The Great Civil War Lie," *New York Times,* June 5, 2013, as well as these two helpful online sources: http://www.newenglandhistoricalsociety.com/justin-morrill-vermonter-raised-u-s-tariffs / and https://en.wikipedia.org/wiki/Morrill_Tariff.
42   **"We do not like slavery but":** Rhodes, *Lectures on the American Civil War,* 154.
42   **Chase knew that floating bonds:** David Kelley Thomson, "Bonds of War: The Evolution of World Financial Markets in the Civil War Era" (PhD diss., University of Georgia, 2016), 69.
42   **"will not long delay":** *Ruffin,* 2:127.
42   **"We are a little uneasy":** *Strong,* 3:143.
42   **Queen Victoria was issuing:** Elizabeth Cobbs Hoffman, "A Dangerous Neutrality," *New York Times,* May 12, 2011.
42   **it entitled the Confederacy:** McPherson, *Battle Cry of Freedom,* 388; Hoffman, "A Dangerous Neutrality."
42   **"Disappointment and exasperation":** *Strong,* 3:145.
42   **an end to friendly relations:** McPherson, *Battle Cry of Freedom,* 389.
42   **By presenting the message verbally:** Hendrick, *Statesmen of the Lost Cause,* 148.

43 **France was more eager:** For French attitudes toward the South at the start of the war, see De Leon, *Secret History of Confederate Diplomacy Abroad*, 14, 24–36, esp. 35; Hoffman, "A Dangerous Neutrality."

43 **Belmont inquired:** Katz, *August Belmont*, 93–94; William H. Seward to August Belmont, May 27, 1861, Belmont Family Papers, box 12. Belmont's engagement in the Union cause was all the more notable because, prewar, he had been mentored by John Slidell, his wife's uncle, a Louisiana senator and now a prominent Confederate.

43 **Belmont sailed for Europe:** Katz, *August Belmont*, 100; August Belmont to Salmon Chase, June 24, 1861, and Salmon Chase to August Belmont, July 1, 1861, Belmont Papers, box 5.

43 **onetime bounty:** Hendrick, *Statesmen of the Lost Cause*, 188.

43 **sold $15 million:** Hendrick, *Statesmen of the Lost Cause*, 188.

43 **Christopher Gustavus Memminger:** The biographical details on Memminger come from Henry D. Capers, *The Life and Times of C.G. Memminger* (Richmond: Everett Waddey, 1893).

44 **earned a reputation as a fierce:** Hendrick, *Statesmen of the Lost Cause*, 188.

44 **limited note issuance:** "Reports of the Secretary of Treasury, Finances of the Confederate States," reprinted in Capers, *Life and Times of C.G. Memminger*, 41.

44 **to pay for stationery:** L. E. Chittenden, *Recollections of President Lincoln and His Administration* (New York: Harper & Brothers, 1891), 258.

44 **Fifth Massachusetts Regiment:** U.S. Department of Treasury, "The Treasury Building: Civil War Fortress," https://www.treasury.gov/connect/blog/Pages/The-Treasury-Building-Civil-War-Fortress.aspx.

44 **parade of office seekers:** "English Letters from America," *New York Times*, Nov. 2, 1861.

44 **"I never worked nearly so hard":** Albert Bushnell Hart, *Salmon Portland Chase* (Boston: Houghton Mifflin, 1899), 215.

45 **Bankers offered a good rate:** Wesley C. Mitchell, "The Suspension of Specie Payments, December 1861," *Journal of Political Economy* 7, no. 3 (1899): 296–98.

45 **Wall Street was buoyant:** "To the Editor of the Herald," *New York Herald*, Mar. 12, 1861; "Financial and Commercial," *New York Herald*, Mar. 16, 1861.

45 **bond prices plunged:** "The Bids of the United States Treasury Notes," *New York Herald*, Apr. 12, 1861; "Financial and Commercial," *New York Herald*, Apr. 13, 1861; "Monetary Affairs," *New York Times*, Apr. 22, 1861.

45 **the Treasury collected just shy:** Mitchell, "The Suspension of Specie Payments," 296. The precise figures for the period were $5.8 million in revenue and $23.4 million in spending.

45 **Chase turned to John Cisco:** Maunsell B. Field, *Memories of Many Men and of Some Women* (New York: Harper and Brothers, 1874), 254–55.

45 **In April, he placed:** Robert T. Patterson, "Government Finance on the Eve of the Civil War," *The Journal of Economic History* 12, no. 1 (1952): 42–43. For the May sale, see Mitchell, "The Suspension of Specie Payments," 298–99.

45 **in 2021 dollars:** Calculation available at http://www.in2013dollars.com/1861-dollars-in-2018?amount=5000000.

46 **the pattern of earlier American wars:** Thomson, "Bonds of War," 53.

46 **Treasury's credit had deteriorated:** Patterson, "Government Finance on the Eve of the Civil War," 43.

46 **Chase reassured himself:** Field, *Memories of Many Men*, 255.

46 **"a long and sanguinary war":** James Garfield to Lucretia Garfield, April 14, 1861, James A. Garfield Papers, reel 2.

46 **he implored Chase to crack down:** *CWL*, 5:292.

46–47 **"decided improvement in finances":** Chase to Lincoln, Apr. 2, 1861, http://www.abrahamlincolnsclassroom.org/abraham-lincoln-in-depth/abraham-lincoln-and-civil-war-finance.

47 **"as yet we have accomplished":** Salmon Chase to Abraham Lincoln, Apr. 25, 1861, in *SPCP*, 3:61.

47 **"ardor and action":** Henry Raymond, "The People Demand Action," *New York Times*, Apr. 23, 1861.

47 **"concerted effort":** Richardson, *The Greatest Nation of the Earth*, 36.

47 **"a farmer at the country crossroads":** Lucius E. Chittenden, *Personal Reminiscences, 1840–1890: Including Some Not Hitherto Published of Lincoln and the War* (New York: Richmond, Croscup, 1893), 93.

47 **He tried to sell bonds:** John G. Nicolay and John Hay, *Abraham Lincoln: A History* (New York: Century, 1886–1890), 4:377.

47   **an American archetype:** See Henrietta M. Larson, *Jay Cooke, Private Banker* (Cambridge: Harvard University Press, 1936), esp. 35.

48   **Clark, Dodge & Company:** Larson, *Jay Cooke, Private Banker*, 34–73; Thomson, "Bonds of War," 44.

48   **"I have got on the right side":** Larson, *Jay Cooke, Private Banker*, 35.

48   **during the Panic of 1857:** Charles W. Calomiris and Larry Schweikart, "The Panic of 1857: Origins, Transmission, and Containment," *The Journal of Economic History* 51, no. 4 (1991): 821.

48   **a "fair fortune":** Larson, *Jay Cooke, Private Banker*, 85, 97.

48   **"I see Chase is in":** Ellis Paxson Oberholtzer, *Jay Cooke: Financier of the Civil War* (Philadelphia: G.W. Jacobs, 1907), 1:132.

48   **"whereby we can all safely make":** Larson, *Jay Cooke, Private Banker*, 102–4.

48   **Chase offered Cooke:** Oberholtzer, *Jay Cooke: Financier*, 1:135–38.

48–49 **opening his home:** Oberholtzer, *Jay Cooke: Financier*, 154.

49   **using newspapers to advertise:** Larson, *Jay Cooke, Private Banker*, 105–8.

49   **"an achievement as great":** Jay Cooke to Henry Cooke, June 13, 1861, in Oberholtzer, *Jay Cooke: Financier*, 1:111.

49   **careful to let Chase know:** Larson, *Jay Cooke, Private Banker*, 105–8.

49   **"The Treasury is now rather":** Salmon Chase to John A. Stevens, June 26, 1861, in *SPCP*, 3:69.

49   **only for sixty days:** Mitchell, "The Suspension of Specie Payments," 299.

Chapter Three: Ways and Means

50   **"All taxes are odious":** *Stevens Papers*, 217.

50   **six times as much:** The Buchanan budgets (fiscal 1858–1861) totaled $264 million, or an average of $66 million per year, excluding debt service (Treasury Secretary, *Annual Reports*).

50   **"We were physically strong":** John Sherman, *Recollections of Forty Years in the House, Senate and Cabinet* (Chicago: Werner, 1895), 1:228. Sherman was specifically referring to some months later—early 1862—but the comment aptly described the war's beginning period as well.

51   **"This is essentially a People's contest":** Message to Congress in Special Session, July 4, 1861, in *CWL*, 4:421–41.

51   **"My political education":** *CWL*, 4:214.

52   **"it might be better":** Adam Rowe, "The Paradox of Union: The Civil War and the Transformation of American Democracy" (PhD diss., University of Chicago, 2018), 285–86.

52   **"Is there, in all republics":** Message to Congress in Special Session, July 4, 1861, 4:421–41.

53   **far more than the United States had spent:** In constant dollars, the American Revolution cost the United States $2.41 billion, the War of 1812 $1.55 billion, and the Mexican War $2.38 billion. See Stephen Daggett, Congressional Research Service, "Costs of Major U.S. Wars," June 2010.

53   **he trimmed Lincoln's request by a fifth:** "The U.S. Treasury: Report of Secretary Chase," *New York Times*, July 6, 1861.

53   **double the previous year's revenues:** Treasury Secretary, *Annual Report*, 1861, p. 37.

53   **Chase's spending forecast:** "The U.S. Treasury: Report of Secretary Chase."

53   **"Do you expect to collect *mileage*":** Ralph Korngold, *Thaddeus Stevens: A Being Darkly Wise and Rudely Great* (New York: Harcourt, Brace, 1955), 128; see also "The U.S. Treasury: Report of Secretary Chase," 126–27, on Stevens's legislative style.

53   **who did not underestimate:** Fawn M. Brodie, *Thaddeus Stevens: Scourge of the South* (New York: W. W. Norton, 1959), 152.

54   **"a protracted and bloody war":** Korngold, *Thaddeus Stevens*, 131.

54   **Within three days:** Samuel W. McCall, *Thaddeus Stevens* (Boston: Houghton Mifflin, 1899), 144.

54   **limited debate to one hour:** James G. Blaine, *Twenty Years of Congress, from Lincoln to Garfield* (Boston: Avery, 1884), 1:1403.

54   **The legislation gave Chase:** J. W. Schuckers, *The Life and Public Services of Salmon Portland Chase* (New York: D. Appleton, 1874), 220–21, 338–39.

54   **Chase immediately used:** Schuckers, *The Life and Public Services*, 234; Lucius E. Chittenden, *Personal Reminiscences 1840–1890: Including Some Not Hitherto Published of Lincoln and the War* (New York: Richmond, Croscup, 1893), 297; Bray Hammond, *Sovereignty and an Empty Purse: Banks and Politics in the Civil War* (Princeton, N.J.: Princeton University Press, 1970), 73, 93.

54   **"greatest care":** "The U.S. Treasury: Report of Secretary Chase."

55 **the prime minister skeptically inquired:** August Belmont to William Seward, July 30, 1861, in August Belmont, *Letters, Speeches and Addresses of August Belmont* (1890; repr., N.p.: Bibliobazaar, 2008), 76.

55 **"It is utterly out of the question":** Schuckers, *The Life and Public Services*, 225–26.

55 **Belmont then traveled to France:** David Kelley Thomson, "Bonds of War: The Evolution of World Financial Markets in the Civil War Era" (PhD diss., University of Georgia, 2016), 73.

55 FORWARD TO RICHMOND: *New York Daily Tribune*, July 8, 1861. See also "On to Richmond," *New York Daily Tribune*, June 29, 1861, and "A Word for President Lincoln," *New York Daily Tribune*, July 18 1861.

55 **Scott sent passes:** Robert J. Cook, *Civil War Senator: William Pitt Fessenden and the Fight to Save the American Republic* (Baton Rouge: Louisiana State University Press, 2011), 136.

55 **rode horseback over a pontoon bridge:** Sherman, *Recollections*, 1:260.

56 **"straggling into the city":** Benjamin Brown French, *Witness to the Young Republic: A Yankee's Journal, 1828–1870*, ed. Donald B. Cole and John J. McDonough (Hanover, N.H.: University Press of New England, 1989), 366.

56 **tragic instances of friendly fire:** Mark R. Wilson, *The Business of Civil War: Military Mobilization and the State* (Baltimore: Johns Hopkins University Press, 2006), 23.

56 **sorrowful state of wartime medical facilities:** Chittenden, *Personal Reminiscences*, 253.

56 **"hotter and more detestable":** *Strong*, 3:172.

56 **"our volunteer system":** *Strong*, 3:174.

56 **"Its superannuated officials":** *Strong*, 3:181.

56 **Lincoln signed a pair of bills:** Walter A. McDougall, *Throes of Democracy: The American Civil War Era 1829–1877* (New York: HarperCollins, 2008), 417–18; James M. McPherson, *Battle Cry of Freedom: The Civil War Era* (New York: Oxford University Press, 1988), 348. Jefferson Davis, adding to an earlier call for 100,000 short-term enlistees, requested 400,000 Confederate troops.

56 **Jacob W. Schuckers:** Schuckers, *The Life and Public Services*, 234.

57 **duty receipts had plunged:** In the quarter ended June 30, 1861 (Lincoln's first full quarter as president), tariff revenues fell to $5.5 million, down from $11.5 million in the corresponding quarter of 1860, and $14.3 million in the 1859 quarter.

57 **duties on coffee and tea:** "The U.S. Treasury: Report of Secretary Chase." See also Leonard P. Curry, *Blueprint for Modern America: Nonmilitary Legislation of the First Civil War Congress* (Nashville: Vanderbilt University Press, 1968), 149–50; Albert Bushnell Hart, *Salmon P. Chase* (Boston: Houghton Mifflin, 1899), 238; Heather Cox Richardson, *The Greatest Nation of the Earth: Republican Economic Policies During the Civil War* (Cambridge: Harvard University Press, 1997), 110.

57 **William Elder:** Arthur M. Lee, "Henry C. Carey and the Republican Tariff," *The Pennsylvania Magazine of History and Biography* 81, no. 3 (1957): 295–96; Marc Egnal, *Clash of Extremes: The Economic Origins of the Civil War* (New York: Farrar, Straus, and Giroux, 2009), 249. Elder would later become Carey's biographer.

57 **Carey also lobbied Lincoln:** Lee, "Henry C. Carey and the Republican Tariff," 293–94.

57 **Morrill reported to Carey:** Lee, "Henry C. Carey and the Republican Tariff," 297.

57 **only two free traders:** Curry, *Blueprint for Modern America*, 150.

57 **Stevens had to force the measure:** Hammond, *Sovereignty and an Empty Purse*, 52–53; Curry, *Blueprint for Modern America*, 151.

57 **worried about the effect of the tariff:** Francis Fessenden, *Life and Public Services of William Pitt Fessenden* (Boston: Houghton Mifflin, 1907), 1:188; "The New Tariff, the Direct Tax, the Income Tax, Virtual Repeal of Sub-Treasury Law," *New York Times*, Aug. 3, 1861.

57 **only just cajoled a majority:** Richardson, *The Greatest Nation of the Earth*, 113.

57 **nearly doubled previous duties:** Reinhard H. Luthin, "Abraham Lincoln and the Tariff," *The American Historical Review* 49, no. 4 (1994): 627.

58 **Chase was only too familiar:** "The U.S. Treasury: Report of Secretary Chase."

58 **to bolster faith:** "Speech on War Financing," July 24, 1861, in *Stevens Papers*, 216.

58 **"many disagreeable things":** "Speech on War Financing," 215.

58 **"It was mainly on account":** "Speech on War Financing," 216.

58 **modeled on that of Albert Gallatin:** Joseph A. Hill, "The Civil War Income Tax," *Quarterly Journal of Economics* 8, no. 4 (1894): 418.

58 **Western legislators opposed it:** "The Civil War Income Tax," 419; Hammond, *Sovereignty and an Empty Purse*, 51–53. See also Joseph J. Thorndike, "An Army of Officials: The Civil War Bureau of Internal Revenue," Tax History Project, Dec. 21, 2001, http://www.taxhistory.org/thp/readings.nsf /ArtWeb/FF949517831B181685256E22007840E8?OpenDocument.

59 **"I cannot go home":** Hill, "The Civil War Income Tax," 419.

59   **"no way of ascertaining":** "Speech on War Financing," 215.

59   **he would vote for it regardless:** "Speech on War Financing," 219.

59   **regarded as provisional:** Thorndike, "An Army of Officials."

59   **"We propose to give personal attention":** *SPCP*, 3:76–77; Cooke's letter was dated July 12, 1861. See also, for Cooke's help to Chase, Ellis Paxson Oberholtzer, *Jay Cooke: Financier of the Civil War* (Philadelphia: G.W. Jacobs, 1907), 1:144.

60   **had to go a roundabout route:** Hammond, *Sovereignty and an Empty Purse*, 73.

60   **Taylor had started out as a merchant:** Daniel Hodas, *The Business Career of Moses Taylor* (New York: New York University Press, 1976), esp. 1–14, 181–84.

61   **uneasy about the Treasury's skimpy tax base:** Maunsell B. Field, *Memories of Many Men and of Some Women* (New York: Harper and Brothers, 1874), 256.

61   **delivered to the sub-Treasury:** Irwin Unger, *The Greenback Era: A Social and Political History of American Finance, 1865–1879* (Princeton, N.J.: Princeton University Press, 1964), 13. For a detailed account of the legislation amending the Independent Treasury Act, see Hammond, *Sovereignty and an Empty Purse*, 62, 63, 65–66, 75, 79, 85, 90–92, 98–104. The amending legislation was confusing and inconsistently interpreted. But almost everyone (aside from Chase) realized that it permitted the Treasury more flexibility. The *New York Times* Aug. 3, 1861, headline declared, VIRTUAL REPEAL OF SUB-TREASURY LAW.

61   **reserves of just over $60 million:** Wesley C. Mitchell, "The Suspension of Specie Payments, December 1861," *Journal of Political Economy* 7, no. 3 (1899): 308, puts the figure at $63.1 million. See also John Niven, *Salmon P. Chase: A Biography* (New York: Oxford University Press, 1995), 265.

61   **deny that Congress had amended the law:** Hammond, *Sovereignty and an Empty Purse*, 79.

61   **drive the price of breakfast:** Schuckers, *The Life and Public Services*, 227.

62   **City's Taylor felt the group could not refuse:** Hodas, *Moses Taylor*, 180.

62   **In mid-August:** The date was Aug. 14, 1861 ("The New Government Loan," *New York Times*, Aug. 15, 1861).

62   **New York bankers pledged:** Hodas, *Moses Taylor*, 180.

62   **could not safely travel east:** Hammond, *Sovereignty and an Empty Purse*, 78.

62   **"you have received":** Oberholtzer, *Jay Cooke: Financier*, 1:152.

62   **"more an Administration than a military disaster":** Salmon Chase to August Belmont, Sept 13, 1861, Belmont Family Papers, box 5.

63   **a private correspondence with several Union generals:** See vol. 3 of *SPCP*. To cite two examples, Chase wrote to John Frémont on Aug. 4, 1861, explaining that he "never ceased to regret" that his suggestions for Frémont's assignment were not adopted; to William Sherman, who had telegrammed his need for funds, Chase on Oct. 13 replied, "I wish I could have said absolutely all requisitions for your troops will be immediately responded to. *It will not be my fault if they are not*" (emphasis added).

63   **Crittenden Resolution:** "Teaching American History," https://teachingamericanhistory.org/library /document/crittenden-resolution.

63–64   **Lincoln took note:** McPherson, *Battle Cry of Freedom*, 365.

64   **Joshua Speed, warned:** McPherson, *Battle Cry of Freedom*, 353.

64   **"How many times":** Brodie, *Thaddeus Stevens: Scourge of the South*, 155.

64   **likened Lincoln's order:** Joseph Medill to Chase, Sept. 15, 1861, in *SPCP*, 3:97.

64   **Chase tried to keep a foot:** Salmon Chase to Jesse Stubbs, Nov. 1, 1861, in *SPCP*, 3:105–8.

65   **"The exchange of provisions":** Schuckers, *The Life and Public Services*, 319.

65   **enacted in July:** The legislation was approved July 13, 1861. See also Hart, *Salmon P. Chase*, 226.

65   **"such trading licenses":** Phil Leigh, "Trading with the Enemy," *New York Times*, Oct. 28, 2012.

65   **Lincoln had several motivations:** Annual Message to Congress, Dec. 3, 1861, in *CWL*, 5:31.

65   **It would relieve mill owners:** Richard H. Abbott, *Cotton and Capital: Boston Businessmen and Antislavery Reform, 1854–1868* (Amherst: University of Massachusetts Press, 1991), 79.

65   **"determined to have the cotton":** *The Diary of Orville Browning*, 488–89, Illinois Historical Collections, https://archive.org/details/diaryoforvillehi20brow/page/488.

65   **little of it was getting to market:** "Monthly Record of Current Events," *Harper's*, Oct. 1861 ("The cotton brokers in the main ports have issued circulars urging planters not to forward cotton to the seaports until the blockade is raised.")

65   **cotton on the New York wharf:** "General Markets," *New York Times*, July 20, 1860; "General Markets," *New York Times*, July 20, 1861.

65   **B. F. Nourse:** See "The Growth of the Cotton Industry in America," https://www.sailsinc.org /durfee/earl2.pdf, 72–73.

66   **"Let commerce follow the flag"**: Salmon Chase to William Mellen, May 29, 1861, in Schuckers, *The Life and Public Services*, 319. Chase often referred to this maxim; see, for instance, Salmon Chase to Henry T. Blow, Sept. 23, 1863, in *SPCP*, 4:143–44.

66   **Chase hired nearly 150 agents**: "The Five-Twenty Loan: Jay Cooke & Co.; Letter from Secretary Chase," *New York Times*, Apr. 1, 1864. In addition to using agents, the Treasury also marketed the notes directly.

66   **He advertised in a score**: Niven, *Chase, A Biography*, 267.

66   **"clergy, draymen"**: Oberholtzer, *Jay Cooke: Financier*, 1:159.

66   **"We bagged over $70,000"**: Oberholtzer, *Jay Cooke: Financier*, 1:159.

66   **In a September 13 article**: Oberholtzer, *Jay Cooke: Financier*, 1:160.

66   **publishing the names**: Oberholtzer, *Jay Cooke: Financier*, 1:159.

67   **refused to up his allowance**: Oberholtzer, *Jay Cooke: Financier*, 1:163; the advertising allowance was $150 per agent.

67   **a trifling fee**: "The Five-Twenty Loan: Jay Cooke & Co.; Letter from Secretary Chase." See also Oberholtzer, *Jay Cooke: Financier*, 1:164, 321. The figure in the text of $6680 was Cooke's fee for $4.2 million in the first note series and $1 million in the second series, so the percentage profit was even smaller than it might appear.

67   **not everybody wanted these notes**: Niven, *Chase: A Biography*, 267; Hammond, *Sovereignty and an Empty Purse*, 93.

67   **Some railroads, and some hotels**: Schuckers, *The Life and Public Services*, 234.

67   **ordered his tellers**: Hammond, *Sovereignty and an Empty Purse*, 94.

67   **stuck with $5 million**: Mitchell, "The Suspension of Specie Payments," 317; Schuckers, *The Life and Public Services*, 227.

67   **Gallatin demanded**: James Gallatin to Salmon Chase, Nov. 14, 1861, William Pitt Fessenden Papers, reel 2; see also Niven, *Chase, A Biography*, 268.

67   **sustain the government in gold**: Mitchell, "The Suspension of Specie Payments," 315–16.

67   **An Ohio colleague of Chase begged him**: Thomson, "Bonds of War," 88.

67   **there was simply not enough gold**: Hammond, *Sovereignty and an Empty Purse*, 110–11.

68   **the public sale was abandoned**: Oberholtzer, *Jay Cooke: Financier*, 1:165.

68   **having suspended gold redemptions**: John Christopher Schwab, *The Confederate States of America, 1861–1865: A Financial and Industrial History of the South During the Civil War* (1901; repr., New York: Burt Franklin, 1968), 124–28. New Orleans banks, the last to go, suspended gold in or about September 1861.

68   **the tax, enacted in August 1861**: Henry D. Capers, *The Life and Times of C.G. Memminger* (Richmond: Everett Waddey, 1893), 340–41; McPherson, *Battle Cry of Freedom*, 438; Michael A. Martorelli, "Financing the Civil War," Essential Civil War Curriculum, https://www.essentialcivilwarcurriculum.com/financing-the-civil-war.html.

68   **Memminger then sought a long-term loan**: "Confederate Bonds," *New York Times*, Aug. 4, 1861; "Southern Finances," *New York Times*, Aug. 29, 1861; Capers, *Life and Times of C.G. Memminger*, 340; "Monthly Record of Current Events," *Harper's*, Oct. 1861.

69   **produce bonds sold briskly**: "Southern Finances"; "Monthly Record of Current Events," Oct. 1861.

69   **sales petered out**: "Confederate Finances," *New York Times*, Aug. 13, 1861; McPherson, *Battle Cry of Freedom*, 438. See also Barbara Hahn and Bruce E. Baker, "Cotton," Essential Civil War Curriculum, https://www.essentialcivilwarcurriculum.com/cotton.html.

69   **authorizing $100 million**: "Southern Finances"; Capers, *Life and Times of C.G. Memminger*, 341; McPherson, *Battle Cry of Freedom*, 439.

69   **"the Confederates feel the need"**: "From Kentucky," *New York Times*, Dec. 28, 1861.

69   **"asks for twice as much"**: Chesnut, 88.

69   **prices had risen**: McPherson, *Battle Cry of Freedom*, 439.

69   **so Richmond authorized**: "Southern Finances"; Capers, *Life and Times of C.G. Memminger*, 341; McPherson, *Battle Cry of Freedom*, 439.

69   **"The currency question perplexes"**: "From Kentucky." The pro-Confederate *Courier* normally was published in Louisville; suppressed by Union authorities, it relocated to Nashville during the war.

70   **"very scarce"**: "Interesting Southern Items," *Cincinnati Daily Press*, Dec. 3, 1861.

70   **"enormous prices"**: *Ruffin*, 2:189.

70   **for a Confederate bond**: *Ruffin*, 2:155.

70   **"We are poor men"**: McPherson, *Battle Cry of Freedom*, 440.

Chapter Four: The Window Shuts

71 **"The lowest abyss":** E. M. Forster, *Howards End* (1910; repr., New York: Dover, 2002), 42.

72 **complained to the governor:** LeRoy Pope Walker to Francis W. Pickens, Aug. 7, 1861, digitized Confederacy Collection, New-York Historical Society.

72 **six hundred runners:** Burton J. Hendrick, *Statesmen of the Lost Cause: Jefferson Davis and His Cabinet* (Boston: Little, Brown, 1939), 214.

72 **shippers could rake in profits:** Eugene R. Dattel, "Cotton and the Civil War," *Mississippi History Now*, http://mshistorynow.mdah.state.ms.us/articles/291/cotton-and-the-civil-war. Among the Confederacy's purchasing agents in Europe were Caleb Huse and Edward C. Anderson.

72 **Small arms, powder, and saltpeter:** Frank E. Vandiver, ed., *Confederate Blockade Running Through Bermuda, 1861–1865* (Austin: University of Texas Press, 1947), xix.

72 **the *Fingal*:** Vandiver, *Confederate Blockade Running Through Bermuda*, xiv.

72 **remittances in cotton:** Vandiver, *Confederate Blockade Running Through Bermuda*, xix.

72 **Britain's liberal interpretation:** See James G. Blaine, *Twenty Years of Congress, from Lincoln to Garfield* (Boston: Avery, 1884), vol. 1, esp. 588–92, noting Britain's "chain of legal artifice."

73 **learned from James De Bow:** *Ruffin*, 2:154.

73 **"These enormous profits":** *Ruffin*, 2:154 (emphasis added).

73 **a favorite from his childhood:** Amy Chambliss, "Edmund Ruffin of Virginia," *The Georgia Review* 14, no. 4 (1960): 418.

73 **sour disapproval:** *Ruffin*, 2:136.

73 **RMS *Trent*:** The *Trent* episode is widely chronicled. See Lucius E. Chittenden, *Personal Reminiscences 1840–1890: Including Some Not Hitherto Published of Lincoln and the War* (New York: Richmond, Croscup, 1893), 135; Hendrick, *Statesmen of the Lost Cause*, 248; James M. McPherson, *Battle Cry of Freedom: The Civil War Era* (New York: Oxford University Press, 1988), 389–90; Walter Coffey, "Mason and Slidell Escape," *The Civil War Months*, https://civilwarmonths.com/2016/10/11/mason-and-slidell-escape.

74 **Wilkes became an instant hero:** Bray Hammond, *Sovereignty and an Empty Purse: Banks and Politics in the Civil War* (Princeton, N.J.: Princeton University Press, 1970), 123.

74 **bristled at the assertion:** "Where Will the Rebellion Leave Us?" *Atlantic Monthly*, Sept. 1861, 236.

74 **"Why has the North":** "Why Has the North Felt Aggrieved with England?" *Atlantic Monthly*, Nov. 1861.

74 **"Not a dozen battles lost":** Irving Katz, *August Belmont: A Political Biography* (New York: Columbia University Press, 1968), 106 (emphasis in original).

74 **"the insult":** *Ruffin*, 2:168.

75 **Sea Island soil produced a fine, long-fibered cotton:** Joseph C. McGowan, "History of Extra-Long-Staple Cottons" (master's thesis, University of Arizona, 1960), 2.

75 **"interesting intelligence from Port Royal":** "News of the Day; The Rebellion," *New York Times*, Dec. 7, 1861.

75 **approximately ten thousand:** Richard H. Abbott, *Cotton and Capital: Boston Businessmen and Antislavery Reform, 1854–1868* (Amherst: University of Massachusetts Press, 1991), 83.

75 **"whipping tree":** "The Freedmen at Port Royal," *Atlantic Monthly*, Sept. 1863, 296; "Life on the Sea Islands," *Atlantic Monthly*, May–June 1864, 672. See also Willie Lee Rose, *Rehearsal for Reconstruction: The Port Royal Experiment* (New York: Oxford University Press, 1976), 12.

75 **Having personally overseen:** Robert J. Brugger, "Redmoor Farewell: The Life and Death of Edmund Ruffin," *VQR*, Summer 1991.

75 **"the most comfortable, happy and cheerful":** Chambliss, "Edmund Ruffin of Virginia," 424.

75 **"This seems to me":** *Ruffin*, 2:173.

75 **On the recommendation:** Rose, *Rehearsal for Reconstruction*, 19.

76 **plantations be leased to private operators:** Abbott, *Cotton and Capital*, 84.

76 **"no less industrious":** Abbott, *Cotton and Capital*, 84.

76 **army consumed most of the food:** Rose, *Rehearsal for Reconstruction*, 20.

76 **"I found 41 bales":** "The War for the Union: Later from Port Royal," *New York Daily Tribune*, Dec. 3, 1861.

76 **"for self-support":** Rose, *Rehearsal for Reconstruction*, 22.

76 **"inaugurate a depreciated paper currency":** James Gallatin to Salmon Chase, Nov. 14, 1861, William Pitt Fessenden Papers, reel 2. See also Daniel Hodas, *The Business Career of Moses Taylor* (New York: New York University Press, 1976), 186.

77 **more than $1.5 million:** J. W. Schuckers, *The Life and Public Services of Salmon Portland Chase* (New York: D. Appleton, 1874), 234.

77   **late in paying bills:** Hammond, *Sovereignty and an Empty Purse*, 125–26. Hammond also cites a letter from the governor of New York, imploring Chase to make "prompt consideration" on his debts.
77   **peddling receivables at a discount:** Hammond, *Sovereignty and an Empty Purse*, 128.
77   **to value the government's paper:** Schuckers, *The Life and Public Services*, 228; Wesley C. Mitchell, "The Suspension of Specie Payments, December 1861," *Journal of Political Economy* 7, no. 3 (1899): 318. Under the loan terms, the banks purchased $50 million face amount of 6 percent, twenty-year bonds for $45.8 million. The reduced price raised the effective interest rate to 7 percent.
77   **resell to investors in Europe:** Gallatin to Chase, Nov. 14, 1861; Mitchell, "The Suspension of Specie Payments," 318.
77   **"to cover the expense":** Mark R. Wilson, *The Business of Civil War: Military Mobilization and the State* (Baltimore: Johns Hopkins University Press, 2006), 130.
78   **each 100,000 men:** McPherson, *Battle Cry of Freedom*, 325.
78   **ordered the states:** Wilson, *The Business of Civil War*, 26, 28–29.
78   **"The public service has suffered":** Wilson, *The Business of Civil War*, 26.
78   **"Quaker guns":** McPherson, *Battle Cry of Freedom*, 362.
78   **"imbecile administration":** Wilson, *The Business of Civil War*, 364–65.
79   **most of the important battles:** After Bull Run, the North was defeated at Wilson's Creek, Lexington (Mo.), Ball's Bluff, and Belmont (Mo.).
79   **"lank and hard-featured":** *Strong*, 3:188.
79   **Lincoln's Annual Message fairly recounted:** Annual Message to Congress, Dec. 3, 1861, in *CWL*, 5:31.
79   **"tedious":** Ted Widmer, "The State of the Union Is Bad," *New York Times*, Dec. 2, 2011.
80   **"There is no appropriate committee":** Leonard P. Curry, *Blueprint for Modern America: Nonmilitary Legislation of the First Civil War Congress* (Nashville: Vanderbilt University Press, 1968), 246.
81   **"labor is the superior of capital":** This and other quotations in this passage are from *CWL*, 5:31.
81   **Recent commentators have seen:** In "The State of the Union Is Bad," Widmer asserted, "That was classic Lincoln—too slow for some, but on his way to the Emancipation Proclamation when circumstances were favorable."
82   **"a fog of calm and confidence":** Hammond, *Sovereignty and an Empty Purse*, 133.
82   **annual budget of $540 million:** Chase's precise forecast was $543.4 million; see Treasury Secretary, *Annual Report*, 1861, p. 21.
82   **forecast only $32 million:** Treasury Secretary, *Annual Report*, 1861, p. 11.
82   **lightly taxed peoples:** McPherson, *Battle Cry of Freedom*, 438.
82   **"It will be seen":** Treasury Secretary, *Annual Report*, 1861, p. 16.
82   **to borrow an additional $650 million:** Treasury Secretary, *Annual Report*, 1861, p. 22. Chase's precise estimate for fiscal years 1862–1863 was $655 million.
82   **not quite a sixth:** Treasury Secretary, *Annual Report*, 1861, pp. 20–22. Chase forecast revenue of $54.6 million for fiscal year 1862 and $95.8 million for 1863, or a total of $150.4 million. Spending for the two years was estimated at a total of $1,018.7 million. Dividing revenue by expenses yields a ratio of 14.8 percent, just under a sixth.
82   **"whether the probable revenue":** Treasury Secretary, *Annual Report*, 1861, p. 15.
83   **taxes for less than 2 percent:** McPherson, *Battle Cry of Freedom*, 439.
83   **his report divulged a plan:** Treasury Secretary, *Annual Report*, 1861, p. 17–20.
83   **He questioned whether bank notes:** Treasury Secretary, *Annual Report*, 1861, p. 17.
83   **the Constitution forbade the *states*:** See art. I, sect. 8 and 10. For an apt discussion of Chase's constitutional views, see Hammond, *Sovereignty and an Empty Purse*, 149.
83   **Congress also was hostile:** Schuckers, *The Life and Public Services*, 292.
83   **he had none:** Albert Bushnell Hart, *Salmon P. Chase* (Boston: Houghton Mifflin, 1899), 235.
84   **he might be forced to resign:** Salmon Chase to Katherine Chase, Oct. 25, 1861, in *SPCP*, 3:102–3.
84   **America and Britain had been through this:** See, e.g., Blaine, *Twenty Years of Congress*, 1:584.
84   **a bellicose British press:** The British reaction was widely reprinted in America, in North and South. See, e.g., "The Trent Affair: Opinion of the Law Officers of the Crown," *New York Times*, Dec. 19, 1861, reprinting excerpts from the London press.
84   **"We know that a message":** *Richmond Daily Dispatch*, Dec. 30, 1861.
85   **panic in the stock market:** "Financial and Commercial," *New York Herald*, Dec. 17, 1861.
85   **"Stocks have experienced":** John J. Cisco to Salmon Chase, Dec. 16, 1861, in *SPCP*, 3:112–13.
85   **"The only question":** *New York Herald*, Dec. 16, 1861.
85   **The group reckoned:** *New York Herald*, Dec. 18, 1861.

85 **balances continued to erode:** Mitchell, "The Suspension of Specie Payments," 314; *New York Herald*, Dec. 17, 1861 reporting "The decline in specie is heavier than was expected."
85 **Some of the banks refused:** "Financial and Commercial," *New York Herald*, Dec. 17, 1861.
85 **"Our total payments today":** Cisco to Chase, Dec. 16, 1861, 3:112–13.
85 **people were hoarding them:** *New York Herald*, Dec. 16, 1861.
85 **"They seemed to vanish":** Chittenden, *Personal Reminiscences*, 299.
85 **a *fourth* loan:** Hammond, *Sovereignty and an Empty Purse*, 154.
85 **Chase was out of ideas:** "Financial and Commercial," *New York Herald*, Dec. 20, 1861.
85 **reported sharp declines:** "Financial and Commercial," *New York Herald*, Dec. 24, 1861.
85 **New York banks were hardest hit:** Mitchell, "The Suspension of Specie Payments," 321.
86 **return the Rebel prisoners from the *Trent*:** For the resolution of the *Trent* affair, see "Opinions in Washington," *Chicago Daily Tribune*, Dec. 23, 1861; Blaine, *Twenty Years of Congress*, 1:581–84; Chittenden, *Personal Reminiscences*, 135–37; McPherson, *Battle Cry of Freedom*, 390–91.
86 **Chase believed that the loyal states:** "Suspension of Specie Payments by the Banks," *New York Times*, Dec. 20, 1861.
86 **closer to $200 million:** Schuckers, *The Life and Public Services*, 291.
86 **seven hundred thousand men:** Samuel W. McCall, *Thaddeus Stevens* (Boston: Houghton Mifflin, 1899), 152–53.
86 **"was not a question for the Government":** *Chicago Daily Tribune*, Dec. 23, 1861.
86 **the Associated Banks reported:** Mitchell, "The Suspension of Specie Payments," 314.
87 **Lincoln's Treasury secretary immediately recognized:** Mitchell, "The Suspension of Specie Payments," 325.
87 **"I deplore exceedingly the suspension":** Salmon Chase to John J. Cisco, Dec. 29, 1861, in *SPCP*, 3:113–14.

Chapter Five: Legal Tender

88 **"The absence of the precious metals":** James Madison, *Selected Writings of James Madison*, ed. Ralph Ketcham (Indianapolis: Hackett, 2006), 297.
88 **Spaulding realized there would not be time:** "The Finances of the Nation," *New York Times*, Jan. 29, 1862.
88 **an investor and director:** Biographical details about Spaulding are from John Jay Knox, *A History of Banking in the United States* (New York: Bradford Rhodes, 1900), 293–94; see also "History of Buffalo: Elbridge Gerry Spaulding," http://buffaloah.com/h/spauld.
89 **a Boston merchant named Samuel Hooper:** Biographical details about Hooper are from *Other Merchants and Sea Captains of Old Boston* (Boston: State Street Trust Co., 1919), 9.
89 **"They [paper bills] are not money":** This and the other Hooper quotations are from Samuel Hooper, *Currency or Money: Its Nature and Uses, and the Effects of the Circulation of Bank-Notes for Currency* (Boston: Little, Brown, 1855), 18.
90 **"depreciation [inflation] is one of the consequences":** Hooper, *Currency or Money*, 25.
90 **"expressed his decided opinion":** Salmon P. Chase, *Inside Lincoln's Cabinet: The Civil War Diaries of Salmon P. Chase*, ed. David Herbert Donald (New York: Longman's Green, 1954), 64. Hooper and Spaulding were accompanied on the visit to Chase by Representative Valentine Horton of Ohio.
90 **Chase was also conferring:** "The Bankers at the Capitol," *New York Times*, Jan. 16, 1862; John Niven, *Salmon P. Chase, A Biography* (New York: Oxford University Press, 1995), 298–99; Daniel Hodas, *The Business Career of Moses Taylor* (New York: New York University Press, 1976), 185; Ralph Korngold, *Thaddeus Stevens: A Being Darkly Wise and Rudely Great* (New York: Harcourt, Brace, 1955), 133–34; Bray Hammond, *Sovereignty and an Empty Purse: Banks and Politics in the Civil War* (Princeton, N.J.: Princeton University Press, 1970), 168–71.
90 **precious metals had been devised:** Hugh McCulloch, *Men and Measures of Half a Century* (New York: Charles Scribner's Sons, 1888), 201.
91 **bankers attempted to cobble together:** See, for example, "The Bankers at the Capitol"; Niven, *Chase: A Biography*, 298–99; Hodas, *Moses Taylor*, 185; Korngold, *Thaddeus Stevens*, 133–34; Hammond, *Sovereignty and an Empty Purse*, 168–71.
91 **a Boston banker telegraphed Chase:** Chase, *Inside Lincoln's Cabinet*, 64. The banker was Samuel Walley of Revere Bank; he was also a former congressman.
91 **"regretting exceedingly":** J. W. Schuckers, *The Life and Public Services of Salmon Portland Chase* (New York: D. Appleton, 1874), 245.
91 **a captain at Bunker Hill:** Knox, *A History of Banking*, 294; "History of Buffalo."

91   **"a measure of necessity"**: "The Finances of the Nation." Regarding the call for taxes, in January Congress approved a resolution to raise $150 million, triple Chase's request.

91   **"The emitting of paper money"**: "Final Version of the Second Report on the Further Provision Necessary for Establishing Public Credit," Dec. 13, 1790, Founders Online, https://founders.archives.gov/documents/Hamilton/01-07-02-0229-0003.

92   **"How do gentlemen expect"**: *Stevens Papers*, 258.

92   **There was extensive debate**: Congress's deliberations were widely covered in the press. For example, see "Proceedings of Congress: Speech of Mr. Pendleton, of Ohio, on the Demand Note Bill," *New York Herald*, Jan. 29, 1862; "House of Representatives," *New York Times*, Jan. 29, 1862.

92   **a "shock" to the mind**: Hammond, *Sovereignty and an Empty Purse*, 182.

92   **"a saturnalia of fraud"**: Theodore E. Burton, *John Sherman* (Boston: Houghton Mifflin, 1908), 101.

92   **Conkling invoked the French maxim**: James G. Blaine, *Twenty Years of Congress, from Lincoln to Garfield* (Boston: Avery, 1884), 1:417.

92   **"It is of doubtful constitutionality"**: Schuckers, *The Life and Public Services*, 245 (emphasis added).

93   **dolefully predicted that within sixty days**: Burton, *John Sherman*, 111.

93   **"that circulating medium"**: *Stevens Papers*, 254; see also *New York Herald*, Feb. 7, 1862.

93   **"Go back to Chase"**: Ward Hill Lamon, *Recollections of Abraham Lincoln, 1847–1865* (Cambridge: University Press, 1911), 219.

93   **"General, what shall I do"**: Montgomery C. Meigs, "General M. C. Meigs on the Conduct of the Civil War," *American Historical Review* 26, no. 2 (1921): 292. Meigs submitted his paper a generation after the war; whether he took down Lincoln's words at the time isn't known.

94   **each was strongly in favor**: Schuckers, *The Life and Public Services*, 247; Hammond, *Sovereignty and an Empty Purse*, 185.

94   **"It is impossible"**: Schuckers, *The Life and Public Services*, 247.

94   **Spaulding complained**: John Sherman, *Recollections of Forty Years in the House, Senate and Cabinet* (Chicago: Werner, 1895), 1:220.

94   **"great aversion"**: Sherman, *Recollections*, 1:220.

94   **"It is true that I came"**: Sherman, *Recollections*, 1:220; "The Financial Measures of the Government: Necessity of Immediate Action," *New York Herald*, Feb. 5, 1862.

94   **"The public exigencies do not admit"**: "News from Washington: Urgent Necessity for the Passage of the Treasury Note Bill," *New York Herald*, Feb. 5, 1862; Sherman, *Recollections*, 1:220.

94   **paying for goods with vouchers**: Mark R. Wilson, *The Business of Civil War: Military Mobilization and the State* (Baltimore: Johns Hopkins University Press, 2006), 111–12.

94   **"My help, who are poor"**: Wilson, *The Business of Civil War*, 129.

94   **vote was expected to be close**: "From Washington," *Chicago Daily Tribune*, Feb. 6, 1862.

95   **adamantly in favor**: "The National Finances," *New York Times*, Feb. 3, 1862; Hammond, *Sovereignty and an Empty Purse*, 203–4.

95   **"selfishly inclined"**: "Affairs at the Capital," *New York Times*, Jan. 26, 1862.

95   **"It would be absurd"**: "Important from Washington," *New York Times*, Feb. 5, 1862.

95   **William Pitt Fessenden**: Biographical details about Fessenden come from Robert J. Cook's fine biography, *Civil War Senator: William Pitt Fessenden and the Fight to Save the American Republic* (Baton Rouge: Louisiana State University Press, 2011), and Michael Todd Landis, "'A Champion Had Come': William Pitt Fessenden and the Republican Party, 1854–60," *American Nineteenth Century History* 9, no. 3 (2008), 269–85.

95   **"lavished praise"**: Cook, *Civil War Senator*, 29.

96   **"a perfect rage"**: Cook, *Civil War Senator*, 38.

96   **grew apart from Webster**: Cook, *Civil War Senator*, 39.

96   **But he missed Portland**: Cook, *Civil War Senator*, 112.

96   **Chase scribbled a personal letter**: Leonard P. Curry, *Blueprint for Modern America: Nonmilitary Legislation of the First Civil War Congress* (Nashville: Vanderbilt University Press, 1968), 189.

96   **with whom Fessenden conferred**: Cook, *Civil War Senator*, 135, 141.

96   **its bonds trading well below par**: Hammond, *Sovereignty and an Empty Purse*, 211.

96   **he was the swing vote**: Curry, *Blueprint for Modern America*, 189.

96   **"I have been engaged"**: Francis Fessenden, *Life and Public Services of William Pitt Fessenden* (Boston: Houghton Mifflin, 1907), 1:194.

97   **it was widely assumed**: This premise that legal tender notes would be temporary runs through the debate. See, e.g., the closing comments of Sherman, an adamant supporter, on Feb. 13, 1862: "After all, there is a mere temporary expedient" (Burton, *John Sherman*, 109). See also Heather Cox Rich-

ardson, *The Greatest Nation of the Earth: Republican Economic Policies During the Civil War* (Cambridge: Harvard University Press, 1997), 79.

97   **He questioned whether the emergency:** Fessenden, *Life and Public Services*, 1:299; "The Proceedings of Congress," *New York Times*, Feb. 13, 1862.

97   **"If the soldier sends the notes":** Blaine, *Twenty Years of Congress*, 1:422.

97   **the *Economist* quickly pronounced:** David Kelley Thomson, "Bonds of War: The Evolution of World Financial Markets in the Civil War Era" (PhD diss., University of Georgia, 2016), 96.

97   **the floor without a recommendation:** Hammond, *Sovereignty and an Empty Purse*, 213.

97   **"in payment of all debts, public and private":** "Important from Washington," *New York Herald*, Feb. 7, 1862.

97   **"effecting its own ruin":** Sherman, *Recollections*, 1:281.

97   **The amendment protected investors:** For additional testimony that this was the motive of the amendment, see Sherman, *Recollections*, 1:275.

98   **pointing out that Boston merchants:** Hammond, *Sovereignty and an Empty Purse*, 216.

98   **Chambers of commerce:** Schuckers, *The Life and Public Services*, 247; Hammond, *Sovereignty and an Empty Purse*, 185.

98   **forcefully prodded by the financier:** Sherman was in close touch with Cooke in the weeks preceding the vote—as was Chase, Sherman's mentor. See Jay Cooke to John Sherman, Jan. 10, 1862, John Sherman Papers, box 44 (in which Cooke pleaded that the bill "must be speedily acted on,"); Cooke to Sherman, Jan. 17, 1862, also in box 44; and Cooke to Sherman, Jan. 29, 1862, box 45.

98   **sponsored the bill:** Richardson, *The Greatest Nation of the Earth*, 78.

98   **"How are we going to get":** "The Proceedings of Congress: Senate," *New York Times*, Feb. 14, 1862.

98   **"lending the Government money":** Sherman, *Recollections*, 1:277.

98   **reckoning that the provision:** Fessenden, *Life and Public Services*, 1:142.

99   **since the war would be over soon:** Curry, *Blueprint for Modern America*, 193.

99   **"if I did not fear":** Chase to Kate Chase, Jan. 20, 1862, in *SPCP*, 3:124–25.

99   **Lincoln had likened to his own:** Don E. Fehrenbacher and Virginia Fehrenbacher, eds., *Recollected Words of Abraham Lincoln* (Stanford, Calif.: Stanford University Press, 1996), 185.

99   **"a miniature Abe Lincoln":** Doug Wead, *All the Presidents' Children: Triumph and Tragedy in the Lives of America's First Families* (New York: Atria, 2003), 90.

99   **The President sobbed:** Fehrenbacher and Fehrenbacher, *Recollected Words of Abraham Lincoln*, 345.

99   **plunged into an absorbing grief:** See Ron Chernow, *Grant*, 481–82 (New York: Penguin Press, 2017); Benjamin Brown French, *Witness to the Young Republic: A Yankee's Journal, 1828–1870*, ed. Donald B. Cole and John J. McDonough (Hanover, N.H.: University Press of New England, 1989), 389.

99   **Spaulding, Hooper, and Stevens:** "Proceedings of Congress: Debate in the House on the Treasury Note Bill; Speech of Mr. Spaulding in Opposition to the Senate's Amendment," *New York Herald*, Feb. 20, 1862. Hooper and Stevens's opposition were widely cited—see, e.g., "House of Representatives," *New York Times*, Feb. 21, 1862.

99   **"simple in its machinery":** *Stevens Papers*, 343.

100 **"cunning scheme" . . . "It creates two classes":** *Stevens Papers*, 345; "House of Representatives," *Chicago Daily Tribune*, Feb. 21, 1862; "House of Representatives," *New York Times*, Feb. 21, 1862.

100 **tried to kill the entire bill:** See *New York Times*, *Chicago Daily Tribune*, and *New York Herald*, all on Feb. 21, 1862.

100 **Stevens fashioned an amendment:** *Stevens Papers*, 345.

100 **"little of any popular distress":** "Another Special Correspondence in America: First Impressions of New York [Correspondence of the *London Spectator*]," *New York Times*, Mar. 9, 1862.

100 **a variety of expedients:** Albert Bushnell Hart, *Salmon P. Chase* (Boston: Houghton Mifflin, 1899), 241–42; Hammond, *Sovereignty and an Empty Purse*, 243–44; Schuckers, *The Life and Public Services*, 269; "Commercial Matters," *New York Daily Tribune*, Mar. 4, 1862.

101 **nearly $2 million worth of certificates:** "News from Washington: Issue of Certificates of Deposit by the Treasury Department," *New York Times*, Mar. 23, 1862.

101 **issued just over $500 million:** Wilson, *The Business of Civil War*, 114.

101 **Confederate Congress was also debating:** John Christopher Schwab, *The Confederate States of America, 1861–1865: A Financial and Industrial History of the South During the Civil War* (1901; repr., New York: Burt Franklin, 1968), 86–92; see also James M. McPherson, *Battle Cry of Freedom: The Civil War Era* (New York: Oxford University Press, 1988), 439.

101 **"threatens greater dangers":** Quoted in "From Kentucky," *New York Times*, Dec. 28, 1861.

101 **"was more to be dreaded":** Quoted in *Bedford* (Pa.) *Inquirer*, Nov. 15, 1861.

102 **an explosion of monetary instruments:** Schwab, *The Confederate States of America,* 149, 153–56.

102 **red-tinted Citizens Bank of Louisiana:** Mark Thornton and Robert B. Ekelund Jr., *Tariffs, Block-ades, and Inflation: The Economics of the Civil War* (Wilmington, Del.: Scholarly Resources, 2004), 62.

102 **a clear preference for Union paper:** "Operations in the West" and "News from Washington," both in *New York Times,* Mar. 28, 1862.

102 **as much as 75 percent:** "The War in the Southwest," *New York Times,* Mar. 16, 1862.

102 **"persons in this city":** Quoted in "Quiet in Nashville: The Union Sentiment Developing; The Memphis Press," *New York Times,* Mar. 6, 1862.

102 **he explicitly forswore legal tender:** C. G. Memminger, "Making Treasury Notes a Legal Tender" (memorandum addressed to L. J. Gartrell, Chairman, Judiciary Committee), Mar. 13, 1862, in Henry D. Capers, *The Life and Times of C.G. Memminger* (Richmond: Everett Waddey, 1893), 488–89.

102 **"the most dangerous of all methods":** C. G. Memminger, Mar. 14, 1862, report to Congress, in "Making Treasury Notes a Legal Tender," 140.

103 **military expenses escalating sharply:** Capers, *Life and Times of C.G. Memminger,* 338.

103 **as high as $200 million:** Schwab, *The Confederate States of America,* 165.

103 **Edmund Ruffin grumbled:** *Ruffin,* 2:216.

103 **$100 in Confederate notes:** *Ruffin,* 2:258.

103 **Memminger requested a tax hike:** Schwab, *The Confederate States of America,* 290.

103 **Infringements on civil liberties:** Schwab, *The Confederate States of America,* 190.

103 **they were bitterly opposed:** Schwab, *The Confederate States of America,* 187, 190–91; McPherson, *Battle Cry of Freedom,* 435.

103 **"ladies in their landaus":** *Chesnut,* 136.

104 **the two worked even more closely:** Robert Douthat Meade, "The Relations Between Judah P. Benjamin and Jefferson Davis: Some New Light on the Working of the Confederate Machine," *The Journal of Southern History* 5, no. 4 (1939): 468–78. Meade observes, "To this day the historians have never been able to determine to what extent each man was responsible for the Confederate policies" (474).

104 **obtaining British and French support:** Robert N. Rosen, *The Jewish Confederates* (Columbia: University of South Carolina Press, 2000), 77–78.

104 **Benjamin urged James Mason:** Blaine, *Twenty Years of Congress,* 1:554.

104 **contacted foreign agents in New Orleans:** Schwab, *The Confederate States of America,* 29.

104 **offering one hundred thousand bales:** Meade, "The Relations Between Benjamin and Davis," 475.

104 **was surely tempted:** Meade, "The Relations Between Benjamin and Davis," 476.

104 **"Wherever the Northern troops advanced":** Schwab, *The Confederate States of America,* 161.

104 **The term "greenback" emerged:** *The New York Times* was relatively late to adopt the term, but it appeared there in "Details of the Rebel Movement," Sept. 9, 1862.

104 **traveled quickly:** Press reports from *Alleghanian* (Ebensburg, Pa.), Apr. 3, 1862; *Holmes County Farmer* (Millersburg, Ohio), May 29, 1862; "From Memphis: Business Prospects and Politics; Various Interesting Items," *Chicago Daily Tribune,* June 30, 1862.

105 **From the outset, greenbacks were exchanged:** William J. Schultz and M. R. Caine, *Financial Development of the United States* (New York: Prentice-Hall, 1937), 324. See also Irwin Unger, *The Greenback Era: A Social and Political History of American Finance, 1865–1879* (Princeton, N.J.: Princeton University Press, 1964), 15.

105 **fell to only seventy-five cents:** Schultz and Caine, *Financial Development of the United States,* 324.

105 **During 1862, prices in the North:** Ethel D. Hoover, "Retail Prices After 1850," in "Conference on Research in Income and Wealth," *Trends in the American Economy in the Nineteenth Century* (New York: National Bureau of Economic Research, 1960), 142.

105 **The government's credit:** Sherman, *Recollections,* 1:279; "The Public Debt and National Credit," *New York Times,* Mar. 17, 1862.

105 **Washington was now able:** "The Public Debt and National Credit."

105 **slightly lower interest rates:** Government 6 percent bonds fetched 87½ in January; by early March they had rallied to 93. See Burton, *John Sherman,* 103, and "The Public Debt and National Credit."

105 **wholesale prices rose at a steadier rate:** See Margaret G. Myers, *A Financial History of the United States* (New York: Columbia University Press, 1970), 171, and Paul R. Auerbach and Michael J. Haupert, "Problems in Analyzing Inflation During the Civil War," *Essays in Economic and Business History* (2002): 58, 65. Wholesale prices in the North rose approximately 10 percent from Fort Sumter to the greenback's debut, and 10 percent more through the end of 1862. According to Auerbach

and Haupert, consumer prices in this period rose by significantly less than wholesale prices, or about 13 percent through the end of 1862.

106 **"The medicine of the Constitution":** John G. Nicolay and John Hay, *Abraham Lincoln: A History* (New York: Century, 1886–1890), 6:233.

106 **Even John Sherman:** Burton, *John Sherman*, 109.

106 **"the legal tender act was the turning point":** Sherman, *Recollections*, 1:279.

Chapter Six: Forgotten Congress

107 **"For me there is no greater name":** Congressional Record, S15146, July 12, 1998.

107 **The enlarged building required:** "Witness Post: Under the Dome," https://henryehooper.blog /witness-post-under-the-dome; Architect of the Capitol reports, "History of the U.S. Capitol Building," https://www.aoc.gov/explore-capitol-campus/buildings-grounds/capitol-building/history; "Capitol Dome," https://www.aoc.gov/explore-capitol-campus/buildings-grounds/capitol-building /capitol-dome. See also "Important from Washington," *New York Times*, Apr. 4, 1862; "News from Washington," *New York Times*, Apr. 16, 1862; *Stevens Papers*, 433.

108 **most prolific in history:** Walter A. McDougall, *Throes of Democracy: The American Civil War Era, 1829–1877* (New York: HarperCollins, 2008), 428.

108 **"second American revolution":** Charles A. Beard and Mary R. Beard, *The Rise of American Civilization* (New York: Macmillan, 1927), 2:52.

108 **"Constitutions are made for peace":** Leonard P. Curry, *Blueprint for Modern America: Nonmilitary Legislation of the First Civil War Congress* (Nashville: Vanderbilt University Press, 1968), 77–78, quoting the *Daily Alta California*.

109 **fidelity to the country:** See, e.g., Sherman's remarks in Congressional Globe, 37th Cong., 3rd Sess., 843.

109 **Homestead Act:** For Republican ideology and the Homestead Act, including its relation to abolitionism, see Heather Cox Richardson, *The Greatest Nation of the Earth: Republican Economic Policies During the Civil War* (Cambridge: Harvard University Press, 1997), 143–54.

109 **Jefferson had proposed:** Gordon S. Wood, *Friends Divided: John Adams and Thomas Jefferson* (New York: Penguin Press, 2017), 109.

109 **promote development as well as immigration:** Richardson, *The Greatest Nation of the Earth*, 162.

109 **"It has long been":** Annual Message to Congress, Dec. 8, 1863, in *CWL*, 7:46.

110 **"Why not a Department of Manufactures?":** "A Privileged Class," *New York Times*, May 10, 1862.

110 **a $3000 annual salary:** "Our Special Washington Dispatches," *New York Times*, May 14, 1862.

110 **championed government support for agriculture:** Richardson, *The Greatest Nation of the Earth*, 144.

110 **not traveled west since the 1830s:** Robert J. Cook, *Civil War Senator: William Pitt Fessenden and the Fight to Save the American Republic* (Baton Rouge: Louisiana State University Press, 2011), 149.

110 **even then he voted against it:** Williamjames Hull Hoffer, *To Enlarge the Machinery of Government: Congressional Debates and the Growth of the American State, 1858–1891* (Baltimore: Johns Hopkins University Press, 2007), 50. Newspaper coverage on the agriculture bill was extensive; see, e.g., "Thirty-Seventh Congress, Second Session," *National Republican* (Washington, D.C.), May 9, 1862; "From Washington," *Chicago Daily Tribune*, May 9, 1862; "XXXVIIth Congress," *Cadiz* (Ohio) *Sentinel*, May 14, 1862.

111 **"great encouragement and assistance":** "The Homestead Bill," *Cleveland Morning Leader*, Mar. 5, 1862.

111 **the son of a blacksmith:** Biographical details on Morrill are from Coy F. Cross II, *Justin Smith Morrill: Father of the Land-Grant Colleges* (East Lansing: Michigan State University Press, 1999), 9–10, 12–15.

111 **a time when less than a quarter of 1 percent:** Thomas D. Snyder, ed., "120 Years of American Education: A Statistical Portrait," U.S. Department of Education, Jan. 1993, 78; the study is available at https://nces.ed.gov/pubs93/93442.pdf. According to this report, in 1869–1870 (the earliest year for which statistics are available), 62,000 Americans were enrolled in colleges out of a total population of 38.5 million. For high school graduation rates, see Cross, *Justin Smith Morrill*, 31.

111 **Morrill wanted colleges to teach:** Cross, *Justin Smith Morrill*, esp. 5, 29, 79–81, 88; Richardson, *The Greatest Nation of the Earth*, 155–60.

112 **Benjamin Wade of Ohio:** *Charles City* (Iowa) *Republican Intelligencer*, May 15, 1862; Curry, *Blueprint for Modern America*, 110.

112 **hundreds of millions of untapped acres:** "Our Heritage, Our Future: The BLM and America's Public Lands," Bureau of Land Management, 2017, 1. Between 1803 and 1867 the United States acquired over 1 billion acres.

112 **sectional rivalry:** See "Agricultural College Bill," *Chicago Daily Tribune*, May 30, 1862, in which a correspondent claimed the bill would "loot the west," and "Agricultural Colleges," *Cleveland Morning Leader*, May 22, 1862, reporting Senator James Lane's comment that the bill would be "ruinous to Kansas." See also Hoffer, *To Enlarge the Machinery of Government*, 50.

112 **"wronging nobody":** "House of Representatives," *New York Times*, June 7, 1862.

112 **amendment limiting the acreage:** "Congress," *New York Times*, June 11, 1862.

112 **approximately seventy institutions:** U.S. Department of Agriculture website, https://nifa.usda .gov/land-grant-colleges-and-universities-partner-website-directory. Multiple colleges within the same institution (e.g., Utah State and Utah State College of Agriculture and Applied Sciences) are counted as one entry.

112 **coeducational and, outside the South:** Cross, *Justin Smith Morrill*, 88.

113 **"The iron horse is panting":** *CWL*, 3:357. The speech was in 1859.

113 **fresh rationale for connecting California:** Curry, *Blueprint for Modern America*, 135; Richardson, *The Greatest Nation of the Earth*, 178.

113 **General Herman Haupt:** Francis A. Lord, *Lincoln's Railroad Man: Herman Haupt* (Rutherford, N.J.: Fairleigh Dickinson University Press, 1969), esp. 11–15, 39–43, 69–73.

113 **Haupt astounded generals:** Lord, *Lincoln's Railroad Man*, 68–78.

113 **"the most remarkable structure":** Lord, *Lincoln's Railroad Man*, 77.

113 **"march of civilization":** "The Pacific Railroad," *New York Times*, May 7, 1862.

113 **"Few will doubt its utility":** Marc Egnal, *Clash of Extremes: The Economic Origins of the Civil War* (New York: Farrar, Straus, and Giroux, 2009), 325.

113 **wasn't one railroad but several:** Congressional Globe, Statues at Large, 37th Cong., 2nd Sess., 494 (hereinafter, Pacific Railway Act). Besides the Union Pacific, the act authorized work "on the same terms and conditions" by the Central Pacific Railroad Company, the Leavenworth, Pawnee and Western Railroad, the Hannibal and St. Joseph Railroad, and the Pacific Railroad Co. of Missouri.

113 **The federal government had no authority:** "The Pacific Railroad Bill," *New York Herald*, June 13, 1862; Richardson, *The Greatest Nation of the Earth*, 181–82, 185–86.

114 **The Union Pacific was to run:** Pacific Railway Act, 493–95.

114 **public or private:** Curry, *Blueprint for Modern America*, 121–25; Maury Klein, *Union Pacific: Birth of a Railroad, 1862–1893* (Garden City, N.Y.: Doubleday, 1987), 10.

114 **private capital would not build:** Curry, *Blueprint for Modern America*, 135. The statement is almost a truism, since private capital *hadn't* built over the many years it had previously been considered. Moreover, only the government could furnish the necessary rights-of-ways.

114 **To induce investment:** Pacific Railway Act, 492–93.

114 **trebled for the most challenging terrain:** Pacific Railway Act, 495.

114 **since the Second Bank of the United States:** Klein, *Union Pacific*, 13.

114 **lobbyists descended:** Curry, *Blueprint for Modern America*, 133; Richardson, *The Greatest Nation of the Earth*, 176, 184.

114 **Thomas Ewing Jr.:** Biographical details come from David G. Taylor, "Thomas Ewing, Jr., and the Origins of the Kansas Pacific Railway Company," *Kansas Historical Quarterly* 42, no. 2 (1976): 155–79; available at Kansas Collection, http://www.kancoll.org/khq/1976/76_2_taylor.htm.

114 **by securing a treaty:** Taylor, "Thomas Ewing, Jr.," 155–79.

115 **Ewing met with Lincoln several times:** Taylor, "Thomas Ewing, Jr.," 155–79.

115 **Shares were promptly distributed:** Taylor, "Thomas Ewing, Jr.," 155–79.

115 **"We have friends":** Curry, *Blueprint for Modern America*, 119.

115 **positioned the main spur in Kansas:** "Summary of Mr. McDougall's Pacific Railroad Bill, Reported to Congress," *Chicago Daily Tribune*, Mar. 9, 1862; "The Pacific Railroad," *New York Times*, May 7, 1862; Taylor, "Thomas Ewing, Jr."

115 **"my interest will be worth":** Taylor, "Thomas Ewing, Jr."

115 **"I am willing to build":** Congressional Globe, 37th Cong., 2nd Sess., 2752.

115 **the Senate version authorized:** Richardson, *The Greatest Nation of the Earth*, 185–87.

115 **precise terminus to be chosen:** Pacific Railway Act, 496.

115 **The LP&W was downgraded:** "Freedom to All the Territories! The Bill Approved by the President! Pacific Railroad Bill Passed the Senate!" *Cleveland Morning Leader*, June 21, 1862; "Thirty-Seventh Congress," *Daily Ohio Statesman* (Columbus), June 20, 1862; "By Telegraph," *Chicago Daily*

Tribune, June 19, 1862. See also Pacific Railway Act, 493–94, 496, as well as Richardson, *The Greatest Nation of the Earth*, 185, and Taylor, "Thomas Ewing, Jr."

116 **Congress narrowed the financial incentive:** Pacific Railway Act, 497; "News from Washington: Passage of the Pacific Railroad Bill," *New York Times*, June 21, 1862; Richardson, *The Greatest Nation of the Earth*, 186.

116 **two nonshareholders:** Pacific Railway Act, 491.

116 **10 percent of costs:** Pacific Railway Act, 497.

116 **wasn't completed by 1876:** Pacific Railway Act, 497.

116 **Fessenden so objected:** Cook, *Civil War Senator*, 163; "Thirty-Seventh Congress," *Daily Ohio Statesman* (Columbus), June 1, 1862.

116 **after it had sold $2 million:** Pacific Railway Act, 490.

116 **side-wheel steamer *Magnolia*:** "The Rebellion," *New York Times*, Mar. 7, 1862.

117 **"The continuation of the Yankee blockade":** *Ruffin*, 2:276.

117 **"New Orleans gone and with it":** *Chesnut*, 139.

117 **But with Davis's strong support:** Frank E. Vandiver, "Jefferson Davis—Leader Without Legend," *The Journal of Southern History* 43, no. 1 (1977): 13.

117 **Plantations switched from cotton:** "Resources of the South," *Atlantic Monthly*, Oct. 1862, 502. According to John Christopher Schwab, *The Confederate States of America, 1861–1865: A Financial and Industrial History of the South During the Civil War* (1901; repr., New York: Burt Franklin, 1968), 279, the cotton harvest in 1862 was something over 1 million bales, compared with 4.5 million bales in 1860.

117 **"tired and tawdry" . . . "excepting the select few":** "The Cotton Famine," *New York Times*, Sept. 16, 1862.

117 **John Beauchamp Jones:** Biographical details about Jones come from *RWCD* (2015), 1:vii, x, xii.

118 **beef was selling at 30 cents:** For the prices of this and the other commodities, see Jones, *RWCD* (2015), 1:89, 112–13.

118 **imposing price ceilings:** James M. McPherson, *Battle Cry of Freedom: The Civil War Era* (New York: Oxford University Press, 1988), 442.

118 **New Yorkers took bets:** *Strong*, 3:215.

118 **"I think it is the precise time":** *CWL*, 5:184–85.

119 **"If the slaves no longer":** *Stevens Papers*, 244.

119 **"carry out to final perfection":** Ralph Korngold, *Thaddeus Stevens: A Being Darkly Wise and Rudely Great* (New York: Harcourt, Brace, 1955), 166.

119 **to demand a larger purpose:** See, e.g., John Sherman to William Tecumseh Sherman, May 19, 1862, in Rachel Sherman Thorndike, ed., *The Sherman Letters: Correspondence Between General and Senator Sherman from 1837 to 1891* (New York: Charles Scribner's Sons, 1894), 150–51, predicting a racial struggle in the cotton states if the war continued.

119 **William Holman:** Congressional Globe, 37th Cong., 2nd Sess., 15.

119 **it forbade army officers:** Egnal, *Clash of Extremes*, 317.

119 **"The federal government":** *Strong*, 3:217.

119 **Stevens prodded and provoked:** Korngold, *Thaddeus Stevens*, 184.

120 **"He is only the *instrument*":** Curry, *Blueprint for Modern America*, 91 (emphasis added).

120 **"the social problem of our time":** "The Freedmen at Port Royal," *Atlantic Monthly*, Sept. 1863, 291.

120 **"definite action" . . . "the chronic but absurd prejudice":** Mary Peabody Mann to Salmon Chase, Apr. 26, 1862, in *SPCP*, 3:184–85.

120 **"The Negroes seem very well":** William H. Reynolds to Salmon Chase, Jan. 1, 1862, in *SPCP*, 3:116–18.

121 **"when properly organized":** "The Negroes at Port Royal; Report of W. L. Pierce, Government Agent, to the Hon. Salmon P. Chase," https://quod.lib.umich.edu/m/moa/AFK4120.0001.001?view=toc, 17.

121 **"Except on Sundays":** "The Negroes at Port Royal," 8.

121 **"Notwithstanding their religious professions":** "The Negroes at Port Royal," 13.

121 **"This delay of payment":** "The Negroes at Port Royal," 31.

122 **"They make no universal charges":** "The Negroes at Port Royal," 14.

122 **"the worst vices" . . . "self-interest":** "The Negroes at Port Royal," 25.

122 **"beneficent system" . . . "a great social question":** "The Negroes at Port Royal," 25.

122 **After getting authorization from Lincoln:** Abraham Lincoln to Salmon Chase, Feb. 15 1862, in *CWL*, 5:132.

122 **The first delegation of pilgrims:** "The Freedmen at Port Royal," 298–99.

122 **"Success or defeat":** "The Freedmen at Port Royal," 298.

122 **"badge of servitude":** "The Freedmen at Port Royal," 299.

123 **Some of the businessmen:** See, e.g., Willie Lee Rose, *Rehearsal for Reconstruction: The Port Royal Experiment* (New York: Oxford University Press, 1976), 142; Richard H. Abbott, *Cotton and Capital: Boston Businessmen and Antislavery Reform, 1854–1868* (Amherst: University of Massachusetts Press, 1991), 85, 91.

123 **Reynolds was overcharging them:** Mansfield French to Salmon Chase, (c. early 1862), in *SPCP*, 3:146–48.

123 **Soldiers cavalierly stole:** E. L. Pierce to Salmon Chase, Mar. 14, 1862, in *SPCP*, 3:149–51.

123 **"I have not found under Colonel Reynolds":** Mansfield French to Salmon Chase, (c. early 1862), in *SPCP*, 3:146–48.

123 **"a most unsuitable man":** E. L. Pierce to Salmon Chase, Mar. 30, 1862, in *SPCP*, 3:154–56.

123 **"I must say frankly":** William H. Reynolds to Salmon Chase, Apr. 1, 1862, in *SPCP*, 3:157–58.

123 **"the Government has not treated"** . . . **"ragged, and even naked":** E. L. Pierce to Salmon Chase, May 8, 1862, in *SPCP*, 3:191–93.

123 **struck him a violent blow:** E. L. Pierce to Salmon Chase, May 7, 1862, in *SPCP*, 3:188–89.

124 **Lincoln feared for their safety:** Salmon Chase to Nettie (Janet) Chase, May 11, 1862, in *SPCP*, 3:193–97.

124 **"and each man, almost":** Salmon Chase to Nettie Chase, May 8, 1862, in Salmon P. Chase, *Inside Lincoln's Cabinet: The Civil War Diaries of Salmon P. Chase*, ed. David Herbert Donald (New York: Longman's Green, 1954) 78–79.

124 **"A man was sometime lucky":** Don E. Fehrenbacher and Virginia Fehrenbacher, eds., *Recollected Words of Abraham Lincoln* (Stanford, Calif.: Stanford University Press, 1996), 452.

124 **"a military necessity":** Hunter's order quoted by Lincoln in *CWL*, 5:222.

125 **"It seems to me":** Salmon Chase to Abraham Lincoln, May 16, 1862, in *CWL*, 5:219.

125 **"No commanding general":** Abraham Lincoln to Salmon Chase, May 17, 1862, in *CWL*, 5:219.

125 **Corresponding with Hunter and with Horace Greeley:** Salmon Chase to David Hunter, May 20, 1862, in *SPCP*, 3:201–2; Salmon Chase to Horace Greeley, May 21, 1862, in *SPCP*, 3:202–3.

125 **"earnest appeal":** "Proclamation Revoking General Hunter's Order of Military Emancipation of May 9, 1862," May 19, 1862, in *CWL*, 5:222–23.

125 **"We are certainly too lenient":** Ellis Paxson Oberholtzer, *Jay Cooke: Financier of the Civil War* (Philadelphia: G.W. Jacobs, 1907), 1:197.

125 **"blind man can see":** Harold Holzer and Norton Garfinkle, *A Just and Generous Nation* (New York: Basic Books, 2015), 127.

125 **"you would be grateful":** "Senator Sumner on President Lincoln" (reprint of June 5, 1862, private letter), *Chicago Daily Tribune*, June 18, 1862.

125 **Duty receipts were also higher:** Boston Custom House to Justin Morrill, Nov. (possibly Nov. 11) 1862, Justin S. Morrill Papers. reel 5. See "Our Customs Revenue: Business of the New York Custom-House," *New York Times*, June 5, 1862. See also J. W. Schuckers, *The Life and Public Services of Salmon Portland Chase* (New York: D. Appleton, 1874), 314.

125 **Newspapers celebrated a bull market:** See, for example, "The Public Debt and the National Credit," and "The Public Credit and Price of Gold," *New York Times*, Mar. 17 and Mar. 24, 1862, respectively.

125 **brisk demand in London:** "Our Credit in London," "Our War Taxes: The British Peace Budget," and "The Public Debt: British Opinion," *New York Times*, Apr. 1, Apr. 21, and June 9, 1862, respectively.

126 **"every thing under the sun":** Maunsell B. Field, *Memories of Many Men and of Some Women* (New York: Harper and Brothers, 1874), 276.

126 **"Every thing on the earth":** Unnamed Dayton correspondent to John Sherman, Mar. 15, 1862, John Sherman Papers, box 47 (emphasis added).

126 **Morrill's bill imposed:** Theodore E. Burton, *John Sherman* (Boston: Houghton Mifflin, 1908), 121.

126 **double taxation:** Congressional Globe, 37th Cong., 2nd Sess., 1196.

126 **185 revenue districts:** Joseph J. Thorndike, "An Army of Officials: The Civil War Bureau of Internal Revenue," Tax History Project, http://www.taxhistory.org/thp/readings.nsf/ArtWeb/FF949517831B181685256E22007840E8?OpenDocument; Richard Franklin Bensel, *Yankee Leviathan: The Origins of Central State Authority in America, 1859–1877* (New York: Cambridge University Press, 1990), 173.

126 **started with three clerks:** Thorndike, "An Army of Officials"; George S. Boutwell, *Reminiscences of Sixty Years in Public Affairs* (New York: McClure, Phillips, 1902), 1:303–4.

126 **A legislative draft:** "Abstract of the Tax Bill," *Indiana State Sentinel* (Indianapolis), Mar. 10, 1862.

127 **"inquisitorial" character:** Congressional Globe, 37th Cong., 2nd Sess., 1196.

127 **"When this vast system":** Congressional Globe, 37th Cong., 2nd Sess., 1227.

127 **"personal declarations":** Joseph A. Hill, "The Civil War Income Tax," *The Quarterly Journal of Economics* 8, no. 4 (1894): 435.

127 **issue summonses and search homes:** Thorndike, "An Army of Officials."

127 **published in local newspapers:** Hill, "The Civil War Income Tax," 436; Thorndike, "An Army of Officials."

127 **taxes for fiscal 1862:** Treasury Secretary, *Annual Report*, 1862, p. 31.

127 **"will there be any more officeholders":** *Stevens Papers,* 283. See also Thorndike, "An Army of Officials."

127 **Some sixty lobbyists:** Curry, *Blueprint for Modern America,* 166–67.

127 **"Everybody wants to see":** *Chicago Daily Tribune,* Mar. 18, 1862.

127 **Sherman's files:** John Sherman Papers, boxes 46, 47, 48, 49. On lobbyists, see also "The Congressional Lobby on the Tax Bill," *New York Herald,* Mar. 15, 1862; "From Washington," *Cleveland Morning Leader,* Mar. 19, 1862; Richardson, *The Greatest Nation of the Earth,* 116.

128 **too high to affect the vast majority:** Hill, "The Civil War Income Tax," 438.

128 **treated farmers more kindly:** Congressional Globe, 37th Cong., 2nd Sess., 1196; see also Jane Flaherty, *The Revenue Imperative: Union Financial Policy During the Civil War* (New York: Routledge, 2016), 2.

128 **The members conducted an interesting debate:** "Proceedings of Congress," May 30, 1862, *Chicago Daily Tribune*; "Matters at the Capital: The Emancipation and Tax Measures," June 6, 1862, *Chicago Daily Tribune.* See also Curry, *Blueprint for Modern America,* 170; Bray Hammond, *Sovereignty and an Empty Purse: Banks and Politics in the Civil War* (Princeton, N.J.: Princeton University Press, 1970), 276–77.

128 **twenty thousand words:** McDougall, *Throes of Democracy,* 433.

128 **even in Richmond:** "Matters Before the Federal Congress," *Richmond Daily Dispatch,* June 19, 1862.

128 **It failed to tackle:** Curry, *Blueprint for Modern America,* 169.

128 **315 amendments:** "Matters at the Capital: The Tax Bill Awaiting Signature," *Chicago Daily Tribune,* June 25, 1862.

128 **"we shall have destroyed":** Congressional Globe, 37th Cong., 2nd Sess., 1196.

128 **American industry was thriving:** See, e.g., McDougall, *Throes of Democracy,* 434.

128 **"it will influence thousands":** Unnamed correspondent to Morrill, n.d. (prior to Mar. 20, 1862), Morrill Papers, reel 5.

129 **The public resented Britain:** See Richardson, *The Greatest Nation of the Earth,* 125.

129 **Henry Carey:** Arthur M. Lee, "Henry C. Carey and the Republican Tariff," *The Pennsylvania Magazine of History and Biography* 81, no. 3 (1957): 299.

129 **It raised duties to record levels:** McDougall, *Throes of Democracy,* 434; Reinhard H. Luthin, "Abraham Lincoln and the Tariff," *The American Historical Review* 49, no. 4 (1994): 628; Burton, *John Sherman,* 118–19.

129 **sliced the "free list":** Luthin, "Abraham Lincoln and the Tariff," 628; Richardson, *The Greatest Nation of the Earth,* 122.

129 **Even farm products were slapped:** Richardson, *The Greatest Nation of the Earth,* 122.

129 **"an Act increasing, temporarily":** "Tariff Act of July 14, 1862" (official printing of tariff acts) (New York: Henry Anstice, 1862), 45.

129 **the Treasury was running out:** John Niven, *Salmon P. Chase: A Biography* (New York: Oxford University Press, 1995), 299.

129 **eight times its prewar level:** Treasury Secretary, *Annual Report,* 1860, p. 22; Treasury Secretary, *Annual Report,* 1862, p. 2. Figures are as of June 30.

129 **borrowing would be difficult:** Schuckers, *The Life and Public Services,* 251.

129 **"give your paper mill another turn":** Fehrenbacher and Fehrenbacher, *Recollected Words of Abraham Lincoln,* 346.

130 **the greenback tumbled:** For the discount to gold in various months, see Schuckers, *The Life and Public Services,* 255, 352.

130 **"starved out":** *Chesnut,* 152.

130 **Both sides suffered horrendous casualties:** McPherson, *Battle Cry of Freedom,* says 30,000 killed or wounded (471). The fighting stretched over a series of encounters known as the Seven Days Battles.

130 **"The darkest day we have seen":** *Strong,* 3:234.

130 **The Treasury secretary contemplated":** Oberholtzer, *Jay Cooke: Financier,* 1:198.
130 **frustrated by Lincoln's continued sufferance:** Oberholtzer, *Jay Cooke: Financier,* 1:197–99.
131 **"Is it the darkest hour":** Oberholtzer, *Jay Cooke: Financier,* 1:198.
131 **As frustration with McClellan:** For the point that impatience with McClellan contributed to the impetus for the Confiscation Act, see Cook, *Civil War Senator,* 146.
131 **"I would seize every foot":** Congressional Globe, 37th Cong., 2nd Sess., 3127.
131 **seemed of dubious legality:** Lincoln to House of Representatives, July 17, 1862, in *CWL,* 5:331. Lincoln wrote, "With great respect, I am constrained to say I think this feature [providing for permanent forfeiture of land] of the act is unconstitutional."
131 **To the fury of the Radicals:** Oberholtzer, *Jay Cooke: Financier,* 1:199.
131 **still with some misgivings:** Lincoln to House of Representatives, July 17, 1862, 5:328–31; see also James G. Blaine, *Twenty Years of Congress, from Lincoln to Garfield* (Boston: Avery, 1884), 1:376.
131 **In practice, neither Confiscation Act:** I am grateful to Frank J. Williams for recounting his conversation with Harold M. Hyman.
131 **Congress adjourned:** "The Adjournment of Congress," *New York Times,* July 18, 1862. On its final day, Lincoln signed the Militia Act, authorizing Black enlistment. This was a military measure more than a bid for racial equality; Blacks were to receive lower pay than whites, and Congress intended that Blacks would work as laborers, not in combat roles.
132 **"The people of the North":** "The Government Credit," *New York Times,* Apr. 21, 1862.
132 **"The two sections":** "The Government Credit."

Chapter Seven: Proclamation

133 **"Chase is a good man":** John Hay, *Inside Lincoln's White House: The Complete Civil War Diary of John Hay,* ed. Michael Burlingame and John R. Turner Ettlinger (Carbondale: Southern Illinois University Press, 1997), 77.
133 **Lincoln thought more about the purse:** Gabor S. Boritt, *Lincoln and the Economics of the American Dream* (Memphis: Memphis State University Press, 1978), 206.
133–134 **each extremely anxious to procure:** William Tecumseh Sherman, *Memoirs of General W. T. Sherman,* 2 vols. (New York: Charles L. Webster, 1892), 1:294.
134 **Chase presented a plan:** Edward Bates, *The Diary of Edward Bates, 1859–1866,* ed. Howard K. Beale (Washington, D.C.: GPO, 1933), 238, referring to the cabinet meeting of Feb. 28, 1862.
134 **Lincoln issued an order:** "Order Relating to Commercial Intercourse," in *CWL,* 5:139.
134 **"all trade with the enemy":** James M. McPherson, *Battle Cry of Freedom: The Civil War Era* (New York: Oxford University Press, 1988), 621–22.
134–135 **"some barter or trading"** . . . **"as a last resort":** McPherson, *Battle Cry of Freedom,* 621–22.
135 **four out of five northern textile mills:** Richard H. Abbott, *Cotton and Capital: Boston Businessmen and Antislavery Reform, 1854–1868* (Amherst: University of Massachusetts Press, 1991, 80.
135 **"physical symptoms of starvation":** "The Distress in Lancashire," *New York Times,* Nov. 26, 1862. The cotton famine was widely reported in the United States. See also Burton J. Hendrick, *Statesmen of the Lost Cause: Jefferson Davis and His Cabinet* (Boston: Little, Brown, 1939), 212.
135 **Seward keenly wanted:** David G. Surdam, "Traders or Traitors: Northern Cotton Trading During the Civil War," *Business and Economic History* 28, no. 2 (1999): 301; Phil Leigh, "Trading with the Enemy," *New York Times,* Oct. 28, 2012.
135 **"We want Cotton badly":** Bates, *Diary of Edward Bates,* 264.
135 **arrived in Memphis:** Sherman, *Memoirs of Gen. W. T. Sherman,* 1:293.
135 **cotton could be procured:** George S. Denison to Salmon Chase, Nov. 29, 1862, in *SPCP,* 3:322–24; see also Leigh, "Trading with the Enemy."
135 **"We cannot carry on war":** Ronald C. White, *American Ulysses: A Life of Ulysses S. Grant* (New York: Random House, 2016), 236.
135 **"has been complicated with the belief":** W. T. Sherman to Salmon Chase, Aug. 11, 1862, in Sherman, *Memoirs of Gen. W. T. Sherman,* 1:294.
136 **funeral procession:** Robert L. O'Connell, *Fierce Patriot: The Tangled Lives of William Tecumseh Sherman* (New York: Random House, 2014), 107–8.
136 **"beyond the sight of the flag-staff":** Sherman to Chase, Aug. 11, 1862, 1:294.
136 **"worse to us than a defeat":** Lee Kennett, *Sherman: A Soldier's Life* (New York: HarperCollins, 2001), 175.

136 **"great disloyalty manifested by the citizens":** John Bordelon, "'Rebels to the Core': Memphians Under William T. Sherman," file:///C:/Users/ElRog/Downloads/Bordelon_John_Rebels_ocr%20 (8).pdf, 7.

136 **travel into and out of Memphis:** "Restrictions on Travel," *New York Times*, Aug. 3, 1862.

136 **Grant directed traders:** Ron Chernow, *Grant* (New York: Penguin Press, 2017), 233.

136 **"Money is as much contraband":** Bordelon, "Rebels to the Core," 26.

136 **ordered that no gold or silver:** "Restrictions on Travel"; Chernow, *Grant*, 232.

136 **Sherman went further:** "News of the Day," *New York Times*, Aug. 6, 1862; Sherman, *Memoirs of Gen. W. T. Sherman*, 1:295. See also Kennett, *Sherman*, 175.

136 **were quickly rescinded:** Chernow, *Grant*, 232; Kennett, *Sherman*, 175; Sherman, *Memoirs of Gen. W. T. Sherman*, 1:295; Bordelon, "Rebels to the Core," 25.

136 **"the country will swarm":** Kennett, *Sherman*, 175.

137 **"the commercial enterprise of the Jews":** Sherman to Chase, Aug. 11, 1862, 1:294–95.

137 **"I found so many Jews":** Chernow, *Grant*, 233.

137 **At least four other Union generals:** White, *American Ulysses*, 251, identified three generals (aside from Sherman and Grant) who traded in anti-Jewish stereotypes. Benjamin Butler, described below, certainly qualified as a fourth.

137 **"a dozen Jewish cotton buyers":** White, *American Ulysses*, 251.

137 **10,000 Jews fought:** Debbie Nathan, "A Very Jewish Civil War," National Archives; also available at https://www.tabletmag.com/jewish-arts-and-culture/194743/a-very-jewish-civil-war.

137 **received more hospitably:** Gareth Russell, *The Ship of Dreams: The Sinking of the Titanic and the End of the Edwardian Era* (New York: Atria, 2019), 147.

137 **"native Southern merchants":** *Richmond Examiner* quoted in "The Situation," *New York Herald*, July 27, 1862.

137 **rapacious commercial practices:** *RWCD* (2015), 1:113, 134, 146, 165, 257. See also Edmund Ruffin's screed of Feb. 2, 1864: "The Jews, as a class, are the most despicable of all our population." *Ruffin*, 3:325–26.

138 **went to great lengths to appoint:** Chernow, *Grant*, 642–43.

138 **"Louisianans to make haste":** Salmon Chase to Benjamin Butler, July 31, 1862, in Benjamin F. Butler, *Private and Official Correspondence of Gen. Benjamin F. Butler During the Period of the Civil War*, ed. Jesse Ames Marshall, 5 vols. (N.p.: Privately published, 1917), 2:132 (hereinafter *Butler Letters*).

138 **was also receiving private reports:** George S. Denison to Salmon Chase, June 28, 1862, in *SPCP*, 3:222–24.

138 **"If some prudential considerations":** Salmon Chase to Benjamin Butler, July 31, 1862, in *SPCP*, 3:234.

138 **cleaned the streets:** McPherson, *Battle Cry of Freedom*, 623.

139 **cotton was purchased with salt:** Albert Bushnell Hart, *Salmon P. Chase* (Boston: Houghton Mifflin, 1899), 226.

139 **Treasury agent and distant Chase relative:** Denison's uncle, Dudley Chase Denison, was Salmon Chase's cousin.

139 **Chase's spy:** Chase wrote Denison on June 28, 1862, "I shall take the liberty of writing private letters to you occasionally" (*SPCP*, 3:222). James Marten called Denison Chase's "personal spy"—see his "The Making of a Carpetbagger: George S. Denison and the South, 1854–1866," *Louisiana History: The Journal of the Louisiana Historical Association* 34, no. 2 (1993): 134.

139 **five thousand sacks of salt:** George S. Denison to Salmon Chase, Oct. 10, 1862, in *Butler Letters*, 2:359.

139 **"Many officers and soldiers":** *Butler Letters*, 2:360.

139 **"They are Jews":** Jonathan D. Sarna and Benjamin Shapell, *Lincoln and the Jews* (New York: Thomas Dunne/St. Martin's, 2015), 142.

139 **the worst offender was a gentile:** George S. Denison to Salmon Chase, Aug. 26, 1862, in *Butler Letters*, 2:299; see also McPherson, *Battle Cry of Freedom*, 624.

139 **"Col. Butler is a brother":** Denison to Chase, Aug. 26, 1862, *Butler Letters*, 2:229.

139 **Chase had heard disquieting reports:** Salmon Chase to Benjamin Butler, June 24, 1862, in *Butler Letters*, 1:623.

139 **Denison noted that eight or nine riverboats:** Denison to Chase, Oct. 10, 1862, 2:355–58.

139 **"will do anything for money":** Denison to Chase, Oct. 10, 1862, 2:355–58.

139 **"So many and seemingly such well-founded":** Salmon Chase to Benjamin Butler, Oct. 29, 1862, in *SPCP*, 3:307–8.

140 **"expressly forbidden"** . . . **"many" expressed:** *SPCP*, 3:307–8. Note that Denison's letter to Chase of Oct. 10, 1862, provided extensive evidence of contraband trade by Butler's officers (*SPCP*, 3:308).

140 **"My brother has been":** Benjamin Butler to Salmon Chase, Nov. 14, 1862, in *Butler Letters*, 2:423.

140 **"People here think":** George S. Denison to Salmon Chase, Nov. 29, 1862, in *SPCP*, 3:322–24.

140 **Denison was later accused:** Marten, "The Making of a Carpetbagger," 154.

141 **reading the tax law:** George S. Boutwell, *Reminiscences of Sixty Years in Public Affairs* (New York: McClure, Phillips, 1902), 1:303.

141 **again falling behind on payments:** Salmon P. Chase, *Inside Lincoln's Cabinet: The Civil War Diaries of Salmon P. Chase*, ed. David Herbert Donald (New York: Longman's Green, 1954), 98. See also Niven, Salmon P. *Chase: A Biography* (New York: Oxford University Press, 1995, 293.

141 **Chase was having no luck:** Heather Cox Richardson, *The Greatest Nation of the Earth: Republican Economic Policies During the Civil War* (Cambridge: Harvard University Press, 1997), 50.

141 **settled into a waiting game:** Chase, *Inside Lincoln's Cabinet*, 93.

141 **"forcible abolition of slavery":** McPherson, *Battle Cry of Freedom*, 502.

141 **Chase visited the White House:** Chase, *Inside Lincoln's Cabinet*, 97–98.

141 **"I also urged":** *Inside Lincoln's Cabinet*, 98. Chase visited Lincoln on the morning of July 22; the cabinet meeting in which Lincoln divulged his plan for a proclamation occurred later the same day.

141 **hoarding gold and silver coins:** "Our New Small Note Currency: The New Postage Stamp Notes Bills for Five, Ten, Twenty-Five and Fifty Cents, in Circulation," *New York Times*, Aug. 29, 1862; Edward K. Spann, *Gotham at War: New York City, 1860–1965* (Wilmington, Del.: Scholarly Resources, 2002), 149.

141 **Lincoln had quipped:** Niven, *Chase, A Biography*, 275–76.

142 **Fessenden made a strong plea:** Robert J. Cook, *Civil War Senator: William Pitt Fessenden and the Fight to Save the American Republic* (Baton Rouge: Louisiana State University Press, 2011), 151.

142 **"Slavery was the cause of this war":** Congressional Globe, 37th Cong., 2nd Sess., 3127.

142 **to preempt more radical action:** See Ralph Korngold, *Thaddeus Stevens: A Being Darkly Wise and Rudely Great* (New York: Harcourt, Brace, 1955), esp. 191–92.

142 **"Broken eggs cannot be mended":** *CWL*, 5:351–52. The letter was forwarded to Lincoln from the financier and Democratic Party operative August Belmont.

142 **"as a practical war measure":** Marc Egnal, *Clash of Extremes: The Economic Origins of the Civil War* (New York: Farrar, Straus, and Giroux, 2009), 318.

142 **"by proclamation":** William E. Gienapp and Erica L. Gienapp, eds., *The Civil War Diary of Gideon Welles* (Urbana: University of Illinois Press, 2014), 1:70–71.

142 **Lincoln divulged his plan:** Chase, *Inside Lincoln's Cabinet*, 99.

143 **"but proposed to issue a Proclamation"** . . . **"cordial support":** Chase, *Inside Lincoln's Cabinet*, 99.

143 **Montgomery Blair:** McPherson, *Battle Cry of Freedom*, 505.

143 **British reaction in mind:** Sven Beckert, *Empire of Cotton: A Global History* (New York: Alfred A. Knopf, 2015), 261–62. Seward worried that the proclamation, by fueling southern resistance, would be seen as lengthening the war, and perhaps provoke the cotton-starved European powers to recognize the Confederacy.

143 **"The Yankees, since the war":** Chesnut, 175.

143 **Lincoln hosted a delegation:** "Address on Colonization to a Deputation of Negroes, August 14, 1862," in *CWL*, 5:370–75. The "substance" of Lincoln's remarks was reported in the next day's *New York Tribune* and in Thaddeus Stevens to Salmon Chase, Aug. 25, 1862, in *Stevens Papers*, 319–20. See also Korngold, *Thaddeus Stevens*, 150; McPherson, *Battle Cry of Freedom*, 508–9.

143 **the first Black guests:** Sean Wilentz, "A Matter of Facts," *The Atlantic*, Jan. 22, 2020.

144 **"as much respect and kindness":** Wilentz, "A Matter of Facts."

144 **deeply offensive to free Black Americans:** David W. Blight, *Frederick Douglass: Prophet of Freedom* (New York: Simon & Schuster, 2018), 238–40, 372–73.

144 **James McPherson has argued:** McPherson, *Battle Cry of Freedom*, 508.

144 **overwhelmingly passed referenda:** "Affairs at the West," *New York Times*, Aug. 14, 1862; see also Mindy Juriga, "The Role of Political Parties in Illinois During the 1862 Illinois Constitutional Convention," Illinois Periodicals Online, https://www.lib.niu.edu/2007/iht14020716.html. As Juriga painfully elaborates, a state convention tasked voters to ratify a new constitution (which they rejected) and, separately, to vote on three articles relating to the status of African Americans. The articles "prohibited persons of color from settling in Illinois, denied them voting rights, and directed the legislature to pass laws necessary to enforce those provisions." The restrictions passed "overwhelmingly."

144 **Lincoln's colonization scheme:** As an example of the extensive coverage, see, "Telegraphic to the Portland Daily Press, Speech of President Lincoln," *Portland* (Me.) *Daily Press*, Aug. 15, 1862.

144 **"oppressors of their race":** Richard Nelson Current, *Old Thad Stevens: A Story of Ambition* (Madison: University of Wisconsin Press, 1942), 168.

144 **Lincoln had been gulled:** Stevens to Chase, Aug. 25, 1862, 319–20.

144 **several Central American countries:** Annual Message to Congress, Dec. 1, 1862, in *CWL*, 5:520.

144 **the U.S. government sponsored:** McPherson, *Battle Cry of Freedom*, 509.

144 **By 1864, Lincoln had dropped:** Tyler Dennett, ed., *Lincoln and the Civil War in the Diaries and Letters of John Hay* (Westport, Conn.: Negro Universities Press, 1972), 203.

144–145 **"How much better":** Chase, *Inside Lincoln's Cabinet*, 112.

145 **"We think you are strangely":** *CWL*, 5:389, from "The Prayer of Twenty Millions," *New York Tribune*, Aug. 20, 1862.

145 **"If I could save the Union":** Abraham Lincoln to Horace Greeley, Aug. 22, 1862, in *CWL*, 5:388; Lincoln's reply appeared in the *Washington Evening Star* on Aug. 23. The *Star* cited that morning's edition of the capital's *Daily National Intelligencer*, apparently where Lincoln directed his reply. Greeley's *Tribune* reprinted the letter on Aug. 25.

145 **"You can form no conception":** John Sherman to W. T. Sherman, Aug. 24, 1862, in *The Sherman Letters Correspondence Between General and Senator Sherman from 1837 to 1891*, ed. Rachel Sherman Thorndike (New York: Charles Scribner's Sons, 1894), 156.

145 **Chase sold a small volume:** Chase, *Inside Lincoln's Cabinet*, 115; he sold $3 to $4 million worth.

145 **He therefore revived his proposal:** Salmon Chase to John Bigelow, Oct. 7, 1862, in *SPCP*, 3:290–94.

146 **"The future does not look promising to me":** J. W. Schuckers, *The Life and Public Services of Salmon Portland Chase* (New York: D. Appleton, 1874), 379. It is true that Chase qualified his pessimism, adding, "It may be brighter than it seems likely to be"—but then, Chase hardly ever issued a remark without qualification.

146 **"hoping to find him well enough":** Salmon Chase to Hiram Barney, Oct. 26, 1862, in *SPCP*, 3:306–7.

146 **"Wrote to Genl. [John] Pope and Genl. Butler":** Chase, *Inside Lincoln's Cabinet*, 103.

146 **"We have as little to do with it":** Salmon Chase to John Sherman, Aug. 29, 1862, in John G. Nicolay and John Hay, *Abraham Lincoln: A History* (New York: Century, 1886–1890), 6:255.

146 **Lincoln declined to act on:** See Chase, *Inside Lincoln's Cabinet*, 107, for Chase's recommendation in the cabinet on Aug. 3, 1862. For further Chase assaults on McClellan, see *Inside Lincoln's Cabinet*, 87, and Niven, *Chase, A Biography*, 292–94.

147 **weak and bungling:** John Niven, "Lincoln and Chase: A Reappraisal," *Journal of the Abraham Lincoln Association* 12, no. 1 (1991).

147 **"half measures":** Salmon Chase to George Denison, Sept. 8, 1862, in *SPCP*, 3:261.

147 **"We have trifled":** Salmon Chase to Kate Chase, July 13, 1862, in *SPCP*, 3:226–27.

147 **"our resources are being exhausted":** Thomas Lamar Coughlin, *Those Southern Lamars: The Stories of Five Illustrious Lamars* (N.p.: Xlibris, 2000), 93–94.

147 **the comfort for writing and reflection:** Robert J. Brugger, "Redmoor Farewell: The Life and Death of Edmund Ruffin," *VQR*, Summer 1991.

147 **"a fruitless attempt":** *Ruffin*, 2:347–48.

147 **Marauding Yankee troops commented:** Amy Chambliss, "Edmund Ruffin of Virginia," *The Georgia Review* 14, no. 4 (1960): 425.

148 **trashed the home:** *Ruffin*, 2:xiii–xiv; Harry Kollatz Jr., "An Unyielding Man," Richmondmag, Apr. 26, 2011, richmondmag.com.

148 **"came across the river":** *Ruffin*, 2:351–52.

148 **Prices of wood and coal:** *RWCD* (2015), 1:89, 138–39, 174, 292.

148 **By October it fetched $2.50:** *RWCD* (2015), 1:112, 146–47; *Ruffin*, 2:216, 347–48.

148 **Only for one "commodity":** *Ruffin*, 2:353. Ruffin reports slave prices had fallen by a quarter.

148 **"the chief cause":** "Financial Weakness in Rebeldom," *New York Times*, Sept. 20, 1862, quoting *Richmond Examiner*.

148 **having topped $210 million:** "The Rebel Currency," *New York Times*, Sept. 26, 1862.

148 **"an evident indisposition":** "Financial Weakness in Rebeldom," quoting *Richmond Examiner*.

149 **"literally overrun with goods":** "Resources of the South," *Atlantic Monthly*, Oct. 1862, 502–10.

149 **"overflowing with merchandize":** "Resources of the South," 502–10.

150 **"vast and pressing importance":** "Resources of the South," 502–10, quoting *Richmond Examiner*.

150 **McClellan was unduly casual:** Niven, *Chase: A Biography*, 293–94.

150 **it withdrew toward the capital:** *Strong*, 3:250.

150 **Chase ordered Treasury clerks:** Chase, *Inside Lincoln's Cabinet*, 117.

150 **further dispiriting the market:** Richardson, *The Greatest Nation of the Earth*, 50.

150 **he thought McClellan's tardiness:** Chase, *Inside Lincoln's Cabinet*, 93. See also Gienapp and Gienapp, *The Civil War Diary of Gideon Welles*, 1:102: "Chase frankly stated he desired it [McClellan's removal], that he deliberately believed McClellan ought to be shot, and should, were he president, be brought to summary punishment."

150 **Modern historians have concluded:** For a brief historiographic summary, see Richard Slotkin, "The McClellan Problem," *New York Times*, Aug, 3, 2012.

150 **"Abe Lincoln is not the style":** *Strong*, 3:256.

150 **"the slave of McClellan":** Cook, *Civil War Senator*, 153.

151 **sought to force the issue:** Gienapp and Gienapp, *The Civil War Diary of Gideon Welles*, 1:100–103. The memo in question was Chase and Stanton's second attempt; for the earlier attempt see *The Civil War Diary of Gideon Welles*, 1:93–95. See also Chase, *Inside Lincoln's Cabinet*, 116–17.

151 **procured signatures from four:** Chase, *Inside Lincoln's Cabinet*, 117; aside from Chase and Stanton, the note was signed by Attorney General Bates and Interior Secretary Caleb Blood Smith. Blair was not consulted; Seward was conveniently out of town.

151 **"disclaimed any movement":** Gienapp and Gienapp, *The Civil War Diary of Gideon Welles*, 1:102. See also Chase, *Inside Lincoln's Cabinet*, 117.

151 **the cabinet was stunned to learn:** Gienapp and Gienapp, *The Civil War Diary of Gideon Welles*, 1:104–5; Chase, *Inside Lincoln's Cabinet*, 118.

151 **The President was supremely distressed:** Gienapp and Gienapp, *The Civil War Diary of Gideon Welles*, 1:105; Chase, *Inside Lincoln's Cabinet*, 119.

151 **"He is a good engineer":** Gienapp and Gienapp, *The Civil War Diary of Gideon Welles*, 1:105.

151 **"The Federals got a very complete":** Lord Palmerston to Lord Russell, Sept. 14, 1862, in James Ford Rhodes, *Lectures on the American Civil War* (New York: Macmillan, 1913), 170.

151 **"an arrangement upon the basis":** James M. McPherson, "No Peace Without Victory, 1861–1865," *American Historical Review*, Feb. 2004, 3.

151 **Throughout September, as Europe:** See, for instance, Chase, *Inside Lincoln's Cabinet*, 131; *Strong*, 3:252; McPherson, "No Peace Without Victory," 3–4.

152 **"There is no doubt that Jefferson Davis":** Rhodes, *Lectures on the American Civil War*, 172–73.

152 **"down-trodden people of Europe":** "The Paisley Reformers and the American Question," *New York Times*, Aug. 13, 1862.

152 **"England will insist":** Edwin De Leon, *Secret History of Confederate Diplomacy Abroad*, ed. William C. Davis (Lawrence: University Press of Kansas, 2005), 126.

152 **bloodiest ever day of fighting:** The National Park Service estimates 2100 Union dead and 1550 Confederate dead (more than on June 6, 1944, or than on any other day of the Civil War) and 23,000 casualties: https://www.nps.gov/anti/learn/historyculture/casualties.htm.

152 **cooled Palmerston's interest:** McPherson, "No Peace Without Victory," 4.

153 **"Thought to myself":** Chase, *Inside Lincoln's Cabinet*, 149.

153 **"I have, as you are aware":** Chase, *Inside Lincoln's Cabinet*, 149–50.

153 **"persons of African descent":** Preliminary Emancipation Proclamation, Sept. 22, 1862, in *CWL*, 5:433–34.

153 **insanity of the slaveholder class:** Hay, *Inside Lincoln's White House*, 40.

153 **"We shout for joy":** Blight, *Frederick Douglass*, 379.

153 **Northern newspapers were mostly positive:** The *New York Daily Tribune* titled its morning-after editorial, "God Bless Abraham Lincoln" (*Strong*, 3:256); the phrase was widely republished.

153–154 **"self-enforcing" . . . "bids fair to become":** "The Hour and the Man," *Atlantic Monthly*, Nov. 1862, 623. For the *Atlantic*'s concern that the freedmen acquire property, see "Resources of the South."

154 **Southerners furiously denounced:** See "Mr. Lincoln's Proclamation," *New York Herald*, Oct. 4, 1862, which excerpted commentary from the South.

154 **"Stocks have declined":** Boritt, *Lincoln and the Economics of the American Dream*, 207–8.

154 **Gold rose to a 20 percent premium:** Ellis Paxson Oberholtzer, *Jay Cooke: Financier of the Civil War* (Philadelphia: G.W. Jacobs, 1907), 1:214.

154 **the Treasury fell four weeks behind:** Salmon Chase to Benjamin Butler, Sept. 23, 1862, in *SPCP*, 3:283–84.

154 **Chase was burning through:** Treasury Secretary, *Annual Report*, 1862, pp. 3–4; figures are for the Sept. 30 quarter.

154 **to buy in any volume:** Schuckers, *The Life and Public Services*, 344–45; John Sherman, *Recollections of Forty Years in the House, Senate and Cabinet* (Chicago: Werner, 1895), 1:321.

154 **Nothing was accomplished:** Salmon Chase to John J. Cisco, Sept. 25, 1862, in *SPCP*, 3:265–66.

154 **Cooke had been nurturing:** Oberholtzer, *Jay Cooke: Financier*, 1:180–84, 187, 210.

155 **"and in this way learned":** Oberholtzer, *Jay Cooke: Financier*, 1:187.

155 **"Please keep out of private letters":** Salmon Chase to Jay Cooke, Aug. 8, 1862, in *SPCP*, 3:249–50. For contemporary criticism of the Chase-Cooke relationship, see Richardson, *The Greatest Nation of the Earth*, 48.

155 **The Philadelphian had quietly been placing:** Oberholtzer, *Jay Cooke: Financier*, 1:217.

155–156 **"among the people":** Oberholtzer, *Jay Cooke: Financier*, 1:218.

156 **"utterly discouraging":** James G. Blaine, *Twenty Years of Congress, from Lincoln to Garfield* (Boston: Avery, 1884), 1:442.

156 **gold hit a high:** Schuckers, *The Life and Public Services*, 255–56.

156 **"By miracles":** Schuckers, *The Life and Public Services*, 457.

156 **"It has seemed to me possible":** Salmon Chase to Jay Cooke, Oct. 23, 1862, in *SPCP*, 3:299–300.

Chapter Eight: Chase's Plan

157 **"The people demand uniformity":** Treasury Secretary, *Annual Report*, 1862, p. 19.

157 **Chase agreed to pay a commission:** See especially Salmon Chase to [House Speaker] Schuyler Colfax, Apr. 1, 1864, in "The Five-Twenty Loan: Jay Cooke & Co., Letter from Secretary Chase," *New York Times*, Apr. 9, 1864, as well as J. W. Schuckers, *The Life and Public Services of Salmon Portland Chase* (New York: D. Appleton, 1874), 344–45, and David K. Thomson, "'Like a Cord Through the Whole Country': Union Bonds and Financial Mobilization for Victory," *The Journal of the Civil War Era* 6, no. 3 (2016): 351.

157 **the first "wire house":** Thomson, "'Like a Cord Through the Whole Country,'" 352.

158 **"Farmers, Merchants, Mechanics, Capitalists":** "Payable in Gold," *Alleghanian* (Ebensburg, Pa.), Nov. 13, 1862.

158 **"payable in gold" . . . "a FIRST MORTGAGE":** "Payable in Gold."

158 **the wisdom of investing:** Heather Cox Richardson, *The Greatest Nation of the Earth: Republican Economic Policies During the Civil War* (Cambridge: Harvard University Press, 1997), 51.

158 **He essentially extorted them:** Michael Hiltzik, *Iron Empires: Robber Barons, Railroads, and the Making of Modern America* (Boston: Houghton Mifflin Harcourt, 2020), 73.

158 **Cooke challenged towns:** Richardson, *The Greatest Nation of the Earth*, 51.

158 **only $14 million . . . $10 million:** Treasury Secretary, *Annual Report*, 1862, pp. 12, 31.

158 **"I am gratified by the success":** Ellis Paxson Oberholtzer, *Jay Cooke: Financier of the Civil War* (Philadelphia: G.W. Jacobs, 1907), 1:221.

159 **the banker was "bound":** Chase to Colfax, Apr. 1, 1864, in "The Five-Twenty Loan: Jay Cooke & Co., Letter from Secretary Chase."

159 **"You must not think me parsimonious":** Oberholtzer, *Jay Cooke: Financier*, 1:222.

159 **Cooke visited Lincoln:** Oberholtzer, *Jay Cooke: Financier*, 1:200–201; Michael Burlingame, *Abraham Lincoln: A Life*, 2 vols. (Baltimore: Johns Hopkins University Press, 2008), 2:429; Rick Beard, "A Terminal Case of the 'Slows,'" *New York Times*, Nov. 5, 2012.

159 **"Will you pardon me for asking":** Abraham Lincoln to George McClellan, Oct. 24, 1864, in *CWL*, 5:474. See also Lincoln to McClellan, Oct. 13, 1864, *CWL*, 5:460–62, in which Lincoln implored the general, "Are you not over-cautious when you assume that you can not do what the enemy is constantly doing?"

159 **"playing false":** William O. Stoddard, *Inside the White House in War Times: Memoirs and Report of Lincoln's Secretary*, ed. Michael Burlingame (Lincoln: University of Nebraska Press, 2000), 80.

159 **Lincoln finally dismissed McClellan:** Abraham Lincoln to Henry Halleck, Nov. 5, 1862, in *CWL*, 5:485.

160 **"The infection of despair":** H. D. Cooke to John Sherman, Oct. 27, 1862, John Sherman Papers, box 52.

160 **The Treasury was behind:** Treasury Secretary, *Annual Report*, 1862, p. 10. See also "Gold Question: A Financial View from a Washington Stand Point," *New York Times*, Oct. 24, 1862; "News from Washington," *New York Times*, Dec. 20, 1862; John Niven, *Salmon P. Chase: A Biography* (New York: Oxford University Press, 1995), 307–8; Schuckers, *The Life and Public Services*, 344–45.

160 **gold premium to 38 percent:** *New York Times*, Oct. 24, 1862.

160 **In late October, the Board of Brokers:** "Financial and Commercial," *New York Herald*, Oct. 23, 1862.

160 **"Large quantities of gold":** "Financial and Commercial," *New York Herald*, Nov. 13, 1862.

160 **"the exclusion of gold":** *New York Herald*, Nov. 17, 1862.

160 **"We are unwilling to lose":** "20th Ward Seymour Club," *New York Herald*, Oct. 5, 1862.

161 **formally sought legislative action:** Annual Message to Congress, Dec. 1, 1862, in *CWL*, 5:518.

161 **"bountiful harvests":** *CWL*, 5:518.

162 **"It is insisted that their presence":** *CWL*, 5:518.

162 **"these United States":** Message to Congress in Special Session, July 4, 1861, *CWL*, 4:421.

162 **"diligent consideration":** Annual Message to Congress, Dec. 1, 1862, 5:518.

163 **the breathtaking sum of $900 million:** Treasury Secretary, *Annual Report*, 1862, p. 6. The exact figure was $899.3 million.

163 **"as injurious as it would be easy":** Treasury Secretary, *Annual Report*, 1862, p. 12.

163 **1600 state-chartered banks:** David M. Gische, "The New York City Banks and the Development of the National Banking System 1860–1870," *The American Journal of Legal History* 23. no 1 (1979): 24.

163 **1400 in the loyal states:** "Our Abominable Currency System," *Chicago Daily Tribune*, Feb 13. 1863.

163 **widespread counterfeiting:** *Thompson's Bank Note Reporter*, quoted in "Our Abominable Currency System."

163 **Chase unfairly blamed:** According to the Treasury's 1862 *Annual Report* (14), there were $167 million of private bank notes extant, compared with, by midsummer, $300 million in greenbacks. Thus, it's unlikely that the bank notes contributed as much to inflation as did Chase's greenbacks.

163 **should control the circulation:** Treasury Secretary, *Annual Report*, 1862, p. 16.

164 **"no mere paper money scheme":** Treasury Secretary, *Annual Report*, 1862, p. 21.

164 **feel a shared interest:** For Chase's thinking on this manifestly ideological purpose, see Treasury Secretary, *Annual Report*, 1862, p. 20.

164 **the "central idea":** Treasury Secretary, *Annual Report*, 1862, p. 17.

164 **his banking reform was unlikely:** Treasury Secretary, *Annual Report*, 1862, p. 24.

164 **enacting it would not be easy:** For initial opposition to the bill in Congress, see "News from Washington," *New York Times*, Dec., 8, 1862, and "News from Washington," *New York Times*, Dec. 18, 1862.

164 **were naturally opposed:** James A. Hamilton to Salmon Chase, Dec. 10, 1862, in *SPCP*, 3:327–28; Salmon Chase to George Opdyke, Dec. 14, 1862, in *SPCP*, 3:338–40.

164 **"cold courtesy":** William E. Gienapp and Erica L. Gienapp, eds., *The Civil War Diary of Gideon Welles* (Urbana: University of Illinois Press, 2014), 1:203.

165 **Lincoln was "fond of" Seward:** Gienapp and Gienapp, *The Civil War Diary of Gideon Welles*, 1:205.

165 **The others were plainly irked:** Gienapp and Gienapp, *Civil War Diary of Gideon Welles*, 1:193, 203.

165 **an exaggerated view of Seward:** See, for instance, Robert J. Cook, *Civil War Senator: William Pitt Fessenden and the Fight to Save the American Republic* (Baton Rouge: Louisiana State University Press, 2011), 154–57; Fawn M. Brodie, *Thaddeus Stevens: Scourge of the South* (New York: W. W. Norton, 1959), 185; Leonard P. Curry, *Blueprint for Modern America: Nonmilitary Legislation of the First Civil War Congress* (Nashville: Vanderbilt University Press, 1968), 216.

165 **"It were a great blessing":** *Stevens Papers*, 328.

165 **"All the wires at the command":** "Our Washington Letter," *Chicago Daily Tribune*, Dec. 27, 1862.

165 **Chase stoked these fears:** Salmon P. Chase, *Inside Lincoln's Cabinet: The Civil War Diaries of Salmon P. Chase*, ed. David Herbert Donald (New York: Longman's Green, 1954), 174. Note that Donald titled this chapter "An Available Candidate."

165 **"an abolitionist like Chase":** John Sherman to William Tecumseh Sherman, Sept. 24, 1862, in Rachel Sherman Thorndike, ed., *The Sherman Letters: Correspondence Between General and Senator Sherman from 1837 to 1891* (New York: Charles Scribner's Sons, 1894), 164–65.

165 **he encouraged the view:** Chase, *Inside Lincoln's Cabinet*, 94, 144, 174; Niven, *Chase: A Biography*, 308.

165 **"back-stairs influence":** Francis Fessenden, *Life and Public Services of William Pitt Fessenden* (Boston: Houghton Mifflin, 1907), 1:234.

166 **a delegation of nine mostly Radical senators:** Fessenden, *Life and Public Services of William Pitt Fessenden*, 1:240–42; John Nicolay and John Hay, *Abraham Lincoln: A History* (New York: Century, 1886–1890), 6:266; Gienapp and Gienapp, *The Civil War Diary of Gideon Welles*, 1:194–95; Curry, *Blueprint for Modern America*, 216–21; Schuckers, *The Life and Public Services*, 473–74.

166 **blunt attack on the executive branch:** After the crisis, *The New York Times* ("The Cabinet Crisis," Dec. 23, 1862) pronounced the senators' actions "directly at war with the independence of the Executive."

166 **Lincoln was shocked:** Gienapp and Gienapp, *The Civil War Diary of Gideon Welles*, 1:195.

166 **"appeared to think":** Nicolay and Hay, *Abraham Lincoln*, 6:265.

166 **trooped back to the White House:** Fessenden, *Life and Public Services*, 1:243–47, 251; Gienapp and Gienapp, *The Civil War Diary of Gideon Welles*, 1:195–97; Niven, *Chase: A Biography*, 311.

167 **"This matter is giving me":** Gienapp and Gienapp, *The Civil War Diary of Gideon Welles*, 1:200.

167 **"Now I can ride":** Nicolay and Hay, *Abraham Lincoln*, 6:270.

167 **He promptly wrote identical letters:** Abraham Lincoln to Salmon Chase and Abraham Lincoln to William Seward, both Dec. 20, 1862, in *CWL*, 6:12.

167 **a tortured disquisition:** *SPCP*, 3:342–43.

167 **"a terrible row in the cabinet":** Oberholtzer, *Jay Cooke: Financier*, 1:223.

167 **Chase's lawyerly revision:** "Preliminary Draft of Final Emancipation Proclamation, Dec. 30, 1862," including Chase's suggested revisions, dated Dec. 31, 1862, in *CWL*, 6:23–25.

167 **Emancipation Proclamation:** *CWL*, 6:28–30; *SPCP*, 3:350–51.

168 **Before the war was over:** The figures come from National Archives, https://www.archives.gov/education/lessons/blacks-civil-war#:~:text=By%20the%20end%20of%20the,30%2C000%20of%20infection%20or%20disease. Nearly 40,000 Black servicemen men died, 30,000 of those from infection or disease.

168 **"If my name ever goes":** Harold Holzer, "A Mighty Act: The 150th Anniversary of the Emancipation Proclamation," *Daily Beast*, Jan. 1, 2013, https://www.thedailybeast.com/a-mighty-act-the-150th-anniversary-of-the-emancipation-proclamation.

168 **"It was not only the Negro":** Don E. Fehrenbacher and Virginia Fehrenbacher, eds., *Recollected Words of Abraham Lincoln* (Stanford, Calif.: Stanford University Press, 1996), 507.

168 **held at the Free Trade Hall:** "Five Days Later from Europe," *New York Times*, Jan. 12, 1863; "Emancipation Meetings in England: The Workingmen of Manchester," *New York Times*, Jan. 15, 1863.

168 **"an instance of sublime Christian heroism":** Jan. 19, 1863, *CWL*, 6:63–64.

168 **"The Emancipation Proclamation has done more":** James M. McPherson, *Battle Cry of Freedom: The Civil War Era* (New York: Oxford University Press, 1988), 566.

168 **gaping federal deficit:** Treasury Secretary, *Annual Report*, 1862, p. 5 (the deficit was then projected at $277 million).

169 **reaching alarming proportions:** Salmon Chase to Pitt Fessenden, Jan. 7, 1863, in *SPCP*, 3:357–59; Salmon Chase to Pitt Fessenden, Jan. 11, 1863, in *SPCP*, 3:367–68. See also the following articles, which all appeared in *New York Times*: "News from Washington: The Finances of the Government," Jan. 12, 1863; "The Financial Condition: Why the Soldiers Have Not Been Paid; Statement of Secretary Chase," Jan. 14, 1863; "The Financial Condition: The Payment of Troops," Jan. 15, 1863.

169 **"operated like magic":** Congressional Globe, 37th Cong., 3rd Sess., 841.

169 **"The people did not care":** Oberholtzer, *Jay Cooke: Financier*, 1:369.

169 **a gold dollar fetched:** "Financial and Commercial," *New York Herald*, Jan. 15, 1863; the precise ratio was $1.46 in greenbacks to a dollar in gold.

169 **"Gold has risen fifteen percent":** "Financial and Commercial, *New York Herald*, Jan. 19, 1863.

169 **"on any terms":** "Financial and Commercial," Jan. 15, 1863.

169 **he expected the Union's debt:** Treasury Secretary, *Annual Report*, 1860, p. 22; Treasury Secretary, *Annual Report*, 1862, p. 2. Chase forecast a debt of $1.74 billion on July 1, 1864, if the war was still on.

169 **the debt in 1860:** The debt on June 30, 1860, was $65 million; after the Revolutionary War it was approximately $75 million.

169 **"Give us the plan and I can borrow":** Bray Hammond, *Sovereignty and an Empty Purse: Banks and Politics in the Civil War* (Princeton, N.J.: Princeton University Press, 1970), 293.

170 **"opiates":** "House of Representatives," *New York Times*, Jan. 14, 1863.

170 **According to Chase:** Chase to Fessenden, Jan. 7, 1863, 3:357–59.

170 **"for the prompt discharge":** "To the Senate and House of Representatives," Jan. 17, 1863, in *CWL*, 6:60–61.

170 **asked Congress to promptly approve:** *CWL*, 6:60–61.

170 **"extraordinary" and "injudicious":** "Our Special Washington Dispatches," *New York Times*, Jan. 20, 1863.

170 **"bound" . . . "so important":** "To the Senate and House of Representatives," 6:60–61.

170 **"every possible support":** "To the Senate and House of Representatives," 6:60–61.

170 **as well as the President:** "To the Senate and House of Representatives," 6:60–61.

170 **"Immense interests are involved":** "The National Finances," *New York Times*, Jan. 14, 1863.

171 **"make himself President any day":** Congressional Globe, 37th Cong., 3rd Sess., 871.

171 **"contravene the State sovereignty":** "The National Finances."

171 **"The choice is really between":** "The Finances of the Country: The Bills Before Congress," *New York Times*, Jan. 14, 1863.

172 **"Why don't you—who can so well":** Schuckers, *The Life and Public Services*, 386–87.

172 **He warned Pitt Fessenden:** Schuckers, *The Life and Public Services*, 385.

172 **pro-reform articles flooded:** Oberholtzer, *Jay Cooke: Financier of the Civil War*, 1:331–32.

172 **"The dollar of America":** Oberholtzer, *Jay Cooke: Financier of the Civil War*, 1:335.

172 **majority of the Finance Committee:** Schuckers, *The Life and Public Services*, 386.

172 **including Fessenden:** Cook, *Civil War Senator*, 158.

172 **one of John Sherman's political campaigns:** Henrietta M. Larson, *Jay Cooke, Private Banker* (Cambridge: Harvard University Press, 1936), 102.

172 **visited his old friend:** Gische, "The New York City Banks," 37.

172 **"Chase appealed to me":** Theodore E. Burton, *John Sherman* (Boston: Houghton Mifflin, 1908), 135.

172 **more than a quarter had defaulted:** Matthew S. Jaremski, "National Banking's Role in U.S. Industrialization, 1850–1900," National Bureau of Economic Research Working Paper, 2 (later published in *The Journal of Economic History* 74, no. 1 [2014], 109–40).

173 **precisely 1 bank:** "National Banking's Role in U.S. Industrialization, 1850–1900," 2.

173 **55 in New York City:** Gische, "The New York City Banks," 26.

173 **Even in Ohio:** John Sherman, *Recollections of Forty Years in the House, Senate and Cabinet* (Chicago: Werner, 1895), 1:290. New England's population in 1860 was one-third larger than Ohio's, 3.13 million to 2.34 million.

173 **"Very little demand will arise":** Congressional Globe, 37th Cong., 3rd Sess., 877.

173 **"This currency . . . will be printed":** Congressional Globe, 37th Cong., 3rd Sess., 843.

173 **"The policy of this country":** Congressional Globe, 37th Cong., 3rd Sess., 843.

173 **for their alleged corruption:** "The Proceedings of Congress," *New York Times*, Feb. 11, 1863.

174 **"facility for excessive expansion":** "The Proceedings of Congress."

174 **onerous reserve requirements:** See Roger Lowenstein, *America's Bank: The Epic Struggle to Create the Federal Reserve* (New York: Penguin Press, 2015), 14–15.

174 **Sherman insisted on the most restrictive:** Congressional Globe, 37th Cong., 3rd Sess., 843. For more on these and other details of the act, see Gische, "The New York City Banks," esp. 38–39, and Jaremski, "National Banking's Role in U.S. Industrialization," 7.

174 **internationally convertible:** Congressional Globe, 37th Cong., 3rd Sess., 843.

174 **called this a "bribe":** Walter A. McDougall, *Throes of Democracy: The American Civil War Era, 1829–1877* (New York: HarperCollins, 2008), 434.

175 **held to only 2 percent:** SPCP, 4:272. See also, e.g., James G. Blaine, *Twenty Years of Congress, from Lincoln to Garfield* (Boston: Avery, 1884), 1:479. The 2 percent tax was finalized six days after the banking bill was enacted, in the revenue bill of Mar. 3, 1863.

175 **arguably trivial:** Rep. Owen Lovejoy of Illinois had proposed a tax of 4 percent, which failed ("House of Representatives," *New York Times*, Jan. 24, 1863).

175 **to arm-wrestle Republican holdouts:** Sherman, *Recollections*, 1:299.

175 **Howe instantly agreed:** Stoddard, *Inside the White House in War Time*, 104–6.

175 **put pressure on Fessenden:** Gabor S. Boritt, *Lincoln and the Economics of the American Dream* (Memphis: Memphis State University Press, 1978), 202; Cook, *Civil War Senator*, 158.

175 **Chase nervously attended the roll call:** "Important from Washington: Passage of Secretary Chase's National Currency Bill by the Senate," *New York Herald*, Feb. 13, 1863.

175 **In the first poll:** "Important from Washington: Passage of Secretary Chase's National Currency Bill by the Senate."

175 **two more senators flipped:** "The Peace Resolutions in New Jersey: Important from Washington; Passage of the Finance Bill Through the Senate," *New York Times*, Feb. 13, 1863; "Mr. Chase's Bill Passes the Senate," *Chicago Daily Tribune*, Feb. 13, 1863; "Important from Washington: Passage of Secretary Chase's National Currency Bill by the Senate." Michigan's Jacob Howard spoke against the bill but voted aye to save it from defeat. Kansas's James Lane, another opponent, declined to vote.

175 **Chase and Lincoln again helped:** The day before the vote, Chase asked Lincoln to intercede with Rep. William Kellogg, an Illinois Republican. Kellogg had been leaning against but voted in favor. See Salmon Chase to Abraham Lincoln, Feb. 19, 1863, in *SPCP*, 3:388.

175 **"the true policy":** "Our National Finances: Remarks of Honorable E. G. Spaulding in the House of Representatives," *New York Times*, Feb. 19, 1863. Chase was pivotal in turning Spaulding's vote.

176 **Wall Street speculators predicting a panic:** "Important New Treasury Measures," *Chicago Daily Tribune*, Feb. 27, 1863.

176 **the gold premium surged:** Schuckers, *The Life and Public Services*, 255; the premium reached that level on Feb. 25, 1863.

177 **"Those who neglect these":** Oberholtzer, *Jay Cooke: Financier*, 1:241. As Paul M. O'Leary ("Repeal of the Greenback Conversion Clause," *American Journal of Economics and Society*, Oct. 1963) explained, after July 1 Chase would have the option of redeeming greenbacks with securities that paid a lower interest rate.

177 **"The laws passed":** John Sherman to William Tecumseh Sherman, Mar. 20, 1863, in Thorndike, *The Sherman Letters*, 194.

Chapter Nine: Cotton for Cash

178 **"Money is the great power":** Ellis Paxson Oberholtzer, *Jay Cooke: Financier of the Civil War* (Philadelphia: G.W. Jacobs, 1907), 1:251, quoting the May 18, 1863, edition.

178 **"Shall we starve?":** *RWCD* (2015), 1:212 (entry for Jan. 17, 1863).

178 **he complained to President Lincoln:** Salmon Chase to Abraham Lincoln, Apr. 22, 1863, in *SPCP*, 3:388.

178 **"Never, as long as I knew him":** Noah Brooks, *Washington in Lincoln's Time* (New York: Century 1895), 57–58.

178 **"fire in the rear":** James M. McPherson, *Battle Cry of Freedom: The Civil War Era* (New York: Oxford University Press, 1988), 591.

178 **prominent northern Democrats:** "The Late Important Anglo-Rebel Diplomatic Correspondence," *New York Herald*, Apr. 1, 1863.

178–179 **arrested Clement Vallandigham:** "Special Dispatch to the *Chicago Daily Tribune*," *Chicago Daily Tribune*, May 7, 1863; McPherson, *Battle Cry of Freedom*, 596.

179 **Joseph Medill:** McPherson, *Battle Cry of Freedom*, 590.

179 **"Lost, lost, all is lost":** William E. Gienapp and Erica L. Gienapp, eds., *The Civil War Diary of Gideon Welles* (Urbana: University of Illinois Press, 2014), 1:293–94.

179 **"But for the daily news":** William E. Dodge to William B. Kinney, Mar. 9 1863, Edmund Clarence Stedman Papers, box 29 (emphasis added).

179 **"a very noble symphony":** *Strong*, 3:267; Strong identified the work as Beethoven's "Symphony in B-flat (no. 2)," however, the Second Symphony was in D major.

179 **10 to 15 percent *per month*:** McPherson (*Battle Cry of Freedom*, 440) says prices doubled in the first six months of 1863, a rate, were it exact, that would translate to 12 percent per month. John Beauchamp Jones's frequent and extensive entries on prices, though anecdotal, roughly agree with this rate.

179 **"All the necessaries of life":** *RWCD* (2015), 1:231.

179 **southern agents in Europe:** John Christopher Schwab, *The Confederate States of America, 1861–1865: A Financial and Industrial History of the South During the Civil War* (1901; repr., New York: Burt Franklin, 1968), 30. The agent J. G. Gibbes was dispatched to Europe, to work with agent James Spence.

180 **He was close to the French court:** Burton J. Hendrick, *Statesmen of the Lost Cause: Jefferson Davis and His Cabinet* (Boston: Little, Brown, 1939), 230.

180 **marry before the war was out:** Phil Leigh, "The Cotton Bond Bubble," *New York Times*, Jan. 30, 2013.

180 **Three-quarters of its arms:** Frank E. Vandiver, ed., *Confederate Blockade Running Through Bermuda, 1861–1865* (Austin: University of Texas Press, 1947), xxviii.

180 **they had lost interest:** Rose Razaghian, "Financial Civil War: The Confederacy's Financial Policies, 1861–1864," Yale ICF Working Paper, No. 04-45, 11.

180 **plunged to 4 percent:** In 1860, Britain's cotton imports from the United States totaled 2.6 million bales. Over 1863 and 1864, it is estimated that imports averaged 100,000 bales per year.

180 **Erlanger demanded an exorbitant fee:** Erlanger initially proposed that he purchase the bonds at 70, a discount of 30 percent (Hendrick, *Statesmen of the Lost Cause*, 220).

180 **Richmond authorized only £3 million:** Henry D. Capers, *The Life and Times of C.G. Memminger* (Richmond: Everett Waddey, 1893), 357–60.

180 **running the blockade from the Bahamas:** According to diplomatic correspondence, unnamed "Erlanger agents" had arrived in Richmond by Dec. 31, 1862—see *Official Records of the Union and Confederate Navies in the War of Rebellion*, series 2, vol. 2, *Navy Department Correspondence, 1861–1865, with Agents Abroad*, 325 (hereinafter *Official Naval Records*); these records are available at http://collections.library.cornell.edu/moa_new/ofre.html. See also Capers, *Life and Times of C.G. Memminger*, 357–58; Robert N. Rosen, *The Jewish Confederates* (Columbia: University of South Carolina Press, 2000), 79. Schwab, *The Confederate States of America*, says explicitly that Erlanger "crossed the Atlantic" (30).

181 **more than $400 million:** Memminger reported $410 million in notes at year end 1862 ("The Rebel Finances," *New York Times*, Feb. 15, 1863); according to Schwab (*The Confederate States of America*, 165), the figure was $450 million.

181 **plausibly $600 million of paper:** Capers, *Life and Times of C.G. Memminger*, 342.

181 **As reported in the *Richmond Daily Dispatch*:** RWCD (2015), 1: 221.

181 **one of history's great inflations:** McPherson, *Battle Cry of Freedom*, 440, estimated that from the beginning of 1861 until two years later, prices rose seven for one.

181 **33 cents in gold:** Schwab, *The Confederate States of America*, 7.

181 **need to issue $200 million:** "The Rebel Finances."

181 **"Bankruptcy stares us in the face":** "The Rebel Finances."

182 **borrow cash from expat southerners:** James D. Bulloch to James H. North, Dec. 18, 1862, *Official Naval Records*, 311–12.

182 **"very, very anxious":** James H. North to Stephon R. Mallory, Feb. 13, 1863, *Official Naval Records*, 361.

182 **"it would be well for us":** Capers, *Life and Times of C.G. Memminger*, 359.

182 **Memminger insisted:** Capers, *Life and Times of C.G. Memminger*, 357–58; Schwab, *The Confederate States of America*, 30.

182 **cotton exports before the war:** Treasury Secretary, *Annual Report*, 1864, p. 246. The $190 million figure is for 1860.

182 **Erlanger appealed to Davis:** Capers, *Life and Times of C.G. Memminger*, 358.

182 **modestly reducing the interest rate:** "One Day Later from Europe: Reports of the Defeat at Vicksburg; Prospects of the Confederate Loan," *New York Daily Tribune*, Apr. 1, 1863; see also Rosen, *Jewish Confederates*, 79.

182 **Congress debated the bond deal:** Hendrick, *Statesmen of the Lost Cause*, 223.

182 **ratified it January 29:** Schwab, *The Confederate States of America*, 31.

182 **returned to Paris in February:** Capers, *Life and Times of C.G. Memminger*, 358.

182 **twenty-year instruments:** For the bond terms and price of cotton in Liverpool, see "One Day Later from Europe"; "Commercial News by the Anglo-Saxon: Liverpool Cotton Market," *New York Times*, Mar. 13, 1863; "Commercial News by the Bohemian: Liverpool Cotton Market," *New York Times*, Mar. 28, 1863; Schwab, *Confederate States of America*, 31–33.

183 **government, which had more than enough surplus cotton:** Hendrick, *Statesmen of the Lost Cause*, 217; Schwab, *The Confederate States of America*, 33.

183 **The offering was wildly popular:** "One Day Later from Europe"; Hendrick, *Statesmen of the Lost Cause*, 224, 225.

183 **purchased the bonds at 77:** Schwab, *The Confederate States of America*, 32.

183 ***Economist* rated the bonds:** Schwab, *The Confederate States of America*, 33.

183 **William Gladstone:** Leigh, "The Cotton Bond Bubble."

183 **Napoleon III's private secretary:** Hendrick, *Statesmen of the Lost Cause*, 223.

183 **$11 million for Richmond:** Erlanger paid 77 percent of £3 million (roughly $15 million), less a 5 percent commission.

183 **absorbed five times that amount:** Schwab, *The Confederate States of America*, 33.

184 **"Cotton is King, at last":** Hendrick, *Statesmen of the Lost Cause*, 225.

184 **to be paid in Paris:** *Official Naval Records*, 417.

184 **established a shipping line:** Leigh, "The Cotton Bond Bubble."

184 **rumors (spread by Richmond):** "One Day Later from Europe."

184 **the same British investment community:** Jane Flaherty, "The Exhausted Condition of the Treasury on the Eve of the Civil War," *Civil War History* 55, no. 2 (2009): 271.

184 **The bonds surged in the aftermarket:** "One Day Later from Europe"; Hendrick, *Statesmen of the Lost Cause*, 225; Schwab, *The Confederate States of America*, 33.

184 **"repudiator":** Hendrick, *Statesmen of the Lost Cause*, 225–28.

184 **15 percent of the total:** Hendrick, *Statesmen of the Lost Cause*, 225–26; Schwab, *The Confederate States of America*, 32–33.

185 **the army's meat ration:** Razaghian, "Financial Civil War," 17.

185 **wild onions:** McPherson, *Battle Cry of Freedom*, 638.

185 **authorities stepped up:** Schwab, *The Confederate States of America*, 202; Richard Franklin Bensel, *Yankee Leviathan: The Origins of Central State Authority in America, 1859–1877* (New York: Cambridge University Press, 1990), 159; McPherson, *Battle Cry of Freedom*, 617.

185 **"tyrannical power":** "A Growl Against Impressment," *New York Times*, Jan. 20, 1863, quoting *Richmond Whig*.

185 **The government established commissions:** Schwab, *The Confederate States of America*, 202; Bensel, *Yankee Leviathan*, 159; McPherson, *Battle Cry of Freedom*, 617.

185 **outstripped his income:** *RWCD* (2015), 1:89, 221, 223, 231, 237, 238, 243. Over the entire war, real wages in the South declined by approximately one-third: see Ralph Andreano, ed., *The Economic Impact of the American Civil War* (Cambridge: Schenkman, 1967), 42–45.

185 **"My youngest daughter":** *RWCD* (2015), 1:243.

185 **"None but the opulent":** *RWCD* (2015), 1:212.

185 **Authorities in Richmond seized flour:** *RWCD* (2015), 1:238.

185–186 **"The gaunt form of wretched famine":** *RWCD* (2015), 1:251.

186 **"We are starving":** McPherson, *Battle Cry of Freedom*, 618. For contemporary reports of this incident, see "The Food Question: The Bread Riot in Richmond," *New York Herald*, Apr. 17, 1863; "Circuit Court," *Richmond Daily Dispatch*, May 6, 1863; "Life in Richmond: Particulars of the Recent Bread Riot," *Chicago Daily Tribune*, May 12, 1863.

186 **riot erupted in Salisbury:** *Ruffin*, 2:613; "From the Army of the Potomac," *Chicago Daily Tribune*, May 11, 1863.

186 **lobbied Davis to consider:** Edwin De Leon, *Secret History of Confederate Diplomacy Abroad*, ed. William C. Davis (Lawrence: University Press of Kansas, 2005), 103.

186 **Congress enacted a bill to induce:** Schwab, *The Confederate States of America*, 52.

186 **Less than 15 percent:** "From the Rebel States: Condition of the Confederate Finances," *New York Times*, Feb. 1, 1863, citing reports in *Richmond Examiner* and *Richmond Whig*. Memminger's year-end report put total Confederate debt on Dec. 31, 1862, at $556 million.

186 **"lamentably small portion":** *Richmond Examiner*, quoted in "The Finances of the Nation: The Financial Condition of England, France, the United States and the Rebel States," *New York Herald*, Jan. 12, 1863.

186–187 **Memminger lobbied governors:** Schwab, *The Confederate States of America*, 48.

187 **"Every man in the community":** Schwab, *The Confederate States of America*, 229.

187 **Congressmen engaged in food speculations:** Schwab, *The Confederate States of America*, 233.

187 **State governments speculated in cotton:** Schwab, *The Confederate States of America*, 233–34.

187 **"Cotton banks":** Schwab, *The Confederate States of America*, 133.

187 **"Money will buy little":** Andreano, *Economic Impact of the American Civil War*, 34–35.

187 **at Memminger's pleading:** Capers, *Life and Times of C.G. Memminger*, 342–43; the tax was enacted in April.

187 **"proper remedy—heavy taxation":** *Ruffin*, 2:581.

187 **Richmond levied a tax:** *Richmond Enquirer*, Apr 24, 1863; "The Confederate Tax Law," *North Carolina Standard*, Apr. 22, 1863; "A Bill for Amendment and Collection of Taxes," *Charlotte Western Democrat*, May 12, 1863. See also Bensel, *Yankee Leviathan*, 160; Schwab, *The Confederate States of America*, 290–95.

187 **three thousand agents:** McPherson, *Battle Cry of Freedom*, 616.

188 **"sought to reach, so far":** "Jeff. Davis' Message," *New York Times*, Dec. 12, 1863.

188 **"compel the country to invest":** *Richmond Enquirer* cited in "An Imperial Despotism," *North Carolina Standard*, May 1, 1863.

188 **"to resist, to the bitter end":** Schwab, *The Confederate States of America*, 296.

188 **"I would like to know":** Andrew B. Hall, Connor Huff, and Shiro Kuriwaki, "When Wealth Encourages Individuals to Fight: Evidence from the American Civil War," Mar. 6, 2017; abstract available at https://osf.io/d4w7j.

188 **slave owners were more likely to fight:** Hall, Huff, and Kuriwaki, "When Wealth Encourages Individuals to Fight: Evidence from the American Civil War."

189 **"We were told"**: "An Imperial Despotism."
189 **Most likely, Erlanger et Compagnie**: Schwab, *The Confederate States of America*, 35; see also Hendrick, *Statesmen of the Lost Cause*, 223–29, 231, and De Leon, *Secret History of Confederate Diplomacy Abroad*, 173.
189 **roughly at the offering price**: Marc D. Weidenmier, "The Market for Confederate Cotton Bonds," *Explorations in Economic History* 37 (2000): 79–80.
189 **"as reported by Mr. Erlanger"**: James Mason to John Slidell, May 14, 1863, *Official Naval Records*, 422.
189 **"We want ironclads"**: Stephen R. Mallory to James D. Bulloch, June 8, 1863, *Official Naval Records*, 435.
189 **The government's grand design**: "Vice President Stephens's Plan to Break the Blockade," *Newbern* (N.C.) *Weekly Progress*, Dec. 20, 1862.
189 **"I fear the Treasury Department is overstating"**: James D. Bulloch to Stephen R. Mallory, June 30, *Official Naval Records*, 447.
189 **only about 40 percent**: Stephen R. Mallory to James D. Bulloch, July 20, 1863, *Official Naval Records*, 467. This may have overstated the Confederacy's take. Weidenmier ("The Market for Confederate Cotton Bonds," 79) says Richmond repurchased more than 45 percent of its bonds; if their average price was 90, they would have expended at least $6 million, leaving $5 million at most. Schwab (*The Confederate States of America*, 35) also says Richmond spent $6 million (in gold) on repurchases.
189 **still desperate for funds**: *Official Naval Records*, 493, 499, 568; see also Leigh, "The Cotton Bond Bubble."
190 **"a grievous disappointment"**: Mallory to Bulloch, *Official Naval Records*, 467.
190 **The only party**: Schwab, *The Confederate States of America*, 35–36.
190 **in the spring they revived**: "The National Finances," *New York Times*, Mar. 28, 1863.
190 **ramped up his use**: Oberholtzer, *Jay Cooke: Financier*, 1:233.
190 **a "nursery maid"**: Oberholtzer, *Jay Cooke: Financier*, 242–44.
190 **"A Day at the Agency"**: See, e.g., *Portland* (Me.) *Daily Press*, Apr. 14, 1863. The *Inquirer* had published it on Apr. 9.
190 **solicit them on paydays**: David K. Thomson, "'Like a Cord Through the Whole Country': Union Bonds and Financial Mobilization for Victory," *The Journal of the Civil War Era* 6, no. 3 (2016): 367.
190 **"If I fight hard enough"**: Oberholtzer, *Jay Cooke: Financier*, 1:246.
190 **"extraordinary demand"**: "The National Finances," *New York Times*, Mar. 28, 1863.
190 **"almost every town and village"**: Oberholtzer, *Jay Cooke: Financier*, 1:238.
191 **"farmers who live in a little cabin"**: Thomson, "'Like a Cord Through the Whole Country,'" 361.
191 **Bonds sold briskly even in border areas**: Oberholtzer, *Jay Cooke: Financier*, 1:245, 250.
191 **President Lincoln purchased**: Thomson, "'Like a Cord Through the Whole Country,'" 358–39.
191 **Lincoln sorely wanted**: Gabor S. Boritt, *Lincoln and the Economics of the American Dream* (Memphis: Memphis State University Press, 1978), 203. See also Lincoln's comments in Annual Message to Congress, Dec. 6, 1864, in *CWL*, 8:136.
191 **were available in two forms**: Thomson, "'Like a Cord Through the Whole Country,'" 351.
191 **purchased by women**: "'Like a Cord Through the Whole Country,'" 358 (also the source for the average investment). It is likely that coupon bonds, being less secure, attracted smaller investments than registered bonds.
191 **lieutenants earned**: "Shotgun's Home of the American Civil War," https://civilwarhome.com/Pay.html.
191 **"utter folly"**: Oberholtzer, *Jay Cooke: Financier*, 1:246.
191–192 **"make gold the barometer"**: Oberholtzer, *Jay Cooke: Financier*, 1:247.
192 **more than $1 million per day**: "From Washington," *Chicago Daily Tribune*, May 2, 1863.
192 **sales often topped $2 million**: Oberholtzer, *Jay Cooke: Financier*, 1:255.
192 **five-twenty sales were paying**: Salmon Chase to William H. Aspinwall and John Murray Forbes, May 14, 1863, in *SPCP*, 4:30.
192 **"The people do not believe"**: "The News," *Chicago Daily Tribune*, May 2, 1863.
192 **Brown's letters were publicized**: Thomson, "'Like a Cord Through the Whole Country,'" 347; "Letter from Spencer Kellogg Brown, the Martyr," *Chicago Daily Tribune*, Oct. 15, 1863. Brown frequently omitted his surname (some sources refer to him as "Spencer Kellogg"). A navy official denied that he was a spy, and his execution, on Sept. 25, 1863, was widely reported.

192 **boosting confidence in the government:** Oberholtzer, *Jay Cooke: Financier,* 1:237–38.
192 **In a parallel to Erlanger:** Thomson, "'Like a Cord Through the Whole Country,'" 366–67.
192 **swelled to $175 million:** Treasury Secretary, *Annual Report,* 1863, p. 28.
192 **three-quarters were sold by Cooke:** Oberholtzer, *Jay Cooke: Financier,* 1:263–64.
192 **criticized Chase for having granted:** Oberholtzer, *Jay Cooke: Financier,* 1:256, 268.
192–193 **In May, he sent a check:** Salmon Chase to Jay Cooke, June 2, 1863, in *SPCP,* 4:52–53.
193 **more than the annual income:** A senator's salary was then $3000.
193 **"As I had not paid for the stock":** Chase to Cooke, June 2, 1863, 4:52–53.
193 **"quite astounded":** Jay Cooke to Salmon Chase, June 3, 1863, in Oberholtzer, *Jay Cooke: Financier,* 1:275.
193 **Chase unwisely asked Cooke:** Oberholtzer, *Jay Cooke: Financier.* The advance went to Mrs. M. L. Bailey, widow of Gamaliel Bailey, editor of the *National Era,* the original publisher, in serial form, of *Uncle Tom's Cabin.*
193 **debt had soared to $1.1 billion:** Treasury Secretary, *Annual Report,* 1863, p. 2 (as of June 30, 1863).
193 **more than able to service it:** See Treasury Secretary, *Annual Report,* 1863, pp. 3, 11 (revenue figure in the text is for fiscal 1863).
193 **"There is not at this date":** Chase to Aspinwall and Forbes, May 14, 1863, 4:30.
194 **Victor Smith, a Chase ally:** Salmon Chase to Abraham Lincoln, May 11, 1863, in *SPCP,* 4:26–27.
194 **"the degree of dissatisfaction":** Abraham Lincoln to Salmon Chase, May 8, 1863, in *CWL,* 6:202.
194 **"greatly pained me":** Chase to Lincoln, May 11, 1863, 4:26–27.
194 **confided to a Springfield chum:** Abraham Lincoln to Anson G. Henry, May 13, 1863, in *CWL,* 6:215.
194 **"Chase, here is a paper":** Maunsell B. Field, *Memories of Many Men and of Some Women* (New York: Harper and Brothers, 1874), 303.

Chapter Ten: Gettysburg Summer

195 **"We are the poor rabble":** *New York Times,* July 15, 1863.
195 **a genuine boom:** See Sean Patrick Adams, "Soulless Monsters and Iron Horses," in *Capitalism Takes Command: The Social Transformation of Nineteenth-Century America,* ed. Michael Zakim and Gary J. Kornblith (Chicago: University of Chicago Press, 2012), 257; Paul R. Auerbach and Michael J. Haupert, "Problems in Analyzing Inflation During the Civil War," *Essays in Economic and Business History* (2002): 65.
195 **the North produced twelve times:** Benjamin T. Arrington, "Industry and Economy During the Civil War," National Park Service, https://www.nps.gov/resources/story.htm%3Fid%3D251.
195–196 **tonnage over the Great Lakes:** Emerson D. Fite, "The Agricultural Development of the West During the Civil War," *Quarterly Journal of Economics* 20, no. 2 (1906): 261.
196 **New York City and the Midwest grew 75 percent:** Edward K. Spann, *Gotham at War: New York City, 1860–1965* (Wilmington, Del.: Scholarly Resources, 2002), 141; the figure is for the period 1860–1864.
196 **Railroad dividends and stock prices:** John F. Stover, *History of the Illinois Central Railroad* (New York: Macmillan, 1975), 102–4; Adams, "Soulless Monsters and Iron Horses," 268. See also Bruce Catton, *The Civil War* (1960; repr., Boston: Houghton Mifflin, 2004), 162.
196 **ninety trains entered Chicago:** Fite, "The Agricultural Development of the West," 262.
196 **Bruce Catton has stressed:** Catton, *The Civil War,* 158–59.
196 **Wheat and corn production:** Fite, "The Agricultural Development of the West," 259–60; "breadbasket states" refers to Illinois, Indiana, Iowa, and Wisconsin, where Fite detailed especially soaring production.
196 **repeated crop failures:** Fite, "The Agricultural Development of the West," 259–60.
196 **northern farms also turned to mechanization:** Fite ("The Agricultural Development of the West," 271) details increased production of farm machinery. Arrington ("Industry and Economy During the Civil War") notes that a single thresher in five minutes matched the output of six men working an hour.
196 **worked longer hours and conscripted children:** Eugene M Lerner, "Money, Prices, and Wages in the Confederacy, 1861–65," *Journal of Political Economy* 63, no. 1 (1955): 31.
196 **In 1863, 176,000 newcomers:** Reuben A. Kessel and Armen A. Alchian, "Real Wages in the North During the Civil War," *The Journal of Law and Economics* 2 (Oct. 1959): 111; most wartime immigrants hailed from England, Ireland, or Germany.
196 **The pace quickened:** Total immigration over the war years (1861–1865) was just over 800,000.

196 **Illinois added:** Fite, "The Agricultural Development of the West," 272–73.

196 **pioneers trekked across the Great Plains:** "The Agricultural Development of the West," 275–76.

196 **annual clip of 23 percent:** Auerbach and Haupert, "Problems in Analyzing Inflation," 65; see also Ethel D. Hoover, "Retail Prices After 1850," in "Conference on Research in Income and Wealth," *Trends in the American Economy in the Nineteenth Century* (New York: National Bureau of Economic Research, 1960), 142. The inflation figure represents the rise in consumer prices for calendar 1863.

196 **wages had fallen 15 percent:** Kessel and Alchian, "Real Wages in the North During the Civil War," 97, citing Wesley C. Mitchell, *Gold, Prices, and Wages Under the Greenback Standard* (Berkeley, Calif.: University Press, 1908). For contemporary testimony of negative real wage growth, see Congressional Globe, 37th Cong., 3rd Sess., 841, and "The Currency: Gold and United States Notes," *New York Times*, Dec. 12, 1862, which observed, "Persons who rely upon salaries or fixed incomes, find the existing state of things especially burdensome."

197 **Workers began to organize:** Spann, *Gotham at War*, 150.

197 **"The Yankees did not whip us":** David K. Thomson, "'Like a Cord Through the Whole Country': Union Bonds and Financial Mobilization for Victory," *The Journal of the Civil War Era* 6, no. 3 (2016): 147.

197 **"Rumors are rife":** Salmon Chase to James A. Garfield, May 14, 1863, in J. W. Schuckers, *The Life and Public Services of Salmon Portland Chase* (New York: D. Appleton, 1874), 467.

197 **"Nothing definite yet as to Lee's programme":** *Strong*, 3:324.

197 **"Stocks must *rise* and gold *fall*":** Edmund Clarence Stedman to Samuel Hallett, Apr. 28, 1863, Edmund Clarence Stedman Papers, box 48.

198 **"Great interest, as you seem":** Samuel Hallett to Edmund Clarence Stedman, Apr. 30, 1863, Stedman Papers, box 48.

198 **"Extra *Herald* with statement":** Samuel Hallett to Edmund Clarence Stedman, May 6, 1863, Stedman Papers, box 48.

198 **Lee's entire force:** *Strong*, 3:326.

198 **"Matters are becoming more serious":** Salmon Chase to Kate Chase, June 25, 1863, in *SPCP*, 4:69–70.

198 **alarmed by the nearness:** Salmon Chase to Kate Chase, June 29, 1863, in *SPCP*, 4:72.

198 **outlined at a war council in Richmond:** Walter A. McDougall, *Throes of Democracy: The American Civil War Era, 1829–1877* (New York: HarperCollins, 2018), 468; James M. McPherson, *Battle Cry of Freedom: The Civil War Era* (New York: Oxford University Press, 1988), 647.

198 **attention of the European powers:** McPherson, *Battle Cry of Freedom*, 651, notes that Rebel diplomats had renewed their efforts to persuade Britain and France to intervene.

198 **"the evils of war":** McDougall, *Throes of Democracy*, 469.

198 **"marauding party":** Ralph Korngold, *Thaddeus Stevens: A Being Darkly Wise and Rudely Great* (New York: Harcourt, Brace, 1955), 211.

198 **"That is not the way":** Korngold, *Thaddeus Stevens: A Being Darkly Wise and Rudely Great*, 212; see also Richard Nelson Current, *Old Thad Stevens: A Story of Ambition* (Madison: University of Wisconsin Press, 1942), 177–83; Hans L. Trefousse, *Thaddeus Stevens: Nineteenth-Century Egalitarian* (Chapel Hill: University of North Carolina Press, 1997), 134–35.

199 **"I think *Lee's* Army, and not *Richmond*":** Abraham Lincoln to Major General Joseph Hooker, June 10, 1863, in *CWL*, 6:258.

199 **But Hooker worried:** McPherson, *Battle Cry of Freedom*, 652.

199 **"one of the great decisive battles":** *Strong*, 3:328.

199 **The gold premium narrowed:** J. W. Schuckers, *The Life and Public Services of Salmon Portland Chase* (New York: D. Appleton, 1874), 356–57, 362; *Strong*, 3:330.

199 **"People downtown very jolly today":** *Strong*, 3:330.

200 **the Erlanger cotton bonds plunged:** Marc D. Weidenmier, "The Market for Confederate Cotton Bonds," *Explorations in Economic History* 37 (2000): 80.

200 **"battles by the score":** *Strong*, 3:330.

200 **Lincoln extremely upset:** John Hay, *Inside Lincoln's White House: The Complete Civil War Diary of John Hay*, ed. Michael Burlingame and John R. Turner Ettlinger (Carbondale: Southern Illinois University Press, 1997), 66.

200 **many enlisted soldiers' terms were expiring:** "The Free Negroes and the War," *New York Herald*, May 28, 1863; Schuckers, *The Life and Public Services*, 467.

200 **three hundred thousand call-ups:** "Important from Washington: Enforcement of the Conscription Law; An Order Issued Calling Out Three Hundred Thousand Conscripts," *New York Herald*, July 9, 1863.

200 **Various communities raised funds:** McPherson, *Battle Cry of Freedom*, 604.

200 **"The government may do":** Alexis de Tocqueville, *Democracy in America* (1835; repr., New York: Bantam Classics, 2000), 809 (emphasis added).

200 **Although three quarters:** McPherson, *Battle Cry of Freedom*, 601; James M. McPherson, *Ordeal by Fire: The Civil War and Reconstruction* (New York: McGraw-Hill, 2001), 182–3.

201 **Recruitment had always been a *state* responsibility:** McPherson, *Battle Cry of Freedom*, 600–601.

201 **"In a Republic neither riches":** *New York Herald*, May 27, 1863; the officer was Major General D. E. Sickles. See also "Mr. Wood's Reply to Senator Williams," *New York Herald*, Apr. 3, 1863.

201 **paired with the baseless charge:** McPherson, *Battle Cry of Freedom*, 609.

201 **"All this folly":** *New York Herald*, Apr. 25, 1863.

201 **"The blood of white men":** *New York Herald*, May 28, 1863.

201 **frequently pointed out the inconsistency:** Albon P. Man Jr., "Labor Competition and the New York Draft Riots of 1863," *The Journal of Negro History* 36, no. 4 (1951): 382.

202 **the city's twelve thousand Blacks:** Man, "Labor Competition and the New York Draft Riots of 1863," 375.

202 **"Every hour sees the black man":** Man, "Labor Competition and the New York Draft Riots of 1863," 376.

202 **mass meeting against "abolitionism":** *New York Herald*, Nov. 9, 1862.

202 **"May not these poor people":** Man, "Labor Competition and the New York Draft Riots of 1863," 380.

202 **appears to have been negligible:** Man, "Labor Competition and the New York Draft Riots of 1863," 385.

202 **not, as was alleged:** Man, "Labor Competition and the New York Draft Riots of 1863," 391.

202 **The longshoremen's trade:** Man, "Labor Competition and the New York Draft Riots of 1863," 392–94.

202 **patronage jobs in the custom house:** Man, "Labor Competition and the New York Draft Riots of 1863," 389.

202 **Irish workers in a tobacco factory:** "Serious Riot in Brooklyn: Attack on a Tobacco Factory in Sedgwick Street; Trouble Between the Negro Laborers and a Party of White Laborers," *New York Herald*, Aug. 5, 1862; "The Northern Allies of Southern Treason," *New York Daily Tribune*, Jan. 24, 1863; Man, "Labor Competition and the New York Draft Riots of 1863," 389–90.

203 **"Burn the damn niggers":** "Serious Riot in Brooklyn."

203 **several solitary Blacks:** "Trying to Kill a Man," *New York Daily Tribune*, Aug. 21, 1862; "General News," *New York Daily Tribune*, Aug. 22, 1862; Man, "Labor Competition and the New York Draft Riots of 1863," 390–91.

203 **complained about inflation:** Man, "Labor Competition and the New York Draft Riots of 1863," 395.

203 **the *Herald* editorialized against:** Man, "Labor Competition and the New York Draft Riots of 1863," 395.

203 **dockworkers at the Erie Railway:** Man, "Labor Competition and the New York Draft Riots of 1863," 396–97.

203 **"Kill the niggers!":** Man, "Labor Competition and the New York Draft Riots of 1863," 397–98.

203 **"the natural climax of the persistent effort":** "The Right to Work," *New York Daily Tribune*, Apr. 14, 1863.

203 **labor leaders called a massive work stoppage:** "The 'Longshoremen's' Strike," *New York Herald*, June 16, 1863. See also reports in the *Herald*, June 13 and June 20, 1863, and in the *New York Daily Tribune*, June 17, 1863, as well as Man, "Labor Competition and the New York Draft Riots of 1863," 398–99.

203 **"obsessed with a fear of competition":** Man, "Labor Competition and the New York Draft Riots of 1863," 405.

203 **murmurings that Democrats might try:** *New York Herald*, Apr. 22, 1863.

204 **publicly denounced Lincoln:** "Speech of Hon. Horatio Seymour," *New York Herald*, July 6, 1863; "The Great Historical Crisis and the Small Politicians," *New York Herald*, July 7, 1863.

204 **"They will lie and steal":** "The Niggerheads and Copperheads in New York," *New York Herald*, July 11, 1863.

204 **running short of fresh recruits:** McPherson, *Battle Cry of Freedom*, 600.

204 NO DRAFT **placards:** Mitchell Snay, *Horace Greeley and the Politics of Reform in Nineteenth Century America* (Lanham, Md.: Rowman & Littlefield, 2011), 146.

204 **Longshoremen canvassed the piers:** Man, "Labor Competition and the New York Draft Riots of 1863," 400–401.

204 **"clubs, stones, brickbats and other missiles":** "The Mob in New York," *New York Times*, July 14, 1863; see also *Strong*, 3:234.

204 **some were pulled off streetcars:** Snay, *Horace Greeley and the Politics of Reform*, 147.

204 **"The mob was in no hurry":** *Strong*, 3:336.

204 **The mob proceeded to the armory:** "The Mob in New York."

204 **Mayor George Opdyke:** *New York Herald*, July 14, 1863.

204 **His home was attacked:** "Miscellaneous Movements," *New York Times*, July 15, 1863; "The Riot Subsiding: A Last Desperate Struggle," *New York Times*, July 17, 1863.

204 **"day of infamy and disgrace":** "The Mob in New York."

204 **the mob set fire . . . went after Greeley:** *Strong*, 3:324; Snay. *Horace Greeley and the Politics of Reform*, 147–48; "The Mob in New York."

204 **the work of loading:** Man, "Labor Competition and the New York Draft Riots of 1863," 401.

204 **Blacks had disappeared from the docks:** "The Riot Subsiding."

204 **posting a sign:** Man, "Labor Competition and the New York Draft Riots of 1863," 401.

205 **some erected barricades:** *Strong*, 3:341; "Miscellaneous Movements."

205 **the attacks were orchestrated by dockworkers:** "The Riot: The Mob Fully Organized," *New York Daily Tribune*, July 16, 1863. See also the report in the *Tribune*, July 21, 1863; "Lessons of the Riot," *New York Times*, July 18, 1863 ("All the evidence goes to show that the plot to resist the draft in New York City had been fully organized previously"); "The Riot Subsiding."

205 **"of fine personal appearance":** "The Riot Subsiding."

205 **railroads and carriages were made to halt:** "Miscellaneous Movements."

205 **"By the authority of the mob":** "The Riot: The Mob Fully Organized."

205 **"The idea has been":** Hamilton Fish to Salmon Chase, July 18, 1863, in *SPCP*, 4:88–90.

205 **such as Brooks Brothers:** *New York Daily Tribune*, July 21, 1863.

205 **"We are the poor rabble":** "A Letter from One of the Rioters," *New York Times*, July 15, 1863.

206 **On Wednesday night:** For the attacks on various African-Americans that day, see "The Riot Subsiding" and "Facts and Incidents of the Riot: The Murder of Colored People in Thompson and Sullivan Streets," *New York Times*, July 16, 1863.

206 **"One could not help wondering":** "The Riot Subsiding."

206 **hung from lampposts:** "Third Day of Mob Rule: More Murder and Destruction; Negro Killed and Hung Up," *New York Sun*, July 16, 1863. See also "The Riot Subsiding"; "The Riot: The Mob Fully Organized."

206 **swelled into the hundreds:** "The Riot in Second Avenue," *New York Times*, July 15, 1863.

206 **Yates hanged himself:** "Inquests upon the Dead: A Colored Man Is Driven to Despair and Suicide," *New York Times*, July 18, 1863.

206 **"I entertain no malice":** "The Riot Subsiding."

206 **Governor Seymour denounced:** "Doings of Gov. Seymour," *New York Times*, July 15, 1863.

207 **"are as orderly and law abiding":** "Board of Aldermen," *New York Times*, July 14, 1863.

207 **Authorities fired:** "Third Day of Mob Rule: More Murder and Destruction; Negro Killed and Hung Up."

207 **more than a hundred rioters dead:** Snay, *Horace Greeley and the Politics of Reform*, 148; McPherson, *Battle Cry of Freedom*, 610.

207 **the President suspended the writ:** "Proclamation Suspending Writ of Habeas Corpus," Sept. 15, 1863, in *CWL*, 6:451.

207 **"mobocratic spirit":** "Address Before the Young Men's Lyceum of Springfield, Ill.," Jan. 27, 1838, *CWL*, 1:115.

207 **"who in no single instance":** Gabor S. Boritt, *Lincoln and the Economics of the American Dream* (Memphis: Memphis State University Press, 1978), 174.

208 **"The most notable feature":** "From Washington," *New York Times*, Mar. 22, 1864.

208 **"I know that in almost every case":** Boritt, *Lincoln and the Economics of the American Dream*, 185.

208 **"That some should be rich":** "From Washington."

208 **"Much complaint is made":** "Opinion on the Draft," in *CWL*, 6:447–48.

209 **funds to exempt draftees:** McPherson, *Battle Cry of Freedom*, 611.

209 **"to pursue unmolested their lawful occupations":** Man, "Labor Competition and the New York Draft Riots of 1863," 403.

209 **He fired a clerk:** "Copperheads in the Basket," *Chicago Daily Tribune*, June 24, 1863.

209 **agitated for equal treatment:** *SPCP*, 4:90–91, 129.

209 **"American blacks must be called":** Schuckers, *The Life and Public Services*, 387–88.

209 **"Why cannot colored people":** Salmon Chase to Jay Cooke, Sept. 1, 1863, in *SPCP*, 4:129.

210 **seeking a more systematic remedy:** Albert Bushnell Hart, *Salmon P. Chase* (Boston: Houghton Mifflin, 1899), 271.

210 **"just and normal relations":** Willie Lee Rose, *Rehearsal for Reconstruction: The Port Royal Experiment* (New York: Oxford University Press, 1976), 208.

210 **the war secretary established:** Richard H. Abbott, *Cotton and Capital: Boston Businessmen and Antislavery Reform, 1854–1868* (Amherst: University of Massachusetts Press, 1991), 160.

210 **"treat poor blacks as we would poor whites":** Abbott, *Cotton and Capital*, 159–60.

210 **Thanks largely to Senator Sumner:** Kate Masur, *An Example for All the Land: Emancipation and the Struggle over Equality in Washington, D.C.* (Chapel Hill: University of North Carolina Press, 2010), 107.

210 **Its preliminary report emphasized:** Rose, *Rehearsal for Reconstruction*, 239.

211 **wide swath of abandoned property:** Records of Civil War Special Agencies of the Treasury Department, (Record Group 366), 1861–1868, National Archives, https://www.archives.gov/research /guide-fed-records/groups/366.html. This expansive territory, including Union-occupied areas of South Carolina, Georgia, and Florida, was established May 1863 and in June designated "Fourth Special Agency" of the U.S. Treasury Department. Subsequently, it was redesignated Fifth Special Agency. See also John Niven, *Salmon P. Chase: A Biography* (New York: Oxford University Press, 1995), 327.

211 **Chase sent his friend Edward Pierce:** Salmon Chase to Galusha Grow, Feb. 18, 1863, in *SPCP*, 3:385–87.

211 **Congress had authorized:** *SPCP*, 4:237; Abbott, *Cotton and Capital*, 140.

211 **converging on Port Royal:** Niven, *Salmon P. Chase: A Biography*, 327.

211 **biblical appellation Gideonites:** See, e.g., "News from Fortress Monroe," *New York Herald*, Aug. 26, 1862; "The Port Royal Negroes," *Daily Ohio Statesman* (Columbus), Jan. 18, 1863; "Notes from a Plantation," *The Free South* (Beaufort, S.C.), Apr. 18, 1863.

211 **"sharp sighted speculators":** Mansfield French to Salmon Chase, Jan. 2, 1863, in *SPCP*, 3:351–52.

211 **newly freed slaves had to prove:** Rose, *Rehearsal for Reconstruction*, 223.

211 **"We find the blacks":** Akiko Ochiai, "The Port Royal Experiment Revisited: Northern Visions of Reconstruction and the Land Question," *The New England Quarterly* 74, no. 1 (2001): 106.

211 **Governor Andrew urged Chase:** John A. Andrew to Salmon Chase, Jan. 3, 1863, in *SPCP*, 3:355–56.

211 **the government went ahead:** Details about the land auction come from *SPCP*, 3:357, and Abbott, *Cotton and Capital*, 141.

211 **As Andrew feared:** Abbott, *Cotton and Capital*, 145.

211 **Philbrick maintained that his venture:** Abbott, *Cotton and Capital*, 142.

212 **donated much of his early profits:** Abbott, *Cotton and Capital*, 141.

212 **purchasing trunks and padlocks:** Abbott, *Cotton and Capital*, 142.

212 **"entirely satisfied" . . . "The negroes will work for a living":** Edward Pierce to Salmon Chase, Apr. 2, 1863, in *SPCP*, 4:3–5.

212 **Black children were enrolled in schools:** Rose, *Rehearsal for Reconstruction*, 229.

212 **"The way to secure the colored people":** William Curtis Noyes to Salmon Chase, Apr. 20, 1863, in *SPCP*, 4:13.

212 **"Many have laid up, little sums":** Mansfield French to Salmon Chase, Aug. 22, 1863, in *SPCP*, 4:113.

212 **Lincoln, on advice from Chase:** "Instructions to Tax Commissioners in South Carolina," Sept. 16, 1863, in *CWL*, 6:453–59. See also Ochiai, "Port Royal Experiment Revisited," 100; Abbott, *Cotton and Capital*, 145.

213 **which had swelled to fifteen thousand:** Ochiai, "Port Royal Experiment Revisited," 100.

213 **Merchants along the Mississippi:** Salmon Chase to George S. Denison, Aug. 26, 1863, in *SPCP*, 4:116.

213 **the British were putting strong pressure:** Sven Beckert, *Empire of Cotton: A Global History* (New York: Alfred A. Knopf, 2014), 261–62.

213 **"as moderate as possible":** Chase to Denison, Aug. 26, 1863, 4:116.

213 **"Clear boats and cargoes":** Salmon Chase, telegraph to customs surveyors, July 23, 1863, in *SPCP*, 4:132.

213 **"No matter what the restrictions":** Ulysses S. Grant to Salmon Chase, July 21, 1863, in Ulysses S. Grant, *The Papers of Ulysses S. Grant*, ed. John Y. Simon et al., 32 vols. (Carbondale: Southern Illinois University Press, 1967–2012), 9:94.

213 **Bates protested in cabinet:** Salmon P. Chase, *Inside Lincoln's Cabinet: The Civil War Diaries of Salmon P. Chase*, ed. David Herbert Donald (New York: Longman's Green, 1954), 187.

213 **St. Louis, where the merchant lobby:** Chase, *Inside Lincoln's Cabinet*, 184.

213 **His new scheme:** Records of Civil War Special Agencies (Record Group 366); Schuckers, *The Life and Public Services*, 326–27.

214 **"You understand these things":** Chase, *Inside Lincoln's Cabinet*, 192.

214 **the record of twenty-seven officers:** *CWL*, 6:397.

214 **"I have received, and read":** Abraham Lincoln to William Kellogg, June 29, 1863, in *CWL*, 6:307.

214 **Lincoln did grant exceptions:** See, for example, *CWL*, 7:63–64. Lincoln granted permission to his wife's half sister, Emilie T. Helm, to transport cotton from Jackson, Mississippi, as well as from Georgia.

214 **According to Confederate naval records:** *Official Naval Records*, 511.

214 **the capture rate had climbed:** McDougall, *Throes of Democracy*, 446.

214 **"I do not think it prudent":** Frank E. Vandiver, ed., *Confederate Blockade Running Through Bermuda 1861–1865* (Austin: University of Texas Press, 1947), 29.

215 **"I regret to state that the Yankees":** Vandiver, *Confederate Blockade Running Through Bermuda*, 52.

215 **more than a thousand captures:** Annual Message to Congress, Dec. 8, 1863, in *CWL*, 7:43; this includes all captures since the imposition of the blockade.

215 **machinery and spare parts:** "Jeff. Davis' Last Appeal for Supplies," *New York Herald*, Apr. 17, 1863.

215 **"It is useless to disguise":** "Intercepted Rebel Correspondence," *New York Times*, Nov. 16, 1863; the letter was seized on one of three ships—*R.E. Lee, Cornubia*, and *Ella and Anna*—that were captured off the coast of Wilmington, North Carolina, in early November.

215 **The unwanted publicity cost De Leon:** Edwin De Leon, *Secret History of Confederate Diplomacy Abroad*, ed. William C. Davis (Lawrence: University Press of Kansas, 2005), xxiii.

215 **Rhett Butler effect:** Mark Thornton and Robert B. Ekelund Jr., *Tariffs, Blockades, and Inflation: The Economics of the Civil War* (Wilmington, Del.: Scholarly Resources, 2004), xxiii.

215 **Quinine, morphine, expensive fabrics:** Thornton and Ekelund, *Tariffs, Blockades, and Inflation*, 38.

215 **twenty-eight times:** Thornton and Ekelund, *Tariffs, Blockades, and Inflation*, 53.

215 **the most of any sea captain:** Thomas E. Taylor, *Running the Blockade: A Personal Narrative of Adventures, Risks, and Escapes During the American Civil War* (London: John Murray, 1896), vii.

215 **"it did not pay merchants":** Taylor, *Running the Blockade*, 18.

215 **Jefferson Davis was furious:** Thornton and Ekelund, *Tariffs, Blockades, and Inflation*, 38.

215 **The government engaged a British partner:** "Intercepted Rebel Correspondence."

215 **a pair of boots:** *RWCD*, 2:48.

216 **"I have lost 20 pounds":** *RWCD*, 2:viii.

216 **"We are a shabby-looking people":** *RWCD*, 2:89.

Chapter Eleven: Chase for President

217 **"Under the sharp discipline":** Annual Message to Congress, Dec. 8, 1863, in *CWL*, 7:40.

218 **Chase had been dropping hints:** Salmon P. Chase, *Inside Lincoln's Cabinet: The Civil War Diaries of Salmon P. Chase*, ed. David Herbert Donald (New York: Longman's Green, 1954), 176.

218 **greeted by hundreds of supporters:** John Niven, *Salmon P. Chase: A Biography* (New York: Oxford University Press, 1995), 336.

218 **"old Greenbacks!":** "'Going Home to Vote': Authentic Speeches of S. P. Chase, Secretary of the Treasury, During His Visit to Ohio," 1863, 4, Chase Papers (LOC), file "Speeches and Writings, 1849–1868."

218 **"It would have been even more right":** "'Going Home to Vote,'" 13.

218 **"the engravers thought me":** "'Going Home to Vote,'" 25.

218 **a fog of self-delusion:** Chase told the Ohio lawyer and journalist Edward D. Mansfield, "The masses seemed to move of themselves"—see his letter of Oct. 18, 1863, in *SPCP*, 4:154.

218 **Radicals such as Horace Greeley:** Horace Greeley to Salmon Chase, Sept. 29, 1863, in *SPCP*, 4:134; Chase, *Inside Lincoln's Cabinet*, 208; Richard Nelson Current, *Old Thad Stevens: A Story of Ambition* (Madison: University of Wisconsin Press, 1942), 186; Henry Ward Beecher to Salmon Chase, Dec. 28, 1863, in *SPCP*, 4:231; "Strife Among Brethren," *New York Times*, Jan. 30, 1864.

218 **all but promised Chase:** Chase, *Inside Lincoln's Cabinet*, 179; the politician was John Covode, previously and also later a congressman.

218 **Jay Cooke & Co. contributed money:** Salmon Chase to Abraham Lincoln, Jan. 13, 1864, in *SPCP*, 4:250–51; Ellis Paxson Oberholtzer, *Jay Cooke: Financier of the Civil War* (Philadelphia: G.W. Jacobs, 1907), 1:363, 388.

218 **Chase and Cooke were still squabbling:** Jay Cooke to Salmon Chase, Nov. 17, 1863, in *SPCP*, 4:187–91.

219 **Cooke added gloss:** Oberholtzer, *Jay Cooke: Financier*, 1:363, 390.

219 **billion-dollar budget:** See Chase's forecast in Treasury Secretary, *Annual Report*, 1864, p. 6.

219 **"a sort of genius":** "Curious Political Developments," *New York Herald*, Sept. 8, 1863.

219 **"has conducted the finances":** "From the Rebel States," *New York Times*, Nov. 11, 1863, quoting *Richmond Examiner*. For other unctuous flattery of Chase, see "From Washington: to the Credit of Secretary Chase," *Chicago Daily Tribune*, July 23, 1863, and "The Approaching Revolution in Our Banking System," *New York Herald*, Sept. 7, 1863.

219 **"only be remedied by the President":** Salmon Chase to Murat Halstead, Sept. 21, 1863, in *SPCP*, 4:142.

219 **the only job he coveted:** Chase, *Inside Lincoln's Cabinet*, 180.

219 **"I really feel as if":** Chase, *Inside Lincoln's Cabinet*, 25.

219 **"advances slowly but yet advances":** Salmon Chase to Horace Greeley, Oct. 9, 1863, in *SPCP*, 4:150–51.

219 **"I can never permit myself":** Salmon Chase to William Sprague, Nov. 26, 1863, in *SPCP*, 4:204–5.

220 **Other seeming supporters:** Greeley to Chase, Sept. 29, 1863, 4:134.

220 **waging a proxy war:** Salmon Chase to N. S. Townshend, Aug. 18, 1863, in Greeley to Chase, Sept. 29, 1863, 4:148*n*; Benjamin Franklin Flanders to Salmon Chase, Jan. 9, 1864, in Greeley to Chase, Sept. 29, 1863, 4:249*n*; James M. McPherson, *Battle Cry of Freedom: The Civil War Era* (New York: Oxford University Press, 1988), 703–5.

220 **a needless political struggle:** See, e.g., Chase to Lincoln, Jan. 13, 1864, 4:250–51; Niven, *Chase: A Biography*, 344–45, 360; Albert Bushnell Hart, *Salmon P. Chase* (Boston: Houghton Mifflin, 1899), 311.

220 **he was similarly overlooking reports:** Niven, *Chase: A Biography*, 354.

220 **"Mother, you are too suspicious!":** Don E. Fehrenbacher and Virginia Fehrenbacher, eds., *Recollected Words of Abraham Lincoln* (Stanford, Calif.: Stanford University Press, 1996), 274. This remark was recalled retrospectively; its accuracy is unknown.

221 **"I suppose he will":** John Hay, *Inside Lincoln's White House: The Complete Civil War Diary of John Hay*, ed. Michael Burlingame and John R. Turner Ettlinger (Carbondale: Southern Illinois University Press, 1997), 103.

221 **"chin-fly":** Fehrenbacher and Fehrenbacher, *Recollected Words of Abraham Lincoln*, 375–76.

221 **the President was truly annoyed:** Niven, *Chase: A Biography*, 340.

221 **When Grant disdained any interest:** Ulysses Grant to Barnabas Burns, Dec. 17, 1863, in Ulysses S. Grant, *The Papers of Ulysses S. Grant*, ed. John Y. Simon et al., 32 vols. (Carbondale: Southern Illinois University Press, 1967–2012), 9:541–44.

221 **"You don't know how deep":** Ron Chernow, *Grant* (New York: Penguin Press, 2017), 329 (emphasis added).

221 **"mingled not a little sadness":** Salmon Chase to William Sprague, Oct. 3, 1863, in *SPCP*, 4:164.

221 **white velvet dress:** "The Nuptials of Miss Kate Chase and ex-Gov. Sprague," *New York Times*, Nov. 15, 1863.

221 **fabulous sum of $50,000:** Niven, *Chase: A Biography*, 340.

221 **Lake Erie grapes:** Oberholtzer, *Jay Cooke: Financier*, 1:301.

222 **Sprague was a large campaign donor:** Oberholtzer, *Jay Cooke: Financier*, 364. Oberholtzer estimates that Sprague contributed $40,000, double the amount spent by Jay Cooke & Co.

222 **he was trailed by whispers:** Willie Lee Rose, *Rehearsal for Reconstruction: The Port Royal Experiment* (New York: Oxford University Press, 1976), 143.

222 **a blockade-running scheme:** See 41st Cong, 3rd Sess., Senate Ex. Doc. no. 10, pt. 3: Letter of the Secretary of War [William W. Belknap]. See also Rose, *Rehearsal for Reconstruction*, 143; Frederick J. Blue, *Salmon P. Chase: A Life in Politics* (Kent, Ohio: Kent State University Press, 1987), 169; Melinda Musil, "Money out of Misery," https://www.historynet.com/money-out-of-misery.htm; Phil Leigh, "Trading with the Enemy," address to Sarasota Civil War Roundtable, Dec. 2, 2014, https://civilwarchat.wordpress.com/2014/12/09/trading-with-the-enemy.

222 **Mary urged Lincoln:** Hay, *Inside Lincoln's White House*, 111.

222 **dispatched a personal note:** Abraham Lincoln to Salmon Chase, Nov. 16, 1863, in *CWL*, 7:15.

222 **"I should like to go":** Salmon Chase to Kate Chase Sprague, Nov. 17, 1863, in *SPCP*, 4:191–92.

222 **"and the spot on which they stood":** "From Gettysburg, Pa: The Consecration of the Battle Cemetery," *Chicago Daily Tribune*, Nov. 21, 1863.

222 **deliberately, and with emphasis:** "The Gettysburgh [*sic*] Celebration," *New York Times*, Nov. 21, 1863.

222 **Newspaper coverage focused:** The *Times* said the crowd "seem to have considered, with President LINCOLN, that it was not what was said here, but what was done here, that deserved their attention." The *Chicago Daily Tribune*, in its first dispatch ("From Gettysburg," Nov. 20, 1863), gave equal weight to the oration of the first speaker, Edward Everett, the choir dirge, and the remarks by Lincoln. Everett spoke for more than two hours. The following day, the *Tribune* reprinted the dirge lyrics as well as Lincoln's address.

223 **"to protect each *State* from invasion":** "Jeff. Davis' Message," *New York Times*, Dec. 12, 1863 (emphasis added).

223 **issuing an order fixing the western boundary:** "Order Concerning Union Pacific Railroad," Nov. 17, 1863, in *CWL*, 7:16; "Order Designating Starting Point of Union Pacific Railroad," Mar. 7, 1864, in *CWL*, 7:228.

223 **Sarah Josepha Hale:** *CWL*, 6:497n.

224 **"Needful diversions of wealth":** "Proclamation of Thanksgiving," Oct. 3, 1863, in *CWL*, 6:496–97.

224 **"beginning a new life":** Annual Message to Congress, Dec. 8, 1863, 7:36–53.

225 **"thronging our foreign consulates":** Annual Message to Congress, Dec. 8, 1863, 7:40.

225 **"source of national wealth and strength":** Annual Message to Congress, Dec. 8, 1863, 7:40.

225 **"It frees the slaves and ignores the negro":** Marc Egnal, *Clash of Extremes: The Economic Origins of the Civil War* (New York: Farrar, Straus, and Giroux, 2009), 328.

225 **"restoration of all rights":** "Proclamation of Amnesty and Reconstruction," Dec. 8, 1863, in *CWL*, 7:54.

225 **"Your party is wrong":** Sidney Blumenthal, *The Political Life of Abraham Lincoln*, vol. 2, *Wrestling with His Angel, 1849–1856* (New York: Simon & Schuster, 2017), 390.

226 **"the foundation of their institutions":** Jordan Lewis Reed, "American Jacobins: Revolutionary Radicalism in the Civil War Era" (PhD diss., University of Massachusetts Amherst, 2009), 199.

226 **the Treasury secretary's quiet encouragement:** Salmon Chase to Thomas J. Durant, Feb. 6, 1864, in *SPCP*, 4:303n; Salmon Chase to Cyrus W. Field, Apr. 6, 1864, in *SPCP*, 4:364. See also Hay, *Inside Lincoln's White House*, 183; McPherson, *Battle Cry of Freedom*, 705.

226 **the President confidentially told Hay:** Fawn M. Brodie, *Thaddeus Stevens: Scourge of the South* (New York: W. W. Norton, 1959), 198.

226 **"whether some of the colored people":** Abraham Lincoln to Michael Hahn, Mar. 13, 1864, in *CWL*, 7:243.

227 **"at work night and day":** Hay, *Inside Lincoln's White House*, 120.

227 **Thomas C. Durant:** Biographical details are from Charles Edgar Ames, *Pioneering the Union Pacific: A Reappraisal of the Builders of the Railroad* (New York: Appleton Century Crofts, 1969), 18–20.

227 **Durant telegraphed Lincoln:** Thomas C. Durant to Lincoln, Oct. 16, 1863, in *CWL*, 6:518n.

227 **Lincoln, impatient for the work to start:** Abraham Lincoln to Thomas C. Durant, Oct. 18, 1863, in *CWL*, 6:525.

227 **charged in a bond forgery:** "The Indiana State Frauds Again," *New York Herald*, June 26, 1862; "The Indiana Frauds: Who are the Greatest Rogues," *Indiana State Sentinel* (Indianapolis), June 30, 1862; "Our New York Correspondence: The Stover Fraud," *Daily State Sentinel* (Indianapolis), July 10, 1862; "General News," *New York Times*, Oct. 7, 1862; *Daily Evansville* (Ind.) *Journal*, Jan. 13, 1862.

227 **reneged on the company's obligations:** Ross, Steel & Co., letter to the editor, *New York Times*, July 16, 1863; "The Union Pacific Railway Embroglio," *Smoky Hill and Republican Union* (Junction City, Kans.), Nov. 14, 1863; David G. Taylor, "Thomas Ewing, Jr., and the Origins of the Kansas Pacific Railway Company," *Kansas Historical Quarterly* 42, no. 2 (1976): 155–79, Kansas Collection, http://www.kancoll.org/khq/1976/76_2_taylor.htm.

227 **without the services of a competent engineer:** Niven, *Chase: A Biography*, 359.

228 **Hallett's only concern:** Hallett went to great lengths to publicize, in self-serving terms, the completion of track. See "Pacific Railroad," *New York Times*, Nov. 19, 1863; "From Kansas: Union Pacific Railway: First Section of Forty Miles Graded," *New York Daily Tribune*, Dec. 3, 1863. The gullible *Tribune* lauded the construction as "an achievement quite unparalleled in the history of railroading."

228 **a friend of Chase's personal secretary:** Niven, *Chase: A Biography*, 359.

228 **Hallett tasked Stedman:** See Samuel Hallett to Edmund Clarence Stedman, Nov. 24, 1863, Edmund Clarence Stedman Papers, box 48; two more Hallett missives to Stedman, both on Dec. 10, 1863, Edmund Clarence Stedman Papers, box 48; Samuel C. Pomeroy to "Whom it May Concern," Jan. 19, 1864, Edmund Clarence Stedman Papers, box 48; Niven, *Chase: A Biography*, 359.

228 **"proceed immediately to Washington":** Hallett to Stedman, Dec. 10, 1863.

228 **"Received my commission from Hallett":** Laura Stedman and George M. Gould, *Life and Letters of Edmund Clarence Stedman* (New York: Moffat, Yard, 1910), 1:327.

228 **"I stood very much in awe of him":** Stedman and Gould, *Life and Letters of Edmund Clarence Stedman*, 1:251.

228 **Included on the committee:** Blue, *Salmon P. Chase*, 222.

228 **his desire for more patronage:** John G. Nicolay and John Hay, *Abraham Lincoln: A History* (New York: Century, 1886–1890), 8:318.

228 **He certainly became aware:** Salmon Chase to Flamen Ball, Feb. 2, 1864, in *SPCP*, 4:274–75. See also Niven, *Chase: A Biography*, 360; Blue, *Salmon P. Chase*, 222.

228 **Pomeroy had a history:** Joseph W. Snell and Don W. Wilson, "The Birth of the Atchison, Topeka and Santa Fe, 1," *Kansas Historical Quarterly* 34, no. 2 (1968): 113–42; *United States Biographical Dictionary* (Chicago: S. Lewis, 1879), Kansas volume, 837–38; Blue, *Salmon P. Chase*, 222; *New York Herald*, Feb. 29, 1864, citing Pomeroy's "deep interest in the Kansas-Pacific Railroad": Territorial Kansas Online (with image of a notice calling a meeting of stockholders, signed by Pomeroy), https://territorialkansasonline.ku.edu/index.php?SCREEN=view_image&document_id =100152&file_name=h000482.

229 **Chase released the bonds:** Niven, *Chase: A Biography*, 360.

229 **Stedman was reassigned:** Stedman and Gould, *Life and Letters of Stedman*, 1:337; see also Niven, *Chase: A Biography*, 360.

229 **sent word of his activities:** Niven, *Chase: A Biography*, 360.

229 **"The history of the world":** Treasury Secretary, *Annual Report*, 1863, p. 14. Chase had copied from Jay Cooke, who had assured him, "There is nothing on record in history" to rival the five-twenty (Oberholtzer, *Jay Cooke: Financier*, 1:313).

229 **"Our reputation is therefore at stake":** Oberholtzer, *Jay Cooke: Financier*, 1:290–91.

229 **twenty-five hundred subagents:** David K. Thomson, "'Like a Cord Through the Whole Country': Union Bonds and Financial Mobilization for Victory," *The Journal of the Civil War Era* 6, no. 3 (2016) says that by the war's end, Cooke employed a slightly larger number—three thousand—agents (352).

229 **just shy of $515 million:** Thomson, "'Like a Cord Through the Whole Country,'" 357. Contemporaneously, Chase reported a slightly slower sales total, $511 million. His figures, and Cooke's fee, are from "The Five-Twenty Loan: Jay Cooke & Co. Letter from Secretary Chase," *New York Times*, Apr. 9, 1864, reprinting Chase's Apr. 1 letter to House Speaker Schuyler Colfax. The government's payments to Jay Cooke & Co. totaled $1.35 million, of which two-thirds was expended on Cooke's subagent network and on advertising, leaving the balance to the firm.

229 **rose to a premium:** Salmon Chase to Cyrus Field, Feb. 17, 1864, in *SPCP*, 4:293–94; "General News," *New York Times*, Feb. 13, 1864.

229 **"Pomeroy undisguised":** Justin Kaplan, *Mr. Clemens and Mark Twain* (New York: Simon & Schuster, 1966), 162.

229–230 **"The entire negotiation":** *SPCP*, 4:243*n*.

230 **Henry Cooke had traded:** Niven, *Chase: A Biography*, 353.

230 **the House voted to seek a full accounting:** "Proceedings of Congress," *Chicago Daily Tribune*, Jan. 6, 1864.

230 **"could not have been as successfully performed":** "The Five-Twenty Loan: Jay Cooke & Co. Letter from Secretary Chase."

230 **He forecasted that:** Treasury Secretary, *Annual Report*, 1863, pp. 6, 8.

230 **hovered around 50 percent:** J. W. Schuckers, *The Life and Public Services of Salmon Portland Chase* (New York: D. Appleton, 1874), 362.

230 **approximately $1.5 billion:** Chase to Field, Feb. 17, 1864, 4:293–94. Chase was referring to the total U.S. debt, as distinct from the portion he had issued—but they amounted to the same, or nearly, as the Buchanan-era debt was less than 5 percent of the total. By June 30, 1864 (when the government's books for the year closed), the debt had risen to $1.74 billion.

230 **Thus, he asked Congress:** Treasury Secretary, *Annual Report*, 1863, pp. 9–10.

230 **Chase warned Pitt Fessenden:** Schuckers, *The Life and Public Services*, 336.

230 **The Cookes had paid a large advance:** Chase to Lincoln, Jan. 13, 1864, 4:250–51; William Orton to Salmon Chase, Jan. 6, 1864, in *SPCP*, 4:246–47. See also Oberholtzer, *Jay Cooke: Financier*, 1:363.

230 **used the Cookes' subscription:** Orton to Chase, Jan. 6, 1864, 4:246–47.

230 **he explained to Lincoln:** Chase to Lincoln, Jan. 13, 1864, 4:250–51.

231 **"yellow-covered-literature":** Orton to Chase, Jan. 6, 1864, 4:246–47.

231 **"Not that any wrong was intended":** Chase to Lincoln, Jan. 13, 1864, 4:250–51.

231 **Once again with backing:** Oberholtzer, *Jay Cooke: Financier*, 1:364.

231 **Chase began writing laborious letters:** Salmon Chase to John T. Trowbridge, Jan 25, 1864, in *SPCP*, 4:263–66.

231 **detectives arrested Albert M. Palmer:** "The Bonds for Blockade-Runners: Further Developments at the Custom-House; Arrest of Albert M. Palmer, Private Secretary to the Collector," *New York Times*, Jan. 8, 1864; *SPCP*, 4:257n.

231 **Lincoln asked Chase whether:** Abraham Lincoln to Salmon Chase, Jan. 11, 1864, in *CWL*, 7:120.

231 **confidence in Barney was "undiminished":** Salmon Chase to Abraham Lincoln, Jan. 12, 1864, in *CWL*, 7:120n.

231 **"Find that Mr. Chase has shockingly mismanaged":** Stedman and Gould, *Life and Letters of Stedman*, 1:337.

231 **"*seem* to indicate the re-nomination":** Chase to Ball, Feb. 2, 1864, 4:274–75 (emphasis in original).

232 **He had used his patronage adroitly:** Blue, *Salmon P. Chase*, 223.

232 **"to go with the current":** Alfred P. Stone to Salmon Chase, Feb. 4, 1864, in *SPCP*, 4:276. Chase, as governor, had appointed Stone state treasurer; during the war he rewarded Stone with the job of revenue collector in Columbus.

232 **"As a mere question of wages withheld":** Akiko Ochiai, "The Port Royal Experiment Revisited: Northern Visions of Reconstruction and the Land Question," *The New England Quarterly* 74, no. 1 (2001): 108.

233 **the two had agreed that the government:** Cory Hartman, "The Useful Life of Mansfield French: A Model of Multivocational Ministry" (thesis, Gordon-Conwell Theological Seminary, 2015), 353.

233 **an official policy of "preemption":** *SPCP*, 4:293n.

233 **Saxton and French encouraged freedmen:** Edward S. Philbrick to Helen Philbrick, Nov. 10, 1863, in *Letters from Port Royal Written at the Time of the Civil War, 1862–1868*, ed. Elizabeth Ware Pearson (Privately published, 1906), 229–30; Hartman, "The Useful Life of Mansfield French," 353–55.

233 **reacted with eager enthusiasm:** Hartman, "The Useful Life of Mansfield French," 355.

233 **160 freed people:** Ochiai, "Port Royal Experiment Revisited," 102.

233 **At Saxton's request:** Edward S. Philbrick to unknown recipient, Jan. 20, 1864, in Pearson, *Letters from Port Royal*, 243–44.

233 **serenaded him on the virtues:** Rose, *Rehearsal for Reconstruction*, 284.

233 **Lincoln gave official sanction:** "Additional Instructions to Direct Tax Commissioners," Dec. 31, 1863, in *CWL*, 7:98–99.

233 **Chase did not fully understand:** Rose, *Rehearsal for Reconstruction*, 284.

234 **"we may see these islands":** Rose, *Rehearsal for Reconstruction*, 283.

234 **"to lose no time":** Ochiai, "Port Royal Experiment Revisited," 105.

234 **Two of the three tax commissioners:** Rose, *Rehearsal for Reconstruction*, 287; Ochiai, "Port Royal Experiment Revisited," 102, 113.

234 **They disputed the legality:** Rose, *Rehearsal for Reconstruction*, 287–88, 292; Ochiai, "Port Royal Experiment Revisited," 103.

234 **He pointed to the superior productivity:** "Cotton Culture by Free Labor," *Portland* (Me.) *Daily Press*, Mar. 24, 1864.

234 **In a public letter, Philbrick boasted:** "Cotton Culture by Free Labor"; "An Experiment with the Freedmen," *Cleveland Morning Leader*, Mar. 8, 1864.

234 **"special privileges to negroes":** Ochiai, "Port Royal Experiment Revisited," 109.

235 **"Never have I seen such joy":** Hartman, "The Useful Life of Mansfield French," 361–62.

235 **only six thousand acres:** "The Useful Life of Mansfield French," 101.

235 **"a correct view":** "An Experiment with the Freedmen."

235 **"the colored man will be the sufferer":** Quincy Adams Gillmore to Salmon Chase, Jan. 31, 1864, in *SPCP*, 4:272–73.

235 **two of the commissioners were refusing:** Rufus Saxton to Salmon Chase, Jan. 22, 1864, in *SPCP*, 4:259–60.

235 **"wild scheme":** William Henry Brisbane to Salmon Chase, Feb. 15, 1864, in *SPCP*, 4:293n.

235 **"beside himself with anger":** Hartman, "The Useful Life of Mansfield French," 362.

236 **all sorts of undeserving folks:** Hartman, "The Useful Life of Mansfield French," 362.

236 **He also pointed out that by selling land:** Rose, *Rehearsal for Reconstruction*, 290.

236 **Brisbane's weightiest assertion:** Hartman, "The Useful Life of Mansfield French," 363.

236 **a notorious drinker:** Rose, *Rehearsal for Reconstruction*, 290–92; Hartman, "The Useful Life of Mansfield French," 365.

236 **Chase suspended Lincoln's instructions:** *SPCP*, 4:293n.

236 **"The willows bend again":** Mansfield French to Salmon Chase, Feb. 15, 1864, in Hartman, "The Useful Life of Mansfield French," 366.

236 **He urged the freedmen:** Rose, *Rehearsal for Reconstruction*, 292.

236 **average price of $11 an acre:** Ochiai, "Port Royal Experiment Revisited," 114.

236 **"Did you know":** William C. Gannett to unknown recipient, Feb. 22, 1864, in Pearson, *Letters from Port Royal*, 254.

236 **bodily evicted by the army:** Ochiai, "Port Royal Experiment Revisited," 115.

237 **Pomeroy Circular:** "The Presidential Question: Circular from the (Self-Appointed) National Executive Committee of the Friends of Mr. Chase," *New York Times*, Feb 23, 1864. For "The Next Presidential Election," see Blue, *Salmon P. Chase*, 222–23; Niven, *Chase: A Biography*, 360, 363.

237 **Ohio's was among them:** Nicolay and Hay, *Abraham Lincoln*, 8:324.

237 **"I should bet on Uncle Abe":** *Strong*, 3:407.

237 **Many newspapers rushed:** See, e.g., *Rutland* (Vt.) *Weekly Herald*, Feb. 25, 1864.

237 **"A Game That Won't Work":** *Chicago Daily Tribune*, Feb. 24, 1864.

238 **"We do not hesitate to say":** *Pittsburgh Gazette*, quoted in *Wheeling* (W. Va.) *Daily Intelligencer*, Feb. 25, 1864.

238 **Chase tried to distance:** Salmon Chase to Abraham Lincoln, Feb. 22, 1864, in *SPCP*, 4:303–5.

238 **responded with a brief note:** Abraham Lincoln to Salmon Chase, Feb. 23, 1864, in *CWL*, 7:200.

238 **"Now, on consideration":** Abraham Lincoln to Salmon Chase, Feb. 29, 1864, in *CWL*, 7:212–13.

238 **"You can have no idea":** Richard C. Parsons to Salmon Chase, Mar. 2, 1864, in *SPCP*, 4:315.

238 **"every honorable man":** "Proceedings of Congress," *New York Times*, Feb. 28, 1864. See also *SPCP*, 4:305; Chase, *Inside Lincoln's Cabinet*, 177.

238 **his "enemies" were intent:** Henry Villard to Salmon Chase, Mar. 7, 1864, in *SPCP*, 4:323.

239 **Early in March, Chase withdrew:** "The News," *Chicago Daily Tribune*, Mar. 11, 1864; "The Declination of Mr. Chase," *New York Times*, Mar. 12, 1864.

239 **"usefulness as Secretary":** Salmon Chase to Nettie Chase, Mar. 15, 1864, in *SPCP*, 4:329.

239 **The Treasury still faced:** *Stevens Papers*, 433, 436–37.

Chapter Twelve: Roast Mutton and Partridge

240 **"To trade with the enemy":** Jacob Thompson to Jefferson Davis, Dec. 23, 1863, in *Davis Papers*, 10:124.

241 **A historian born during Davis's lifetime:** Frank E. Vandiver, "Jefferson Davis—Leader Without Legend," *The Journal of Southern History* 43, no. 1 (1977): 4; the historian was Elisabeth Brown Cutting.

241 **"that this great war":** Vandiver, "Jefferson Davis—Leader Without Legend," 15 (emphasis in original).

241 **"We have been united":** Vandiver, "Jefferson Davis—Leader Without Legend," 15.

241 **In staggered elections:** James M. McPherson, *Battle Cry of Freedom: The Civil War Era* (New York: Oxford University Press, 1988), 691–92.

242 **"few deadly enemies":** *RWCD* (2015), 2:12.

242 **"The famine [in Richmond] is caused":** *Strong*, 3:371–72.

242 **fastest rate of the war:** John Christopher Schwab, *The Confederate States of America, 1861–1865: A Financial and Industrial History of the South During the Civil War* (1901; repr., New York: Burt Franklin, 1968), 54.

242 **revenues amounted to $601 million:** Schwab, *The Confederate States of America, 1861–1865*, 55.

242 **10 percent per month:** Eugene M. Lerner, "Money, Prices, and Wages in the Confederacy, 1861–65," *Journal of Political Economy* 63, no. 1 (1955): 23; Lerner said this pattern held for thirty-one consecutive months, which equates to a general price increase of 1800 percent.

242 **soared to $220:** "The Markets," *Richmond Enquirer*, Apr. 2, 1861; *RWCD* (1866), 1:278, 2:133.

242 **far faster than the rise in wages:** Lerner, "Money, Prices, and Wages in the Confederacy," 31, 33, 36.

242 **"It is nothing unusual to see":** "The Battle in Georgia: The Rebel Accounts of It; Miscellaneous," *New York Times*, Sept. 25, 1863, quoting *Richmond Whig*.

242 **currency was now supplemented:** *Stevens Papers*, 34.

242 **Memminger even saw fit:** *RWCD* (2015), 2:91.

242 **The best estimate for the growth:** Mark Thornton and Robert B. Ekelund Jr, *Tariffs, Blockades, and Inflation: The Economics of the Civil War* (Wilmington, Del.: Scholarly Resources, 2004), 33; see also Lerner, "Money, Prices, and Wages in the Confederacy," 21.

243 *residents shipped notes back:* Lerner, "Money, Prices, and Wages in the Confederacy," 20.

243 *eighteen* **times higher:** Paul R. Auerbach and Michael J. Haupert, "Problems in Analyzing Inflation During the Civil War," *Essays in Economic and Business History* (2002): 67.

243 **The best indicator of monetary instability:** *RWCD* (2015), 2:2, 89, 139; *Ruffin*, 3:45, 139, 400; Rose Razaghian, "Financial Civil War: The Confederacy's Financial Policies, 1861–1864," Yale ICF Working Paper, No. 04-45, 29; Schwab, *The Confederate States of America*, 133; Auerbach and Haupert, "Problems in Analyzing Inflation," 67.

243 **farmers switched to cotton and tobacco:** Razaghian, "Financial Civil War," 13.

243 **"We have accounts of corn":** *RWCD* (2015), 2:91; see also 113.

243 **Right under the President's nose:** *RWCD* (2015), 2:68, 89–90.

243 **anyone with a product to sell:** Lerner, "Money, Prices, and Wages in the Confederacy," 38.

244 **While blaming high prices:** *RWCD* (1866), 2:122, 139.

244 **"Without such 'short cuts' ":** *RWCD* (2015), 2:88.

244 **The wealthy purchased property:** "The War in Virginia," *New York Times*, Mar 6, 1864, reprinting *Richmond Examiner*, Feb 23, 1864.

244 **They stopped selling meat:** *RWCD* (1866), 2:95.

244 **"The cotton trade is carried on":** D. B. Dobbins to Jefferson Davis, n.d. [c. Dec. 1863], in *Davis Papers*, 10:117.

244 **"You cannot consider it":** Thompson to Davis, Dec. 23, 1863, 10:123.

244 **"The passion for speculation":** *RWCD* (1866), 2:63–64.

244 **the army reduced to half rations:** Razaghian, "Financial Civil War," 17; *RWCD* (1866), 2:136–37; McPherson, *Battle Cry of Freedom*, 617.

244 **"Everywhere the people are clamorous":** *RWCD* (1866), 2:103.

244 **"in preference to anything else":** *RWCD* (1866), 2:96.

245 **Lack of tradesmen:** Lerner, "Money, Prices, and Wages in the Confederacy," 31, 34.

245 **"a number of our most important":** Lerner, "Money, Prices, and Wages in the Confederacy," 35.

245 **In Manchester, Virginia:** *Richmond Enquirer*, June 21, 1864.

245 **The government similarly exerted:** Jefferson Davis to Joseph E. Johnston, Jan. 13, 1864, in *Davis Papers*, 10:171.

245 **southern generals demanded:** James Longstreet to Jefferson Davis, Feb. 25, 1864, in *Davis Papers*, 10:261; Robert E. Lee to Jefferson Davis, Jan. 11, 1864, in *Davis Papers*, 10:168.

245 **In an extreme case:** *RWCD* (1866), 2:188–89.

245 **Refugees were streaming north:** *Chicago Daily Tribune*, Jan. 14, 1864.

245 **peace or starvation:** *RWCD* (2015), 2:123; Jones repeatedly invoked the prospect of famine, e.g., 2:89, 142, 151–52, 169.

245 **Richmond was plagued by robberies:** *RWCD* (2015), 2:119, 166.

245 **Thanks to human scavengers:** *RWCD* (1866), 2:156.

245 **A sea captain:** Captain Roberts [pseud. for Augustus Charles Hobart-Hampden], *Never Caught: Personal Adventures Connected with Twelve Successful Trips in Blockade-Running During the American Civil War, 1863–1864* (1867; repr, N.p. Hardpress, 2012), 25.

245 **laid a Christmas dinner:** *Chesnut*, 234.

246 **"It is a sad Christmas":** *RWCD* (1866), 2:119.

246 **inflation in the price of substitutes:** *RWCD* (1866), 1:144, 182, 218–19, 387, and 2:85.

246 **Confederate officers died:** McPherson, *Battle Cry of Freedom*, 330.

246 **Just as worrisome:** "European News: Additional from Our Foreign Files; Utterances on the American Question," *New York Times*, Dec. 27, 1863, citing near "open revolt" in various southern states.

246 **"The crime is with the planters":** David Williams, "Southern Unionism," Essential Civil War Curriculum, https://www.essentialcivilwarcurriculum.com/southern-unionism.html.

246 **bands of deserters congealed:** Williams, "Southern Unionism."

246 **"We are fighting each other":** Williams, "Southern Unionism."

246 **"The ladies were all dressed":** Roberts, *Never Caught*, 47–48.

247 **"the army can do without whiskey":** "Distilling the Tithes," *North Carolina Standard*, Jan. 1, 1864.

247 **"We might as well be under":** *Wilmington* (N.C.) *Journal*, Jan. 28, 1864.

247 **"I fear we are on the eve":** *Davis Papers*, 10:163.

247 **"the evils and abuses":** Zebulon B. Vance to Jefferson Davis, Dec. 3, 1863, in *Davis Papers*, 10:99.

247 **"ruthless" conscription:** Zebulon B. Vance to Jefferson Davis, Feb. 9, 1864, in *Davis Papers*, 10:227.

247 **"an over-earnest desire":** Jefferson Davis to Zebulon B. Vance, Jan. 8, 1864, in *Davis Papers*, 10:161.

247 **"the bloodiest field of the South":** "Interview with North Carolina Delegation," Jan. 23, 1864, in *Davis Papers*, 10:199–200.

247 **"I warned you":** Jefferson Davis to Zebulon B. Vance, Feb. 28, 1864, in *Davis Papers*, 10:267.

248 **resentment curdled into prejudice:** W. L. Cunningham to Jefferson Davis, Jan. 16. 1864, in *Davis Papers*, 10:177; *Ruffin*, 3:325–36.

248 **"In all else we have":** "News from Washington: General Toombs on the Rebel Currency," *New York Times*, Aug. 28, 1863, quoting Augusta *Constitutionalist*.

248 **Early in 1864, Toombs declared:** "The News," *Chicago Daily Tribune*, Feb. 10, 1864.

248 **officers quietly suggested:** *Davis Papers*, 10:178–79n; see also Vandiver, "Jefferson Davis—Leader Without Legend," 14.

248 **"a dreaded weakness":** Shelby Foote, *The Civil War: A Narrative* (New York: Random House, 1963), 2:953–54.

248 **Davis told his wife:** Foote, *The Civil War*, 2:955.

249 **his servant Cornelius:** *RWCD* (1866), 2:150.

249 **"monstrous proposition":** Foote, *The Civil War*, 2:954.

249 **"his most dangerous & abominable principles":** *Ruffin*, 3:302, 312–13.

249 **the war secretary commanded Cleburne:** Foote, *The Civil War*, 2:954.

249 **"There is no reason for distrust":** "The Rebel Finances: A Letter from Secretary Memminger," *New York Times*, Sept., 1, 1863, quoting from Memminger's letter of Aug. 24, 1863, to R. M. T. Hunter.

250 **gold sewn by his mother:** Jan Whitaker, "Isidor Straus, 1845–1912," https://www.immigrantentrepreneurship.org/entries/isidor-straus/#_edn7; Straus was in New York en route to Liverpool.

250 **"Buy real estate, land, houses and lots":** Gareth Russell, *The Ship of Dreams: The Sinking of the Titanic and the End of the Edwardian Era* (New York: Atria, 2019), 153.

250 **plunged to nine cents to the dollar:** Schwab, *The Confederate States of America*, 36.

250 **plummeted to less than forty cents:** Mark D. Weidenmier, "The Market for Confederate Cotton Bonds," *Explorations in Economic History* 37 (2000): 85, 87. The cotton bonds were quoted, as usual, in British sterling.

250 **the Confederacy's debt:** Schwab, *The Confederate States of America*, 55.

250 **Davis settled on "compulsory funding":** "From the Rebel States: Proposed Reduction of the Currency," *New York Times*, Dec. 20, 1863, quoting *Richmond Examiner* of Dec. 11, 1863. See also Schwab, *The Confederate States of America*, 59–60.

250–251 **Opposition was vehement:** Jefferson Davis, "Message to Congress," Dec. 7, 1863, in *Davis Papers*, 10:103; Vandiver, "Jefferson Davis—Leader Without Legend," 17.

251 **Critics accused Davis:** "Interview with North Carolina Delegation," Jan. 23, 1864, in *Davis Papers*, 10:199; *RWCD* (1866), 2:116.

251 **The Rebel Congress met:** *RWCD* (1866), 2:116, 137.

251 **An Act to Fund, Tax and Limit the Currency:** *Raleigh Daily Confederate*, Feb. 20, 1864; see also "The Funding Act," *Charlotte Western Democrat*, Mar. 22, 1864; Schwab, *The Confederate States of America*, 59–66. Very small bills ($5 and under) were treated less severely; penalties for not exchanging very large bills ($100 and up) were greater. The bonds paid 4 percent interest.

251 **more than $700 million:** The precise total of monetary instruments in circulation is unknown; Davis said the total just of Treasury notes was "more than $600 million": "Message to Congress," 10:103; Lerner reports just over $825 million in Confederate notes as of January 1864 and nearly $1.1 billion in all monetary instruments, including notes: Lerner, "Money, Prices, and Wages in the Confederacy," 21.

251 **Congress legislated a tax:** "The Tax Act of February 17, 1864," *Charlotte Western Democrat* (quoting *Richmond Enquirer*), Mar. 22, 1864.

251 **two-thirds of the Confederacy's taxable property:** "Jeff Davis' Message," Dec. 12, 1863; Razaghian, "Financial Civil War," 18.

251 **The immediate reaction to the currency law:** *Richmond Examiner*, Feb. 29, 1864.

251 **"a sensible decline"**: "Southern News," *New York Times*, Mar. 26, 1864, quoting *Augusta* (Ga.) *Chronicle and Sentinel*.

251 **Before long, people were swapping:** "Southern News."

252 **"prices are tumbling"**: "Rebel Repudiation—Rebel Currency," *New York Times*, Apr. 5, 1864.

252 **money in the city was "tight"**: "Southern News," quoting *Lynchburg* (Va.) *Republican*.

252 **A later reconstruction:** See InflationData.com, https://inflationdata.com/articles/confederate -inflation.

252 **"our currency, under the salutary provisions"**: "Southern News," quoting *Richmond Whig*.

252 **a general deflation:** Accounts of the timing of the effects of currency reform differ. Contemporary sources suggest an immediate effect, with prices falling in March 1864 and rebounding later in the spring. Lerner says they started falling in May and remained depressed through December: "Money, Prices, and Wages in the Confederacy," 25. All sources agree that the respite from inflation was temporary. Lerner also says that, by April 1865 (when the war ended) the price index reached 92 times its prewar base, which meant there was epic inflation over the final year ("Money, Prices, and Wages in the Confederacy," 24).

252 **The share of revenue raised:** Razaghian, "Financial Civil War," 18, 29. Razaghian's computation includes the effect of two later tax bills, both enacted in June 1864.

252 **"a remarkable achievement"**: "Financial Civil War," 18.

252 **Richmond could not spare:** Jefferson Davis to Christopher M. Memminger, Jan. 12, 1864, in *Davis Papers*, 10:170.

252 **Evasion was rampant:** Razaghian, "Financial Civil War," 18.

252 **fresh emissions of the dreaded notes:** "Rebel Repudiation—Rebel Currency."

252 **Distribution of the new notes started:** Schwab, *The Confederate States of America*, 67.

253 **widened draft eligibility:** The provision permitting hiring of substitutes was eliminated on Dec. 28, 1863, and other rules were tightened on Feb. 17, 1864: see *Davis Papers*, 10:183n. Conscription in the South initially applied to white males between the ages of eighteen and thirty-five; a second act raised eligibility to forty-five; the 1864 bill widened eligibility to between seventeen and fifty.

253 **save for the risible exception:** Schwab, *The Confederate States of America*, 162.

253 **The most extreme proposal:** Alexander M. Clayton to Jefferson Davis, Dec. 26, 1863, in *Davis Papers*, 10:135–36.

253 **Richmond's agents in Europe:** *Davis Papers*, 10:110; Razaghian, "Financial Civil War," 14.

253 **The new law compelled blockade runners:** *Davis Papers*, 10:301n; Richard Franklin Bensel, *Yankee Leviathan: The Origins of Central State Authority in America, 1859–1877* (New York: Cambridge University Press, 1990), 180; Thornton and Ekelund, *Tariffs, Blockades, and Inflation*, 50–54.

253 **Cotton in Liverpool fetched ten times:** In February 1864, cotton in Liverpool fetched 27 English pence. If those pence were converted to U.S. money (at the going rate of roughly 10 greenbacks to 1 pound sterling), they would have been worth just over $1 U.S., or enough to purchase *ten* pounds of cotton in the South. Cotton similarly fetched more than $1 per pound in New York. See "Financial and Commercial," *New York Times*, Feb. 5, 1864; *Davis Papers*, 10:126–27n.

254 **Several states were already:** *Davis Papers*, 10:301n.

254 **Governor Vance vehemently protested:** Zebulon B. Vance to Jefferson Davis, Mar. 17, 1864, in *Davis Papers*, 10:283.

254 **"then all the ships engaged"**: Jefferson Davis to Zebulon B. Vance, Mar. 26, 1864, in *Davis Papers*, 10:299–301.

254 **Augustus Charles Hobart-Hampden:** Roberts, *Never Caught*, 2, 13, 15, 51; Francis I. W. Jones, "This Fraudulent Trade: Confederate Blockade-Running from Halifax During the American Civil War," *Northern Mariner* 9, no. 4 (1999): 37. See also "Important Bills Approved by the President," *New York Times*, Feb. 24, 1864, quoting *Richmond Examiner* of Feb. 10, 1864.

255 **"a sense of Confederateness"**: Vandiver, "Jefferson Davis—Leader Without Legend," 17.

255 **The same fidelity to planters:** Razaghian points out that Davis was aware of the threat to food supplies posed by nonfood crops as early as 1863 and essentially ignored it: Razaghian, "Financial Civil War," 13.

255 **He "overmobilized"**: Lerner, "Money, Prices, and Wages in the Confederacy," 28.

255 **David Williams points out:** Williams, "Southern Unionism."

Chapter Thirteen: Exit Secretary

256 **"The greatest financial Secretary"**: John G. Nicolay and John Hay, *Abraham Lincoln: A History* (New York: Century, 1886–1890), 9:103.

256 **his master bond salesman, Jay Cooke:** Salmon P. Chase, *Inside Lincoln's Cabinet: The Civil War Diaries of Salmon P. Chase,* ed. David Herbert Donald (New York: Longman's Green, 1954), 212.

257 **"To arrest this depreciation":** Salmon Chase to Thaddeus Stevens, Apr. 11, 1864, in J. W. Schuckers, *The Life and Public Services of Salmon Portland Chase* (New York: D. Appleton, 1874), 401.

257 **The Treasury secretary was a bullionist:** See, e.g., Salmon Chase to S. Dewitt Bloodgood, May 9, 1864, in Schuckers, *The Life and Public Services of Salmon Portland Chase,* 402.

257 **"Chase is a man of ability":** John Sherman to William Tecumseh Sherman, Apr. 17, 1864, in Rachel Sherman Thorndike, ed., *The Sherman Letters: Correspondence Between General and Senator Sherman from 1837 to 1891* (New York: Charles Scribner's Sons, 1894), 233.

257 *"influenced by the rapid rise":* "General News," *New York Times,* Apr. 13, 1864 (emphasis added). For coffee, sugar, and pork prices, see "Plundering Trade Combinations," *New York Times,* Apr. 17, 1864.

257 **Representative James Brooks toted:** Schuckers, *The Life and Public Services,* 301–2.

257 **modern research shows:** See Ethel D. Hoover, "Retail Prices After 1850," in "Conference on Research in Income and Wealth," *Trends in the American Economy in the Nineteenth Century* (New York: National Bureau of Economic Research, 1960), 142.

257–258 **significantly higher than in wages:** Reuben A. Kessel and Armen A. Alchian, "Real Wages in the North During the Civil War," *The Journal of Law and Economics* 2 (Oct. 1959): 97.

258 **Over the entirety of 1864:** Kessel and Alchian calculate inflation in 1864 at 21.4 percent, up from 19.7 percent in 1863 ("Real Wages in the North During the Civil War," 97). Hoover has consumer prices rising at 26.7 percent in 1864, compared with 23 percent the preceding year ("Retail Prices After 1850," 142).

258 **Chase was also to blame:** See Chase, *Inside Lincoln's Cabinet,* 44, 212.

258 **"The war languishes":** *Strong,* 3:422 (emphasis in original).

258 **tripled the tax on spirits:** *Report of the Commissioner of Internal Revenue,* June 30, 1864, 2–3; the tax was enacted on Mar. 7, 1864.

258 **total contribution of tax revenues should *double*:** Salmon Chase to Cyrus W. Field, Feb. 17, 1864, in *SPCP,* 4:293; Salmon Chase to Horace Greeley, Apr. 6, 1864, in *SPCP,* 4:366; Salmon Chase to William Fessenden, June 20, 1864, in *SPCP,* 4:399.

258 **"men on the temperance side":** "House of Representatives: From Washington," *New York Times,* Feb. 24, 1864.

258–259 **to tax them out of existence:** Salmon Chase to Cyrus W. Field, Apr. 6, 1864, in *SPCP,* 4:364. See also Salmon Chase to Joshua Leavitt, Mar. 31, 1864, in Schuckers, *The Life and Public Services,* 400, in which Chase bluntly expresses his aim "to tax the local bank circulation out of existence"; and Salmon Chase to Thaddeus Stevens, Apr. 11, 1864, in *SPCP,* 4:372.

259 **He wrote to Joseph Medill:** Salmon Chase to Joseph Medill, Jan. 30, 1864, in *SPCP,* 4:271–72.

259 **Chase's justification:** Salmon Chase to William Dodge, Mar. 31, 1864, in *SPCP,* 4:360.

259 **"What can I do?":** Chase to Greeley, Apr. 6, 1874, 4:366–67.

259 **Since the volume of government issues:** Mark Thornton and Robert B. Ekelund Jr. note that at the start of the war, state bank notes totaled twelve times the volume of government currency; by 1864 the total of U.S. Notes (greenbacks) alone was roughly double that of bank notes: *Tariffs, Blockades, and Inflation: The Economics of the Civil War* (Wilmington, Del.: Scholarly Resources, 2004), 62.

259 **Telegrams poured into the Treasury:** Schuckers, *The Life and Public Services,* 358.

259 **"Stock and gold gambling":** William O. Stoddard, *Inside the White House in War Times: Memoirs and Reports of Lincoln's Secretary,* ed. Michael Burlingame (Lincoln: University of Nebraska Press, 2000), xvii.

259 **President Lincoln exclaimed:** Don E. Fehrenbacher and Virginia Fehrenbacher, eds., *Recollected Words of Abraham Lincoln* (Stanford, Calif.: Stanford University Press, 1996), 84.

259 **he treated Stoddard with compassion:** Burlingame, introduction to Stoddard, *Inside the White House in War Times,* xviii.

259 **He misread speculators:** See, e.g., "Taxation: An Important Letter from Secretary Chase," *New York Times,* Apr. 18, 1864, reprinting Salmon Chase to William P. Fessenden, Apr. 12, 1864.

259 **was said to be exceedingly anxious:** "The Gold Bill," *New York Herald,* Mar. 2, 1864.

260 **"When a man asks five dollars":** *Stevens Papers,* 439.

260 **"They are not debts":** *Stevens Papers,* 444.

260 **Cisco argued that the threat:** John J. Cisco to Salmon Chase, Mar. 21, 1864, in *SPCP,* 4:353–55.

260 **"hold the whip":** Ellis Paxson Oberholtzer, *Jay Cooke: Financier of the Civil War* (Philadelphia: G.W. Jacobs, 1907), 1:400.

260 **"It is of immense importance":** Salmon Chase to Jay Cooke, Apr. 10, 1864, in *SPCP,* 4:369.

260 **"Panic in stocks this morning":** Laura Stedman and George M. Gould, *Life and Letters of Edmund Clarence Stedman* (New York: Moffat, Yard, 1910), 1:340–43.

261 **Chase had already made a desperate pronouncement:** William E. Gienapp and Erica L. Gienapp eds., *The Civil War Diary of Gideon Welles* (Urbana: University of Illinois Press, 2014), 1:389.

261 **He begged Lincoln:** Salmon Chase to Abraham Lincoln, Apr. 14, 1864, in *SPCP*, 4:375.

261 **On April 14:** Schuckers, *The Life and Public Services*, 358.

261 **soared to 90 percent:** Gienapp and Gienapp, *The Civil War Diary of Gideon Welles*, 1:391.

261 **furiously unloaded the Treasury's bullion:** To saturate the market with yet more gold, Chase paid the May interest ahead of schedule (*The Civil War Diary of Gideon Welles*, 1:392).

261 **"Gold has been oscillating madly":** *Strong*, 3:428.

261 **New York banks were desperately short:** "General News," *New York Times*, Apr. 19, 1864.

261 **A well-known speculator:** *Strong*, 3:429; "General News." The speculator was Anthony Morse.

261 **Chase had expended $11 million:** Schuckers, *The Life and Public Services*, 358; Albert Bushnell Hart, *Salmon P. Chase* (Boston: Houghton Mifflin, 1899), 284.

261 **"There is panic and smash":** *Strong*, 3:429.

261 **With the gold premium having retreated:** "General News," *New York Times*, Apr. 21, 1864.

261 **"It seems to me that I":** Oberholtzer, *Jay Cooke: Financier*, 1:405.

262 **would empty its vault:** Senator Sherman calculated that vaults of the Treasury and the private banks in New York held a surplus of just over $40 million (*Chicago Daily Tribune*, Mar. 14, 1864).

262 **"there will be no need to fear":** Salmon Chase to Abraham Lincoln, Apr. 14, 1864, in *SPCP*, 4:375.

262 **raking in three times the taxes collected:** John Sherman, *Recollections of Forty Years in the House, Senate and Cabinet* (Chicago: Werner, 1895), 1:304; Kessel and Alchian, "Real Wages in the North," 109.

262 **Tariff collections had surged:** Kessel and Alchian, "Real Wages in the North," 109.

262 **climbed to $2.5 million a day:** Salmon Chase to Richard Smith, May 27, 1864, in Schuckers, *The Life and Public Services*, 403.

262 **Chase again fell behind on requisitions:** Sumner Welles to Salmon Chase, May 20, 1864, in *SPCP*, 4:386.

262 **the Republican press supported him:** See, e.g., "Taxation," Apr. 15, 1864, *New York Times*; "Is It Imbecility or Treachery?" *New York Times*, Apr. 16, 1864; "Congress: The People; Taxation," *New York Times*, Apr. 19, 1864.

262 **internal revenue eclipsed the tariff:** The two sources, respectively, produced $110 million and $102 million: Treasury Secretary, *Annual Report*, 1864, p. 73. See also Kessel and Alchian, "Real Wages in the North," 109.

262 **Luxury items:** "The Copperhead Vote in Congress on the Tax Bill," *New York Times*, May 4, 1864. Enthusiasm for taxing luxuries was also evident in the tariff legislation; see "The New Tariff Bill Reported in the House; Heavily Increased Duties on Articles of Luxury," *New York Herald*, May 28, 1864.

262 **Chase's commissioner of internal revenue urged:** Sheldon D. Pollack, "The First National Income Tax, 1861–1872," *Tax Lawyer* 67, no. 2 (2014): 13. The commissioner was Joseph J. Lewis, who had replaced George Boutwell.

262 **Representative Augustus Frank:** "Proceedings of Congress," *New York Times*, Apr. 27, 1864; Joseph. J. Thorndike, "An Army of Officials: The Civil War Bureau of Internal Revenue," Tax History Project, http://www.taxhistory.org/thp/readings.nsf/ArtWeb/FF949517831B181685256E22007840E8?OpenDocument.

263 **between 10 and 15 percent of Union households:** Thorndike, "An Army of Officials." Thorndike cited estimates ranging from 1.3 percent to 20 percent.

263 **Pitt Fessenden, whose roots:** Heather Cox Richardson, *The Greatest Nation of the Earth: Republican Economic Policies During the Civil War* (Cambridge: Harvard University Press, 1997), 131.

263 **"spirit of agrarianism":** Pollack, "The First National Income Tax," 13.

263 **"It is seizing property":** Thorndike, "An Army of Officials."

263 **"Let not him who is houseless":** "From Washington," *New York Times*, Mar. 22, 1864.

264 **Republican legislators were more:** Pollack, "The First National Income Tax," 13, 14.

264 **Morrill argued that steeper duties:** Douglas A. Irwin, *Clashing over Commerce: A History of U.S. Trade Policy* (Chicago: University of Chicago Press, 2017), 213. The text omits the emergency tariff approved in April 1864, but only for sixty days (see "Congress on Taxation: Its Freaks and Fallacies," *New York Times*, Apr. 28, 1864, and "Congress," *New York Times*, Apr. 29, 1864).

264 **"If you concur with me":** Salmon Chase to Abraham Lincoln, Apr. 15, 1864, in *SPCP*, 4:375–77 (emphasis added).

264 **"Suppose you change":** Abraham Lincoln to Salmon Chase, May 18, 1864, in *CWL*, 7:347.

264 **His political enemies:** See, e.g., Ambrose W. Thompson to Abraham Lincoln, Apr. 3, 1864, in *CWL*, 7:285n, in which the shipbuilder advised Lincoln that a banker's loan in Europe "would crush the Chase faction."

264 **Blair was delivering:** "Frank Blair's Attack on Secretary Chase and General Fremont," *New York Herald*, Apr. 24, 1864. See also *SPCP*, 4:380n; Gienapp and Gienapp, *The Civil War Diary of Gideon Welles*, 398; Schuckers, *The Life and Public Services*, 347.

265 **sex and champagne bacchanalia:** Gienapp and Gienapp, *The Civil War Diary of Gideon Welles*, 354n, 401n; *SPCP*, 4:385n; Schuckers, *The Life and Public Services*, 250.

265 **"knew that another beehive was knocked over":** Hart, *Salmon P. Chase*, 314.

265 **He considered withdrawing:** Hart, *Salmon P. Chase*, 314.

265 **Chase erupted:** Salmon Chase to Jay Cooke, May 5, 1864, in *SPCP*, 4:379–80; Schuckers, *The Life and Public Services*, 350–51.

265 **"a frightful rage":** *SPCP*, 4:380n.

265 **"the Convention will not be regarded":** Salmon Chase to John Brough, May 19, 1864, in *SPCP*, 4:384–85.

265 **"perhaps the busiest":** Sherman, *Recollections*, 1:331.

265 **the immigration bill:** The act was signed on July 14, 1864. For a synopsis, see Jason Silverman, "Lincoln's 'Forgotten' Act to Encourage Immigration," July 1, 2016, http://www.lincolncottage.org/lincolns-forgotten-act-to-encourage-immigration.

266 ***The New York Times* felt compelled:** "Growth of the American Nation: The Nationality of the [word unclear] Philosophy of National Growth Elements Which Compose the American Nation; Their Homogeneousness Compared with Europe; The Irish in America," *New York Times*, May 8, 1864.

266 **"four millions of human beings":** "Proceedings of Congress," *New York Times*, Apr. 9, 1864.

266 **"the day in which the nation":** "Proceedings of Congress," *New York Times*, Apr. 7, 1864.

266–267 **The Senate approved the amendment:** "The Constitutional Amendment," *New York Times*, Apr. 9, 1864.

267 **slavery was the optimal condition:** "House of Representatives: The Anti-Slavery Amendment," *New York Times*, June 16, 1864. The congressman was Fernando Wood, the former New York City mayor.

267 **"When the war began":** "Address at Sanitary Fair, Baltimore," Apr. 18, 1864, in *CWL*, 7:301–3.

267 **Sanitary fairs were held:** "The Fair: Commencement of the Third Week Today," *New York Herald*, Apr. 18, 1864; "The Sword Contest," *Chicago Daily Tribune*, Apr. 21, 1864. For the founding of the U.S. Sanitary Commission, see "The Great Insurrection," *New York Times*, June 17, 1861.

268 **the politically powerful state banks still outnumbered:** Bray Hammond, *Sovereignty and an Empty Purse: Banks and Politics in the Civil War* (Princeton, N.J.: Princeton University Press, 1970), 345.

268 **an incentive *not* to convert:** *Chicago Daily Tribune*, Apr. 6, 1864; *Chicago Daily Tribune*, Apr. 7, 1864; "News from Washington: Defeat of the National Bank Bill in the House," *New York Herald*, Apr. 7, 1864. See also *Stevens Papers*, 451n; Oberholtzer, *Jay Cooke: Financier*, 1:357.

268 **"adventurous speculators":** Treasury Secretary, *Annual Report*, 1863, p. 58.

268 **By the end of 1863:** Treasury Secretary, *Annual Report*, 1863, p. 49; the exact total was 134.

268 **mostly small ones:** Treasury Secretary, *Annual Report*, 1863, p. 56; David M. Gische, "The New York City Banks and the Development of the National Banking System 1860–1870," *The American Journal of Legal History* 23. no. 1 (1979): 45.

268 **only $4 million worth:** *Stevens Papers*, 451n; Henrietta M. Larson, *Jay Cooke, Private Banker* (Cambridge: Harvard University Press, 1936), 142. By comparison, the total of state bank currency was $239 million.

268 **New York banks posed:** Gische, "The New York City Banks," 38–59.

268 **volume had soared to $115 million:** Schuckers, *The Life and Public Services*, 301.

269 **Institutions in the city:** Gische, "The New York City Banks," 42–43.

269 **Under National Banking:** Gische, "The New York City Banks," 39.

269 **the New Yorkers actively conspired:** Oberholtzer, *Jay Cooke: Financier*, 1:344.

269 **"Let the Associated Banks":** Gische, "The New York City Banks," 43.

269 **quickly raised $5 million:** Oberholtzer, *Jay Cooke: Financier*, 1:341–42, 345–46.

269 **"New York opposes the scheme":** Oberholtzer, *Jay Cooke: Financier*, 1:347.

269 **Chase and McCulloch:** Gische, "The New York City Banks," 48–49.

269 **"They think they can now get along":** Gische, "The New York City Banks."

270 **Chase's draconian plan:** Chase pushed for his plan right until the bill was signed. See Salmon Chase to John Sherman, May 26, 1864, in *SPCP*, 4:390; Salmon Chase to Richard Smith, May 27, 1864, in *SPCP*, 4:392; Salmon Chase to Frederick Kuhne, June 1, 1864, in *SPCP*, 4:395. See also Hart, *Salmon P. Chase*, 280.

270 **"far beyond the end of the Civil War":** Gische, "The New York City Banks," 51.

270 **"a vast moneyed power":** "House of Representatives," *New York Times*, Apr. 6, 1864.

270 **"an immense accumulation":** Gische, "The New York City Banks," 53.

270 **Chase and McCulloch buttonholed Sherman:** Gische, "The New York City Banks," 53–54.

270 **Sherman promptly flipped:** Gische, "The New York City Banks," 53–54.

270 **Reserve requirements were reduced:** Gische, "The New York City Banks," 52, 54. The amended law required country banks to keep a reserve of only 15 percent; big-city banks were required to keep only half of their reserves in their vaults; the rest could be parked elsewhere, including in New York.

270 **The Bank of Commerce won:** Gische, "The New York City Banks," 51–52.

271 **"gave legal status to the pyramiding":** Gische, "The New York City Banks," 54.

271 **"There is nothing more important":** Fehrenbacher and Fehrenbacher, *Recollected Words of Abraham Lincoln*, 143.

271 **He told one of the promoters:** Charles Edgar Ames, *Pioneering the Union Pacific: A Reappraisal of the Builders of the Railroad* (New York: Appleton Century Crofts, 1969), 30.

271 **thirty-one miles had been completed:** "The Pacific Railroad," *Chicago Daily Tribune*, June 7, 1864.

272 **"I hardly know what to do":** Thaddeus Stevens to Simon Stevens, Apr. 18, 1864, *Stevens Papers*, 455–56.

272 **an investor in the Kansas line:** Richardson, *The Greatest Nation of the Earth*, 198.

272 **the President said his experience:** Ames, *Pioneering the Union Pacific*, 30.

272 **In a brutal coda:** *White Cloud Kansas Chief*, July 28, 1864; "The Late Samuel Hallett; Meagre Particulars of His Death," *New York Times*, Aug. 4, 1864; "Samuel Hallett Killed," *New York Daily Tribune*, Aug. 6, 1864. See also David G. Taylor, "Thomas Ewing, Jr. and the Origins of the Kansas Pacific Railway Company," *Kansas Historical Quarterly* 42, no. 2 (1976): 155–79; available at Kansas Collection, http://www.kancoll.org/khq/1976/76_2_taylor.htm.

273 **"I am willing to appropriate":** Marc Egnal, *Clash of Extremes: The Economic Origins of the Civil War* (New York: Farrar, Straus, and Giroux, 2009), 247 (emphasis added). Sherman said this in 1860.

273 **Joseph Stewart:** Maury Klein, *Union Pacific: Birth of a Railroad, 1862–1893* (Garden City, N.Y.: Doubleday, 1987), 32; Ames, *Pioneering the Union Pacific*, 28; Richardson, *The Greatest Nation of the Earth*, 201.

273 **"bad . . . unprincipled men":** Richardson, *The Greatest Nation of the Earth*, 203.

273 **"while the real management is in the hands":** *Stevens Papers*, 494n.

273 **"I believe the company":** *Stevens Papers*, 493n.

274 **A Story of Ambition:** Richard Nelson Current, *Old Thad Stevens: A Story of Ambition* (Madison: University of Wisconsin Press, 1942).

274 **he unabashedly worked to quash:** Current, *Old Thad Stevens: A Story of Ambition*, 196.

274 **"one of the greatest enterprises of the age":** Fawn M. Brodie, *Thaddeus Stevens: Scourge of the South* (New York: W. W. Norton, 1959), 183.

274 **"If the bill passes":** Speech on Union Pacific, June 21, 1864, in *Stevens Papers*, 487.

274 **"The gentleman lives in the West":** *Stevens Papers*, 487.

275 **"all in favor of the United States":** *Stevens Papers*, 494n; see also Brodie, *Thaddeus Stevens*, 183.

275 **George Francis Train:** William Robinson Petrowski, *The Kansas Pacific: Study in Railroad Promotion* (New York: Arno Press, 1981), 92.

275 **Congress, in its haste:** Ames, *Pioneering the Union Pacific*, 30; Richardson, *The Greatest Nation of the Earth*, 205.

275 **Congress significantly expanded:** Richardson, *The Greatest Nation of the Earth*, 202.

275 **Stevens, by then deceased, was not implicated:** Brodie, *Thaddeus Stevens*, 185.

276 **the Republicans would be better served:** Current, *Old Thad Stevens*, 197.

276 **at the behest of Lincoln's commander:** David W. Blight, *Frederick Douglass: Prophet of Freedom* (New York: Simon & Schuster, 2018), 430–31.

276 **Stevens strove for a plank:** "The Presidency: The New Republican Platform," *New York Herald*, June 9, 1864.

276 **The platform was penned:** Ted Widmer, "Disunion: 'A Very Mad-Man,'" *New York Times*, Mar. 19, 2011.

276 **Whiggish economic planks:** *CWL*, 7:382n.

276 **"prepared to go further":** "National Union Convention," *New York Times*, June 8, 1864.

277 **the waving of hats:** *CWL*, 7:382*n*.

277 **William Lloyd Garrison:** James M. McPherson, *Battle Cry of Freedom: The Civil War Era* (New York: Oxford University Press, 1988), 716.

277 **unconditional surrender:** *CWL*, 7:382*n*.

277 **"rank demagogue" and a "scoundrel":** Ralph Korngold, *Thaddeus Stevens: A Being Darkly Wise and Rudely Great* (New York: Harcourt, Brace, 1955), 226.

277 **In a portent of the power:** "The National Union Convention," *New York Times*, June 7, 1864.

277 **"I now perceive its importance":** "The Baltimore Nomination: Mr. Lincoln's Acceptance; Address of Gov. Dennison; The Platform; Its Indorsement by the President," *New York Times*, June 10, 1864.

277 **"grinding away":** Chase, *Inside Lincoln's Cabinet*, 210.

277 **"Many a man has gone crazy":** Walter A. McDougall, *Throes of Democracy: The American Civil War Era, 1829–1877* (New York: HarperCollins, 2018), 478.

277 **the boldface headline:** "Grant!" *New York Herald*, May 12, 1864.

277 **Lincoln fretted that such bulletins:** McPherson, *Battle Cry of Freedom*, 731.

277 **heavy rains slowed Grant's advance:** Chase to Brough, May 19, 1864, 4:384–85.

278 **"the long, lean, lank figure":** *Strong*, 3:442.

278 **"the feeling downtown":** *Strong*, 3:447.

278 **John Cisco had predicted:** *Strong*, 3:434.

278 **"My anxiety is very great":** Chase to Brough, May 19, 1864, 4:384–85.

278 **rebounded to 180:** "General News," *New York Times*, Apr. 29, 1864.

278 **Chase responded predictably:** Salmon Chase to Jay Cooke, May 30, 1864, in Oberholtzer, *Jay Cooke: Financier*, 1:407.

278 **"seriously embarrassed":** Gideon Welles to Salmon Chase, May 20, 1864, in *SPCP*, 4:386.

278 **"Your letter of yesterday":** Salmon Chase to John Cisco, May 24, 1864, in *SPCP*, 4:387.

278 **seeking to establish a base:** *Strong*, 3:456*n*.

279 **"no advantage whatever":** Ulysses S. Grant, *Personal Memoirs of U. S. Grant* (New York: Charles L. Webster, 1892), 344.

279 **Lincoln stuck by his determined general:** John Hay, *Inside Lincoln's White House: The Complete Civil War Diary of John Hay*, ed. Michael Burlingame and John R. Turner Ettlinger (Carbondale: Southern Illinois University Press, 1997), 195.

279 **gold had risen to 197:** *Strong*, 3:458; "General News," *New York Times*, June 10, 1864.

279 **"People are blue":** *Strong*, 3:458.

279 **"It galls me":** Salmon Chase to Horace Greeley, June 10, 1864, in *SPCP*, 4:396.

279 **struggling to sell barely $10 million:** Schuckers, *The Life and Public Services*, 349.

279 **His expenses were running:** Treasury Secretary, *Annual Report*, 1864, p. 6.

279 **He was even considering:** In late June 1864, Chase did try to sell 6 percent bonds: see Richardson, *The Greatest Nation of the Earth*, 59.

279 **"The price of gold must & shall":** Chase to Greeley, June 10, 1864, 4:396.

279 **Fifteen thousand locals:** "The President in Philadelphia," *New York Herald*, June 17, 1864.

279 **"from whence he will never be dislodged":** "Speech at Great Central Sanitary Fair, Philadelphia," June 16, 1864, in *CWL*, 7:394–95.

280 **Strong joyfully reported:** *Strong*, 3:459.

280 **"Why won't Congress see it?":** Salmon Chase to John Murray Forbes, June 25, 1864, in *SPCP*, 4:404.

280 **a tax of 10 or even 20 percent:** Frederick J. Blue, *Salmon P. Chase: A Life in Politics* (Kent, Ohio: Kent State University Press, 1987), 164.

280 **Publicly, and for dramatic effect:** "Original and Selected," *Portland* (Me.) *Daily Press*, June 18, 1864.

280 **"There is not the slightest reason":** Hart, *Salmon P. Chase*, 286.

280 **the aim was to prevent "gambling":** Richardson, *The Greatest Nation of the Earth*, 97.

280 **suspend not only the laws of trade:** "House of Representatives: The Contract with the Overland Mail Company; The Gold Bill," *New York Times*, June 15, 1864.

280 **"ignoramuses":** *SPCP*, 4:403*n*. See also, on the gold bill, Gienapp and Gienapp, *The Civil War Diary of Gideon Welles*, 1:427–28; Chase, *Inside Lincoln's Cabinet*, 212; Sherman, *Recollections*, 1:333.

280 **By June 21, gold had risen:** *Strong*, 3:460.

281 **Bankers begged the government:** Chase, *Inside Lincoln's Cabinet*, 212–13.

281 **"Pauperism probably awaits me":** *Strong*, 3:460.

281 **As cotton climbed to $1.20:** Francis Fessenden, *Life and Public Services of William Pitt Fessenden* (Boston: Houghton Mifflin, 1907), 1:344.

281 **price of the Confederate cotton bonds:** Mark D. Weidenmier, "The Market for Confederate Cotton Bonds," *Explorations in Economic History* 37 (2000): 83, 85, 87.

281 **"I am daily more dissatisfied":** Gienapp and Gienapp, *The Civil War Diary of Gideon Welles*, 1:432.

281 **Gold surged to 230:** *The Civil War Diary of Gideon Welles*, 1:428; *Strong*, 3:460.

281 **A delegation of New York financiers:** Chase, *Inside Lincoln's Cabinet*, 212–13.

281 **a bill was introduced for repeal:** Richardson, *The Greatest Nation of the Earth*, 98.

281 **The gold price slightly receded:** Schuckers, *The Life and Public Services*, 360–61.

281 **One credulous English investor:** Weidenmier, "The Market for Confederate Cotton Bonds," 94.

282 **"Well, I backed down again":** Fehrenbacher and Fehrenbacher, *Recollected Words of Abraham Lincoln*, 159.

282 **The President had similarly relented:** Hay, *Inside Lincoln's White House*, 73.

282 **Edwin D. Morgan:** Biographical details about Morgan are drawn from "Mr. Lincoln's White House: Visitors from Congress, Edwin D. Morgan," http://www.mrlincolnswhitehouse.org /residents-visitors/visitors-from-congress/visitors-congress-edwin-d-morgan-1811-1883.

282 **"I can not, without much embarrassment":** Abraham Lincoln to Salmon Chase, June 28, 1864, in *CWL*, 7:412–13.

282 **"Oh, for more faith":** *SPCP*, 4:466.

282 **"the difficulty does not":** Lincoln to Chase, June 28, 1864, 7:413.

283 **"an open revolt":** Lincoln to Chase, June 28, 1864, 7:414.

283 **"I trust you will act":** Salmon Chase to Abraham Lincoln, June 28, 1864, in *SPCP*, 4:406.

283 **Cisco promptly telegraphed:** *CWL*, 7:414n.

283 **Chase relayed the welcome news:** Salmon Chase to Abraham Lincoln, June 29, 1864, in *CWL*, 7:414n.

283 **The public debt had swelled:** Treasury Secretary, *Annual Report*, 1864, pp. 7–8.

283 **"The day has been":** Chase, *Inside Lincoln's Cabinet*, 219.

283 **He dusted off:** Fessenden, *Life and Public Services*, 1:314; Richardson, *The Greatest Nation of the Earth*, 59.

283 **Purchases of artillery horses:** Robert J. Cook, *Civil War Senator: William Pitt Fessenden and the Fight to Save the American Republic* (Baton Rouge: Louisiana State University Press, 2011), 174; Fessenden, *Life and Public Services*, 1:346–47.

283 **Chase was writing the committee chairs:** *SPCP*, 4:411n.

283 **consulting with Representative Morrill:** Chase, *Inside Lincoln's Cabinet*, 223, 219.

283 **He huddled with the Senate Finance Committee:** "News from Washington," *New York Times*, June 29, 1864.

283 **It sent the gold price soaring:** "General News," *New York Times*, June 29, 1864.

283 **"The Confederates give":** "Progress of the War," *New York Times*, June 29, 1864, quoting *The Times* of London.

284 **"my wife happened to be":** Maunsell B. Field, *Memories of Many Men and of Some Women* (New York: Harper and Brothers, 1874), 301–2.

284 **He picked up the enclosure:** Field, *Memories of Many Men and of Some Women*, 298–302. Field heard this from Lincoln shortly after June 30.

284 **"Your resignation of the office":** Abraham Lincoln to Salmon Chase, June 30, 1864, in *CWL*, 7:419.

284 **"We no longer have a Secretary!":** Field, *Memories of Many Men*, 298.

284 **"I had found a good deal":** Chase, *Inside Lincoln's Cabinet*, 223–24.

285 **"that I am too earnest":** Chase, *Inside Lincoln's Cabinet*, 231.

285 **"official life":** Chase, *Inside Lincoln's Cabinet*, 225.

285 **He continued to fret:** Chase, *Inside Lincoln's Cabinet*, 223.

285 **"My grand objects":** Schuckers, *The Life and Public Services*, 405.

285 **Hooper was so depressed:** Nicolay and Hay, *Abraham Lincoln*, 9:98.

285 **Gold soared to 245:** "News of the Day," *New York Times*, July 1, 1864.

285 **His choice, David Tod:** Abraham Lincoln to David Tod, June 30, 1864, in *CWL*, 7:420. Secretary Welles, reflecting general alarm over Tod's nomination, wrote in his diary, "The President's course is a riddle."

285 **"If you decline":** Nicolay and Hay, *Abraham Lincoln*, 9:99.

285 **"utterly exhausted":** Cook, *Civil War Senator*, 172.

Chapter Fourteen: Staggering Transformation

286　**"A centralization of power":** "The Dead Lion; The Thirty-Seventh Congress—What It Was and What It Did," *New York Times*, Mar. 9, 1863.

286　**Congress adopted a graduated income tax:** See, e.g., Joseph J. Thorndike, "An Army of Officials: The Civil War Bureau of Internal Revenue," Tax History Project, http://www.taxhistory.org /thp/readings.nsf/ArtWeb/FF949517831B181685256E22007840E8?OpenDocument; John Sherman, *Recollections of Forty Years in the House, Senate and Cabinet* (Chicago: Werner, 1895), 1:331; Heather Cox Richardson, *The Greatest Nation of the Earth: Republican Economic Policies During the Civil War* (Cambridge: Harvard University Press, 1997), 132–33; "The Internal Revenue Bill," *New York Herald*, June 27, 1864.

286　**Under the new law:** Treasury Secretary, *Annual Report*, 1864, p. 6; Treasury Secretary, *Annual Report*, 1865, p. 18 ($210 million was collected in fiscal 1865).

286　**raising the average duty to 47 percent:** Theodore E. Burton, *John Sherman* (Boston: Houghton Mifflin, 1908, 119; see also Richardson, *The Greatest Nation of the Earth*, 133. The previous rate on dutiable goods was 37 percent.

286　**"It provided for an increase":** Sherman, *Recollections*, 1:331.

287　**Over the entire war:** James M. McPherson, *Battle Cry of Freedom: The Civil War Era* (New York: Oxford University Press, 1988), 443.

287　**World War I:** Carlos Lozada, "The Economics of World War I," National Bureau of Economic Research *Digest*, January 2005, 3–4. "Taxes" include both internal and external.

287　**"almost unlimited sources of revenue":** Sherman, *Recollections*, 1:332.

287　**industry in the North was thriving:** McPherson, *Battle Cry of Freedom*, 816–18; Paul R. Auerbach and Michael J. Haupert, "Problems in Analyzing Inflation During the Civil War," *Essays in Economic and Business History* (2002): 65.

287　**rate of business incorporation:** Sean Patrick Adams, "Soulless Monsters and Iron Horses," in *Capitalism Takes Command*, ed. Michael Zakim and Gary J. Kornblith (Chicago: University of Chicago Press, 2012), 257.

287　**jockeyed for oil leases:** "The Pennsylvania Oil Regions: 'Rich as Mud,'" *New York Times*, Dec. 20, 1864.

287　**manufacturing was greater in 1864:** McPherson, *Battle Cry of Freedom*, 817.

287　**Exports were vibrant:** Treasury Secretary, *Annual Report*, 1864, pp. 249–50.

287　**Farther uptown, New York opened:** *Strong*, 3:490.

287　**two "distinct" sewing machines:** "An American Invention," *Chicago Daily Tribune*, Dec. 11, 1864; "Local Matters," *Chicago Daily Tribune*, Dec. 11, 1864.

288　**the United States had expended:** Burton, *John Sherman*, 114. Burton says the United States spent $1.8 billion from 1789 through June 30, 1861, and $3.35 billion from then to June 30, 1865.

288　**some thirty-two varieties:** *John Sherman*, 128.

288　**Rebel General Jubal Early:** McPherson, *Battle Cry of Freedom*, 756–57; Ron Chernow, *Grant* (New York: Penguin Press, 2017), 419; Walter A. McDougall, *Throes of Democracy: The American Civil War Era, 1829–1877* (New York: HarperCollins, 2018), 480.

288　**Fessenden by then was in New York:** Arthur Livermark to Pitt Fessenden, July 25, 1864, William Pitt Fessenden Papers, reel 2; "General News," *New York Times*, July 13, 1864; "News from Washington . . . Secretary Fessenden's Visit to New York," *New York Times*, July 18, 1864.

288　**But the banks had lent:** Robert J. Cook, *Civil War Senator: William Pitt Fessenden and the Fight to Save the American Republic* (Baton Rouge: Louisiana State University Press, 2011), 175.

288　**"I am pained to see":** Published letter [correspondent and newspaper illegible], August 1864, Fessenden Papers, reel 3.

288–289　**Congress had authorized the Treasury to issue:** Treasury Secretary, *Annual Report*, 1864, p. 20; Francis Fessenden, *Life and Public Services of William Pitt Fessenden* (Boston: Houghton Mifflin, 1907), 1:369. The authorization was for $200 million, on June 30, 1864.

289　**He could have issued:** Additional five-twenties were similarly authorized on June 30, 1864.

289　**wary of pledging too much gold:** Treasury Secretary, *Annual Report*, 1864, pp. 10, 23. For 1865, Fessenden projected gold revenue from customs at $70 million; most of that—$56 million—was already committed to bondholders.

289　**an attractive interest rate:** For the notes' investment appeal, see Treasury Secretary, *Annual Report*, 1864, p. 20, 22, 23; Fessenden, *Life and Public Services*, 1:338; Henrietta M. Larson, *Jay Cooke, Private Banker* (Cambridge: Harvard University Press, 1936), 163; "7-30-10 Notes and 5-20 Bonds," *New York Times*, Dec. 6, 1864.

289 **"It is *your* war"**: Cook, *Civil War Senator*, 175–76 (emphasis in original). See also Fessenden, *Life and Public Services*, 1:339; "From Washington: Mr. Fessenden's Financial Policy," *New York Times*, July 26, 1864.

289 **But the war years had wearied**: Cook, *Civil War Senator*, 143, 149; Maunsell B. Field, *Memories of Many Men and of Some Women* (New York: Harper and Brothers, 1874), 306; John Niven, *Salmon P. Chase: A Biography* (New York: Oxford University Press, 1995), 257; Fessenden, *Life and Public Services*, 1:317, 325; Sherman, *Recollections*, 1:338.

289 **He had been considering**: Joseph A. Ware to Pitt Fessenden, June 27, 1864, Fessenden Papers, reel 2.

289 **"More depends on you"**: Unknown writer [illegible] to Fessenden, July 9, 1864, Fessenden Papers, reel 2.

289 **The gold price, though receded**: "General News," *New York Times*, Aug. 18, 1864; *Strong*, 3:464, 477.

290 **"Grant must do that"**: Ellis Paxson Oberholtzer, *Jay Cooke: Financier of the Civil War* (Philadelphia: G.W. Jacobs, 1907), 1:412.

290 **"I sigh for State Street"**: Fessenden, *Life and Public Services*, 1:325.

290 **Barely a month into the job**: "General News," *New York Times*, Aug. 13, 1864; "Junketing Congressional Committee Down East," *New York Herald*, Aug. 4, 1864; "Secretary Fessenden," *New York Times*, Aug. 5, 1864. See also William E. Gienapp and Erica L. Gienapp, eds., *The Civil War Diary of Gideon Welles* (Urbana: University of Illinois Press, 2014), 1:467.

290 **increasingly intimate**: Cook, *Civil War Senator*, 176, 182–83.

290 **sales of the seven-thirty**: Fessenden, *Life and Public Services*, 1:342.

290 **"The people are not awake"**: Cook, *Civil War Senator*, 176.

290 **Fessenden reckoned**: Fessenden, *Life and Public Services*, 1:330, 369; this calculation applied to Secretary Fessenden's first trimester, or until October 1, 1864.

290 **he papered the country**: Fessenden also issued "compound notes," a blended security with aspects of debt and currency; see J. W. Schuckers, *The Life and Public Services of Salmon Portland Chase* (New York: D. Appleton, 1874), 412–14.

290 **"certificates of indebtedness"**: Fessenden, *Life and Public Services*, 1:313, 334–35, 345, 354, 373; Richardson, *The Greatest Nation of the Earth*, 61; Mark R. Wilson, *The Business of Civil War: Military Mobilization and the State* (Baltimore: Johns Hopkins University Press, 2006), 115; see also *Cleveland Morning Leader*, Oct. 18, 1864.

290 **permitted unpaid bills to accumulate**: Cook, *Civil War Senator*, 174; Fessenden, *Life and Public Services*, 1:369.

290 **"The pressure for money was unceasing"**: Fessenden, *Life and Public Services*, 1:371.

290 **Congress authorized**: Fessenden, *Life and Public Services*, 345; Salmon P. Chase, *Inside Lincoln's Cabinet: The Civil War Diaries of Salmon P. Chase*, ed. David Herbert Donald (New York: Longman's Green, 1954), 228–29.

291 **"The President told me yesterday"**: John Hay, *Inside Lincoln's White House: The Complete Civil War Diary of John Hay*, ed. Michael Burlingame and John R. Turner Ettlinger (Carbondale: Southern Illinois University Press, 1997), 217.

291 **the Union's trade balance**: Treasury Secretary, *Annual Report*, 1864, p. 242. From a record $58.8 million in 1861, the trade surplus declined in 1862, spiked in 1863 thanks to wheat exports, and plunged to $12.2 million in 1864.

291 **The bullion held in New York banks**: Treasury Secretary, *Annual Report*, 1864, p. 185.

291 **He seems to have been overly impressed**: Cook, *Civil War Senator*, 179.

291 **Edward Atkinson**: Richard H. Abbott, *Cotton and Capital: Boston Businessmen and Antislavery Reform, 1854–1868* (Amherst: University of Massachusetts Press, 1991), 159.

291 **"tainted with treason"**: William Tecumseh Sherman, *Memoirs of General W. T. Sherman*, 2 vols. (1885; repr. New York: Charles L. Webster, 1892), 1:265.

291 **resorted to economic warfare**: Chernow, *Grant*, 476; McPherson, *Battle Cry of Freedom*, 823.

291 **Union exported significantly more bullion**: Treasury Secretary, *Annual Report*, 1864, pp. 183, 185, 243.

291 **"What direction the gold product takes"**: Treasury Secretary, *Annual Report*, 1864, p. 183–85.

292 **In August, the Union general cut**: McPherson, *Battle Cry of Freedom*, 777–78.

292 **"One can almost hear"**: *Chesnut*, 274; see also *Chesnut*, 280.

292 **"no material aid will be derived"**: Eugene M. Lerner, "The Monetary and Fiscal Programs of the Confederate Government, 1861–65," *Journal of Political Economy* 62, no. 6 (1954): 511–12.

292 **Taxes in kind:** *Raleigh Daily Confederate*, May 4, 1864. See also Richard Franklin Bensel, *Yankee Leviathan: The Origins of Central State Authority in America, 1859–1877* (New York: Cambridge University Press, 1990), 159; Lerner, "The Monetary and Fiscal Programs," 513.

292 **"The army . . . is abundantly furnished":** "An Intercepted Rebel Mail," *New York Times*, July 7, 1864.

292 **Fessenden's cotton-trading policy:** See, e.g., Gienapp and Gienapp, *The Civil War Diary of Gideon Welles*, 1:499–500; Cook, *Civil War Senator*, 180.

292 **"the sinews of war":** Gienapp and Gienapp, *The Civil War Diary of Gideon Welles*, 1:533.

293 **Confederate government, which now owned much:** "Cotton: As a Basis for Confederate Currency," *New York Times*, Sept. 25, 1864.

293 **Many of the Treasury agents:** Cook, *Civil War Senator*, 181–82; David G. Surdam, "Traders or Traitors: Northern Cotton Trading During the Civil War," *Business and Economic History* 28, no. 2 (1999).

293 **Fessenden naïvely expressed his shock:** Edward Bates, *The Diary of Edward Bates, 1859–1866*, ed. Howard K. Beale (Washington, D.C.: GPO, 1933), 414.

293 **"Fessenden certainly knows":** Gienapp and Gienapp, *The Civil War Diary of Gideon Welles*, 1:570.

293 **However, responsibility for the policy:** See, e.g., "Executive Order Relative to the Purchase of Products of Insurrectionary States," Sept. 24, 1864, in *CWL*, 8:20–22.

293 **"Let us be thankful":** Abraham Lincoln to Edward R. S. Canby, Dec. 12, 1864, in *CWL*, 8:164.

293 **favors to friends or politicos:** See, e.g., "Recommendation for James Hughes," Oct. 22, 1864, in *CWL*, 8:73, and the plea by John Forney, who wrote Lincoln on behalf of Morris L. Hallowell, an "upright and influential" Cincinnati merchant who was "ruined by the Rebellion," requesting permission for Hallowell to receive Arkansas cotton in payment of a debt. Lincoln advised Fessenden that Hallowell has "a very meritorious cotton-case." (Oct. 3, 1864, *CWL*, 8:35). See also "Recommendation for Mrs. Charlotte Hough," Oct. 3, 1864, in *CWL*, 8:35, and *CWL*, 8:35*n*.

293 **Lincoln's endorsement helped:** "Passes for James W. Singleton," Jan 5, 1865, in *CWL*, 8:200. See also *CWL*, 8:200*n*, citing Browning's Dec. 24, 1864, diary entry recording a conference with Lincoln "about letting Genl Singleton go to Richmond for the purpose of purchasing cotton &c." Browning added in a Jan. 5 entry that he spoke with Lincoln about "permitting Singleton to go South [for] a scheme out of which he, Singleton, Judge [James] Hughes of the Court of Claims, [N.Y.] Senator Morgan, myself and some others, hope to make some money." Finally, see Abraham Lincoln to Ulysses S. Grant, Feb. 7, 1865, in *CWL*, 8:267, and Abraham Lincoln to Ulysses S. Grant, Mar. 8, 1865, in *CWL*, 8:343–44, as well as nn on 8:267, 344, 353.

293 **Leonard Swett:** Abraham Lincoln to William Pitt Fessenden, Sept. 16, 1864, in *CWL*, 8:7 (asking that Swett's partner be appointed cotton agent in Vicksburg). See also *CWL*, 8:8*n*, and Surdam, "Traders or Traitors."

293 **"a worthy gentleman and a friend":** "Recommendation for James Hughes," 8:73. Also worth citing is Lincoln's August 1864 recommendation on behalf of A. J. Hamilton, a Texas Unionist with Seward's backing: see Abraham Lincoln to Edward R. S. Canby, Aug. 9, 1864, in *CWL*, 7:488–89; *CWL*, 8:93–94*n*; Gienapp and Gienapp, *The Civil War Diary of Gideon Welles*, 1:516–17. Welles wrote in his diary, "The President seemed embarrassed [by the favor to Hamilton] but said he believed it was all right." Apparently, either Lincoln or Seward clung to a hope that the cotton scheme would convert "important" Rebels to the Union—a hope that went unfulfilled.

293 **"all kinds of Merchandize":** "Endorsement Concerning Allison C. Poorman," May 15, 1864, in *CWL*, 7:342.

293 **Lincoln requested safe transport:** "Pass for James Harrison," Dec. 22, 1864, in *CWL*, 8:177, and *CWL*, 8:177*n*.

294 **"frequent complaints":** Abraham Lincoln to Edward R. S. Canby, July 25, 1864, in *CWL*, 7:457.

294 **Napoleon J. T. Dana:** *CWL*, 8:202*n*.

294 **Dana's order prompted:** Abraham Lincoln to Napoleon J. T. Dana, Jan. 6, 1865, in *CWL*, 8:201.

294 **"extensive regions lay open":** Don E. Fehrenbacher and Virginia Fehrenbacher, eds., *Recollected Words of Abraham Lincoln* (Stanford, Calif.: Stanford University Press, 1996), 483.

294 **"I do not wish [cotton] to take precedence":** Lincoln to Canby, Dec. 12, 1864, 8:163–64.

294 **Having approved a large shipment:** Abraham Lincoln to Ulysses S. Grant, Feb. 7, 1865, in *CWL*, 8:267.

294 **"You [Grant] must be allowed":** Abraham Lincoln to Ulysses S. Grant, n.d. [after Feb. 7, 1865], in *CWL*, 8:267.

294 **"loaded with sugar and coffee":** *CWL*, 8:267–68*n*.

295 **"Grant has lost prestige":** Oberholtzer, *Jay Cooke: Financier*, 1:415.

295 **Harrington . . . refuted the charge:** "News from Washington: The President's Salary," *New York Times*, Oct. 21, 1864; "President Lincoln's Salary: A Copperhead Lie Squelched," *Cleveland Morning Leader*, Oct. 24, 1864.

295 **After his death, his estate:** Joseph J. Thorndike, "Abraham Lincoln Paid Income Taxes—But He Didn't Have to," Tax History Project, July 2, 2013, at http://www.taxhistory.org/thp/readings.nsf /ArtWeb/4481BB3C2C09C77C85257BE400723DF9?OpenDocument.

295 **"negro mania":** McPherson, *Battle Cry of Freedom*, 768–69.

296 **"We are fighting for independence":** *Burlington* (Vt.) *Free Press*, July 29, 1864. The journalist (also a businessman) was James R. Gilmore, who often went by the name Edmund Kirke. He described his trip in a letter to the *Boston Transcript*, published July 22, 1864; other accounts appeared in the *New York Herald* (July 24, 1864), *Atlantic Monthly* (Sept. 1864), and elsewhere.

296 **Horace Greeley, who in 1862:** On Aug. 20, 1862, a *New York Tribune* editorial assailed Lincoln as "strangely and disastrously remiss" for failing to advance emancipation and for a "mistaken deference to Rebel slavery."

296 **peace talks without preconditions:** Hay, *Inside Lincoln's White House*, 224–27.

296 **"our bleeding, bankrupt, almost dying":** *CWL*, 7:435n.

296 **In mid-July, Greeley involved himself:** See, e.g., Mitchell Snay, *Horace Greeley and the Politics of Reform in Nineteenth Century America* (Lanham, Md.: Rowman & Littlefield, 2011), 152.

296 **"wretched finances":** Strong, 3:470.

296 **"an impossibility":** McPherson, *Battle Cry of Freedom*, 761.

296 **Even Thaddeus Stevens declined:** Richard Current, *Old Thad Stevens: A Story of Ambition* (Madison: University of Wisconsin Press, 1942), 202.

296 **"The conviction is general":** James L. McDonough, *William Tecumseh Sherman: In the Service of My Country; A Life* (New York: W. W. Norton, 2016), 548.

297 **"One of the bluest":** Strong, 3:471.

297 **Lincoln "is already beaten":** Strong, 3:477n; see also Chernow, *Grant*, 439.

297 **"negroes, like other people":** Abraham Lincoln to Charles D. Robinson, Aug. 17, 1864 (unsent draft), in *CWL*, 7:499–500.

297 **Lincoln didn't send this letter:** *CWL*, 7:501–2n.

297 **"The tide is setting":** *CWL*, 7:517–18n (emphasis in original).

298 **"upon the restoration of the Union":** Abraham Lincoln to Henry J. Raymond, Aug. 24, 1864, in *CWL*, 7:517.

298 **"would be worse than losing":** *CWL*, 7:518n. The secretary was John G. Nicolay.

298 **He penned the thought:** "Memorandum Concerning His Probable Failure of Re-Election," Aug. 23, 1864, in *CWL*, 7:514.

298 **sales of the seven-thirty broke:** "News from Washington," *New York Times*, Aug. 30, 1864; "News from Washington," *New York Times*, Aug. 31, 1864.

298 **"Money comes in very slowly":** Cook, *Civil War Senator*, 182–83.

298 **"I do not think":** Oberholtzer, *Jay Cooke: Financier*, 1:434.

298 **issued certificates to suppliers:** Fessenden, *Life and Public Services*, 1:334, 342, 348, 352, 370.

298 **Like his predecessor:** Fessenden issued more than $70 million in so-called temporary loans, which were callable any time on ten days' notice. Fessenden, *Life and Public Services*, 1:335, 348.

298 **swell to $247 million:** Fessenden, *Life and Public Services*, 1:334, 342, 348; the sum was equivalent to 40 percent of the total outstanding Union currency—i.e., of greenbacks, National Bank Notes, and state bank notes.

299 **an embarrassing discount:** Fessenden, *Life and Public Services*, 334, 342, 348, 352, 370.

299 *The Times* **of London judged:** "The Rebel Loan," *New York Times*, Sept. 21, 1864.

299 **above 80 percent of par:** Marc D. Weidenmier, "The Market for Confederate Cotton Bonds," *Explorations in Economic History* 37 (2000): 87.

299 **"immediate efforts . . . for a cessation":** The 1864 Democratic platform is available at https://www .presidency.ucsb.edu/documents/1864-democratic-party-platform.

299 **"Oh, for a great victory":** Fessenden, *Life and Public Services*, 1:342–43.

299 **Seventy million were printed:** John Christopher Schwab, *The Confederate States of America, 1861–1865: A Financial and Industrial History of the South During the Civil War* (1901; repr., New York: Burt Franklin, 1968), 67.

299 **Their value collapsed:** Rose Razaghian, "Financial Civil War: The Confederacy's Financial Policies, 1861–1864," Yale ICF Working Paper, No. 04-45, 29. See also *Ruffin*, 3:660; McPherson, *Battle Cry of Freedom*, 778.

299 **The government manufactured so many bills:** Razaghian, "Financial Civil War," 13.

300 **set up makeshift printing:** Lerner, "The Monetary and Fiscal Programs," 521.

300 **Trenholm, the new Treasury secretary:** "Our Southern Files: Financial Condition of the Rebel States," *New York Times*, Sept. 12, 1864; "The Finances of the Rebel Confederacy," *New York Times*, Nov. 13, 1864.

300 **Farmers and tradespeople refused:** "New Way to Pay Public Debts," *New York Times*, Oct. 27, 1864; "Confederate Credit and Discredit," *New York Times*, Sept. 14, 1864.

300 **"the wealthy consume their capital":** *Richmond Enquirer*, Sept. 23, 1864.

300 **Greeley did a volte-face:** Snay, *Horace Greeley and the Politics of Reform*, 151.

300 **Chase campaigned for his former boss:** Niven, *Chase: A Biography*, 373.

300 **"ever erred":** Hans L. Trefousse, *Thaddeus Stevens: Nineteenth-Century Egalitarian* (Chapel Hill: University of North Carolina Press, 1997), 149.

300 **Fessenden had reluctantly decided:** Fessenden, *Life and Public Services*, 1:348.

300 **the Treasury secretary offered $32 million:** Treasury Secretary, *Annual Report*, 1864, p. 21. The first offering (which slightly oversold) furnished $33 million; the second, in October, $40 million.

300 **"It is a great success":** Fessenden, *Life and Public Services*, 1:348–49.

300 **The biggest purchaser:** Cook, *Civil War Senator*, 183.

300 **also strong in Europe:** Treasury Secretary, *Annual Report*, 1864, p. 14; "The Financial Success of the Government," *Cleveland Morning Leader*, Sept 12, 1864; *Strong*, 3:500n.

301 **Fessenden's thoughts turned to Europe:** Cook, *Civil War Senator*, 183; Fessenden, *Life and Public Services*, 1:352.

301 **gradually accelerated:** David Kelley Thomson, "Bonds of War: The Evolution of World Financial Markets in the Civil War Era" (PhD diss., University of Georgia, 2016), 158, 162.

301 **The two had fashioned:** Cook, *Civil War Senator*, 141.

301 **lobbying for the chief justice job:** Chase, *Inside Lincoln's Cabinet*, 240.

301 **three-quarters of active soldiers:** James M. McPherson, "No Peace Without Victory, 1861–1865," *American Historical Review*, February 2004, 14; the figure reflects votes cast by soldiers in military camps.

301 **"Mr. Lincoln has steadily drawn":** James Russell Lowell, "The President's Policy," *North American Review* 98 (Jan. 1864).

302 **Lincoln's appeal continued to be weakest:** McPherson, *Battle Cry of Freedom*, 805.

302 **He was concerned that the court:** Fehrenbacher and Fehrenbacher, *Recollected Words of Abraham Lincoln*, 38.

302 **Chase would presumably support him:** Chase had commented the previous spring, "I do not agree with you in thinking that the constitution prohibits the issue of legal tender notes": Salmon Chase to Jesse Baldwin, May 18, 1864, in *SPCP*, 4:383–84.

302 **"Probably no other man":** Michael Burlingame, ed., *With Lincoln in the White House: Letters, Memoranda, and Other Writings of John G. Nicolay, 1860–1865* (Carbondale: Southern Illinois University Press, 2000), 166.

303 **Lincoln's Annual Message:** Annual Message to Congress, Dec. 6, 1864, in *CWL*, 8:136–53.

303 **"condition of prosperity":** *CWL*, 8:145.

303 **"material resources":** *CWL*, 8:151.

303 **"venture[d] to recommend":** *CWL*, 8:149.

303 **more than $2 billion:** "From Washington: The National Finances," *New York Times*, Feb. 14, 1865.

303 **thirty times larger:** Treasury Secretary, *Annual Report*, 1860, p. 6; Treasury Secretary, *Annual Report*, 1861, p. 23.

303 **"a substantial branch of national":** "Annual Message to Congress," 8:143.

303 **"Men readily perceive":** "Annual Message to Congress," 8:143.

303 **"The more nearly this property":** "Annual Message to Congress," 8:143.

304 **"enable every prudent person":** "Annual Message to Congress," 8:143.

304 **Fessenden asked Congress to impose:** Treasury Secretary, *Annual Report*, 1864, p. 24.

304 **Five hundred and eighty-four banks:** "Annual Message to Congress," 8:143.

304 **one hundred in New York State:** Annual Report of Comptroller of the Currency, in Treasury Secretary, *Annual Report*, 1864, p. 46; see also David M. Gische, "The New York City Banks and the Development of the National Banking System 1860–1870," *The American Journal of Legal History* 23. no. 1 (1979): 57–58.

305 **The negotiations were difficult:** Oberholtzer, *Jay Cooke: Financier*, 1:444–45, 453–58, 460–61.

305 **The banker recruited Sherman:** Oberholtzer, *Jay Cooke: Financier*, 461–62.

305 **Their sales amounted to a trickle:** Fessenden sold $100 million of the ten-forties over his first twenty-seven weeks, or just over $525,000 a day (Fessenden, *Life and Public Services,* 1:359), and $771,000 per day of the seven-thirties prior to signing Cooke. Federal expenses were on the order of $2 million a day; in addition, Fessenden faced substantial debt repayments.

305 **"I have very little doubt":** Oberholtzer, *Jay Cooke: Financier,* 1:462–63; Cooke's informant was John A. Stewart, who had replaced Cisco.

305 **"disappointingly small":** Oberholtzer, *Jay Cooke: Financier,* 1:469.

305 **Fessenden quietly arranged:** "By Telegraph: Mr. Fessenden Unanimously Nominated," *Portland* (Me.) *Daily Press,* Jan. 6, 1865; "Hood's Escape . . . The Maine Senatorship," *New York Times,* Jan. 6, 1865.

305 **The price of wheat:** Razaghian, "Financial Civil War," 13.

305 **A barrel of flour:** *RWCD* (1866), 2:386.

306 **One scholar calculates:** Eugene M. Lerner, "Money, Prices, and Wages in the Confederacy, 1861–65," *Journal of Political Economy* 63, no. 1 (1955): 24–25; after dipping earlier in 1864, inflation in the South seems to have reaccelerated rapidly in the fall.

306 **"the thin and haggard cheek":** "Savannah: The Relief Movement," *New York Herald,* Jan. 29, 1965.

306 **set up headquarters at his other plantation:** Amy Chambliss, "Edmund Ruffin of Virginia," *The Georgia Review* 14, no. 4 (1960): 431.

306 **Sensing the downfall:** *Ruffin,* 3:745.

306 **He suffered recurring doubts:** *Ruffin,* 3:xxix, xxx.

306 **"The deep waters are closing over us":** *Chesnut,* 295.

306 **had to stop paying the troops:** Lerner, "The Monetary and Fiscal Programs," 521; see also Unsigned letter to Jefferson Davis, Sept. 7, 1864, in *Davis Papers,* 11:19.

306 **already on tight rations:** Lerner, "The Monetary and Fiscal Programs," 518.

306 **wanted even for soap:** *RWCD* (1866), 2:406.

306 **one-seventh of the market price:** "Confederate Confessions," *New York Times,* Nov. 15, 1864; see also *Ruffin,* 3:616–17.

306 **Farmers, when they could, refused to sell:** "Confederate Confessions."

306 **"Cotton, Bacon or Salted Pork":** *Raleigh Daily Confederate,* Jan. 20, 1865.

307 **"payable in provisions, or in cotton cloth":** *Raleigh Daily Confederate,* Jan. 17, 1865.

307 **impressment agents scavenging the countryside:** See, e.g., *Ruffin,* 3:717.

307 **"Our whole male population":** "From the South: Spirit of the Southern Press; Furious Tirades Against Davis," *New York Times,* Jan. 19, 1865, quoting *Charlottesville* (Va.) *Chronicle.*

307 **"prolific of mischiefs":** Lerner, "The Monetary and Fiscal Programs," 521.

307 **He acknowledged that the recent reforms:** Lerner, "The Monetary and Fiscal Programs," 522.

307 **"We want a measure of value":** "The Rebel Finances; A Letter from Secretary Trenholm," *New York Times,* Dec. 18, 1864.

307 **"the Treasury will be completely empty":** Lerner, "The Monetary and Fiscal Programs," 521.

307 **The only buyers in bulk:** The N.C. Railroad Co. repeatedly advertised that it was seeking to hire five hundred Negroes; see, e.g., *Raleigh Daily Confederate,* Jan. 6, 1865.

307 NEGROES FOR HIRE AND SALE: See, e.g., *Richmond Daily Dispatch.*

308 **rewards for runaways:** *Richmond Daily Dispatch* of Jan. 13, 1865, advertised rewards for multiple runaways at, respectively, $25 (for a nine-year-old boy), $250, $300, and $500; see also "Wanted: The Negro Caught" in that newspaper's Jan. 6, 1865, edition.

308 **Similar rewards were quoted for horses:** *Raleigh Daily Confederate,* Jan. 12, 1865, offering $500; *Richmond Daily Dispatch,* Jan. 16, 1865, offering $300.

308 **the equivalent of four barrels of flour:** On Feb. 11, 1865, Jones cited a slave price of five thousand in notes: *RWCD* (1866), 2:417. His most recent quote for flour, on Jan. 18, was $1250.

308 **General Lee advised:** Allen C. Guelzo, "Robert E. Lee and Slavery," Encyclopedia Virginia, https://www.encyclopediavirginia.org/Lee_Robert_E_and_Slavery#start_entry; see also *Davis Papers,* v. 11.

308 **unfit for soldiering:** "The Impolicy of the Proposed Plan of Arming the Slave Population of the South," *Richmond Enquirer,* Nov. 2, 1864.

308 **"abolition doctrine":** *North Carolina Standard,* Jan. 18, 1865.

308 **"If slaves will make good soldiers":** Howell Cobb to James A. Seddon, Jan. 8, 1865, Encyclopedia Virginia, https://www.encyclopediavirginia.org/Letter_from_Howell_Cobb_to_James_A_Seddon_January_8_1865.

308 **southern newspapers were openly debating:** "How to Reinforce the Army," *Charlotte Western Democrat*, Sept. 20, 1864; "Arming the Slaves," *North Carolina Standard*, Nov. 4, 1864; and "Negro Soldiers," *Edgefield (S.C.) Advertiser*, Jan. 18, 1865.

308 **"One thing is evident":** "Conscription of Negroes," *Raleigh Daily Confederate*, Jan. 12, 1865, quoting Wilmington *Carolinian*.

308 **"as a reward for faithful service":** Frank E. Vandiver, "Jefferson Davis—Leader Without Legend," *The Journal of Southern History* 43, no. 1 (1977): 13–14.

308 **Early in 1865, Lee publicly endorsed:** *North Carolina Standard*, Feb. 21, 1865.

308 **With Davis's support:** McPherson, *Battle Cry of Freedom*, 836–37.

309 **"The negro is free":** Sherman, *Memoirs of Gen. W. T. Sherman*, 250. For Sherman's order, see *Memoirs of Gen. W. T. Sherman*, 247–50; Chernow, *Grant*, 471; McPherson, *Battle Cry of Freedom*, 841–42; Willie Lee Rose, *Rehearsal for Reconstruction: The Port Royal Experiment* (New York: Oxford University Press, 1976), 325–27, 330.

309 **"Federal troops, white and colored":** "Fort Fisher: Details of the Victory," *New York Times*, Jan. 19, 1865.

309 **"No more cotton goes out":** "Wilmington: The Rebel Accounts," *New York Herald*, Jan. 20, 1865, quoting *Richmond Enquirer*.

309 **"cannot fight and stay at home":** "Speech to One Hundred Fortieth Indiana Regiment," Mar. 17, 1865 (newspaper version), in *CWL*, 8:362.

310 **By March, Richmond was suffering:** *Richmond Daily Dispatch*, Mar. 31, 1865.

310 **The society doyenne:** *Chesnut*, 317.

310 **quoted at one seventy-sixth:** "The Gold Market," *Richmond Daily Dispatch*, Jan. 21, 1865.

310 **General Lee himself:** Chernow, *Grant*, 514.

310 **Even the cotton bonds:** Weidenmier, "The Market for Confederate Cotton Bonds," 85, 87.

310 **"We have to reach the bottom":** "Speech to One Hundred Fortieth Indiana Regiment," Mar. 17, 1865, 8:361.

310 **Lincoln urged his Treasury secretary:** Gabor S. Boritt, *Lincoln and the Economics of the American Dream* (Memphis: Memphis State University Press, 1978), 206.

310 **Perhaps embarrassed at having awarded:** The terms were disclosed in Fessenden's Jan. 28, 1865, letter to Cooke: see Oberholtzer, *Jay Cooke: Financier*, 1:471–73.

310 **vigorous arm-twisting by Lincoln:** McDougall, *Throes of Democracy*, 487.

311 **"the original disturbing cause":** "Response to a Serenade," Feb. 1, 1865, in *CWL*, 8:254; see also "The Abolition of Slavery: The Amendment Ratified by Rhode Island, Michigan and Illinois; Speech of Mr. Lincoln on the Constitutional Amendment," *New York Herald*, Feb. 3, 1865.

311 **Demand for Union paper soared:** Thomson, "Bonds of War," 185–86.

311 **Cooke was besting Fessenden's target:** "U.S. Bond Sales," *Cleveland Morning Leader*, Feb. 7, 1865. Sales of the seven-thirties topped $3 million a day. The previous November, Fessenden told Cooke he needed to sell $1.5 to $2 million a day.

311 **Cooke literally bought:** David K. Thomson, "'Like a Cord Through the Whole Country': Union Bonds and Financial Mobilization for Victory," *The Journal of the Civil War Era* 6, no. 3 (2016): 364.

311 **"needlewomen" and "mechanics":** Oberholtzer, *Jay Cooke: Financier*, 1:486.

311 **Chase purchased $20,000 worth:** Oberholtzer, *Jay Cooke: Financier*, 1:488–89.

311 **On February 15, sales reached:** "Immense Sale of Seven-Thirties," *New York Times*, Feb. 16, 1865.

311 **three thousand small investors:** "The Seven-Thirty Loan," *New York Times*, Feb. 17, 1865.

311 **Black recruits in Pennsylvania:** Thomson, "'Like a Cord Through the Whole Country,'" 362.

311 **southerners in occupied Arkansas and Louisiana:** "The Finances," *New York Times*, Apr. 8, 1865.

311 **"Night agencies":** Thomson, "'Like a Cord Through the Whole Country,'" 365.

311 **The seven-thirty reached:** Thomson, "'Like a Cord Through the Whole Country,'" 366.

311 **"more than all the generals":** Oberholtzer, *Jay Cooke: Financier*, 1:494–95.

312 **"The efforts of the Yankees":** "The South: Rebel News, Rumors and Speculations," *New York Times*, Feb. 24, 1865, quoting *Richmond Examiner*.

312 **Sales of the seven-thirty skyrocketed:** Oberholtzer, *Jay Cooke: Financier*, 1:507–8.

312 **An estimated thirty thousand people:** Chernow, *Grant*, 475.

312 **"Mud, (and such mud!)":** [Walt Whitman], "Washington: The Last Hours of Congress—Washington Crowds, and the President," *New York Times*, Mar. 12, 1865.

312 **a spiritual journey:** McDougall, *Throes of Democracy*, 489.

312 **"wear as well as"**: John Williams, "Twenty-Four Tense Hours in Abraham Lincoln's Life," *New York Times*, Feb. 23, 2020.

313 **"All knew"**: "Second Inaugural Address," in *CWL*, 8:332–33.

313 **After the inauguration**: McCulloch took office on Mar. 9.

313 **"Hurry up the sales"**: Oberholtzer, *Jay Cooke: Financier*, 1:513; see also 1:508–12.

313 **the gold price had barely budged**: "General News," *New York Times*, Jan. 28, 1865; "Evening Exchange," *New York Times*, Feb. 26, 1865.

313 **"We must accept the fact"**: "The Gold Question," *New York Times*, Feb. 26, 1865.

313 **Through the first week of March**: "Monetary Affairs," *New York Times*, Mar. 9, 1865; "Local News," *New York Times*, Mar. 25, 1865.

314 **Wall Street cried "panic"**: "Local News," *New York Times*, Mar. 19, 1865; "The Financial Panic," *New York Times*, Mar. 22, 1865.

314 **$4 or $5 million worth a day**: "7-30 Loan," *Cleveland Morning Leader*, Mar. 15, 1865; "From Kentucky . . . The Seven-Thirty Loan," *New York Times*, Mar. 16, 1865; "The New 7-30 Loan," *Cleveland Morning Leader*, Mar. 17, 1865.

314 **the roads at Petersburg improving**: "From the Petersburg Front," *Richmond Whig*, Mar. 22, 1865. See also "The News," *Richmond Daily Dispatch*, Mar. 22, 1865; *"From the Army Before Richmond,"* Portland (Me.) *Daily Press*, Mar. 22, 1865.

314 **"the nation is able to bear"**: Richardson, *The Greatest Nation of the Earth*, 64.

314 **towering sum of $2.68 billion**: Treasury Secretary, *Annual Report*, 1865, p. 18; Treasury Secretary, *Annual Report*, 1860, p. 22.

314 **Yet with all its borrowing**: Recall that at the end of the Buchanan administration, the United States had struggled to raise funds at 12 percent interest. By 1865, the Union's 6 percent bonds were trading at a premium.

314 **thousands of claims for homesteads**: Rick Beard, "Westward, Ho!" *New York Times*, May 20, 2012; 26,500 claims had been filed by the war's end.

315 **"We simply must begin with"**: "Last Public Address," Apr. 11, 1865, in *CWL*, 8:400–401 ("mould" is used in the original). In this speech, Lincoln discussed his thoughts on Reconstruction.

315 **he told an Alabaman**: Fehrenbacher and Fehrenbacher, *Recollected Words of Abraham Lincoln*, 30.

315 **he wanted southerners back at work**: *Recollected Words of Abraham Lincoln*, 404.

315–316 **"great enterprise"**: "Annual Message to Congress," Dec. 6, 1864, 8:146, 147–48.

316 **"Tell the miners for me"**: Boritt, *Lincoln and the Economics of the American Dream*, 226.

316 **thinking of relocating to California**: Fehrenbacher and Fehrenbacher, *Recollected Words of Abraham Lincoln*, 55.

Chapter Fifteen: Epilogue

317 **"It must be admitted"**: *Strong*, 3:580.

317 **"I am stunned"**: *Strong*, 582.

317 **"The middle-class country"**: "Abraham Lincoln, (15 April 1865) Eulogy by Ralph Waldo Emerson," https://www.rwe.org/abraham-lincoln-15-april-1865-eulogy-by-ralph-waldo-emerson.

318 **"for Lincoln the vital test"**: Richard Hofstadter, *The American Political Tradition and the Men Who Made It* (1948; repr., New York: Vintage, 1989), 135.

318 **80 percent inflation**: This figure refers to consumer prices. Many scholars give a range of values, generally coalescing around 75–80 percent. See Mark R. Wilson, *The Business of Civil War: Military Mobilization and the State* (Baltimore: Johns Hopkins University Press, 2006), 299; Paul R. Auerbach and Michael J. Haupert, "Problems in Analyzing Inflation During the Civil War," *Essays in Economic and Business History* (2002): 65; James M. McPherson, *Battle Cry of Freedom: The Civil War Era* (New York: Oxford University Press, 1988), 447; Walter A. McDougall, *Throes of Democracy: The American Civil War Era, 1829–1877* (New York: HarperCollins, 2018), 457. According to Auerbach and Haupert, *wholesale* prices in the North doubled during the war.

318 **greenbacks amounted to only a sixth**: Bray Hammond, *Sovereignty and an Empty Purse: Banks and Politics in the Civil War* (Princeton, N.J.: Princeton University Press, 1970), 252.

318 **two world wars**: According to the Bureau of Labor Statistics ("One Hundred Years of Price Change: The Consumer Price Index and the American Inflation Experience"), from Dec. 1916 to June 1920, consumer prices rose by just over 80 percent. Price indices during World War II were distorted by the imposition of price controls. According to the BLS, prices rose 76 percent from 1941 to 1951, a

period that captures the inflation after the expiration of controls as well as a subsequent deflation. According to "U.S. Inflation Calculator," inflation from 1940 to 1948 was 72 percent.

318 **9000 percent:** Eugene M. Lerner says the price index in the South rose 92 times: see "Money, Prices, and Wages in the Confederacy, 1861–65," *Journal of Political Economy* 63, no. 1 (1955): 24.

318 **moved to retire greenbacks:** Jeffry A. Frieden, *Currency Politics: The Political Economy of Exchange Rate Policy* (Princeton, N.J.: Princeton University Press, 2014), 68.

318 **some $431 million:** Treasury Secretary, *Annual Report*, 1865, p. 96.

318 **McCulloch quickly reduced:** Treasury Secretary, *Annual Report*, 1868, p. 24.

318 **enacted a law to stop McCulloch:** Frieden, *Currency Politics*, 71–72.

319 **The debate over the greenback:** See, e.g., *Currency Politics*, 62–72.

319 **"A fearless and sagacious secretary":** Mark A. Neels, "'A Just Application of Democratic Principles': The Fiscal Conservatism of Salmon P. Chase," *Journal of the Abraham Lincoln Association* 39, no. 1 (2018): 44.

319 **As Treasury secretary, Chase had stated:** Salmon Chase to Jesse Baldwin, May 18, 1864, in *SPCP*, 4, 383–84. Chase's exact words are worth quoting: "I do not agree with you in thinking that the Constitution prohibits the issue of legal tender notes." See also John Sherman, *Recollections of Forty Years in the House, Senate and Cabinet* (Chicago: Werner, 1895), 1:344*n*.

319 **"For more than a quarter of a century":** Neels, "'A Just Application of Democratic Principles,'" 32.

319 **a wealthy Kentuckian:** *Hepburn v. Griswold*, 75 U.S. 603 (1870).

320 **the reconstituted court reversed:** *Knox v. Lee*, 79 U.S. 457 (1871).

321 **Defaults were rare:** Matthew S. Jaremski, "National Banking's Role in U.S. Industrialization, 1850–1900," National Bureau of Economic Research Working Paper, 2 (later published in *The Journal of Economic History* 74, no. 1 [2014], 109–40).

321 **the interior suffered money shortages:** David M. Gische, "The New York City Banks and the Development of the National Banking System 1860–1870," *The American Journal of Legal History* 23. no 1 (1979): 62.

321 **Banks became the veritable engine:** Jaremski, "National Banking's Role," 3, reporting that counties with banks industrialized more rapidly.

321 **thirty years of *deflation*:** Milton Friedman and Anna Schwartz, *A Monetary History of the United States, 1867–1960* (Princeton, N.J.: Princeton University Press, 1963), 24, 41, 91.

321 **more concentrated in New York:** Gische, "The New York City Banks," 60. See also Robert P. Sharkey in David T. Gilchrist and W. David Lewis, eds., *Economic Change in the Civil War Era*, ed. David T. Gilchrist and W. David Lewis (Greenville, Del.: Eleutherian Mills-Hagley Foundation, 1965), 25–28.

322 **the Republicans solidly aligned:** Duties remained at a highly protectionist level until the Woodrow Wilson era: see Douglas A. Irwin, *Clashing over Commerce: A History of U.S. Trade Policy* (Chicago: University of Chicago Press, 2017), 254–56; Marc Egnal, *Clash of Extremes: The Economic Origins of the Civil War* (New York: Farrar, Straus, and Giroux, 2009), 370.

322 **the government reaped large surpluses:** Treasury Secretary, *Annual Report*, 1870, p. iii.

322 **a choice that epitomized the party's retreat:** See, e.g., Joseph J. Thorndike, "An Army of Officials: The Civil War Bureau of Internal Revenue," Tax History Project, http://www.taxhistory.org/thp /readings.nsf/ArtWeb/FF949517831B181685256E22007840E8?OpenDocument.

322 **The Lincoln administration bequeathed:** See, e.g., "An Army of Officials: The Civil War Bureau of Internal Revenue" and Richard Franklin Bensel, *Yankee Leviathan: The Origins of Central State Authority in America, 1859–1877* (New York: Cambridge University Press, 1990), 248.

322 **allocating $30 million annually:** Treasury Secretary, *Annual Report*, 1872, p. viii.

322 **a swiftly escalating sum:** In 1872, annual pension expenses were estimated at $30 million (Treasury Secretary, *Annual Report*, 1872, p. viii); in 1892 they were $135 million (Treasury Secretary, *Annual Report*, 1892, p. xxi).

323 **Federal budgets:** Treasury Secretary, *Annual Reports*, various years. The figures do not include debt repayments.

323 **To pay for this expanded state:** Treasury Secretary, *Annual Reports*, various years. Internal taxes in the mid-1890s reached $150 million, the same order of magnitude as the tariff.

323 **The seven-thirty Treasury drive raised $830 million:** Treasury Secretary, *Annual Report*, 1865, p. 17.

323 **the largest financing in the country's history:** Ellis Paxson Oberholtzer, *Jay Cooke: Financier of the Civil War* (Philadelphia: G.W. Jacobs, 1907), 1:478, 507.

323 **Improbably, they continued to trade:** Marc D. Weidenmier, "The Market for Confederate Cotton Bonds," *Explorations in Economic History* 37 (2000): 94.

323 **The U.S. debt peaked:** Treasury Secretary, *Annual Report*, 1870, p. xxv; Treasury Secretary, *Annual Report*, 1880, p. iv.

324 **government had deeded 270 million acres:** Rick Beard, "Westward, Ho!" *New York Times*, May 20, 2012.

324 **1.7 million students:** Congressional Research Service, "The U.S. Land-Grant University System: An Overview," Aug. 29, 2019, 3.

325 **number and diversity of line items:** Treasury Secretary, *Annual Report*, 1892, p. xxiii.

325 **Illinois senator Lyman Trumbull:** Adam Rowe, "The Paradox of Union: The Civil War and the Transformation of American Democracy" (PhD diss., University of Chicago, 2018), 281, 288–89.

325 **"such title as the United States can convey":** "Law Creating the Freedmen's Bureau," Freedmen and Southern Society Project, http://www.freedmen.umd.edu/fbact.htm.

326 **"If we do not furnish them":** Donald K. Pickens, "The Republican Synthesis and Thaddeus Stevens," *Civil War History* 31, no. 1 (1985): 72.

326 **"government existed to protect property":** Pickens, "The Republican Synthesis and Thaddeus Stevens," 66.

326 **"freedom and famine":** David W. Blight, *Frederick Douglass: Prophet of Freedom* (New York: Simon & Schuster, 2018), 556.

326 **Congress moved cautiously on land reform:** Pickens, "The Republican Synthesis and Thaddeus Stevens," 71.

326 **"We shall not approach":** Egnal, *Clash of Extremes*, 332.

326 **the administration restored lands to previous owners:** Egnal, *Clash of Extremes*, 332.

326 **"With help and striving, the Negro":** "The Freedmen's Bureau," *Atlantic Monthly*, March 1901, 354–65.

327 **Blacks in Georgia acquired:** "The Freedmen's Bureau"; the figure for Black ownership was tallied in 1874. Georgia's total farmland was 26 million acres, as per U.S. Census Bureau, "Agriculture, Year Ending June 1, 1860," 1860, 22, 26.

327 **defected to the Liberal Republican Party:** Egnal, *Clash of Extremes*, 336.

327 **Only about 10 percent:** Gary M. Walton and Hugh Rockoff, *History of the American Economy*, 11th ed. (Mason, Ohio: South-Western/Cengage Learning, 2010), 256–57.

327 **a state of legal adjudication:** Willie Lee Rose, *Rehearsal for Reconstruction: The Port Royal Experiment* (New York: Oxford University Press, 1976), 350.

327 **Johnson granted a blanket amnesty:** "President Johnson's Amnesty Proclamation," *New York Times*, May 30, 1865.

327 **"Secesh are coming back thick":** Rose, *Rehearsal for Reconstruction*, 346.

328 **Johnson ordered Howard:** Rose, *Rehearsal for Reconstruction*, 352–53.

328 **the President's meaning was clear:** Rose, *Rehearsal for Reconstruction*, 353.

328 **"Why, General Howard":** Rose, *Rehearsal for Reconstruction*, 353.

328 **U.S. military forces:** Rose, *Rehearsal for Reconstruction*, 377.

328 **Freedmen in the islands closest:** Rose, *Rehearsal for Reconstruction*, 385–86.

328 **excise taxes on whiskey and tobacco:** In 1885, federal internal revenue totaled $112 million, of which $67.5 million derived from excise taxes on spirits and $26.4 million on tobacco: Treasury Secretary, *Annual Report*, 1885, p. xxxvii.

328 **the South received less than 10 percent:** I'm indebted to Adam Rowe, who unearthed this nugget from a musty edition of C. Vann Woodward's *Reunion and Reaction: The Compromise of 1877 and the End of Reconstruction* (Boston: Little, Brown, 1951), 58–59.

329 **excluded Confederate soldiers:** National Archives and Records Administration, https://www.archives.gov/files/research/military/civil-war/confederate/confederate-pensions.pdf.

329 **fallen to half that of 1860:** McPherson, *Battle Cry of Freedom*, 818–19.

329 **Over the same decade, the southern share:** McPherson, *Battle Cry of Freedom*, 819.

329 **plunged in the South by 40 percent:** Walton and Rockoff, *History of the American Economy*, 249–50; the drop in commodity production occurred from 1860 to 1870.

329 **personal income per capita in Dixie:** Kris James Mitchener and Ian W. McClean, "U.S. Regional Growth and Convergence, 1880–1980," *Journal of Economic History* 59, no. 4 (1999): 1033, 1019.

329 **incomes grew at only half the rate:** Walton and Rockoff, *History of the American Economy*, 250; their figures refer to per capita income over the period 1879–1899.

330 **most southerners worked on farms:** Just under 40 percent of the U.S. population lived on farms in 1900, and 60 percent of the U.S. population was rural (Carolyn Dimitri, Anne Effland, and Neilson Conklin, "The Twentieth Century Transformation of U.S. Agriculture and Farm Policy," USDA Economic Research Service, Economic Information Bulletin no. 3, June 2005, 3). The share in the South was vastly higher. For instance, fully 90 percent of North Carolina was rural in 1900 (U.S. Census Bureau, "Statistics for North Carolina, Supplement for North Carolina," 1910, 570).

330 **30 percent less than in 1860:** Walton and Rockoff, *History of the American Economy*, 252–53.

330 **Southern farmers worked with inferior tools:** Mitchener and McClean, "U.S. Regional Growth and Convergence," 1032.

330 **cotton production did not return to its previous high:** *Statistical Abstract of the United States*, 1896 (19th number), 282.

330 **surprisingly primitive:** "Agriculture 1950, Changes in Agriculture 1900 to 1950," 69, https:// www2.census.gov/prod2/decennial/documents/41667073v5p6ch4.pdf.

330 **As late as 1920:** "Agriculture 1950, Changes in Agriculture 1900 to 1950," 80. Also evidencing lack of investment, farm values in the South were only 40 percent of the U.S. average (*Statistical Abstract of the United States*, 1896, 337).

330 **Southern industry:** Walton and Rockoff, *History of the American Economy*, 252–53.

330 **Three decades after the war:** *Statistical Abstract of the United States*, 1898 (21st number), 356.

330 **national banks in the eleven:** *Statistical Abstract of the United States*, 1896, 54–55.

330 **Three-quarters of northern children:** These educational measurements come from *Statistical Abstract of the United States*, 1898, 379–80; "southern" schools refer to those in the former Confederacy; "northern" denote those in nonslave states at the time of the war.

331 **In 1940, per capita income:** Mitchener and McClean, "U.S. Regional Growth and Convergence," 1019. As late as 1953 (ninety years after the Emancipation Proclamation), median income for males was $3221 in the entire United States but only $2317 in the South, according to the U.S. Census Bureau.

332 **"more than sufficed all the needs":** Phil Leigh, "The Cotton Bond Bubble," *New York Times*, Jan. 30, 2013.

332 **Benjamin "cheerfully start[ed] all over":** Ruth Bader Ginsburg, "Four Louisiana Giants in the Law," Memorial Lecture Series, Loyola University New Orleans, Feb. 4, 2002, http://www.laed .uscourts.gov/court-history/law-giants.

332 **"Like Moses and Washington":** Widely quoted from Jay Cooke, "Jay Cooke's Memoir" (manuscript), Baker Business Special Collections, Harvard University, Cambridge, Mass., 2.

333 **she was often compared:** Mary A. DeCredico's biography (*Mary Boykin Chesnut: A Confederate Woman's Life* [Lanham, Md.: Rowman & Littlefield, 2002], xv) says "the record of her life could have served as a model for Margaret Mitchell as she created her much-loved heroine." See also Anna Braunscheidel, "Will the Real Miss Scarlett Please Stand Up: How the Life of Mary Boykin Chesnut Can Be Considered a Model for Margaret Mitchell's Scarlett O'Hara" (master's thesis, Clemson University, 2012).

334 **novelized but also acclaimed:** William Styron called it "a great epic drama of our greatest national tragedy"; the 1981 edition, edited by the historian C. Vann Woodward, won the Pulitzer Prize.

334 **"whole remaining capital":** For Edmund Ruffin's final musings and his preparation for suicide, see *Ruffin*, 3:xxi, xxvi, xvii, 392, 577, 602, 797, 829, 830, 846, 848, 935, 945–46.

334 **the acidic Tidewater soils:** Robert J. Brugger, "Redmoor Farewell: The Life and Death of Edmund Ruffin," *VQR*, Summer 1991.

334 **In his room upstairs:** Brugger, "Redmoor Farewell." See also "The Suicide of Ruffin: The Man Who Fired the First Gun on Fort Sumter Blows His Brains Out; He Prefers Death to Living Under the Government of the United States," *New York Times*, June 22, 1865; Harry Kollatz Jr., "An Unyielding Man," Richmondmag, Apr. 26, 2011, richmondmag.com.

Illustration Credits

page 1 (top): Abraham Lincoln: president-elect, by Samuel G. Alschuler, 1860. Library of Congress, Prints and Photographs Division, LC-USZ62-15984.

page 1 (bottom left): Portrait of Salmon P. Chase, by Henry Ulke, U.S. Department of the Treasury.

page 1 (bottom right): Justin Smith Morrill of Vermont, created between 1855 and 1865. Brady-Handy photograph collection, Library of Congress, Prints and Photographs Division, LC-DIG-cwpbh-01804.

page 2 (top left): Thaddeus Stevens of Pennsylvania, created between 1860 and 1875. Brady-Handy photograph collection, Library of Congress, Prints and Photographs Division, LC-DIG-cwpbh-00460.

page 2 (right): Portrait of Jay Cooke taken during the Civil War (exact date unknown), by Wenderoth & Taylor. *The Century* magazine, vol. 73.

page 2 (bottom left): Journalist and abolitionist Horace Greeley wearing hat, created between 1860 and 1872. Library of Congress, Prints and Photographs Division, LC-DIG-ppmsca-49763.

page 3 (top): A one-dollar legal tender note from the Series 1862–1863 greenback issue, by National Banknote Company. National Numismatic Collection, National Museum of American History.

page 3 (bottom): Courtesy of the collection of the Massachusetts Historical Society. William Pitt Fessenden, from Portraits of American Abolitionists (a collection of images of individuals representing a broad spectrum of viewpoints in the slavery debate), Mass. Historical Society. Photo. 81.235.

page 4 (top): Elevation of dome of U.S. Capitol, by Thomas Ustick Walter, 1859. Library of Congress, Prints and Photographs Division, LC-USZ62-4701.

page 4 (bottom): Map of the central portion of the United States showing the lines of the proposed Pacific railroads, New York, c. 1857. Library of Congress, Geography and Map Division, G3701.P3 185-.M3.

page 5 (top): Camp scene at Fort Monroe, Virginia, by George Stacy, 1861. Library of Congress, Prints and Photographs Division, LC-DIG-stereo-1s01795, LC-DIG-stereo-2s01795.

page 5 (middle): The slave market, Atlanta, by George N. Barnard, created 1864 (or earlier). Library of Congress, Prints and Photographs Division, LC-DIG-stereo-1s02513, LC-DIG-stereo-2s02513.

page 5 (bottom): Webb Ship Yard, Archive Photos/Stringer via Getty Images.

page 6 (top): Jefferson Davis, created between 1855 and 1865. Brady-Handy photograph collection, Library of Congress, Prints and Photographs Division, LC-DIG-cwpbh-00879.

page 6 (middle): Senator Judah P. Benjamin of Louisiana, half-length portrait, c. 1856. Library of Congress, Prints and Photographs Division, LC-DIG-ppmsca-05642.

page 6 (bottom): Two-dollar Confederate note, by B. Duncan (Columbia, South Carolina), printers for the Confederate States Department of the Treasury, 1862. National Numismatic Collection, National Museum of American History.

page 7 (top): Portrait of Mary Boykin Chesnut, National Park Service.

page 7 (bottom): Edmund Rubbin [i.e., Edmund Ruffin], created between 1860 and 1875. Brady-Handy photograph collection, Library of Congress, Prints and Photographs Division, LC-DIG-cwpbh-00486.

page 8 (top): Slave quarters, Port Royal, South Carolina, by Timothy H. O'Sullivan, 1862. Civil war photographs, 1861–1865, Library of Congress, Prints and Photographs Division, LC-DIG-cwpb-00806, LC-DIG-cwpb-00805.

page 8 (bottom): African Americans working, Charleston, South Carolina: cotton warehouse, carrying cotton, c. 1879. Library of Congress, Prints and Photographs Division, LC-USZ62-68073.